Preface

The Butterworths Planning Law Handbook is being launched with the intention of providing for all practitioners and students concerned with town and country planning the same kind of assistance as the existing handbooks provide in other fields, but on a more modest scale.

Planning law is a bulky subject, though its limits are not precisely fixed. They can embrace compulsory purchase and compensation, and must do if the compensation–betterment question is still to be taken seriously, as well as new towns and town development, recreation and the countryside, and similar subjects. But to keep this new handbook within more modest limits the decision has been taken to confine it to the Town and Country Planning Act 1971, various other Acts most closely connected with that Act, and then the main statutory instruments made under those provisions (especially the Use Classes Order 1987 and the General Development Order 1977).

Statutory branches of law are not of course confined to statute but expand by judicial and quasi-judicial interpretation through ever-increasing case law. A handbook of statutes cannot provide the whole picture, but Part I of this book is intended as a brief introduction to planning law in its entirety; however a casebook should be consulted for a more detailed consideration of the relevant case law. Certainly the cases mean very little unless the statutory provisions have been studied first.

The law is as enacted down to the beginning of 1987, in England and Wales but not Scotland, though the Scots legislation is strictly parallel with it. There are sure to be further legislation changes in due course, whatever government is in office, and it is to be hoped that it will be practicable to issue further editions of the Handbook to bring the present readers up to date in respect of them. Readers' suggestions as to the scope and format of this edition would be greatly welcomed.

April 1987   Keith Davies

BUTTERWORTHS PLANNING LAW HANDBOOK

Edited by

KEITH DAVIES, JP, MA, LLM, *Barrister*
Professor of Law in the University of Reading

LONDON
BUTTERWORTHS
1987

United Kingdom	Butterworth & Co (Publishers) Ltd, 88 Kingsway, LONDON WC2B 6AB and 61A North Castle Street, EDINBURGH EH2 3LJ
Australia	Butterworths Pty Ltd, SYDNEY, MELBOURNE, BRISBANE, ADELAIDE, PERTH, CANBERRA and HOBART
Canada	Butterworths. A division of Reed Inc, TORONTO and VANCOUVER
New Zealand	Butterworths of New Zealand Ltd, WELLINGTON and AUCKLAND
Singapore	Butterworth & Co (Asia) Pte Ltd, SINGAPORE
South Africa	Butterworth Publishers (Pty) Ltd, DURBAN and PRETORIA
USA	Butterworths Legal Publishers, ST PAUL, Minnesota, SEATTLE, Washington, BOSTON, Massachusetts, AUSTIN, Texas and D & S Publishers, CLEARWATER, Florida

ISBN 0 406 50580 2

Typeset, printed and bound in Great Britain by
William Clowes Limited, Beccles and London

PUBLISHER'S NOTE

This handbook contains statutory materials which are up to date to 1st January 1987. Wherever possible, subsequent developments have been incorporated or are reproduced in the Appendix and cross-referred to in the annotations to the relevant provisions.

CONTENTS

APPENDIX   NEW LEGISLATION

Index

PART I

INTRODUCTION TO PLANNING LAW

INTRODUCTION TO PLANNING LAW

I THE PUBLIC PLANNING SYSTEM

A Authorities

Modern land use planning is a nationwide system of control by public authorities of how land is to be used and developed by particular landowners and developers, whether private or public.

A Minister of Town and Country Planning was first appointed in 1943, and his duties have now been inherited in substance by the Secretary of State for the Environment. Local planning authorities administer the system of planning control in detail; and the council of a county is the county planning authority for the county and the council of a district is the district planning authority for the district. London borough councils and the City of London Corporation are the local planning authorities for Greater London. Joint planning boards may be set up as necessary. Authorities are empowered to delegate routine administration to their officers. The Town and Country Planning Act 1971, as subsequently amended, and statutory instruments made thereunder, contain the bulk of the relevant law, subject to interpretation by the courts.

B Development Plans

Development of land must, in general, conform with development plans made in draft (after a survey) and constantly reviewed by local planning authorities. But other factors may justify divergence from these plans in particular cases.

Provision is made for publicity and the hearing of objections before plans formally come into effect, and alterations to and withdrawal of plans after they have come into effect. There will normally be a public local inquiry into objections. Different sorts of plans are authorised, but all aim at avoiding random decision-making by owners and authorities.

II THE MEANING OF 'DEVELOPMENT'

A The General Concept

The concept of 'development' is fundamental to planning law. 'Development' of land is controlled by a system of planning permissions, and the law which regulates it rests on the statutory definition of 'development' in s 22 of the Town and Country Planning Act 1971, as amplified by the Town and Country Planning (Use Classes) Order 1972.

In accordance with this definition it can be said that land will undergo 'development' either because its physical state is altered by 'operations' (building, engineering, mining, etc) or because there is 'material change of use'. Often there is both an 'operation' and a 'material change of use', as when a house is built on farm land. Every case has to be considered, according to its circumstances, as a question of fact and degree, as the courts frequently point out. The Use Classes Order, however, provides that specified changes of use are not development, ie they are not to be regarded as 'material'.

B The Planning Unit

It is important to take a realistic view of the unit of property to which the question of development control is to be related in any particular case. Planning units should normally be units of ownership of land rather than sub-divisions of such units.

There may be multiple uses of a 'unit' of land, sometimes with a separate area for each, sometimes with predominant and ancillary uses, sometimes with seasonal changes.

III PLANNING PERMISSIONS, APPEALS AND AGREEMENTS

A Automatic Permissions

By the authority of s 24 of the Town and Country Planning Act 1971 the Secretary of State has made general and special development orders giving automatic permission for various kinds of development. The Town and Country Planning General Development Order 1977 (the 'GDO'), as amended, among other things lists 30 classes of permitted development, subject to various elaborate qualifications of detail. But art 4 of the Order empowers the Secretary of State to direct, or consent to, a withdrawal of the automatic permission in general or specific cases, without giving any owner affected a chance to object; though if any such withdrawal is followed by a specific refusal of permission there is a right to compensation.

Other articles in the GDO prescribe in detail the procedure to be followed in regard to making specific planning applications. These need to be made if it is proposed to carry out any development which is not automatically permitted under a development order or already authorised in any other way.

B Specific Permissions

Section 23 of the 1971 Act dispenses with the need for any planning permission at all in certain special cases and permission is 'deemed' to be granted in certain other special cases. It is also dispensed with to a large extent in designated parts of run-down urban areas known as 'enterprise zones'. Apart from these cases, the section states that planning permission is 'required' for carrying out development.

Sections 25–29 of the Act of 1971, supplemented by provisions in the GDO govern the procedure for making specific planning applications. These are normally dealt with by the district (or London borough) planning authority, which may grant them, with or without conditions, or refuse them. Planning permissions normally 'enure for the benefit of the land' and may be retrospective. But they can be temporary, or restricted to a particular person. Special rules apply to development by local planning authorities themselves, or by the Crown, or on Crown land by other persons.

There is no obligation to carry out development authorised by a planning permission. But, if it is carried out, there is no right to continue or begin or revert to any use of the land (or any operation on it) which is inconsistent with what is authorised. Any further change of use (including a reversion to a previous use) if 'material', or any further operation, will constitute fresh development.

A change made in the terms of a planning permission before the authorised development takes place would amount to a fresh planning permission, which would need to be granted by the authority in the same manner as the first permission. But if a change in the terms of a permission is no more than a trivial variation this is treated as being within the terms of the permission itself and it is lawful for local planning authorities to empower their officers to decide when any such proposed variation is trivial and agree with a developer that it should be made.

Fees are in general payable for making planning applications; but this rule is subject to various exemptions.

C Time Limits and Outline Permissions

A normal requirement in planning permissions is that the development must begin with a stated time. This is now regulated by statutory rules which pay special attention to 'outline' permissions. Article 5 of the GDO gives discretion to the local planning authority to grant an application for 'outline' permission if the development comprises a building operation. Any such permission is a decision in principle, leaving details ('reserved matters') to be dealt with in subsequent applications.

Subject to express substitution by a planning authority of different periods, there is, in normal planning permissions, a standard five-year deadline for beginning development; but in the case of 'outline' permissions there is to be a standard three-year deadline for seeking approval for all 'reserved matters' (ie permission in detail) followed by a standard two-year deadline for beginning development after obtaining such approval, or alternatively an overall deadline of five years, whichever is longer. And where these conditions apply, local planning authorities have a further power to serve a 'completion notice', needing Ministerial confirmation, which requires development to be completed within a specified period of not less than a year.

D Planning Conditions

Conditions imposed by planning authorities must be reasonable and must be imposed for proper planning purposes, both in principle and in detail: if not, they are ultra vires and consequently invalid. Subject to this, the authorities have complete discretion in deciding what conditions to impose. The validity or invalidity of a condition is a question of law for the courts to decide, in contrast to its desirability, which is a policy question for the planning authorities to decide.

If a condition is invalidated by the court, does the permission survive without the condition; or is the permission also invalidated? This question is essentially one of planning policy, and for that reason it would be more in accordance with the rationale of the legislation for the court to remit the case to the planning authority. But in fact the courts have taken to deciding this question themselves. Yet in reality it is artificial to separate conditions from permissions, except for the purposes of testing their validity. It is the project of development as a whole which needs to be considered in each case, in order to decide as a question of policy whether its implementation is desirable in the public interest; and the making of policy decisions, if intra vires, is within the competence of the appropriate planning authorities, not of the courts.

E 'Called In' Applications and Appeals

An applicant may appeal from an unfavourable decision of the local planning authority to the Secretary of State, or the latter may 'call in' a planning application of his own accord and decide it instead of allowing the local planning authority to do so. A local planning authority's decision may be challenged in the High Court within three months by way of judicial review. A decision of the Secretary of State may also be challenged in the High Court, but only within six weeks by a special procedure under the Town and Country Planning Act itself. These challenges in the High Court can, of course, only be made on legal grounds, not policy grounds.

Time limits (normally two months) are imposed on local planning authorities; if they fail to give a decision in due time, an appeal lies as if from a refusal.

Hearings of appeals by way of public local inquiry before an inspector are part of the normal procedure, and are governed by statutory regulations and by the rules of natural justice. In many cases inspectors not only conduct inquiries but decide the appeals themselves. The 'calling in' procedure, though it normally only occurs in cases of special concern, includes applications comprising 'reserved matters' after 'outline' permissions.

F Revocation and Discontinuance Orders

A planning permission may be withdrawn wholly by a revocation or partly by a modification order so long as development has not taken place; but, if it has, a discontinuance order is necessary to put an end to it.

In each of these cases a hearing must be given to objections. In default of compliance with a discontinuance order the authority concerned may enter and do the work themselves, and criminal penalties may also be imposed. But local planning authorities must pay full compensation for loss occasioned by these orders, even if made by the Secretary of State under his default powers. Special but related procedures apply to orders for the discontinuance (or suspension) of mineral operations.

G Agreements and Determinations

Quite apart from applications for planning permission, a landowner or developer and a local planning authority may enter into a planning agreement, which allows the question of future use and development of land to be agreed on a general basis and not merely in relation to a particular project as when a planning application is submitted. Each agreement may be enforced as if it were a restrictive covenant without the need for a benefit to be annexed to land. An authority will often bargain for some public benefit to be provided by the developer as part of the agreement: this is informally known as 'planning gain'.

There is also a procedure enabling applicants to require a local planning authority to 'determine' whether proposed acts on land are 'development' or not, and, if they are, whether planning permission must be applied for. The Secretary of State may 'call in' such requests, and may hear appeals against unfavourable 'determinations'. These decisions may be challenged in the High Court in the same way as decisions on planning applications and appeals.

IV BREACH OF PLANNING CONTROL

A Enforcement Notices and Stop Notices

The carrying out of development without the grant of the necessary planning permission is a 'breach of planning control'. Local planning authorities which consider it 'expedient' to do so in any particular case may issue an 'enforcement notice' and serve a copy on each owner, occupier or other person involved. The notice must specify the breach and the steps required to be taken to put it right. It must also specify: (i) a period of not less than 28 days before it is to take effect; and (ii) a period for compliance. An authority may also serve a 'stop notice' prohibiting specified acts from being done in furtherance of the breach during the first of those two periods, that being the time in which an appeal may be made to the Secretary of State against the enforcement notice (which will be suspended while it is contested). A stop notice is appropriate where the planning authority fears that a developer will contest an enforcement notice and press on with an unauthorised development in the hope of presenting a 'fait accompli' which the authority may be reluctant to reverse. But the authority serving a stop notice may in some circumstances incur liability to pay compensation.

Enforcement notices can only be served in respect of any 'operations', or of any 'material change' of use to use as a single dwelling, which have been carried out within the past four years, but can be served in respect of other 'material changes of use' which have been carried out at any time after 1963.

B Enforcement Appeals and Sanctions

Appeals against enforcement notices may be made to the Secretary of State on one or more of eight specified grounds. These are not exhaustive, and the possibility of challenge in legal proceedings on other grounds remains; but the eight specified grounds cannot normally be invoked against a local planning authority in any proceedings other than an appeal to the Secretary of State. He can uphold, quash or vary the notice appealed against, and may correct any defect in it so long as this does not prejudice any party affected. His decision is itself subject to an appeal to the High Court on a point of law.

Planning authorities may, in default of compliance with an enforcement notice, carry out themselves 'the works specified'. Criminal penalties are also prescribed.

It is also possible in some circumstances to apply to a local planning authority for an 'established use certificate'. This is intended to serve as conclusive proof, in the event of an enforcement appeal, that specified uses of land are authorised.

Many leading cases on planning law which reach the courts arise out of enforcement notices. The courts have usually tended to interpret them very strictly, for example in regard to time limits or to the technical accuracy of complaints which they contain. But purely technical points should not interfere with proper enforcement.

V PRESERVATION OF AMENITY

A The General Concept

'Amenity' is second only in importance to 'development' as a basic concept in planning law. But whereas 'development' refers to physical acts and changes on land, 'amenity' (which is not defined) refers to the effect of the state of the land on people. The question is: how far can that effect be made or kept pleasurable? In fact, the control of development and the safeguarding of amenity are two sides of the same coin, and planning authorities, in shaping their policies, must keep both concepts constantly in balance.

Any aspect of land use may include questions of amenity. Planning law concentrates upon five main aspects.

B Trees

Local planning authorities may 'in the interests of amenity' make a 'tree preservation order' to protect any specified tree or trees or area of woodland, subject to confirmation by the Secretary of State except in uncontested cases. This applies to the protected tree or trees a code of planning control similar to ordinary planning control, including applications, appeals, revocation and enforcement, but substituting consents to fell or lop for planning permissions to develop. Authorities have a general duty to see that consents to fell protected trees are matched as far as possible by a requirement to replace them by replanting. But it is common to include conditions for preserving or replanting trees in ordinary planning permission.

Tree preservation orders are, in effect, special ad hoc extensions of planning control, and it is important not to confuse the procedure for making them with the procedure for obtaining consents under them when made. They can be worded so as to apply to future trees to be planted in accordance with a planning condition of the kind referred to above. Interfering with protected trees is a criminal offence; but they can be felled or lopped in cases of danger or nuisance.

C   Buildings of Special Interest and Conservation Areas

The Secretary of State has a duty, subject to expert consultation, to compile and maintain lists of buildings of special architectural or historic interest, referred to as 'listed buildings'. Carrying out works to any 'listed building' which would 'affect its character' as such, whether by demolition or lesser interferences, requires a 'listed building consent' from the local planning authority. Such works are in themselves not 'development', though in many cases works are both development and interference with the special character of a listed building at one and the same time.

Contravention of 'listed building' control is a criminal offence. Provision is also made for 'listed building' enforcement notices and purchase notices and also for payment of compensation for refusals of consent for works not amounting to demolition or development which reduce the value of the property. A compulsory purchase order can be made if the owner has first been given by the local planning authority a notice to put the listed building into proper repair and has failed to comply. Any building not listed may be given temporary protection for six months by means of a 'building preservation notice' while the local planning authority request the Secretary of State to consider listing it.

Churches (but not parsonages) and ancient monuments are excluded from these provisions. Each local authority keeps a copy of the list of buildings in its area.

Local planning authorities also have a duty to consider designating any parts of their areas which are 'of special architectural or historic interest the character or appearance of which it is desirable to preserve or enhance'. These 'conservation areas' are, in effect, areas especially rich in listed (or listable) buildings; and the duty of local planning authorities in respect of them may be expressed under three heads: (i) evolving a specific policy for safeguarding amenity generally in each area; (ii) publicising planning applications within each area; (iii) consulting preservation societies and other interested bodies as appropriate. Where buildings in a conservation area are listable but not listed, listed building consent is nevertheless required for demolishing them.

D   Advertisements

The Secretary of State is empowered to make regulations controlling 'the display of advertisements so far as appears ... to be expedient in the interests of amenity or public safety'. The details include a system of consents; and in many cases consent is 'deemed' to be granted, under the regulations, for the general run of routine, modest-sized advertisements, within specified limits. But 'areas of special control' may be declared, in which express consents are only available for specified kinds of advertisement. Contravention of the regulations is a criminal offence.

E   Caravan Sites

The Caravan Sites and Control of Development Act 1960 (as amended) gives local authorities control over the use of land for caravan sites by means of a licensing system.

The conditions contained in a 'site licence' are more important than the granting of the licence, because the licence normally follows automatically upon a planning permission and lasts as long as that permission. The conditions may be imposed for certain specified purposes, which pertain to public health as well as amenity; but those which have no connection with these purposes will almost certainly be 'ultra vires'.

Appeal against site licence conditions, or against a decision or refusal to vary them, lies to a magistrates' court, on the ground that they are 'unduly burdensome'. There are various categories of exemption from control, such as use in the garden of a house, or occasional and intermittent use, and also use for seasonal and temporary workers, and circus and fairground showmen.

F Waste Land and Dumping

Local planning authorities which consider that amenity in their area or nearby is 'adversely affected by the condition of land' can serve a notice on the owner and occupier specifying 'steps for remedying the condition of the land' to be taken within a prescribed period. Appeal lies to a magistrates' court, with a further appeal to the Crown Court, but the authority may, in default of compliance, do the specified works themselves at the defaulter's expense. Authorities also have powers to deal with dumping of refuse and abandoned vehicles.

VI COMPULSORY PURCHASE IN PLANNING

A Planning Purposes

Local authorities, if so authorised by the Secretary of State, may compulsorily purchase land for 'planning purposes'. This usually means urban redevelopment or 'urban renewal', otherwise known as 'positive' planning. If authorities want to carry out redevelopment themselves instead of disposing of land to private developers, the consent of the Secretary of State is needed for that also. In the period since the Second World War a somewhat similar function in the form of planning and developing New Towns away from existing urban areas has been given to independent bodies known as 'development corporations'. More recently 'urban development corporations' have been set up to carry out urban renewal in designated inner city areas which are in need of regeneration, such as the dockland area of London.

B Purchase notices

Owners of land which is 'incapable of reasonably beneficial use in its existing state', and which cannot be made capable of reasonably beneficial use because of either a refusal of planning permission or a grant of planning permission which is subject to burdensome conditions, may serve a 'purchase notice' on the local authority requiring them to buy the property. The procedure under these notices amounts to 'compulsory purchase in reverse', that is to say, at the instance of the vendor and not of the acquiring authority. No CPO is needed. Compensation is payable as for an ordinary compulsory purchase. 'Owners' do not, however, include ground landlords, or tenants paying a full rent.

For a purchase notice to take effect after rejection by the local authority it has to be confirmed by the Secretary of State, to whom in such a case it is automatically referred. But he must not do so merely because the land would otherwise be less valuable, since this applies to nearly all cases of planning refusals: in effect, the land must be virtually useless as a result of the adverse decision. His own decision in this, as in other planning procedures, is in turn open to challenge on legal grounds in the High Court.

C   Blight Notices

If owner-occupiers of land (freeholders, or leaseholders with three or more years to run, but not owners of high-value non-residential property), or residential landlords, are unable to sell at a fair market price because of the prospect that the land may be compulsorily purchased, they can serve a 'blight notice' on the public authority responsible, requiring that authority to buy the property. A rateable value limit is imposed on property other than residential or agricultural.

The authority can object by serving a counter-notice alleging that the claimant is not qualified, or that they do not intend to acquire the land; the dispute must then be settled by the Lands Tribunal. Blight notices, like purchase notices, amount to 'compulsory purchase in reverse' and, as with purchase notices, no CPO is needed and compensation follows the normal rules. But whereas purchase notices arise from adverse decisions, blight notices arise from adverse proposals.

VII   BETTERMENT

A   Taxation of Development Value

'Development value' must be distinguished from the 'existing use value' of land and also from the actual cost of development. The price of land after it has been developed will represent an aggregation of all three items of value. Development value of land over and above existing use value depends on genuine suitability and market demand for development, plus planning permission. The argument goes that, unlike existing use value or actual development, an owner has not paid for it, but (in a sense) the community has. Two questions arise. First: Should there be compensation for loss of 'betterment' (development value) by reason of planning control? Second: Should 'betterment' be retained by owners who do have the benefit of it or should all or any of it go to the community? The first question has been dealt with by the law on planning compensation, the second by taxation of betterment.

Various attempts have been made to tax 'betterment' for the community, the most recent being Development Land Tax. This tax having now been abolished, development value has for tax purposes fallen to be treated like any other capital gain.

B   Planning Compensation

On the other hand there is no general entitlement to compensation for loss of development value on 'betterment', by reason of adverse planning decisions. Compensation is, however, payable in some cases.

Full compensation for loss is allowed as of right, payable by the local planning authority, where an existing right to development value is lost by reason of revocation, modification or discontinuance, but not where a refusal of planning permission prevents the right from being obtained at the outset. Even in the latter case, however, full compensation is allowed as of right in certain cases (on a decision of the Secretary of State, not of a local planning authority). The development restricted must not be 'new' or substantial, but merely marginal to 'existing use' as listed in the eight categories within Pts I and II of the Eighth Schedule (as amended) of the Town and Country Planning Act 1971. The value of all such development must normally be included in compensation for compulsory purchase. Planning compensation, however, is only payable where development within Pt II, not Pt I, is restricted, the remedy for Pt I restrictions being to serve a purchase notice (assuming that the requirements for it are satisfied).

But compensation is payable in some cases even for refusal of planning permission for 'new development'. It is payable only to the extent that a special asset known as the 'unexpended balance of established development value' (the 'UXB') attaches to the claimant's interest in the land; though, even where this is so, there are many cases where the right is excluded. It is payable by the Secretary of State (as distinct from the varieties of planning compensation already discussed, which are payable by local planning authorities).

The 'unexpended balance' represents an owner's established claim to loss (in effect) of 'new' development value which was made originally under the Town and Country Planning Act 1947, but adjusted and converted into an asset attached to the land by virtue of the Town and Country Planning Act 1954. It is used up at any time as a result of the realising of development value either by the receipt of planning or compulsory purchase compensation or by the actual carrying out of 'new' development. If 'UXB' compensation of over £20 is paid, a notice must be registered as a local land charge. If permission is then granted for certain substantial kinds of development, that compensation will have to be repaid before development begins. The value of any 'unexpended balance' remains at 1947 prices, increased by one-seventh.

Disputes over planning compensation go to the Lands Tribunal.

VIII PURCHASERS AND PLANNING

Conveyancers often need to spend more time investigating the planning aspects of land transactions than the pure conveyancing aspects. A purchaser's solicitor should normally, as a matter of course, apply for an official search of the relevant local land charges registers, which will disclose any restrictive orders of a public nature which affect the property. In addition, there are the local lists of buildings of special interest, and also registers of planning applications and application for consent to display advertisements, which are all available for public inspection and should be inspected if the circumstances warrant it.

IX PLANNING AND THE COURTS

Although planning authorities can sue and be sued in *private* law actions in their capacity as corporations, planning law is itself part of *public* law. Persons and bodies entrusted with public functions must act *intra vires*—ie within the proper limits of those functions. When their activities are *ultra vires* anyone with a relevant 'legitimate expectation' that they will act correctly can challenge the validity of those activities in the High Court by bringing proceedings for judicial review, or special statutory proceedings in lieu (eg under Part XII of the Town and Country Planning Act 1971), to invalidate wrongful acts or omissions. Planning authorities in their turn can if necessary enforce their control 'in the public interest' by seeking injunctions, or bringing special statutory proceedings (civil or criminal) as appropriate.

PART II
PRIMARY LEGISLATION

LOCAL GOVERNMENT ACT 1985
(c 51)

An Act to abolish the Greater London Council and the metropolitan county councils; to transfer their functions to the local authorities in their areas and, in some cases, to other bodies; and to provide for other matters consequential on, or connected with, the abolition of those councils.　　　　　[16 July 1985]

PART I
ABOLITION OF GREATER LONDON COUNCIL AND METROPOLITAN COUNTY COUNCILS

1. Abolition of GLC and metropolitan county councils

(1) On the date on which this subsection comes into force—

    (*a*)　the Greater London Council; and

    (*b*)　the metropolitan county councils, shall cease to exist.

(2) The date on which subsection (1) above comes into force is in this Act referred to as the "abolition date" and shall be 1st April 1986.　　　　**[1]**

NOTES
    Commencement: 1 April 1986.

PART II
TRANSFER OF FUNCTIONS TO LONDON BOROUGH COUNCILS, METROPOLITAN DISTRICT COUNCILS AND OTHER EXISTING AUTHORITIES

Town and country planning etc

4. Development plans

(1) Part I of Schedule 1 to this Act shall apply instead of Part II of the Town and Country Planning Act 1971 (development plans) to the area of any local planning authority in Greater London or a metropolitan county and shall come into force in any such area on such day after the abolition date as may be appointed in relation to that area by an order made by the Secretary of State.

(2) Part II of that Schedule shall have effect with respect to development plans in any such area as is mentioned in subsection (1) above from the abolition date until a unitary development plan for that area becomes operative under Part I of that Schedule and with respect to other transitional matters.

(3) The said Act of 1971 and the provisions of Schedule 1 to this Act shall have effect as if that Schedule were contained in that Act.　　　　**[2]**

NOTES
    Commencement: 1 April 1986.

5. Joint planning committee for Greater London

(1) The local planning authorities in Greater London shall not later than the abolition date establish a joint committee to discharge the functions mentioned in subsection (2) below.

(2) The joint committee shall—

(*a*) consider and advise those authorities on matters of common interest relating to the planning and development of Greater London;

(*b*) inform the Secretary of State of the views of those authorities concerning such matters including any such matters as to which he has requested their advice;

(*c*) inform the local planning authorities for areas in the vicinity of Greater London, or any body on which those authorities and the local planning authorities in Greater London are represented, of the views of the local planning authorities in Greater London concerning any matters of common interest relating to the planning and development of Greater London and those areas;

and the committee may, if it thinks fit, contribute towards the expenses of any such body as is mentioned in paragraph (*c*) above.

(3) The expenses of the joint committee which have been incurred with the approval of at least two-thirds of the local planning authorities in Greater London shall be defrayed by those authorities in such proportions as they may decide or, in default of a decision by them, as the Secretary of State may determine.

(4) In this section references to the local planning authorities in Greater London are to the authorities which are the local planning authorities in Greater London for the purposes of Part II of the Town and Country Planning Act 1971 or section 4 above.   [3]

NOTES
Commencement: 1 April 1986.

SCHEDULES
SCHEDULE 1

Section 4

DEVELOPMENT PLANS

PART I
UNITARY DEVELOPMENT PLANS

Survey of planning areas

1.—(1) The local planning authority—

(*a*) shall keep under review the matters which may be expectd to affect the development of their area or the planning of its development; and

(*b*) may, if they think fit, institue a survey or surveys of their area or any part of their area for examining those matters.

(2) Without prejudice to the generality of sub-paragraph (1) above, the matters to be kept under review or examined under that sub-paragraph shall include—

(*a*) principal physical and economic characteristics of the area of the authority (including the principal purposes for which land is used) and, so far as they may be expected to affect that area, of any neighbouring areas;

(*b*) the size, composition and distribution of the population of that area (whether resident or otherwise);

(*c*) without prejudice to paragraph (*a*) above, the communications, transport system and traffic of that area and, so far as they may be expected to affect that area, of any neighbouring areas;

(*d*) any considerations not mentioned in any of the foregoing paragraphs which may be expected to affect any matters mentioned in them;

(*e*) such other matters as may be prescribed or as the Secretary of State may in a particular case direct;

(*f*) any changes already projected in any of the matters mentioned in any of the foregoing paragraphs and the effect which those changes are likely to have on the development of that area or the planning of such development.

(3) A local planning authority shall, for the purpose of discharging their functions under this paragraph of keeping under review and examining any matters relating to the area of another such authority, consult with that other authority about those matters.

Preparation of unitary development plan

2.—(1) The local planning authority shall, after the coming into force of this paragraph in their area and within such period (if any) as the Secretary of State may direct, prepare for their area a plan to be known as a unitary development plan.

(2) A unitary development plan shall comprise two parts, namely—

(*a*) Part I which shall consist of a written statement formulating the authority's general policies in respect of the development and other use of land in their area (including measures for the improvement of the physical environment and the management of traffic); and

(*b*) Part II which shall consist of—

(i) a written statement formulating in such detail as the authority think appropriate (and so as to be readily distinguishable from the other contents of the plan) their proposals for the development or other use of land in their area or for any description of development or other use of such land;

(ii) a map showing those proposals on a geographical basis;

(iii) a reasoned justification of the general policies in Part I and of the proposals in Part II; and

(iv) such diagrams, illustrations or other descriptive or explanatory matter in respect of the general policies in Part I or the proposals in Part II as the authority think appropriate or as may be prescribed.

(3) A unitary development plan shall also contain such other matters as may be prescribed or as the Secretary of State may in any particular case direct.

(4) In formulating the general policies in Part I of a unitary development plan the authority shall have regard—

(*a*) to any strategic guidance given by the Secretary of State to assist them in the preparation of the plan;

(*b*) to current national and regional policies;

(*c*) to the resources likely to be available; and

(*d*) to such other matters as the Secretary of State may direct the authority to take into account.

(5) The proposals in Part II of a unitary development plan shall be in general conformity with Part I.

(6) Part II of a unitary development plan may designate any part of the authority's area as an action area, that is to say, an area which they have selected for the commencement during a prescribed period of comprehensive treatment by development, redevelopment or improvement (or partly by one and partly by another method) and if an area is so designated that Part of the plan shall contain a description of the treatment proposed by the authority.

(7) In preparing a unitary development plan the authority shall take into account the provisions of any scheme under paragraph 3 of Schedule 32 to the Local Government, Planning and Land Act 1980 relating to land in their area which has been designated under that Schedule as an enterprise zone.

Publicity in connection with preparation of unitary development plan

3.—(1) When preparing a unitary development plan for their area and before finally determining its contents the local planning authority shall take such steps as will in their opinion secure—

(a) that adequate publicity is given in their area to the matters which they propose to include in the plan;

(b) that persons who may be expected to desire an opportunity of making representations to the authority with respect to those matters are made aware that they are entitled to an opportunity of doing so; and

(c) that such persons are given an adequate opportunity of making such representations;

and the authority shall consider any representations made to them within the prescribed period.

(2) Where the local planning authority have prepared a unitary development plan they shall, before adopting it, make copies of it available for inspection at their office and at such other places as may be prescribed and send a copy to the Secretary of State; and each copy made available for inspection shall be accompanied by a statement of the time within which objections to the plan may be made to the authority.

(3) The copy of a unitary development plan sent to the Secretary of State under sub-paragraph (2) above shall be accompanied by a statement—

(a) of the steps which the authority have taken to comply with sub-paragraph(1) above; and

(b) of the authority's consultations with, and their consideration of the views of, other persons.

(4) If, on considering the statement submitted with and the matters contained in a unitary development plan and any other information provided by the local planning authority, the Secretary of State is not satisfied that the purposes of paragraphs (a) to (c) of sub-paragraph (1) above have been adequately achieved by the steps taken by the authority in compliance with that sub-paragraph, he may, within twenty-one days of the receipt of the statement, direct the authority not to take further steps for the adoption of the plan without taking such further action as he may specify in order better to achieve those purposes and satisfying him that they have done so.

(5) A local planning athority who are given directions by the Secretary of State under sub-paragraph (4) above shall—

(a) forthwith withdraw the copies of the unitary development plan made available for inspection as required by sub-paragraph (2) above; and

(b) notify any person by whom objections to the plan have been made to the authority that the Secretary of State has given such directions as aforesaid.

Withdrawal of unitary development plan

4.—(1) A unitary development plan may be withdrawn by the local planning authority at any time before it is adopted by the authority or approved by the Secretary of State and shall be withdrawn by the authority if the Secretary of State so directs.

(2) Where a unitary development plan is withdrawn the authority shall—

(a) withdraw the copies made available for inspection and sent to the Secretary of State under paragraph 3(2) above; and

(b) give notice that tha plan has been withdrawn to every person who has made an objection to it.

(3) In determining the steps to be taken by a local planning authority to secure the purposes of paragraphs (a) to (c) of sub-paragraph (1) of paragraph 3 above the authority and the Secretary of State may take into account any steps taken to secure those purposes in connection with any unitary development plan which the authority have previously withdrawn.

(4) Where a unitary development plan is withdrawn the copies of the plan shall be treated as never having been made available under paragraph 3(2) above.

Adoption of unitary development plan by local planning authority

5.—(1) After the expiry of the period afforded for making objections to a unitary development plan or, if such objections have been duly made during that period, after considering those objections, the local planning authority may, subject to the following provisions of this paragraph and paragraph 7 below, by resolution adopt the plan either as originally prepared or as modified to take account—

(*a*) of those objections;
(*b*) of any other objections made to the plan;
(*c*) of any other considerations which appear to the authority to be material.

(2) A unitary development plan shall not be adopted unless Part II of the plan is in general conformity with Part I.

(3) Where an objection to a unitary development plan has been made by the Minister of Agriculture, Fisheries and Food and the local planning authority do not propose to modify the plan to take account of the objection the authority—

(*a*) shall send the Secretary of State particulars of the objection and a statement of their reasons for not modifying the plan to take account of it; and
(*b*) shall not adopt the plan unless the Secretary of State authorises them to do so.

(4) Subject to the following provisions of this Schedule and to section 242 of the Town and Country Planning Act 1971, a unitary development plan shall become operative on the date on which it is adopted.

Local inquiries and hearings prior to adoption

6.—(1) For the purposes of considering objections to a unitary development plan the local planning authority may, and shall in the case of objections made in accordance with regulations under this Part of this Schedule, cause a local inquiry or other hearing to be held by a person appointed by the Secretary of State or, in such cases as may be prescribed by regulations under this Part of this Schedule, by the authority themselves; and—

(*a*) subsections (2) and (3) of section 250 of the Local Government Act 1972 (power to summon and examine witnesses) shall apply to an inquiry held under this paragraph as they apply to an inquiry under that section; and
(*b*) the Tribunals and Inquiries Act 1971 shall apply to a local inquiry or other hearing held under this paragraph as it applies to a statutory inquiry held by the Secretary of State but as if in section 12(1) of that Act (statement of reasons for decisions) the reference to any decision taken by the Secretary of State were a reference to a decision taken by a local authority.

(2) Regulations made for the purposes of this paragraph may—

(*a*) make provision with respect to the appointment and qualifications for appointment of persons to hold a local inquiry or other hearing under this paragraph, including provision enabling the Secretary of State to direct a local planning authority to appoint a particular person or one of a specified list or class of persons;
(*b*) make provision with respect to the remuneration and allowances of a person appointed for that purpose.

(3) No local inquiry or other hearing need be held under this paragraph if all persons who have made objections have indicated in writing that they do not wish to appear.

[*Direction to reconsider proposals*

6A.—(1) After a copy of a unitary development plan has been sent to the Secretary of State and before it is adopted by the local planning authority, the Secretary of State may, if it appears to him that the plan is unsatisfactory, direct the authority to consider modifying the proposals in such respects as are indicated in the direction.

(2) An authority to whom a direction is given shall not adopt the plan unless they satisfy the Secretary of State that they have made the modifications necessary to conform with the direction or the direction is withdrawn.]

Calling in of unitary development plan for approval by Secretary of State

7.—(1) At any time after a copy of a unitary development plan has been sent to the Secretary of State under paragraph 3(2) above and before it is adopted by the local planning authority, the Secretary of State may direct that the whole or part of the plan shall be submitted to him for his approval, and in that event—

(a) the authority shall not take any further steps for the adoption of the plan until the Secretary of State has given his decision on the plan or the relevant part of it; and

(b) the plan or the relevant part of it shall not have effect unless approved by him and shall not require adoption under the foregoing provisions of this Schedule.

(2) Where particulars of an objection to a unitary development plan have been sent to the Secretary of State under paragraph 5(3) above, then, unless he is satisfied that the Minister of Agriculture, Fisheries and Food no longer objects to the plan, it shall be the duty of the Secretary of State to give a direction in respect of it under sub-paragraph (1) above.

(3) Sub-paragraph (1)(a) above applies in particular to holding or proceeding with a local inquiry or other hearing in respect of the plan under paragraph 6 above; and at any such inquiry or hearing which is subsequently held or resumed a local planning authority shall not be obliged to afford any person an opportunity of being heard in respect of any objection which has been heard at an examination, local inquiry or other hearing under paragraph 9 below or which the Secretary of State states that he has considered in making his decision.

Approval of unitary development plan by the Secretary of State

8.—(1) Subject to paragraph 9 below, the Secretary of State may after considering a plan or part of a plan submitted to him under paragraph 7(1) above either approve it in whole or in part and with or without modifications or reservations or reject it.

(2) In considering a plan or part of a plan submitted to him as aforesaid the Secretary of State may take into account any matters which he thinks relevant, whether or not they were taken into account in the plan or that part of it.

(3) The Secretary of State shall give to a local planning authority such statement as he considers appropriate of the reasons governing his decision on any plan or part of a plan submitted to him.

(4) Where the whole or part of Part I of a unitary development plan is approved by the Secretary of State with modifications, the local planning authority shall, before adopting the remainder of the plan, make such modifications in Part II as may be directed by the Secretary of State for bringing it into general conformity with Part I and, in the absence of any such direction, shall make such modifications for that purpose in Part II as appear to the authority to be required.

(5) Subject to section 242 of the Town and Country Planning Act 1971, a plan or part of a plan which is approved by the Secretary of State under this paragraph shall become operative on such day as he may appoint.

Local inquiry, public examination and consultation by Secretary of State

9.—(1) Subject to sub-paragraph (3) below, before deciding whether or not to approve a plan or part of a plan submitted to him under paragraph 7(1) above, the Secretary of State shall consider any objection to it so far as made in accordance with regulations under this Part of this Schedule.

(2) Subject to sub-paragraph (3) below, where—

(a) the whole of a unitary development plan; or

(b) the whole or part of Part II of Such a plan; or

(c) the whole or part of Part I together with any part of Part II, or the whole of Part II together with any part of Part I, of such a plan,

is submitted as aforesaid, then, if any objections have been made to the plan or the relevant part of it as aforesaid, the Secretary of State shall before deciding whether to approve it cause a local inquiry or other hearing to be held for the purpose of considering those objections.

(3) The Secretary of State need not under sub-paragraph (1) above consider any objections which have already been considered by the local planning authority and need not cause a local inquiry or other hearing to be held under sub-paragraph (2) above if that authority have already held a local inquiry or other hearing into the objections under paragraph 6 above or the Secretry of State, on taking the plan or the relevant part of it into consideration, decides to reject it.

(4) Where the whole or part of Part I of a unitary development plan (but not the whole or any part of Part II) is submitted to the Secretary of State under paragraph 7(1) above he may cause a person or persons appointed by him for the purpose to hold an examination in public of such matters affecting the Secretary of State's consideration of the part of the plan submitted to him as he considers ought to be so examined.

(5) The Secretary of State may, after consultation with the Lord Chancellor, make regulations with respect to the procedure to be followed at any examination under sub-paragraph (4) above.

(6) The Secretary of State shall not be required to secure to any local planning authority or other person a right to be heard at an examination under sub-paragraph (4) above, and the bodies and persons who may take part shall be such only as he may, whether before or during the course of the examination, in his discretion invite to do so; but the person or persons holding the examination shall have power, exercisable either before or during the course of the examination, to invite additional bodies or persons to take part if it appears to him or them desirable to do so.

(7) An examination under sub-paragraph (4) above shall constitute a statutory inquiry for the purposes of section 1(1)(c) of the Tribunals and Inquiries Act 1971 but shall not constitute such an inquiry for any other purpose of that Act.

(8) On considering a plan or part of a plan submitted to him under paragraph 7(1) above the Secretary of State may consult with or consider the views of any local planning authority or other person but shall not be under any obligation to do so except as provided in the foregoing provisions of this paragraph.

Alteration of unitary development plan

10.—(1) [Subject to paragraph 10A below,] a local planning authority may at any time, and shall if so directed by the Secretary of State, make proposals for the alteration or replacement of a unitary development plan adopted or approved for their area under the foregoing provisions of this Part of this Schedule but, except in pursuance of such a direction, a local planning authority shall not without the consent of the Secretary of State make proposals under this paragraph in respect of any plan or part of a plan if that plan or any part of it has been approved by him under those provisions.

(2) Paragraphs 2 to 9 above (other than sub-paragraph (1) of paragraph 2) shall apply in relation to the making of proposals under this paragraph and to any alteration or replacement so proposed as they apply to the preparation of a unitary development plan under paragraph 2 and to a plan prepared under that paragraph.

(3) As soon as practicable after—

(a) an order has been made under paragraph 5 of Schedule 32 to the Local Government, Planning and Land Act 1980 (designation of enterprise zone); or

(b) a notification has been given under paragraph 11(1) of that Schedule (approval of modification of enterprise zone scheme),

the local planning authority for an area in which the zone is wholly or partly situated shall review any unitary development plan for that area in the light of the provisions of the scheme or modified scheme under that Schedule and prepare proposals under this paragraph for any consequential alterations to the plan which they consider necessary.

[*Short procedure for certain alterations*

10A.—(1) Where a local planning authority propose to alter or replace a unitary development plan and it appears to them that the issues involved are not of sufficient importance to warrant the full procedure set out in paragraph 3(1) and (2), they may instead proceed as follows.

(2) They shall prepare the relevant documents, that is, the proposed alterations or replacement plan, and shall make a copy of them available for inspection at their office and at such other places as may be prescribed and send a copy to the Secretary of State.

(3) Each copy of the documents made available for inspection shall be accompanied by a statement of the time within which representations or objections may be made.

(4) They shall then take such steps as may be prescribed for the purpose of—

   (a) advertising the fact that the documents are available for inspection, and the places and times at which and period during which they may be inspected, and
   (b) inviting the making of representations or objections in accordance with regulations;

and they shall consider any representations made to them within the prescribed period.

(5) The documents sent by the local planning authority to the Secretary of State under sub-paragraph (2) above shall be accompanied by a statement of the steps which the authority are taking to comply with sub-paragraph (4) above.

(6) If, on considering the statement submitted with and the matters contained in the documents sent to him under sub-paragraph (2) above and any other information provided by the local planning authority, the Secretary of State is not satisfied with the steps taken by the authority he may, within twenty-one days of the receipt of the statement, direct the authority not to take further steps for the adoption of their proposals without—

   (a) proceeding in accordance with paragraph 3(1) and (2) above, or
   (b) taking such further action as he may specify,

and satisfying him that they have done so.

(7) A local planning authority who are given directions by the Secretary of State under sub-paragraph (6) above shall—

   (a) forthwith withdraw the copies of documents made available for inspection as required by sub-paragraph (2) above; and
   (b) notify any person by whom objections to the proposals have been made to the authority that the Secretary of State has given such directions as aforesaid.

(8) Where a local planning authority proceed in accordance with this paragraph, the references in paragraphs 4(2)(a) and (4) and 7(1) to copies made available or sent to the Secretary of State under paragraph 3(2) shall be construed as references to copies made available or sent to the Secretary of State under sub-paragraph (2) of this paragraph.]

Disregard of certain representations

11. Notwithstanding anything in the foregoing provisions of this Part of this Schedule, neither the Secretary of State nor a local planning authority shall be required to consider representations or objections with respect to a unitary development plan or any proposals for the alteration or replacement of such a plan if it appears to the Secretary of State or the authority, as the case may be, that those representations or objections are in substance representations or objections with respect to things done or proposed to be done in pursuance of—

   (a) an order or scheme under section 10, 14, 16, 18, 106(1) or (3) or 108(1) of the Highways Act 1980;
   (b) an order or scheme under any provision replaced by the provisions mentioned in paragraph (a) above, namely, an order or scheme under section 7, 9, 11, 13

or 20 of the Highways Act 1959, section 3 of the Highways (Miscellaneous Provisions) Act 1961 or section 1 or 10 of the Highways Act 1971; or

(c) an order under section 1 of the New Towns Act 1981.

Joint unitary development plans

12.—(1) A joint unitary development plan may be prepared by two or more local planning authorities in Greater London or by two or more local planning authorities in a metropolitan county; and the foregoing provisions of this Part of this Schedule shall, in relation to any such joint plan, have effect subject to the following provisions of this paragraph.

(2) The local plannning authorities shall jointly take such steps as will in their opinion secure—

(a) that adequate publicity is given in their areas to the matters proposed to be included in the plan;

(b) that persons who may be expected to desire an opportunity of making representations to any of the authorities are made aware that they are entitled to an opportunity of doing so; and

(c) that such persons are given an adequate opportunity of making such representations;

and the authorities shall consider any representations made to them within the prescribed period.

(3) Sub-paragraph (1) of paragraph 3 above shall not apply in relation to a joint unitary development plan and references in sub-paragraphs (3) and (4) of that paragraph and in paragraph 4(3) above to sub-paragraph (1) of paragraph 3 and the purposes of paragraphs (a) to (c) of that sub-paragraph shall include references to sub-paragraph (2) above and the purposes of paragraphs (a) to (c) of that sub-paragraph.

(4) Each of the local planning authorities by whom a joint unitary development plan is prepared shall have the duty imposed by sub-paragraph (2) of paragraph 3 above of making copies of the plan available for inspection, and objections to the plan may be made to any of those authorities and the statement required by that sub-paragraph to accompany copies of the plan shall state that objections may be so made.

(5) It shall be for each of the local planning authorities by whom a joint unitary development plan is prepared to adopt the plan under paragraph 5(1) above and they may do so as respects any part of their area to which the plan relates, but any modifications subject to which the plan is adopted must have the agreement of all those authorities.

(6) Where a unitary development plan has been prepared jointly the power of making proposals in respect of the plan under paragraph 10 above may be exercised as respects their respective areas by any of the authorities by whom it was prepared and the Secretary of State may under that paragraph direct any of them to make proposals as respects their respective areas.

(7) In relation to any proposals made jointly under paragraph 10 above the reference in sub-paragraph (2) of that paragraph to paragraphs 2 to 9 above shall include a reference to sub-paragraph (2) above.

[(7) In relation to any proposals made jointly under paragraph 10 above, the references—

(a) in sub-paragraph (2) of that paragraph to paragraphs 2 to 9 above, and

(b) in paragraph 10A(1) above to paragraph 3(1) above,

shall include a reference to sub-paragraph (2) above.

(7A) In relation to such joint proposals the references in paragraph 10A above to the local planning authority shall be construed as references to the authorities acting jointly, except that—

(a) each of the authorities shall have the duty under sub-paragraph (2) of making copies of the relevant documents available for inspection, and (*b*) representations or objections may be made to any of the authorities, and the statement required by sub-paragraph (3) of that paragraph shall state that objections may be so made.]

(8) The date of the coming into operation of a unitary development plan prepared jointly by two or more local planning authorities or for the alteration or replacement of such a plan in pursuance of proposals so prepared shall be a date jointly agreed by those authorities.

Default powers

13.—(1) Where, by virtue of any of the foregoing provisions of this Part of this Schedule, any unitary development plan or proposals for the alteration or replacement of such a plan are required to be prepared, or steps are required to be taken for the adoption of any such plan or proposals, then—

(*a*) if at any time the Secretary of State is satisfied, after holding a local inquiry or other hearing, that the local planning authority are not taking the steps necessary to enable them to prepare or adopt such a plan or proposals within a reasonable period; or

(*b*) in a case where a period is specified for the preparation or adoption of any such plan or proposals if no such plan or proposals have been prepared or adopted within that period,

the Secretary of State may prepare and make the plan or any part of it or, as the case may be, alter or replace it, as he thinks fit.

(2) Where under this paragraph anything which ought to have been done by a local planning authority is done by the Secretary of State, the foregoing provisions of this Part of this Schedule shall, so far as practicable, apply with any necessary modifications in relation to the doing of that thing by the Secretary of State and the thing so done.

(3) Where the Secretary of State incurs expenses under this paragraph in connection with the doing of anything which should have been done by a local planning authority, so much of those expenses as may be certified by the Secretary of State to have been incurred in the performance of functions of that authority shall on demand be repaid by that authority to the Secretary of State.

Regulations and directions

14.—(1) Without prejudice to the foregoing provisions of this Part of this Schedule, the Secretary of State may make regulations with respect to the form and content of unitary development plans and with respect to the procedure to be followed in connection with their preparation, withdrawal, adoption, submission, approval, making, alteration or replacement; and such regulations may in particular—

(*a*) provide for publicity to be given to the results of any review or survey carried out under paragraph 1 above;

(*b*) provide for the notice to be given of, or the publicity to be given to, matters included or proposed to be included in any unitary development plan, and the approval, adoption or making of any such plan or any alteration or replacement of it or to any other prescribed procedural step, and for publicity to be given to the procedure to be followed as aforesaid;

(*c*) make provision with respect to the making and consideration of representations with respect to matters to be included in, or objections to, any such plan or proposals for its alteration or replacement;

(*d*) without prejudice to paragraph (*b*) above, provide for notice to be given to particular persons of the approval, adoption, alteration or replacement of any plan if they have objected to the plan and have notified the local planning authority of their wish to receive notice, subject (if the regulations so provide) to the payment of a reasonable charge;

(*e*) require or authorise a local planning authority to consult with, or consider the views of, other persons before taking any precribed procedural step;

(*f*) require a local planning authority, in such cases as may be prescribed or in such particular cases as the Secretary of State may direct, to provide persons making a request in that behalf with copies of any plan or document which has been made public for the purpose mentioned in paragraphs 3(1)(*a*) or 12(2)(*a*) above or has been made available for inspection under paragraph 3(2) above, subject (if the regulations so provide) to the payment of a reasonable charge;

(*g*) provide for the publication and inspection of any unitary development plan which has been adopted, approved or made or any document approved, adopted or made altering or replacing any such plan, and for copies of any such plan or document to be made available on sale.

(2) Regulations under this paragraph may make different provision for different cases.

(3) Subject to the foregoing provisions of this Part of this Schedule and to any regulations under this paragraph, the Secretary of State may give directions to any local planning authority or to local planning authorities generally,—

(*a*) for formulating the procedure for the carrying out of their functions under this Part of this Schedule;

(*b*) for requiring them to give him such information as he may require for carrying out any of his functions under this Part of this Schedule.

Meaning of "development plan" in Greater London and metropolitan counties

15.—(1) For the purposes of the Town and Country Planning Act 1971, any other enactment relating to town and country planning, the Land Compensation Act 1961 and the Highways Act 1980, the development plan for any district in Greater London or a metropolitan county (whether the whole or part of the area of a local planning authority) shall be taken as consisting of—

(*a*) the provisions of the unitary development plan for the time being in force for that area or the relevant part of it, together with a copy of the local planning authority's resolution of adoption or the Secretary of State's notice of approval or, where part of the plan has been adopted and the remainder approved, copies of the resolution and the notice; and

(*b*) any alteration to that plan, together with a copy of the authority's resolution of adoption, or the Secretary of State's notice of approval, of the alteration or, where part of the alteration has been adopted and the remainder approved, copies of the resolution and the notice.

16. ...

17.—(1) In paragraphs (*bb*) and (*bc*) of section 192(1) of the Town and Country Planning Act 1971 the references to a unitary development plan shall include references to—

(*a*) a unitary development plan of which copies have been made available for inspection under paragraph 3(2) above;

(*b*) proposals for the alteration or replacement of a unitary development plan of which copies have been made available for inspection under that provision as applied by paragraph 10(2) above; and

(*c*) modifications proposed to be made by the local planning authority or the Secretary of State to any such plan or proposals as are mentioned in paragraph (*a*) or (*b*) above, being modifications of which notice has been given in accordance with regulations under Part I of this Schedule.

(2) No blight notice shall be served by virtue of this paragraph at any time after the copies of the plan or proposals made available for inspection have been withdrawn under paragraph 3(5) or 4(2) above but paragraph 4(4) above shall not invalidate any blight notice served by virtue of this paragraph before the withdrawal of copies of the plan or proposals.

(3) No blight notice shall be served by virtue of this paragraph after the relevant plan or alterations have come into force (whether in their original form or with modifications) or the local planning authority have decided to abandon, or the Secretary of State has decided to reject, the plan or alterations and notice of the decision has been given by advertisement.

(4) Section 68(6) of the Land Compensation Act 1973 (right to serve substituted counter-notice where the relevant plan or alterations come into force) shall apply also to a blight notice served by virtue of this paragraph.

(5) References in sub-paragraph (1) above to anything done under the provisions there mentioned include references to anything done under those provisions as they apply by virtue of paragraph 13(2) above.

(6) In relation to land falling within the said section 192(1) by virtue of this paragraph "the appropriate enactment" for the purposes of sections 192 to 207 of the said Act of 1971 shall be determined in accordance with subsection (2) of section 206 of that Act as if references in that subsection to the development plan were references to such plan, proposals or modifications as are mentioned in sub-paragraph (1)(*a*), (*b*) or (*c*) above. **[4]**

NOTES
Commencement: To be appointed.
Paras 6A, 10A: prospectively added by the Housing and Planning Act 1986, s 41(3), Sch 10, Part II, paras 2, 4, as from a day to be appointed.
Para 10: in sub-para (1) words in square brackets prospectively added by the Housing and Planning Act 1986, s 41(3), Sch 10, Part II, para 3, as from a day to be appointed.
Para 12: sub-para (7) prospectively substituted by new paras (7), (7A) by the Housing and Planning Act 1986, s 49, Sch 11, Part I, para 26, as from a day to be appointed.
Para 16: amends the Town and Country Planning Act 1972, ss 192(1), 194(2)(*d*), 242(1)(*a*), 244, 255(2)(*a*), 266(1)(*a*), 280(1)(*a*), 290(1).

PART II
TRANSITIONAL PROVISIONS

Continuation of structure plans, local plans and old development plans

18.—(1) Subject to paragraphs 19 and 20 below—

(*a*) the structure plan,
(*b*) any local plan; and
(*c*) any old development plan,

which at the abolition date is in force in the area of a local planning authority in Greater London or a metropolitan county (or in that and other areas) shall continue in force in respect of the area of that authority until a unitary development plan for that area becomes operative under Part I of this Schedule or, where parts of a unitary development plan become operative on different dates, until every part of it has become operative.

(2) A plan which continues in force by virtue of this paragraph shall, while it continues in force, be treated for the purposes of the Town and Country Planning Act 1971, any other enactment relating to town and country planning, the Land Compensation Act 1961 and the Highways Act 1980 as being, or being comprised in, the development plan in respect of the area in question.

(3) In this paragraph "structure plan", in relation to Greater London, means the Greater London Development Plan and "old development plan" means any plan which is in force in the area in question on the abolition date by virtue of Schedule 7 to the said Act of 1971.

Revocation of structure plan

19.—(1) Where under Part I of this Schedule the Secretary of State approves all or any of Part I of a unitary development plan he may by order—

(*a*) wholly or partly revoke a structure plan continued in force by paragraph 18 above, either in its application to the whole of the area of a local planning authority or in its application to part of that area; and
(*b*) make such consequential amendments to that plan as appear to him to be necessary or expedient.

(2) Before making an order under this paragraph the Secretary of State shall consult the local planning authority for the area to which the unitary development plan relates.

Local plans between abolition date and coming into force of Part I of this Schedule

20.—(1) This paragraph has effect with respect to the application of Part II of the said Act of 1971 in relation to the area of a local planning authority in Greater London or a metropolitan county between the abolition date and the coming into force in that area of Part I of this Schedule.

(2) The said Part II shall not apply except for sections 6 and 21(3), paragraph 2 of Schedule 4 and the provisions relating to the preparation, alteration, repeal or replacement of local plans by local planning authorities which are London borough councils or metropolitan district councils *and, in respect of those matters, those provisions shall not include—*

(a) sections 12(1A) and 14(5) to (7) and any other provision relating to those provisions; and
(b) section 15A.

[(2A) In respect of the matters referred to in sub-paragraph (2) the following provisions (which relate to county planning authorities) do not apply to metropolitan district councils, namely, sections 11A, 11B(4), 12(3) and (4)(c), 12A(2)(c), 15, 15A and 15B(2).]

(3) In section 15(1) and (2) the references to a local plan adopted by a local planning authority shall—

(a) in the case of a local planning authority which is a London borough council, include a local plan adopted by the Greater London Council and in force in respect of the area of that authority on the abolition date;
(b) in the case of a local planning authority which is a metropolitan district council, include a local plan adopted by the metropolitan county council and in force in the area of that authority on that date.

[(3) In section 15(1) and (2) (alteration of local plans), as applying in Greater London, the reference to a local plan adopted by a local planning authority includes, in the case of a London borough council, a local plan adopted by the Greater London Council and in force in respect of the area of that authority on the abolition date.

(3A) A metropolitan district council may at any time—

(a) make proposals for the preparation, alteration, repeal or replacement of a local plan adopted by them or adopted by the metropolitan county council and in force in the area of that authority on the abolition date;
(b) with the consent of the Secretary of State, make proposals for the alteration, repeal or replacement of a local plan approved by him.]

(4) On the coming into force in any area of Part I of this Schedule, any local plan or proposal for the alteration, repeal or replacement of a local plan which—

(a) has been prepared by a London borough council or metropolitan district council (or by such a council jointly with one or more other such councils); but
(b) has not been adopted or approved,

shall be treated as having been abandoned by that council or those councils.

Incorporation of current local plan in unitary development plan

21.—(1) A unitary development plan shall include any local plan which is in force in respect of the area in question at the time when the unitary development plan is prepared but subject to such alterations, if any, as may be specified in Part II of the unitary development plan; and a unitary development plan shall as respects any such local plan indicate the extent, if any, to which it is subject to alteration in accordance with Part II of the unitary development plan.

(2) This paragraph shall not be construed as enabling any objections to be made to any part of a unitary development plan which consists of provisions of a local plan that are not subject to alterations as aforesaid.

Publicity in connection with local plan

22. In determining the steps to be taken by a local planning authority or local planning authorities to secure the purposes of paragraph 3(1)(*a*) to (*c*) or paragraph 12(2)(*a*) to (*c*) above in relation to proposals made in respect of a unitary development plan, the authority or authorities may under those provisions, and the Secretary of State may under paragraph 3(4) above, take into account any steps taken by the authority or authorities to secure those purposes in relation to the same or similar or similar proposals made in respect of a local plan.

Pending proposals by GLC or metropolitan county council

23.—(1) Any proposals for the alteration, or for the repeal and replacement, of a structure plan which have been prepared by the Greater London Council or a metropolitan county council before the abolition date but have not been approved by the Secretary of State shall be treated as having been withdrawn by that council.

(2) Subject to sub-paragraph (3) below, any local plan or proposal for the alteration, repeal or replacement of a local plan which has been prepared by the Greater London Council or a metropolitan county council before the abolition date but has not been adopted or approved shall be treated as having been abandoned by that council.

(3) Where before the abolition date the Secretary of State has directed that any local plan or any such proposals as are mentioned in sub-paragraph (2) above shall not have effect unless approved by him, he shall continue to consider the plan or the proposals and give his decision thereon as if the plan or proposals had been prepared and submitted by the London borough or metropolitan district council whose area is affected by the plan or proposals or, where the areas of two or more such councils are affected, as if the plan or proposals had been a joint plan or joint proposals prepared by those councils.

(4) In the case of any such local plan or proposals as are mentioned in sub-paragraph (2) above the grounds on which the Secretary of State may give such a direction as is mentioned in sub-paragraph (3) above shall include the ground that he considers it desirable that the plan or proposals should, instead of being treated as abandoned, be dealt with by him in accordance with sub-paragraph (3) above. **[5]**

NOTES
Commencement: 1 April 1986.
Para 20: words in italics prospectively repealed and words in square brackets prospectively substituted or added by the Housing and Planning Act 1986, s 49, Sch 11, Part I, para 27.

HOUSING AND PLANNING ACT 1986
(c 63)

(The substantive provisions of this Act which are within the scope of this Handbook are set out below; those which contain amendments and repeals are set out in the Appendix.)

ARRANGEMENT OF SECTIONS

PART II
SIMPLIFIED PLANNING ZONES

England and Wales

An Act to make further provision with respect to housing, planning and local inquiries; to provide financial assistance for the regeneration of urban areas; and for connected purposes   [7 November 1986]

PART II

SIMPLIFIED PLANNING ZONES

England and Wales

25. Simplified planning zones in England and Wales

(1) ...

(2) After Schedule 8 to the Town and Country Planning Act 1971 insert as Schedule 8A the Schedule set out in Part I of Schedule 6 to this Act which contains provision with respect to the making and alteration of simplified planning zone schemes and other related matters.

(3) The Town and Country Planning Act 1971 also has effect subject to the consequential amendments specified in Part II of Schedule 6 to this Act.   **[6]**

NOTES
Commencement: To be appointed.
Sub-s (1): adds the Town and Country Planning Act 1971, ss 24A-E.

PART VI

MISCELLANEOUS PROVISIONS

England and Wales

40. Listed buildings and conservation areas

The enactments relating to listed buildings and conservation areas are amended in accordance with Part I of Schedule 9 with respect to the following matters—

    (a) the treatment of free-standing objects and structures within the curtilage of a listed building;
    (b) the scope of the exception for urgent works to a listed building;

(c) the grant of listed building consent subject to the subsequent approval of detail;

(d) applications for the variation or discharge of conditions attached to listed building consent;

(e) the extent of the exemption accorded to ecclesiastical buildings;

(f) dangerous structure orders in respect of listed buildings;

(g) the power of a local authority, the Secretary of State or the Historic Buildings and Monuments Commission for England to carry out urgent works for the preservation of a building;

(h) the control of demolition in a conservation area;

(i)   the form of an application for listed building consent; and

(j)   the powers of the Secretary of State with respect to applications for listed building consent.   [7]

NOTES
Commencement: 1 April 1987.
Commencement order. SI 1987 No 348.

41. Local plans and unitary development plans

(1) In Part II of the Town and Country Planning Act 1971 (development plans), the sections set out in Part I of Schedule 10 are substituted, except as to Greater London, for sections 10C to 15B (local plans), the main changes being—

(a) to provide for the co-ordination by county planning authorities, of the process of making, altering, repealing or replacing local plans;

(b) to provide a short procedure for altering a local plan where the issues are not of sufficient importance to warrant the full procedure; and

(c) to enable the Secretary of State to direct a local planning authority to reconsider proposals for making, altering, repealing or replacing a local plan; and

(d) to omit provisions which are spent in consequence of the approval of structure plans for the whole of England and Wales.

(2) The substituted sections have effect in relation to metropolitan counties until the coming into force of Part I of Schedule 1 to the Local Government Act 1985 (unitary development plans), but subject to the provisions of Part II of that Schedule.

(3) Part of Schedule 1 to the Local Government Act 1985 (unitary development plans) is amended in accordance with Part II of Schedule 10 to this Act, so as to—

(a) provide a short procedure for altering a unitary development plan where the issues are not of sufficient importance to warrant the full procedure; and

(b) enable the Secretary of State to direct a local planning authority to reconsider proposals for making, altering or replacing a unitary development plan.   [8]

NOTES
Commencement: To be appointed.

42. Recovery of Minister's costs in connection with inquiries

(1) The following provisions of this section apply where a Minister is authorised under or by virtue of any of the following statutory provisions to recover costs incurred by him in relation to an inquiry—

(*a*) section 250(4) of the Local Government Act 1972 (general provision as to costs of inquiries),

(*b*) section 96(5) of the Land Drainage Act 1976 (cost of inquiry under that Act),

(*c*) section 129(1)(*d*) of the Road Traffic Regulation Act 1984 (costs of inquiry under that Act),

(*d*) paragraph 9(2) of Schedule 22 to the Housing Act 1985 (costs of inquiry in connection with acquisition of land for clearance),

(*e*) any other statutory provision to which this section is applied by order of the Minister.

(2) What may be recovered by the Minister is the entire administrative cost of the inquiry, so that, in particular—

(*a*) there shall be treated as costs incurred in relation to the inquiry such reasonable sum as the Minister may determine in respect of the general staff costs and overheads of his department, and

(*b*) there shall be treated as costs incurred by the Minister holding the inquiry any costs incurred in relation to the inquiry by any other Minister or government department and, where appropriate, such reasonable sum as the Minister or department may determine in respect of general staff costs and overheads.

(3) The cost of an inquiry which does not take place may be recovered by the Minister from any person who would have been a party to the inquiry to the same extent, and in the same way, as the cost of an inquiry which does not take place.

(4) The Minister may by regulations prescribe for any description of inquiry a standard daily amount and where any inquiry of that description does take place what may be recovered is—

(*a*) the prescribed standard amount in respect of each day (or an appropriate proportion of that amount in respect of a part of a day) on which the inquiry sits or the person appointed to hold the inquiry is otherwise engaged on work connected with the inquiry,

(*b*) costs actually incurred in connection with the inquiry on travelling or subsistence allowances or the provision of accommodation or other facilities for the inquiry,

(*c*) any costs attributable to the appointment of an assessor to assist the person appointed to hold the inquiry, and

(*d*) any legal costs or disbursements incurred or made by or on behalf of the Minister in connection with the inquiry.

(5) An order or regulations under this section shall be made by statutory instrument which shall be subject to annulment in pursuance of a resolution of either House of Parliament.

(6) An order applying this section to a statutory provision may provide for the consequential repeal of so much of that provision, or any other provision, as restricts the sum recoverable in the inquiry or is otherwise inconsistent with the application of the provisions of this section. **[9]**

NOTES
Commencement: To be appointed.

43. Compulsory acquisition of land on behalf of parish or community councils

. . . **[10]**

NOTES
Commencement: To be appointed.
This section substitutes the Local Government Act 1972, s 125.

44. Overhead electricity lines

(1), (2) . . .

(3) Section 149(3)(*a*) of the Local Government, Planning and Land Act 1980 (power of Secretary of State to confer functions of local planning authority on urban development corporation) has effect in relation to-

section 21 of the Electricity (Supply) Act 1919, and
section 34 of the Electricity Act 1957, so far as applying to an application for consent or authorisation under section 10(*b*) of the Schedule to the Electric Lighting (Clauses) Act 1899,

as it has effect in relation to the provisions listed in Part I of Schedule 29 to the 1980 Act. **[11]**

NOTES
Commencement: 7 January 1987.
Commencement order: SI 1986 No 2262.
Sub-s (1): substitutes the Electricity (Supply) Act 1919, s 21.
Sub-s (2): adds the Electricity Act 1975, s 34(1A).

45. Control of advertisements: experimental areas

. . .   **[12]**

NOTES
Commencement: 7 January 1987.
Commencement order: SI 1986 No 2262.
This section revises the Town and Country Planning Act 1971, s 63.

46. Land adversely affecting amenity of neighbourhood

. . .   **[13]**

NOTES
Commencement: 7 January 1987.
Commencement order: SI 1986 No 2262.
This section substitutes the Town and Country Planning Act 1971, s 65.

47. Areas which may be designated urban development areas

. . .   **[14]**

NOTES
Commencement: 7 January 1987.
Commencement order: SI 1986 No 2262.
This section amends the Local Government, Planning and Land Act 1980, s 134.

48. Repeal of unnecessary enactments

(1) . . .

(2) The repeal does not affect the operation—
(*a*) of section 52 of the Requisitioned Land and War Works Act 1945 or paragraph 10 of the Schedule to the Requisitioned Land and War Works Act 1948 in relation to undertakings given before the repeal;

(*b*) of sections 250 to 252 of the 1971 Act in relation to land for which approval for the purposes of regulations under section 250 was sought before 1st April 1986. **[15]**

NOTES
Commencement: 7 January 1987.
Commencement order: SI 1986 No 2262.
Sub-s (1): repeals the Requisitioned Land and War Works Act 1945, s 52; the Requisitioned Land and War Works Act 1948, Schedule, para 10 and the Town and Country Planning Act 1971, ss 66-72, 250-252.

49. Minor and consequential amendments; repeals

(1) The Town and Country Planning Act 1971, and certain related enactments, are amended in accordance with Part I of Schedule 11 with respect to the following matters—

(*a*) the operation of the Use Classes Order on the subdivision of the planning unit;
(*b*) the provision which may be made by development orders;
(*c*) the construction of references to certain documents relating to access for the disabled;
(*d*) applications to vary or revoke conditions attached to planning permission;
(*e*) the procedure on appeals and applications disposed of without a local inquiry or hearing;
(*f*) purchase notices;
(*g*) local inquiries;
(*h*) the determination of appeals by inspectors; and
(*i*) daily penalties for offences;

and that Part also contains amendments consequential on the provisions of this Part.

(2) The enactments specified in Part III of Schedule 12 are repealed to the extent specified. **[16]**

NOTES
Commencement: 7 November 1986 (certain purposes); 7 January 1987 (certain purposes); 2 March 1987 (certain purposes); 1 April 1987 (certain purposes); to be appointed (remaining purposes).
Commencement orders: SI 1986 No 2262; SI 1987 No 304; SI 1987 No 348.

SCHEDULES
SCHEDULE 6

Section 25(2)

SIMPLIFIED PLANNING ZONES: FURTHER PROVISIONS

PART I
SCHEDULE TO BE INSERTED IN THE TOWN AND COUNTRY PLANNING ACT 1971

. . .
[17]

NOTES
Commencement: To be appointed.
This Part is added as the Town and Country Planning Act 1971, Sch 8A.

Section 25(3)

SIMPLIFIED PLANNING ZONES: FURTHER PROVISIONS

PART II

CONSEQUENTIAL AMENDMENTS - ENGLAND AND WALES

...   **[18]**

NOTES
    Commencement: To be appointed.
    This Part contains amendments only.

SCHEDULE 9

Section 40

LISTED BUILDINGS AND CONSERVATION AREAS

PART I

ENGLAND AND WALES

1. (1) ...

    (2) Where by virtue of this paragraph an object or structure ceases to be treated as
part of a listed building—

    (*a*) liabilities incurred before the commencement of this paragraph by reason of
        the object or structure being so treated cease to have effect, and
    (*b*) a condition attached to a listed building consent ceases to have effect if, or to
        the extent that, it could not have been attached if this paragraph had been in
        force;

except for the purposes of criminal proceedings begun before the commencement of this
paragraph.

    2.–12. ...   **[19]**

NOTES
    Commencement: 1 April 1987.
    Commencement order: SI 1987 No 348.
    Words omitted contain amendments only.

SCHEDULE 10

Section 41(1)

LOCAL PLANS AND UNITARY DEVELOPMENT PLANS

PART I

SECTIONS 11 TO 15B OF THE TOWN AND COUNTRY PLANNING ACT 1971 (C 78), AS
SUBSTITUTED

...   **[20]**

NOTES
    Commencement: To be appointed.
    This Part is substituted as the Town and Country Planning Act 1971, ss 11-15B in place of
previous ss 10C-15B.

Section 41(3)

LOCAL PLANS AND UNITARY DEVELOPMENT PLANS

PART II

UNITARY DEVELOPMENT PLANS

...   **[21]**

NOTES
Commencement: To be appointed.
This Part amends the Local Government Act 1985, Sch 1, Part I.

SCHEDULE 11

Section 49

PLANNING—MINOR AND CONSEQUENTIAL AMENDMENTS

PART I

ENGLAND AND WALES

[22]

NOTES
Commencement: 7 January 1987 (in part); to be appointed (remainder).
Commencement order: SI 1986 No 2262.
This Part contains amendments only.

TOWN AND COUNTRY PLANNING ACT 1971
(c 78)

ARRANGEMENT OF SECTIONS

PART I

ADMINISTRATION

PART IV

ADDITIONAL CONTROL IN SPECIAL CASES

Buildings of special architectural or historic interest

Trees

Advertisements

Waste land

Industrial development

Office development

PART V

ENFORCEMENT OF CONTROL UNDER PARTS III AND IV

Development requiring planning permission

PART VI

ACQUISITION AND APPROPRIATION OF LAND AND RELATED PROVISIONS

Acquisition and appropriation of land

PART VII

COMPENSATION FOR PLANNING DECISIONS RESTRICTING NEW DEVELOPMENT

PART VIII

COMPENSATION FOR OTHER PLANNING RESTRICTIONS

Revocation or modification of planning permission

Other restrictions

Supplementary provisions

PART IX

PROVISIONS ENABLING OWNER TO REQUIRE PURCHASE OF HIS INTEREST

Interests affected by planning decisions or orders

An Act to consolidate certain enactments relating to town and country planning in England and Wales with amendments to give effect to recommendations of the Law Commission　　　　　　　　　　　　　　　　[28 October 1971]

PART I

ADMINISTRATION

1. Local planning authorities

[(1) Subject to the provisions of this section—

(*a*) in a non-metropolitan county, the council of the county is the county planning authority for the county and the council of a district is the district planning authority for the district;

(*b*) the council of a metropolitan district is the local planning authority for the district; and

(*c*) the council of a London borough is the local planning authority for the borough.]

(2) If it appears to the Secretary of State that it is expedient that a joint board should be established as the county planning authority for the areas or parts of the areas of any two or more county councils or as the district planning authority for the areas or parts of the areas of any two or more district councils, he may by order constitute those areas or parts as a united district for the purposes of this Act, and constitute a joint board (in this Act referred to as a "joint planning board") as the county planning authority or the district planning authority, as the case may be, for that united district:

Provided that the Secretary of State shall not make such an order except after holding a local inquiry unless all the councils concerned have consented to the making of the order.

(2A) References in this Act to a local planning authority shall, except as respects [a metropolitan county] Greater London and the National Parks, be construed as references to a county planning authority and a district planning authority, and the foregoing provision shall have effect subject to section 183 of and Part I of Schedule 16 to the Local Government Act 1972.]

[(2B) In this Act "mineral planning authority" means—

(*a*) in respect of a site in a non-metropolitan county, the county planning authority; and

(*b*) in respect of a site in a metropolitan district or London borough, the local planning authority.]

(3) The provisions of Schedule 1 to this Act shall have effect with respect to the constitution of joint planning boards.

(4) Where a joint planning board is constituted for a united district, references in this Act to the area of a local planning authority—

(*a*) in relation to the board, shall be construed as references to that district; and

(*b*) in relation to any local planning authority being the council of a county or [district] of which part (but not the whole) is included in [the united district], shall be construed as references to so much of the county or [district] as is not so included.

(5) Regulations under this Act may make such provision consequential upon or supplementary to the provisions of this section as appears to the Secretary of State to be necessary or expedient.

(6) The preceding provisions of this section, and the provisions of Schedule 1 to this Act, shall have effect subject to the provisions of [Part I of Schedule 17 to the Local Government Act 1972].   **[23]**

NOTES

Commencement: 1 April 1986 (sub-ss (1), (2B)); 1 April 1974 (sub-ss (2), (2A)); 1 April 1972 (remainder).

This section derived from the Town and Country Planning Act 1962, s 2.

Sub-s (1): substituted by the Local Government Act 1985, s 3(1).

Sub-s (2): substituted by the Local Government Act 1972, s 182(1).

Sub-s (2A): new sub-s (2A) substituted by the Housing and Planning Act 1986, s 49(1), Sch 11, Part I, para 14. See Appendix.

Sub-s (2A): substituted by the Local Government Act 1972, s 182(1); amended by the Local Government Act 1985, s 3(2).

Sub-s (2B): added by the Town and Country Planning (Minerals) Act 1981, s 2(2); substituted by the Local Government Act 1985, s 3(3).

Sub-ss (4), (6): amended by the Local Government Act 1972, s 182(3), Sch 16, Part I, para 43.

(New ss 1A–1B prospectively inserted by the Housing and Planning Act 1986, s 30. See Appendix.)

PART II

DEVELOPMENT PLANS

Survey and Structure Plan

6. Survey of planning areas

(1) It shall be the duty of the local planning authority to institute a survey of their area, in so far as they have not already done so, examining the matters which may be expected to affect the development of that area or the planning of its development and in any event to keep all such matters under review.

(2) Notwithstanding that the local planning authority have carried out their duty under subsection (1) of this section, the authority may, if they think fit, . . . institute a fresh survey of their area examining the matters mentioned in that subsection.

(3) Without prejudice to the generality of the preceding provisions of this section, the matters to be examined and kept under review thereunder shall include the following, that is to say—

   (a) the principal physical and economic characteristics of the area of the authority (including the principal purposes for which land is used) and, so far as they may be expected to affect that area, of any neighbouring areas;

   (b) the size, composition and distribution of the population of that area (whether resident or otherwise);

   (c) without prejudice to paragraph (a) of this subsection, the communications, transport system and traffic of that area and, so far as they may be expected to affect that area, of any neighbouring areas;

   (d) any considerations not mentioned in any of the preceding paragraphs which may be expected to affect any matters so mentioned;

   (e) such other matters as may be prescribed or as the Secretary of State may in a particular case direct;

   (f) any changes already projected in any of the matters mentioned in any of the preceding paragraphs and the effect which those changes are likely to have on the development of that area or the planning of such development.

(4) A local planning authority shall, for the purpose of discharging their functions under this section of examining and keeping under review any matters relating to the area of another such authority, consult with that other authority about those matters.

(5) Subsection (1) of this section shall, as respects any period during which this section is in operation in part only of the area of a local planning authority, be construed as requiring a local planning authority to institute a survey of that part of that area and to keep under review matters affecting only that part of that area; and subsection (2) of this section shall, whether or not this section is in operation in the whole of such an area, have effect as if the power thereby conferred included power for a local planning authority to institute . . . a fresh

survey of part only of their area; and references in subsection (3) of this section
to the area of a local planning authority or any neighbouring areas shall be
construed accordingly.   **[24]**

NOTES
Commencement: 28 October 1971–1 August 1974.
Words omitted repealed by the Local Government, Planning and Land Act 1980, s 194, Sch 34.

7. Preparation of structure plans

[(1) The local planning authority shall, within such period from the commencement of this section within their area as the Secretary of State may direct,
prepare and submit to the Secretary of State for his approval a structure plan
for their area complying with the provisions of subsection (1A) of this section.

(1A) The structure plan for any area shall be a written statement—

  (a) formulating the local planning authority's policy and general proposals
       in respect of the development and other use of land in that area
       (including measures for the improvement of the physical environment
       and the management of traffic); and
  (b) containing such other matters as may be prescribed or as the Secretary
       of State may in any particular case direct.]

(4) In formulating their policy and general proposals under [subsection
(1A)(a)] of this section, the local planning authority shall secure that the policy
and proposals are justified by the results of their survey under section 6 of this
Act and by any other information which they may obtain and shall have
regard—

  (a) to current policies with respect to the economic planning and
       development of the region as a whole;
  (b) to the resources likely to be available for the carrying out of the
       proposals of the structure plan; and
  (c) to such other matters as the Secretary of State may direct them to take
       into account.

(5) . . .

[(6) The written statement shall be illustrated by such diagram or diagrams
as may be prescribed, which shall be treated as forming part of the plan.]

[(6A) The structure plan shall be accompanied by an explanatory
memorandum summarising the reasons which in the opinion of the local
planning authority justify each and every policy and general proposal formulated
in the plan, stating the relationship thereof to expected development and other
use of land in neighbouring areas where relevant and containing such other
matters as may be prescribed; and the explanatory memorandum may contain
such illustrative material as the local planning authority think appropriate.]

(7) At any time before the Secretary of State has under section 9 of this Act
approved a structure plan with respect to the whole of the area of a local
planning authority, the authority may with his consent, and shall, if so directed
by him, prepare and submit to him for his approval a structure plan relating to
part of that area; and where the Secretary of State has given a consent or
direction for the preparation of a structure plan for part of such an area,
references in this Part of this Act to such an area shall, in relation to a structure
plan, be construed as including references to part of that area.   **[25]**

NOTES

Commencement: 28 October 1971–1 August 1974.

Sub-ss (1), (1A): substituted for sub-ss (1)-(3) by the Local Government, Planning and Land Act 1980, s 89, Sch 14, para 2.

Sub-s (4): amended by the Local Government (Miscellaneous Provisions) act 1982, s 47, Sch 6, para 7.

Sub-s (5): repealed by the Local Government, Planning and Land Act 1980, ss 89, 194, Sch 14, para 2, Sch 34, Part X.

Sub-s (6): substituted by the Local Government, Planning and Land Act 1980, s 89, Sch 14, para 2.

Sub-s (6A): added by the Local Government, Planning and Land Act 1980, s 89, Sch 14, para 2.

8. Publicity in connection with preparation of structure plans

(1) When preparing a structure plan for their area and before finally determining its content for submission to the Secretary of State, the local planning authority shall take such steps as will in their opinion secure—

[(a) that adequate publicity is given in their area to the matters which they propose to include in the plan and to the proposed content of the explanatory memorandum relating to each such matter;]

(b) that persons who may be expected to desire an opportunity of making representations to the authority with respect to those matters are made aware that they are entitled to an opportunity of doing so; and

(c) that such persons are given an adequate opportunity of making such representations;

and the authority shall consider any representations made to them within the prescribed period.

(2) Not later than the submission of a structure plan to the Secretary of State, the local planning authority shall make copies of the plan as submitted to the Secretary of State [and of the explanatory memorandum] available for inspection at their office and at such other places as may be prescribed; and each copy shall be accompanied by a statement of the time within which objections to the plan may be made to the Secretary of State.

(3) A structure plan submitted by the local planning authority to the Secretary of State for his approval shall be accompanied by a statement containing such particulars, if any, as may be prescribed—

(a) of the steps which the authority have taken to comply with subsection (1) of this section; and

(b) of the authority's consultations with, and consideration of the views of, other persons with respect to those matters.

(4) If after considering the statement submitted with, and the matters included in, the structure plan and any other information provided by the local planning authority, the Secretary of State is satisfied that the purposes of paragraphs (a) to (c) of subsection (1) of this section have been adequately achieved by the steps taken by the authority in compliance with that subsection, he shall proceed to consider whether to approve the structure plan; and if he is not so satisfied, he shall return the plan to the authority and direct them—

(a) to take such further action as he may specify in order better to achieve those purposes; and

(b) after doing so, to resubmit the plan with such modifications, if any, as they then consider appropriate and, if so required by the direction, to do so within a specified period.

(5) Where the Secretary of State returns the structure plan to the local planning authority under subsection (4) of this section, he shall inform the

authority of his reasons for doing so and, if any person has made to him an objection to the plan, shall also inform that person that he has returned the plan.

(6) A local planning authority who are given directions by the Secretary of State under subsection (4) of this section shall forthwith withdraw the copies of the plan made available for inspection as required by subsection (2) of this section.

(7) Subsections (2) to (6) of this section shall apply, with the necessary modifications, in relation to a structure plan resubmitted to the Secretary of State in accordance with directions given by him under subsection (4) as they apply in relation to the plan as originally submitted. **[26]**

NOTES
Commencement: 28 October 1971–1 August 1974.
Amended by the Local Government, Planning and Land Act 1980, s 89, Sch 14.

9. Approval or rejection of structure plan by Secretary of State

(1) The Secretary of State may, after considering a structure plan submitted (or resubmitted) to him, either approve it (in whole or in part and with or without modifications or reservations) or reject it.

(2) In considering any such plan the Secretary of State may take into account any matters which he thinks are relevant, whether or not they were taken into account in the plan as submitted to him.

[(3) Where on taking any such plan into consideration the Secretary of State does not determine then to reject it, he shall, before determining whether or not to approve it—

> (a) consider any objections to the plan, so far as they are made in accordance with regulations under this Part of this Act, and
> (b) cause a person or persons appointed by him for the purpose to hold an examination in public of such matters affecting his consideration of the plan as he considers ought to be so examined.

(4) The Secretary of State may after consultation with the Lord Chancellor make regulations with respect to the procedure to be followed at any examination under subsection (3) of this section.

[(4A) Subsection (4) of this section shall come into operation on a day appointed by an order made by the Secretary of State.]

(5) The Secretary of State shall not be required to secure to any local planning authority or other person a right to be heard at any examination under the said subsection (3), and the bodies and persons who may take part therein shall be such only as he may, whether before or during the course of the examination, in his discretion invite to do so:

Provided that the person or persons holding the examination shall have power, exercisable either before or during the course of the examination, to invite additional bodies or persons to take part therein if it appears to him or them desirable to do so.

(6) An examination under subsection (3)(b) of this section shall constitute a statutory inquiry for the purposes of section 1(1)(c) of the Tribunals and Inquiries Act 1971, but shall not constitute such an inquiry for any other purpose of that Act.

(7) On considering a structure plan the Secretary of State may consult with, or consider the views of, any local planning authority or other person, but shall not be under any obligation to do so.

(8) On exercising his powers under subsection (1) of this section in relation to any structure plan, the Secretary of State shall give such statement as he considers appropriate of the reasons governing his decision.]   **[27]**

NOTES
Commencement: To be appointed (sub-s (4)); 28 October 1971–1 August 1974 (remainder).
First amendment made by the Town and Country Planning (Amendment) Act 1972, s 3(1); second amendment made by the Local Government, Planning and Land Act 1980, s 89, Sch 14.

10. Alteration of structure plans

[(1) At any time after the approval of a structure plan for their area or part of their area a local planning authority may submit to the Secretary of State and shall, if so directed by the Secretary of State, submit to him within a period specified in the direction, proposals for such alterations to that plan as appear to them to be expedient or as the Secretary of State may direct, as the case may be, and any such proposals may relate to the whole or part of the area to which the plan relates.

(2) At any time after the approval of the structure plan for their area or any part of their area a local planning authority may submit proposals for its repeal and replacement to the Secretary of State.

(3) An authority submitting a proposal under subsection (2) of this section for the repeal and replacement of a structure plan shall at the same time submit to the Secretary of State the structure plan with which they propose that it shall be replaced.

(4) Proposals under subsection (1) or (2) of this section shall be accompanied by an explanatory memorandum summarising—

    (a) in the case of proposals under subsection (1) of this section, the reasons which in the opinion of the local planning authority justify the alterations which they are proposing; and

    (b) in the case of proposals under subsection (2) of this section, the reasons which in their opinion justify the repeal and replacement of the structure plan.

(5) The explanatory memorandum shall also state the relationship of the proposals to general proposals for the development and other use of land in neighbouring areas which may be expected to affect the area to which the proposals relate.

(6) The explanatory memorandum—

    (a) shall also contain any information on which the proposals are based; and

    (b) may contain such illustrative material as the local planning authority think appropriate.

(7) Subject to subsection (8) of this section, sections 8 and 9 of this Act [and paragraph 8 of Schedule 16 to the Local Government Act 1972] shall apply, with any necessary modifications, in relation to the proposals as they apply in relation to a structure plan.

(8) Section 9(3)(b) of this Act shall not apply in any case where it appears to the Secretary of State, on consideration of proposals for the alteration or repeal

and replacement of a structure plan, that no matters which require an examination in public arise—

(*a*) from the proposals; or

(*b*) from any structure plan submitted with them under subsection (3) of this section.]   **[28]**

NOTES

Commencement: 13 November 1980.

Substituted by the Local Government, Planning and Land Act 1980, s 89, Sch 14.

Sub-s (7): amended by the Local Government (Miscellaneous Provisions) Act 1982, s 47, Sch 6, para 7.

10B. Withdrawal of plans, and effect of steps taken in connection with plans withdrawn or not submitted

[(1) A structure plan submitted to the Secretary of State for his approval may be withdrawn by the local planning authority, or the local planning authorities or any of them, submitting it by a notice in that behalf given to the Secretary of State at any time before he has approved it, and shall in that event be treated as never having been submitted.

(2) On the withdrawal of a structure plan, the authority or authorities preparing it shall also withdraw the copies of the plan which they have made available for inspection in accordance with section 8(2) of this Act, and shall give notice that the plan has been withdrawn to every person who has made an objection thereto.

(3) In determining the steps to be taken by them to secure the purposes of paragraphs (*a*) to (*c*) of section 8(1) of this Act, the local planning authority or authorities preparing a structure plan for any area may take into account any steps taken to secure those purposes in connection with any other structure plan, being one which either was not submitted to the Secretary of State for his approval or was so submitted and then withdrawn; and the authority or authorities submitting for approval by the Secretary of State a plan in the case of which they have taken any steps into account by virtue of this subsection shall give particulars of those steps in their statement to him under subsection (3) of the said section 8, and the Secretary of State may treat the steps as having been taken by them in connection with that plan in determining under subsection (4) of that section whether he is satisfied that the said purposes have been adequately achieved in relation thereto.]   **[29]**

NOTES

Commencement: 21 August 1972–1 August 1974.

Added by the Town and Country Planning (Amendment) Act 1972, s 2.

10C. Development plan schemes

[(1) The functions of a local planning authority of preparing local plans under section 11 of this Act shall, subject to the following provisions of this section, be exercisable by the district planning authority.

(2) . . . it shall be the duty of the county planning authority in consultation with the district planning authorities to make, and thereafter to keep under review and amend, if they think fit, a scheme (to be known as a development plan scheme) for the preparation of local plans for those areas in the county in which sections 11 to 15 of this Act are in force, except any part of the county included in a National Park, and—

(*a*) the scheme shall designate the local planning authority or authorities (whether county or district) by whom local plans are to be prepared for any such area and provide for the exercise of all functions of a local planning authority under those sections in relation to any such plan exclusively by the authority designated in relation to that plan; and

(*b*) references in those sections to a local planning authority shall be construed accordingly.

(3) A development plan scheme may include such incidental, consequential, transitional or supplementary provision as may appear to the county planning authority to be necessary or proper for the purposes or in consequence of the provisions of the scheme and for giving full effect thereto, and, without prejudice to the foregoing provision, shall—

(*a*) specify the title and nature of each local plan for the area in question and the part or parts of the area to which it is to apply and give an indication of its scope;

(*b*) set out a programme for the preparation of the several local plans for that area; and

(*c*) where appropriate indicate the relationship between the several local plans for that area, specifying those which should be prepared concurrently with the structure plan for that area.

(4) As soon as practicable after making or amending a development plan scheme the county planning authority shall send a copy of the scheme or the scheme as amended, as the case may be, to the Secretary of State.

(5) A structure plan prepared by a county planning authority may provide, to the extent that provision to the contrary is not made by a development plan scheme, for the preparation of local plans exclusively by the county planning authority and, where it so provides, shall also provide for the exercise exclusively by that authority of all other functions of a local planning authority under sections 11 to 15 of this Act, and any provision included in a structure plan by virtue of this subsection shall be treated for the purposes of the other provisions of this section as if it were contained in a development plan scheme.

[(6) Where a district planning authority make representations to the Secretary of State that they are dissatisfied with a development plan scheme, the Secretary of State may amend the scheme, and any amendment so made shall have effect as if made by the county planning authority.]]   **[30]**

NOTES

Commencement: 1 August 1974 (except as to Greater London).

Added by the Local Government Act 1972, s 183(2); amended by the Local Government, Planning and Land Act 1980, ss 89, 194, Schs 14, 34.

This section and ss 11–15B prospectively substituted by new ss 11–15B except as to Greater London and, in relation to metropolitan counties, subject to the Housing and Planning Act 1986, s 41(2), by s 41(1) of, and Sch 10, Part I to, that Act. See Appendix.

Local plans

11. Preparation of local plans

[(1) Where a county planning authority are in course of preparing a structure plan for their area, or have prepared for their area a structure plan which has not been approved or rejected by the Secretary of State, the local planning authority to whom it falls to prepare a local plan for any part of that area may, if they think it desirable, prepare a local plan for all or any of that part of the area.

(2) Where a structure plan for the area of a county planning authority has

been approved by the Secretary of State, the local planning authority to whom it falls to prepare a local plan for any part of that area shall as soon as practicable consider, and thereafter keep under review, the desirability of preparing and, if they consider it desirable and they have not already done so, shall prepare one or more local plans for all or any of that part of the area.]

(3) A local plan shall consist of a map and a written statement and shall—

(*a*) formulate in such detail as the [local planning authority] authority think appropriate the authority's proposals for the development and other use of land in that part of their area or for any description of development or other use of such land (including in either case such measures as the authority think fit for the improvement of the physical environment and the management of traffic); and

(*b*) contain such matters as may be prescribed . . . .

(4) Different local plans may be prepared for different purposes for the same part of any area.

[(4A) Without prejudice to subsections (1), (2) and (4) of this section, the local planning authority may prepare a local plan for any part of their area (in this section referred to as an "action area") which they have selected for the commencement during a prescribed period of comprehensive treatment, by development, redevelopment or improvement of the whole or part of the area selected, or partly by one and partly by another method.

(4B) A local plan prepared for an action area under subsection (4A) of this section shall indicate the nature of the treatment selected for the action area.]

(5) A local plan for any area shall contain, or be accompanied by, such diagrams, illustrations and descriptive matter as the local planning authority think appropriate for the purpose of explaining or illustrating the proposals in the plan, or as may be prescribed, . . . ; and any such diagrams, illustrations and descriptive matter shall be treated as forming part of the plan.

(6) . . .

(7) Without prejudice to the preceding provisions of this section, the local planning authority shall, if the Secretary of State gives them a direction in that behalf with respect to a part of an area for which a structure plan has been, or is in course of being, prepared, as soon as practicable prepare for that part a local plan of such nature as may be specified in the direction.

(8) Directions under subsection (7) of this section may be given by the Secretary of State either before or after he approves the structure plan; but no such directions shall require a local planning authority to take any steps to comply therewith until the structure plan has been approved by him.

(9) In formulating their proposals in a local plan the local planning authority shall secure that the proposals conform generally to the structure plan as it stands for the time being (whether or not it has been approved by the Secretary of State) and shall have regard to any information and any other considerations which appear to them to be relevant, or which may be prescribed, or which the Secretary of State may in any particular case direct them to take into account.

[(9A) For the purpose of discharging their functions under this section a district planning authority may, in so far as it appears to them necessary to do so having regard to the survey made by the county planning authority under section 6 of this Act, examine the matters mentioned in subsections (1) and (3) of that section so far as relevant to their area.]

(10) Before giving a direction under . . . this section to a local planning authority, the Secretary of State shall consult the authority with respect to the proposed direction.

(11) Where a local planning authority are required by this section to prepare a local plan, they shall take steps for the adoption of the plan.

[(12) . . .]   **[31]**

NOTES
Commencement: 28 October 1971–1 August 1974.
Sub-ss (1), (2): substituted, except as to Greater London, by the Local Government Act 1972, s 182, Sch 16.
Sub-s (3): amended, except as to Greater London, by the Local Government Act 1972, s 182, Sch 16; words omitted repealed by the Local Government, Planning and Land Act 1980, s 194, Sch 34.
Sub-ss (4A), (4B): added by the Local Government, Planning and Land Act 1980, s 89, Sch 14.
Sub-s (5): words omitted repealed by the Local Government, Planning and Land Act 1980, s 194, Sch 34.
Sub-s (6): repealed by the Local Government, Planning and Land Act 1980, s 89, Sch 14.
Sub-s (9A): added, except as to Greater London, by the Local Government Act 1972, s 182, Sch 16.
Sub-s (10): words omitted repealed by the Local Government, Planning and Land Act 1980, s 194, Sch 34.
Sub-s (12): repealed by the Local Government Act 1972, s 272, Sch 30.
Prospectively substituted as noted to s 10C above.

12. Publicity in connection with preparation of local plans

(1) A local planning authority who propose to prepare a local plan shall take such steps as will in their opinion secure—

  [(a) that adequate publicity is given in the area in question . . . to the matters proposed to be included in the plan;]
  (b) that persons who may be expected to desire an opportunity of making representations to the authority with respect to those matters are made aware that they are entitled to an opportunity of doing so; and
  (c) that such persons are given an adequate opportunity of making such representations;

and the authority shall consider any representations made to them within the prescribed period.

  [(1A) A county or district planning authority to whom it falls to prepare a local plan for any part of their area shall—

  (a) consult the district planning authority or the county planning authority, as the case may be, with respect to the contents of the plan;
  (b) afford the latter authority a reasonable opportunity to express their views;
  (c) take those views into consideration.]

  [(2) When a local planning authority have prepared a local plan and [subject to section 15A of this Act] the Secretary of State has approved the structure plan so far as it applies to the area of that local plan and, in a case where the local planning authority are required to obtain a certificate under section 14 of this Act, they have obtained that certificate, they shall before adopting the local plan or submitting it for approval under that section make copies of it available for inspection at their office . . . and send a copy to the Secretary of State and to the district or county planning authority, as the case may require; and each copy made available for inspection shall be accompanied by a statement of the time within which objections to the local plan may be made to the local planning authority.]

(3) A copy of a local plan sent to the Secretary of State under subsection (2) of this section shall be accompanied by a statement . . .

(a) of the steps which the authority have taken to comply with subsection (1) of this section; and

(b) of the authority's consultations with, and their consideration of the views of, other persons.

(4) If, on considering the statement submitted with, and the matters included in, the local plan and any other information provided by the local planning authority, the Secretary of State is not satisfied that the purposes of paragraphs (a) to (c) of subsection (1) of this section have been adequately achieved by the steps taken by the authority in compliance with that subsection, he may, within twenty-one days of the receipt of the statement, direct the authority not to take any further steps for the adoption of the plan without taking such further action as he may specify in order better to achieve those purposes and satisfying him that they have done so.

(5) A local planning authority who are given directions by the Secretary of State under subsection (4) of this section shall—

(a) forthwith withdraw the copies of the local plan made available for inspection as required by subsection (2) of this section; and

(b) notify any person by whom objections to the local plan have been made to the authority that the Secretary of State has given such directions as aforesaid.   **[32]**

NOTES
Commencement: 28 October 1971–1 August 1974.
Sub-s (1): para (a) substituted, except as to Greater London, by the Local Government Act 1972, s182; Sch 16; words omitted repealed by the Local Government, Planning and Land Act 1980, s 194, Sch 34.
Sub-s (1A): added, except as to Greater London, by the Local Government Act 1972, s 182, Sch 16.
Sub-s (2): substituted, except as to Greater London, by the Local Government Act 1972, s 182, Sch 16; amendment made and words omitted repealed by the Local Government, Planning and Land Act 1980, ss 88(2), 194, Sch 34.
Sub-s (3): words omitted repealed by the Local Government, Planning and Land Act 1980, s 194, Sch 34.
Prospectively substituted as noted to s 10C above.

13. Inquiries, etc with respect to local plans

(1) For the purpose of considering objections made to a local plan the local planning authority may, and shall in the case of objections so made in accordance with regulations under this Part of this Act, cause a local inquiry or other hearing to be held by a person appointed by the Secretary of State or, in such cases as may be prescribed by regulations under this Part of this Act, by the authority themselves, and—

(a) subsections (2) and (3) of section 290 of the Local Government Act 1933 (power to summon and examine witnesses) shall apply to an inquiry held under this section as they apply to an inquiry held under that section;

(b) the Tribunals and Inquiries Act 1971 shall apply to a local inquiry or other hearing held under this section as it applies to a statutory inquiry held by the Secretary of State, but as if in section 12(1) of that Act (statement of reasons for decisions) the reference to any decision taken by the Secretary of State were a reference to a decision taken by a local authority.

(2) Regulations made for the purposes of subsection (1) of this section may—

(*a*) make provision with respect to the appointment and qualifications for appointment of persons to hold a local inquiry or other hearing under that subsection, including provision enabling the Secretary of State to direct a local planning authority to appoint a particular person, or one of a specified list or class of persons;

(*b*) make provision with respect to the remuneration and allowances of a person appointed for the said purpose.

[(3) The requirement for a local inquiry or other hearing to be held shall not apply if all persons who have made an objection have indicated in writing that they do not wish to appear.] **[33]**

NOTES
Commencement: 28 October 1971–1 August 1974.
Amended by the Local Government, Planning and Land Act 1980, s 89, Sch 14.
Prospectively substituted as noted to s 10C above.

14. Adoption and approval of local plans

[(1) After the expiry of the period afforded for making objections to a local plan or, if such objections have been duly made during that period, after considering the objections so made, the local planning authority may, subject to section 12 of this Act and subsections (1A), (2) and (3) of this section, by resolution adopt the plan either as originally prepared or as modified so as to take account—

(*a*) of the objections so made;

(*b*) of any other objections made to the plan;

(*c*) of any other considerations which appear to the authority to be material.

(1A) Where—

(*a*) an objection to the plan has been made by the Minister of Agriculture, Fisheries and Food (in this section referred to as "the Minister"); and

(*b*) the local planning authority do not propose to modify the plan to take account of that objection,

the authority—

(i) shall send the Secretary of State particulars of the Minister's objection, together with a statement of their reasons for not modifying the plan to take account of it; and

(ii) shall not adopt the plan unless the Secretary of State authorises them to do so.]

(2) [Subject to section 15A of this Act, the] local planning authority shall not adopt a local plan unless it conforms [and, in the case of a local plan prepared by a district planning authority, a certificate is issued under subsection (5) or (7) of this section that it conforms] generally to the structure plan as approved by the Secretary of State.

(3) After copies of a local plan have been sent to the Secretary of State and before the plan has been adopted by the local planning authority, the Secretary of State may direct that the plan shall not have effect unless approved by him.

[(3A) Subject to subsection (3B) of this section, where particulars of an objection to a local plan made by the Minister have been sent to the Secretary of State under subsection (1A) of this section, it shall be the duty of the Secretary of State to direct that the plan shall not have effect unless approved by him.

(3B) The Secretary of State need not give a direction under subsection (3A) of this section if he is satisfied that the Minister no longer objects to the plan.]

[(4) Where the Secretary of State gives a direction under subsection (3) [or (3A)] of this section, the local planning authority shall submit the plan accordingly to him for his approval, and

    (*a*) the Secretary of State may, after considering the plan, either approve it (in whole or in part and with or without modifications or reservations) or reject it;

    (*b*) in considering the plan, the Secretary of State may take into account any matters which he thinks are relevant, whether or not they were taken into account in the plan as submitted to him;

    (*c*) subject to paragraph (*d*) of this subsection, where on taking the plan into consideration the Secretary of State does not determine then to reject it, he shall, before determining whether or not to approve it—

        (i) consider any objections to the plan, so far as they are made in accordance with regulations under this Part of this Act;

        (ii) afford to any persons whose objections so made are not withdrawn an opportunity of appearing before, and being heard by, a person appointed by him for the purpose; and

        (iii) if a local inquiry or other hearing is held, also afford the like opportunity to the authority and such other persons as he thinks fit;

    (*d*) before deciding whether or not to approve the plan the Secretary of State shall not be obliged to consider any objections thereto if objections thereto have been considered by the authority, or to cause an inquiry or other hearing to be held into [any objections thereto] if any such inquiry or hearing has already been held at the instance of the authority;

    (*e*) without prejudice to paragraph (*c*) of this subsection, on considering the plan the Secretary of State may consult with, or consider the views of, any local planning authority or other persons, but shall not be under an obligation to consult with, or consider the views of, any other authority or persons or, except as provided by that paragraph, to afford an opportunity for the making of any objections or other representations, or to cause any local inquiry or other hearing to be held; and

    (*f*) after the giving of the direction the authority shall have no further power or duty to hold a local inquiry or other hearing under section 13 of this Act in connection with the plan.]

[(5) Where a district planning authority have prepared a local plan for any part of their area the structure plan for which has been approved by the Secretary of State, they shall request the county planning authority to certify that the local plan conforms generally to the structure plan and, subject to subsection (6) below, the county planning authority shall, within the period of one month from their receipt of the request or such longer period as may be agreed between them and the district planning authority, consider the matter and, if satisfied that the local plan does so conform, issue a certificate to that effect; and if it appears to the county planning authority that the local plan does not so conform in any respect, they shall, during or as soon as practicable after the end of that period, refer the question whether it so conforms in that respect to the Secretary of State to be determined by him.

(6) The Secretary of State may in any case by direction to a county planning authority reserve for his own determination the question whether a local plan conforms generally to a structure plan.

(7) Where on determining a question referred to or reserved for him under subsection (5) or (6) of this section the Secretary of State is of opinion that a local plan conforms generally to the relevant structure plan in the relevant respect or, as the case may be, all respects he may issue, or direct the county planning authority to issue, a certificate to that effect, and where he is of the contrary opinion, he may direct the district planning authority to revise the local plan in such respects as he thinks appropriate so as to secure that it will so conform and thereupon those subsections and the preceding provisions of this subsection shall apply to the revised plan.]

[(8) Where there is a conflict between any of the provisions of a local plan which has been adopted or approved under this section and the provisions of a structure plan which has been approved under section 9 of this Act, the provisions of the local plan shall be taken to prevail for all purposes:

Provided that where the local plan is specified in such a list as is mentioned in subsection (2)(ii) or (3)(ii) of section 15B of this Act, the provisions of this subsection shall not apply until such time as a proposal for the alteration of the local plan or for its repeal and replacement with a new plan has been adopted or has been approved by the Secretary of State.]   **[34]**

NOTES
 Commencement: 28 October 1971–1 August 1974.
 Sub-ss (1), (1A): substituted by the Local Government, Planning and Land Act 1980, s 89, Sch 14.
 Sub-s (2): first amendment made by the Local Government, Planning and Land Act 1980, s 88(2); second amendment made, except as to Greater London, by the Local Government Act 1972, s 182, Sch 16.
 Sub-ss (3A), (3B): added by the Local Government, Planning and Land Act 1980, s 89, Sch 14.
 Sub-s (4): substituted by the Town and Country Planning (Amendment) Act 1972, s 3(2); amended by the Local Government, Planning and Land Act 1980, s 89, Sch 14.
 Sub-ss (5)–(7): added, except as to Greater London, by the Local Government Act 1972, s 182, Sch 16.
 Sub-s (8): added by the Local Government, Planning and Land Act 1980, s 89, Sch 4.
 Prospectively substituted as noted to s 10C above.

15. Alteration of local plans

(1) A local planning authority may at any time make proposals for the alteration, repeal or replacement of a local plan adopted by them and may at any time, with the consent of the Secretary of State, make proposals for the alteration, repeal or replacement of a local plan approved by him.

(2) Without prejudice to subsection (1) of this section, a local planning authority shall, if the Secretary of State gives them a direction in that behalf with respect to a local plan adopted by them or approved by him, as soon as practicable prepare proposals of a kind specified in the direction, being proposals for the alteration, repeal or replacement of the plan.

(3) [Subject to subsection (4) of this section and to section 15A of this Act] sections 11(9) to (11), 12, 13 and 14 of this Act shall apply in relation to the making of proposals for the alteration, repeal or replacement of a local plan under this section, and to alterations to a local plan so proposed, as they apply

in relation to the preparation of a local plan under section 11 of this Act and to a local plan prepared thereunder, . . .

[(4) The requirement in section 13 of this Act for a local inquiry or other hearing to be held shall not apply if all persons who have made an objection have indicated in writing that they do not wish to appear.]   **[35]**

NOTES
Commencement: 28 October 1971–1 August 1974.
Sub-s (3): amendment in square brackets made by the Local Government (Miscellaneous Provisions) Act 1982, s 47, Sch 6, para 7; words omitted repealed by the Town and Country Planning (Amendment) Act 1972, s 3(3).
Sub-s (4): added by the Local Government, Planning and Land Act 1980, s 89, Sch 14.
Prospectively substituted as noted to s 10C above.

15A. Local plans—expedited procedure

[(1) Where—

    (*a*) a local planning authority have prepared a local plan; and

    (*b*) the Secretary of State gives them a direction authorising them to take such steps preliminary to its adoption as are mentioned in section 12(2) of this Act; and

    (*c*) at the time when he gives them that direction he has not approved the structure plan so far as it relates to the area of the local plan,

they may take those steps and adopt the local plan, whether or not the Secretary of State approves the structure plan first.

(2) Where—

    (*a*) a local planning authority have prepared proposals for the repeal of a local plan and its replacement with a new local plan; and

    (*b*) the Secretary of State gives them a direction authorising them to take such steps preliminary to its repeal and replacement as are mentioned in section 12(2) of this Act; and

    (*c*) at the time when he gives them that direction he has not approved the structure plan so far as it relates to the area of the new local plan,

they may take those steps and repeal the existing plan and adopt the new one, whether or not the Secretary of State approves the structure plan first.

(3) Where—

    (*a*) a local planning authority have prepared proposals—

        (i) for the alteration of a local plan; or

        (ii) for the repeal of a local plan without its replacement with a new plan; and

    (*b*) the Secretary of State gives them a direction authorising them to take such steps preliminary to the alteration or, as the case may be, the repeal of the local plan as are mentioned in section 12(2) of this Act; and

    (*c*) at the time when he gives them that direction he has not approved the structure plan so far as it relates to the area of the local plan,

they may take those steps and adopt the proposals, whether or not the Secretary of State approves the structure plan first.

(4) The powers conferred by subsections (1) to (3) of this section may be exercised by a district planning authority notwithstanding that they have not obtained a certificate under section 14(5) or (7) of this Act, but subject to the other provisions of that section and to the provisions of sections 12 and 13 of this Act.

(5) Before adopting—

   (*a*) a local plan; or

   (*b*) proposals for the repeal or alteration of a local plan,

in exercise of the powers conferred on them by this section, a local planning authority shall make such modifications to the plan (if any) as may be necessary to make it conform generally to the structure plan as it stands for the time being.

(6) Where this section applies, if the Secretary of State has approved the structure plan so far as it relates to the area of the local plan, but proposals for its alteration, repeal or replacement, so far as it relates to that area, have been prepared and submitted to the Secretary of State, he may direct that such of the provisions of this Act [specified in subsection (7)] of this section as are applicable shall have effect as respects the local planning authority's exercise of their powers under this section as if the proposals for alteration, repeal or replacement of the structure plan had been approved by him.

(7) The provisions of this Act mentioned in subsection [(6) of this section] are—

   (*a*) section 11(9);

   (*b*) paragraph 11(4)(*a*) of Schedule 4; and

   (*c*) section 14(2) and (5) to (7).

(8) If the Secretary of State thinks fit, a direction under subsection (6) of this section may specify modifications which the local planning authority are to make to a local plan or to proposals for the alteration, repeal or replacement of such a plan before adopting the plan or the proposals, for the purpose of bringing the local plan into general conformity with the structure plan as it will be after alteration, or, if the structure plan is to be repealed and replaced, for the purpose of bringing the local plan into general conformity with the new structure plan as it stands for the time being.

(9) Before giving a direction under this section, the Secretary of State shall consult—

   (*a*) every county planning authority and district planning authority whose area includes any land to which the local plan relates; or

   (*b*) if the land to which the local plan relates is in Greater London, the Greater London Council and every London borough council in whose area the land is situated.]   **[36]**

NOTES

   Commencement: 13 November 1980.

   Added by the Local Government, Planning and Land Act 1980, s 88(1).

   Sub-ss (6), (7): amended by the Local Government (Miscellaneous Provisions) Act 1982, s 47, Sch 6, para 7.

   Prospectively substituted as noted to s 10C above.

15B. Conformity between plans—supplementary

[(1) It shall be the duty of a county planning authority—

   (*a*) on the approval of a structure plan, to consider whether any local plan which has been adopted for part of the area to which the structure plan relates, or which has been approved by the Secretary of State for part of that area, conforms generally to the structure plan; and

   (*b*) on the approval of proposals for the alteration of a structure plan, to consider whether any local plan which has been adopted for an area affected by the alterations, or which has been approved by the

Secretary of State for such an area, conforms generally to the structure plan as altered.

(2) Not later than the expiration of the period of one month from the date on which the county planning authority receive notice of the Secretary of State's approval of a structure plan they shall send—

(*a*) to the Secretary of State; and

(*b*) to every district planning authority who prepared for any part of the area to which the structure plan relates a local plan which has been adopted or which has been approved by the Secretary of State,

a copy—

(i) of a list specifying every such local plan as is mentioned in subsection (1)(*a*) of this section which they certify to conform generally to the structure plan; and

(ii) of a list specifying every such plan which in their opinion does not so conform.

(3) Not later than the expiration of the period of one month from the date on which the county planning authority receive notice of the Secretary of State's approval of proposals for the alteration of a structure plan, they shall send—

(*a*) to the Secretary of State; and

(*b*) to every district planning authority who prepared a local plan which has been adopted or which has been approved by the Secretary of State and which is for an area which will be affected by the alterations,

a copy—

(i) of a list specifying every such local plan as is mentioned in subsection (1)(*b*) of this section which they certify to conform generally to the structure plan as altered; and

(ii) of a list specifying every such plan which in their opinion does not so conform.]   **[37]**

NOTES

Commencement: 13 November 1980.
Added by the Local Government, Planning and Land Act 1980, s 88(1).
Prospectively substituted as noted to s 10C above.

Supplementary provisions

16. Disregarding of representations with respect to development authorised by or under other enactments

Notwithstanding anything in the preceding provisions of this Act, neither the Secretary of State nor a local planning authority shall be required to consider representations or objections with respect to a structure plan, a local plan or any proposal to alter, repeal or replace any such plan if it appears to the Secretary of State or the authority, as the case may be, that those representations or objections are in substance representations or objections with respect to things done or proposed to be done in pursuance of—

(*a*) an order or scheme under [section 10, 14, 16, 18, 106(1), 106(3) or 108(1) of the Highways Act 1980 (trunk road orders, special road schemes, orders or schemes for bridges over or tunnels under navigable waters, orders for diversion of navigable waters, and supplementary orders relating to trunk roads, classified roads or special roads)];

[(*b*) an order or scheme under any provision replaced by the provisions of the Highways Act 1980 mentioned in paragraph (*a*) above (namely, an order or scheme under section 7, 9, 11, 13 or 20 of the Highways Act 1959, section 3 of the Highways (Miscellaneous Provisions) Act 1961 or section 1 or 10 of the Highways Act 1971);]

(*c*) ...

(*d*) an order under section 1 of the New Towns Act 1965 (designation of sites of new towns).   **[38]**

NOTES
Commencement: 28 October 1971–1 August 1974.
Amended by the Highways Act 1980, s 343, Sch 24.

17. Default powers of Secretary of State

(1) Where, by virtue of any of the preceding provisions of this Part of this Act, any survey is required to be carried out, or any structure or local plan or proposals for the alteration, repeal or replacement thereof are required to be prepared or submitted to the Secretary of State, or steps are required to be taken for the adoption of any such plan or proposals, then—

(*a*) if at any time the Secretary of State is satisfied, after holding a local inquiry or other hearing, that the [relevant] local planning authority are not carrying out the survey or are not taking the steps necessary to enable them to submit or adopt such a plan or proposals within a reasonable period; or

(*b*) in a case where a period is specified for the submission or adoption of any such plan or proposals, if no such plan or proposals have been submitted or adopted within that period,

the Secretary of State may carry out the survey or prepare and make a structure plan or local plan or, as the case may be, alter, repeal or replace it, as he thinks fit.

(2) Where under subsection (1) of this section the Secretary of State has power to do anything which should have been done by a local planning authority, he may, if he thinks fit, authorise any other local planning authority who appear to the Secretary of State to have an interest in the proper planning of the area of the first-mentioned authority to do that thing.

(3) Where under this section anything which ought to have been done by a local planning authority is done by the Secretary of State or another such authority, the preceding provisions of this Part of this Act shall, so far as applicable, apply with any necessary modifications in relation to the doing of that thing by the Secretary of State and the latter authority and the thing so done.

(4) Where the Secretary of State incurs expenses under this section in connection with the doing of anything which should have been done by a local planning authority, so much of those expenses as may be certified by the Secretary of State to have been incurred in the performance of functions of that authority shall on demand be repaid by that authority to the Secretary of State.

(5) Where under this section anything which should have been done by one local planning authority is done by another such authority, any expenses reasonably incurred in connection with the doing of that thing by the latter authority, as certified by the Secretary of State, shall be repaid to the latter authority by the former authority.   **[39]**

NOTES
Commencement: 28 October 1971–1 August 1974.

Amended, except as to Greater London, by the Local Government Act 1972, s 182, Sch 16.

18. Supplementary provisions as to structure and local plans

(1) Without prejudice to the preceding provisions of this Part of this Act, the Secretary of State may make regulations with respect to the form and content of structure and local plans and with respect to the procedure to be followed in connection with their preparation, submission, withdrawal, approval, adoption, making, alteration, repeal and replacement; and in particular any such regulations may—

(a) provide for the publicity to be given to the report of any survey carried out by a local planning authority under section 6 of this Act;

(b) provide for the notice to be given of, or the publicity to be given to, matters included or proposed to be included in any such plan, and the approval, adoption or making of any such plan or any alteration, repeal or replacement thereof or to any other prescribed procedural step, and for publicity to be given to the procedure to be followed as aforesaid;

(c) make provision with respect to the making and consideration of representations with respect to matters to be included in, or objections to, any such plan or proposals for its alteration, repeal or replacement;

(d) without prejudice to paragraph (b) of this subsection, provide for notice to be given to particular persons of the approval, adoption or alteration of any plan, if they have objected to the plan and have notified the [relevant] local planning authority of their wish to receive notice, subject (if the regulations so provide) to the payment of a reasonable charge for receiving it;

(e) require or authorise a local planning authority to consult with, or consider the views of, other persons before taking any prescribed procedural step;

(f) require a local planning authority, in such cases as may be prescribed or in such particular cases as the Secretary of State may direct, to provide persons making a request in that behalf with copies of any plan or document which has been made public for the purpose mentioned in section 8(1)(a) or 12(1)(a) of this Act or has been made available for inspection under section 8(2) or 12(2) of this Act, subject (if the regulations so provide) to the payment of a reasonable charge therefor;

(g) provide for the publication and inspection of any structure plan or local plan which has been approved, adopted or made, or any document approved, adopted or made altering, repealing or replacing any such plan, and for copies of any such plan or document to be made available on sale.

(2) Regulations under this section may extend throughout England and Wales or to specified areas only and may make different provisions for different cases.

(3) Subject to the preceding provisions of this Part of this Act and to any regulations under this section, the Secretary of State may give directions to any local planning authority, or to local planning authorities generally,—

(a) for formulating the procedure for the carrying out of their functions under this Part of this Act;

(b) for requiring them to give him such information as he may require for carrying out any of his functions under this Part of this Act.

(4) Subject to the provisions of section 242 of this Act, a structure plan or local plan or any alteration, repeal or replacement thereof shall become operative on a date appointed for the purpose in the relevant notice of approval, resolution of adoption or notice of the making, alteration, repeal or replacement of the plan. **[40]**

NOTES
    Commencement: 28 October 1971.
    Amended, except as to Greater London, by the Local Government Act 1972, s 182, Sch 16.
    Sub-s (1): prospectively amended, except as to Greater London, by the Housing and Planning Act 1986, s 49(1), Sch 11, Part I, para 15. See Appendix.

19. Application of Part II to Greater London

[Schedule 4 to this Act shall have effect with respect to surveys, joint surveys, action areas, local plans and joint local plans in and around Greater London and generally with respect to the operation for London of Part II of this Act.]
[41]

NOTES
    Commencement: 12 October 1973.
    Substituted by the Town and Country Planning (Amendment) Act 1972, s 4(1).

20. Meaning of "development plan"

(1) For the purposes of this Act, any other enactment relating to town and country planning, the Land Compensation Act 1961 and [the Highways Act 1980], the development plan for any district outside Greater London (whether the whole or part of the area of a local planning authority) shall be taken as consisting of—

   (*a*) the provisions of the structure plan for the time being in force for that area or the relevant part of that area, together with the Secretary of State's notice of approval of the plan;

   (*b*) any alterations to that plan, together with the Secretary of State's notices of approval thereof;

   (*c*) any provisions of a local plan for the time being applicable to the district, together with a copy of the authority's resolution of adoption or, as the case may be, the Secretary of State's notice of approval of the local plan; and

   (*d*) any alterations to that local plan, together with a copy of the authority's resolutions of adoption or, as the case may be, the Secretary of State's notices of approval thereof.

(2) For the said purposes the development plan for any district in Greater London (whether the whole or part of a London borough) shall be taken as consisting of—

   [(*a*) the provisions of the Greater London development plan as in force for the time being, together with the notices given from time to time by the Secretary of State indicating his approval of any feature or element of the plan;

   (*b*) any alterations to that plan, together with the Secretary of State's notices of approval thereof;]

   (*c*) any provisions of a local plan for the time being applicable to the district, together with a copy of the resolution of adoption of the relevant council or, as the case may be, the Secretary of State's notice of approval of the local plan; and

   (*d*) any alterations to that local plan, together with a copy of the resolutions of adoption of the relevant council or, as the case may be, the Secretary of State's notices of approval thereof.

(3) References in subsections (1) and (2) of this section to the provisions of any plan, notices of approval, alterations and resolutions of adoption shall, in relation to a district forming part of the area to which they are applicable, be respectively construed as references to so much of those provisions, notices, alterations and resolutions as is applicable to the district.

(4) References in subsections (1) to (3) of this section to notices of approval shall in relation to any plan or alteration made by the Secretary of State under section 17 of this Act be construed as references to notices of the making of the plan or alteration.

(5) This section has effect subject to Schedule 7 and Part I of Schedule 23 to this Act. [42]

NOTES

Commencement: 9 June 1975–17 November 1980 (certain areas, in part); to be appointed (remaining areas).

Commencement orders: SI 1975 Nos 780, 781, 1276, 1277; 1976 Nos 105, 815, 1163; 1977 Nos 470, 1363, 1769; 1978 Nos 557, 725, 727; 1979 Nos 140, 200, 201, 329, 891, 1043, 1187, 1485, 1622, 1624, 1626, 1628; 1980 Nos 2, 41, 65, 101, 174, 300, 458, 460, 492, 575, 577, 828, 932, 963, 1098, 1155, 1209, 1403, 1451, 1547, 1559, 1634.

First amendment made by the Highways Act 1980, s 343, Sch 24; second amendment made by the Town and Country Planning (Amendment) Act 1972, s 4(2).

21. Commencement of Part II and interim provisions

[(1) Subject to subsection (2) below, on the date on which a structure plan becomes operative—

(*a*) the following provisions of this Act, namely—

(i) section 20, and

(ii) the first paragraph of Part I of Schedule 23 (amendment of the Land Compensation Act 1961),

shall come into operation in the area to which the structure plan relates, and

(*b*) the following provisions of this Act, namely—

(i) Part I of Schedule 5, and

(ii) Schedule 6,

shall cease to have effect in that area.

(2) Where by virtue of section 15A of this Act a local plan becomes operative before the structure plan—

(*a*) the following provisions of this Act, namely—

(i) section 20, except paragraphs (*a*) and (*b*) of subsection (1), and

(ii) the first paragraph of Part I of Schedule 23,

shall come into operation in the area to which the local plan relates on the date on which that plan becomes operative;

(*b*) the following provisions of this Act, namely—

(i) Part I of Schedule 5, and

(ii) Schedule 6,

shall cease to have effect in that area on that date; and

(*c*) paragraphs (*a*) and (*b*) of section 20(1) of this Act shall come into operation on the date on which the structure plan becomes operative, in so far as they apply to the area to which the structure plan relates.

(3) Schedule 7 to this Act shall have effect as respects the transition from Schedules 5 and 6 to this Act to the preceding provisions of this Part of this Act.

(4) Any reference in this Part of this Act to the commencement of any provision of this Part of this Act shall be construed in accordance with subsections (5) to (7) of this section.

(5) If a day was appointed for the coming into operation of any such provision before the coming into operation of section 89 of the Local Government, Planning and Land Act 1980, any such reference shall be construed as a reference to the day so appointed.

(6) If different days were so appointed for the coming into operation of any such provision in different areas, any such reference shall, in relation to any area, be construed as a reference to the day appointed for the coming into operation of that provision in that area.

(7) If any such provision comes into operation in any area on the date on which a structure plan becomes operative, any such reference shall, in relation to that area, be construed as a reference to that date.

(7A) The Secretary of State for the time being having general responsibility in planning matters in relation to England shall, for England, and the Secretary of State for the time being having such responsibility in relation to Wales shall, for Wales, each maintain and keep up to date a register showing, in such a way as to enable members of the public to obtain the information for themselves—

(a) the provisions of this Part of this Act which have come into operation in relation to any area and the dates on which they came into operation in relation to it; and

(b) whether, in the case of a particular area, any transitional provision was made by an order under this section before the coming into operation of section 89 of the Local Government, Planning and Land Act 1980.]

(8) The register maintained under this section by the Secretary of State for the time being having general responsibility in planning matters in relation to England shall be kept at his principal offices in London, and the register so maintained by the Secretary of State for the time being having general responsibility in planning matters in relation to Wales shall be kept at his principal offices in Cardiff; and both registers shall be available for inspection by the public at reasonable hours.   **[43]**

NOTES

Commencement: 28 October 1971 (certain purposes); 1 April 1972 (remainder).
Amended by the Local Government, Planning and Land Act 1980, s 89, Sch 14.

PART III

GENERAL PLANNING CONTROL

Meaning of development and requirement of planning permission

22. Meaning of "development" and "new development"

(1) In this Act, except where the context otherwise requires, "development", subject to the following provisions of this section, means the carrying out of building, engineering, mining or other operations in, on, over or under land, or the making of any material change in the use of any buildings or other land.

(2) The following operations or uses of land shall not be taken for the purposes of this Act to involve development of the land, that is to say—

(a) the carrying out of works for the maintenance, improvement or other alteration of any building, being works which affect only the interior of the building or which do not materially affect the external appearance of the building and (in either case) are not works for making good war damage or works begun after 5th December 1968 for the alteration of a building by providing additional space therein below ground;

(b) the carrying out by a local highway authority of any works required for the maintenance or improvement of a road, being works carried out on land within the boundaries of the road;

(c) the carrying out by a local authority or statutory undertakers of any works for the purpose of inspecting, repairing or renewing any sewers, mains, pipes, cables or other apparatus, including the breaking open of any street or other land for that purpose;

(d) the use of any buildings or other land within the curtilage of a dwellinghouse for any purpose incidental to the enjoyment of the dwellinghouse as such;

(e) the use of any land for the purposes of agriculture or forestry (including afforestation) and the use for any of those purposes of any building occupied together with land so used;

(f) in the case of buildings or other land which are used for a purpose of any class specified in an order made by the Secretary of State under this section, the use thereof for any other purpose of the same class.

(3) For the avoidance of doubt it is hereby declared that for the purposes of this section—

(a) the use as two or more separate dwellinghouses of any building previously used as a single dwellinghouse involves a material change in the use of the building and of each part thereof which is so used;

(b) the deposit of refuse or waste materials on land involves a material change in the use thereof, notwithstanding that the land is comprised in a site already used for that purpose, if either the superficial area of the deposit is thereby extended, or the height of the deposit is thereby extended and exceeds the level of the land adjoining the site.

[(3A) For the purposes of this Act mining operations include—

(a) the removal of material of any description—

(i) from a mineral-working deposit;

(ii) from a deposit of pulverised fuel ash or other furnace ash or clinker; or

(iii) from a deposit of iron, steel or other metallic slags; and

(b) the extraction of minerals from a disused railway embankment.]

(4) Without prejudice to any regulations made under the provisions of this Act relating to the control of advertisements, the use for the display of advertisements of any external part of a building which is not normally used for that purpose shall be treated for the purposes of this section as involving a material change in the use of that part of the building.

(5) In this Act "new development" means any development other than development of a class specified in Part I or Part II of Schedule 8 to this Act; and the provisions of Part III of that Schedule shall have effect for the purposes of Parts I and II thereof.   **[44]**

NOTES
    Commencement: 19 May 1986 (sub-s (3A)); 1 April 1972 (remainder).
    Commencement order: SI 1986 No 760.
    This section derived from the Town and Country Planning Act 1962, s 12.
    Sub-s (2): amended by the Housing and Planning Act 1986, s 49(1), Sch 11, Part I, para 1. See
Appendix.
    Sub-s (3A): added by the Town and Country Planning (Minerals) Act 1981, s 1(1).

23. Development requiring planning permission

(1) Subject to the provisions of this section, planning permission is required for
the carrying out of any development of land.

(2) Where on 1st July 1948 (in this Act referred to as "the appointed day")
land was being temporarily used for a purpose other than the purpose for which
it was normally used, planning permission is not required for the resumption of
the use of the land for the last-mentioned purpose before 6th December 1968.

(3) Where on the appointed day land was normally used for one purpose
and was also used on occasions, whether at regular intervals or not, for another
purpose, planning permission is not required—

  (*a*) in respect of the use of the land for that other purpose on similar
    occasions before 6th December 1968; or
  (*b*) in respect of the use of the land for that other purpose on similar
    occasions on or after that date if the land has been used for that other
    purpose on a least one similar occasion since the appointed day and
    before the beginning of 1968.

(4) Where land was unoccupied on the appointed day, but had before that
day been occupied at some time on or after 7th January 1937, planning
permission is not required in respect of any use of the land begun before 6th
December 1968 for the purpose for which the land was last used before the
appointed day.

(5) Where planning permission to develop land has been granted for a
limited period, planning permission is not required for the resumption, at the
end of that period, of the use of the land for the purpose for which it was
normally used before the permission was granted.

(6) In determining, for the purposes of subsection (5) of this section, what
were the purposes for which land was normally used before the grant of planning
permission, no account shall be taken of any use of the land begun in
contravention of the provisions of this Part of this Act or in contravention of
previous planning control.

(7) Notwithstanding anything in subsections (2) to (4) of this section, the
use of land as a caravan site shall not, by virtue of any of those subsections, be
treated as a use for which planning permission is not required, unless the land
was so used on one occasion at least during the period of two years ending with
9th March 1960.

(8) Where by a development order planning permission to develop land has
been granted subject to limitations, planning permission is not required for the
use of that land which (apart from its use in accordance with that permission) is
the normal use of that land, unless the last-mentioned use was begun in
contravention of the provisions of this Part of this Act or in contravention of
previous planning control.

(9) Where an enforcement notice has been [issued] in respect of any
development of land, planning permission is not required for the use of that
land for the purpose for which (in accordance with the provisions of this Part of

this Act) it could lawfully have been used if that development had not been carried out.

(10) For the purposes of this section a use of land shall be taken to have been begun in contravention of previous planning control if it was begun in contravention of the provisions of Part III of the Act of 1947 or of Part III of the Act of 1962.   **[45]**

NOTES
Commencement: 1 April 1972.
Sub-s (9): amended by the Local Government (Miscellaneous Provisions) Act 1982, s 47, Sch 6, para 7.
Act of 1947: Town and Country Planning Act 1947.
Act of 1962: Town and Country Planning Act 1962.

Development orders

24. Development orders

(1) The Secretary of State shall by order (in this Act referred to as a "development order") provide for the granting of planning permission.

(2) A development order may either—

(*a*) itself grant planning permission for development specified in the order, or for development of any class so specified; or

(*b*) in respect of development for which planning permission is not granted by the order itself, provide for the granting of planning permission by the local planning authority (or, in the cases hereinafter provided, by the Secretary of State) on an application in that behalf made to the local planning authority in accordance with the provisions of the order.

(3) A development order may be made either as a general order applicable (subject to such exceptions as may be specified therein) to all land, or as a special order applicable only to such land [or descriptions of land] as may be so specified.

(4) Planning permission granted by a development order may be granted either unconditionally or subject to such conditions or limitations as may be specified in the order.

(5) Without prejudice to the generality of subsection (4) of this section—

(*a*) where planning permission is granted by a development order for the erection, extension or alteration of any buildings, the order may require the approval of the local planning authority to be obtained with respect to the design or external appearance of the buildings;

(*b*) where planning permission is granted by a development order for development of a specified class, the order may enable the Secretary of State or the local planning authority to direct that the permission shall not apply either in relation to development in a particular area or in relation to any particular development.

(6) Any provision of a development order whereby permission is granted for the use of land for any purpose on a limited number of days in a period specified in that provision shall (without prejudice to the generality of references in this Act to limitations) be taken to be a provision granting permission for the use of land for any purpose subject to the limitation that the land shall not be used for any one purpose in pursuance of that provision on more than that number of days in that period.

(7) For the purpose of enabling development to be carried out in accordance with planning permission, or otherwise for the purpose of promoting proper development in accordance with the development plan, a development order may direct that any enactment to which this subsection applies, or any regulations, orders or byelaws made at any time under any such enactment, shall not apply to any development specified in the order, or shall apply thereto subject to such modifications as may be so specified.

(8) Subsection (7) of this section applies—

(*a*) to any enactment passed before 6th August 1947 (being the date of the passing of the Act of 1947); and

(*b*) to any enactment contained in [the Highways Act 1980] being an enactment [(derived from the Highways Act 1959)] which re-enacts (with or without modifications) any such enactment as is mentioned in paragraph (*a*) of this subsection. **[46]**

NOTES
Commencement: 1 April 1972.
First amendment made by the Local Government, Planning and Land Act 1980, s 90, Sch 15; second and third amendments made by the Highways Act 1980, s 343, Sch 24.
Sub-s (3): new sub-s (3) substituted by the Housing and Planning Act 1986, s 49(1), Sch 11, Part I, para 2(1). See Appendix.

(New ss 24A–24E prospectively inserted by the Housing and Planning Act 1986, s 25(1). See Appendix.)

Applications for planning permission

25. Form and content of applications

Any application to a local planning authority for planning permission shall be made in such manner as may be prescribed by regulations under this Act, and shall include such particulars, and be verified by such evidence, as may be required by the regulations or by directions given by the local planning authority thereunder. **[47]**

NOTES
Commencement: 1 April 1972.

26. Publication of notices of applications

(1) Provision may be made by a development order for designating the classes of development to which this section applies, and this section shall apply accordingly to any class of development which is for the time being so designated.

(2) An application for planning permission for development of any class to which this section applies shall not be entertained by the local planning authority unless it is accompanied—

(*a*) by a copy of a notice of the application, in such form as may be prescribed by a development order, and by such evidence as may be so prescribed that the notice has been published in a local newspaper circulating in the locality in which the land to which the application relates is situated; and

(*b*) by one or other of the following certificates, signed by or on behalf of the applicant, that is to say—

(i) a certificate stating that he has complied with subsection (3) of this section and when he did so; or

(ii) a certificate stating that he has been unable to comply with it because he has not such rights of access or other rights in respect of the land as would enable him to do so, but that he has taken such reasonable steps as are open to him (specifying them) to acquire those rights and has been unable to acquire them.

(3) In order to comply with this subsection a person must—

(a) post on the land a notice, in such forms as may be prescribed by a development order, stating that the application for planning permission is to be made; and

(b) leave the notice in position for not less than seven days in a period of not more than one month immediately preceding the making of the application to the local planning authority.

(4) The said notice must be posted by affixing it firmly to some object on the land, and must be sited and displayed in such a way as to be easily visible and legible by members of the public without going on the land.

(5) The applicant shall not be treated as unable to comply with subsection (3) of this section if the notice is, without any fault or intention of his, removed, obscured or defaced before the seven days referred to in subsection (3)(b) of this section have elapsed, so long as he has taken reasonable steps for its protection and, if need be, replacement; and, if he has cause to rely on this subsection, his certificate under subsection (2)(b) of this section shall state the relevant circumstances.

(6) The notice mentioned in subsection (2)(a) or required by subsection (3) of this section shall (in addition to any other matters required to be contained therein) name a place within the locality where a copy of the application for planning permission, and of all plans and other documents submitted with it, will be open to inspection by the public at all reasonable hours during such period as may be specified in the notice, not being a period of less than twenty-one days beginning with the date on which the notice is published or first posted, as the case may be.

(7) An application for planning permission for development of any class to which this section applies shall not be determined by the local planning authority before the end of the period of twenty-one days beginning with the date of the application.

(8) If any person issues a certificate which purports to comply with the requirements of subsection (2)(b) of this section and which contains a statement which he knows to be false or misleading in a material particular, or recklessly issues a certificate which purports to comply with those requirements and which contains a statement which is false or misleading in a material particular, he shall be guilty of an offence and liable on summary conviction to a fine not exceeding [level 3 on the standard scale].

(9) Any certificate issued for the purpose of this section shall be in such form as may be prescribed by a development order. **[48]**

NOTES
Commencement: 1 April 1972.
Sub-s (8): maximum fine increased and converted to a level on the standard scale by the Criminal Justice Act 1982, ss 37, 38, 46.

27. Notification of applications to owners and agricultural tenants

(1) Without prejudice to section 26 of this Act, a local planning authority shall not entertain any application for planning permission unless it is accompanied

by one or other of the following certificates signed by or on behalf of the applicant, that is to say—

[(*a*) a certificate stating that, at the beginning of the period of twenty-one days ending with the date of the application, no person (other than the applicant) was the owner of any of the land to which the application relates;]

(*b*) a certificate stating that the applicant has given the requisite notice of the application to all the persons (other than the applicant) who, at the beginning of the period of twenty-one days ending with the date of the application, were owners of any of the land to which the application relates, and setting out the names of those persons, the addresses at which notice of the application was given to them respectively, and the date of service of each such notice;

(*c*) a certificate stating that the applicant is unable to issue a certificate in accordance with either of the preceding paragraphs, that he has given the requisite notice of the application to such one or more of the persons mentioned in the last preceding paragraph as are specified in the certificate (setting out their names, the addresses at which notice of the application was given to them respectively, and the date of the service of each such notice), that he has taken such steps as are reasonably open to him (specifying them) to ascertain the names and addresses of the remainder of those persons and that he has been unable to do so;

[(*cc*) in the case of an application for planning permission for development consisting of the winning and working of minerals by underground mining operations, a certificate stating—

(i) that the applicant has given the requisite notice of the application to such one or more of the persons mentioned in paragraph (*b*) of this subsection as are specified in the certificate, and setting out the names of those persons, the addresses at which notice of the application was given to them respectively, and the date of service of each such notice;

(ii) that there is no person mentioned in paragraph (*b*) of this subsection whom the applicant knows to be such a person and whose name and address is known to the applicant but to whom he has not given the requisite notice of the application; and

(iii) that he has complied with subsection (2A) of this section and when he did so;]

(*d*) a certificate stating that the applicant is unable to issue a certificate in accordance with paragraph (*a*) of this subsection, that he has taken such steps as are reasonably open to him (specifying them) to ascertain the names and addresses of the persons mentioned in paragraph (*b*) of this subsection and that he has been unable to do so.

[(1A) Subject to subsection (1B) of this section, subsection (1) of this section shall have effect as respects notice of an application for planning permission for development consisting of the winning and working of minerals as if any person entitled to an interest in a mineral in the land to which the application relates were an owner of the land.

(1B) Subsection (1) of this section shall not have effect as provided by subsection (1A) of this section in relation to a person entitled to an interest in—

(*a*) oil, gas or coal; or

(*b*) gold or silver.]

(2) Any such certificate as is mentioned in paragraph (*c*)[, paragraph (*cc*)] or paragraph (*d*) of subsection (1) of this section shall also contain a statement that the requisite notice of the application, as set out in the certificate, has on a date specified in the certificate (being a date not earlier than the beginning of the period mentioned in paragraph (*b*) of that subsection) been published in a local newspaper circulating in the locality in which the land in question is situated.

[(2A) In order to comply with this subsection the applicant must—

(*a*) post the requisite notice of the application, sited and displayed in such a way as to be easily visible and legible by members of the public, in at least one place in every parish or community within which there is situated any part of the land to which the application relates; and

(*b*) leave the notice in position for not less than seven days in the period of 21 days immediately preceding the making of the application to the local planning authority.

(2B) The applicant shall not be treated as unable to comply with subsection (2A) of this section if the notice is, without any fault or intention of his, removed, obscured or defaced before the seven days referred to in subsection (2A)(*b*) of this section have elapsed, so long as he has taken reasonable steps for its protection and, if need be, replacement; and, if he has cause to rely on this subsection, his certificate under subsection (1)(*cc*) of this section shall state the relevant circumstances.

(2C) The notice required by subsection (2A) of this section shall (in addition to any other matters required to be contained in it) name a place within the area of the local planning authority to whom the application is made where a copy of the application for planning permission, and of all plans and other documents submitted with it, will be open to inspection by the public at all reasonable hours during such period as may be specified in the notice, being a period of not less than 21 days beginning with the date on which the notice is first posted.]

(3) In addition to any other matters required to be contained in a certificate issued for the purposes of this section, every such certificate shall contain one or other of the following statements, that is to say—

(*a*) a statement that none of the land to which the application relates constitutes or forms part of an agricultural holding;

(*b*) a statement that the applicant has given the requisite notice of the application to every person (other than the applicant) who, at the beginning of the period of twenty-one days ending with the date of the application, was a tenant of any agricultural holding any part of which was comprised in the land to which the application relates, and setting out the name of each such person, the address at which notice of the application was given to him, and the date of service of that notice.

(4) Where an application for planning permission is accompanied by such a certificate as is mentioned in subsection (1)(*b*), (*c*) or (*d*) of this section, or by a certificate containing a statement in accordance with subsection (3)(*b*) of this section, the local planning authority shall not determine the application before the end of the period of twenty-one days beginning with the date appearing from the certificate to be the latest of the dates of service of notices as mentioned in the certificate, or the date of publication of a notice as therein mentioned, whichever is the later.

(5) If any person issues any certificate which purports to comply with the requirements of this section and which contains a statement which he knows to be false or misleading in a material particular, or recklessly issues a certificate which purports to comply with those requirements and which contains a statement which is false or misleading in a material particular, he shall be guilty of an offence and liable on summary conviction to a fine not exceeding [level 3 on the standard scale].

(6) Any certificate issued for the purposes of this section shall be in such form as may be prescribed by a development order; and any reference in any provision of this section to the requisite notice, where a form of notice is prescribed by a development order for the purposes of that provision, is a reference to a notice in that form.

(7) In this section "owner", in relation to any land, means a person [who is for the time being the estate owner in respect of the fee simple in the land or is entitled to a tenancy of the land granted or extended for a term of years certain of which not less than seven years remain unexpired], and "agricultural holding" has the same meaning as in the *Agricultural Holdings Act 1948* [Agricultural Holdings Act 1986].   [49]

NOTES
    Commencement: 22 February 1982 (sub-ss (1A), (1B), (2A)-(2C)); 1 April 1972 (remainder).
    This section derived from the Town and Country Planning Act 1962, s 16.
    Sub-s (1): para (*a*) substituted by the Local Government, Planning and Land Act 1980, s 90, Sch 15; para (*cc*) added by the Town and Country Planning (Minerals) Act 1981, s 4(1).
    Sub-ss (1A), (1B), (2A)–(2C): added by the Town and Country Planning (Minerals) Act 1981, s 4(2), (4).
    Sub-s (2): amended by the Town and Country Planning (Minerals) Act 1981, s 4(3).
    Sub-s (5): maximum fine increased and converted to a level on the standard scale by the Criminal Justice Act 1982, ss 37, 38, 46.
    Sub-s (7): first amendment in square brackets made by the Local Government, Planning and Land Act 1980, s 90, Sch 15; words in italics repealed with savings and subsequent words in square brackets substituted with savings by the Agricultural Holdings Act 1986, ss 99, 100, Sch 13, para 3, Sch 14, para 50.

28. Publicity for applications affecting conservation areas

(1) This section applies where an application for planning permission for any development of land is made to a local planning authority and . . . —

   (*a*) the development would, in the opinion of the authority, affect the character or appearance of a conservation area; [or
   (*aa*) the development would, in the opinion of the authority, affect the setting of a listed building.]

(2) [[In Greater London or a metropolitan county the local planning authority, in any part of a National Park outside a metropolitan county] the county planning authority and elsewhere the district planning authority] shall—

   (*a*) publish in a local newspaper circulating in the locality in which the land is situated; and
   (*b*) for not less than seven days display on or near the land,

a notice indicating the nature of the development in question and naming a place within the locality where a copy of the application, and of all plans and other documents submitted with it, will be open to inspection by the public at all reasonable hours during the period of twenty-one days beginning with the date of publication of the notice under paragraph (*a*) of this subsection.

[(2A) In a case where the land is situated in England, the local, county or district planning authority (as the case may be) shall send a copy of the notice to the Historic Buildings and Monuments Commission for England.

(2B) Where the Secretary of State, after consulting with the Commission, notifies a local, county or district planning authority in writing that subsection (2A) of this section shall not affect the authority as regards any notice relating to any kind of application specified in the notification, then that subsection shall not affect the authority as regards any such noise.

(2C) The Secretary of State shall send to the Commission a copy of any notification made under subsection (2B) of this section.]

(3) The application shall not be determined by the local planning authority before both the following periods have elapsed, namely—

(*a*) the period of twenty-one days referred to in subsection (2) of this section; and

(*b*) the period of twenty-one days beginning with the date on which the notice required by that subsection to be displayed was first displayed.

[50]

NOTES

Commencement: 1 October 1984 (sub-ss (2A)-(2C)); 1 April 1972 (remainder).
Commencement order: SI 1984 No 208.
This section derived from the Civic Amenities Act 1967, s 1(6), and the Town and Country Planning Act 1968, s 57.
Sub-s (1): words omitted repealed by the Local Government Act 1974, s 42(2), Sch 8; amendment in square brackets made by the Town and Country Amenities Act 1974, s 4(1).
Sub-s (2): first amendment in square brackets made by the Local Government Act 1972, s 182, Sch 16; second amendment in square brackets made by the Local Government Act 1985, s 6, Sch 2, para 1.
Sub-ss (2A)-(2C): added by the National Heritage Act 1983, s 33, Sch 4, para 15.

Determination by local planning authorities of applications for planning permission

29. Determination of applications

(1) Subject to the provisions of sections 26 to 28 of this Act, and to the following provisions of this Act, where an application is made to a local planning authority for planning permission, that authority, in dealing with the application, shall have regard to the provisions of the development plan, so far as material to the application, and to any other material considerations, and—

(*a*) subject to sections 41, 42, 70 and 77 to 80 of this Act, may grant planning permission, either unconditionally or subject to such conditions as they think fit; or

(*b*) may refuse planning permission.

(2) In determining any application for planning permission for development of a class to which section 26 of this Act applies, the local planning authority shall take into account any representations relating to that application which are received by them before the end of the period of twenty-one days beginning with the date of the application.

(3) Where an application for planning permission is accompanied by such a certificate as is mentioned in subsection (1)(*b*), (*c*) or (*d*) of section 27 of this Act, or by a certificate containing a statement in accordance with subsection (3)(*b*) of that section, the local planning authority—

(*a*) in determining the application, shall take into account any representations relating thereto which are made to them, before the end of the period mentioned in subsection (4) of that section, by any person who satisfies them that he is an owner of any land to which the application relates or that he is the tenant of an agricultural holding any part of which is comprised in that land; and

(b) shall give notice of their decision to every person who has made representations which they were required to take into account in accordance with the preceding paragraph.

(4) In determining any application for planning permission to which section 28 of this Act applies, the local planning authority shall take into account any representations relating to the application which are received by them before the periods mentioned in subsection (3) of that section have elapsed.

(5) Before a local planning authority grant planning permission for the use of land as a caravan site, they shall, unless they are also the authority having power to issue a site licence for that land, consult the local authority having that power.

(6) In this section "site licence" means a licence under Part I of the Caravan Sites and Control of Development Act 1960 authorising the use of land as a caravan site and "owner" and "agricultural holding" have the same meanings as in section 27 of this Act.   **[51]**

NOTES
Commencement: 1 April 1972.
Sub-s (1): amended by the Housing and Planning Act 1986, s 49(1), Sch 11, Part I, para 16. See Appendix.

29A. Duty to draw attention to certain provisions for benefit of disabled

[(1) When granting planning permission for any development which will result in the provision—

(a) of a building or premises to which section 4 of the Chronically sick and Disabled Persons Act 1970 applies (buildings or premises to which the public are to be admitted whether on payment or otherwise);

(b) of any of the following, being in each case, premises in which persons are employed to work,—

(i) office premises, shop premises and railway premises to which the Offices, Shops and Railway Premises Act 1963 applies;

(ii) premises which are deemed to be such premises for the purposes of that Act; or

(iii) factories as defined by section 175 of the Factories Act 1961,

the local planning authority shall draw the attention of the person to whom the permission is granted—

(i) to the relevant provisions of the Chronically Sick and Disabled Persons Act 1970; and

(ii) to the Code of Practice for Access for the Disabled to Buildings.

(2) In subsection (1) of this section—

"the relevant provisions of the Chronically Sick and Disabled Persons Act 1970" means—

(a) for the purposes of paragraph (a), sections 4 and 7;

(b) for the purposes of paragraph (b), sections 7 and 8A; and

"the Code of Practice for Access for the Disabled to Buildings" means the British Standards Institution code of practice referred to as BS 5810: 1979.

(3) Section 28 of the Chronically Sick and Disabled Persons Act 1970 (power to define certain expressions for the purposes of provisions of that Act) shall have effect as if any reference in it to a provision of that Act included a reference to this section.] **[52]**

NOTES

Commencement: 27 October 1981.

Added by the Disabled Persons Act 1981, s 3.

Sub-s (1): new para (ii) substituted by the Housing and Planning Act 1986, s 49(1), Sch 11, Part I, para 3(1). See Appendix.

Sub-s (2): repealed in part by the Housing and Planning Act 1986, s 49(2), Sch 12, Part III. See Appendix.

Sub-s (3): repealed by the Housing and Planning Act 1986, s 49(2), Sch 12, Part III. See Appendix.

29B. Duty to draw attention to certain provisions for benefit of disabled— educational buildings

(1) When granting planning permission for any development which will result in the provision of a building intended for the purposes—

> (*a*) of a university, university college or college, or of a school or hall of a university; or
>
> (*b*) of a school within the meaning of the Education Act 1944, a teacher training college maintained by a local education authority in England or Wales or any other institution providing further education pursuant to a scheme under section 42 of that Act,

the local planning authority shall draw the attention of the person to whom the permission is granted—

> > (i) to sections 7 and 8 of the Chronically Sick and Disabled Persons Act 1970; and
> >
> > (ii) to the Design Note.

(2) In subsection (1) of this section "the Design Note" means Design Note 18 "Access for the Physically Disabled to Educational Buildings", published on behalf of the Secretary of State.

(3) Section 28 of the Chronically Sick and Disabled Persons Act 1970 (power to define certain expressions for the purposes of provisions of that Act) shall have effect as if any reference in it to a provision of that Act included a reference to this section.] **[53]**

NOTES

Commencement: 27 October 1981.

Added by the Disabled Persons Act 1981, s 3.

Sub-s (1): new para (ii) substituted by the Housing and Planning Act 1986, s 49(1), Sch 11, Part I, para 3(2). See Appendix.

Sub-ss (2) and (3): repealed by the Housing and Planning Act 1986, s 49(2), Sch 12, Part III. See Appendix.

30. Conditional grant of planning permission

(1) Without prejudice to the generality of section 29(1) of this Act, conditions may be imposed on the grant of planning permission thereunder—

> (*a*) for regulating the development or use of any land under the control of the applicant (whether or not it is land in respect of which the application was made) or requiring the carrying out of works on any such land, so far as appears to the local planning authority to be expedient for the purposes of or in connection with the development authorised by the permission;
>
> (*b*) for requiring the removal of any buildings or works authorised by the permission, or the discontinuance of any use of land so authorised, at the end of a specified period, and the carrying out of any works required for the reinstatement of land at the end of that period.

(2) [Subject to section 44A(6) of this Act, any] planning permission granted

subject to such a condition as is mentioned in subsection (1)(*b*) of this section is in this Act referred to as "planning permission granted for a limited period".

(3) Where—

(*a*) planning permission is granted for development consisting of or including the carrying out of building or other operations subject to a condition that the operations shall be commenced not later than a time specified in the condition (not being a condition attached to the planning permission by or under section 41 or 42 of this Act); and

(*b*) any building or other operations are commenced after the time so specified,

the commencement and carrying out of those operations do not constitute development for which that permission was granted.   **[54]**

NOTES
Commencement: 1 April 1972.
Sub-s (2): amended by the Town and Country Planning (Minerals) Act 1981, s 34, Sch 1.

30A. Aftercare conditions on permission for winning and working of minerals

[(1) Where planning permission for development consisting of the winning and working of minerals is granted subject to a restoration condition, it may be granted subject also to any such aftercare condition as the mineral planning authority think fit.

(2) In this Act—

"restoration condition" means a condition requiring that after operations for the winning and working of minerals have been completed, the site shall be restored by the use of any or all of the following, namely, subsoil, topsoil and soil-making material; and

"aftercare condition" means a condition requiring that such steps shall be taken as may be necessary to bring land to the required standard for whichever of the following uses is specified in the condition, namely—

(*a*) use for agriculture;
(*b*) use for forestry; or
(*c*) use for amenity.

(3) An aftercare condition may either—

(*a*) specify the steps to be taken; or
(*b*) require that the steps be taken in accordance with a scheme (in this section referred to as an "aftercare scheme") approved by the mineral planning authority.

(4) A mineral planning authority may approve an aftercare scheme in the form in which it is submitted to them or may modify it and approve it as modified.

(5) The steps that may be specified in an aftercare condition or an aftercare scheme may consist of planting, cultivating, fertilising, watering, draining or otherwise treating the land.

(6) Where a step is specified in a condition or a scheme, the period during which it is to be taken may also be specified, but no step may be required to be taken after the expiry of the aftercare period.

(7) In subsection (6) of this section "the aftercare period" means a period of

five years from compliance with the restoration condition or such other maximum period after compliance with that condition as may be prescribed; and in respect of any part of a site, the aftercare period shall commence on compliance with the restoration condition in respect of that part.

(8) The power to prescribe maximum periods conferred by subsection (7) of this section includes power to prescribe maximum periods differing according to the use specified.

(9) In a case where—

(*a*) the use specified is a use for agriculture; and

(*b*) the land was in use for agriculture at the time of the grant of the planning permission or had previously been used for that purpose and had not at the time of the grant been used for any authorised purpose since its use for agriculture ceased; and

(*c*) the Minister has notified the mineral planning authority of the physical characteristics of the land when it was last used for agriculture,

the land is brought to the required standard when its physical characteristics are restored, so far as it is practicable to do so, to what they were when it was last used for agricultue.

(10) In any other case where the use specified is a use for agriculture, the land is brought to the required standard when it is reasonably fit for that use.

(11) Where the use specified is a use for forestry, the land is brought to the required standard when it is reasonably fit for that use.

(12) Where the use specified is a use for amenity, the land is brought to the required standard when it is suitable for sustaining trees, shrubs or plants.

(13) Before imposing an aftercare condition, the mineral planning authority shall consult—

(*a*) the Minister, where they propose that the use specified in the condition shall be a use for agriculture; and

(*b*) the Forestry Commission, where they propose that the use so specified shall be a use for forestry,

as to whether it is appropriate to specify that use.

(14) Where after consultations required by subsection (13) of this section the mineral planning authority are satisfied that the use that they ought to specify is a use for agriculture or for forestry, they shall consult—

(*a*) where it is for agriculture, the Minister; and

(*b*) where it is for forestry, the Forestry Commission,

with regard to whether the steps to be taken should be specified in the aftercare condition or in an aftercare scheme.

(15) The mineral planning authority shall also consult the Minister or the Forestry Commission, as the case may be,—

(*a*) as to the steps to be specified in an aftercare condition which specifies a use for agriculture or for forestry; and

(*b*) before approving an aftercare scheme submitted in accordance with an aftercare condition which specifies such a use.

(16) The mineral planning authority shall also, from time to time as they

consider expedient, consult the Minister or the Commission, as the case may be, as to whether the steps specified in an aftercare condition or an aftercare scheme are being taken.

(17) On the application of any person with an interest in land in respect of which an aftercare condition has been imposed the mineral planning authority, if they are satisfied that the condition has been complied with, shall issue a certificate to that effect.

(18) A person who has complied with an aftercare condition but who has not himself carried out any operations for the winning and working of minerals in, on or under the land shall be entitled, subject to any condition to the contrary contained in a contract which is enforceable against him by the person who last carried out such operations, to recover from that person any expenses reasonably incurred in complying with the aftercare condition.

(19) In this section—

"authorised" means authorised by planning permission;
"forestry" means the growing of a utilisable crop of timber; and
"the Minister" means—

(i) in relation to England, the Minister of Agriculture, Fisheries and Food; and
(ii) in relation to Wales, the Secretary of State.]   [55]

NOTES
Commencement: 22 February 1982.
Added by the Town and Country Planning (Minerals) Act 1981, s 5.

31. Directions etc as to method of dealing with applications

(1) Subject to the provisions of section 29(2) to (5) of this Act, provision may be made by a development order for regulating the manner in which applications for planning permission to develop land are to be dealt with by local planning authorities, and in particular—

(a) for enabling the Secretary of State to give directions restricting the grant of planning permission by the local planning authority, either indefinitely or during such period as may be specified in the directions, in respect of any such development, or in respect of development of any such class, as may be so specified;

(b) for authorising the local planning authority, in such cases and subject to such conditions as may be prescribed by the order, or by directions given by the Secretary of State thereunder, to grant planning permission for development which does not accord with the provisions of the development plan;

[(c) for requiring that, before planning permission for any development is granted or refused, local planning authorities prescribed by the order or by directions given by the Secretary of State thereunder shall consult with such authorities or persons as may be so prescribed;]

(d) for requiring the local planning authority to give to any applicant for planning permission, within such time as may be prescribed by the order, such notice as may be so prescribed as to the manner in which his application has been dealt with;

[(dd) for requiring the local planning authority to give any applicant for any consent, agreement or approval required by a condition imposed on a grant of planning permission notice of their decision on his application, within such time as may be so prescribed;]

(*e*) for requiring the local planning authority to give to the Secretary of State, and to such other persons as may be prescribed by or under the order, such information as may be so prescribed with respect to applications for planning permission made to the authority, including information as to the manner in which any such application has been dealt with.

(2), (3) . . .   **[56]**

NOTES
Commencement: 1 April 1972.
First amendment made by the Local Government Act 1972, s 182, Sch 16; second amendment made by the Local Government, Planning and Land Act 1980, s 90, Sch 15; words omitted repealed by the Local Government Act 1974, s 42(2), Sch 8.

(New s 31A inserted by the Housing and Planning Act 1986, s 49(1), Sch 11, Part I, para 4. See Appendix.)

32. Permission to retain buildings or works or continue use of land

(1) An application for planning permission may relate to buildings or works constructed or carried out, or a use of land instituted, before the date of the application, whether—

    (*a*) the buildings or works were constructed or carried out, or the use instituted, without planning permission or in accordance with planning permission granted for a limited period; or

    (*b*) the application is for permission to retain the buildings or works, or continue the use of the land, without complying with some condition subject to which a previous planning permission was granted.

(2) Any power to grant planning permission to develop land under this Act shall include power to grant planning permission for the retention on land of buildings or works constructed or carried out, or for the continuance of a use of land instituted, as mentioned in subsection (1) of this section; and references in this Act to planning permission to develop land or to carry out any development of land, and to applications for such permission, shall be construed accordingly:

Provided that this subsection shall not affect the construction of section 26, 28, 29(2) or (4) or 59, of sections 66 to 86 or of Part VII of this Act.

(3) Any planning permission granted in accordance with subsection (2) of this section may be granted so as to take effect from the date on which the buildings or works were constructed or carried out, or the use was instituted, or (in the case of buildings or works constructed or a use instituted in accordance with planning permission granted for a limited period) so as to take effect from the end of that period, as the case may be.   **[57]**

NOTES
Commencement: 1 April 1972.
Sub-s (2): repealed in part by the Housing and Planning Act 1986, s 49(2), Sch 12, Part III. See Appendix.

33. Provisions as to effect of planning permission

(1) Without prejudice to the provisions of this Part of this Act as to the duration, revocation or modification of planning permission, any grant of planning permission to develop land shall (except in so far as the permission otherwise provides) enure for the benefit of the land and of all persons for the time being interested therein.

(2) Where planning permission is granted for the erection of a building, the grant of permission may specify the purposes for which the building may be

used; and if no purpose is so specified, the permission shall be construed as including permission to use the building for the purpose for which it is designed.   **[58]**

NOTES
    Commencement: 1 April 1972.

34. Registers of applications and decisions

(1) Every local planning authority shall keep, in such manner as may be prescribed by a development order, a register containing such information as may be so prescribed with respect to applications for planning permission made to that authority, including information as to the manner in which such applications have been dealt with.

[(1A) . . .]

(2) A development order may make provision for the register to be kept in two or more parts, each part containing such information relating to applications for planning permission made to the authority as may be prescribed by the order, and may also make provision—

   (*a*) for a specified part of the register to contain copies of applications and of any plans or drawings submitted therewith; and
   (*b*) for the entry relating to any application, and every thing relating thereto, to be removed from that part of the register when the application (including any appeal arising out of it) has been finally disposed of, without prejudice to the inclusion of any different entry relating thereto in another part of the register.

(3) Every register kept under this section shall be available for inspection by the public at all reasonable hours.   **[59]**

NOTES
    Commencement: 1 April 1972.
    Sub-s (1): prospectively amended by the Housing and Planning Act 1986, s 25(3), Sch 6, Part II, para 1. See Appendix.
    Sub-s (1A): repealed by the Local Government, Planning and Land Act 1980, s 194, Sch 34.

Secretary of State's powers in relation to planning applications and decisions

35. Reference of applications to Secretary of State

(1) The Secretary of State may give directions requiring applications for planning permission, or for the approval of any local planning authority required under a development order, to be referred to him instead of being dealt with by local planning authorities.

(2) A direction under this section—

   (*a*) may be given either to a particular local planning authority or to local planning authorities generally; and
   (*b*) may relate either to a particular application or to applications of a class specified in the direction.

(3) Any application in respect of which a direction under this section has effect shall be referred to the Secretary of State accordingly.

(4) Subject to subsection (5) of this section, where an application for planning permission is referred to the Secretary of State under this section, the following provisions of this Act, that is to say, sections 26(2) and (7), 27, 29(1) to (3) [, 30(1) and 30A] shall apply, with any necessary modifications, as they

apply to an application for planning permission which falls to be determined by the local planning authority.

(5) Before determining an application referred to him under this section, other than an application for planning permission referred to a Planning Inquiry Commission under section 48 of this Act, the Secretary of State shall, if either the applicant or the local planning authority so desire, afford to each of them an opportunity of appearing before, and being heard by, a person appointed by the Secretary of State for the purpose.

(6) The decision of the Secretary of State on any application referred to him under this section shall be final.   **[60]**

NOTES
Commencement: 1 April 1972.
Sub-s (4): amended by the Town and Country Planning (Minerals) Act 1981, s 34, Sch 1, and by the Housing and Planning Act 1986, s 49(1), Sch 11, Part I, para 17. See Appendix.

36. Appeals against planning decisions

(1) Where an application is made to a local planning authority

[(a) for planning permission to develop land;
(b) for any consent, agreement or approval of that authority required by a condition imposed on a grant of planning permission; or
(c) for any approval of that authority required under a development order,

and that permission, consent, agreement] or approval is refused by that authority or is granted by them subject to conditions, the applicant, if he is aggrieved by their decision, may by notice under this section appeal to the Secretary of State.

(2) Any notice under this section shall be served within such time (not being less than twenty-eight days from the date of notification of the decision to which it relates) and in such manner as may be prescribed by a development order.

(3) Where an appeal is brought under this section from a decision of a local planning authority, the Secretary of State, subject to the following provisions of this section, may allow or dismiss the appeal, or may reverse or vary any part of the decision of the local planning authority, whether the appeal relates to that part thereof or not, and may deal with the application as if it had been made to him in the first instance.

(4) Before determining an appeal under this section, other than an appeal referred to a Planning Inquiry Commission under section 48 of this Act, the Secretary of State shall, if either the applicant or the local planning authority so desire, afford to each of them an opportunity of appearing before, and being heard by, a person appointed by the Secretary of State for the purpose.

(5) Subject to subsection (4) of this section, the following provisions of this Act, that is to say, sections 27, 29(1) and (3) and [, 30(1) and 30A] shall apply, with any necessary modifications, in relation to an appeal to the Secretary of State under this section as they apply in relation to an application for planning permission which falls to be determined by the local planning authority.

(6) The decision of the Secretary of State on any appeal under this section shall be final.

(7) If before or during the determination of an appeal under this section in respect of an application for planning permission to develop land, the Secretary of State forms the opinion that, having regard to the provisions of sections

29(1), 30(1), 67 and 74 of this Act and of the development order and to any directions given under that order, planning permission for that development—

    (*a*) could not have been granted by the local planning authority; or

    (*b*) could not have been granted by them otherwise than subject to the conditions imposed by them,

he may decline to determine the appeal or to proceed with the determination.

    (8) Schedule 9 to this Act applies to appeals under this section, including appeals under this section as applied by or under any other provision of this Act.   **[61]**

NOTES

    Commencement: 1 April 1972.

    Sub-s (1): amended by the Local Government, Planning and Land Act 1980, s 90, Sch 15.

    Sub-s (5): amended by the Town and Country Planning (Minerals) Act 1981, s 34, Sch 1, and by the Housing and Planning Act 1986, s 49(1), Sch 11, Part I, para 17. See Appendix.

    Sub-s (7): amended by the Housing and Planning Act 1986, s 49(1), Sch 11, Part I, para 18. See Appendix.

---

37. Appeal in default of planning decision

Where [any such application as is mentioned in section 36(1) of this Act is made to a local planning authority], then unless within such period as may be prescribed by the development order, or within such extended period as may at any time be agreed upon in writing between the applicant and the local planning authority, the local planning authority either—

    (*a*) give notice to the applicant of their decision on the application; or

    (*b*) give notice to him that the application has been referred to the Secretary of State in accordance with directions given under section 35 of this Act,

the provisions of section 36 of this Act shall apply in relation to the application as if the permission or approval to which it relates had been refused by the local planning authority, and as if notification of their decision had been received by the applicant at the end of the period prescribed by the development order, or at the end of the said extended period, as the case may be.   **[62]**

NOTES

    Commencement: 1 April 1972.

    Amended by the Local Government, Planning and Land Act 1980, s 90, Sch 15.

---

38. Review of planning decisions where compensation claimed

(1) The provisions of this section and of section 39 of this Act shall have effect where, in accordance with the provisions of Part VII of this Act, one or more claims for compensation in respect of a planning decision have been transmitted to the Secretary of State, and the claim, or (if there is more than one) one or more of the claims, has not been withdrawn.

    (2) If, in the case of a planning decision of the local planning authority, it appears to the Secretary of State that, if the application for permission to develop the land in question had been referred to him for determination, he would have made a decision more favourable to the applicant, the Secretary of State may give a direction substituting that decision for the decision of the local planning authority.

    (3) If, in an case, it appears to the Secretary of State that planning permission could properly be granted (either unconditionally or subject to certain conditions) for some development of the land in question other than the development to which the application for planning permission related, the

Secretary of State may give a direction that the provisions of this Act shall have effect in relation to that application and to the planning decision—

(a) as if the application had included an application for permission for that other development, and the decision had included the grant of planning permission (unconditionally or subject to the said conditions, as the case may be) for that development; or

(b) as if the decision had been a decision of the Secretary of State and had included an undertaking to grant planning permission (unconditionally or subject to the said conditions, as the case may be) for that development,

as may be specified in the direction.

(4) The reference in subsection (2) of this section to a decision more favourable to the applicant shall be construed—

(a) in relation to a refusal of permission, as a reference to a decision granting the permission, either unconditionally or subject to conditions, and either in respect of the whole of the land to which the application for permission related or in respect of part of that land; and

(b) in relation to a grant of permission subject to conditions, as a reference to a decision granting the permission applied for unconditionally or subject to less stringent conditions. **[63]**

NOTES
Commencement: 1 April 1972.

39. Provisions supplementary to s 38

(1) Before giving a direction under section 38 of this Act the Secretary of State shall give notice in writing of his proposed direction to the local planning authority to whose decision that direction relates, and to any person who made, and has not since withdrawn, a claim for compensation in respect of that decision; and, if so required by the local planning authority or by any such person, shall afford to each of them an opportunity to appear before, and be heard by, a person appointed by the Secretary of State for the purpose.

(2) In giving any direction under section 38 of this Act, the Secretary of State shall have regard to the provisions of the development plan for the area in which the land in question is situated, in so far as those provisions are material to the development of that land, and shall also have regard to the local circumstances affecting the proposed development, including the use which prevails generally in the case of contiguous or adjacent land, and to any other material considerations.

(3) Where the Secretary of State gives a direction under section 38 of this Act, he shall give notice of the direction to the local planning authority to whose decision the direction relates, and to every person (if any) who made, and has not since withdrawn, a claim for compensation in respect of that decision. **[64]**

NOTES
Commencement: 1 April 1972.

Deemed planning permission

40. Development by local authorities and statutory undertakers with authorisation of government department

(1) Where the authorisation of a government department is required by virtue of an enactment in respect of development to be carried out by a local authority, or by statutory undertakers not being a local authority, that department may, on granting that authorisation, direct that planning permission for that development shall be deemed to be granted, subject to such conditions (if any) as may be specified in the directions.

(2) The provisions of this Act (except Parts VII and XII thereof) shall apply in relation to any planning permission deemed to be granted by virtue of directions under this section as if it had been granted by the Secretary of State on an application referred to him under section 35 of this Act.

(3) For the purposes of this section development shall be taken to be authorised by a government department if—

    (*a*) any consent, authority or approval to or for the development is granted by the department in pursuance of an enactment;

    (*b*) a compulsory purchase order is confirmed by the department authorising the purchase of land for the purpose of the development;

    (*c*) consent is granted by the department to the appropriation of land for the purpose of the development or the acquisition of land by agreement for that purpose;

    (*d*) authority is given by the department for the borrowing of money for the purpose of the development, or for the application for that purpose of any money not otherwise so applicable; or

    (*e*) any undertaking is given by the department to pay a grant in respect of the development in accordance with an enactment authorising the payment of such grants,

and references in this section to the authorisation of a government department shall be construed accordingly.   [65]

NOTES
Commencement: 1 April 1972.

Duration of planning permission

41. Limit of duration of planning permission

(1) Subject to the provisions of this section, every planning permission granted or deemed to be granted shall be granted or, as the case may be, be deemed to be granted, subject to the condition that the development to which it relates must be begun not later than the expiration of—

    (*a*) five years beginning with the date on which the permission is granted or, as the case may be, deemed to be granted; or

    (*b*) such other period (whether longer or shorter) beginning with the said date as the authority concerned with the terms of the planning permission may direct, being a period which the authority considers appropriate having regard to the provisions of the development plan and to any other material considerations.

(2) If planning permission is granted without the condition required by subsection (1) of this section, it shall be deemed to have been granted subject to

the condition that the development to which it relates must be begun not later than the expiration of five years beginning with the date of the grant.

(3) Nothing in this section applies—

   (*a*) to any planning permission granted by a development order;

[(*aa*) to any planning permission granted by an enterprise zone scheme;]

   (*b*) to any planning permission granted for a limited period;

[(*bb*) to any planning permission for development consisting of the winning and working of minerals which is granted (or deemed to be granted) subject to a condition that the development to which it relates must be begun before the expiration of a specified period after the completion of other development consisting of the winning and working of minerals which is already being carried out by the applicant for the planning permission.]

   (*c*) to any planning permission granted under section 32 of this Act on an application relating to buildings or works completed, or a use of land instituted, before the date of the application; or

   (*d*) to any outline planning permission, as defined by section 42 of this Act.   **[66]**

NOTES

Commencement: 1 April 1972.

Sub-s (3): para (*aa*) added by the Local Government, Planning and Land Act 1980, s 179, Sch 32; para (*bb*) added by the Town and Country Planning (Minerals) Act 1981, s 6; prospectively amended by the Housing and Planning Act 1986, s 25(3), Sch 6, Part II, para 2. See Appendix.

42. Outline planning permission

(1) In this section and section 41 of this Act "outline planning permission" means planning permission granted, in accordance with the provisions of a development order, with the reservation for subsequent approval by the local planning authority or the Secretary of State of matters (referred to in this section as "reserved matters") not particularised in the application.

(2) Subject to the provisions of this section, where outline planning permission is granted for development consisting in or including the carrying out of building or other operations, it shall be granted subject to conditions to the following effect—

   (*a*) that, in the case of any reserved matter, application for approval must be made not later than the expiration of three years beginning with the date of the grant of outline planning permission; and

   (*b*) that the development to which the permission relates must be begun not later than whichever is the later of the following dates—

      (i) the expiration of five years from the date of the grant of outline planning permission; or

     (ii) the expiration of two years from the final approval of the reserved matters or, in the case of approval on different dates, the final approval of the last such matter to be approved.

(3) If outline planning permission is granted without the conditions required by subsection (2) of this section, it shall be deemed to have been granted subject to those conditions.

(4) The authority concerned with the terms of an outline planning permission may, in applying subsection (2) of this section, substitute, or direct that there be substituted, for the periods of three years, five years or two years referred to in that subsection such other periods respectively (whether longer or shorter) as they consider appropriate.

(5) The said authority may, in applying the said subsection, specify, or direct that there be specified, separate periods under paragraph (*a*) of the subsection in relation to separate parts of the development to which the planning permission relates; and, if they do so, the condition required by paragraph (*b*) of the subsection shall then be framed correspondingly by reference to those parts, instead of by reference to the development as a whole.

(6) In considering whether to exercise their powers under subsections (4) and (5) of this section, the said authority shall have regard to the provisions of the development plan and to any other material considerations. **[67]**

NOTES
Commencement: 1 April 1972.

43. Provisions supplementary to ss 41 and 42

(1) For the purposes of sections 41 and 42 of this Act, development shall be taken to be begun on the earliest date on which any specified operation comprised in the development begins to be carried out.

(2) In subsection (1) of this section "specified operation" means any of the following, that is to say—

 (*a*) any work of construction in the course of the erection of a building;
 (*b*) the digging of a trench which is to contain the foundations, or part of the foundations, of a building;
 (*c*) the laying of any underground main or pipe to the foundations, or part of the foundations, of a building or to any such trench as is mentioned in the last preceding paragraph;
 (*d*) any operation in the course of laying out or constructing a road or part of a road;
 (*e*) any change in the use of any land, where that change constitutes material development.

(3) In subsection (2)(*e*) of this section "material development" means any development other than—

 (*a*) development for which planning permission is granted by a general development order for the time being in force and which is carried out so as to comply with any condition or limitation subject to which planning permission is so granted;
 (*b*) development falling within any of paragraphs 1, 2, 3 and 5 to 8 of Schedule 8 to this Act, as read with Part III of that Schedule; and
 (*c*) development of any class prescribed for the purposes of this subsection;

and in this subsection "general development order" means a development order made as a general order applicable (subject to such exceptions as may be specified therein) to all land in England and Wales.

(4) The authority referred to in sections 41(1)(*b*) and 42(4) of this Act is the local planning authority or the Secretary of State, in the case of planning permission granted by them, and in the case of planning permission under section 40 of this Act is the department on whose direction planning permission is deemed to be granted.

(5) For the purposes of section 42 of this Act, a reserved matter shall be treated as finally approved when an application for approval is granted or, in a case where the application is made to the local planning authority and there is an appeal to the Secretary of State against the authority's decision on the

application and the Secretary of State grants the approval, on the date of the determination of the appeal.

(6) Where a local planning authority grant planning permission, the fact that any of the conditions of the permission are required by the provisions of sections 41 or 42 of this Act to be imposed, or are deemed by those provisions to be imposed, shall not prevent the conditions being the subject of an appeal under section 36 of this Act against the decision of the authority.

(7) In the case of planning permission (whether outline or other) having conditions attached to it by or under section 41 or 42 of this Act—

(a) development carried out after the date by which the conditions of the permission require it to be carried out shall be treated as not authorised by the permission; and

(b) an application for approval of a reserved matter, if it is made after the date by which the conditions require it to be made, shall be treated as not made in accordance with the terms of the permission.   [68]

NOTES
Commencement: 1 April 1972.

44. Termination of planning permission by reference to time limit

(1) The following provisions of this section shall have effect where, by virtue of section 41 or 42 of this Act, a planning permission is subject to a condition that the development to which the permission relates must be begun before the expiration of a particular period and that development has been begun within that period but the period has elapsed without the development having been completed.

(2) If the local planning authority are of opinion that the development will not be completed within a reasonable period, they may serve a notice (in this section referred to as a "completion notice") stating that the planning permission will cease to have effect at the expiration of a further period specified in the notice, being a period of not less than twelve months after the notice takes effect.

(3) A completion notice—

(a) shall be served on the owner and on the occupier of the land and on any other person who in the opinion of the local planning authority will be affected by the notice; and

(b) shall take effect only if and when it is confirmed by the Secretary of State, who may in confirming it substitute some longer period for that specified in the notice as the period at the expiration of which the planning permission is to cease to have effect.

(4) If, within such period as may be specified in a completion notice (not being less than twenty-eight days from the service thereof) any person on whom the notice is served so requires, the Secretary of State, before confirming the notice, shall afford to that person and to the local planning authority an opportunity of appearing before, and being heard by, a person appointed by the Secretary of State for the purpose.

(5) If a completion notice takes effect, the planning permission therein referred to shall at the expiration of the period specified in the notice, whether the original period specified under subsection (2) of this section or a longer period substituted by the Secretary of State under subsection (3) of this section,

be invalid except so far as it authorises any development carried out thereunder up to the end of that period.

(6) The local planning authority may withdraw a completion notice at any time before the expiration of the period specified therein as the period at the expiration of which the planning permission is to cease to have effect; and if they do so they shall forthwith give notice of the withdrawal to every person who was served with the completion notice.   [69]

NOTES
Commencement: 1 April 1972.

44A. Limit of duration of planning permission for winning and working of minerals

[(1) Every planning permission for development consisting of the winning and working of minerals shall be subject to a condition as to the duration of the development.

(2) Except where a condition is specified under subsection (3) of this section the condition in the case of planning permission granted or deemed to be granted after the date of the commencement of section 7 of the Town and Country Planning (Minerals) Act 1981 is that the development must cease not later than the expiration of the period of sixty years beginning with the date of the permission.

(3) An authority granting planning permission after the date of the commencement of the said section 7 or directing after that date that planning permission shall be deemed to be granted may specify a longer or shorter period than sixty years, and if they do so, the condition is that the development must cease not later than the expiration of a period of the specified length beginning with the date of the permission.

(4) A longer or shorter period than sixty years may be prescribed for the purposes of subsections (2) and (3) of this section.

(5) The condition in the case of planning permission granted or deemed to have been granted before the commencement of section 7 of the Town and Country Planning (Minerals) Act 1981 is that the development must cease not later than the expiration of the period of sixty years beginning with the date of the commencement of that section.

(6) A condition to which planning permission for development consisting of the winning and working of minerals is subject by virtue of this section is not to be regarded for the purposes of this Act as a condition such as is mentioned in subsection (1)(*b*) of section 30 of this Act.

(7) Where planning permission for development consisting of the winning and working of minerals is granted by the mineral planning authority, any condition to which it is subject by virtue of this section is to be regarded for the purposes of section 36 of this Act as a condition imposed by a decision of the local planning authority, and may accordingly be the subject of an appeal under that section.]   [70]

NOTES
Commencement: 22 February 1982.
Added by the Town and Country Planning (Minerals) Act 1981, s 7.

Revocation or modification of planning permission

45. Power to revoke or modify planning permission

(1) If it appears to the local planning authority, having regard to the development plan and to any other material considerations, that it is expedient to revoke or modify any permission to develop land granted on an application made under this Part of this Act, the authority, subject to the following provisions of this section, may by order revoke or modify the permission to such extent as (having regard to those matters) they consider expedient.

(2) Except as provided in section 46 of this Act, an order under this section shall not take effect unless it is confirmed by the Secretary of State; and the Secretary of State may confirm any such order submitted to him either without modification or subject to such modifications as he considers expedient.

(3) Where a local planning authority submit an order to the Secretary of State for his confirmation under this section, the authority shall serve notice on the owner and on the occupier of the land affected and on any other person who in their opinion will be affected by the order; and if within such period as may be specified in that notice (not being less than twenty-eight days from the service thereof) any person on whom the notice is served so requires, the Secretary of State, before confirming the order, shall afford to that person and to the local planning authority an opportunity of appearing before, and being heard by, a person appointed by the Secretary of State for the purpose.

(4) The power conferred by this section to revoke or modify permission to develop land may be exercised—

 (*a*) where the permission relates to the carrying out of building or other operations, at any time before those operations have been completed;
 (*b*) where the permission relates to a change of the use of any land, at any time before the change has taken place:

Provided that the revocation or modification of permission for the carrying out of building or other operations shall not affect so much of those operations as has been previously carried out.

[(5) References to the local planning authority in this section are to be construed, in relation to development consisting of the winning and working of minerals, as references to the mineral planning authority.

(6) An order under this section may include any such aftercare condition as the mineral planning authority think fit if—

 (*a*) it also includes a restoration condition; or
 (*b*) a restoration condition has previously been imposed in relation to the land by virtue of any provision of this Act.

(7) Subsections (3) to (19) of section 30A of this Act shall apply in relation to an aftercare condition so imposed as they apply in relation to such a condition imposed under that section.]   **[71]**

NOTES
  Commencement: 19 May 1986 (sub-ss (5)-(7)); 1 April 1972 (remainder).
  Commencement order: SI 1986 No 760.
  Sub-ss (1)-(4) derived from the Town and Country Planning Act 1962, s 27.
  Sub-ss (5)—(7): added by the Town and Country Planning (Minerals) Act 1981, s 8.
  See further: Town and Country Planning (Compensation for Restrictions on Mineral Working)
Regulations 1985, SI 1985 No 698, regs 3, 6.

46. Unopposed revocation or modification

(1) The following provisions shall have effect where the local planning authority have made an order under section 45 of this Act but have not submitted the order to the Secretary of State for confirmation by him, and—

> (*a*) the owner and the occupier of the land and all persons who in the authority's opinion will be affected by the order have notified the authority in writing that they do not object to the order; ...

(2) The authority shall advertise in the prescribed manner the fact that the order has been made, and the advertisement shall specify—

> (*a*) the period (not being less than twenty-eight days from the date on which the advertisement first appears) within which persons affected by the order may give notice to the Secretary of State that they wish for an opportunity of appearing before, and being heard by, a person appointed by the Secretary of State for the purpose; and
>
> (*b*) the period (not being less than fourteen days from the expiration of the period referred to in paragraph (*a*) of this subsection) at the expiration of which, if no such notice is given to the Secretary of State, the order may take effect by virtue of this section and without being confirmed by the Secretary of State.

(3) The authority shall also serve notice to the same effect on the persons mentioned in subsection (1)(*a*) of this section, ...

(4) The authority shall send a copy of any advertisement published under subsection (2) of this section to the Secretary of State, not more than three days after the publication.

(5) If within the period referred to in subsection (2)(*a*) of this section no person claiming to be affected by the order has given notice to the Secretary of State as aforesaid, and the Secretary of State has not directed that the order be submitted to him for confirmation, the order shall, at the expiration of the period referred to in subsection (2)(*b*) of this section, take effect by virtue of this section and without being confirmed by the Secretary of State as required by section 45(2) of this Act.

(6) This section does not apply to an order revoking or modifying a planning permission granted or deemed to have been granted by the Secretary of State under this Part of this Act or under Part IV or V thereof; nor does it apply to an order modifying any conditions to which a planning permission is subject by virtue of section 41 or 42 of this Act. **[72]**

NOTES
> Commencement: To be appointed (sub-ss (1A)-(14)); 1 April 1972 (remainder).
> Words omitted repealed by the Local Government Act 1974, s 42(2), Sch 8.

Reference of certain matters to Planning Inquiry Commission or independent tribunal

47. Constitution of Planning Inquiry Commission

(1) The Secretary of State may constitute a Planning Inquiry Commission to inquire into and report on any matter referred to them under section 48 of this Act.

(2) Any such commission shall consist of a chairman and not less than two nor more than four other members appointed by the Secretary of State.

(3) The Secretary of State may pay to the members of any such commission such remuneration and allowances as he may with the consent of the Minister for the Civil Service determine, and may provide for each such commission such officers or servants, and such accommodation, as appears to him expedient to provide for the purpose of assisting the commission in the discharge of their functions.

(4) The validity of any proceedings of any such commission shall not be affected by any vacancy among the members of the commission or by any defect in the appointment of any member.

(5) . . .

(6) The "Secretary of State", in relation to any matter affecting both England and Wales, means in subsections (1) and (2) of this section the Secretaries of State for the time being having general responsibility in planning matters in relation to England and in relation to Wales acting jointly, and in subsection (3) of this section one of those Secretaries of State authorised by the other to act on behalf of both of them for the purposes of that subsection.   **[73]**

NOTES
Commencement: 1 April 1972.
Words omitted repealed by the House of Commons Disqualification Act 1975, s 10(2), Sch 3.

48. References to a Planning Inquiry Commission

(1) The following matters may, in the circumstances mentioned in subsection (2) of this section, be referred to a Planning Inquiry Commission, that is to say—

    (*a*) an application for planning permission which the Secretary of State has under section 35 of this Act directed to be referred to him instead of being dealt with by a local planning authority;

    (*b*) an appeal under section 36 of this Act (including that section as applied by or under any other provision of this Act);

    (*c*) a proposal that a government department should give a direction under section 40 of this Act that planning permission shall be deemed to be granted for development by a local authority or by statutory undertakers which is required by any enactment to be authorised by that department;

    (*d*) a proposal that development should be carried out by or on behalf of a government department.

(2) Any of the matters mentioned in subsection (1) of this section may be referred to any such commission under this section if it appears expedient to the responsible Minister or Ministers that the question whether the proposed development should be permitted to be carried out should be the subject of a special inquiry on either or both of the following grounds—

    (*a*) there are considerations of national or regional importance which are relevant to the determination of that question and require evaluation, but a proper evaluation thereof cannot be made unless there is a special inquiry for the purpose;

    (*b*) the technical or scientific aspects of the proposed development are of so unfamiliar a character as to jeopardise a proper determination of that question unless there is a special inquiry for the purpose.

(3) Two or more of the matters mentioned in subsection (1) of this section may be referred to the same commission under this section if it appears to the

responsible Minister or Ministers that they relate to proposals to carry out development for similar purposes on different sites.

(4) Where a matter referred to a commission under this section relates to a proposal to carry out development for any purpose at a particular site, the responsible Minister or Ministers may also refer to the commission the question whether development for that purpose should instead be carried out at an alternative site.

(5) The responsible Minister or Ministers shall, on referring a matter to a commission under this section, state in the reference the reasons therefor and may draw the attention of the commission to any points which seem to him or them to be relevant to their inquiry.

(6) A commission inquiring into a matter referred to them under this section shall—

   (a) identify and investigate the considerations relevant to, or the technical or scientific aspects of, that matter which in their opinion are relevant to the question whether the proposed development should be permitted to be carried out and assess the importance to be attached to those considerations or aspects;

   (b) thereafter, if the applicant, in the case of a matter mentioned in subsection (1)(a), (b) or (c) of this section, or the local planning authority in any case so desire, afford to each of them, and, in the case of an application or appeal mentioned in the said subsection (1)(a) or (b), to any person who has made representations relating to the subject matter of the application or appeal which the authority are required to take into account under section 29(2) or (3) of this Act, an opportunity of appearing before and being heard by one or more members of the commission;

   (c) report to the responsible Minister or Ministers on the matter referred to them.

(7) Any such commission may, with the approval of the Secretary of State and at his expense, arrange for the carrying out (whether by the commission themselves or by others) of research of any kind appearing to them to be relevant to a matter referred to them for inquiry and report.

In this subsection "the Secretary of State", in relation to any matter affecting both England and Wales, means the Secretary of State for the time being having general responsibility in planning matters in relation to England or the Secretary of State for the time being having such responsibility in relation to Wales acting, by arrangements between the two of them, on behalf of both.

(8) Schedule 10 to this Act shall have effect for the construction of references in this section and in section 49 of this Act to "the responsible Minister or Ministers".   [74]

NOTES
Commencement: 1 April 1972.

49. Procedure on reference to a Planning Inquiry Commission

(1) A reference to a Planning Inquiry Commission of a proposal that development should be carried out by or on behalf of a government department may be made at any time and a reference of any other matter mentioned in section 48 of this Act may be made at any time before, but not after, the determination of the relevant application referred under section 35 of this Act

or the relevant appeal under section 36 of this Act or, as the case may be, the giving of the relevant direction under section 40 of this Act, notwithstanding that an inquiry or other hearing has been held into the proposal by a person appointed by any Minister for the purpose.

(2) Notice of the making of a reference to any such commission shall be published in the prescribed manner, and a copy of the notice shall be served on the local planning authority for the area in which it is proposed that the relevant development shall be carried out, and—

   (*a*) in the case of an application for planning permission referred under section 35 of this Act or an appeal under section 36 of this Act, on the applicant and any person who has made representations relating to the subject matter of the application or appeal which the authority are required to take into account under section 29(2) or (3) of this Act;
   (*b*) in the case of a proposal that a direction should be given under section 40 of this Act with respect to any development, on the local authority or statutory undertakers applying for authorisation to carry out that development.

(3) A Planning Inquiry Commission shall, for the purpose of complying with section 48(6)(*b*) of this Act, hold a local inquiry; and they may hold such an inquiry, if they think it necessary for the proper discharge of their functions, notwithstanding that neither the applicant nor the local planning authority desire an opportunity of appearing and being heard.

(4) Where a Planning Inquiry Commission are to hold a local inquiry under subsection (3) of this section in connection with a matter referred to them, and it appears to the responsible Minister or Ministers, in the case of some other matter falling to be determined by a Minister of the Crown and required or authorised by an enactment other than this section to be the subject of a local inquiry, that the two matters are so far cognate that they should be considered together, he or, as the case may be, they may direct that the two inquiries be held concurrently or combined as one inquiry.

(5) An inquiry held by such a commission under this section shall be treated for the purposes of the Tribunals and Inquiries Act 1971 as one held by a Minister in pursuance of a duty imposed by a statutory provision.

(6) Subsections (2) to (5) of section 290 of the Local Government Act 1933 (evidence and costs at local inquiries) shall apply in relation to an inquiry held under subsection (3) of this section as they apply in relation to an inquiry caused to be held by a department under subsection (1) of that section, with the substitution for references to a department (other than the first reference in subsection (4)) of references to the responsible Minister or Ministers.

(7) Subject to the provisions of this section and to any directions given to them by the responsible Minister or Ministers, a Planning Inquiry Commission shall have power to regulate their own procedure.   **[75]**

NOTES
Commencement: 1 April 1972.

Additional powers of control

51. Orders requiring discontinuance of use or alteration or removal of buildings or works

(1) If it appears to a local planning authority that it is expedient in the interests of the proper planning of their area (including the interests of amenity), regard being had to the development plan and to any other material considerations—

    (*a*) that any use of land should be discontinued, or that any conditions should be imposed on the continuance of a use of land; or

    (*b*) that any buildings or works should be altered or removed,

the local planning authority may by order require the discontinuance of that use, or impose such conditions as may be specified in the order on the continuance thereof, or require such steps as may be so specified to be taken for the alteration or removal of the buildings or works, as the case may be.

[(1A) For the purposes of this section development consisting of the winning and working of minerals in, on or under any land is to be treated as a use of that land.

(1B) References in this section to the local planning authority are to be construed, in relation to development consisting of the winning and working of minerals, as references to the mineral planning authority.

(1C) Subsection (1) of this section shall have effect in relation to the mineral planning authority as if—

    (*a*) the words "or

        (*c*) that any plant or machinery used for the winning and working of minerals should be altered or removed,"

    were added at the end of paragraph (*b*); and

    (*b*) the words "or plant or machinery" were inserted after the words "buildings or works", in the second place where those words occur.

(1D) Where development consisting of the winning and working of minerals is being carried out in, on or under any land, the conditions which an order under this section may impose include a restoration condition.

(1E) An order under this section may include any such aftercare condition as the mineral planning authority think fit if—

    (*a*) it also includes a restoration condition; or

    (*b*) a restoration condition has previously been imposed in relation to the land by virtue of any provision of this Act.

(1F) Subsections (3) to (8) and (11) to (19) of section 30A of this Act shall apply in relation to an aftercare condition imposed under this section as they apply in relation to such a condition imposed under that section.

(1G) In a case where—

    (*a*) the use specified is a use for agriculture; and

    (*b*) the land was in use for agriculture immediately before development consisting of the winning and working of minerals began to be carried out in, on or under it or had previously been used for agriculture and had not been used for any authorised purpose since its use for agriculture ceased; and

(c) the Minister has notified the mineral planning authority of the physical characteristics of the land when it was last used for agriculture,

the land is brought to the required standard when its physical characteristics are restored, so far as it is practicable to do so, to what they were when it was last used for agriculture.

(1H) In any other case where the use specified is a use for agriculture, the land is brought to the required standard when it is reasonably fit for that use.]

(2) Any order under this section may grant planning permission for any development of the land to which the order relates, subject to such conditions as may be specified in the order; and the provisions of section 45 of this Act shall apply in relation to any planning permission granted by an order under this section as they apply in relation to planning permission granted by the local planning authority on an application made under this Part of this Act.

(3) The power conferred by subsection (2) of this section shall include power, by an order under this section, to grant planning permission, subject to such conditions as may be specified in the order—

(a) for the retention, on the land to which the order relates, of buildings or works constructed or carried out before the date on which the order was submitted to the Secretary of State; or

(b) for the continuance of a use of that land instituted before that date;

and subsection (3) of section 32 of this Act shall apply to planning permission granted by virtue of this subsection as it applies to planning permission granted in accordance with subsection (2) of that section.

(4) An order under this section shall not take effect unless it is confirmed by the Secretary of State, either without modification or subject to such modifications as he considers expedient.

(5) The power of the Secretary of State under this section to confirm an order subject to modifications shall include power—

(a) to modify any provision of the order granting planning permission, as mentioned in subsection (2) or subsection (3) of this section;

(b) to include in the order any grant of planning permission which might have been included in the order as submitted to the Secretary of State.

(6) Where a local planning authority submit an order to the Secretary of State for his confirmation under this section, that authority shall serve notice on the owner and on the occupier of the land affected, and on any other person who in their opinion will be affected by the order; and if within the period specified in that behalf in the notice (not being less than twenty-eight days from the service thereof) any person on whom the notice is served so requires, the Secretary of State, before confirming the order, shall afford to that person and to the local planning authority an opportunity of appearing before, and being heard by, a person appointed by the Secretary of State for the purpose.

(7) Where an order under this section has been confirmed by the Secretary of State, the local planning authority shall serve a copy of the order on the owner and occupier of the land to which the order relates.

(8) Where the requirements of an order under this section will involve the displacement of persons residing in any premises, it shall be the duty of the local planning authority, in so far as there is no other residential accommodation

suitable to the reasonable requirements of those persons available on reasonable terms, to secure the provision of such accommodation in advance of the displacement.

(9) In the case of planning permission granted by an order under this section, the authority referred to in sections 41(1)(*b*) and 42(4) of this Act is the local planning authority making the order or, where the Secretary of State in confirming the order exercises his powers under subsection (5) of this section, the Secretary of State. **[76]**

NOTES
   Commencement: 19 May 1986 (sub-ss (1A)-(1H)); April 1972 (remainder).
   Commencement order: SI 1986 No 760.
   This section derived from the Town and Country Planning Act 1962, s 28, and the Town and Country Planning Act 1968, s 67(2).
   Sub-ss (1A)-(1H): added by the Town and Country Planning (Minerals) Act 1981, s 9.
   See further: Town and Country Planning (Compensation for Restrictions on Mineral Working) Regulations 1985, SI 1985 No 698, regs 4, 6.

51A. Prohibition of resumption of winning and working minerals

[(1) Where it appears to the mineral planning authority—

> (*a*) that development consisting of the winning and working of minerals has been carried out in, on or under any land; but
> (*b*) that it has permanently ceased,

the mineral planning authority may by order—

> > (i) prohibit the resumption of such development; and
> > (ii) impose, in relation to the site, any such requirement as is specified in subsection (3) of this section.

(2) The mineral planning authority may assume that development consisting of the winning and working of minerals has permanently ceased only when—

> (*a*) no such development has been carried out to any substantial extent anywhere in, on or under the site of which the land forms part for a period of at least two years; and
> (*b*) it appears to the mineral planning authority, on the evidence available to them at the time when they make the order, that resumption of such development in, on or under the land is unlikely.

(3) The requirements mentioned in subsection (1) of this section are—

> (*a*) a requirement to alter or remove plant or machinery which was used for the purpose of the winning and working of minerals or for any purpose ancillary to that purpose;
> (*b*) a requirement to take such steps as may be specified in the order, within such period as may be so specified, for the purpose of removing or alleviating any injury to amenity which has been caused by the winning and working of minerals, other than injury due to subsidence caused by underground mining operations;
> (*c*) a requirement that any condition subject to which planning permission for development consisting of the winning and working of minerals was granted or which has been imposed by virtue of any provision of this Act shall be complied with; and
> (*d*) a restoration condition.

(4) An order under this section may include any such aftercare condition as the mineral planning authority think fit if—

> (*a*) it also includes a restoration condition; or

(b) a restoration condition has previously been imposed in relation to the site by virtue of any provision of this Act.

(5) Subsections (3) to (8) and (11) to (19) of section 30A of this Act shall apply in relation to an aftercare condition imposed under this section as they apply in relation to such a condition imposed under that section.

(6) In a case where—

(a) the use specified is a use for agriculture; and
(b) the land was in use for agriculture immediately before development consisting of the winning and working of minerals began to be carried out in, on or under it or had previously been used for agriculture and had not been used for any authorised purpose since its use for agriculture ceased; and
(c) the Minister has notified the mineral planning authority of the physical characteristics of the land when it was last used for agriculture,

the land is brought to the required standard when its physical characteristics are restored, so far as it is practicable to do so, to what they were when it was last used for agriculture.

(7) In any other case where the use specified is a use for agriculture, the land is brought to the required standard when it is reasonably fit for that use.

(8) An order under this section shall not take effect unless it is confirmed by the Secretary of State, either without modification or subject to such modifications as he considers expedient.

(9) Where a mineral planning authority submit an order under this section to the Secretary of State for his confirmation under this section, that authority shall serve notice of the order on any person who is an owner or occupier of any of the land to which the order relates, and on any other person who in their opinion will be affected by the order; and if within the period specified in that behalf in the notice (not being less than twenty-eight days from the service thereof) any person on whom the notice is served so requires, the Secretary of State, before confirming the order, shall afford to that person and to the mineral planning authority an opportunity of appearing before, and being heard by, a person appointed by the Secretary of State for that purpose.

(10) Where an order under this section has been confirmed by the Secretary of State, the mineral planning authority shall serve a copy of the order on every person who was entitled to be served with notice under subsection (9) of this section.

(11) On an order under this section taking effect any planning permission for the development to which the order relates shall cease to have effect but without prejudice to the power of the mineral planning authority, on revoking the order, to make a further grant of planning permission for development consisting of the winning and working of minerals.]   [77]

NOTES
Commencement: 19 May 1986.
Commencement order: SI 1986 No 760.
Added by the Town and Country Planning (Minerals) Act 1981, s 10.
See further: Town and Country Planning (Compensation for Restrictions on Mineral Working) Regulations 1985, SI 1985 No 698, regs 4, 5.

51B. Orders after suspension of winning and working of minerals

[(1) Where it appears to the mineral planning authority—

    (*a*) that development consisting of the winning and working of minerals has been carried out in, on or under any land; but

    (*b*) that it has been temporarily suspended,

the mineral planning authority may by order (in this Act referred to as a "suspension order") require that steps shall be taken for the protection of the environment.

(2) The mineral planning authority may assume that development consisting of the winning and working of minerals has been temporarily suspended only when—

    (*a*) no such development has been carried out to any substantial extent anywhere in, on or under the site of which the land forms part for a period of at least twelve months; but

    (*b*) it appears to the mineral planning authority, on the evidence available to them at the time when they make the order, that a resumption of such development in, on or under the land is likely.

(3) In this Act "steps for the protection of the environment" means steps for the purpose—

    (*a*) of preserving the amenities of the area in which the land in, on or under which the development was carried out is situated during the period while operations for the winning and working of minerals in, on or under it are suspended;

    (*b*) of protecting that area from damage during that period; or

    (*c*) of preventing any deterioration in the condition of the land during that period.

(4) A suspension order shall specify a period, commencing with the date on which it is to take effect, within which any requried step for the protection of the environment is to be taken and may specify different periods for the taking of different steps.

(5) At any time when a suspension order is in operation the mineral planning authority may by order (in this Act referred to as a "supplementary suspension order") direct—

    (*a*) that steps for the protection of the environment shall be taken in addition to or in substitution for any of the steps which the suspension order or a previous supplementary suspension order specified as required to be taken; or

    (*b*) that the suspension order or any supplementary suspension order shall cease to have effect.]   **[78]**

NOTES
    Commencement: 19 May 1986.
    Commencement order: SI 1986 No 760.
    Added by the Town and Country Planning (Minerals) Act 1981, s 10.
    See further: Town and Country Planning (Compensation for Restrictions on Mineral Working) Regulations 1985, SI 1985 No 698, regs 4, 5.

51C. Confirmation and coming into operation of suspension orders

[(1) Subject to subsection (2) of this section, a suspension order or a supplementary suspension order shall not take effect unless it is confirmed by the Secretary of

State, either without modification or subject to such modifications as he considers expedient.

(2) A supplementary suspension order revoking a suspension order or a previous supplementary suspension order and not requiring that any fresh step shall take effect without confirmation.

(3) Subsection (9) of section 51A of this Act shall have effect in relation to a suspension order or supplementary suspension order submitted to the Secretary of State for his confirmation as it has effect in relation to an order submitted to him for his confirmation under that section.

(4) Where a suspension order or supplementary suspension order has been confirmed by the Secretary of State, the mineral planning authority shall serve a copy of the order on every person who was entitled to be served with notice by virtue of subsection (3) of this section.]   **[79]**

NOTES
    Commencement: 19 May 1986.
    Commencement order: SI 1986 No 760.
    Added by the Town and Country Planning (Minerals) Act 1981, s 10.

51D. Registration of suspension orders as local land charges

[A suspension order or a supplementary suspension order shall be a local land charge.]   **[80]**

NOTES
    Commencement: 19 May 1986.
    Commencement order: SI 1986 No 760.
    Added by the Town and Country Planning (Minerals) Act 1981, s 10.

51E. Reviews of suspension orders

[(1) It shall be the duty of a mineral planning authority—

    (*a*) to undertake in accordance with the following provisions of this section reviews of suspension orders and supplementary suspension orders which are in operation in their area; and

    (*b*) to determine whether they should make, in relation to any land to which a suspension order or supplementary suspension order applies,—

        (i) an order under section 51A of this Act; or
        (ii) a supplementary suspension order.

(2) The first review of a suspension order shall be undertaken not more than five years from the date on which the order takes effect.

(3) Each subsequent review shall be undertaken not more than five years after the previous review.

(4) If a supplementary suspension order is in operation for any part of the area for which a suspension order is in operation, they shall be reviewed together.

(5) If a mineral planning authority have made a supplementary suspension order which requires the taking of steps for the protection of the environment in substitution for all the steps required to be taken by a previous order under section 51B of this Act, the authority shall undertake reviews of the

supplementary suspension order in accordance with subsections (6) and (7) of this section.

(6) The first review shall be undertaken not more than five years from the date on which the order takes effect.

(7) Each subsequent review shall be undertaken not more than five years after the previous review.

(8) The duties to undertake reviews imposed by this section are in addition to and not in substitution for the duties imposed by section 264A of this Act.]

[81]

NOTES
Commencement: 19 May 1986.
Commencement order: SI 1986 No 760.
Added by the Town and Country Planning (Minerals) Act 1981, s 10.

51F. Resumption of winning and working of minerals after suspension order

[(1) Nothing in a suspension order or a supplementary suspension order shall prevent the recommencement of development consisting of the winning and working of minerals in, on, or under the land in relation to which the order is in effect; but no person shall recommence such development without first giving the mineral planning authority notice of his intention to do so.

(2) A notice under subsection (1) of this section shall specify the date on which the person giving the notice intends to recommence development consisting of the winning and working of minerals.

(3) The mineral planning authority shall revoke the order if development consisting of the winning and working of minerals has recommenced to a substantial extent in, on or under the land in relation to which the order is in effect.

(4) If the authority do not revoke the order before the end of the period of two months from the date specified in the notice under subsection (1) of this section, the person who gave that notice may apply to the Secretary of State for the revocation of the order.

(5) Notice of an application under subsection (4) of this section shall be given by the applicant to the mineral planning authority.

(6) If he is required to do so by the person who gave the notice or by the mineral planning authority, the Secretary of State, before deciding whether to revoke the order, shall afford to that person and to the mineral planning authority an opportunity of appearing before, and being heard by, a person appointed by the Secretary of State for the purpose.

(7) If the Secretary of State is satisfied that development consisting of the winning and working of minerals in, on or under the land has recommenced to a substantial extent, he shall revoke the order.

(8) If the Secretary of State revokes an order by virtue of subsection (7) of this section, he shall give notice of its revocation to the person who applied to him for the revocation and to the mineral planning authority.]   **[82]**

NOTES
Commencement: 19 May 1986.
Commencement order: SI 1986 No 760.
Added by the Town and Country Planning (Minerals) Act 1981, s 10.

52. Agreements regulating development or use of land

(1) A local planning authority may enter into an agreement with any person interested in land in their area for the purpose of restricting or regulating the development or use of the land, either permanently or during such period as may be prescribed by the agreement; and any such agreement may contain such incidental and consequential provisions (including provisions of a financial character) as appear to the local planning authority to be necessary or expedient for the purposes of the agreement.

(2) An agreement made under this section with any person interested in land may be enforced by the local planning authority against persons deriving title under that person in respect of that land, as if the local planning authority were possessed of adjacent land and as if the agreement had been expressed to be made for the benefit of such land.

(3) Nothing in this section or in any agreement made thereunder shall be construed—

    (*a*) as restricting the exercise, in relation to land which is the subject of any such agreement, of any powers exercisable by any Minister or authority under this Act so long as those powers are exercised in accordance with the provisions of the development plan, or in accordance with any directions which may have been given by the Secretary of State as to the provisions to be included in such a plan; or

    (*b*) as requiring the exercise of any such powers otherwise than as mentioned in paragraph (*a*) of this subsection.

(4) The power of a local planning authority to make agreements under this section may be exercised also—

    (*a*) in relation to land in a county district, by the council of that district;

    (*b*) in relation to land in the area of a joint planning board, by the council of the county or county borough in which the land is situated,

and references in this section to a local planning authority shall be construed accordingly.   **[83]**

NOTES

    Commencement: 1 April 1972.

Determination whether planning permission required

53. Applications to determine whether planning permission required

(1) If any person who proposes to carry out any operations on land, or to make any change in the use of land, wishes to have it determined whether the carrying out of those operations, or the making of that change, would constitute or involve development of the land, and, if so, whether an application for planning permission in respect thereof is required under this Part of this Act, having regard to the provisions of the development order [and of any enterprise zone scheme], he may, either as part of an application for planning permission, or without any such application, apply to the local planning authority to determine that question.

(2) The provisions of sections 24, 29(1), 31(1), 34(1) and (3) and 35 to 37 of this Act shall, subject to any necessary modifications, apply in relation to any

application under this section, and to the determination thereof, as they apply in relation to applications for planning permission and to the determination of such applications. **[84]**

NOTES
Commencement: 1 April 1972.
Amended by the Local Government, Planning and Land Act 1980, s 179, Sch 32.
Sub-s (1): prospectively amended by the Housing and Planning Act 1986, s 25(3), Sch 6, Part II, para 3. See Appendix.

PART IV

ADDITIONAL CONTROL IN SPECIAL CASES

Buildings of special architectural or historic interest

54. Lists of buildings of special architectural or historic interest

(1) For the purposes of this Act and with a view to the guidance of local planning authorities in the performance of their functions under this Act in relation to buildings of special architectural or historic interest, the Secretary of State shall compile lists of such buildings, or approve, with or without modifications, such lists compiled by [the Historic Buildings and Monuments Commission for England (in this section referred to as "the Commission") or by] other persons or bodies of persons, and may amend any list so compiled or approved.

[The Secretary of State shall not approve under this subsection any list compiled by the Commission if the list contains any building situated outside England.]

(2) In considering whether to include a building in a list compiled or approved under this section, the Secretary of State may take into account not only the building itself but also—

(a) any respect in which its exterior contributes to the architectural or historic interest of any group of buildings of which it forms part; and

(b) the desirability of preserving, on the ground of its architectural or historic interest, any feature of the building consisting of a man-made object or structure fixed to the building or forming part of the land and comprised within the curtilage of the building.

(3) Before compiling or approving, with or without modifications, any list under this section, or amending any list thereunder the Secretary of State shall consult with [the Commission and with such other] persons or bodies of persons as appear to him appropriate as having special knowledge of, or interest in, buildings of architectural or historic interest.

[The Secretary of State shall consult with the Commission under this subsection only in relation to buildings which are situated in England.]

(4) As soon as may be after any list has been compiled or approved under this section, or any amendments of such a list have been made, a copy of so much of the list as relates to any . . . London borough or county district, or of so much of the amendments as relates thereto, as the case may be, certified by or on behalf of the Secretary of State to be a true copy thereof, shall be deposited with [the proper officer of the borough or district council and, outside Greater London, with the proper officer of the county planning authority whose area or any part of whose area includes the district, or any part of it, and where the district council are not the district planning authority, the proper officer of that authority].

(5) A copy of anything required by subsection (4) of this section to be deposited with the [proper officer of a London borough shall be deposited also with the chief officer of the Commission].

(6) Any copy deposited under subsection (4) of this section shall be registered [a local land charge, and for the purposes of the Local Land Charges Act 1975 the council with whom a copy is deposited shall be treated as the originating authority as respects the charge thereby constituted].

(7) As soon as may be after the inclusion of any building in a list under this section, whether on the compilation or approval of the list or by the amendment thereof, or as soon as may be after any such list has been amended by the exclusion of any building therefrom, the council of the . . . London borough or county district in whose area the building is situated, on being informed of the fact by the Secretary of State, shall serve a notice in the prescribed form on every owner and occupier of the building, stating that the building has been included in, or excluded from, the list, as the case may be.

(8) The Secretary of State shall keep available for public inspection, free of charge at reasonable hours and at a convenient place, copies of all lists and amendments of lists compiled, approved or made by him under this section; and every authority [or body with whose officer] copies of any list or amendments are deposited under this section shall similarly keep available copies of so much of any such list or amendment as relates to buildings within their area [or, in the case of the Commission, in Greater London.]

(9) In this Act "listed building" means a building which is for the time being included in a list compiled or approved by the Secretary of State under this section; and, for the purposes of the provisions of this Act relating to listed buildings and building preservation notices, any object or structure fixed to a building, or forming part of the land and comprised within the curtilage of a building, shall be treated as part of the building.

(10) Every building which immediately before 1st January 1969 was subject to a building preservation order under Part III of the Act of 1962 but was not then included in a list compiled or approved under section 32 of that Act, shall be deemed to be a listed building; but the Secretary of State may at any time direct, in the case of any building, that this subsection shall no longer apply to it and the council of the . . . London borough or county district in whose area the building is situated, on being notified of the Secretary of State's direction, shall give notice of it to the owner and occupier of the building.

(11) Before giving a direction under subsection (10) of this section in relation to a building, the Secretary of State shall [(subject to subsection (12) of this section)] consult with

[(a) in Greater London [or a metropolitan county], the local planning authority;
(b) in [any part of a National Park outside a metropolitan county], the county planning authority;
(c) elsewhere the district planning authority; and
(d) in any case the owner and the occupier of the building.]

[(12) Where a direction mentioned in subsection (11) of this section relates to a building situated in England, that subsection shall not apply but the Secretary of State shall consult with the Commission, who shall in turn consult with the persons mentioned in paragraphs (a) to (d) of that subsection.]   **[85]**

NOTES
Commencement: 1 April 1984 (sub-s (12)); 1 April 1972 (remainder).
Commencement order: SI 1984 No 208.
   This section derived from the Town and Country Planning Act 1962, s 32, the London Government Act 1963, s 28(1), the Civic Amenities Act 1967, s 11, and the Town and Country Planning Act 1968, ss 40(1), (3), (10), (11), 54, Sch 9, para 17.
   Sub-ss (1), (3): amended by the National Heritage Act 1983, s 33, Sch 4, para 16(2), (3).
   Sub-ss (4), (7), (10): amended by the Local Government Act 1972, ss 182, 272(1), Schs 16, 30.
   Sub-ss (5), (8): amended by the Local Government Act 1985, s 6, Sch 2, para 1.
   Sub-s (6): amended by the Local Land Charges Act 1975, s 17(2), Sch 1.
   Sub-s (9): amended by the Housing and Planning Act 1986, s 40, Sch 9, Part I, para 1(1). See Appendix.
   Sub-s (11): first amendment in square brackets made by the National Heritage Act 1983, s 33, Sch 4, para 16(4); paras (*a*)-(*d*) substituted by the Local Government Act 1972, s 182, Sch 16, para 28(2); in paras (*a*), (*b*) amendments in square brackets made by the Local Government Act 1985, s 6, Sch 2, para 1.
   Sub-s (12): added by the National Heritage Act 1983, s 33, Sch 4, para 16(5).

54A. Issue of certificate that building is not intended to be listed

[(1) Where—

   (*a*) application has been made for planning permission for any development involving the alteration, extension or demolition of a building; or

   (*b*) any such planning permission has been granted,

the issue by the Secretary of State, on the application of any person of a certificate stating that he does not intend to list the building shall have the effect specified in subsection (2) of this section.

(2) The effect of the issue under subsection (1) of this section of a certificate stating that the Secretary of State does not intend to list a building is to preclude him for a period of 5 years from the date of issue of the certificate, from exercising in relation to that building any of the powers conferred on him by section 54 of this Act, and to preclude the local planning authority from serving a notice in relation to it under section 58 of this Act.

(3) Notice of an application made under subsection (1) above shall be given to the local planning authority within whose area the building is situated at the same time that the application is submitted to the Secretary of State.

[(4) In this section "local planning authority" shall, in relation to a building in Greater London, include the Historic Buildings and Monuments Commission for England.]   **[86]**

NOTES
Commencement: 1 April 1986 (sub-s (4)); 13 November 1980 (remainder).
Added by the Local Government, Planning and Land Act 1980, s 90, Sch 15.
Sub-s (4): substituted by the Local Government Act 1985, s 6, Sch 2, para 1.

55. Control of works for demolition, alteration or extension of listed buildings

(1) Subject to this Part of this Act, if a person executes or causes to be executed any works for the demolition of a listed building or for its alteration or extension in any manner which would affect its character as a building of special architectural or historic interest, and the works are not authorised under [subsection (2) of this section], he shall be guilty of an offence.

(2) Works for the demolition of a listed building, or for its alteration or extension, are authorised under this Part of this Act . . . if—

   (*a*) the local planning authority or the Secretary of State have granted written consent . . . for the execution of the works and the works are executed in accordance with the terms of the consent and of any conditions attached to the consent under section 56 of this Act; and

(*b*) in the case of demolition, notice of the proposal to execute the works has been given to the Royal Commission and thereafter either—

    (i) for a period of at least one month following the grant of listed building consent, and before the commencement of the works, reasonable access to the building has been made available to members or officers of the Commission for the purpose of recording it; or

    (ii) the Commission have, by their Secretary or other officer of theirs with authority to act on the Commission's behalf for the purposes of this section, stated in writing that they have completed their recording of the building or that they do not wish to record it.

[(2A) If written consent is granted by the local planning authority or the Secretary of State for the retention of works for the demolition of a listed building, or for its alteration or extension, which have been executed without consent under subsection (2) of this section, the works are authorised under this Part of this Act from the grant of the consent under this subsection.]

(3) In subsection (2) of this section "the Royal Commission" means, in relation to England, the Royal Commission on Historical Monuments (England) and, in relation to Wales, the Royal Commission on Ancient and Historical Monuments (Wales and Monmouthshire); but the Secretary of State may, in relation to either England or Wales, or both, by order provide that the said subsection shall, in the case of works executed or to be executed on or after such date as may be specified in the order, have effect with the substitution for the reference to the Royal Commission of a reference to such other body as may be so specified.

[(3A) Consent under subsection (2) or (2A) of this section is referred to in this Part of this Act as "listed building consent".]

(4) Without prejudice to subsection (1) of this section, if a person executing or causing to be executed any works in relation to a listed building under a listed building consent fails to comply with any condition attached to the consent under section 56 of this Act, he shall be guilty of an offence.

(5) A person guilty of an offence under this section shall be liable—

(*a*) on summary conviction to imprisonment for a term not exceeding three months or a fine not exceeding [the prescribed sum], or both; or

(*b*) on conviction on indictment to imprisonment for a term not exceeding twelve months or a fine, or both;

and, in determining the amount of any fine to be imposed on a person convicted on indictment, the court shall in particular have regard to any financial benefit which has accrued or appears likely to accrue to him in consequence of the offence.

(6) In proceedings for an offence under this section it shall be a defence to prove that the works were urgently necessary in the interests of safety or health, or for the preservation of the building, and that notice in writing of the need for the works was given to the local planning authority as soon as reasonably practicable.   **[87]**

NOTES

Commencement: 13 November 1980 (sub-ss (2A), (3A)); 1 April 1972 (remainder).

This section derived from the Town and Country Planning Act 1968, s 40(2), (4)-(8).

Sub-s (1): amended by the Local Government, Planning and Land Act 1980, s 90, Sch 15.

Sub-s (2): words omitted repealed by the Local Government, Planning and Land Act 1980, s 194, Sch 34.

Sub-ss (2A), (3A): added by the Local Government, Planning and Land Act 1980, s 90, Sch 15.

Sub-s (4): repealed in part by the Housing and Planning Act 1986, s 49(1), Sch 11, Part I, para 19 and s 49(2), Sch 12, Part III. See Appendix.

Sub-s (5): amended by the Magistrates' Courts Act 1980, s 32(2).

Sub-s (6): new sub-s (6) substituted except in relation to any works carried out before 1 April 1987 by the Housing and Planning Act 1986, s 40, Sch 9, Part I, para 2(1). See Appendix.

56. Provisions supplementary to s 55

(1) Section 55 of this Act shall not apply to works for the demolition, alteration or extension of—

> (a) an ecclesiastical building which is for the time being used for ecclesiastical purposes or would be so used but for the works; or
>
> [(b) a building for the time being included in the schedule of monuments compiled and maintained under section 1 of the Ancient Monuments and Archaeological Areas Act 1979.]

For the purposes of this subsection, a building used or available for use by a minister of religion wholly or mainly as a residence from which to perform the duties of his office shall be treated as not being an ecclesiastical building.

(2) ...

(3) In considering whether to grant planning permission for development which [affects a listed building or its setting], and in considering whether to grant listed building consent for any works, the local planning authority or the Secretary of State, as the case may be, shall have special regard to the desirability of preserving the building [or its setting] or any features of special architectural or historic interest which it possesses.

[(4) Listed building consent may be granted subject to conditions.

(4A) Without prejudice to the generality of subsection (4) of this section, the conditions subject to which listed building consent may be granted], include conditions with respect to—

> (a) the preservation of particular features of the building, either as part of it or after severance therefrom;
>
> (b) the making good, after the works are completed, of any damage caused to the building by the works;
>
> (c) the reconstruction of the building or any part of it following the execution of any works, with the use of original materials so far as practicable and with such alterations of the interior of the building as may be specified in the conditions.

[(5) Listed building consent for the demolition of a listed building may be granted subject to a condition that the building shall not be demolished before a contract for the carrying out of works of redevelopment of the site has been made, and planning permission has been granted for the redevelopment for which the contract provides.]

(6) Part I of Schedule 11 to this Act shall have effect with respect to applications to local planning authorities for listed building consent, the reference of such applications to the Secretary of State and appeals against decisions on such applications; and Part II of that Schedule shall have effect with respect to the revocation of listed building consent by a local planning authority or the Secretary of State. **[88]**

NOTES
Commencement: 1 April 1972.
Sub-s (1): amended by the Ancient Monuments and Archaeological Areas Act 1979, s 64(2),
Sch 4.
Sub-ss (2)–(5): amended by the Local Government, Planning and Land Act 1980, s 90, Sch 15.
New sub-s (4B) inserted by the Housing and Planning Act 1986, s 40, Sch 9, Part I, para 3(1).
See Appendix.

56A. Limit of duration of listed building consent

[(1) Subject to the provisions of this section, every listed building consent shall be granted subject to the condition that the works to which it relates must be begun not later than the expiration of—

    (*a*) five years beginning with the date on which the consent is granted; or

    (*b*) such other period (whether longer or shorter) beginning with the said date as the authority granting the consent may direct, being a period which the authority considers appropriate having regard to any material considerations.

(2) If listed building consent is granted without the condition required by subsection (1) of this section, it shall be deemed to have been granted subject to the condition that the works to which it relates must be begun not later than the expiration of five years beginning with the date of the grant.

(3) If listed building consent was granted before 1st January 1978 and without the condition required by subsection (1) of this section, it shall be deemed to have been granted subject to the condition that the works to which it relates must be begun not later than the expiration of three years beginning with the date on which paragraph 11 of Schedule 15 to the Local Government, Planning and Land Act 1980 came into force.

(4) If listed building consent was granted on or after 1st January 1978 but before the date on which paragraph 11 of Schedule 15 to the Local Government, Planning and Land Act 1980 came into force, and was granted without the condition required by subsection (1) of this section, it shall be deemed to have been granted subject to the condition that the works to which it relates must be begun not later than the expiration of five years beginning with the date on which the said paragraph 11 came into force.

(5) Nothing in this section applies to any consent to the retention of works granted under section 55(2A) of this Act.]   **[89]**

NOTES
Commencement: 13 November 1980.
Added by the Local Government, Planning and Land Act 1980, s 90, Sch 15.

(New s 56B inserted by the Housing and Planning Act 1986, s 40, Sch 9, Part I, para 4. See Appendix.)

(New s 56C inserted except in relation to certain applications, notices or complaints made or served before 1 April 1987 (as to which see SI 1987 No 348, art 3(2)) by the Housing and Planning Act 1986, s 40, Sch 9, Part I, para 6. See Appendix.)

57. Acts causing or likely to result in damage to listed buildings

(1) Where a building, not being a building excluded by section 56(1) of this Act from the operation of section 55, is included in a list compiled or approved under section 54 of this Act, then, if any person who, but for this section, would be entitled to do so, does or permits the doing of any act which causes or is likely to result in damage to the building (other than an act for the execution of excepted works) and he does or permits it with the intention of causing such damage, he shall be guilty of an offence and liable on summary conviction to a fine not exceeding [level 3 on the standard scale].

(2) In subsection (1) of this section "excepted works" means works authorised by planning permission granted or deemed to be granted in pursuance of an application under this Act and works for which listed building consent has been given under this Act.

(3) Where a person convicted of an offence under this section fails to take such reasonable steps as may be necessary to prevent any damage or further damage resulting from the offence, he shall be guilty of a further offence and liable on summary conviction to a fine not exceeding £20 for each day on which the failure continues.   **[90]**

NOTES
Commencement: 1 April 1972.
Sub-s (1): maximum fine increased and converted to a level on the standard scale by the Criminal Justice Act 1982, ss 37, 38, 46.
Sub-s (3): amended by the Housing and Planning Act 1986, s 49(1), Sch 11, Part I, para 13. See Appendix.

58. Building preservation notice in respect of building not listed

(1) If it appears to the [local planning authority, other than a county planning authority,], in the case of a building in their area which is not a listed building, that it is of special architectural or historic interest and is in danger of demolition or of alteration in such a way as to affect its character as such, they may (subject to subsection (2) of this section) serve on the owner and occupier of the building a notice (in this section referred to as a "building preservation notice")—

    (a) stating that the building appears to them to be of special architectural or historic interest and that they have requested the Secretary of State to consider including it in a list compiled or approved under section 54 of this Act; and

    (b) explaining the effect of subsections (3) and (4) of this section.

(2) A building preservation notice shall not be served in respect of an excepted building, that is to say—

    (a) an ecclesiastical building which is for the time being used for ecclesiastical purposes; or

    [(b) a building for the time being included in the schedule of monuments compiled and maintained under section 1 of the Ancient Monuments and Archaeological Areas Act 1979.]

For the purposes of this subsection, a building used or available for use by a minister of religion wholly or mainly as a residence from which to perform the duties of his office shall be treated as not being an ecclesiastical building.

(3) A building preservation notice shall come into force as soon as it has been served on both the owner and occupier of the building to which it relates and shall remain in force for six months from the date when it is served or, as the case may be, last served; but it shall cease to be in force if, before the expiration of that period, the Secretary of State either includes the building in a list compiled or approved under section 54 of this Act or notifies the [local] planning authority in writing that he does not intend to do so.

(4) While a building preservation notice is in force with respect to a building, the provisions of this Act (other than section 57) shall have effect in relation to it as if the building were a listed building; and if the notice ceases to be in force (otherwise than by reason of the building being included in a list compiled or approved under the said section 54) the provisions of Part III of Schedule 11 to this Act shall have effect with respect to things done or occurring under the notice or with reference to the building being treated as listed.

(5) If, following the service of a building preservation notice, the Secretary of State notifies the [local] planning authority that he does not propose to include the building in a list compiled or approved under section 54 of this Act, the authority—

(*a*) shall forthwith give notice of the Secretary of State's decision to the owner and occupier of the building; and

(*b*) shall not, within the period of twelve months beginning with the date of the Secretary of State's notification, serve another such notice in respect of the said building.

[(6) If it appears to the [local] planning authority to be urgent that a building preservation notice should come into force, they may, instead of serving the notice on the owner and occupier of the building to which it relates, affix the notice conspicuously to some object on the building; and this shall be treated for all the purposes of this section and of Schedule 11 to this Act as service of the said notice, in relation to which subsection (1)(*b*) of this section shall be taken to include a reference to this subsection.]

[(7) The Historic Buildings and Monuments Commission for England shall, as respects any London borough, have concurrently with the council of that borough the functions of a local planning authority under this section; and references to the local planning authority shall be construed accordingly.]   **[91]**

NOTES
Commencement: 1 April 1986 (sub-s (7)); 27 July 1972 (sub-s (6)); 1 April 1972 (remainder).
This section derived from the Town and Country Planning Act 1968, s 48.
Sub-ss (1), (3), (5): amended by the Local Government Act 1985, s 6, Sch 2, para 1.
Sub-s (2): amended by the Ancient Monuments and Archaeological Areas Act 1979, s 64(2), Sch 4.
Sub-s (6): added by the Town and Country Planning (Amendment) Act 1972, s 7(1); amended by the Local Government Act 1985, s 6, Sch 2, para 1.
Sub-s (7): added by the Local Government Act 1985, s 6, Sch 2, para 1.

58A. Special provision for listed buildings in Greater London

[(1) Without prejudice to his powers by virtue of section 31(1) of this Act the Secretary of State may by regulations provide for any application for planning permission to which this section applies to be referred to the Historic Buildings and Monuments Commission for England before it is dealt with by the local planning authority.

(2) This section applies to an application for planning permission for any development in Greater London which would, in the opinion of the local planning authority to which the application is made, involve the demolition, in whole or in part, or a material alteration, of a listed building.

(3) Regulations under this section may provide—

(*a*) for the giving to the referring authority by the Commission of directions as to the manner in which an application is to be dealt with; and

(*b*) that an application which satisfies such conditions as may be specified in the regulations need not be referred to the Commission.]   **[92]**

NOTES
Commencement: 1 April 1986.
Added by the Local Government Act 1985, s 6, Sch 2, para 1(6).

(New s 58AA inserted by the Housing and Planning Act 1986, s 40, Sch 9, Part I, para 5(1). See Appendix.)

(New ss 58B–58N prospectively inserted by the Housing and Planning Act 1986, s 31. See Appendix. For transitional provisions see s 34 of the 1986 Act. See Appendix.)

Trees

59. Planning permission to include appropriate provision for preservation and planting of trees

It shall be the duty of the local planning authority—

(*a*) to ensure, whenever it is appropriate, that in granting planning permission for any development adequate provision is made, by the imposition of conditions, for the preservation or planting of trees; and

(*b*) to make such orders under section 60 of this Act as appear to the authority to be necessary in connection with the grant of such permission, whether for giving effect to such conditions or otherwise.

[93]

NOTES
    Commencement: 1 April 1972.

60. Tree preservation orders

(1) [Subject to subsection (1A) below, if] it appears to a local planning authority that it is expedient in the interests of amenity to make provision for the preservation of trees or woodlands in their area, they may for that purpose make an order (in this Act referred to as a "tree preservation order") with respect to such trees, groups of trees or woodlands as may be specified in the order; and, in particular, provision may be made by any such order—

(*a*) for prohibiting (subject to any exemptions for which provision may be made by the order) the cutting down, topping, lopping [uprooting, wilful damage,] or wilful destruction of trees except with the consent of the local planning authority, and for enabling that authority to give their consent subject to conditions;

(*b*) for securing the replanting, in such manner as may be prescribed by or under the order, of any part of a woodland area which is felled in the course of forestry operations permitted by or under the order;

(*c*) for applying, in relation to any consent under the order, and to applications for such consent, any of the provisions of this Act falling within subsection (2) of this section, subject to such adaptations and modifications as may be specified in the order.

[(1A) A county planning authority may only make an order under subsection (1) of this section—

(*a*) if they make it in pursuance of section 59(*b*) of this Act;

(*b*) if it relates to land which does not lie wholly within the area of a single district planning authority;

(*c*) if it relates to land in which the county planning authority hold an interest; or

(*d*) if it relates to land in a National Park.]

(2) References in this Act to provisions thereof falling within this subsection are references to—

(*a*) the provisions of Part III of this Act relating to planning permission and to applications for planning permission, except sections 25, 26, 27, 28, 29(2) to (6), 34(2), 38, 39, 41 to 44 and 47 to 49 of this Act; and

(*b*) such of the provisions of Part IX of this Act as are therein stated to be provisions falling within this subsection;

(*c*) section 270 of this Act.

(3) A tree preservation order may be made so as to apply, in relation to trees to be planted pursuant to any such conditions as are mentioned in section 59(*a*) of this Act, as from the time when those trees are planted.

[(4) A tree preservation order shall not take effect until it is confirmed by the local planning authority and the local planning authority may confirm any such order either without modification or subject to such modifications as they consider expedient.]

(5) Provision may be made by regulations under this Act with respect to the form of tree preservation orders, and the procedure to be followed in connection with the submission and confirmation of such orders; and the regulations may (without prejudice to the generality of this subsection) make provision as follows—

> (a) that, before a tree preservation order is [confirmed by the local planning authority], notice of the making of the order shall be given to the owners and occupiers of land affected by the order and to such other persons, if any, as may be specified in the regulations;
>
> (b) that objections and representations with respect to the order, if duly made in accordance with the regulations, shall be considered before the order is confirmed by [the local planning authority];
>
> (c) ... and
>
> (d) that copies of the order, when confirmed by ... the authority, shall be served on such persons as may be specified in the regulations.

(6) Without prejudice to any other exemptions for which provision may be made by a tree preservation order, no such order shall apply to the cutting down, [uprooting] topping or lopping of trees which are dying or dead or have become dangerous, or the cutting down, [uprooting] topping or lopping of any trees in compliance with any obligations imposed by or under an Act of Parliament or so far as may be necessary for the prevention or abatement of a nuisance.

(7) In relation to land in respect of which the Forestry Commissioners have made advances under section 4 of the Forestry Act 1967 or in respect of which there is in force a forestry dedication covenant entered into with the Commissioners under section 5 of that Act, a tree preservation order may be made only if—

> (a) there is not in force in respect of the land a plan of operations or other working plan approved by the Commissioners under such a covenant; and
>
> (b) the Commissioners consent to the making of the order.

(8) Where a tree preservation order is made in respect of land to which subsection (7) of this section applies, the order shall not have effect so as to prohibit, or to require any consent for, the cutting down of a tree in accordance with a plan of operations or other working plan approved by the Forestry Commissioners, and for the time being in force, under such a covenant as is mentioned in that subsection or under a woodlands scheme made under the powers contained in the said Act of 1967.

(9) In the preceding provisions of this section references to provisions of the Forestry Act 1967 include references to the corresponding provisions (replaced by that Act) in the Forestry Acts 1919 to 1951.

(10) The preceding provisions of this section shall have effect subject to the provisions—

> (a) of section 2(4) of the Opencast Coal Act 1958 (land comprised in an authorisation under that Act which is affected by a tree preservation order); and

(*b*) of section 15 of the Forestry Act 1967 (licences under that Act to fell
trees comprised in a tree preservation order).   **[94]**

NOTES

Commencement: 1 April 1972.

Sub-s (1): para (*a*) amended by the Town and Country Amenities Act 1974, s 10; other
amendments made by the Local Government, Planning and Land Act 1980, s 90, Sch 15.

Sub-ss (4), (5): amended by the Local Government, Planning and Land Act 1980, ss 90, 194,
Schs 15, 34.

Sub-s (6): amended by the Town and Country Amenities Act 1974, s 10.

61. Provisional tree preservation orders

(1) If it appears to a local planning authority that a tree preservation order
proposed to be made by that authority should take effect immediately without
previous confirmation, they may include in the order as made by them a
direction that this section shall apply to the order.

(2) Notwithstanding section 60(4) of this Act, an order which contains such
a direction shall take effect provisionally on such date as may be specified
therein and shall continue in force by virtue of this section until—

(*a*) the expiration of a period of six months beginning with the date on
which the order was made; or

(*b*) the date on which the order is confirmed . . .

(3) . . .   **[95]**

NOTES

Commencement: 1 April 1972.

Words omitted repealed by the Local Government, Planning and Land Act 1980, ss 90, 194,
Schs 15, 34.

61A. Trees in conservation areas

[(1) Subject to the provisions of this section, any person who, in relation to a
tree to which this section applies, does any act which might by virtue of section
60(1)(*a*) above be prohibited by a tree preservation order shall be guilty of an
offence.

(2) Subject to the provisions of this section, this section applies to any tree
in a conservation area but in respect of which no tree preservation order is for
the time being in force.

(3) It shall be a defence for a person charged with an offence under
subsection (1) above to prove—

(*a*) that he served notice of his intention to do the act in question, with
sufficient particulars to identify the tree, on the council of the district
or London borough in whose area the tree is or was situated; and

(*b*) that he did the act in question—

(i) with the consent of the local planning authority in whose area
the tree is or was situated, or

(ii) after the expiry of the period of six weeks from the date of the
notice but before the expiry of the period of two years from that
date.

(4) The Secretary of State may by regulations direct that this section shall
not apply in such cases as may be specified in the regulations.

(5) Without prejudice to the generality of subsection (4) above, the

regulations may be framed so as to exempt from the application of this section cases defined by reference to all or any of the following matters, namely—

(a) acts of such descriptions or done in such circumstances or subject to such conditions as may be specified in the regulations;

(b) trees in such conservation areas as may be so specified;

(c) trees of a size or species so specified; or

(d) trees belonging to persons or bodies of a description so specified;

and the regulations may, in relation to any matter by reference to which an exemption is conferred by them, make different provision for different circumstances.

(6) Regulations under subsection (4) above may in particular, but without prejudice to the generality of that subsection, exempt from the application of this section cases exempted from section 60 above by subsection (6) of that section.

(7) It shall be the duty of the council of a district or a London borough to compile and keep available for public inspection free of charge at all reasonable hours and at a convenient place a register, containing such particulars as the Secretary of State may determine of notices under this section affecting trees in their area.

(8) If any tree to which this section applies is removed, uprooted or destroyed in contravention of this section or is removed, uprooted or destroyed or dies at a time when its cutting down or uprooting is authorised only by virtue of the provisions of such regulations under subsection (4) above as are mentioned in subsection (6) above, it shall be the duty of the owner of the land, unless on his application the local planning authority dispense with this requirement, to plant another tree of an appropriate size and species at the same place as soon as he reasonably can.

(9) The duty imposed by subsection (8) above on the owner of any land shall attach to the person who is from time to time the owner of the land and may be enforced as provided by section 103 of this Act and not otherwise.] [96]

NOTES
Commencement: 12 March 1975.
Added by the Town and Country Amenities Act 1974, s 8.

62. Replacement of trees

(1) If any tree in respect of which a tree preservation order is for the time being in force, *other than a tree to which the order applies as part of a woodland*, is removed [uprooted] or destroyed in contravention of the order or [, except in the case of a tree to which the order applies as part of a woodland,] is removed [uprooted] or destroyed or dies at a time when its cutting down [or uprooting] is authorised only by virtue of the provisions of section 60(6) of this Act relating to trees which are dying or dead or have become dangerous, it shall be the duty of the owner of the land, unless on his application the local planning authority dispense with this requirement, to plant another tree of an appropriate size and species at the same place as soon as he reasonably can.

[(1A) In respect of trees in a woodland it shall be sufficient for the purposes of this section to replace the trees removed, uprooted or destroyed by planting the same number of trees either on or near the land on which the trees removed, uprooted or destroyed stood or on such other land as may be agreed between the local planning authority and the owner of the land, and (in either case) in such places as may be designated by the local planning authority.]

(2) In relation to any tree planted pursuant to this section, the relevant tree preservation order shall apply as it applied to the original tree.

(3) The duty imposed by subsection (1) of this section on the owner of any land shall attach to the person who is from time to time the owner of the land and may be enforced as provided by section 103 of this Act and not otherwise.

[97]

NOTES

Commencement: 22 September 1985 (sub-s (1A)); 1 April 1972 (remainder).

This section derived from the Civic Amenities Act 1967, s 13(1)-(3).

Sub-s (1): words in italics repealed with savings and second words in square brackets added with savings by the Town and Country Planning (Amendment) Act 1985, ss 1(2), 3(4); other amendments made by the Town and Country Amenities Act 1974, s 10.

Sub-s (1A): added with savings by the Town and Country Planning (Amendment) Act 1985, ss 1(3), 3(4).

Advertisements

63. Control of advertisements

(1) Subject to the provisions of this section, provision shall be made by regulations under this Act for restricting or regulating the display of advertisements so far as appears to the Secretary of State to be expedient in the interests of amenity or public safety.

(2) Without prejudice to the generality of subsection (1) of this section, any such regulations may provide—

(*a*) for regulating the dimensions, appearance and position of advertisements which may be displayed, the sites on which advertisements may be displayed, and the manner in which they are to be affixed to the land;

(*b*) for requiring the consent of the local planning authority to be obtained for the display of advertisements, or of advertisements of any class specified in the regulations;

(*c*) for applying, in relation to any such consent and to applications for such consent, any of the provisions of this Act falling within section 60(2) thereof, subject to such adaptations and modifications as may be specified in the regulations;

(*d*) for the constitution, for the purposes of the regulations, of such advisory committees as may be prescribed by the regulations, and for determining the manner in which the expenses of any such committee are to be defrayed.

[(3) Regulations made for the purposes of this section may make different provision with respect to different areas, and in particular may make special provision—

(*a*) with respect to conservation areas; and

(*b*) with respect to areas defined for the purposes of the regulations as areas of special control, being either rural areas or areas other than rural areas which appear to the Secretary of State to require special protection on grounds of amenity;

and, without prejudice to the generality of this subsection, the regulations may prohibit the display in an area of special control of all advertisements except advertisements of such classes (if any) as may be prescribed.]

(4) Areas of special control for the purposes of regulations under this section may be defined by means of orders made or approved by the Secretary of State in accordance with the provisions of the regulations.

(5) Where the Secretary of State is authorised by the regulations to make or approve any such order as is mentioned in subsection (4) of this section, the regulations shall provide for the publication of notice of the proposed order in such manner as may be prescribed by the regulations, for the consideration of objections duly made thereto, and for the holding of such inquiries or other hearings as may be so prescribed, before the order is made or approved.

(6) Regulations made under this section may be made so as to apply to advertisements which are being displayed on the date on which the regulations come into force, or to the use for the display of the advertisements of any site which was being used for that purpose on that date; but any regulations made in accordance with this subsection shall provide for exempting therefrom—

(a) the continued display of any such advertisement; and
(b) the continued use for the display of advertisements of any such site,

during such period as may be prescribed in that behalf by the regulations, and different periods may be so prescribed for the purposes of different provisions of the regulations.

(7) Without prejudice to the generality of the powers conferred by the preceding provisions of this section, regulations made for the purposes of this section may provide that any appeal from the decision of the local planning authority, on an application for their consent under the regulations, shall be to an independent tribunal constituted in accordance with the regulations, instead of being an appeal to the Secretary of State; and subsection (2) of section 50 of this Act shall apply to any tribunal so constituted as it applies to any tribunal constituted in accordance with subsection (1) of that section.   **[98]**

NOTES
Commencement: 1 April 1972.
Amended by the Town and Country Amenities Act 1974, s 3(1).
New sub-s (3) substituted and new sub-ss (3A) and (3B) inserted by the Housing and Planning Act 1986, s 45. See Appendix.

64. Application for planning permission not needed for advertisements complying with regulations

Where the display of advertisements in accordance with regulations made under section 63 of this Act involves development of land, planning permission for that development shall be deemed to be granted by virtue of this section, and no application shall be necessary in that behalf under Part III of this Act.   **[99]**

NOTES
Commencement: 1 April 1972.

Waste land

65. Proper maintenance of waste land

(1) If it appears to a [district planning authority or the council of a London borough] that the amenity of any part of their area, or of any adjoining area, is seriously injured by the condition of any garden, vacant site or other open land in their area, . . . [they] may serve on the owner and occupier of the land a notice

requiring such steps for abating the injury as may be specified in the notice to be taken within such period as may be so specified.

(2) Subject to the provisions of Part V of this Act, a notice under this section shall take effect at the end of such period (not being less than twenty-eight days after the service thereof) as may be specified in the notice.   **[100]**

NOTES
Commencement: 1 April 1972.
Amendments in square brackets made by the Local Government, Planning and Land Act 1980, s 90, Sch 15; words omitted repealed by the Local Government Act 1974, s 42(2), Sch 8.
New s 65 substituted by the Housing and Planning Act 1986, s 46. See Appendix.

Industrial development

66. Meaning of "industrial building"

(1) In this Part of this Act "industrial building" means a building used or designed for use—

    (*a*) for the carrying on of any process for or incidental to any of the following purposes, that is to say—

        (i) the making of any article or of part of any article; or

        (ii) the altering, repairing, ornamenting, finishing, cleaning, washing, freezing, packing or canning, or adapting for sale, or breaking up or demolition, of any article; or

        (iii) without prejudice to the preceding sub-paragraphs, the getting, dressing or preparation for sale of minerals or the extraction or preparation for sale of oil or brine;

    (*b*) for the carrying on of scientific research,

being a process or research carried on in the course of a trade or business.

(2) For the purposes of subsection (1) of this section, premises which—

    (*a*) are used or designed for use for providing services or facilities ancillary to the use of other premises for the carrying on of any such process or research as is mentioned in that subsection; and

    (*b*) are or are to be comprised in the same building or the same curtilage as those other premises,

shall themselves be treated as used or designed for use for the carrying on of such a process or, as the case may be, of such research.

(3) In this section—

    "article" means an article of any description, including a ship or vessel;
    "building" includes a part of a building;
    "scientific research" means any activity in the fields of natural or applied science for the extension of knowledge.   **[101]**

NOTES
Commencement: 1 April 1972.
This section and ss 67–72 repealed by the Housing and Planning Act 1986, s 48(1)(*b*) and s 49(2), Sch 12, Part III. See Appendix.

67. Industrial development certificates

(1) Subject to the provisions of this section and of section 68 of this Act, an application to the local planning authority for permission to develop land by—

    (*a*) the erection thereon of an industrial building of one of the prescribed classes; or

    (*b*) a change of use whereby premises, not being an industrial building of one of the prescribed classes, will become such an industrial building, shall be of no effect unless a certificate (in this Act referred to as an "industrial development certificate") is issued under this section by the Secretary of State, certifying that the development in question can be carried out consistently with the proper distribution of industry, and a copy of the certificate is furnished to the local planning authority together with the application.

(2) Subject to subsection (5) of this section, an industrial development certificate shall be required for the purposes of an application for planning permission made as mentioned in section 32(1) of this Act if the circumstances are such that, in accordance with subsection (1) of this section, such a certificate would have been required if the application had been for planning permission to construct the building, or to institute the use of land, which the application seeks permission to retain or continue or (as the case may be) seeks permission to retain or continue without complying with a condition previously imposed, and the provisions of this section shall have effect in relation to that application accordingly.

(3) In considering whether any development for which an industrial development certificate is applied for can be carried out consistently with the proper distribution of industry, the Secretary of State shall have particular regard to the need for providing appropriate employment in development areas.

(4) An industrial development certificate shall not be required for the extension of an industrial building if the extension, taken by itself, would not be an industrial building of one of the prescribed classes, but (subject to the provisions of section 68 of this Act) an industrial development certificate shall be required for the extension of any building if the extension, taken by itself, would be such an industrial building.

(5) An industrial development certificate shall not be required for the purposes of an application for planning permission to retain a building or continue a use of land after the end of any period specified in, or otherwise without complying with, a condition subject to which a previous planning permission was granted if the condition in question is not one subject to which the previous planning permission was granted in accordance with the provisions of section 70 of this Act or subject to which that planning permission is by virtue of that section deemed to have been granted.

(6) The preceding provisions of this section shall have effect without prejudice to any provisions for restricting the granting of planning permission by local planning authorities which are included in a development order by virtue of section 31(1) of this Act.

(7) In this section—

"the prescribed classes" means such classes or descriptions of industrial buildings as may be prescribed by regulations made for the purposes of this section by the Secretary of State;
["development area" means any area specified as such by an order made, or having effect as if made, under section 1 of the Industrial Development Act 1982].

and any reference to an application made as mentioned in section 32(1) of this Act includes a reference to an application which by virtue of section 88(7) or 95(6) of this Act is deemed to have been made for such planning permission as is mentioned in the said section 88(7) or, as the case may be, the said section 95(6). **[102]**

NOTES
Commencement: 1 April 1972.
Sub-s (7): definition "development area" substituted by the Industrial Development 1982, s 19,
Sch 2, para 7(1).
Repealed as noted to s 66 above.

68. Exemption of certain classes of development

(1) Notwithstanding anything in section 67 of this Act, but subject to section 69 of this Act, an industrial development certificate shall not be required if the industrial floor space to be created by the development in question (in this section referred to as "the proposed development"), together with any other industrial floor space created or to be created by any related development, does not exceed [50,000] square feet, excluding, where an industrial development certificate has been issued in respect of any related development, any floor space created or to be created by that development or by development carried out, or for which planning permission has been granted, before the issue of that certificate.

(2) Regulations made for the purposes of section 67 of this Act by the Secretary of State may direct that no industrial development certificate shall be required in respect of the erection, in any area prescribed by or under the regulations, of industrial buildings of any such class or description as may be so prescribed, or in respect of a change of use whereby premises in any such area, not being an industrial building of a class or description so prescribed, will become an industrial building of such a class or description.

(3) In this section "industrial floor space" means floor space comprised in an industrial building or industrial buildings of any of the prescribed classes.

(4) For the purposes of subsection (1) of this section development shall, in relation to an application for planning permission (in this section referred to as "the relevant application"), be taken to be "related development" if—

(a) it related, or is to relate, to the same building as that to which the proposed development is to relate (in this subsection referred to as the "relevant building"); or

(b) it related, or is to relate, to a building which is, or is to be, contiguous or adjacent to the relevant building, and it was, or is to be, development comprised in, or for the purposes of, the same scheme or project or for the purposes of the same undertaking as the proposed development,

and (in either case) it fulfils one or other of the conditions mentioned in subsection (5) of this section.

(5) The said conditions are—

(a) that it is development for which, before the date of the relevant application, planning permission has been granted by a planning decision made on or after 1st April 1960;

(b) that it is development which has been initiated on or after 1st April 1960 but before the date of the relevant application and is not development for which planning permission has been granted by a planning decision made on or after 1st April 1960;

(c) that it is development in respect of which an application to the local planning authority for planning permission either is pending on the date of the relevant application or is made on that date.

(6) For the purposes of subsection (5)(c) of this section, an application is pending on a particular date if—

(a) it is made before that date and not withdrawn; and

(b) no planning decision on that application has been made before that date.

(7) In subsection (4) of this section and in this subsection "building" does not include a part of a building; and any reference in subsection (4) of this section to development relating to a building is a reference to the erection, extension, alteration or re-erection of the building or a change of use of the whole or part of the building.

(8) In this section "the prescribed classes" has the same meaning as in section 67 of this Act.   **[103]**

NOTES
Commencement: 1 April 1972.
Amended by the Town and Country Planning (Industrial Development Certificates: Exemption) Order 1979, SI 1979 No 839.
Repealed as noted to s 66 above.

69. Power to vary exemption limit as to industrial floor space

(1) The Secretary of State may by order direct that subsection (1) of section 68 of this Act shall be amended by substituting, for the number of square feet specified in the subsection as originally enacted or as previously amended under this subsection, such number of square feet as may be specified in the order being not less than 1,000 square feet.

(2) Any amendment made by an order under this section may be made so as to have effect either in relation to the whole of England and Wales or in relation only to a part of England and Wales specified in the order.

(3) Any amendment made by such an order shall have effect—

(a) in relation to applications for planning permission relating to land in any area to which the order applies which are made on or after the date on which the order comes into operation; and

(b) in relation to applications relating to land in such an area which have been made before that date, other than any application on which a planning decision has been made before that date.

(4) Where in accordance with subsection (3) of this section an amendment made by such an order has effect in relation to an application for planning permission made before the date on which the order comes into operation, so much of section 67(1) of this Act as requires a copy of an industrial development certificate to be furnished to the local planning authority together with the application shall have effect in relation to that application with the substitution, for the words "together with the application", of the words "as soon as practicable after the certificate is issued".

(5) In this section any reference to land in any area to which an order under this section applies shall be construed as a reference to land of which any part is in that area.   **[104]**

NOTES
Commencement: 1 April 1972.
Repealed as noted to s 66 above.

70. Restrictions or conditions attached to certificates

(1) An industrial development certificate in respect of any development may be issued subject to such restrictions on the making of an application for planning permission for that development (whether as to the period within which, or the persons by whom, such an application may be made, or otherwise) as the

Secretary of State considers appropriate having regard to the proper distribution of industry; and where an industrial development certificate in respect of any development is issued subject to any such restrictions, and an application for planning permission for that development is made which does not comply with those restrictions, the provisions of section 67 of this Act shall apply in relation to that application as if no such certificate had been issued.

(2) Without prejudice to subsection (1) of this section, an industrial development certificate may be issued either unconditionally or subject to such conditions as the Secretary of State considers appropriate having regard to the proper distribution of industry; and any reference in this section to conditions attached to an industrial development certificate is a reference to conditions subject to which such a certificate is issued.

(3) Without prejudice to the generality of subsection (2) of this section, conditions may be attached to an industrial development certificate—

    (*a*) for requiring the removal of any building or the discontinuance of any use of land to which the certificate relates at the end of a specified period and the carrying out of any works required for the reinstatement of land at the end of that period;

    (*b*) restricting the amount of office floor space (as defined in section 85 of this Act) to be contained in any building to which the certificate relates, or precluding it from containing any office floor space (as so defined);

and conditions of the kind mentioned in paragraph (*b*) of this subsection may be framed so as to apply (either or both) to the building as originally erected or as subsequently extended or altered.

(4) In so far as any of the conditions attached to an industrial development certificate are of such a description that (apart from this section) they could not have been imposed under this Act, this Act shall apply in relation to any application for planning permission for the purposes of which that certificate is required, and to any planning permission granted on such an application, as if the powers conferred by this Act included power to impose conditions of that description.

(5) Where conditions are attached to an industrial development certificate, and, on an application for planning permission for the purposes of which that certificate is required, planning permission is granted, the authority granting the permission shall grant it subject to those conditions, with or without other conditions.

(6) Planning permission to which subsection (5) of this section applies shall not be invalid by reason only that the requirements of that subsection are not complied with; but where any such planning permission is granted without complying with the requirements of that subsection the planning permission shall be deemed to have been granted subject to the conditions attached to the industrial development certificate, or (if any other conditions were imposed by the authority granting the permission) to have been granted subject to the conditions attached to the certificate in addition to the other conditions.   **[105]**

NOTES
    Commencement: 1 April 1972.
    Repealed as noted to s 66 above.

71. Provisions as to conditions imposed under s 70

(1) This section applies to any condition subject to which planning permission is granted in accordance with the provisions of section 70 of this Act, or subject

to which planning permission is by virtue of that section deemed to have been granted, whether it is a condition which could have been imposed apart from that section or not.

(2) If the planning permission is or was granted by the local planning authority, the Secretary of State shall not be required to entertain an appeal under section 36 of this Act from the decision of the local planning authority, in so far as that decision relates or related to any condition to which this section applies.

(3) If any condition imposed by an authority granting planning permission is inconsistent with any condition to which this section applies, the last-mentioned condition shall prevail so far as it is inconsistent with the condition so imposed.

(4) Where on an application made as mentioned in section 32(1) of this Act (as modified by section 67 of this Act) planning permission is granted (either unconditionally or subject to conditions) for a building to be retained, or a use of a building to be continued, without complying with a condition to which this section applies (that condition being one subject to which a previous planning permission was granted or is deemed to have been granted), nothing in section 70 of this Act or in the foregoing provisions of this section shall be construed as preventing the subsequent planning permission from operating so as to extinguish or modify that condition, as the case may be.   **[106]**

NOTES
Commencement: 1 April 1972.
Repealed as noted to s 66 above.

72. Provision for cases where certificate withheld

(1) Where such an application as is mentioned in subsection (1) or (2) of section 67 of this Act is, by virtue of those subsections, of no effect by reason that the requirements of those subsections are not fulfilled, the local planning authority shall consider whether, if those requirements had been fulfilled, they would nevertheless have refused the permission sought by the application, either in respect of the whole or in respect of part of the land to which the application relates; and if they are of the opinion that they would so have refused that permission, they shall serve on the applicant a notice in writing to that effect.

(2) Where a notice is served under subsection (1) of this section in respect of the whole or part of any land, it shall operate, for the purposes of sections 38 and 39 of this Act, as if the application for planning permission had been an effective application and the notice had been a planning decision of the local planning authority refusing that permission in respect of that land or that part thereof, as the case may be; and the provisions of those sections (if in those circumstances they would have been applicable) shall have effect accordingly.
                                                                              [107]

NOTES
Commencement: 1 April 1972.
Repealed as noted to s 66 above.

Office development

86. Temporary operation of these provisions

[(1) These provisions (other than this section) shall cease to have effect at the end of the period of [seventeen] years beginning with 5th August 1965, or, if Her Majesty by Order in Council so provides, on such earlier date as is specified in the Order; and if these provisions cease to have effect on a date specified as aforesaid, references therein to the end of the said period of [seventeen] years shall be read as references to that date.]

(2) Where immediately before the end of that period any planning permission has effect subject to a condition subject to which the planning permission is by virtue of these provisions deemed to have been granted, the planning permission shall, as from the end of that period, have effect free from that condition.

(3) Where immediately before the end of that period any planning permission has effect subject to a condition imposed by the authority granting the permission in circumstances where that authority was required by these provisions to impose that condition, then unless the condition is the subject of a certificate under section 82(3) of this Act, the planning permission shall, as from the end of that period, have effect free from that condition.

(4) An enforcement notice to which paragraph 4 of Schedule 12 to this Act applies shall not operate so as to prevent or restrict the doing of anything after the end of that period.

(5) Subject to the preceding provisions of this section, at the end of that period section 38(2) of the Interpretation Act 1889 (effect of repeals) shall apply as if these provisions had, as from the end of that period, been repealed by another Act.   **[108]**

NOTES
Commencement: 1 April 1972.
Repealed by the Housing and Planning Act 1986, s 49(2), Sch 12, Part III. See Appendix.
Sub-s (1): substituted by the Town and Country Planning (Amendment) Act 1972, s 5(1); amended by the Control of Office Development Act 1977, s 1.

PART V

ENFORCEMENT OF CONTROL UNDER PARTS III AND IV

Development requiring planning permission

87. Power to issue enforcement notice

[(1) Where it appears to the local planning authority that there has been a breach of planning control after the end of 1963, then, subject to the following provisions of this section, the authority, if they consider it expedient to do so having regard to the provisions of the development plan and to any other material considerations, may issue a notice requiring the breach to be remedied and serve copies of the notice in accordance with subsection (5) of this section.

(2) A notice under this section is referred to in this Act as an "enforcement notice".

(3) There is a breach of planning control—

(a) if development has been carried out, whether before or after the commencement of this Act, without the grant of the planning permission required in that behalf in accordance with Part III of the Act of 1962 or Part III of this Act; or

(b) if any conditions or limitations subject to which planning permission was granted have not been complied with.

(4) An enforcement notice which relates to a breach of planning control consisting in—

(*a*) the carrying out without planning permission of building, engineering, mining or other operations in, on, over or under land; or

(*b*) the failure to comply with any condition or limitation which relates to the carrying out of such operations and subject to which planning permission was granted for the development of that land; or

(*c*) the making without planning permission of a change of use of any building to use as a single dwelling-house; or

(*d*) the failure to comply with a condition which prohibits or has the effect of preventing a change of use of a building to use as a single dwelling-house,

may be issued only within the period of four years from the date of the breach.

(5) A copy of an enforcement notice shall be served, not later than 28 days after the date of its issue and not later than 28 days before the date specified in the notice as the date on which it is to take effect—

(*a*) on the owner and on the occupier of the land to which it relates; and

(*b*) on any other person having an interest in that land, being an interest which in the opinion of the authority is materially affected by the notice.

(6) An enforcement notice shall specify the matters alleged to constitute a breach of planning control.

(7) An enforcement notice shall also specify—

(*a*) any steps which are required by the authority to be taken in order to remedy the breach;

(*b*) any such steps as are referred to in subsection (10) of this section and are required by the authority to be taken.

(8) An enforcement notice shall specify the period within which any such step as is mentioned in subsection (7) of this section is to be taken and may specify different periods for the taking of different steps.

(9) In this section "steps to be taken in order to remedy the breach" means (according to the particular circumstances of the breach) steps for the purpose—

(*a*) of restoring the land to its condition before the development took place; or

(*b*) of securing compliance with the conditions or limitations subject to which planning permission was granted,

including—

(i) the demolition or alteration of any buildings or works;

(ii) the discontinuance of any use of land; and

(iii) the carrying out on land of any building or other operations.

(10) The steps mentioned in subsection (7)(*b*) of this section are steps for the purpose—

(*a*) of making the development comply with the terms of any planning permission which has been granted in respect of the land; or

(*b*) of removing or alleviating any injury to amenity which has been caused by the development.

(11) Where the matters which an enforcement notice alleges to constitute a breach of planning control include development which has involved the making of a deposit of refuse or waste materials on land, the notice may require that the

contour of the deposit shall be modified by altering the gradient or gradients of its sides in such manner as may be specified in the notice.

(12) The Secretary of State may by regulations direct—

    (a) that enforcement notices shall specify matters additional to those which they are required to specify by this section; and

    (b) that every copy of an enforcement notice served under this section shall be accompanied by an explanatory note giving such information as may be specified in the regulations with regard to the right of appeal conferred by section 88 of this Act.

(13) Subject to section 88 of this Act, an enforcement notice shall take effect on a date specified in it.

(14) The local planning authority may withdraw an enforcement notice (without prejudice to their power to issue another) at any time before it takes effect.

(15) If they do so, they shall forthwith give notice of the withdrawal to every person who was served with a copy of the notice.

(16) Where—

    (a) an enforcement notice has been issued in respect of development consisting of the erection of a building or the carrying out of works without the grant of planning permission; and

    (b) the notice has required the taking of steps for a purpose mentioned in subsection (10)(b) of this section; and

    (c) the steps have been taken,

for the purposes of this Act planning permission for the retention of the building or works as they are as a result of compliance with the notice shall be deemed to have been granted on an application for such permission made to the local planning authority.] **[109]**

NOTES
Commencement: 27 August 1981.
Substituted by the Local Government and Planning (Amendment) Act 1981, s 1, Schedule.
Act of 1962: Town and Country Planning Act 1962.

88. Appeal against enforcement notice

[(1) A person having an interest in the land to which an enforcement notice relates may, at any time before the date specified in the notice as the date on which it is to take effect, appeal to the Secretary of State against the notice, whether or not a copy of it has been served on him.

(2) An appeal may be brought on any of the following grounds—

    (a) that planning permission ought to be granted for the development to which the notice relates or, as the case may be, that a condition or limitation alleged in the enforcement notice not to have been complied with ought to be discharged;

    (b) that the matters alleged in the notice do not constitute a breach of planning control;

    (c) that the breach of planning control alleged in the notice has not taken place;

    (d) in the case of a notice which, by virtue of section 87(4) of this Act, may be issued only within the period of four years from the date of the breach of planning control to which the notice relates, that that period had elapsed at the date when the notice was issued;

(*e*) in the case of a notice not falling within paragraph (*d*) of this subsection, that the breach of planning control alleged by the notice occurred before the beginning of 1964;

(*f*) that copies of the enforcement notice were not served as required by section 87(5) of this Act;

(*g*) that the steps required by the notice to be taken exceed what is necessary to remedy any breach of planning control or to achieve a purpose specified in section 87(10) of this Act;

(*h*) that the period specified in the notice as the period within which any step is to be taken falls short of what should reasonably be allowed.

(3) An appeal under this section shall be made by notice in writing to the Secretary of State.

(4) A person who gives notice under subsection (3) of this section shall submit to the Secretary of State, either when giving the notice or within such time as may be prescribed by regulations under subsection (5) of this section, a statement in writing—

(*a*) specifying the grounds on which he is appealing against the enforcement notice; and

(*b*) giving such further information as the regulations may prescribe.

(5) The Secretary of State may by regulations prescribe the procedure which is to be followed on appeals under this section, and in particular, but without prejudice to the generality of this subsection—

(*a*) may prescribe the time within which an appellant is to submit a statement under subsection (4) of this section and the matters on which information is to be given in such a statement;

(*b*) may require the local planning authority to submit, within such time as may be prescribed, a statement indicating the submissions which they propose to put forward on the appeal;

(*c*) may specify the matters to be included in such a statement;

(*d*) may require the authority or the appellant to give such notice of an appeal under this section as may be prescribed, being notice which in the opinion of the Secretary of State is likely to bring the appeal to the attention of persons in the locality in which the land to which the enforcement notice relates is situated;

(*e*) may require the authority to send to the Secretary of State, within such period from the date of the bringing of the appeal as may be prescribed, a copy of the enforcement notice and a list of the persons served with copies of it.

(6) The Secretary of State—

(*a*) may dismiss an appeal if the appellant fails to comply with subsection (4) of this Section within the time prescribed by regulations under subsection (5); and

(*b*) may allow an appeal and quash the enforcement notice if the local planning authority fail to comply with any requirement of regulations made by virtue of paragraph (*b*), (*c*) or (*e*) of subsection (5) of this section within the period prescribed by the regulations.

(7) Subject to subsection (8) below, the Secretary of State shall, if either the appellant or the local planning authority so desire, afford to each of them an

opportunity of appearing before, and being heard by, a person appointed by the Secretary of State for the purpose.

(8) The Secretary of State shall not be required to afford such an opportunity if he proposes to dismiss an appeal under paragraph (*a*) of subsection (6) of this section or to allow an appeal and quash the enforcement notice under paragraph (*b*) of that subsection.

(9) If—

   (*a*) a statement under subsection (4) of this section specifies more than one ground on which the appellant is appealing against an enforcement notice; but

   (*b*) the appellant does not give information required under paragraph (*b*) of that subsection in relation to each of the specified grounds within the time prescribed by regulations under subsection (5) of this section,

the Secretary of State may determine the appeal without considering any of the specified grounds as to which the appellant has failed to give such information within that time.

(10) Where an appeal is brought under this section, the enforcement notice shall be of no effect pending the final determination or the withdrawal of the appeal.

(11) Schedule 9 to this Act applies to appeals under this section, including appeals under this section as applied by regulations under any other provision of this Act.] **[110]**

NOTES

Commencement: 27 August 1981.

Substituted by the Local Government and Planning (Amendment) Act 1981, s 1, Schedule.

88A. Appeals against enforcement notices — general supplementary provisions

[(1) On the determination of an appeal under section 88 of this Act, the Secretary of State shall give directions for giving effect to the determination, including, where appropriate, directions for quashing the enforcement notice or for varying its terms.

(2) On such an appeal the Secretary of State may correct any informality, defect or error in the enforcement notice, or give directions for varying its terms, if he is satisfied that the correction or variation can be made without injustice to the appellant or to the local planning authority.

(3) Where it would otherwise be a ground for determining such an appeal in favour of the appellant that a person required to be served with a copy of the enforcement notice was not served, the Secretary of State may disregard that fact if neither the appellant nor that person has been substantially prejudiced by the failure to serve him.] **[111]**

NOTES

Commencement: 27 August 1981.

Substituted by the Local Government and Planning (Amendment) Act 1981, s 1, Schedule.

88B. Appeals against enforcement notices — supplementary provisions relating to planning permission

[(1) On the determination of an appeal under section 88 of this Act, the Secretary of State may—

(*a*) grant planning permission for the development to which the enforcement notice relates or for part of that development or for the development of part of the land to which the enforcement notice relates;

(*b*) discharge any condition or limitation subject to which planning permission was granted;

(*c*) determine any purpose for which the land may, in the circumstances obtaining at the time of the determination, be lawfully used having regard to any past use of it and to any planning permission relating to it.

(2) In considering whether to grant planning permission under subsection (1) of this section, the Secretary of State shall have regard to the provisions of the development plan, so far as material to the subject matter of the enforcement notice, and to any other material considerations; and any planning permission granted by him under that subsection may—

(*a*) include permission to retain or complete any buildings or works on the land, or to do so without complying with some condition attached to a previous planning permission;

(*b*) be granted subject to such conditions as the Secretary of State thinks fit;

and where under that subsection he discharges a condition or limitation, he may substitute another condition or limitation for it, whether more or less onerous.

(3) Where an appeal against an enforcement notice is brought under section 88 of this Act, the appellant shall be deemed to have made an application for planning permission for the development to which the notice relates and, in relation to any exercise by the Secretary of State of his powers under subsection (1) of this section—

(*a*) any planning permission granted under that subsection shall be treated as granted on that application;

(*b*) in relation to a grant of planning permission or a determination under that subsection, the Secretary of State's decision shall be final; and

(*c*) for the purposes of section 34 of this Act, the decision shall be treated as having been given by the Secretary of State in dealing with an application for planning permission made to the local planning authority.

(4) On an appeal under section 88 of this Act against an enforcement notice relating to anything done in contravention of a condition to which section 71 of this Act applies, the Secretary of State shall not be required to entertain the appeal in so far as the appellant claims that planning premission free from that condition ought to be granted.] **[112]**

NOTES
Commencement: 27 August 1981.
Substituted by the Local Government and Planning (Amendment) Act 1981, s 1, Schedule.
Sub-s (4): repealed by the Housing and Planning Act 1986, s 49(2), Sch 12, Part III. See Appendix.

89. Penalties for non-compliance with enforcement notice

(1) Subject to the provisions of this section, [where a copy of an enforcement notice has been served on the person who, at the time when the copy was served on him, was the owner of the land to which the notice] relates, then, if any steps required by the notice to be taken (other than the discontinuance of a use of land) have not been taken within the period allowed for compliance with the

notice, that person shall be liable on summary conviction to a fine not exceeding [the prescribed sum] or on conviction on indictment to a fine.

(2) If a person against whom proceedings are brought under subsection (1) of this section has, at some time before the end of the period allowed for compliance with the notice, ceased to be the owner of the land, he shall, upon information duly laid by him, and on giving to the prosecution not less than three clear days' notice of his intention, be entitled to have the person who then became the owner of the land (in this section referred to as "the subsequent owner") brought before the court in the proceedings.

(3) If, after it has been proved that any steps required by the enforcement notice have not been taken within the period allowed for compliance with the notice, the original defendant proves that the failure to take those steps were attributable, in whole or in part, to the default of the subsequent owner—

    (*a*) the subsequent owner may be convicted of the offence; and

    (*b*) the original defendant, if he further proves that he took all reasonable steps to secure compliance with the enforcement notice, shall be acquitted of the offence.

(4) If, after a person has been convicted under the preceding provisions of this section, he does not as soon as practicable do everything in his power to secure compliance with the enforcement notice, he shall be guilty of a further offence and liable—

    (*a*) on summary conviction to a fine not exceeding [£100] for each day following his first conviction on which any of the requirements of the enforcement notice (other than the discontinuance of the use of land) remain unfulfilled; or

    (*b*) on conviction on indictment to a fine.

(5) Where, by virtue of an enforcement notice, a use of land is required to be discontinued, or any conditions or limitations are required to be complied with in respect of a use of land or in respect of the carrying out of operations thereon, then if any person uses the land or causes or permits it to be used, or carries out those operations or causes or permits them to be carried out, in contravention of the notice, he shall be guilty of an offence, and shall be liable on summary conviction to a fine not exceeding [the prescribed sum], or on conviction on indictment to a fine; and if the use is continued after the conviction he shall be guilty of a further offence and liable on summary conviction to a fine not exceeding [£100] for each day on which the use is so continued, or on conviction on indictment to a fine.

(6) Any reference in this section to the period allowed for compliance with an enforcement notice is a reference to the period specified in the notice for compliance therewith or such extended period as the local planning authority may allow for compliance with the notice. **[113]**

NOTES

    Commencement: 1 April 1972.

    This section derived from the Town and Country Planning Act 1962, s 47.

    Sub-s (1): first amendment made by the Local Government and Planning (Amendment) Act 1981, s 1, Schedule; second amendment made by the Magistrates' Courts Act 1980, s 32(2).

    Sub-s (4): amended by the Local Government and Planning (Amendment) Act 1981, s 1, Schedule, and by the Housing and Planning Act 1986, s 49(1), Sch 11, Part I, para 13. See Appendix.

    Sub-s (5): first amendment made by the Magistrates' Courts Act 1980, s 32(2); second amendment made by the Local Government and Planning (Amendment) Act 1981, s 1, Schedule; amended by the Housing and Planning Act 1986, s 49(1), Sch 11, Part I, para 13. See Appendix.

90. Stop notices

[(1) Where in respect of any land the local planning authority—

(*a*) have served [a copy of] an enforcement notice requiring a breach of planning control to be remedied; but

(*b*) consider it expedient to prevent, before the expiry of the period allowed for compliance with the notice, the carrying out of any activity which is, or is included in, a matter alleged by the notice to constitute the breach,

then, subject to the following provisions of this section, they may at any time before the notice takes effect serve a ... notice (in this Act referred to as a "stop notice") referring to, and having annexed to it a copy of, the enforcement notice and prohibiting the carrying out of that activity on the land, or on any part of it specified in the stop notice.

(2) A stop notice shall not prohibit—

(*a*) the use of any building as a dwellinghouse, or

(*b*) the use of land as the site for a caravan occupied by any person as his only or main residence (and for this purpose "caravan" has the same meaning as it has for the purposes of Part I of the Caravan Sites and Control of Development Act 1960), or

(*c*) the taking of any steps specified in the enforcement notice as required to be taken in order to remedy the breach of planning control;

and where the period during which an activity has been carried out on land (whether continuously or otherwise) began more than twelve months earlier, a stop notice shall not prohibit the carrying out of that activity on that land unless it is, or is incidental to, building, engineering, mining or other operations or the deposit of refuse or waste materials.

(3) A stop notice shall not take effect (and so cannot be contravened) until such date as it may specify, being a date not earlier than three nor later than twenty-eight days from the day on which it is first served on any person.

(4) A stop notice shall cease to have effect when—

(*a*) the enforcement notice is withdrawn or quashed, or

(*b*) the period allowed for compliance with the enforcement notice expires, or

(*c*) notice of the withdrawal of the stop notice is first served under subsection (6) of this section;

and a stop notice shall also cease to have effect if or to the extent that the activities prohibited by it cease, on a variation of the enforcement notice, to be included in the matters alleged by the enforcement notice to constitute a breach of planning control.

(5) A stop notice may be served by the local planning authority on any person who appears to them to have an interest in the land or to be engaged in any activity prohibited by the notice; and where a stop notice has been served in respect of any land, the authority may display there a notice (in this section referred to as a "site notice") stating that a stop notice has been served and that any person contravening it may be prosecuted for an offence under this section, giving the date when the stop notice takes effect and indicating its requirements.

(6) The local planning authority may at any time withdraw a stop notice (without prejudice to their power to serve another) by serving notice to that effect on persons served with the stop notice and, if a site notice was displayed

in respect of the stop notice, displaying a notice of the withdrawal in place of the site notice.

(7) If any person contravenes, or causes or permits the contravention of, a stop notice—

(*a*) after a site notice has been displayed, or

(*b*) if a site notice has not been displayed, more than two days after the stop notice has been served on him,

then, subject to subsection (8) of this section, he shall be guilty of an offence and liable on summary conviction to a fine not exceeding [the prescribed sum], or on conviction on indictment to a fine; and if the offence is continued after conviction he shall be guilty of a further offence and liable on summary conviction to a fine not exceeding [£100] for each day on which the offence is continued, or on conviction on indictment to a fine.

(8) In proceedings for an offence under this section it shall be a defence for the accused to prove that the stop notice was not served on him and that he did not know, and could not reasonably have been expected to know, of its existence.

(9) A stop notice shall not be invalid by reason that [a copy of] the enforcement notice to which it relates was not served as required by section [87(5)] of this Act if it is shown that the local planning authority took all such steps as were reasonably practicable to effect proper service.

(10) Any reference in this section to the period allowed for compliance with an enforcement notice shall be construed in accordance with section 89(6) of this Act.] **[114]**

NOTES

Commencement: 22 August 1977.

Substituted by the Town and Country Planning (Amendment) Act 1977, s 1.

Sub-ss (1), (9): amended by the Local Government and Planning (Amendment) Act 1981, s 1, Schedule.

Sub-s (7): first amendment made by the Magistrates' Courts Act 1980, s 32(2); second amendment made by the Local Government and Planning (Amendment) Act 1981, s 1, Schedule; amended by the Housing and Planning Act 1986, s 49(1), Sch 11, Part I, para 13. See Appendix.

91. Execution and cost of works required by enforcement notice

(1) If, within the period specified in an enforcement notice for compliance therewith, or within such extended period as the local planning authority may allow, any steps [which by virtue of section 87(7)(*a*) of this Act are] required by the notice to be taken (other than the discontinuance of a use of land) have not been taken, the local planning authority may enter the land and take those steps, and may recover from the person who is then the owner of the land any expenses reasonably incurred by them in doing so.

(2) Any expenses incurred by the owner or occupier of any land for the purpose of complying with an enforcement notice [a copy of which has been] served in respect of any breach of planning control (as defined in section [87(3)] of this Act) and any sums paid by the owner of any land under subsection (1) of this section in respect of expenses incurred by the local planning authority in taking steps required by such a notice to be taken, shall be deemed to be incurred or paid for the use and at the request of the person by whom the breach of planning control was committed.

(3) Regulations made under this Act may provide that, in relation to any steps required to be taken by an enforcement notice, all or any of the enactments specified in subsection (4) of this section shall apply, subject to such adaptations

and modifications as may be specified in the regulations, including, in the case of the enactment specified in paragraph (*b*) of that subsection, adaptations and modifications for the purpose of affording to the owner of land to which an enforcement notice relates the right, as against all other persons interested in the land, to comply with the requirements of the enforcement notice.

(4) The said enactments are the following provisions of the Public Health Act 1936, that is to say—

> (*a*) section 276 (power of local authorities to sell materials removed in executing works under that Act subject to accounting for the proceeds of sale);
> (*b*) section 289 (power to require the occupier of any premises to permit works to be executed by the owner of the premises);
> (*c*) . . . ; and
> (*d*) section 294 (limit on liability of persons holding premises as agents or trustees in respect of the expenses recoverable under that Act).

(5) Any regulations made in accordance with subsection (3) of this section may provide for the charging on the land of any expenses recoverable by a local authority under subsection (1) of this section.   **[115]**

NOTES
Commencement: 1 April 1972.
Amendments in square brackets made by the Local Government and Planning (Amendment) Act 1981, s 1 Schedule; words omitted repealed by the Local Government Act 1972, s 42(2), Sch 8.

92. Effect of planning permission on enforcement notice

(1) If, after the service of [a copy of] an enforcement notice, planning permission is granted for the retention on land of buildings or works, or for the continuance of a use of land, to which the enforcement notice relates, the enforcement notice shall cease to have effect in so far as it requires steps to be taken for the demolition or alteration of those buildings or works, or the discontinuance of that use, as the case may be.

(2) If the planning permission granted as mentioned in subsection (1) of this section is granted so as to permit the retention of buildings or works, or the continuance of a use of land, without complying with some condition subject to which a previous planning permission was granted, the enforcement notice shall cease to have effect in so far as it requires steps to be taken for complying with that condition.

(3) The preceding provisions of this section shall be without prejudice to the liability of any person for an offence in respect of a failure to comply with the enforcement notice before the relevant provision of the enforcement notice ceased to have effect.   **[116]**

NOTES
Commencement: 1 April 1972.
Sub-s (1): amended by the Local Government and Planning (Amendment) Act 1981, s 1, Schedule.

92A. Register of enforcement and stop notices

[(1) Every district planning authority and [the council of every metropolitan district or London borough] shall keep, in such manner as may be prescribed by a development order, a register containing such information as may be so prescribed with respect—

(*a*) to enforcement notices; and

(*b*) to stop notices,

which relate to land in their area and to which this section applies.

(2) This section applies to enforcement notices issued and stop notices served after the date on which there expired the period of four months beginning with the date on which the Local Government and Planning (Amendment) Act 1981 was passed.

(3) A development order may make provision—

(*a*) for the entry relating to any enforcement notice or stop notice, and everything relating to any such notice, to be removed from the register in such circumstances as may be specified in the order;

(*b*) for requiring a county planning authority to supply to a district planning authority such information as may be so specified with regard to enforcement notices issued and stop notices served by the county planning authority; . . .

(*c*) . . .

(4) Every register kept under this section shall be available for inspection by the public at all reasonable hours.] **[117]**

NOTES

Commencement: 27 November 1981.

Added by the Local Government and Planning (Amendment) Act 1981, s 1, Schedule.

Sub-s (1): amended by the Local Government Act 1985, s 3(4).

Sub-s (3): in paras (*b*) and (*c*) words omitted repealed by the Local Government Act 1985, s 102, Sch 17.

93. Enforcement notice to have effect against subsequent development

(1) Compliance with an enforcement notice, whether in respect of—

(*a*) the [completion,] demolition or alteration of any buildings or works; or

(*b*) the discontinuance of any use of land,

or in respect of any other requirements contained in the enforcement notice, shall not discharge the enforcement notice.

(2) Without prejudice to subsection (1) of this section, any provision of an enforcement notice requiring a use of land to be discontinued shall operate as a requirement that it shall be discontinued permanently, to the extent that it is in contravention of Part III of this Act; and accordingly the resumption of that use at any time after it has been discontinued in compliance with the enforcement notice shall to that extent be in contravention of the enforcement notice.

(3) Without prejudice to subsection (1) of this section, if any development is carried out on land by way of reinstating or restoring buildings or works which have been demolished or altered in compliance with an enforcement notice, the notice shall, notwithstanding that its terms are not apt for the purpose, be deemed to apply in relation to the buildings or works as reinstated or restored as it applied in relation to the buildings or works before they were demolished or altered; and, subject to subsection (4) of this section, the provisions of section 91(1) and (2) of this Act, shall apply accordingly.

(4) Where, at any time after an enforcement notice takes effect—

    (*a*) any development is carried out on land by way of reinstating or restoring buildings or works which have been demolished or altered in compliance with the notice; and

    (*b*) the local planning authority propose, under section 91(1) of this Act, to take any steps required by the enforcement notice for the demolition or alteration of the buildings or works in consequence of the reinstatement or restoration,

the local planning authority shall, not less than twenty-eight days before taking any such steps, serve on the owner and occupier of the land a notice of their intention to do so.

    (5) A person who, without the grant of planning permission in that behalf, carries out any development on land by way of reinstating or restoring buildings or works which have been demolished or altered in compliance with an enforcement notice shall be guilty of an offence, and shall be liable on summary conviction to a fine not exceeding [level 5 on the standard scale]; and no person shall be liable under any of the provisions of section 89(1) to (4) of this Act for failure to take any steps required to be taken by an enforcement notice by way of demolition or alteration of what has been so reinstated or restored.   **[118]**

NOTES

    Commencement: 1 April 1972.

    Sub-s (1): amended by the Local Government and Planning (Amendment) Act 1981, s 1, Schedule.

    Sub-s (5): maximum fine increased by the Local Government and Planning (Amendment) Act 1981, s 1, Schedule, and converted to a level on the standard scale by the Criminal Justice Act 1982, ss 37, 46.

---

94. Certification as to established use

    (1) For the purposes of this Part of this Act, a use of land is established if—

    (*a*) it was begun before the beginning of 1964 without planning permission in that behalf and has continued since the end of 1963; or

    (*b*) it was begun before the beginning of 1964 under a planning permission in that behalf granted subject to conditions or limitations, which either have never been complied with or have not been complied with since the end of 1963; or

    (*c*) it was begun after the end of 1963 as the result of a change of use not requiring planning permission and there has been, since the end of 1963, no change of use requiring planning permission.

    (2) Where a person having an interest in land claims that a particular use of it has become established, he may apply to the local planning authority for a certificate (in this Act referred to as an "established use certificate") to that effect:

    Provided that no such application may be made in respect of the use of land as a single dwellinghouse, or of any use not subsisting at the time of the application.

    (3) An established use certificate may be granted (either by the local planning authority or, under section 95 of this Act, by the Secretary of State)—

    (*a*) either for the whole of the land specified in the application, or for a part of it;

    (*b*) in the case of an application specifying two or more uses, either for all those uses or for some one or more of them.

    (4) On an application to them under this section, the local planning

authority shall, if and so far as they are satisfied that the applicant's claim is made out, grant to him an established use certificate accordingly; and if and so far as they are not so satisfied, they shall refuse the application.

(5) Where an application is made to a local planning authority for an established use certificate, then unless within such period as may be prescribed by a development order, or within such extended period as may at any time be agreed upon in writing between the applicant and the local planning authority, the authority give notice to the applicant of their decision on the application, then, for the purposes of section 95(2) of this Act, the application shall be deemed to be refused.

(6) Schedule 14 to this Act shall have effect with respect to established use certificates and applications therefor and to appeals under section 95 of this Act.

(7) An established use certificate shall, as respects any matters stated therein, be conclusive for the purposes of an appeal to the Secretary of State against an enforcement notice [a copy of which has been] served in respect of any land to which the certificate relates, but only where [the copy of] the notice is served after the date of the application on which the certificate was granted.

(8) If any person, for the purpose of procuring a particular decision on an application (whether by himself or another) for an established use certificate or on an appeal arising out of such an application—

(*a*) knowingly or recklessly makes a statement which is false in a material particular; or

(*b*) with intent to deceive, produces, furnishes, sends or otherwise makes use of any document which is false in a material particular; or

(*c*) with intent to deceive, withholds any material information,

he shall be guilty of an offence and liable on summary conviction to a fine not exceeding [the prescribed sum] or, on conviction on indictment, to imprisonment for a term not exceeding two years or a fine, or both. **[119]**

NOTES
Commencement: 1 April 1972.
This section derived from the Town and Country Planning Act 1968, s 17.
Sub-s (7): amended by the Local Government and Planning (Amendment) Act 1981, s 1, Schedule.
Sub-s (8): amended by the Magistrates' Courts Act 1980, s 32(2).

95. Grant of certificate by Secretary of State on referred application or appeal against refusal

(1) The Secretary of State may give directions requiring applications for established use certificates to be referred to him instead of being dealt with by local planning authorities; and, on any such application being referred to him in accordance with such directions, section 94(4) of this Act shall apply in relation to the Secretary of State as it applies in relation to the local planning authority in the case of an application determined by them.

(2) Where an application is made to a local planning authority for an established use certificate and is refused, or is refused in part, the applicant may by notice under this subsection appeal to the Secretary of State; and on any such appeal the Secretary of State shall—

(*a*) if and so far as he is satisfied that the authority's refusal is not well-founded, grant to the appellant an established use certificate

accordingly or, as the case may be, modify the certificate granted by
the authority on the application; and

(*b*) if and so far as he is satisfied that the authority's refusal is well-
founded, dismiss the appeal.

(3) On an application referred to him under subsection (1) of this section or
on an appeal to him under subsection (2) of this section, the Secretary of State
may, in respect of any use of land for which an established use certificate is not
granted (either by him or by the local planning authority), grant planning
permission for that use or, as the case may be, for the continuance of that use
without complying with some condition subject to which a previous planning
permission was granted.

(4) Before determining an application or appeal under this section the
Secretary of State shall, if either the applicant or appellant (as the case may be)
or the local planning authority so desire, afford to each of them an opportunity
of appearing before, and being heard by, a person appointed by the Secretary
of State for the purpose.

(5) The decision of the Secretary of State on an application referred to him,
or on an appeal, under this section shall be final.

(6) In the case of any use of land for which the Secretary of State has power
to grant planning permission under this section, the applicant or appellant shall
be deemed to have made an application for such planning permission; and any
planning permission so granted shall be treated as granted on the said
application.

(7) Schedule 9 to this Act applies to appeals under this section.   **[120]**

NOTES
  Commencement: 1 April 1972.

Listed buildings

96. Power to issue listed building enforcement notice

[(1) Where it appears to the local planning authority that any works have been
or are being executed to a listed building in their area and are such as to involve
a contravention of section 55(1) or (4) of this Act, they may, if they consider if
expedient to do so having regard to the effect of the works on the character of
the building as one of special architectural or historic interest, issue a notice—

(*a*) specifying the alleged contravention; and
(*b*) requiring such steps as may be specified in the notice to be taken
within such period as may be so specified—

(i) for restoring the building to its former state; or
(ii) where the authority consider that such restoration would not be
reasonably practicable, or would be undesirable, for executing
such further works specified in the notice as they consider
necessary to alleviate the effect of the works which were carried
out without listed building consent; or
(iii) for bringing the building to the state in which it would have been
if the terms and conditions of any listed building consent which
has been granted for the works had been complied with.

(2) A notice under this section is referred to in this Act as a "listed building
enforcement notice".

(3) A copy of a listed building enforcement notice shall be served, not later than 28 days after the date of its issue and not later than 28 days before the date specified in the notice as the date on which it is to take effect—

(*a*) on the owner and on the occupier of the building to which it relates; and

(*b*) on any other person having an interest in that building, being an interest which in the opinion of the authority is materially affected by the notice.

(4) Subject to section 97 of this Act, a listed building enforcement notice shall take effect on a date specified in it.

(5) The local planning authority may withdraw a listed building enforcement notice (without prejudice to their power to issue another) at any time before it takes effect.

(6) If they do so, they shall forthwith give notice of the withdrawal to every person who was served with a copy of the notice.

(7) Where a listed building enforcement notice imposes any such requirement as is mentioned in subsection (1)(*b*)(ii) of this section, listed building consent shall be deemed to be granted for any works of demolition, alteration or extension of the building executed as a result of compliance with the notice.]

[121]

NOTES

Commencement: 27 August 1981.

Substituted by the Local Government and Planning (Amendment) Act 1981, s 1, Schedule.

97. Appeal against listed building enforcement notice

[(1) A person having an interest in the building to which a listed building enforcement notice relates may, at any time before the date specified in the notice as the date on which it is to take effect, appeal to the Secretary of State against the notice on any of the following grounds—

(*a*) that the building is not of special architectural or historic interest;

(*b*) that the matters alleged to constitute a contravention of section 55 of this Act do not involve such a contravention;

(*c*) that the contravention of that section alleged in the notice has not taken place;

(*d*) that the works were urgently necessary in the interest of safety or health or for the preservation of the building;

(*e*) that listed building consent ought to be granted for the works, or that any relevant condition of such consent which has been granted ought to be discharged, or different conditions substituted;

(*f*) that copies of the notice were not served as required by section 96(3) of this Act;

(*g*) except in relation to such a requirement as is mentioned in section 96(1)(*b*)(ii) or (iii) of this Act, the requirements of the notice exceed what is necessary for restoring the building to its condition before the works were carried out;

(*h*) that the period specified in the notice as the period within which any step required thereby is to be taken falls short of what should reasonably be allowed;

(*i*) that the steps required by the notice for the purpose of restoring the character of the building to its former state would not serve that purpose;

(*j*) that steps required to be taken by virtue of section 96(1)(*b*)(ii) of this Act exceed what is necessary to alleviate the effect of the works executed to the building;

(*k*) that steps required to be taken by virtue of section 96(1)(*b*)(iii) of this Act exceed what is necessary to bring the building to the state in which it would have been if the terms and conditions of the listed building consent had been complied with.

(2) An appeal under this section shall be made by notice in writing to the Secretary of State.

(3) A person who gives notice under subsection (2) of this section shall submit to the Secretary of State, either when giving the notice or within such time as may be prescribed under subsection (4) of this section, a statement in writing—

(*a*) specifying the grounds on which he is appealing against the listed building enforcement notice; and

(*b*) giving such further information as the regulations may prescribe.

(4) The Secretary of State may by regulations prescribe the procedure which is to be followed on appeals under this section, and in particular, but without prejudice to the generality of this subsection, may make any such provision in relation to appeals under this section as may be made in relation to appeals under section 88 of this Act by regulations under subsection (5) of that section.

(5) The Secretary of State—

(*a*) may dismiss an appeal if the appellant fails to comply with subsection (3) of this section within the time prescribed by regulations under subsection (4); and

(*b*) may allow an appeal and quash the listed building enforcement notice if the local planning authority fail to comply with any requirement of regulations under this section corresponding to regulations made by virtue of subsection (5)(*b*), (*c*) or (*e*) of section 88 of this Act within the period prescribed by the regulations.

(6) Subject to subsection (7) of this section, the Secretary of State shall, if either the appellant or the local planning authority so desire, afford to each of them an opportunity of appearing before and being heard by a person appointed by the Secretary of State for the purpose.

(7) The Secretary of State shall not be required to afford such an opportunity if he proposes to dismiss an appeal under paragraph (*a*) of subsection (5) of this section or to allow an appeal and quash the listed building enforcement notice under paragraph (*b*) of that subsection.

(8) If—

(*a*) a statement under subsection (3) of this section specifies more than one ground on which the appellant is appealing against a listed building enforcement notice; but

(*b*) the appellant does not give information required under paragraph (*b*) of that subsection in relation to each of the specified grounds within the time prescribed by regulations under subsection (4) of this section,

the Secretary of State may determine the appeal without considering any of the specified grounds as to which the appellant has failed to give such information within that time.

(9) Where an appeal is brought under this section, the listed building

enforcement notice shall be of no effect pending the final determination or the withdrawal of the appeal.

(10) Schedule 9 to this Act applies to appeals under this section.] **[122]**

NOTES

Commencement: 27 August 1981.

Substituted by the Local Government and Planning (Amendment) Act 1981, s 1, Schedule.

Sub-s (1): amended by the Housing and Planning Act 1986, s 40, Sch 9, Part I, para 2(2). See Appendix.

97A. Appeals against listed building enforcement notices — supplementary

[(1) On the determination of an appeal under section 97 of this Act, the Secretary of State shall give directions for giving effect to the determination, including, where appropriate, directions for quashing the listed building enforcement notice or for varying its terms.

(2) On such an appeal the Secretary of State may correct any informality, defect or error in the listed building enforcement notice, or give directions for varying its terms, if he is satisfied that the correction or variation can be made without injustice to the appellant or to the local planning authority.

(3) Where it would otherwise be a ground for determining such an appeal in favour of the appellant that a person required to be served with a copy of the listed building enforcement notice was not served, the Secretary of State may disregard that fact if neither the appellant nor that person has been substantially prejudiced by the failure to serve him.

(4) On the determination of such an appeal the Secretary of State may—

    (*a*) grant listed building consent for the works to which the listed building enforcement notice relates or for part only of those works;

    (*b*) discharge any condition or limitation subject to which listed building consent was granted and substituted any other condition, whether more or less onerous;

    (*c*) if he thinks fit, exercise—

        (i) his power under section 54 of this Act to amend any list compiled or approved under that section by removing from it the building to which the appeal relates; or

        (ii) his power under subsection (10) of that section to direct that that subsection shall no longer apply to the building.

(5) Any listed building consent granted by the Secretary of State under subsection (4) of this section shall be treated as granted on an application for the like consent under Part I of Schedule 11 to this Act, and the Secretary of State's decision in relation to the grant shall be final.] **[123]**

NOTES

Commencement: 27 August 1981.

Substituted by the Local Government and Planning (Amendment) Act 1981, s 1, Schedule.

98. Penalties for non-compliance with listed building enforcement notice

(1) Subject to the provisions of this section, where a listed building enforcement notice has been served on the person who, at the time when the notice was served on him, was the owner of the building to which it relates, then, if any steps required by the notice to be taken have not been taken within the period allowed for compliance with the notice, that person shall be guilty of an offence and liable on summary conviction to a fine not exceeding [the prescribed sum], or on conviction on indictment to a fine.

(2) If a person against whom proceedings have been brought under subsection (1) of this section has, at some time before the end of the period allowed for compliance with the notice, ceased to be the owner of the building, he shall, upon information duly laid by him, and on giving to the prosecution not less than three clear days' notice of his intention, be entitled to have the person who then became the owner of the building (in this section referred to as "the subsequent owner") brought before the court in the proceedings.

(3) If, after it has been proved that any steps required by the notice have not been taken within the period allowed for compliance with the notice, the original defendant proves that the failure to take those steps was attributable, in whole or in part, to the default of the subsequent owner—

> (a)   the subsequent owner may be convicted of the offence; and
> (b)   the original defendant, if he further proves that he took all reasonable steps to secure compliance with the notice, shall be acquitted of the offence.

(4) If, after a person has been convicted under the preceding provisions of this section, he does not as soon as practicable do everything in his power to secure compliance with the notice, he shall be guilty of a further offence and be liable—

> (a)   on summary conviction to a fine not exceeding [£100] for each day following his first conviction on which any of the requirements of the notice remain unfulfilled; or
> (b)   on conviction on indictment to a fine.

(5) Any reference in this section to the period allowed for compliance with a listed building enforcement notice is a reference to the period specified in the notice as that within which the steps specified in the notice are required thereby to be taken, or such extended period as the local planning authority may allow for taking them.   **[124]**

NOTES

Commencement: 1 April 1972.

This section derived from the Town and Country Planning Act 1968, s 45.

Sub-s (1): amended by the Magistrates' Courts Act 1980, s 32(2).

Sub-s (4): amended by the Local Government and Planning (Amendment) Act 1981, s 1, Schedule, and by the Housing and Planning Act 1986, s 49(1), Sch 11, Part I, para 13. See Appendix.

99. Execution and cost of works required by listed building enforcement notice

(1) If, within the period specified in a listed building enforcement notice as that within which the steps specified in the notice are required thereby to be taken, or within such extended period as the local planning authority may allow, any steps required by the notice to be taken have not been taken, the authority may enter the land and take those steps, and may recover from the person who is then the owner of the land any expenses reasonably incurred by them in doing so.

(2) Any expenses incurred by the owner or occupier of a building for the purpose of complying with a listed building enforcement notice, and any sums paid by the owner of a building under subsection (1) of this section in respect of expenses incurred by the local planning authority in taking steps required by such a notice to be taken, shall be deemed to be incurred or paid for the use and at the request of the person who carried out the works to which the notice relates.

(3) The provisions of section 91(3) and (4) of this Act shall apply in relation

to a listed building enforcement notice as they apply in relation to an enforcement notice; and any regulations made by virtue of this subsection may provide for the charging on the land on which the building stands of any expenses recoverable by a local planning authority under subsection (1) of this section.   **[125]**

NOTES
Commencement: 1 April 1972.

99A. Effect of listed building consent on listed building enforcement notice

[(1) If, after the issue of a listed building enforcement notice, consent is granted under section 55(2A) of this Act for the retention of any work to which the listed building enforcement notice relates, the listed building enforcement notice shall cease to have effect in so far as it requires steps to be taken which would involve the works not being retained in accordance with the consent.

(2) If the consent is granted so as to permit the retention of works without complying with some condition subject to which a previous listed building consent was granted, the listed building enforcement notice shall cease to have effect in so far as it requires steps to be taken for complying with that condition.

(3) The preceding provisions of this section shall be without prejudice to the liability of any person for an offence in respect of a failure to comply with the listed building enforcement notice before the relevant provisions of that notice ceased to have effect.]   **[126]**

NOTES
Commencement: 13 November 1980.
Added by the Local Government, Planning and Land Act 1980, s 90, Sch 15.

99B. Concurrent functions in London

[The Historic Buildings and Monuments Commission for England shall, as respects any London borough, have concurrently with the council of that borough the functions of a local planning authority under sections 96 to 99A of this Act; and references to the local planning authority in those provisions, or in section 88 of this Act as applied for the purpose of any of those provisions, shall be construed accordingly.]   **[127]**

NOTES
Commencement: 1 April 1986.
Added by the Local Government Act 1985, s 6, Sch 2, para 1(7).

100. Enforcement by the Secretary of State

[(1) If it appears to the Secretary of State, after consultation with the local planning authority ... , to be expedient that a listed building enforcement notice should be issued in respect of any land, he may issue such a notice; and any notice so issued by the Secretary of State shall have the like effect as a notice issued by the local planning authority.

[Where the land is situated in England, the Secretary of State shall also consult with the Historic Buildings and Monuments Commission for England before he serves a notice under this subsection.]

(2) In relation to a listed building enforcement notice issued by the Secretary

of State, the provisions of section 99 of this Act shall apply as if for any reference in that section to the local planning authority there were substituted a reference to the Secretary of State.] **[128]**

NOTES
Commencement: 27 August 1981.
Substituted by the Local Government and Planning (Amendment) Act 1981, s 1, Schedule.
Sub-s (1): words omitted repealed by the Local Government Act 1985, s 102, Sch 17; amendment in square brackets made by the National Heritage Act 1983, s 33, Sch 4, para 17.

101. Urgent works for preservation of unoccupied buildings

[(1) This section applies to any unoccupied building which satisfies one of the conditions specified in subsection (2) below but is not an excepted building as defined in section 58(2) above.

(2) The conditions mentioned in subsection (1) above are—

(*a*) that the building is a listed building;
(*b*) that a direction that this section shall apply to the building has been given under subsection (3) below.

(3) If it appears to the Secretary of State, in the case of a building which is not a listed building but is situated in a conservation area, that it is important to preserve it for the purpose of maintaining the character or appearance of the conservation area, he may direct that this section shall apply to it.

[Before making a direction under this subsection in relation to a building situated in England, the Secretary of State shall consult with the Historic Buildings and Monuments Commission for England (in this section referred to as "the Commission").]

(4) If it appears to a local authority [or the Commission] that any works are urgently necessary for the preservation of a building to which this section applies and which is situated in their area [or, in the case of the Commission, in Greater London,], they may execute the works, after giving the owner of the building not less than seven days' notice in writing of their intention to do so.

(5) If it appears to the Secretary of State that any works are urgently necessary for the preservation of a building to which this section applies, he may execute the works, after giving the owner of the building not less than seven days' notice in writing of his intention to do so.

[(5A) If it appears to the Secretary of State that any works are urgently necessary for the preservation of a building to which this section applies and which is situated in England, and if he would (apart from this subsection) act as mentioned in subsection (5) above, he shall (instead of so acting) authorise the Commission to execute such works as are specified in the authorisation.

(5B) In that case, the Commission may execute the works after giving the owner of the building not less than seven days notice in writing of their intention to do so.]

(6) The local authority [or the Commission,] or, as the case may be, the Secretary of State may give notice to the owner of the building requiring him to pay the expenses of any works executed under subsection (4) or (5) above [and the Secretary of State may give notice to the owner of the building requiring him to pay the expenses of any works executed under subsection (5B) above]; and if such a notice is given by the local authority [or the Commission,] or the

Secretary of State, the amount specified in the notice shall be recoverable from the owner, subject to subsections (7) to (9) below.

(7) Within 28 days of the date of a notice under subsection (6) above, the owner may represent to the Secretary of State—

(*a*) that the amount specified in the notice is unreasonable; or
(*b*) that recovery of it would cause him hardship; or
(*c*) that some or all of the works were unnecessary for the building's preservation.

(8) The Secretary of State shall determine the extent, if any, to which representations under subsection (7) above are justified.

(9) The Secretary of State shall give the owner and the local authority [(and the Commission, in a case where they have executed the works concerned)] notice of any determination under subsection (8) above and of the reasons for it, and of the amount (if any) which is to be recoverable from the owner; and no sum shall be recoverable from him unless it is so notified.]   **[129]**

NOTES
Commencement: 1 April 1984 (sub-ss (5A), (5B)); 31 August 1974 (remainder).
Commencement order: SI 1984 No 208.
Substituted by the Town and Country Amenities Act 1974, s 5.
Sub-ss (3), (9): amended by the National Heritage Act 1983, s 33, Sch 4, para 18(2), (5).
Sub-s (4): amended by the Local Government Act 1985, s 6, Sch 2, para 1.
Sub-ss (5A), (5B): added by the National Heritage Act 1983, s 33, Sch 4, para 18(3).
Sub-s (6): first and third words in square brackets added by the Local Government Act 1985, s 6, Sch 2, para 1; second words in square brackets added by the National Heritage Act 1983, s 33, Sch 4, para 18(4).

(New ss 101 and 101A substituted except in relation to works commenced before 1 April 1987 for s 101 above by the Housing and Planning Act 1986, s 40, Sch 9, Part I, para 7. See Appendix.)
(New s 101B prospectively inserted by the Housing and Planning Act 1986, s 32. See Appendix.)

Trees

102. Penalties for non-compliance with tree preservation order
[(1) If any person, in contravention of a tree preservation order, cuts down, uproots or wilfully destroys a tree, or wilfully damages, tops or lops a tree in such a manner as to be likely to destroy it, he shall be guilty of an offence and shall be liable—

(*a*) on summary conviction to a fine not exceeding [the prescribed sum] or twice the sum which appears to the court to be the value of the tree, whichever is the greater; or
(*b*) on conviction on indictment, to a fine, and, in determining the amount of any fine to be imposed on a person convicted on indictment, the court shall in particular have regard to any financial benefit which has accrued or appears likely to accrue to him in consequence of the offence.]

(2) If any person contravenes the provisions of a tree preservation order otherwise than as mentioned in subsection (1) of this section, he shall be guilty of an offence and liable on summary conviction to a fine not exceeding [level 4 on the standard scale].

(3) If, in the case of a continuing offence under this section, the contravention is continued after the conviction, the offender shall be guilty of a further offence

and liable on summary conviction to an additional fine not exceeding [£5] for each day on which the contravention is so continued.

[(4) This section shall apply to an offence under section 61A above as it applies to a contravention of a tree preservation order.]   **[130]**

NOTES
   Commencement: 31 August 1974 (sub-ss (1), (4)); 1 April 1972 (remainder).
   This section derived from the Town and Country Planning Act 1962, s 62(1).
   Sub-s (1): substituted by the Town and Country Amenities Act 1974, s 10; amended by the Magistrates' Courts Act 1980, s 32(2).
   Sub-s (2): maximum fine increased and converted to a level on the standard scale by the Criminal Justice Act 1982, ss 37, 38, 46.
   Sub-s (3): amended by the Town and Country Amenities Act 1974, s 10.
   Sub-s (4): added by the Town and Country Amenities Act 1974, s 10.

103. Enforcement of duties as to replacement of trees

(1) If it appears to the local planning authority that the provisions of section 62 of this Act, or any conditions of a consent given under a tree preservation order which require the replacement of trees, are not complied with in the case of any tree or trees, that authority may, at any time within four years from the date of the alleged failure to comply with the said provisions or conditions, serve on the owner of the land a notice requiring him, within such period as may be specified in the notice, to plant a tree or trees of such size and species as may be so specified.

(2) Subject to the following provisions of this section, a notice under this section shall take effect at the end of such period, not being less than twenty-eight days after the service   of the notice, as may be specified in the notice.

(3) A person on whom a notice under this section is served may, at any time within the period specified in the notice as the period at the end of which it is to take effect, appeal to the Secretary of State against the notice on any of the following grounds—

   (a) that the provisions of the said section 62 or the conditions aforesaid are not applicable or have been complied with;
   (b) that the requirements of the notice are unreasonable in respect of the period or the size or species of trees specified therein;
   (c) that the planting of a tree or trees in accordance with the notice is not required in the interests of amenity or would be contrary to the practice of good forestry;
   (d) that the place on which the tree is or trees are required to be planted is unsuitable for that purpose;

. . .

[(3A) An appeal under this section shall be made by notice in writing to the Secretary of State.

(3B) The notice shall indicate the grounds of the appeal and state the facts on which it is based.

(3C) On any such appeal the Secretary of State shall, if either the appellant or the local planning authority so desire, afford to each of them an opportunity of appearing before, and being heard by, a person appointed by the Secretary of State for the purpose.

(3D) Where an appeal is brought under this section, the notice under subsection (1) of this section shall be of no effect pending the final determination or the withdrawal of the appeal.

(3E) On the determination of an appeal under this section, the Secretary of State shall give directions for giving effect to the determination, including, where appropriate, directions for quashing the notice under subsection (1) of this section or for varying its terms.

(3F) On such an appeal the Secretary of State may correct any informality, defect or error in the notice under subsection (1) of this section, or give directions for varying its terms, if he is satisfied that the correction or variation can be made without injustice to the appellant or the local planning authority.]

(4) Schedule 9 to this Act applies to appeals under subsection (3) of this section.

(5) In section 91 of this Act, and in regulations in force under that section, references to an enforcement notice and an enforcement notice [a copy of which has been] served in respect of any breach of planning control shall include references to a notice under this section; and in relation to such a notice the reference in subsection (2) of that section to the person by whom the breach of planning control was committed shall be construed as a reference to any person, other than the owner, responsible for the cutting down, destruction or removal of the original tree or trees.   **[131]**

NOTES
   Commencement: 1 April 1972.
   Amended by the Local Government and Planning (Amendment) Act 1981, s 1, Schedule.

Waste land

104. Penalties for non-compliance with notice as to waste land

[(1) The provisions of this section shall have effect where a notice has been served under section 65 of this Act.

(2) Subject to the following provisions of this section, if any owner or occupier of the land on whom the notice was served fails to take any steps required by the notice within the period specified in it for compliance with it, he shall be guilty of an offence and liable on summary conviction to a fine not exceeding [level 3 on the standard scale].

(3) If a person against whom proceedings are brought under subsection (2) of this section as the owner of the land has, at some time before the end of the period allowed for compliance with the notice, ceased to be the owner, he shall, upon information duly laid by him, and on giving to the prosecution not less than three clear days' notice of his intention, be entitled to have the person who then became the owner brought before the court in the proceedings.

(4) If a person against whom proceedings are brought under subsection (2) of this section as the occupier of the land has, at some time before the end of the period allowed for compliance with the notice, ceased to be the occupier, he shall, upon information duly laid by him, and on giving to the prosecution not less than three clear days' notice of his intention, be entitled to have any person who then became the occupier brought before the court in the proceedings.

(5) If—
   (*a*) a person against whom proceedings are brought under subsection (2) of this section as the occupier of the land has, at some time before the

end of the period allowed for compliance with the notice, ceased to be the occupier; and
(*b*) nobody then became the occupier,

he shall, upon information duly laid by him, and giving to the prosecution not less than three clear days' notice of his intention, be entitled to have the person who is the owner at the date of the notice brought before the court in the proceedings.

(6) If, after it has been proved that any steps required by the notice under section 65 of this Act have not been taken within the period allowed for compliance with that notice, the original defendant proves that the failure to take those steps was attributable, in whole or in part, to the default of a person specified in a notice under this section—

(*a*) that person may be convicted of the offence; and
(*b*) the original defendant shall be acquitted of the offence if he further proves that he took all reasonable steps to ensure compliance with the notice.

(7) If, after a person as been convicted under the preceding provisions of this section, he does not as soon as practicable do everything in his power to secure compliance with the notice, he shall be guilty of a further offence and liable on summary conviction to a fine not exceeding £20 for each day following his first conviction on which any of the requirements of the notice remain unfulfilled.

(8) Any reference in this section to the period allowed for compliance with a notice is a reference to the period specified in the notice for compliance with it or to such extended period as the local planning authority who served the notice may allow for compliance with it.] **[132]**

NOTES
Commencement: 27 August 1981.
Substituted by the Local Government and Planning (Amendment) Act 1981, s 1, Schedule.
Sub-s (2): maximum fine converted to a level on the standard scale by the Criminal Justice Act 1982, ss 37, 46.
Sub-s (7): amended by the Housing and Planning Act 1986, s 49(1), Sch 11, Part I, para 13. See Appendix.

105. Appeal to magistrates' court against notice as to waste land

(1) A person on whom a notice under section 65 of this Act is served, or any other person having an interest in the land to which the notice relates, may, at any time within the period specified in the notice as the period at the end of which it is to take effect, appeal against the notice on any of the following grounds—

(*a*) that the condition of the land to which the notice relates does not seriously injure the amenity of any part of the area of the local planning authority who served the notice, or of any adjoining area;
(*b*) that the condition of the land to which the notice relates is attributable to, and such as results in the ordinary course of events from, the carrying on of operations or a use of land which is not in contravention of Part III of this Act;
(*c*) that the land to which the notice relates does not constitute a garden, vacant site or other open land in the area of the local planning authority who served the notice;
(*d*) that the requirements of the notice exceed what is necessary for preventing the condition of the land from seriously injuring the

amenity of any part of the area of the local planning authority who served the notice, or of any adjoining area;

(*e*) that the period specified in the notice as the period within which any steps required by the notice are to be taken falls short of what should reasonably be allowed.

(2) Any appeal under this section shall be made to a magistrates' court acting for the petty sessions area in which the land in question is situated.

(3) Where an appeal is brought under this section, the notice to which it relates shall be of no effect pending the final determination or withdrawal of the appeal.

(4) On an appeal under this section the magistrates' court may correct any informality, defect or error in the notice if satisfied that the informality, defect or error is not material.

(5) On the determination of an appeal under this section the magistrates' court shall give directions for giving effect to their determination, including, where appropriate, directions for quashing the notice or for varying the terms of the notice in favour of the appellant.   **[133]**

NOTES
Commencement: 1 April 1972.
Sub-s (1): paras (*a*) and (*d*) amended by the Housing and Planning Act 1986, s 49(1), Sch 11, Part I, para 20; para (*c*) repealed by the Housing and Planning Act 1986, s 49(1), Sch 11, Part I, para 20 and s 49(2), Sch 12, Part III. See Appendix.

106. Further appeal to the Crown Court

Where an appeal has been brought under section 105 of this Act, an appeal against the decision of the magistrates' court thereon may be brought to the Crown Court by the appellant or by the local planning authority [who served the notice in question under section 65 of this Act].   **[134]**

NOTES
Commencement: 1 April 1972.
Amended by the Local Government and Planning (Amendment) Act 1981, s 1, Schedule.

107. Execution and cost of works required by notice as to waste land

(1) If, within the period specified in a notice under section 65 of this Act in accordance with subsection (1) of that section, or within such extended period as the local planning authority [who served the notice] may allow, any steps required by the notice to be taken have not been taken, the local planning authority [who served the notice] may enter the land and take those steps, and may recover from the person who is then the owner of the land any expenses reasonably incurred by them in doing so.

(2) Any expenses incurred by the owner or occupier of any land for the purpose of complying with a notice under section 65 of this Act, and any sums paid by the owner of any land under subsection (1) of this section in respect of expenses incurred by the local planning authority [who served the notice] in taking steps required by such a notice to be taken, shall be deemed to be incurred or paid for the use and at the request of the person who caused or permitted the land to come to be in the condition in which it was when the notice was served.

(3) The provisions of section 91(3) and (4) of this Act shall apply in relation to a notice under section 65 of this Act as they apply in relation to an enforcement

notice; and regulations made by virtue of this subsection may provide for the charging on the land of any expenses recoverable by a local authority under subsection (1) of this section.   **[135]**

NOTES
Commencement: 1 April 1972.
Amended by the Local Government and Planning (Amendment) Act 1981, s 1, Schedule.

Other controls

108. Enforcement of orders under s 51 [Enforcement of Orders under sections 51, 51A and 51B]

[(1) Any person who, without the grant of planning permission in that behalf,—

(*a*) uses land, or causes or permits land to be used—

  (i) for any purpose for which an order under section 51 of this Act has required that its use shall be discontinued; or
  (ii) in contravention of any condition imposed by such an order by virtue of subsection (1) of that section; or

(*b*) resumes, or causes or permits to be resumed, development consisting of the winning and working of minerals the resumption of which an order under section 51A of this Act has prohibited; or

(*c*) contravenes, or causes or permits to be contravened, any such requirement as is specified in section 51A(3) or (4) of this Act,

shall be guilty of an offence.

(2) Any person who contravenes any requirement of a suspension order or a supplementary suspension order or who causes or permits any requirement of such an order to be contravened shall be guilty of an offence.

(3) Any person guilty of an offence under this section shall be liable—

(*a*) on summary conviction to a fine not exceeding the statutory maximum; and

(*b*) on conviction on indictment, to a fine.

(4) If—

(*a*) any step required by an order under section 51 of this Act to be taken for the alteration or removal of any buildings or works or any plant or machinery; or

(*b*) any step required by an order under section 51A of this Act to be taken—

  (i) for the alteration or removal of plant or machinery; or
  (ii) for the removal or alleviation of any injury to amenity; or

(*c*) any step for the protection of the environment required to be taken by a suspension order or a supplementary suspension order,

has not been taken within the period specified in the order, or within such extended period as the local planning authority may allow, the local planning authority may enter the land and take that step, and may recover from the person who is then the owner of the land any expenses reasonably incurred by them in doing so; and section 276 of the Public Health Act 1936 shall apply in relation to any works executed by a local planning authority under this subsection as it applies in relation to works executed by a local authority under that Act.

(5) The references to the local planning authority in subsection (4) of this section are to be construed as references to the mineral planning authority—

(*a*) in relation to an order under section 51 of this Act requiring that any buildings or works or plant or machinery used for the winning and working of minerals shall be altered or removed; and

(*b*) in relation to any step required to be taken as mentioned in paragraphs (*b*) and (*c*) of subsection (4) of this section.

(6) It shall be a defence for a person charged with an offence under this section to prove that he took all reasonable measures and exercised all due diligence to avoid commission of the offence by himself or by any person under his control.

(7) If in any case the defence provided by subsection (6) of this section involves an allegation that the commission of the offence was due to the act or default of another person or due to reliance on information supplied by another person, the person charged shall not, without the leave of the court, be entitled to rely on the defence unless, within a period ending seven clear days before the hearing, he has served on the prosecutor a notice in writing giving such information identifying or assisting in the identification of the other person as was then in his possession.]   **[136]**

NOTES
   Commencement: 19 May 1986.
   Commencement order: SI 1986 No 760.
   This section, as originally enacted, derived from the Town and Country Planning Act 1962, s 61.
   Substituted by the Town and Country Planning (Minerals) Act 1981, s 11.

109. Enforcement of control as to advertisements

(1) The matters for which provision may be made by regulations under section 63 of this Act shall include provision for enabling the local planning authority to require the removal of any advertisement which is being displayed in contravention of the regulations, or the discontinuance of the use for the display of advertisements of any site which is being so used in contravention of the regulations, and for that purpose for applying any of the provisions of this Part of this Act with respect to enforcement notices or the provisions of section 177 of this Act, subject to such adaptations and modifications as may be specified in the regulations.

(2) Without prejudice to any provisions included in regulations made under section 63 of this Act by virtue of subsection (1) of this section, if any person displays an advertisement in contravention of the provisions of the regulations he shall be guilty of an offence and liable on summary conviction to a fine of such amount as may be prescribed by the regulations, not exceeding [level 3 on the standard scale] and, in the case of a continuing offence, [£20] for each day during which the offence continues after conviction.

(3) For the purposes of subsection (2) of this section, and without prejudice to the generality thereof, a person shall be deemed to display an advertisement if—

(*a*) the advertisement is displayed on land of which he is the owner or occupier; or

(*b*) the advertisement gives publicity to his goods, trade, business or other concerns:

Provided that a person shall not be guilty of an offence under that subsection by reason only that an advertisement is displayed on land of which he is the owner or occupier, or that his goods, trade, business or other concerns are given publicity by the advertisement, if he proves that it was displayed without his knowledge or consent.   **[137]**

NOTES
Commencement: 1 April 1972.
Sub-s (2): fines increased by the Local Government and Planning (Amendment) Act 1981, s 1, Schedule, and first-mentioned maximum fine converted to a level on the standard scale by the Criminal Justice Act 1982, ss 37, 46; amended by the Housing and Planning Act 1986, s 49(1), Sch 11, Part I, para 13. See Appendix.

109A. Power to remove or obliterate placards and posters

[(1) Subject to subsections (2) and (3) of this section, the council of a district or a London borough may remove or obliterate any placard or poster—

  (*a*) which is displayed in their area; and
  (*b*) which, in their opinion, is so displayed in contravention of the advertisement regulations.

(2) Subsection (1) of this section does not authorise the removal or obliteration of a placard or poster displayed within a building to which there is no public right of access.

(3) Subject to subsection (4) of this section, a council shall not exercise any power conferred by subsection (1) of this section where a placard or poster identifies the person who displayed it or caused it to be displayed unless they have first given him notice in writing—

  (*a*) that in their opinion it is displayed in contravention of the advertisement regulations; and
  (*b*) that they intend to remove or obliterate it on the expiry of a period specified in the notice.

(4) A council may exercise a power conferred by subsection (1) of this section without giving the person who displayed the placard or poster notice under subsection (3) of this section if the placard or poster does not give his address and the council do not know it and are unable to ascertain it after reasonable inquiry.

(5) The period to be specified in a notice under subsection (3) of this section shall be a period of not less than two days from the date of service of the notice.

(6) In this section "the advertisement regulations" means regulations made or having effect as if made under section 63 of this Act.]   **[138]**

NOTES
Commencement: 13 July 1982.
Added by the Local Government (Miscellaneous Provisions) Act 1982, s 36.

Supplementary provisions

110. Supplementary provisions as to appeals to Secretary of State under Part V

(1) Subsection (5) of section 290 of the Local Government Act 1933 (which authorises a government department holding an inquiry under that section to make orders with respect to the costs of the parties) shall apply in relation to any proceedings before the Secretary of State on an appeal under this Part of this Act as if those proceedings were an inquiry held by the Secretary of State under the said section 290.

(2) Where under this Part of this Act any person has appealed to the Secretary of State or (in accordance with section 105 of this Act) to a magistrates' court against a notice, neither that person nor any other shall be entitled, in any other proceedings instituted after the making of the appeal, to claim that the notice was not duly served on the person who appealed.   **[139]**

NOTES
Commencement: 1 April 1972.
Sub-s (1): prospectively repealed by the Housing and Planning Act 1986, s 49(2), Sch 12, Part III. See Appendix.

111. Recovery of expenses of local planning authority under Part V

Where by virtue of any of the preceding provisions of this Part of this Act any expenses are recoverable by a local planning authority, those expenses shall be recoverable as a simple contract debt in any court of competent jurisdiction.
          [140]

NOTES
Commencement: 1 April 1972.

PART VI

ACQUISITION AND APPROPRIATION OF LAND AND RELATED PROVISIONS

Acquisition and appropriation of land

112. Compulsory acquisition of land in connection with development and for other planning purposes

[(1) A local authority to whom this section applies shall, on being authorised to do so by the Secretary of State, have power to acquire compulsorily—

   (a) any land which is in their area and which is suitable for and is required in order to secure the carrying out of one or more of the following activities, namely, development, re-development and improvement;

   (b) any land which is in their area and which is required for a purpose which it is necessary to achieve in the interests of the proper planning of an area in which the land is situated.

(1A) A local authority and the Secretary of State in considering for the purposes of subsection (1)(a) above whether land is suitable for development, re-development or improvement shall have regard—

   (a) to the provisions of the development plan, so far as material;

   (b) to whether planning permission for any development on the land is in force; and

   (c) to any other considerations which, on an application for planning permission for development on the land, would be material for the purpose of determining that application.

(1B) Where a local authority exercise their power under subsection (1) of this section in relation to any land, they shall, on being authorised to do so by the Secretary of State, have power to acquire compulsorily—

   (a) any land adjoining that land which is required for the purpose of executing works for facilitating its development or use; or

   (b) where that land forms part of a common or open space or fuel or field garden allotment, any land which is required for the purpose of being given in exchange for the land which is being acquired.

(1C) It is immaterial by whom the local authority propose that any activity or purpose mentioned in subsection (1) or (1B)(a) of this section should be undertaken or achieved (and in particular the local authority need not propose to undertake an activity or to achieve that purpose themselves).]

(2) Where under subsection (1) of this section the Secretary of State has power to authorise a local authority to whom this section applies to acquire any land compulsorily he may, after the requisite consultation, authorise the land to be so acquired by another authority, being a local authority within the meaning of this Act.

(3) Before giving an authorisation under subsection (2) of this section, the Secretary of State shall—

(a) ...

(b) where the land is in a county district, consult with the councils of the county and the county district;

(c) where the land is in a London borough, consult with the council of the borough and with the Greater London Council.

(4) The [Acquisition of Land Act 1981] shall apply to the compulsory acquisition of land under this section . . .

(5) The local authorities to whom this section applies are the councils of counties, . . . and county districts, the Greater London Council and the councils of London boroughs.   **[141]**

NOTES
Commencement: 1 April 1972.
Sub-s (1): substituted by the Local Government, Planning and Land Act 1980, s 91.
Sub-ss (1A)–(1C): added by the Local Government, Planning and Land Act 1980, s 91.
Sub-ss (3), (5): words omitted repealed by the Local Government Act 1972, s 272, Sch 30.
Sub-s (4): amended by the Acquisition of Land Act 1981, s 34, Schs 4, 6.

113. Compulsory acquisition of land by Secretary of State for the Environment

(1) The Secretary of State for the Environment may acquire compulsorily any land necessary for the public service.

(2) The power of acquiring land compulsorily under this section shall include power to acquire an easement or other right over land by the grant of a new right:

Provided that this subsection shall not apply to an easement or other right over any land which would for the purposes of the [Acquisition of Land Act 1981] form part of a common, open space or fuel or field garden allotment.

(3) The [Acquisition of Land Act 1981] shall apply to any compulsory acquisition by the Secretary of State for the Environment under this section . . .   **[142]**

NOTES
Commencement: 1 April 1972.
Amended by the Acquisition of Land Act 1981, s 34, Schs 4, 6.

114. Compulsory acquisition of listed building in need of repair

(1) Where it appears to the Secretary of State, in the case of a building to which this section applies, that reasonable steps are not being taken for properly preserving it, the Secretary of State may authorise the council of the county, . . . or county district in which the building is situated or, in the case of a building situated in Greater London, [the Historic Buildings and Monuments Commis-

sion for England] or the London borough council, to acquire compulsorily under this section the building and any land comprising or contiguous or adjacent to it which appears to the Secretary of State to be required for preserving the building or its amenities, or for affording access to it, or for its proper control or management.

(2) Where it appears to the Secretary of State, in the case of a building to which this section applies, that reasonable steps are not being taken for properly preserving it, he may be authorised under this section to acquire compulsorily the building and any land comprising or contiguous or adjacent to it which appears to him to be required for the purpose mentioned in subsection (1) of this section.

(3) This section applies to any listed building, not being an excepted building as defined in section 58(2) of this Act.

[(3A) The Secretary of State shall consult with the Historic Buildings and Monuments Commission for England before he makes or confirms a compulsory purchase order for the acquisition by virtue of this section of any building situated in England [, other than an order for the acquisition of a building by the Commission.]]

(4) The Secretary of State shall not make or confirm a compulsory purchase order for the acquisition of any building by virtue of this section unless he is satisfied that it is expedient to make provision for the preservation of the building and to authorise its compulsory acquisition for that purpose.

(5) The [Acquisition of Land Act 1981] shall apply to the compulsory acquisition of land under this section . . .

(6) Any person having an interest in a building which it is proposed to acquire compulsorily under this section may, within twenty-eight days after the service of the notice required by [section 12 of the Acquisition of Land Act 1981], apply to a magistrates' court acting for the petty sessions area within which the building is situated for an order staying further proceedings on the compulsory purchase order; and, if the court is satisfied that reasonable steps have been taken for properly preserving the building, the court shall make an order accordingly.

(7) Any person aggrieved by the decision of a magistrates' court on an application under subsection (6) of this section may appeal against the decision to the Crown Court.   [143]

NOTES
   Commencement: 1 April 1984 (sub-s (3A)); 1 April 1972 (remainder).
   Commencement order: SI 1984 No 208.
   This section derived from the Town and Country Planning Act 1968, s 50.
   Sub-s (1): words omitted repealed by the Local Government Act 1972, s 272, Sch 30; amendment in square brackets made by the Local Government Act 1985, s 6, Sch 2, para 1.
   Sub-s (3A): added by the National Heritage Act 1983, s 33, Sch 4, para 19; amended by the Local Government Act 1985, s 6, Sch 2, para 1.
   Sub-ss (5), (6): amended by the Acquisition of Land Act 1981, s 34, Schs 4, 6.

115. Repairs notice as preliminary to compulsory acquisition under s 114

(1) [The compulsory purchase of a building under section 114 of this Act shall not be started by a council or by the Historic Buildings and Monuments Commission for England (in this section referred to as "the Commission") or by the Secretary of State] unless at least two months previously they have served

on the owner of the building, and not withdrawn, a notice under this section (in this section referred to as a "repairs notice")—

    (*a*) specifying the works which they consider .reasonably necessary for the proper preservation of the building; and

    (*b*) explaining the effect of sections 114 to 117 of this Act.

(2) Where a council [, the Commission] or the Secretary of State have served a repairs notice, the demolition of the building thereafter shall not prevent them from being authorised under section 114 of this Act to acquire compulsorily the site of the building, if the Secretary of State is satisfied that he would have confirmed or, as the case may be, would have made a compulsory purchase order in respect of the building had it not been demolished.

(3) A council [, the Commission] or the Secretary of State may at any time withdraw a repairs notice served by them; and if they do so, they shall forthwith give notice of the withdrawal to the person who was served with the notice.

[(3A) The Secretary of State shall consult with [the Commission] before he serves or withdraws a repairs notice in relation to a building situated in England.]

(4) For the purposes of this section a compulsory acquisition is started when the council [, the Commission] or the Secretary of State, as the case may be, serve the notice required by [section 12 of the Acquisition of Land Act 1981].

[144]

NOTES

    Commencement: 1 April 1984 (sub-s (3A)); 1 April 1972 (remainder).

    Commencement order: SI 1984 No 208.

    This section derived from the Town and Country Planning Act 1968, s 51(1)-(3), (5).

    Sub-ss (1)-(3): amended by the Local Government Act 1985, s 6, Sch 2, para 1.

    Sub-s (3A): added by the National Heritage Act 1983, s 33, Sch 4, para 20; amended by the Local Government Act 1985, s 6, Sch 2, para 1.

    Sub-s (4): first amendment in square brackets made by the Local Government Act 1985, s 6, Sch 2, para 1; final amendment in square brackets made by the Acquisition of Land Act 1981, s 34(1), Sch 4.

116. Compensation on compulsory acquisition of listed building

Subject to section 117 of this Act, for the purpose of assessing compensation in respect of any compulsory acquisition of land including a building which, immediately before the date of the compulsory purchase order, was listed, it shall be assumed that listed building consent would be granted for any works for the alteration or extension of the building, or for its demolition, other than works in respect of which such consent has been applied for before the date of the order and refused by the Secretary of State, or granted by him subject to conditions, the circumstances having been such that compensation thereupon became payable under section 171 of this Act.   **[145]**

NOTES

    Commencement: 1 April 1972.

117. Minimum compensation in case of listed building deliberately left derelict

(1) [Where a council or the Historic Buildings and Monuments Commission for England propose to acquire a building compulsorily under section 114 of this Act and] they are satisfied that the building has been deliberately allowed to fall into disrepair for the purpose of justifying its demolition and the development or re-development of the site or any adjoining site, [they] may include in the

compulsory purchase order as submitted to the Secretary of State for confirmation . . . a direction for minimum compensation; . . .

(2) Subject to the provisions of this section, where the Secretary of State acquires a building compulsorily under section 114 of this Act, he may, if he is satisfied as mentioned in subsection (1) of this section, include a direction for minimum compensation in the compulsory purchase order.

(3) The notice required to be served in accordance with [section 12 of the Acquisition of Land Act 1981] (notices stating effect of compulsory purchase order or, as the case may be, draft order) shall, without prejudice to so much of that paragraph as requires the notice to state the effect of the order, include a statement that the authority have [included in the order] a direction for minimum compensation or, as the case may be, that the Secretary of State has included such a direction in the draft order prepared by him in accordance with [Schedule 1 to the said Act of 1981] and shall in either case explain the meaning of the expression "direction for minimum compensation".

(4) A direction for minimum compensation, in relation to a building compulsorily acquired, is a direction that for the purpose of assessing compensation it is to be assumed, notwithstanding anything to the contrary in the Land Compensation Act 1961 or this Act, that planning permission would not be granted for any development or re-development of the site of the building and that listed building consent would not be granted for any works for the demolition, alteration or extension of the building other than development or works necessary for restoring it to, and maintaining it in, a proper state of repair; and if a compulsory purchase order is confirmed or made with the inclusion of such a direction, the compensation in respect of the compulsory acquisition shall be assessed in accordance with the direction.

(5) Where [a council or the Historic Buildings and Monuments Commission for England] include in a compulsory purchase order made by them . . . a direction for minimum compensation, or the Secretary of State includes such a direction in a draft compulsory purchase order prepared by him, any person having an interest in the building may, within twenty-eight days after the service of the notice required by [section 12 of the Acquisition of Land Act 1981], apply to a magistrates' court acting for the petty sessions area in which the building is situated for an order that . . . a direction for minimum compensation . . . be not included in the compulsory purchase order as [confirmed or] made by the Secretary of State; and if the court is satisfied that the building has not been deliberately allowed to fall into disrepair for the purpose mentioned in subsection (1) of this section, the court shall make the order applied for.

(6) A person aggrieved by the decision of a magistrates' court on an application under subsection (5) of this section may appeal against the decision to the Crown Court.

(7) The rights conferred by subsections (5) and (6) of this section shall not prejudice those conferred by section 114(6) and (7) of this Act. **[146]**

NOTES

Commencement: 1 April 1972.

This section derived from the Town and Country Planning Act 1968, s 53.

Sub-s (1): amendments in square brackets made by the Local Government Act 1985, s 6, Sch 2, para 1; words omitted repealed by the Local Government Act 1974, s 35, Sch 6.

Sub-s (3): amended by the Acquisition of Land Act 1981, s 34(1), Sch 4.

Sub-s (5): first amendment in square brackets made by the Local Government Act 1985, s 6, Sch

2, para 1; words omitted repealed and third words in square brackets substituted by the Local Government Act 1974, s 35, Sch 6; second words in square brackets substituted by the Acquisition of Land Act 1981, s 34(1), Sch 4.

118. Extinguishment of rights over land compulsorily acquired

(1) Subject to the provisions of this section, upon the completion by the acquiring authority of a compulsory acquisition of land under this Part of this Act, all private rights of way and rights of laying down, erecting, continuing or maintaining any apparatus on, under or over the land shall be extinguished, and any such apparatus shall vest in the acquiring authority.

(2) Subsection (1) of this section shall not apply to any right vested in, or apparatus belonging to, statutory undertakers for the purpose of the carrying on of their undertaking [or to any right conferred by or in accordance with the telecommunications code on the operator of a telecommunications code system or to any telecommunication apparatus kept installed for the purposes of any such system.].

(3) In respect of any right or apparatus not falling within subsection (2) of this section, subsection (1) of this subsection shall have effect subject—

    (a) to any direction given by the acquiring authority before the completion of the acquisition that subsection (1) of this section shall not apply to any right or apparatus specified in the direction; and

    (b) to any agreement which may be made (whether before or after the completion of the acquisition) between the acquiring authority and the person in or to whom the right or apparatus in question is vested or belongs.

(4) Any person who suffers loss by the extinguishment of a right or the vesting of any apparatus under this section shall be entitled to compensation from the acquiring authority.

(5) Any compensation payable under this section shall be determined in accordance with the Land Compensation Act 1961.   **[147]**

NOTES

Commencement: 1 April 1972.

This section derived from the Town and Country Planning Act 1962, s 70.

Sub-s (2): amended by the Telecommunications Act 1984, s 109, Sch 4, para 53.

119. Acquisition of land by agreement

(1) The council of any county, ... London borough or county district may acquire by agreement—

    (a) any land which they require for any purpose for which a local authority may be authorised to acquire land under section 112 of this Act;

    (b) any building appearing to them to be of special architectural or historic interest; and

    (c) any land comprising or contiguous or adjacent to such a building which appears to the Secretary of State to be required for preserving the building or its amenities, or for affording access to it, or for its proper control or management.

(2) ...

(3) The provisions of Part I of the Compulsory Purchase Act 1965 (so far as applicable), other than sections 4 to 8, section 10 and section 31, shall apply in relation to the acquisition of land under this section.

(4) ... **[148]**

NOTES
Commencement: 1 April 1972.
This section derived from the Town and Country Planning Act 1962, s 71 and the London Government Act 1963, s 29(3).
Sub-s (1): amended by the Local Government Act 1980, s 118, Sch 30.
Sub-s (2): repealed by the Local Government, Planning and Land Act 1980, s 118, Sch 23.
Sub-s (4): repealed by SI 1986 No 452, art 5.

120. Acquisition of land for purposes of exchange

Without prejudice to the generality of the powers conferred by the preceding provisions of this Part of this Act, any power of a local authority to acquire land thereunder, whether compulsorily or by agreement, shall include power to acquire land required for giving in exchange—

    (*a*) for land appropriated under section 121 of this Act; or

    (*b*) for Green Belt land, within the meaning of the Green Belt (London and Home Counties) Act 1938, appropriated in accordance with that Act for any purpose specified in a development plan. **[149]**

NOTES
Commencement: 1 April 1972.

121. Appropriation of land forming part of common etc

(1) Any local authority may be authorised, by an order made by that authority and confirmed by the Secretary of State, to appropriate for any purpose for which that authority can be authorised to acquire land under any enactment any land for the time being held by them for other purposes, being land which is or forms part of a common, ... or fuel or field garden allotment (including any such land which is specially regulated by any enactment, whether public general or local or private), other than land which is Green Belt land within the meaning of the Green Belt (London and Home Counties) Act 1938.

    (2) [Section 19 of the Acquisition of Land Act 1981] (special provision with respect to compulsory purchase orders under that Act relating to land forming part of a common, open space or fuel or field garden allotment) shall apply to an order under this section authorising the appropriation of land as it applies to a compulsory purchase order under that Act.

    (3) ...

    (4) Where land appropriated under this section was acquired under an enactment incorporating the Lands Clauses Acts, any works executed on the land after the appropriation has been effected shall, for the purposes of section 68 of the Lands Clauses Consolidation Act 1845 and section 10 of the Compulsory Purchase Act 1965 be deemed to have been authorised by the enactment under which the land was acquired.

    (5) On an appropriation of land by a local authority under this section, where—

    (*a*) the authority is not an authority to whom Part II of the Act of 1959 applies; or

    (*b*) the land was immediately before the appropriation held by the authority for the purposes of a grant-aided function within the meaning of the Act of 1959, or is appropriated by the authority for the purposes of such a function, there shall be made in the accounts of the local authority such adjustments as the Secretary of State may direct.

(6) On an appropriation under this section which does not fall within subsection (5) of this section, there shall be made such adjustment of accounts as is required by section 24(1) of the Act of 1959.   **[150]**

NOTES
Commencement: 1 April 1972.
Sub-s (1): words omitted repealed by the Local Government, Planning and Land Act 1980, s 118, Sch 23.
Sub-s (2): amended by the Acquisition of Land Act 1981, s 34(1), Sch 4.
Sub-s (3): repealed by the Local Government Act 1972, s 272, Sch 30.
Act of 1959: Town and Country Planning Act 1959.

Powers exercisable in relation to land held for planning purposes, and other related powers

122. Appropriation of land held for planning purposes

(1) Where any land has been acquired or appropriated by a local authority for planning purposes and is for the time being held by the authority for the purposes for which it was so acquired or appropriated, the authority (subject to the following provisions of this section) may appropriate the land for any purpose for which they are or may be authorised in any capacity to acquire land by virtue of or under any enactment not contained in this Part of this Act.

[(2) The consent of the Secretary of State shall be requisite to any appropriation under this section of land which, immediately before the appropriation, is land which consists or forms part of a common, or formerly consisted or formed part of a common, and is held or managed by a local authority in accordance with a local Act.

(2A) Any such consent may be given either in respect of a particular appropriation or in respect of appropriations of any class, and may be given either subject to or free from any conditions or limitations.

(2B) Before appropriating under this section any land which consists of or forms part of an open space, a local authority—

(*a*) shall publish a notice of their intention to do so for at least two consecutive weeks in a newspaper circulating in their area; and
(*b*) shall consider any objections to the proposed appropriation which may be made to them.]

(4) In relation to any appropriation under this section—

(*a*) subsection (2) of section 163 of the Local Government Act 1933 (which relates to the operation of section 68 of the Lands Clauses Consolidation Act 1845 and section 10 of the Compulsory Purchase Act 1965); and
(*b*) subsections (5) and (6) of section 121 of this Act,

shall have effect as they have effect in relation to appropriations under those sections respectively.

(5) In relation to any such land as is mentioned in subsection (1) of this section, this section shall have effect to the exclusion of the provisions of section 163(1) of the Local Government Act 1933.   **[151]**

NOTES
Commencement: 1 April 1972.
Amended by the Local Government, Planning and Land Act 1980, s 118, Sch 23.

123. Disposal of land held for planning purposes

(1) Where any land had been acquired or appropriated by a local authority for planning purposes, and is for the time being held by the authority for the purposes for which it was so acquired or appropriated, the authority may dispose of the land to such person, in such manner and subject to such conditions as may appear to them to be expedient in order to secure the best use of that or other land and any buildings or works which have been, or are to be, erected, constructed or carried out thereon, whether by themselves or by any other person, or to secure the erection, construction or carrying out thereon of any buildings or works appearing to them to be needed for the proper planning of the area of the authority.

[(2) The consent of the Secretary of State shall be requisite to any disposal under this section—

    (*a*) of land which, immediately before the disposal, is land which consists or forms part of a common, or formerly consisted or formed part of a common, and is held or managed by a local authority in accordance with a local Act; or

    (*b*) where the disposal is to be for a consideration less than the best that can reasonably be obtained and is not—

        (i) the grant of a term of seven years or less; or

        (ii) the assignment of a term of years of which seven years or less are unexpired at the date of the assignment.

(2A) Before disposing under this section of any land which consists of or forms part of an open space, a local authority—

    (*a*) shall publish a notice of their intention to do so for at least two consecutive weeks in a newspaper circulating in their area; and

    (*b*) shall consider any objections to the proposed disposal which may be made to them.]

(7) In relation to land acquired or appropriated for planning purposes for a reason mentioned in section 112(1)(*a*) to (*c*) of this Act the powers conferred by this section on a local authority, and on the Secretary of State in respect of the giving of consent to disposals under this section, shall be so exercised as to secure, so far as may be practicable, to persons who were living or carrying on business or other activities on any such land which the authority have acquired as mentioned in subsection (1) of this section, who desire to obtain accommodation on such land, and who are willing to comply with any requirements of the authority as to the development and use of such land, an opportunity to obtain thereon accommodation suitable to their reasonable requirements, on terms settled with due regard to the price at which any such land has been acquired from them.

In this subsection "development" includes redevelopment.

(8) Subject to the provisions of section 27 of the Act of 1959 (which enables capital money in certain cases to be applied without the consent or approval of a Minister which would otherwise be required), section 166 of the Local Government Act 1933 (which relates to the application of capital money received from the disposal of land) shall have effect in relation to capital money

received in respect of transactions under this section as it has effect in relation to capital money received in respect of such transactions as are mentioned in that section.

(9) In relation to any such land as is mentioned in subsection (1) of this section, this section shall have effect to the exclusion of sections 164 and 165 of the Local Government Act 1933.   **[152]**

NOTES

Commencement: 1 April 1972.
Amended by the Local Government, Planning and Land Act 1980, s 118, Sch 23.
Act of 1959: Town and Country Planning Act 1959.

124. Development of land held for planning purposes

(1) The functions of a local authority shall include power for the authority, notwithstanding any limitation imposed by law on the capacity of the authority by virtue of its constitution, to erect, construct or carry out any building or work on any land to which this section applies, not being a building or work for the erection, construction or carrying out of which, whether by that local authority or by any other person, statutory power exists by virtue of, or could be conferred under, an alternative enactment.

(2) This section applies to any land which has been acquired or appropriated by a local authority for planning purposes and is for the time being held by the authority for the purposes for which it was so acquired or appropriated.

(3), (4) . . .

(5) The functions of a local authority shall include power for the authority, notwithstanding any such limitation as is mentioned in subsection (1) of this section, to repair, maintain and insure any buildings or works on land to which this section applies, and generally to deal therewith in a proper course of management.

(6) A local authority may, . . . enter into arrangements with an authorised association for the carrying out by the association of any operation which, apart from the arrangements, the local authority would have power under this section to carry out, on such terms (including terms as to the making of payments or loans by the authority to the association) as may be specified in the arrangements:

Provided that nothing in this section shall be construed as authorising such an association to carry out any operation which they would not have power to carry out apart from this subsection.

(7) Nothing in this section shall be construed as authorising any act or omission on the part of a local authority which is actionable at the suit of any person on any grounds other than such a limitation as is mentioned in subsection (1) of this section.

(8) In this section "alternative enactment" means any enactment which is not contained in this Part of this Act . . . in section 2, 5 or 6 of the Local Authorities (Land) Act 1963, or in [section 14(1) or (4) or 17(3) of the Industrial Development Act 1982]; and "authorised association" means any society, company or body of persons . . . whose objects include the promotion, formation or management of garden cities, garden suburbs or garden villages, and the erection, improvement or management of buildings for the working classes and

others, and which does not trade for profit or whose constitution forbids the issue of any share or loan capital with interest or dividend exceeding the rate for the time being fixed by the Treasury. **[153]**

NOTES
Commencement: 1 April 1972.
Sub-ss (3), (4): repealed by the Local Government Act 1974, s 42(2), Sch 8.
Sub-s (6): words omitted repealed by the Local Government Act 1974, s 42(2), Sch 8.
Sub-s (8): first words omitted repealed by the Local Employment Act 1972, s 22(1), Sch 3; amendment in square brackets made by the Industrial Development Act 1982, s 19, Sch 2, para 7(2); second words omitted repealed by the Local Government Act 1974, s 42(2), Sch 8.

125. Special provisions as to features and buildings of architectural and historic interest

(1) In the exercise of the powers of appropriation, disposal and development conferred by the provisions of sections 122, 123 and 124(1) of this Act, a local authority shall have regard to the desirability of preserving features of special architectural or historic interest, and in particular, listed buildings; ...

(2) ...

(3) In this section ... "development" includes redevelopment.

(4) This section is without prejudice to the provisions of section 277(5) of this Act. **[154]**

NOTES
Commencement: 1 April 1972.
Words omitted repealed by the Local Government Act 1974, s 42, Sch 8.

126. Management etc of listed buildings acquired by local authority or Secretary of State

(1) Where a local authority acquire any building or other land under section 114(1) or 119(1)(*b*) of this Act [or the Historic Buildings and Monuments Commission for England acquire any building or other land under the said section 114(1)], they may make such arrangements as to its management, use or disposal as they consider appropriate for the purpose of its preservation.

(2) Where the Secretary of State acquires any building or other land under section 114(2) of this Act, subsection (3) of section 5 of the Historic Buildings and Ancient Monuments Act 1953 (management, custody and disposal), except so much of it as refers to subsection (4) of that section, shall apply in relation thereto as it applies in relation to property acquired under that section. **[155]**

NOTES
Commencement: 1 April 1972.
This section derived from the Civic Amenities Act 1967, s 8.
Sub-s (1): amended by the Local Government Act 1985, s 6, Sch 2, para 1.

127. Power to override easements and other rights

(1) The erection, construction or carrying out, or maintenance, of any building or work on land which has been acquired or appropriated by a local authority for planning purposes, whether done by the local authority or by a person deriving title under them, is authorised by virtue of this section if it is done in accordance with planning permission, notwithstanding that it involves interference with an interest or right to which this section applies, or involves a breach of a restriction as to the user of land arising by virtue of a contract:

Provided that nothing in this subsection shall authorise interference with any right of way or right of laying down, erecting, continuing or maintaining apparatus on, under or over land, being a right vested in or belonging to statutory undertakers for the purpose of the carrying on of their undertaking [or a right conferred by or in accordance with the telecommunications code on the operator of a telecommunications code system.].

(2) This section applies to the following interests and rights, that is to say, any easement, liberty, privilege, right or advantage annexed to land and adversely affecting other land, including any natural right to support.

(3) In respect of any interference or breach in pursuance of subsection (1) of this section, compensation shall be payable under section 63 or 68 of the Lands Clauses Consolidation Act 1845 or under section 7 or 10 of the Compulsory Purchase Act 1965 to be assessed in the same manner and subject to the same rules as in the case of other compensation under those sections in respect of injurious affection where the compensation is to be estimated in connection with a purchase under those Acts or the injury arises from the execution of works on land acquired under those Acts.

(4) Where a person deriving title under the local authority by whom the land in question was acquired or appropriated is liable to pay compensation by virtue of subsection (3) of this section, and fails to discharge that liability, the liability shall be enforceable against the local authority:

Provided that nothing in this subsection shall be construed as affecting any agreement between the local authority and any other person for indemnifying the local authority against any liability under this subsection.

(5) Nothing in this section shall be construed as authorising any act or omission on the part of any person which is actionable at the suit of any person on any grounds other than such an interference or breach as is mentioned in subsection (1) of this section.   **[156]**

NOTES
> Commencement: 1 April 1972.
> This section derived from the Town and Country Planning Act 1962, s 81.
> Sub-s (1): amended by the Telecommunications Act 1984, s 109, Sch 4, para 53.

128. Use and development of consecrated land and burial grounds

(1) Any consecrated land, whether or not including a building, which has been acquired by a Minister, a local authority or statutory undertakers under this Part of this Act or compulsorily under any other enactment, or which has been appropriated by a local authority for planning purposes, may, subject to the following provisions of this section—

> (a) in the case of land acquired by a Minister, be used in any manner by him or on his behalf for any purpose for which he acquired the land; and
>
> (b) in any other case, be used by any person in any manner in accordance with planning permission,

notwithstanding any obligation or restriction imposed under ecclesiastical law or otherwise in respect of consecrated land:

Provided that this subsection does not apply to land which consists or forms part of a burial ground.

(2) Any use of consecrated land authorised by subsection (1) of this section,

and the use of any land, not being consecrated land, acquired or appropriated as therein mentioned which at the time of acquisition or appropriation included a church or other building used or formerly used for religious worship or the site thereof, shall be subject to compliance with the prescribed requirements with respect to the removal and reinterment of any human remains, and the disposal of monuments and fixtures and furnishings; and, in the case of consecrated land, shall be subject to such provisions as may be prescribed for prohibiting or restricting the use of the land, either absolutely or until the prescribed consent has been obtained, so long as any church or other building used or formerly used for religious worship, or any part thereof, remains on the land.

(3) Any regulations made for the purposes of subsection (2) of this section—

(a) shall contain such provisions as appear to the Secretary of State to be requisite for securing that any use of land which is subject to compliance with the regulations shall, as nearly as may be, be subject to the like control as is imposed by law in the case of a similar use authorised by an enactment not contained in this Act or by a Measure, or as it would be proper to impose on a disposal of the land in question otherwise than in pursuance of an enactment or Measure;

(b) shall contain requirements relating to the disposal of any such land as is mentioned in subsection (2) of this section such as appear to the Secretary of State requisite for securing that the provisions of that subsection shall be complied with in relation to the use of the land; and

(c) may contain such incidental and consequential provisions (including provision as to the closing of registers) as appear to the Secretary of State to be expedient for the purposes of the regulations.

(4) Any land consisting of a burial ground or part of a burial ground, which has been acquired or appropriated as mentioned in subsection (1) of this section, may—

(a) in the case of land acquired by a Minister, be used in any manner by him or on his behalf for any purpose for which he acquired the land; and

(b) in any other case, be used by any person in any manner in accordance with planning permission,

notwithstanding anything in any enactment relating to burial grounds or any obligation or restriction imposed under ecclesiastical law or otherwise in respect of burial grounds:

Provided that this subsection shall not have effect in respect of any land which has been used for the burial of the dead until the prescribed requirements with respect to the removal and reinterment of human remains, and the disposal of monuments, in or upon the land have been complied with.

(5) Provision shall be made by any regulations made for the purposes of subsection (2) of this section and the proviso to subsection (4) of this section—

(a) for requiring the persons in whom the land is vested to publish notice of their intention to carry out the removal and reinterment of any human remains or the disposal of any monuments;

(b) for enabling the personal representatives or relatives of any deceased person themselves to undertake the removal and reinterment of the remains of the deceased and the disposal of any monument commemorating the deceased, and for requiring the persons in whom the land is vested to defray the expenses of such removal, reinterment and disposal, not exceeding such amount as may be prescribed;

(c) for requiring compliance with such reasonable conditions (if any) as may be imposed, in the case of consecrated land, by the bishop of the diocese, with respect to the manner of removal, and the place and manner of reinterment of any human remains, and the disposal of any monuments, and with any directions given in any case by the Secretary of State with respect to the removal and reinterment of any human remains.

(6) Subject to the provisions of any such regulations, no faculty shall be required for the removal and reinterment in accordance with the regulations of any human remains, or for the removal or disposal of any monuments, and the provisions of section 25 of the Burial Act 1875 (prohibition of removal of human remains without the licence of the Secretary of State except in certain cases) shall not apply to a removal carried out in accordance with the regulations.

(7) Nothing in this section shall be construed as authorising any act or omission on the part of any person which is actionable at the suit of any person on any grounds other than contravention of any such obligation, restriction or enactment as is mentioned in subsection (1) or subsection (4) of this section.

(8) In this section "burial ground" includes any churchyard, cemetery or other ground, whether consecrated or not, which has at any time been set apart for the purposes of interment, and "monument" includes a tombstone or other memorial.   **[157]**

NOTES
Commencement: 1 April 1972.

129. Use and development of land for open spaces

(1) Any land being, or forming part of, a common, open space or fuel or field garden allotment, which has been acquired by a Minister, a local authority or statutory undertakers under this Part of this Act or compulsorily under any other enactment, or which has been appropriated by a local authority for planning purposes, may—

(a) in the case of land acquired by a Minister, be used in any manner by him or on his behalf for any purpose for which he acquired the land; and

(b) in any other case, be used by any person in any manner in accordance with planning permission,

notwithstanding anything in any enactment relating to land of that kind, or in any enactment by which the land is specially regulated.

(2) Nothing in this section shall be construed as authorising any act or omission on the part of any person which is actionable at the suit of any person on any grounds other than contravention of any such enactment as is mentioned in subsection (1) of this section.   **[158]**

NOTES
Commencement: 1 April 1972.

130. Displacement of persons from land acquired or appropriated

(1), (2) . . .

(3) If the Secretary of State certifies that possession of a house which has

been acquired or appropriated by a local authority for planning purposes, and is for the time being held by the authority for the purposes for which it was acquired or appropriated, is immediately required for those purposes, nothing in the Rent Act 1968 shall prevent the acquiring or appropriating authority from obtaining possession of the house.

(4), (5) . . . **[159]**

NOTES

Commencement: 1 April 1972.

Words omitted repealed by the Land Compensation Act 1973, s 86, Sch 3.

131. Constitution of joint body to hold land acquired for planning purposes

(1) If it appears to the Secretary of State, after consultation with the local authorities concerned, to be expedient that any land acquired by a local authority for planning purposes should be held by a joint body, consisting of representatives of that authority and of any other local authority, he may by order provide for the establishment of such a joint body and for the transfer to that body of the land so acquired.

(2) Any order under this section providing for the establishment of a joint body may make such provision as the Secretary of State considers expedient with respect to the constitution and functions of that body, including provisions—

    (*a*) for incorporating the joint body;

    (*b*) for conferring on them, in relation to land transferred to them as mentioned in subsection (1) of this section, any of the powers conferred on local authorities by this Part of this Act in relation to land acquired and held by such authorities for the purposes of this Part of this Act;

    (*c*) for determining the manner in which their expenses are to be defrayed.

(3) Regulations under this Act may make such provision consequential upon or supplementary to the provisions of this section as appears to the Secretary of State to be necessary or expedient. **[160]**

NOTES

Commencement: 1 April 1972.

Supplementary provisions

132. Modification of incorporated enactments for purposes of Part VI

(1) Where it is proposed that land should be acquired compulsorily under section 112 or 113 of this Act, and a compulsory purchase order relating to that land is submitted to the confirming authority in accordance with [Part II of the Acquisition of Land Act 1981], or as the case may be, is made in draft by the Secretary of State for the Environment in accordance with [Schedule 1 to that Act], the confirming authority or that Secretary of State, as the case may be, may disregard for the purposes of that Schedule any objection to the order or draft which, in the opinion of that authority or Secretary of State, amounts in substance to an objection to the provisions of the development plan defining the proposed use of that or any other land.

(2) Where a compulsory purchase order authorising the acquisition of any land under section 112 of this Act is submitted to the Secretary of State in accordance with [Part II of the Acquisition of Land Act 1981], then if the Secretary of State—

(*a*) is satisfied that the order ought to be confirmed so far as it relates to part of the land comprised therein; but

(*b*) has not for the time being determined whether it ought to be confirmed so far as it relates to any other such land,

he may confirm the order so far as it relates to the land mentioned in paragraph (*a*) of this subsection, and give directions postponing consideration of the order, so far as it relates to any other land specified in the directions, until such time as may be so specified.

(3) Where the Secretary of State gives directions under subsection (2) of this section, the notices required by [section 15 of the Acquisition of Land Act 1981] to be published and served shall include a statement of the effect of the directions.

(4) In construing the Compulsory Purchase Act 1965 in relation to any of the provisions of this Part of this Act—

(*a*) references to the execution of the works shall be construed as including references to any erection, construction or carrying out of buildings or works authorised by section 127 of this Act;

(*b*) in relation to the erection, construction or carrying out of any buildings or works so authorised, references in section 10 of the said Act of 1965 to the acquiring authority shall be construed as references to the person by whom the buildings or works in question are erected, constructed or carried out; and

(*c*) references to the execution of the works shall be construed as including also references to any erection, construction or carrying out of buildings or works on behalf of a Minister or statutory undertakers on land acquired by that Minister or those undertakers, where the buildings or works are erected, constructed or carried out for the purposes for which the land was acquired.   **[161]**

NOTES
Commencement: 1 April 1972.
Amended by the Acquisition of Land Act 1981, s 34(1), Sch 4.

133. Interpretation of Part VI

(1) In this Part of this Act any reference to the acquisition of land for planning purposes is a reference to the acquisition thereof under section 112 or 119 of this Act or section 68 or 71 of the Act of 1962 and any reference to the appropriation of land for planning purposes is a reference to the appropriation thereof for purposes for which land can be or could have been acquired under those sections.

(2) In relation to a local authority or body corporate, nothing in sections 127 to 129 of this Act shall be construed as authorising any act or omission on their part in contravention of any limitation imposed by law on their capacity by virtue of the constitution of the authority or body.

(3) Any power conferred by section 128 or 129 of this Act to use land in a manner therein mentioned shall be construed as a power so to use the land, whether it involves the erection, construction or carrying out of any building or work, or the maintenance of any building or work, or not.   **[162]**

NOTES
Commencement: 1 April 1972.
Act of 1962: Town and Country Planning Act 1962.

PART VII

COMPENSATION FOR PLANNING DECISIONS RESTRICTING NEW DEVELOPMENT

Unexpended balance of established development value

134. Scope of Part VII

(1) The provisions of this Part of this Act shall have effect for enabling compensation to be claimed in respect of planning decisions whereby permission for the carrying out of new development of land to which this section applies is refused or is granted subject to conditions.

(2) This section applies to any land in respect of which planning permission is refused or is granted subject to conditions, by a planning decision if, at the time of the planning decision, that land, or part of that land, has an unexpended balance of established development value.

(3) In accordance with the proviso to subsection (2) of section 32 of this Act, that subsection does not apply for the purposes of this Part of this Act.

(4) In this Part of this Act "interest" (where the reference is to an interest in land) means the fee simple or a tenancy of the land, and does not include any other interest therein; [and "local planning authority", in relation to a planning decision, means the authority who made the decision]. **[163]**

NOTES
Commencement: 1 April 1972.
Amended by the Local Government Act 1972, s 182, Sch 16.

135. Derivation of unexpended balance from claims under Part VI of Act of 1947

(1) In determining, for the purposes of this Part of this Act, whether land has an unexpended balance of established development value, regard shall be had to claims made, in pursuance of Part VI of the Act of 1947, for payments under the scheme provided for by section 58 of that Act (that is to say, the scheme which, but for the provisions of section 2 of the Town and Country Planning Act 1953, would have fallen to be made under the said section 58, providing for payments in respect of interests in land depreciated in value by virtue of the provisions of the Act of 1947).

(2) Where such a claim was made in respect of an interest in land, that claim shall for the purposes of this Part of this Act be taken to have been established in respect of that land under Part VI of the Act of 1947 if an amount was determined under the said Part VI as being the development value of the interest to which the claim related, and payment in respect of that interest would not have been excluded—

    (*a*) by section 63 of the Act of 1947 (which excluded claims where the development value was small in proportion to the area, or to the restricted value, of the land); or

    (*b*) by any of sections 82 to 85 of that Act (which related to certain land belonging to local authorities, development corporations and statutory undertakers, and to land held on charitable trusts); or

    (*c*) by section 84 of that Act as applied by regulations under section 90 of that Act (which related to the National Coal Board).

(3) In this Part of this Act "established claim" means a claim which by virtue of subsection (2) of this section is to be taken to have been established as therein mentioned, and references to the establishment of a claim shall be

construed accordingly; and "the claim area", in relation to an established claim, means the land in respect of which the claim is by virtue of that subsection to be taken to have been established.

(4) References in this Part of this Act to the benefit of an established claim—

(a) in relation to any time before the passing of the Town and Country Planning Act 1953, whether before or after the making of the claim, or before or after the establishment thereof, shall be construed as references to the prospective right, under and subject to the provisions of the scheme referred to in subsection (1) of this section, to receive a payment in respect of the interest in land to which the claim related; and

(b) in relation to any time after the passing of the said Act of 1953, shall be construed as references to such prospective right to the satisfaction of the claim as subsisted by virtue of section 2 of that Act immediately before 1st January 1955 (being the date of the commencement of the Act of 1954);

and references to part of the benefit of an established claim shall be construed accordingly.

(5) References in this Part of this Act to the amount of an established claim are references to the amount determined under Part VI of the Act of 1947 as being the development value of the interest in land to which the claim related.

(6) In this section any reference to Part VI of the Act of 1947 includes a reference to the provisions of the said Part VI as modified by Schedule 1 to the Act of 1954.   **[164]**

NOTES
Commencement: 1 April 1972.
Act of 1947: Town and Country Planning Act 1947.
Act of 1954: Town and Country Planning Act 1954.

136. Original unexpended balance of established development value

(1) In this Part of this Act "original unexpended balance of established development value", in relation to any land, means the unexpended balance of established development value which that land had immediately after the time when, in accordance with section 138 of this Act, the adjustment of claim holdings is deemed to have been completed.

(2) For the purposes of this Part of this Act land shall be taken to have had such a balance if, immediately after the time referred to in subsection (1) of this section—

(a) there were subsisting one or more claim holdings whose area consisted of that land, or included that land together with other land; and

(b) there was not subsisting any claim holding whose area consisted of part only of that land, whether with or without other land.

(3) Where subsection (2) of this section applies, there shall be attributed to the land referred to in that subsection—

(a) the value of any claim holding having an area consisting of that land; and

(b) such fraction of the value of any claim holding whose area included that land as attached to that land,

and the original unexpended balance of established development value of that land shall be taken to have been an amount equal to eight-sevenths of the amount or aggregate amount so attributed. **[165]**

NOTES
Commencement: 1 April 1972.

137. Claim holdings, their areas and values

(1) Subject to the provisions of this section and of section 138 of this Act, in this Part of this Act—

(a) "claim holding" means the benefit of an established claim, references to the area of a claim holding are references to the land which, in relation to the established claim constituting that holding, is the claim area, and references to the value of a claim holding are references to the amount of the established claim constituting that holding; and

(b) references to the fraction of the value of a claim holding which attached to a part of the area of the holding are references to so much of the amount of the established claim of which that holding represents the benefit or part of the benefit (in this section referred to as "the relevant established claim") as was properly attributable to that part of the area of the holding.

(2) In the case of a claim holding where—

(a) the area of the holding is the same as the claim area of the relevant established claim; but

(b) the value of the claim holding is, by virtue of the adjustment of claim holdings, less than the amount of the relevant established claim,

the amount of any such fraction as is referred to in subsection (1)(b) of this section shall be treated as reduced proportionately.

(3) In the case of a claim holding where—

(a) the area of the holding consists of part only of the claim area of the relevant established claim; and

(b) the value of the holding is, by virtue of the adjustment of claim holdings, less or greater than so much of the amount of the relevant established claim as was properly attributable to the area of the holding,

the amount of any such fraction as is referred to in subsection (1)(b) of this section shall be treated as reduced, or (as the case may be) increased, proportionately.

(4) For the purposes of this section, the part of the amount of the relevant established claim which was properly attributable to any land forming part of the claim area shall be taken to have been so much of the amount of that claim as might reasonably be expected to have been attributed to that land if the authority determining that amount had been required to apportion it, in accordance with the same principles as applied to its determination, between that land and the residue of the claim area. **[166]**

NOTES
Commencement: 1 April 1972.

138. Adjustment of claim holdings

(1) The provisions of Schedule 15 to this Act shall have effect for the purposes of this Part of this Act; and any reference in this Part of this Act to the adjustment of claim holdings is a reference to the operation of those provisions.

(2) For the purposes of this Part of this Act the adjustment of claim holdings shall be deemed to have been completed on 1st January 1955.   **[167]**

NOTES
   Commencement: 1 April 1972.

139. General provision for continuance of original unexpended balance

Where in accordance with section 136 of this Act land had an original unexpended balance of established development value, then, subject to the following provisions of this Part of this Act, that land shall be taken—

   (*a*) to have continued to have that balance until the commencement of this Act; and
   (*b*) to continue to have that balance at all times thereafter.   **[168]**

NOTES
   Commencement: 1 April 1972.

140. Reduction or extinguishment of balance in consequence of compensation

(1) Where at any time compensation becomes payable under this Part of this Act, or became payable under Part II of the Act of 1954 or Part VI of the Act of 1962, in respect of depreciation of the value of an interest in land by a planning decision, then, for the purpose of determining whether that land or any part thereof has or had an unexpended balance of established development value at any subsequent time, the amount of the compensation shall be deducted from the original unexpended balance of established development value of that land, and the original unexpended balance of that land or that part thereof shall be treated as having been reduced or extinguished accordingly immediately before that subsequent time.

(2) Subsection (1) of this section shall have effect subject to the provisions of this Part of this Act relating to the recovery of compensation on subsequent development.   **[169]**

NOTES
   Commencement: 1 April 1972.
   Act of 1954: Town and Country Planning Act 1954.
   Act of 1962: Town and Country Planning Act 1962.

141. Reduction or extinguishment of balance on initiation of new development

(1) Where in accordance with section 136 of this Act land had an original unexpended balance of established development value, and at any time on or after the appointed day (whether before or after the commencement of this Act) any new development of that land is or was initiated, then (subject to the following provisions of this section) for the purpose of determining whether that land or any part thereof has or had an unexpended balance of established development value at any subsequent time—

   (*a*) if the development relates or related only to that land the value of that development (ascertained, with reference to that subsequent time, in accordance with the provisions of Schedule 16 to this Act); or (*b*) if the development relates or related to that land together with other land, so much of the value of that development (so ascertained) as is or was attributable to that land,

shall be deducted from the original unexpended balance of established development value of that land, and the original unexpended balance of that land or that part thereof shall be treated as having been reduced or extinguished accordingly immediately before that subsequent time.

(2) Subsection (1) of this section shall not apply to any land if, in respect of any interest therein, a payment has become or becomes payable under section 59 of the Act of 1947 (which provided for payments in respect of certain war-damaged land).

(3) For the purposes of subsection (1) of this section no account shall be taken of any development initiated before 1st January 1955, if—

(*a*) a development charge under Part VII of the Act of 1947 was determined to be payable in respect thereof, or would have fallen to be so determined but for any exemption conferred by regulations under that Part of that Act, or by any provisions of Part VIII of that Act; or

(*b*) in a certificate issued under section 58 of the Act of 1954 (which related to monopoly value of licensed premises) it was certified that a development charge could have been determined to be payable in respect of that development if the circumstances referred to in subsection (1)(*a*) or (*b*) of that section had not existed.   **[170]**

NOTES
Commencement: 1 April 1972.
Act of 1947: Town and Country Planning Act 1947.
Act of 1954: Town and Country Planning Act 1954.

142. Reduction or extinguishment of balance on acquisition of land under compulsory powers

(1) Where in the case of—

(*a*) a compulsory acquisition to which this section applies; or

(*b*) a sale of an interest in land by agreement in circumstances corresponding to such an acquisition,

any of the land in which the interest acquired or sold subsists or subsisted has or had an unexpended balance of established development value immediately before the relevant date (in this section referred to as "the relevant balance") the following provisions of this section shall have effect for the purpose of determining whether that land or any part thereof has or had an unexpended balance of established development value at any subsequent time.

(2) This section applies—

(*a*) to every compulsory acquisition of an interest in land in pursuance of a notice to treat served on or after 30th October 1958, whether before or after the commencement of this Act; and

(*b*) to every compulsory acquisition of an interest in land, in pursuance of a notice to treat served on or after 1st January 1955 but before the said 30th October, by an authority possessing compulsory purchase powers, being at that time a government department or local or public authority within the meaning of the Acquisition of Land (Assessment of Compensation) Act 1919, or a person or body of persons to whom that Act applied as it applied to such a department or authority.

(3) Unless, immediately after the acquisition or sale, there is or was outstanding some interest (other than an excepted interest) in the land to which some person other than the acquiring authority is or was entitled, the original unexpended balance of established development value of that land shall be treated as having been extinguished immediately before the subsequent time referred to in subsection (1) of this section.

(4) If, immediately after the acquisition or sale, there is or was such an outstanding interest (other than an excepted interest) as is mentioned in subsection (3) of this section, there shall be deducted from the said original balance an amount equal to any part of the relevant balance which is or was not attributable to any such outstanding interest, and the original unexpended balance of established development value of the land or the part thereof in question shall be treated as having been reduced or extinguished accordingly immediately before that subsequent time.

(5) For the purposes of this section any question as to the portion of the relevant balance which is or was attributable to an interest in land—

(*a*) in relation to a compulsory acquisition to which this section applies, shall be determined in accordance with the provisions of Schedule 17 to this Act; and

(*b*) in relation to a sale of an interest in land by agreement in circumstances corresponding to such an acquisition, shall be determined in accordance with the provisions of that Schedule as those provisions would apply if the sale had been a compulsory acquisition in pursuance of a notice to treat served on the relevant date.

(6) Any reference in this section or in section 143 of this Act to a sale of an interest in land by agreement in circumstances corresponding to a compulsory acquisition to which this section applies is a reference to a sale thereof—

(*a*) to an authority possessing compulsory purchase powers, in pursuance of a contract made on or after 30th October 1958, whether before or after the commencement of this Act; or

(*b*) to such an authority possessing compulsory purchase powers as is mentioned in subsection (2)(*b*) of this section, in pursuance of a contract made on or after 1st January 1955 but before the said 30th October.

(7) In this section "the relevant date" means the date of service of the notice to treat or the date of the contract in pursuance of which the interest was sold, as the case may be, and "excepted interest" means the interest of any such person as is mentioned in section 20(1) of the Compulsory Purchase Act 1965 (which relates to persons having no greater interest than as tenant for a year or from year to year).   **[171]**

NOTES
Commencement: 1 April 1972.

143. Reduction or extinguishment of balance in consequence of severance or injurious affection

(1) Where in connection with—

(*a*) a compulsory acquisition to which section 142 of this Act applies; or

(*b*) a sale of an interest in land by agreement in circumstances corresponding to such an acquisition,

compensation is or was payable, or an amount is or was included in the purchase price, in respect of an interest in land other than the relevant land (in this section referred to as "the interest affected"), for damage sustained by reason that the relevant land is or was severed from other land held therewith, or that any other land (whether held with the relevant land or not) is or was injuriously affected, then (subject to the following provisions of this section) for the purpose of determining whether that other land or any part thereof has or had an unexpended balance of established development value at any subsequent time, there shall be deducted from the original unexpended balance of established development value of that other land an amount calculated in accordance with the following provisions of this section, and the original unexpended balance of that land, or of the part thereof in question, as the case may be, shall be treated as having been reduced or extinguished accordingly immediately before that subsequent time.

(2) In the case of an acquisition or sale in pursuance of a notice to treat served, or contract made, on or after 30th October 1958, the amount to be deducted, as mentioned in subsection (1) of this section, shall be the amount (if any) by which the compensation payable, or amount included in the purchase price, as therein mentioned exceeds or exceeded the compensation which would have been so payable, or the amount which would have been so included, if the extent of the damage sustained in respect of the other land in question had fallen to be ascertained on the assumption that planning permission would not be granted for any new development of that land, but would be granted for any development thereof other than new development.

(3) The following provisions of this section shall have effect with respect to any such acquisition or sale as is mentioned in subsection (1) of this section, being an acquisition or sale in pursuance of a notice to treat served, or contract made, before 30th October 1958; and any such acquisition or sale is hereinafter referred to as an acquisition or sale to which this subsection applies.

(4) No such deduction as is mentioned in subsection (1) of this section shall be made in the case of an acquisition or sale to which subsection (3) of this section applies unless—

 (a) where it was a compulsory acquisition, an amount was paid by way of compensation as mentioned in the said subsection (1);
 (b) the amount which was so paid, or in the case of a sale by agreement, was included in the purchase price as mentioned in the said subsection (1) (hereafter in this section referred to as "the sum paid for severance or injurious affection") exceeded the loss of immediate value of the interest affected; and
 (c) where it was a sale by agreement, the other land in question was held with the relevant land.

(5) Subject to subsection (4) of this section, the amount to be deducted as mentioned in subsection (1) of this section, in the case of an acquisition or sale to which subsection (3) of this section applies, shall be the amount by which the sum paid for severance or injurious affection exceeded the loss of immediate value of the interest affected.

(6) The following provisions of this subsection shall have effect, in the case of an acquisition or sale to which subsection (3) of this section applies, where so much (if any) of the sum paid for severance or injurious affection as was attributable to the loss of immediate value of the interest affected was less than the depreciation in restricted value of that interest, that is to say—

 (a) the amount of the difference shall be ascertained; and

(*b*) for the purpose of determining whether, at any time after the acquisition or sale, the land in which the interest affected subsisted or any part thereof had or has an unexpended balance of established development value (whether or not that land or any part thereof would apart from this subsection have had an original unexpended balance of established development value) a claim holding with an area consisting of that land and a value equal to seven-eighths of the amount of the difference shall be deemed to have subsisted immediately after the time when the adjustment of claim holdings was completed.

(7) In this section—

"the loss of immediate value" means the amount (if any) by which the difference in the value of the interest affected before and immediately after the acquisition or sale, exceeded the loss of development value;

"the loss of development value" means the amount (if any) by which the value of the interest affected immediately before the acquisition or sale, if calculated on the assumption that, until such time as the land in which that interest subsisted might reasonably be expected to become ripe for new development, no use whatever could be made of that land, would have exceeded the value of that interest immediately after the acquisition or sale if calculated on the like assumption;

"the depreciation in restricted value" means the amount (if any) by which the value of the interest affected, immediately after the acquisition or sale, would have been less than the value of that interest immediately before the acquisition or sale, if both values were calculated on the assumption that planning permission would not be granted for any new development of that land, but would be granted for any development thereof other than new development;

"the relevant land", in relation to an acquisition or sale, means the land in which the interest acquired or sold subsisted.   **[172]**

NOTES
Commencement: 1 April 1972.

144. Supplementary provisions as to deductions from original balance

(1) Where, immediately after the time when the adjustment of claim holdings was completed, any land taken as a whole had an original unexpended balance of established development value, and at any time thereafter (whether before or after the commencement of this Act) an act or event occurs or has occurred in relation to part of that land such that, in accordance with any of the preceding provisions of this Part of this Act, an amount is required to be deducted from the original unexpended balance of that part of that land for the purpose of determining whether it has or had an unexpended balance of established development value at any subsequent time, then (without prejudice to the operation of any of the preceding provisions of this Part of this Act with respect to any part of the land taken separately) the land taken as a whole shall be treated as not having (or as not having had) any such balance at that subsequent time.

(2) Where in accordance with any of the preceding provisions of this Part of this Act an amount is required to be deducted from the original unexpended balance of established development value of any land, there shall be attributed to the various parts of that land so much of that amount as might reasonably be expected to have been attributed thereto if the authority determining the

amount had been required to apportion it between those parts in accordance with the same principles as applied to its determination.

(3) Where two or more acts or events occur or have occurred in relation to the same land (whether before or after the commencement of this Act) such that, in accordance with any of the preceding provisions of this Part of this Act, an amount is required to be deducted from the original unexpended balance of established development value of that land or any part thereof, those provisions shall apply cumulatively, and the requisite deduction from the original unexpended balance of established development value of that land shall be made by reference to each of those acts or events. **[173]**

NOTES
    Commencement: 1 April 1972.

145. Provision of information relating to unexpended balance

(1) Subject to the provisions of this section, the Secretary of State shall, on application being made to him by any person, and may if he thinks fit without any such application, issue a certificate in the prescribed form with respect to any land stating whether any of that land had an original unexpended balance of established development value, and, if so—

    (a) giving a general statement of what was taken by the Central Land Board, for the purposes of Part VI of the Act of 1947, to be the state of that land on the appointed day; and

    (b) specifying (subject to any outstanding claims under Part I or Part V of the Act of 1954) the amount of that original balance.

(2) Any such certificate issued with respect to any land may, if the Secretary of State thinks fit, contain additional information with respect to acts or events in consequence of which, in accordance with any of the preceding provisions of this Part of this Act, an amount is required to be deducted from the original unexpended balance of established development value of any of that land.

(3) Where, at any time on or after 1st January 1955 (whether before or after the commencement of this Act), a notice to treat has been served with a view to the compulsory acquisition of an interest in land by an authority possessing compulsory purchase powers, that authority may apply to the Secretary of State for, and shall be entitled to the issue of, a certificate showing the unexpended balance of established development value (if any) of any of that land immediately before the service of that notice.

(4) Where the issue of a certificate under this section with respect to any land involves a new apportionment, or, in the case of a certificate under subsection (3) of this section, involves the calculation of a deduction from the original unexpended balance of established development value by virtue of section 141 of this Act, then—

    (a) except in the case of a certificate under subsection (3) of this section, or of a certificate which the Secretary of State proposes to issue without any application being made for it, the certificate shall not be issued otherwise than on the application of a person who is for the time being entitled to an interest in that land;

    (b) before issuing the certificate, the Secretary of State shall give notice in writing to any person entitled to an interest in land appearing to him to be an interest which will be substantially affected by the apportionment or calculation, giving particulars of the proposed apportionment or calculation, and stating that objections or other representations with respect thereto may be made to the Secretary of State within the period of thirty days from the date of the notice; and

(c) the certificate shall not be issued before the end of that period, and if within that period an objection to the proposed apportionment or calculation has been made by any person to whom notice has been given under paragraph (b) of this subsection, or by any other person who establishes that he is entitled to an interest in land which is substantially affected by the apportionment or calculation, and that objection has not been withdrawn, subsection (5) of this section shall have effect.

(5) Where by virtue of subsection (4)(c) of this section this subsection is to have effect, then—

(a) if within a further period of thirty days the person by whom any such objection was made requires the dispute to be referred to the Lands Tribunal, the dispute shall be so referred, and the certificate shall not be issued until either the Tribunal has decided the matter or the reference to the Tribunal has been withdrawn;

(b) the certificate may be issued before the end of the said further period if every such objection has been withdrawn;

(c) the certificate shall be issued at the end of that further period, notwithstanding that every such objection has not been withdrawn, if no requirement has within that period been made under paragraph (a) of this subsection.

(6) Where, on a reference to the Lands Tribunal under this section, it is shown that a new apportionment relates partly to the same matters as a previous apportionment, and is consistent with that previous apportionment in so far as it relates to those matters, the Tribunal shall not vary the new apportionment in such a way as to be inconsistent with the previous apportionment in so far as it relates to those matters.

(7) A certificate under subsection (3) of this section shall be conclusive evidence of the unexpended balance shown therein; and a certificate under subsection (1) of this section shall be sufficient proof of any facts stated therein unless the contrary is shown.

(8) An application for a certificate under this section shall be made in such form and manner as may be prescribed, and shall be accompanied by sufficient particulars, including a map if necessary, to enable the land to be identified, and, where a new apportionment will be involved, particulars of the nature of the applicant's interest, and such information as to the nature of any other interest in the land, and as to the name and address of the person entitled to that other interest, as may be known to the applicant.

(9) On any application under subsection (1) of this section the applicant shall pay in the prescribed manner a fee of twenty-five new pence, and, if the application involves a new apportionment, the certificate shall not be issued until the applicant has paid in the prescribed manner a further fee of seventy-five new pence.

(10) In this section "new apportionment" means an apportionment which relates wholly or partly to any matter to which no previous apportionment related.   **[174]**

NOTES

Commencement: 1 April 1972.

Act of 1947: Town and Country Planning Act 1947.

Act of 1954: Town and Country Planning Act 1954.

Right to compensation

146. General provision as to right to compensation

Subject to the provisions of this Part of this Act, a person shall be entitled to compensation under this Part of this Act in respect of a planning decision whereby planning permission for the carrying out of new development of land is refused, or is granted subject to conditions, if—

(a) at the time of the decision he is entitled to an interest in any land to which the decision relates which has an unexpended balance of established development value; and

(b) the value of that interest, or, in the case of an interest extending to other land, the value of that interest in so far as it subsists in such land as is referred to in the preceding paragraph, is depreciated by the decision. **[175]**

NOTES
Commencement: 1 April 1972.

147. Planning decisions not ranking for compensation

(1) Compensation under this Part of this Act shall not be payable—

(a) in respect of the refusal of planning permission for any development which consists of or includes the making of any material change in the use of any buildings or other land; or

(b) in respect of any decision made on an application in pursuance of regulations under section 63 of this Act for consent to the display of advertisements.

(2) Compensation under this Part of this Act shall not be payable in respect of the imposition, on the granting of planning permission to develop land, of any condition relating to—

(a) the number or disposition of buildings on any land;

(b) the dimensions, design, structure or external appearance of any building, or the materials to be used in its construction;

(c) the manner in which any land is to be laid out for the purposes of the development, including the provision of facilities for the parking, loading, unloading or fuelling of vehicles on the land;

(d) the use of any buildings or other land; or

(e) the location or design of any means of access to a highway, or the materials to be used in the construction of any such means of access,

or in respect of any condition subject to which permission is granted for the winning and working of minerals.

In this subsection "means of access to a highway" does not include a service road.

(3) Compensation under this Part of this Act shall not be payable in respect of the application to any planning permission of any of the conditions referred to in sections 41 and 42 of this Act or in respect of the imposition of any condition to which section 71 or 82 of this Act applies.

(4) Compensation under this Part of this Act shall not be payable in respect of the refusal of permission to develop land, if the reason or one of the reasons

stated for the refusal is that development of the kind proposed would be premature by reference to either or both of the following matters, that is to say—

    (*a*) the order of priority (if any) indicated in the development plan for the area in which the land is situated for development in that area;

    (*b*) any existing deficiency in the provision of water supplies or sewerage services, and the period within which any such deficiency may reasonably be expected to be made good:

[Provided that this subsection shall not apply if the reason or one of the reasons so stated is that that development would be premature by reference to the matters mentioned in paragraph (*a*) of this subsection and the planning decision refusing the permission is made on an application made more than seven years after the date of a previous planning decision whereby permission to develop the same land was refused for the same reason, or for reasons which included the same reason.]

(5) Compensation under this Part of this Act shall not be payable in respect of the refusal of permission to develop land, if the reason or one of the reasons stated for the refusal is that the land is unsuitable for the proposed development on account of its liability to flooding or to subsidence.

(6) For the purposes of this section, a planning decision whereby permission to develop land is granted subject to a condition prohibiting development on a specified part of that land shall be treated as a decision refusing the permission with respect to that part of the land.   **[176]**

NOTES

    Commencement: 1 April 1972.

    Sub-s (3): repealed in part by the Housing and Planning Act 1986, s 49(2), Sch 12, Part III. See Appendix.

    Sub-s (4): amended by the Water Act 1973, s 40(2), Sch 8.

148. No compensation if certain other development permitted

(1) Compensation under this Part of this Act shall not be payable in respect of a planning decision whereby permission is refused for the development of land if, notwithstanding that refusal, there is available with respect to that land planning permission for development to which this section applies:

Provided that, where such permission is available with respect to part only of the land, this section shall have effect only in so far as the interest subsists in that part.

(2) Where a claim for compensation under this Part of this Act is made in respect of an interest in any land, planning permission for development to which this section applies shall be taken for the purposes of this section to be available with respect to that land or a part thereof if, immediately before the Secretary of State gives notice of his findings in respect of that claim, there is in force with respect to that land, or that part thereof, a grant of, or an undertaking by the Secretary of State to grant, planning permission for some such development, subject to no conditions other than such as are mentioned in section 147(2) of this Act.

(3) This section applies to any development of a residential, commercial or industrial character, being development which consists wholly or mainly of the construction of houses, flats, shop or office premises, or industrial buildings (including warehouses), or any combination thereof.   **[177]**

NOTES
Commencement: 1 April 1972.

149. Further exclusions from compensation

(1) Where an interest in any land has (whether before or after the commencement of this Act) been compulsorily acquired by, or sold to, an authority possessing compulsory purchase powers (not being statutory undertakers or the National Coal Board), that authority, and any person deriving title from that authority under a disposition made by that authority on or at any time after the appointed day, shall not be entitled to compensation under this Part of this Act in respect of a planning decision made after the service of the notice to treat, or after the making of the contract of sale, as the case may be, by reason that the value of that interest, or of any interest created (whether immediately or derivatively) out of that interest, is depreciated by the decision.

(2) Subsection (1) of this section shall apply to land which has at any time on or after the appointed day (whether before or after the commencement of this Act) been appropriated by a local authority for a purpose for which the authority could have been authorised to acquire the land compulsorily, as it applies to land in which an interest has been acquired as mentioned in that subsection, with the substitution, for the reference to the service of the notice to treat, of a reference to the appropriation.

(3) Where at the relevant date any land was or is operational land of statutory undertakers, or land of the National Coal Board of a class specified in regulations made under section 90 of the Act of 1947 or under section 273 of this Act, the statutory undertakers or the National Coal Board, as the case may be, and any person deriving title from those undertakers or that Board, shall not be entitled to compensation under this Part of this Act, in respect of a planning decision made after the relevant date, by reason that the value of any interest in that land is depreciated by that decision.

In this subsection "the relevant date", in relation to land which was such operational land or land of the National Coal Board as is mentioned in this subsection on 1st January 1955, means that day, and, in relation to land which (whether before or after the commencement of this Act) became or becomes such operational land or land of the National Coal Board on a date subsequent to the said 1st January, means that subsequent date.

(4) A person shall not be entitled to compensation under this Part of this Act in respect of depreciation of the value of an interest in land by a planning decision if he is entitled to compensation by virtue of section 165 of this Act in respect of depreciation of the value of that interest by that decision.   [178]

NOTES
Commencement: 1 April 1972.
Act of 1947: Town and Country Planning Act 1947.

150. Grant of planning permission treated as subject to notional condition

(1) The provisions of this section shall have effect where—

  (a) on an application for planning permission for the carrying out of new development of land, a planning decision is made whereby the permission is granted, whether unconditionally or subject to conditions; and

  (b) the Secretary of State certifies that he is satisfied that particular buildings or works to which the application related were only included therein because the applicant had reason to believe that permission for the other development to which the application related (in this section referred to as "the principal development") would not have been granted except subject to a condition requiring the erection or construction of those buildings or works.

(2) Where subsection (1) of this section applies, then for the purposes of this Part of this Act—

(a)   the application shall be deemed to have included, in place of those buildings or works, such other development of the land on which the buildings or works were to be erected or constructed as might reasonably have been expected to have been included having regard to the principal development; and

(b)   the permission shall be deemed to have been granted for the principal development subject to a condition requiring the erection or construction of those buildings or works.   **[179]**

NOTES
Commencement: 1 April 1972.

151. Notice under s 72 treated as planning decision

Where a notice under section 72(1) of this Act is served in respect of the whole or part of any land, the provisions of this Part of this Act shall have effect as if the application, in consequence of which the notice is served, had been an effective application for planning permission, and as if the notice had been a planning decision of the local planning authority refusing that permission in respect of that land or that part thereof, as the case may be.   **[180]**

NOTES
Commencement: 1 April 1972.
Repealed by the Housing and Planning Act 1986, s 49(2), Sch 12, Part III. See Appendix.

Measure of compensation

152. General provisions as to amount of compensation

(1) Where a person is entitled to compensation under this Part of this Act in respect of depreciation by a planning decision of the value of an interest in land, the amount of the compensation, subject to the following provisions of this section, shall be whichever is the lesser of the following amounts, that is to say—

(a)   the amount by which the value of that interest (if it is an interest subsisting only in land to which this section applies), or (if it is an interest extending to other land) the amount by which the value of the interest in so far as it subsists in land to which this section applies, is depreciated by the decision; and

(b)   the amount of the unexpended balance of established development value, immediately before the decision, of so much of the land in which the interest subsists as is land to which this section applies.

(2) Land to which this section applies, in relation to a planning decision, is land which—

(a)   constitutes or forms part of the decision area; and

(b)   at the time of the decision has an unexpended balance of established development value.

(3) If, in the case of any land to which this section applies, compensation is

payable under this Part of this Act in respect of two or more interests in that land by reason of the same planning decision, and the aggregate amount of compensation payable apart from this subsection in respect of those interests would exceed the amount mentioned in paragraph (*b*) of subsection (1) of this section, the amount mentioned in that paragraph shall be allocated between those interests in proportion to the depreciation of the value of each of them respectively, and the amount of the compensation payable in respect of any of those interests shall be the sum so allocated to that interest.

(4) Where the land constituting the decision area, taken as a whole, does not satisfy both of the following conditions, that is to say—

(*a*) that at the time of the decision it has an unexpended balance of established development value; and

(*b*) that every interest subsisting therein, the value of which is depreciated by the decision, subsists in the whole of that land,

the provisions of subsection (5) of this section shall have effect for the purpose of assessing the compensation payable under this Part of this Act in respect of any interest subsisting in that land or any part thereof.

(5) Where this subsection applies in relation to an interest in land—

(*a*) the depreciation of the value of the interest by the planning decision shall first be ascertained with reference to the whole of the land which constitutes or forms part of the decision area and is land in which that interest subsists;

(*b*) the land referred to in paragraph (*a*) of this subsection shall then be treated as divided into as many parts as may be requisite to ensure that each such part consists of land which either satisfies both of the conditions mentioned in subsection (4) of this section or is not land which, at the time of the decision, has an unexpended balance of established development value; and

(*c*) the depreciation of the value of the interest, ascertained in accordance with paragraph (*a*) of this subsection, shall then be apportioned between those parts, according to the nature of those parts and the effect of the planning decision in relation to each of them,

and the amount of the compensation shall be the aggregate of the amounts which would be payable by virtue of the preceding provisions of this section if the planning decision had been made separately with respect to each of those parts.

(6) In this section "the decision area" in relation to a planning decision means the aggregate of the land to which the decision relates. **[181]**

NOTES
Commencement: 1 April 1972.

153. Assessment of depreciation

(1) For the purposes of this Part of this Act, the value of an interest in land, or of an interest in so far as it subsists in particular land, shall be taken to be depreciated by a planning decision (in this section referred to as "the relevant decision") if, and to the extent to which, that value, calculated in accordance with the following provisions of this section, falls short of what that value, so calculated, would have been if the relevant decision had been a decision to the contrary effect.

(2) Subject to the following provisions of this section, any such value shall for the purposes of this section be calculated—

(a) as at the time of the relevant decision; but

(b) as affected by that decision, by any grant of planning permission made after that decision and in force immediately before the Secretary of State gives notice of his findings on the claim for compensation in respect of that decision, and by any undertaking to grant planning permission so in force; and

(c) on the assumption that, after the relevant decision, and apart from any such permission or undertaking as is mentioned in paragraph (b) of this subsection, planning permission would not be granted for any new development of the land in question, but would be granted for any development thereof other than new development.

(3) If in consequence of another planning decision or of an order, being a decision or order made—

(a) before the relevant decision; and

(b) either in respect of the whole or part of the land to which the relevant decision relates, or in respect of land which includes the whole or part of that land,

compensation to which this subsection applies has become or becomes payable in respect of that other planning decision or that order, the calculation to be made under this section shall be made as if that other planning decision had been a decision to the contrary effect, or that order had not been made, as the case may be.

(4) Subsection (3) of this section applies—

(a) to any compensation payable under this Part of this Act, or under Part II or Part V of the Act of 1954 or Part VI of the Act of 1962; and

(b) to so much of any compensation payable under section 164 of this Act or section 118 of the Act of 1962, or under the provisions of those sections as applied by section 165 of this Act or section 119 of the Act of 1962 respectively, and so much of any compensation to which Part IV of the Act of 1954 applied, as is or was payable in respect of loss or damage consisting of depreciation of the value of an interest in land.

(5) In this section "a decision to the contrary effect"—

(a) in relation to a decision refusing permission, means a decision granting the permission subject to such condition (if any) of a description falling within subsection (2) of section 147 of this Act as the authority making the decision might reasonably have been expected to impose if the permission had not been refused; and

(b) in relation to a decision granting the permission subject to conditions, means a decision granting the permission applied for subject only to such of those conditions (if any) as fell within subsection (2) of that section.   **[182]**

NOTES

Commencement: 1 April 1972.

Claims for, and payment of, compensation

154. General provisions as to claims for compensation

(1) Compensation under this Part of this Act shall not be payable unless a claim for it is duly made in accordance with the provisions of this section.

(2) A claim for compensation under this Part of this Act shall not have effect unless it is made before the end of the period of six months beginning with the date of the planning decision to which it relates:

Provided that the Secretary of State may in any particular case (either before, on or after the date on which the time for claiming would otherwise have expired) allow an extended, or further extended, period for making such a claim.

(3) Regulations made under this section may—

    (a) require claims for compensation under this Part of this Act to be made in a form prescribed by the regulations;

    (b) require a claimant to provide such evidence in support of the claim, and such information as to the interest of the claimant in the land to which the claim relates, and as to the interests of other persons therein which are known to the claimant, as may be so prescribed.

(4) Any claim for such compensation in respect of a planning decision shall be sent to the local planning authority; and it shall be the duty of that authority, as soon as may be after receipt of a claim, to transmit the claim to the Secretary of State, and to furnish the Secretary of State with—

    (a) any evidence or other information provided by the claimant in accordance with regulations made under this section; and

    (b) such other information (if any) as may be required by or under regulations made under this section, being information appearing to the Secretary of State to be relevant to the exercise of his powers under the provisions of Part III of this Act relating to the review of planning decisions where compensation is claimed.

(5) Where a claim is transmitted to the Secretary of State under subsection (4) of this section—

    (a) if it appears to the Secretary of State that the development to which the planning decision related was not new development, or that at the time of the planning decision no part of the land to which the claim relates had an unexpended balance of established development value, or that compensation is excluded by section 147 or 148 of this Act, the Secretary of State shall notify the claimant accordingly, stating on which of those grounds it appears to him that compensation is not payable, and inviting the claimant to withdraw the claim;

    (b) unless the claim is withdrawn, the Secretary of State shall give notice of the claim to every other person (if any) appearing to him to have an interest in the land to which the planning decision related. **[183]**

NOTES
Commencement: 1 April 1972.

155. Effect on claims of direction under s 38

(1) Where, in accordance with section 39(3) of this Act, the Secretary of State gives notice of a direction under section 38 of this Act to a person who has made a claim for compensation in respect of the planning decision to which that direction relates, that person, if he does not withdraw the claim, may, at any time within thirty days after the service on him of the Secretary of State's notice, give notice to the Secretary of State modifying the claim.

(2) Subject to any modification by virtue of a notice given by a claimant under subsection (1) of this section, where the Secretary of State gives a direction

under section 38 of this Act in respect of a decision of a local planning authority, any claim made in respect of that decision shall have effect as if it had been made in respect of the decision which, by virtue of the direction, is substituted for the decision of the authority, or, as the case may be, as if it had been made in respect of the decision of the authority as modified by the direction.   **[184]**

NOTES
Commencement: 1 April 1972.

156. Determination of claims

(1) Provision shall be made by regulations under this section—

(a) for requiring claims for compensation under this Part of this Act to be determined by the Secretary of State in such manner as may be prescribed by the regulations;

(b) for regulating the practice and procedure to be followed in connection with the determination of such claims;

(c) for requiring the Secretary of State, on determining any such claim, to give notice of his findings to the claimant, and to every other person (if any) who has made a claim for compensation under this Part of this Act in respect of the same planning decision, and, if his findings include an apportionment, to give particulars of the apportionment to any other person entitled to an interest in land appearing to the Secretary of State to be an interest substantially affected by the apportionment.

(2) Subject to subsection (3) of this section, provision shall be made by regulations under this section—

(a) for enabling the claimant or any other person to whom notice of the Secretary of State's findings has been given in accordance with subsection (1) of this section, if he wishes to dispute the findings, and any other person to whom particulars of an apportionment included in those findings have been so given, or who establishes that he is entitled to an interest in land which is substantially affected by such an apportionment, if he wishes to dispute the apportionment, to require the findings, or, as the case may be, the apportionment, to be referred to the Lands Tribunal;

(b) for enabling the claimant and every other person to whom notice of any findings or apportionment has been given as mentioned in paragraph (a) of this subsection to be heard by the Tribunal on any reference under this section of those findings or of that apportionment, as the case may be; and

(c) for requiring the Tribunal, on any such reference, either to confirm or to vary the Secretary of State's findings or the apportionment, as the case may be, and to notify the parties of the decision of the Tribunal.

(3) Where on a reference to the Lands Tribunal under this section it is shown that an apportionment relates wholly or partly to the same matters as a previous apportionment, and is consistent with that previous apportionment in so far as it relates to those matters, the Tribunal shall not vary the apportionment in such a way as to be inconsistent with the previous apportionment in so far as it relates to those matters.   **[185]**

NOTES
Commencement: 1 April 1972.

157. Payment of compensation

Where compensation is determined under section 156 of this Act to be payable, the Secretary of State shall pay the compensation to the person entitled thereto in accordance with the preceding provisions of this Part of this Act. **[186]**

NOTES
Commencement: 1 April 1972.

Subsequent recovery of compensation

158. Apportionment and registration of compensation

(1) Where, on a claim for compensation under this Part of this Act in respect of a planning decision, the Secretary of State determines that compensation is payable and that the amount of the compensation exceeds £20, the Secretary of State shall (if it appears to him to be practicable to do so) apportion the amount of the compensation between different parts of the land to which the claim for compensation relates, and shall include particulars of the apportionment in the notice of his findings under section 156 of this Act.

(2) In carrying out an apportionment under subsection (1) of this section the Secretary of State shall divide the land into parts, and shall distribute the compensation between those parts, according to the way in which the different parts of the land appear to him to be differently affected by the planning decision.

(3) On a reference to the Lands Tribunal under section 156 of this Act, unless the decision of the Tribunal will not affect the amount of the compensation or any apportionment thereof by the Secretary of State, the preceding provisions of this section shall apply with the substitution, for references to the Secretary of State, of references to the Lands Tribunal.

(4) Where, on a claim for compensation under this Part of this Act in respect of a planning decision, compensation has become payable of an amount exceeding £20, the Secretary of State shall cause notice of that fact, specifying the planning decision and the land to which the claim for compensation relates, and the amount of the compensation and any apportionment thereof under this section, to be deposited with the council of the ... London borough or county district in which the land is situated, and, if that council is not the local planning authority, with the local planning authority.

(5) Notices deposited under this section shall be registered [local land charges, and for the purposes of the Local Land Charges Act 1975 the council with whom any such notice is deposited shall be treated as the originating authority as respects the charge thereby constituted.]

(6) In relation to compensation specified in a notice registered under this section, references in this Part of this Act to so much of the compensation as is attributable to a part of the land to which the notice relates shall be construed in accordance with the following provisions, that is to say—

(a) if the notice does not include an apportionment under the preceding provisions of this section, the amount of the compensation shall be treated as distributed rateably according to area over the land to which the notice relates;

(b) if the notice includes such an apportionment, the compensation shall be treated as distributed in accordance with that apportionment as between the different parts of the land by reference to which the apportionment is made; and so much of the compensation as, in accordance with the apportionment, is attributed to a part of the land shall be treated as distributed rateably according to area over that part of the land.   **[187]**

NOTES
Commencement: 1 April 1972.
Words omitted repealed by the Local Government Act 1972, s 272(1), Sch 30.
Amendment in square brackets made by the Local Land Charges Act 1975, s 17, Sch 1.

159. Recovery of compensation on subsequent development

(1) No person shall carry out any new development to which this section applies, on land in respect of which a notice (hereafter in this Part of this Act referred to as a "compensation notice") is registered under section 158 of this Act, until such amount (if any) as is recoverable under this section in respect of the compensation specified in the notice has been paid or secured to the satisfaction of the Secretary of State.

(2) Subject to the following provisions of this section, this section applies to any new development—

(a) which is development of a residential, commercial or industrial character and consists wholly or mainly of the construction of houses, flats, shop or office premises, or industrial buildings (including warehouses), or any combination thereof; or

(b) which consists in the winning and working of minerals; or

(c) to which, having regard to the probable value of the development, it is in the opinion of the Secretary of State reasonable that this section should apply.

(3) This section shall not apply to any development by virtue of subsection (2)(c) of this section if, on an application made to him for the purpose, the Secretary of State has certified that, having regard to the probable value of the development, it is not in his opinion reasonable that this section should apply thereto.

(4) Where the compensation specified in the compensation notice became payable in respect of the imposition of conditions on the granting of permission to develop land, this section shall not apply to the development for which that permission was granted.   **[188]**

NOTES
Commencement: 1 April 1972.

160. Amount recoverable, and provisions for payment or remission thereof

(1) Subject to the following provisions of this section, the amount recoverable under section 159 of this Act in respect of the compensation specified in a compensation notice—

(a) if the land on which the development is to be carried out (in this subsection referred to as "the development area") is identical with, or includes (with other land) the whole of, the land comprised in the compensation notice, shall be the amount of compensation specified in that notice;

(b) if the development area forms part of the land comprised in the compensation notice, or includes part of that land together with other land not comprised in that notice, shall be so much of the amount of the compensation specified in that notice as is attributable to land comprised in that notice and falling within the development area.

(2) Where, in the case of any land in respect of which a compensation notice has been registered, the Secretary of State is satisfied, having regard to the probable value of any proper development of that land, that no such development is likely to be carried out unless he exercises his powers under this subsection, he may, in the case of any particular development, remit the whole or part of any amount otherwise recoverable under section 159 of this Act; and where part only of any such amount has been remitted, he shall cause the compensation notice to be amended by substituting therein, for the statement of the amount of the compensation, in so far as it is attributable to that land, a statement of the amount which has been remitted under this subsection.

(3) Where, in connection with the development of any land, an amount becomes recoverable under section 159 of this Act in respect of the compensation specified in a compensation notice, then, except where, and to the extent that, payment of that amount has been remitted under subsection (2) of this section, no amount shall be recoverable under section 159 of this Act in respect of that compensation, in so far as it is attributable to that land, in connection with any subsequent development thereof.

(4) No amount shall be recoverable under section 159 of this Act in respect of any compensation by reference to which a sum has become recoverable by the Secretary of State under section 257 of this Act.

(5) An amount recoverable under section 159 of this Act in respect of any compensation shall be payable to the Secretary of State, and—

> (*a*) shall be so payable either as a single capital payment or as a series of instalments of capital and interest combined, or as a series of other annual or periodical payments, of such amounts, and payable at such times, as the Secretary of State may direct, after taking into account any representations made by the person by whom the development is to be carried out; and
>
> (*b*) except where the amount is payable as a single capital payment, shall be secured by that person in such manner (whether by mortgage, convenant or otherwise) as the Secretary of State may direct.

(6) If any person initiates any new development to which section 159 of this Act applies in contravention of subsection (1) of that section, the Secretary of State may serve a notice on him specifying the amount appearing to the Secretary of State to be the amount recoverable under that section in respect of the compensation in question, and requiring him to pay that amount to the Secretary of State within such period, not being less than three months after the service of the notice, as may be specified in the notice.   **[189]**

NOTES
 Commencement: 1 April 1972.

161. Amount recovered not to be deducted from unexpended balance

(1) Where an amount has become recoverable under section 159 of this Act in respect of the compensation specified in a compensation notice the following provisions of this section shall have effect for the purpose of determining any question as to the unexpended balance of established development value of any land at any subsequent time.

(2) Except where, and to the extent that, payment of that amount has been

remitted under section 160 of this Act, so much (if any) of that compensation as is attributable to that land shall, for the purpose mentioned in subsection (1) of this section, be treated as not having become payable, and accordingly (notwithstanding anything in section 140 of this Act) shall not be deducted from that balance.   **[190]**

NOTES
Commencement: 1 April 1972.

Supplementary provisions

162. Mortgages, rentcharges and settlements

(1) Regulations made under this section may make provision as to the exercise of the right to claim compensation under this Part of this Act, and as to the person to whom such compensation or any part thereof is to be paid, and as to the application of any such compensation or any part thereof, in cases where apart from this section, the right to claim the compensation is exercisable by reference to an interest in land which is subject to a mortgage, or to a rentcharge, or to the trusts of a settlement, or which was so subject at a time specified in the regulations.

(2) In relation to any case where, by virtue of any such regulations, compensation or a part thereof is to be paid to the owner of a rentcharge, the regulations may apply all or any of the provisions of section 25 of the War Damage Act 1943 (rights of owners of rentcharges as to payments for war damage) subject to such adaptations and modifications as may be prescribed by the regulations, and may provide for disputes arising under the regulations, so far as they relate to rentcharges, to be referred to the Lands Tribunal for determination by that tribunal.   **[191]**

NOTES
Commencement: 1 April 1972.

163. Calculation of value

(1) In calculating value for any of the purposes of this Part of this Act—

    (*a*) rules (2) to (4) of the rules set out in section 5 of the Land Compensation Act 1961 shall apply with the necessary modifications; and

    (*b*) if the interest to be valued is subject to a mortgage, it shall be treated as if it were not subject to the mortgage:

Provided that rule (3) of those rules shall not apply for the purposes of Schedule 16 to this Act.

(2) Where, for the purposes of any of the provisions of this Part of this Act, value falls to be calculated by reference to the duration of a tenancy, and, by reason of any option or other contractual right with respect to the determination, renewal or continuance of the tenancy, the date of expiry of the tenancy is not ascertainable with certainty, that date shall be taken to be such as appears reasonable and probable having regard to the interests of the party by whom the option is exercisable, or in whose favour the right operates, and to any other material considerations subsisting at the time when the calculation of value falls to be made.   **[192]**

NOTES
Commencement: 1 April 1972.

PART VIII

COMPENSATION FOR OTHER PLANNING RESTRICTIONS

Revocation or modification of planning permission

164. Compensation where planning permission revoked or modified

(1) [Subject to section 164A of this Act, where] planning permission is revoked or modified by an order under section 45 of this Act, . . . , then if, on a claim made to the local planning authority within the time and in the manner prescribed by regulations under this Act, it is shown that a person interested in the land [or a person who is without an interest in the land itself but has an interest in minerals in, on or under it]—

(a) has incurred expenditure in carrying out work which is rendered abortive by the revocation or modification; or

(b) has otherwise sustained loss or damage which is directly attributable to the revocation or modification,

the local planning authority shall pay to that person compensation in respect of that expenditure, loss or damage.

(2) For the purposes of this section, any expenditure incurred in the preparation of plans for the purposes of any work, or upon other similar matters preparatory thereto, shall be taken to be included in the expenditure incurred in carrying out that work.

(3) Subject to subsection (2) of this section, no compensation shall be paid under this section in respect of any work carried out before the grant of the permission which is revoked or modified, or in respect of any other loss or damage (not being loss or damage consisting of depreciation of the value of an interest in land) arising out of anything done or omitted to be done before the grant of that permission.

(4) In calculating, for the purposes of this section, the amount of any loss or damage consisting of depreciation of the value of an interest in land, it shall be assumed that planning permission would be granted for development of the land of any class specified in Schedule 8 to this Act.

(5) In this Part of this Act any reference to an order under section 45 of this Act includes a reference to an order under the provisions of that section as applied by section 51(2) of this Act.   **[193]**

NOTES

Commencement: 1 April 1972.

Sub-s (1): first words in square brackets substituted by the Town and Country Planning (Minerals) Act 1981, s 34, Sch 1; words omitted repealed by the Local Government Act 1974, s 42, Sch 8; second words in square brackets added by the Town and Country Planning (Minerals) Act 1981, s 12.

164A. Compensation for certain orders under s 45 relating to mineral working to be on special basis

[(1) Where mineral compensation requirements are satisfied in relation to an order under section 45 of this Act, section 164 of this Act shall have effect subject to mineral compensation modifications.

(2) Subject of subsection (4) of this section, mineral compensation requirements are satisfied in relation to an order under section 45 of this Act if—

(a) the order modifies planning permission for development consisting of the winning and working of minerals; and
(b) the order does not—

    (i) impose any restriction on the winning and working of minerals; or

    (ii) modify or replace any such restriction subject to which the planning permission was granted or which was imposed by a relevant order; and

(c) the mineral planning authority carried out special consultations about the making and terms of the order before they made it; and
(d) either—

    (i) the permission was granted not less than five years before the date of the order; or

    (ii) the conditions specified in subsection (3) of this section are satisfied.

(3) The conditions mentioned in subsection (2)(d)(ii) of this section are—

(a) that the planning permission which the order modifies was granted before the commencement of section 30A of this Act; and
(b) that the order—

    (i) imposes an aftercare condition; and

    (ii) does not impose any other condition.

(4) Where the mineral planning authority—

(a) make an order under section 45 of this Act modifying planning permission for development consisting of the winning and working of minerals; and
(b) have previously made a relevant order or orders,

mineral compensation requirements are not satisfied in relation to the order mentioned in paragraph (a) of this subsection unless it was made more than five years after the order previously made or the last such order.]   **[194]**

NOTES
Commencement: 17 September 1982.
Commencement order: SI 1982 No 1177.
Added by the Town and Country Planning (Minerals) Act 1981, s 13.

165. Application of s 164 to special cases of refusal or conditional grant of planning permission

(1) The provisions of this section shall have effect where—

(a) planning permission for the development of land has been granted by a development order; and
(b) that permission is withdrawn, whether by the revocation or amendment of the order by the issue of directions under powers in that behalf conferred by the order; and
(c) on an application made in that behalf under Part III of this Act, planning permission for that development is refused, or is granted subject to conditions other than those previously imposed by the development order.

[(1A) Where planning permission granted by a development order is withdrawn by revocation or amendment of the order subsection (1) of this section applies only if the application referred to in paragraph (c) is made before the end of the period of twelve months beginning with the date on which the revocation or amendment came into operation.]

(2) In any case falling within subsection (1) of this section, the provisions of section 164 of this Act shall apply as if the planning permission granted by the development order—

(a) had been granted by the local planning authority under Part III of this Act; and

(b) had been revoked or modified by an order under section 45 of this Act,

and the provisions of section 166 (except subsection (5)(b) thereof) and of sections 167 and 168 of this Act shall apply as if references therein to an order under section 45 of this Act were references to the planning decision whereby the planning permission in question is refused, or is granted subject to conditions other than those previously imposed by the development order.

(3) This section shall not apply in relation to planning permission for the development of operational land of statutory undertakers.

(4) No compensation shall be payable under this section in respect of the imposition of any condition to which section 71 or 82 of this Act applies. **[195]**

NOTES

Commencement: 9 May 1985 (sub-s (1A), certain purposes); 1 April 1972 (remainder).

This section derived from the Town and Country Planning Act 1962, s 119, and the Town and Country Planning Act 1968, s 71(3).

Sub-s (1A): added by the Town and Country Planning (Compensation) Act 1985, s 1(1).

Sub-s (4): repealed by the Housing and Planning Act 1986, s 49(2), Sch 12, Part III. See Appendix.

166. Registration and apportionment of compensation for depreciation

(1) Where compensation becomes payable under the preceding provisions of this Part of this Act, and includes compensation for depreciation of an amount exceeding £20, the local planning authority shall (if it appears to them to be practicable to do so) apportion the amount of the compensation for depreciation between different parts of the land to which the claim for that compensation relates, and give particulars of any such apportionment to the claimant and to every other person (if any) entitled to an interest in land which appears to the authority to be substantially affected by the apportionment.

(2) In carrying out an apportionment under subsection (1) of this section, the local planning authority shall divide the land into parts, and shall distribute the compensation for depreciation between those parts, according to the way in which different parts of the land appear to the authority to be differently affected by the order in consequence of which the compensation is payable.

(3) Section 156(2) of this Act, and any regulations made by virtue thereof, shall have effect with respect to any such apportionment (subject to any necessary modifications) as they have effect with respect to an apportionment under section 158(1) of this Act.

(4) On a reference to the Lands Tribunal by virtue of subsection (3) of this section, subsections (1) and (2) of this section, so far as they relate to the making of an apportionment, shall apply with the substitution, for references to the local planning authority, of references to the Lands Tribunal.

(5) Where compensation becomes payable under the preceding provisions of this Part of this Act, and includes compensation for depreciation exceeding £20, the local planning authority shall give notice thereof to the Secretary of

State, specifying the amount of the compensation for depreciation and any apportionment thereof under this section; and subsections (4) to (6) of section 158 of this Act shall have effect with respect thereto as they have effect with respect to compensation under Part VII of this Act, subject, however, to any necessary modifications, and, in particular, with the substitution—

    (a) for references to the compensation mentioned in that section, of references to the compensation for depreciation specified in the notice; and

    (b) for references to the planning decision, of references to the order under section 45 of this Act in consequence of which the compensation is payable.

(6) In this section and in section 167 of this Act " compensation for depreciation" means so much of any compensation payable under the preceding provisions of this Part of this Act as is payable in respect of loss or damage consisting of depreciation of the value of an interest in land, and "interest" (where the reference is to an interest in land) means the fee simple or a tenacy of the land and does not include any other interest therein.   **[196]**

NOTES
    Commencement: 1 April 1972.

167. Contribution by Secretary of State towards compensation in certain cases

(1) Where a notice under section 166 of this Act is given to the Secretary of State in consequence of the making of an order under section 45 of this Act, and the circumstances are such that, if the permission revoked or modified by the order had been refused, or, as the case may be, had been granted as so modified, at the time when it was granted, compensation under Part VII of this Act could have been claimed and would have been payable by the Secretary of State, the Secretary of State may, subject to the provisions of this section, pay to the local planning authority a contribution of the amount appearing to him to be the amount of compensation which would have been so payable by him under Part VII of this Act.

(2) The amount of any such contribution shall not exceed—

    (a) the amount of the compensation for depreciation paid by the local planning authority; or

    (b) the unexpended balance of established development value, at the date of the making of the order, of the land in respect of which that compensation was paid.

(3) Regulations made under this section shall make provision, in relation to cases where the Secretary of State proposes to pay a contribution under this section—

    (a) for requiring the Secretary of State to give notice of his proposal to persons entitled to such interests as may be prescribed in the land to which the proposal relates, and to such other persons (if any) as may be determined in accordance with the regulations to be affected by the proposal;

    (b) for enabling persons to whom notice of the proposal is given to object to the proposal, on the grounds that compensation would not have been payable as mentioned in subsection (1) of this section, or that the amount of the compensation so payable would have been less than the amount of the proposed contribution;

(c) for enabling any person making such an objection to require the matter in dispute to be referred to the Lands Tribunal for determination; and

(d) where a contribution under this section is paid, for applying (with any necessary modifications) the provisions of Part VII of this Act at to the reduction or extinguishment of the unexpended balance of established development value of land, as if the contribution had been a payment of compensation under that Part of this Act.   **[197]**

NOTES
Commencement: 1 April 1972.

168. Recovery, on subsequent development, of compensation under s 164

(1) In relation to notices registered under the provisions of section 158 of this Act, as applied by the preceeding provisions of this Part of this Act, sections 159 and 160 of this Act shall have effect as they have effect in relation to compensation notices registered as therein mentioned:

Provided that, in a case where the compensation under section 164 of this Act specified in such a notice became payable in respect of an order modifying planning permission, the said sections shall not apply to development in accordance with that permission as modified by the order.

(2) Subject to subsection (3) of this section, any sum recovered by the Secretary of State under section 159 of this Act, as applied by subsection (1) of this section, shall be paid to the local planning authority who paid the compensation to which that sum relates.

(3) In paying any such sum to the local planning authority, the Secretary of State shall deduct therefrom—

(a) the amount of any contribution paid by him under section 167 of this Act in respect of the compensation to which the sum relates;

(b) the amount of any grant paid by him under Part XIII of this Act in respect of that compensation:

Provided that, if the sum recovered by the Secretary of State is an instalment of the total sum recoverable, or is recovered by reference to development of part of the land in respect of which the compensation was payable, any deduction to be made under paragraph (a) or paragraph (b) of this subsection shall be a deduction of such amount as the Secretary of State may determine to be the proper proportion of the amount referred to in that paragraph.

(4) For the purposes of sections 159 and 160 of this Act, in their application by virtue of this section to compensation calculated under section 164 of this Act, the expression "new development" shall include—

(a) any development of a class specified in paragraph 1 or 3 of Schedule 8 to this Act which is carried out otherwise than subject to the condition set out in Schedule 18 to this Act; and

(b) any development excluded by subsection (2) of section 278 of this Act from that Schedule in its application to any determination to which subsection (1) of the said section 278 applies.   **[198]**

NOTES
Commencement: 1 April 1972.

Other restrictions

169. Compensation for planning decisions restricting development other than new development

(1) The provisions of this section shall have effect where, on an application for planning permission to carry out development of any class specified in Part II of Schedule 8 to this Act, the Secretary of State, either on appeal or on the reference of the application to him for determination, refuses the permission or grants it subject to conditions.

(2) If, on a claim made to the local planning authority within the time and in the manner prescribed by regulations under this Act, it is shown that the value of the interest of any person in the land is less than it would have been if the permission had been granted, or had been granted unconditionally, as the case may be, the local planning authority shall pay to that person compensation of an amount equal to the difference.

(3) In determining, for the purposes of subsection (2) of this section, whether or to what extent the value of an interest in land is less than it would have been if the permission had been granted, or had been granted unconditionally—

    (a) it shall be assumed that any subsequent application for the like planning permission would be determined in the same way; but

    (b) if, in the case of a refusal of planning permission, the Secretary of State, on refusing that permission, undertook to grant planning permission for some other development of the land in the event of an application being made in that behalf, regard shall be had to that undertaking; and

    (c) no account shall be taken of any prospective use which would contravene the condition set out in Schedule 18 to this Act.

(4) Where, on such an application as is mentioned in subsection (1) of this section, planning permission is granted by the Secretary of State subject to conditions for regulating the design or external appearance of buildings, or the size or height of buildings, the Secretary of State, if it appears to him to be reasonable to do so having regard to the local circumstances, may direct that those conditions shall be disregarded, either altogether or to such extent as may be specified in the direction, in assessing the compensation (if any) payable under this section.

(5) Where, in the case of an application for planning permission to carry out any such development as is mentioned in subsection (1) of this section, a notice under section 72(1) of this Act is served in respect of the whole or part of the land to which the application relates, the preceding provisions of this section shall have effect as if the application had been an effective application for planning permission, and as if that permission had been refused, as mentioned in subsection (1) of this section, in respect of that land or that part thereof, as the case may be.

(6) For the purposes of subsection (1) of this section—

    (a) paragraph 3 of Schedule 8 to this Act shall be construed as not extending to works involving any increase in the cubic content of a building erected after the appointed day (including any building resulting from the carrying out of such works as are described in paragraph 1 of that Schedule); and (*b*) paragraph 7 of that Schedule shall not apply to any such building.

[(6A) For the purposes of subsection (1) of this section paragraph 3 of Schedule 8 to this Act shall be construed as not extending to the enlargement of a building which was in existence on the appointed day if—

    (*a*) the building contains two or more separate dwellings divided horizontally from each other or from some other part of the building; and

    (*b*) the enlargement would result in either an increase in the number of such dwellings contained in the building or an increase of more than one-tenth in the cubic content of any such dwelling contained in the building.]

(7) For the purposes of this section the conditions referred to in sections 41 and 42 of this Act shall be disregarded and no compensation shall be payable under this section in respect of the imposition of any condition to which section 71 or 82 of this Act applies.

(8) No compensation shall be payable under this section in respect of an interest in land in respect of which a purchase notice is served. **[199]**

NOTES
Commencement: 23 January 1985 (sub-s (6A)); 1 April 1972 (remainder).
  This section derived from the Town and Country Planning Act 1962, s 123, the Town and Country Planning Act 1963, s 1(2), the Control of Office and Industrial Development Act 1965, s 8(5), the Industrial Development Act 1966, s 24(4), and the Town and Country Planning Act 1968, s 67(7).
  Sub-s (5): repealed by the Housing and Planning Act 1986, s 49(2), Sch 12, Part III. See Appendix.
  Sub-s (6A): added by the Town and Country Planning (Compensation) Act 1985, s 1(2).
  Sub-s (7): repealed in part by the Housing and Planning Act 1986, s 49(2), Sch 12, Part III. See Appendix.

170. Compensation in respect of orders under s 51

(1) [Subject to section 170B of this Act, the] provisions of this section shall have effect where an order is made under section 51 of this Act, requiring a use of land to be discontinued, or imposing conditions on the continuance thereof, or requiring any buildings or works on land to be altered or removed.

(2) If, on a claim made to the local planning authority within the time and in the manner prescribed by regulations under this Act, it is shown that any person has suffered damage in consequence of the order by depreciation of the value of an interest [to which he is entitled in the land or in minerals in, on or under it, or by being disturbed in his enjoyment of the land or of minerals in, on or under it], that authority shall pay to that person compensation in respect of that damage.

(3) Without prejudice to subsection (2) of this section, any person who carries out any works in compliance with the order shall be entitled, on a claim made as mentioned in that subsection, to recover from the local planning authority compensation in respect of any expenses reasonably incurred by him in that behalf.

(4) Any compensation payable to a person under this section by virtue of such an order as is mentioned in subsection (1) of this section shall be reduced by the value to him of any timber, apparatus or other materials removed for the purpose of complying with the order. **[200]**

NOTES
Commencement: 1 April 1972.
  This section derived from the Town and Country Planning Act 1962, s 124.
  Sub-s (1): amended by the Town and Country Planning (Minerals) Act 1981, s 34, Sch 1.
  Sub-s (2): amended by the Town and Country Planning (Minerals) Act 1981, s 14.

170A. Compensation in respect of orders under s 51A and suspension orders

[Subject of section 170B of this Act, the provisions of section 170 of this Act shall apply where an order is made under section 51A of this Act or a suspension order or supplementary suspension order is made as they apply where an order is made under section 51 of this Act.]   **[201]**

NOTES
   Commencement: 19 May 1986.
   Commencement order: SI 1986 No 760.
   Added by the Town and Country Planning (Minerals) Act 1981, s 15.

170B. Compensation on special basis

[(1) Where mineral compensation requirements are satisfied in relation to an order under section 51 or 51A of this Act, or in relation to a suspension order or supplementary suspension order, section 170 or 170A of this Act shall have effect subject to mineral compensation modifications.

(2) Subject to subsection (6) of this section, mineral compensation requirements are satisfied in relation to an order under section 51 of this Act if—

   (*a*) the order—

      (i) imposes any conditions on the continuance of the use of land for the winning and working of minerals; or

      (ii) requires that any buildings or works or plant or machinery used for the winning and working of minerals shall be altered or removed; and

   (*b*) the conditions specified in subsection (5) of this section are satisfied.

(3) Subject to subsection (6) of this section, mineral compensation requirements are satisfied in relation to an order under section 51A of this Act if the conditions specified in subsection (5)(*a*) and (*c*) of this section are satisfied.

(4) Mineral compensation requirements are satisfied in relation to a suspension order or supplementary suspension order if the conditions specified in subsection (5)(*c*) of this section are satisfied.

(5) The conditions mentioned in subsections (2)(*b*), (3) and (4) of this section are—

   (*a*) that development consisting of the winning and working of minerals began not less than five years before the date of the order;

   (*b*) that the order does not—

      (i) impose any restriction on the winning and working of minerals; or

      (ii) modify or replace any such restriction subject to which planning permission for development consisting of the winning and working of minerals was granted or which was imposed by a relevant order; and

   (*c*) that the mineral planning authority carried out special consultations about the making and terms of the order before they made it.

(6) Where the mineral planning authority—

   (*a*) make—

     (i) an order under section 51 of this Act which imposes any such conditions or makes any such requirement as is mentioned in subsection (2)(*a*) of this section; or

     (ii) an order under section 51A of this Act; and

  (*b*) have previously made a relevant order or orders,

mineral compensation requirements are not satisfied in relation to the order mentioned in paragraph (*a*) of this subsection unless it was made more than five years after the order previously made or the last such order.] **[202]**

NOTES
    Commencement: 17 September 1982.
    Commencement order: SI 1982 No 1177
    Added by the Town and Country Planning (Minerals) Act 1981, s 15.

171. Compensation for refusal of consent to alteration, etc of listed building

(1) The provisions of this section shall have effect where an application is made for listed building consent for the alteration or extension of a listed building and—

  (*a*) either the works do not constitute development or they do so but the development is such that planning permission therefore is granted by a development order; and

  (*b*) the Secretary of State, either on appeal or on the reference of the application to him, refuses such consent or grants it subject to conditions.

(2) If, on a claim made to the local planning authority within the time and in the manner prescribed by regulations under this Act, it is shown that the value of the interest of any person in the land is less than it would have been if listed building consent had been granted, or had been granted unconditionally, as the case may be, the local planning authority shall pay to the person compensation of an amount equal to the difference.

(3) In determining, for the purposes of subsection (2) of this section, whether or to what extent the value of an interest in land is less than it would have been if the permission had been granted, or has been granted unconditionally—

  (*a*) it shall be assumed that any subsequent application for the like consent would be determined in the same way; but

  (*b*) if, in the case of a refusal of listed building consent, the Secretary of State, on refusing that consent, undertook to grant such consent for some other works to the building in the event of an application being made in that behalf, regard shall be had to that undertaking.

(4) No compensation shall be payable under this section in respect of an interest in land in respect of which a purchase notice is served, whether under section 180, 188 or 190 of this Act, being a purchase notice which takes effect.

[203]

NOTES
    Commencement: 1 April 1972.

172. Compensation where listed building consent revoked or modified

(1) Where listed building consent is revoked or modified by an order under paragraph 10 of Schedule 11 to this Act (other than an order which takes effect by virtue of paragraph 12 of that Schedule and without being confirmed by the Secretary of State), then if on a claim made to the local planning authority

within the time and in the manner prescribed by regulations under this Act, it is shown that a person interested in the building—

(*a*) has incurred expenditure in carrying out works which are rendered abortive by the revocation or modification; or

(*b*) has otherwise sustained loss or damage which is directly attributable to the revocation or modification,

the authority shall pay to that person compensation in respect of that expenditure, loss or damage.

(2) For the purposes of this section, any expenditure incurred in the preparation of plans for the purposes of any works, or upon other similar matters preparatory thereto, shall be taken to be included in the expenditure incurred in carrying out those works.

(3) Subject to subsection (2) of this section, no compensation shall be paid under this section in respect of any works carried out before the grant of the listed building consent which is revoked or modified, or in respect of any other loss or damage (not being loss or damage consisting of depreciation of the value of an interest in land) arising out of anything done or omitted to be done before the grant of that consent.　　　　　　　　　　　　　　　　　　　　　　　**[204]**

NOTES
　Commencement: 1 April 1972.

173. Compensation for loss or damage caused by service of building preservation notice

(1) The provisions of this section shall have effect as respects compensation where a building preservation notice is served.

(2) The local planning authority shall not be under any obligation to pay compensation under section 171 of this Act, in respect of any refusal of listed building consent or its grant subject to conditions, unless and until the building is included in a list compiled or approved by the Secretary of State under section 54 of this Act; but this subsection shall not prevent a claim for such compensation being made before the building is so included.

(3) If the building preservation notice ceases to have effect without the building having been included in a list so compiled or approved, then, subject to a claim in that behalf being made to the local planning authority within the time and in the manner prescribed by regulations under this Act, any person who at the time when the notice was served had an interest in the building shall be entitled to be paid compensation by the authority in respect of any loss or damage directly attributable to the effect of the notice.

(4) The loss or damage in respect of which compensation is payable under subsection (3) of this section shall include a sum payable in respect of a breach of contract caused by the necessity of discontinuing or countermanding any works to the building on account of the building preservation notice being in force with respect thereto.　　　　　　　　　　　　　　　　　　　　**[205]**

NOTES
　Commencement: 1 April 1972.

174. Compensation in respect of tree preservation orders

The matters for which provision may under section 60 of this Act be made by a tree preservation order include the payment by the local planning authority, subject to such exceptions and conditions as may be specified in the order, of compensation in respect of loss or damage caused or incurred in consequence of the refusal of any consent required under the order, or of the grant of any such consent subject to conditions. **[206]**

NOTES
Commencement: 1 April 1972.

175. Compensation in respect of requirement as to replanting of trees

(1) The provisions of this section shall have effect where, in pursuance of provision made by a tree preservation order, a direction is given, by the local planning authority or the Secretary of State, for securing the replanting of all or any part of a woodland area which is felled in the course of forestry operations permitted by or under the order.

(2) If the Forestry Commissioners decide not to make any advance under section 4 of the Forestry Act 1967 in respect of the replanting and come to that decision on the ground that the direction frustrates the use of the woodland area for the growing of timber or other forest products for commercial purposes and in accordance with the rules or practice of good forestry, the local planning authority exercising functions under the tree preservation order shall be liable, on the making of a claim in accordance with this section, to pay compensation in respect of such loss or damage, if any, as is caused or incurred in consequence of compliance with the direction.

(3) The Forestry Commissioners shall, at the request of the person under a duty to comply with the direction, give a certificate stating whether they have decided not to make any such advance and, if so, the grounds of their decision.

(4) A claim for compensation under this section must be served on the local planning authority within twelve months from the date on which the direction was given, or where an appeal has been made to the Secretary of State against the decision of the local planning authority, from the date of the decision of the Secretary of State on the appeal, but subject in either case to such extension of that period as the local planning authority may allow. **[207]**

NOTES
Commencement: 1 April 1972.

176. Compensation for restrictions on advertising

Where, for the purpose of complying with any regulations made under section 63 of this Act, works are carried out by any person—

(a) for removing an advertisement which was being displayed on 1st August 1948; or

(b) for discontinuing the use for the display of advertisements of a site used for that purpose on that date,

that person shall, on a claim made to the local planning authority within the time and in the manner prescribed by regulations under this Act, be entitled to recover from that authority compensation in respect of any expenses reasonably incurred by him in that behalf. **[208]**

NOTES
Commencement: 1 April 1972.

177. Compensation for loss due to stop notice

[(1) A person who, when a stop notice under section 90 of this Act is first served, has an interest in or occupies the land to which the stop notice relates shall, in any of the circumstances mentioned in subsection (2) of this section, be entitled to be compensated by the local planning authority in respect of any loss or damage directly attributable to the prohibition contained in the notice (or, in a case within paragraph (*b*) of that subsection, so much of that prohibition as cease to have effect).]

(2) A person shall be entitled to compensation under subsection (1) of this section in respect of a prohibition contained in a stop notice in any of the following circumstances:—

[(*a*) the enforcement notice is quashed on grounds other than those mentioned in paragraph (*a*) of section [88(2)] of this Act;
(*b*) the enforcement notice is varied, otherwise than on the grounds mentioned in that paragraph, so that the matters alleged to constitute a breach of planning control cease to include one or more of the activities prohibited by the stop notice;]
(*c*) the enforcement notice is withdrawn by the local planning authority otherwise than in consequence of the grant by them of planning permission for the development to which the notice relates or for its retention or continuance without compliance with a condition or limitation subject to which a previous planning permission was granted;
(*d*) the stop notice is withdrawn.

(3) . . .

(4) A claim for compensation under this section shall be made to the local planning authority within the time and in the manner prescribed by regulations under this Act.

(5) The loss or damage in respect of which compensation is payable under this section in respect of a prohibition shall include a sum payable in respect of a breach of contract caused by the taking of action necessary to comply with the prohibition . . . .

[(6) In the assessment of compensation under this section, account shall be taken of the extent (if any) to which the claimant's entitlement is attributable to his failure to comply with a notice under section 284 of this Act or to any mis-statement made by him in response to such a notice.]   **[209]**

NOTES
Commencement: 1 April 1972.
Amended by the Town and Country Planning (Amendment) Act 1977, s 2; further amended by the Local Government (Miscellaneous Provisions) Act 1982, s 47, Sch 6, para 7.

Supplementary provisions

178. General provisions as to compensation for depreciation under Part VIII

(1) For the purpose of assessing any compensation to which this section applies, the rules set out in section 5 of the Land Compensation Act 1961 shall, so far as applicable and subject to any necessary modifications, have effect as they have effect for the purpose of assessing compensation for the compulsory acquisition of an interest in land.

(2) [Subject to regulations under section 178A of this Act, this] section

applies to any compensation which, under the preceding provisions of this Part of this Act other than section 174, 175 or 177 is payable in respect of depreciation of the value of an interest in land.

(3) Where an interest in land is subject to a mortgage—

(*a*) any compensation to which this section applies, which is payable in respect of depreciation of the value of that interest, shall be assessed as if the interest were not subject to the mortgage;

(*b*) a claim for any such compensation may be made by any mortgagee of the interest, but without prejudice to the making of a claim by the person entitled to the interest;

(*c*) no compensation to which this section applies shall be payable in respect of the interest of the mortgagee (as distinct from the interest which is subject to the mortgage); and

(*d*) any compensation to which this section applies which is payable in respect of the interest which is subject to the mortgage shall be paid to the mortgagee, or, if there is more than one mortgagee, to the first mortgagee, and shall in either case be applied by him as if it were proceeds of sale.   **[210]**

NOTES

Commencement: 1 April 1972.

This section derived from the Town and Country Planning Act 1962, s 127.

Sub-s (2): words in square brackets substituted by the Town and Country Planning (Minerals) Act 1981, s 34, Sch 1.

Applied by SI 1986 No 225.

178A. Regulations as to compensation in respect of orders relating to mineral working— meaning of "mineral compensation modifications"

[(1) The Secretary of State may by regulations made with the consent of the Treasury direct that sections 164, 170, 178, 237 and 238 of this Act shall have effect, where mineral compensation requirements are satisfied, subject, in such cases as may be specified in the regulations, to such modifications as may be so specified.

(2) Any such regulations shall make provision as to circumstances in which compensation is not to be payable.

(3) Any such regulations shall make provision—

(*a*) for the modification of the basis on which any amount to be paid by way of compensation is to be assessed; or

(*b*) for the assessment of any such amount on a basis different from that on which it would otherwise have been assessed.

(4) Regulations made by virtue of subsection (3)(*a*) of this section in relation to compensation where an order is made under section 45 or 51 of this Act shall provide that the amount of the compensation under section 164 or, as the case may be, 170 of this Act, shall be reduced—

(*a*) by the prescribed sum; or

(*b*) by a sum equal to the prescribed percentage of the appropriate sum.

(5) In subsection (4) of this section "the appropriate sum" means the product of the sum which represents the annual value of the right to win and work minerals at the site to which the order relates and a multiplier which the Secretary of State considers appropriate having regard to the period at the expiration of which the minerals in, on or under that site might be expected to

be exhausted if they continued to be extracted at the rate which has been assumed for the purpose of calculating the annual value of the right to win and work them.

(6) The prescribed percentage shall not be more than 10 per cent.

(7) The annual value of the right to win and work the minerals shall be calculated in the prescribed manner.

(8) In this Act "mineral compensation modifications" means modifications specified in regulations made by virtue of this section.

(9) Regulations under this section—

(a) may make different provision for different cases; and
(b) may include such incidental or supplementary provisions as the Secretary of State considers expedient.

(10) No regulations under this section shall have effect until approved by resolution of each House of Parliament.

(11) Before making any such regulations the Secretary of State shall consult such persons or bodies of persons as appear to him to be representative—

(a) of persons carrying out mining operations;
(b) of owners of interests in land containing minerals; and
(c) of mineral planning authorities.]   **[211]**

NOTES
Commencement: 17 September 1982.
Commencement order: SI 1982 No 1177.
Added by the Town and Country Planning (Minerals) Act 1981, s 16.

178B. Orders relating to mineral working— meaning of "special consultations"

[(1) Any reference in this Act to a mineral planning authority carrying out special consultations about the making and terms of an order before they make it is a reference to their carrying out consultations—

(a) subject to subsection (2) of this section, with any person who has an interest—

(i) in the land to which the order will relate; or
(ii) in minerals in, on or under that land; and

(b) with the relevant authority.

(2) The duty to consult imposed by subsection (1)(a) of this section is only a duty to consult persons whom the mineral planning authority are able to trace by taking reasonable steps to do so.

(3) In subsection (1)(b) above "the relevant authority" means—

(a) if the land to which the order will relate is outside Greater London, the district council in whose area it is situated; and
(b) if it is in Greater London—

(i) where the order is to be made by a London borough council, the Greater London Council; and
(ii) where it is to be made by the Greater London Council, the London borough council in whose area the land is situated.][212]

NOTES
Commencement: 17 September 1982.
Commencement order: SI 1982 No 1177.

Added by the Town and Country Planning (Minerals) Act 1981, s 16.

178C. Orders relating to mineral working — meaning of "restriction on the winning and working of minerals" and "relevant order"

[(1) In this Act "restriction on the winning and working of minerals" means—

    (*a*) in relation to planning permission granted for development consisting of the winning and working of minerals, a condition subject to which the permission was granted and which made provision to which this section applies; and

    (*b*) in relation to an order under section 45 or 51 of this Act, a term of the order which made such provision.

  (2) This section applies to—

    (*a*) any provision—

      (i) for the period before the expiration of which developement consisting of the winning and working of minerals was to be begun;

      (ii) for the size of the area to be used for the winning and working of minerals;

      (iii) for the depth to which operations for the winning and working of minerals were to extend;

      (iv) for the rate at which any particular mineral was to be extracted; or

      (v) for the period at the expiration of which the winning and working of minerals was to cease; and

    (*b*) any provision whose effect is in any way to restrict the total quantity of minerals to be extracted.

  (3) In this Act "relevant order", in relation to any land, means an order under section 45, 51 or 51A of this Act.] **[213]**

NOTES
    Commencement: 17 September 1982.
    Commencement order: SI 1982 No 1177.
    Added by the Town and Country Planning (Minerals) Act 1981, s 16.

179. Determination of claims for compensation

(1) Except in so far as may be otherwise provided by any tree preservation order or by any regulations made under this Act, any question of disputed compensation under this Part of this Act [including any question of disputed compensation under section 164, 170, 178, 237 or 238 of this Act as modified by regulations under section 178A of this Act] shall be referred to and determined by the Lands Tribunal.

  (2) In relation to the determination of any such question, the provisions of sections 2 and 4 of the Land Compensation Act 1961 shall apply, subject to any necessary modifications and to the provisions of any regulations made under this Act. **[214]**

NOTES
    Commencement: 1 April 1972.
    This section derived from the Town and Country Planning Act 1962, s 128 and the Countryside Act 1968, s 25(5).
    Sub-s (1): amended by the Town and Country Planning (Minerals) Act 1981, s 17.

PART IX

PROVISIONS ENABLING OWNER TO REQUIRE PURCHASE OF HIS INTEREST

Interests affected by planning decisions or orders

180. Purchase notice on refusal or conditional grant of planning permission

(1) Where, on an application for planning permission to develop any land, permission is refused or is granted subject to conditions, then if any owner of the land claims—

(*a*) that the land has become incapable or reasonably beneficial use in its existing state; and

(*b*) in a case where planning permission was granted subject to conditions, that the land cannot be rendered capable of reasonably beneficial use by the carrying out of the permitted development in accordance with those conditions; and

(*c*) in any case, that the land cannot be rendered capable of reasonably beneficial use by the carrying out of any other development for which planning permission has been granted or for which the local planning authority or the Secretary of State has undertaken to grant planning permission,

he may, within the time and in the manner prescribed by regulations under this Act, serve on the council of the . . . , London borough or county district in which the land is situated a notice requiring that council to purchase his interest in the land in accordance with the following provisions of this Part of this Act.

(2) Where, for the purpose of determining whether the conditions specified in subsection (1)(*a*) to (*c*) of this section are fulfilled in relation to any land, any question arises as to what is or would in any particular circumstances be a reasonably beneficial use of that land, then, in determining that question for that purpose, no account shall be taken of any prospective use of that land which would involve the carrying out of new development or which would contravene the condition set out in Schedule 18 to this Act.

(3) In the application of Schedule 8 to this Act for the purposes of any determination under subsection (2) of this section—

(*a*) paragraph 3 of that Schedule shall be construed as not extending to works involving any increase in the cubic content of a building erected after the appointed day (including any building resulting from the carrying out of such works as are described in paragraph 1 of that Schedule); and

(*b*) paragraph 7 of that Schedule shall not apply to any such building.

(4) For the purposes of this section the conditions referred to in sections 41 and 42 of this Act shall be disregarded, and no account shall be taken of any condition to which section 71 or 82 of this Act applies.

(5) A person on whom there has been served a repairs notice under section 115 of this Act shall not in any case be entitled to serve a purchase notice under this section in respect of the building in question until the expiration of three months beginning with the date of the service of the repairs notice; and if during that period the council or the Secretary of State start the compulsory acquisition of the building in the exercise of their powers under section 114 of this Act, that person shall not be so entitled unless and until the compulsory acquisition is discontinued.

(6) For the purposes of subsection (5) of this section a compulsory acquisition—

  (a) is started when the council or the Secretary of State, as the case may be, serve the notice required by paragraph 3(1)(b) of Schedule 1 to the Acquisition of Land (Authorisation Procedure) Act 1946; and

  (b) is discontinued, in the case of acquisition by a council, when they withdraw the compulsory purchase order or the Secretary of State decides not to confirm it and, in the case of acquisition by the Secretary of State, when he decides not to make the compulsory purchase order.

(7) A notice under this section, or under any other provision of this Part of this Act to which this subsection is applied, is in this Act referred to as a "purchase notice". **[215]**

NOTES
Commencement: 1 April 1972.
Words omitted repealed by the Local Government Act 1972, s 272, Sch 30.
Sub-s (4): repealed in part by the Housing and Planning Act 1986, s 49(2), Sch 12, Part III. See Appendix.

181. Action by council on whom purchase notice is served

(1) The council on whom a purchase notice is served under section 180 of this Act shall, before the end of the period of three months beginning with the date of service of that notice, serve on the owner by whom the purchase notice was served a notice stating either—

  (a) that the council are willing to comply with the purchase notice; or

  (b) that another local authority or statutory undertakers specified in the notice under this subsection have agreed to comply with it in their place; or

  (c) that, for reasons specified in the notice under this subsection, the council are not willing to comply with the purchase notice and have not found any other local authority or statutory undertakers who will agree to comply with it in their place, and that they have transmitted a copy of the purchase notice to the Secretary of State, on a date specified in the notice under this subsection, together with a statement of the reasons so specified.

(2) Where the council on whom a purchase notice is served by an owner have served on him a notice in accordance with subsection (1)(a) or (b) of this section, the council, or the other local authority or statutory undertakers specified in the notice, as the case may be, shall be deemed to be authorised to acquire the interest of the owner compulsorily in accordance with the relevant provisions, and to have served a notice to treat in respect thereof on the date of service of the notice under that subsection.

(3) Where the council on whom a purchase notice is served by an owner propose to serve on him a notice in accordance with subsection (1)(c) of this section, they shall transmit a copy of the purchase notice to the Secretary of State, together with a statement of their reasons.

(4) In this section "the relevant provisions" means the provisions of Part VI of this Act or, in the case of statutory undertakers, any statutory provision (however expressed) under which they have power, or may be authorised, to purchase land compulsorily for the purposes of their undertaking. **[216]**

NOTES
Commencement: 1 April 1972.
Sub-s (1): amended by the Housing and Planning Act 1986, s 49(1), Sch 11, Part I, para 5(1)(a). See Appendix.
Sub-s (3): amended by the Housing and Planning Act 1986, s 49(1), Sch 11, Part I, para 5(1)(b). See Appendix.

182. Procedure on reference of purchase notice to Secretary of State

(1) Where a copy of a purchase notice is transmitted to the Secretary of State under section 181(3) of this Act, the Secretary of State shall consider whether to confirm the notice or to take other action under section 183 of this Act in respect thereof.

(2) Before confirming a purchase notice or taking any other action under section 183 of this Act in respect thereof, the Secretary of State shall give notice of his proposed action—

> (*a*) to the person by whom the purchase notice was served;
> (*b*) to the council on whom the purchase notice was served;
> (*c*) to the local planning authority for the area in which the land is situated; and
> (*d*) if the Secretary of State proposes to substitute any other local authority or statutory undertakers for the council on whom the purchase notice was served, to that other local authority or those statutory undertakers.

(3) If, within such period as may be specified in a notice under subsection (2) of this section, being a period of not less than twenty-eight days from the service of that notice, any of the persons, authorities or statutory undertakers on whom that notice is served so requires, the Secretary of State, before confirming the purchase notice or taking any other action under section 183 of this Act in respect thereof, shall afford to those persons, authorities and undertakers an opportunity of appearing before, and being heard by, a person appointed by the Secretary of State for the purpose.

(4) Where the Secretary of State has given notice under subsection (2) of this section of his proposed action, and any of the persons, authorities and statutory undertakers concerned have appeared before and been heard by a person appointed by the Secretary of State for the purpose, and it then appears to the Secretary of State to be expedient to take action under section 183 of this Act otherwise than in accordance with the notice given by him, the Secretary of State may take that action accordingly.   **[217]**

NOTES
Commencement: 1 April 1972.

183. Action by Secretary of State in relation to purchase notice

(1) Subject to the following provisions of this section and to section 184 of this Act, if the Secretary of State is satisfied that the conditions specified in section 180(1)(*a*) to (*c*) of this Act are fulfilled in relation to a purchase notice, he shall confirm the notice.

(2) If it appears to the Secretary of State to be expedient to do so, he may, in lieu of confirming the purchase notice, grant planning permission for the development in respect of which the application was made, or, where planning permission for that development was granted subject to conditions, revoke or amend those conditions so far as appears to him to be required in order to enable the land to be rendered capable of reasonably beneficial use by the carrying out of that development.

(3) If it appears to the Secretary of State that the land, or any part of the land, could be rendered capable of reasonably beneficial use within a reasonable time by the carrying out of any other development for which planning permission ought to be granted, he may, in lieu of confirming the purchase notice, or in lieu of confirming it so far as it relates to that part of the land, as the case may be,

direct that planning permission for that development shall be granted in the event of an application being made in that behalf.

(4) If it appears to the Secretary of State, having regard to the probable ultimate use of the land, that it is expedient to do so, he may, if he confirms the notice, modify it, either in relation to the whole or in relation to any part of the land to which it relates, by substituting another local authority or statutory undertakers for the council on whom the notice was served.

(5) In section 182 of this Act, any reference to the taking of action by the Secretary of State under this section is a reference to the taking by him of any such action as is mentioned in subsections (1) to (4) of this section, or to the taking by him of a decision not to confirm the purchase notice either on the grounds that any of the conditions referred to in subsection (1) of this section are not fulfilled or by virtue of section 184 of this Act.   **[218]**

NOTES
Commencement: 1 April 1972.

184. Power to refuse to confirm purchase notice where land has restricted use by virtue of previous planning permission

(1) This section shall have effect where, on an application for planning permission to develop any land which has a restricted use by virtue of a previous planning permission, permission is refused or granted subject to conditions and an owner of the land serves a purchase notice under section 180 of this Act.

(2) For the purposes of this section, land is to be treated as having a restricted use by virtue of a previous planning permission if it is part of a larger area in respect of which planning permission was previously granted (and has not been revoked) and either—

(*a*) it remains a condition of the planning permission (however expressed) that that part shall remain undeveloped or be preserved or laid out in a particular way as amenity land in relation to the remainder; or

(*b*) the planning permission was granted on an application which contemplated (expressly or by necessary implication) that the part should not be comprised in the development for which planning permission was sought, or should be preserved or laid out as aforesaid.

(3) If a copy of the purchase notice is transmitted to the Secretary of State under section 181(3) of this Act the Secretary of State, although satisfied that the land has become incapable of reasonably beneficial use in its existing state, shall nevertheless not be required under section 183(1) of this Act to confirm the notice if it appears to him that the land ought, in accordance with the previous planning permission, to remain undeveloped or, as the case may be, remain or be preserved or laid out as amenity land in relation to the remainder of the large area for which that planning permission was granted.   **[219]**

NOTES
Commencement: 1 April 1972.
Sub-s (1): amended by the Housing and Planning Act 1986, s 49(1), Sch 11, Part I, para 6(*a*). See Appendix.
Sub-s (3): amended by the Housing and Planning Act 1986, s 49(1), Sch 11, Part I, para 6(*b*). See Appendix.

185. Power to refuse to confirm purchase notice in respect of office premises

(1) This section applies to any purchase notice served on or after 5th November 1964 (whether before or after the passing of this Act) in respect of land within the metropolitan region, or served on or after 5th August 1965 (whether before or after the passing of this Act) in respect of land which, at the date of service

of the notice, is within a controlled area as defined in section 81(2) of this Act outside the metropolitan region, where either—

(a) planning permission for the carrying out on that land, or part of it, of development to which section 74 of this Act applies was granted before 5th August 1965, but by virtue of paragraph 1(4) of Schedule 12 to this Act that planning permission is for the time being deemed not to have effect; or

(b) the purpose for which that land, or part of it, is or was used at the date of service of the notice, or was last used before that date, is or was that of a building containing office premises.

(2) In relation to a purchase notice to which this section applies, the provisions of this Act shall have effect as if, after subsection (4) of section 183 of this Act, there were inserted the following subsection—

"(4A) Where the purchase notice is one to which section 185 of this Act applies, the Secretary of State may, if he thinks fit, determine not to confirm the notice without taking any such action as is mentioned in subsections (2) to (4) of this section",

and as if, in subsection (5) of that section, after the words "by virtue of" there were inserted the words "subsection (4A) of this section or".

(3) Where in pursuance of subsection (4A) of the said section 183 (as modified by subsection (2) of this section) the Secretary of State has determined not to confirm a purchase noticed to which this section applies, and on a subsequent date the land to which that notice related ceases to be within an area to which section 74 of this Act applies—

(a) a further purchase notice may be served on or after that date in respect of the planning decision to which the previous notice related; and

(b) for the purposes of any regulations made under this Act as to the time within which a purchase notice may be served, the service of such a further purchase notice shall not be treated as out of time if it is served within the period which would be applicable in accordance with those regulations if the planning decision referred to in the preceding paragraph had been made on that subsequent date.

(4) In determining, for the purposes of subsection (1)(b) of this section, for what purpose any land is used, or was last used, as the case may be, no account shall be taken—

(a) of any use in accordance with planning permission granted for a limited period; or

(b) of any use in respect of which, before the date of service of the purchase notice, an enforcement notice had been served and had become effective; or

(c) of any use of land at a time when it is or was not covered by a building.

(5) For the purposes of this section "office premises" has the meaning assigned by section 73(4) of this Act and this section shall have effect as if it were included in sections 73 to 86 of this Act.

(6) Notwithstanding subsection (5) of this section, subsection (3) of this section shall not cease to have effect at the end of the period mentioned in section 86 of this Act; and in relation to any land which, immediately before the end of that period, is land within an area to which section 74 of this Act

applies, any reference in that subsection to the date on which the land ceases to be within such an area shall be construed as a reference to the end of that period. **[220]**

NOTES
Commencement: 1 April 1972.
Repealed by the Housing and Planning Act 1986, s 49(2), Sch 12, Part III. See Appendix.

186. Effect of Secretary of State's action in relation to purchase notice

(1) Where the Secretary of State confirms a purchase notice, the council on whom the purchase notice was served (or, if under section 183(4) of this Act the Secretary of State modified the purchase notice by substituting another local authority or statutory undertakers for that council, that other local authority or those statutory undertakers) shall be deemed to be authorised to acquire the interest of the owner compulsorily in accordance with the relevant provisions and to have served a notice to treat in respect thereof on such date as the Secretary of State may direct.

(2) If, before the end of the relevant period, the Secretary of State has neither confirmed the purchase notice nor taken any such action in respect thereof as is mentioned in section 183(2) or (3) of this Act, and has not notified the owner by whom the notice was served that he does not propose to confirm the notice, the notice shall be deemed to be confirmed at the end of that period, and the council on whom the notice was served shall be deemed to be authorised to acquire the interest of the owner compulsorily in accordance with the relevant provisions and to have served a notice to treat in respect thereof at the end of that period.

(3) For the purposes of subsection (2) of this section the relevant period is whichever of the following periods first expires, that is to say—

    (*a*) the period of nine months beginning with the date of service of the purchase notice; and

    (*b*) the period of six months beginning with the date on which a copy of the purchase notice was transmitted to the Secretary of State.

(4) Where the Secretary of State has notified the owner by whom a purchase notice has been served of a decision on his part to confirm, or not to confirm, the notice (including any decision not to confirm the notice in respect of part of the land to which it relates, and including any decision to grant any permission, or give any direction, in lieu of confirming the notice, either wholly or in part) and that decision of the Secretary of State is quashed under the provisions of Part XII of this Act, the purchase notice shall be treated as cancelled, but the owner may serve a further purchase notice in its place.

(5) For the purposes of any regulations made under this Act as to the time within which a purchase notice may be served, the service of a purchase notice under subsection (4) of this section shall not be treated as out of time if the notice is served within the period which would be applicable in accordance with those regulations if the planning decision, in consequence of which the notice is served, had been made on the date on which the decision of the Secretary of State was quashed as mentioned in subsection (4) of this section.

(6) In this section "the relevant provisions" has the same meaning as in section 181 of this Act. **[221]**

NOTES
Commencement: 1 April 1972.
Sub-s (3): amended by the Housing and Planning Act 1986, s 49(1), Sch 11, Part I, para 7(1). See Appendix.
New sub-s (3A) inserted by the Housing and Planning Act 1986, s 49(1), Sch 11, Part I, para 7(1). See Appendix.

187. Special provisions as to compensation where purchase notice served

(1) Where by virtue of section 164 of this Act compensation is payable in respect of expenditure incurred in carrying out any work on land, then, if a purchase notice is served in respect of an interest in that land, any compensation payable in respect of the acquisition of that interest in pursuance of the purchase notice shall be reduced by an amount equal to the value of the works in respect of which compensation is payable by virtue of that section.

(2) Where a purchase notice served in respect of an interest in land does not take effect, or does not take effect in relation to a part of the land, by reason that the Secretary of State gives a direction under section 183(3) of this Act, then if, on a claim made to the local planning authority within the time and in the manner prescribed by regulations under this Act it is shown that the permitted development value of that interest (or, as the case may be, of that interest so far as it relates to that part of the land) is less than its existing use value, the local planning authority shall pay to the person entitled to that interest compensation of an amount which (subject to the following provisions of this section) shall be equal to the difference.

(3) If the planning permission which, by the direction referred to in subsection (2) of this section, is required to be granted would be granted subject to conditions for regulating the design or external appearance of buildings, or the size of height of buildings, or for regulating the number of buildings to be erected on the land, the Secretary of State, if it appears to him to be reasonable to do so having regard to the local circumstances, may direct that those conditions shall be disregarded, either altogether or to such extent as may be specified in the direction, in assessing any compensation payable under subsection (2) of this section.

(4) Sections 178 and 179 of this Act shall have effect in relation to compensation under subsection (2) of this section as they have effect in relation to compensation to which those sections apply.

(5) In this section "permitted development value", in relation to an interest in land in respect of which a direction is given under section 183(3) of this Act, means the value of that interest calculated with regard to that direction, but on the assumption that no planning permission would be granted otherwise than in accordance with that direction, and "existing use value", in relation to such an interest, means the value of that interest as (for the purpose of ascertaining the compensation payable on an acquisition thereof in pursuance of the purchase notice) that value would have been assessed in accordance with the provisions of the Acquisition of Land (Assessment of Compensation) Act 1919, as modified by the provisions of sections 51 to 54 of the Act of 1947, if no enactment repealing, modifying or superseding any of those provisions had been passed after the passing of the Act of 1947.   **[222]**

NOTES
Commencement: 1 April 1972.
Act of 1947: Town and Country Planning Act 1947.

188. Purchase notice in respect of order revoking or modifying planning permission

(1) Where by an order under section 45 of this Act planning permission in respect of any land is revoked, or is modified by the imposition of conditions, then if any owner of the land claims—

    (*a*) that the land has become incapable of reasonably beneficial use in its existing state; and

    (*b*) in a case where the planning permission was modified by the imposition of conditions, that the land cannot be rendered capable of reasonably beneficial use by the carrying out of the permitted development in accordance with those conditions; and

    (*c*) in any case, that the land cannot be rendered capable of reasonably beneficial use by the carrying out of any other developmemt for which planning permission has been granted or for which the local planning authority or the Secretary of State has undertaken to grant planning permission,

he may, within the time and in the manner prescribed by regulations under this Act, serve on the council of the . . . , London borough or county district in which the land is situated a notice requiring that council to purchase his interest in the land in accordance with the preceding provisions of this Part of this Act.

(2) Section 180(7) of this Act shall apply to this section; and, subject to subsection (3) of this section, sections 180(2), 181 to 184, 186 and 187 of this Act shall apply to a notice served by virtue of subsection (1) of this section as they apply to a notice served by virtue of section 180(1) of this Act.

(3) In the application of subsection (2) of section 180 of this Act to a purchase notice served by virtue of subsection (1) of this section, that subsection shall apply as if the words "or which would contravene the condition set out in Schedule 18 to this Act" were omitted; and in the application of section 183 of this Act to a purchase notice served as aforesaid, that section shall apply as if the following subsection were substituted for subsection (2) thereof—

"(2) If it appears to the Secretary of State to be expedient to do so, he may, in lieu of confirming the purchase notice, cancel the order revoking the planning permission, or, where the order modified the permission by the imposition of conditions, revoke or amend those conditions so far as appears to him to be required in order to enable the land to be rendered capable of reasonably beneficial use by the carrying out of the development in respect of which the permission was granted".   **[223]**

NOTES
    Commencement: 1 April 1972.
    Words omitted repealed by the Local Government Act 1972, s 272, Sch 30.

189. Purchase notice in respect of order requiring discontinuance of use or alteration or removal of buildings or works

(1) If any person entitled to an interest in land in respect of which an order is made under section 51 of this Act claims—

    (*a*) that by reason of the order the land is incapable of reasonably beneficial use in its existing state; and

    (*b*) that it cannot be rendered capable of reasonably beneficial use by the carrying out of any development for which planning permission has been granted, whether by that order or otherwise,

he may, within the time and in the manner prescribed by regulations under this Act, serve on the council of the . . . , London borough or county district in which the land is situated a notice requiring that council to purchase his interest in the land in accordance with the preceding provisions of this Part of this Act.

(2) Section 180(7) of this Act shall apply to this section; and, subject to

subsection (3) of this section, sections 180(2), 181 to 184, 186 and 187 of this Act shall apply to a notice served by virtue of subsection (1) of this section as they apply to a notice served by virtue of section 180(1) of this Act.

(3) In the application of subsection (2) of section 180 of this Act to a purchase notice served by virtue of subsection (1) of this section, that subsection shall apply as if the words "or which would contravene the condition set out in Schedule 18 to this Act" were omitted; and in the application of section 183 of this Act to a purchase notice served as aforesaid, that section shall have effect subject to the following modifications, that is to say—

(a) in subsection (1), for the reference to the conditions therein mentioned, there shall be substituted a reference to the conditions specified in subsection (1)(a) and (b) of this section; and

(b) the following subsection shall be substituted for subsection (2)—

"(2) If it appears to the Secretary of State to be expedient to do so, he may, in lieu of confirming the purchase notice, revoke the order under section 51 of this Act, or, as the case may be, amend that order so far as appears to him to be required in order to prevent the land from being rendered incapable of reasonably beneficial use by the order".

(4) Where a purchase notice in respect of an interest in land is served in consequence of such an order as is mentioned in subsection (1) of this section, then if—

(a) that interest is acquired in accordance with the preceding provisions of this Part of this Act; or

(b) compensation is payable in respect of that interest under section 187(2) of this Act,

no compensation shall be payable in respect of that order under section 170 of this Act.

(5) Except as provided by this section, no purchase notice shall be served in respect of an interest in land while the land is incapable of reasonably beneficial use by reason only of such an order as is mentioned in subsection (1) of this section. **[224]**

NOTES
Commencement: 1 April 1972.
Words omitted repealed by the Local Government Act 1972, s 272, Sch 30.

190. Purchase notice on refusal or conditional grant of listed building consent

(1) Where, on an application for listed building consent in respect of a building, consent is refused or is granted subject to conditions or, by an order under Part II of Schedule 11 to this Act, listed building consent is revoked or modified, then if any owner of the land claims—

(a) that the land has become incapable of reasonably beneficial use in its existing state; and

(b) in a case where consent was granted subject to conditions with respect to the execution of the works or, as the case may be, was modified by the imposition of such conditions, that the land cannot be rendered capable of reasonably beneficial use by the carrying out of the works in accordance with those conditions; and

(c) in any case that the land cannot be rendered capable of reasonably beneficial use by the carrying out of any other works for which listed building consent has been granted or for which the local planning authority or the Secretary of State has undertaken to grant such consent,

he may, within the time and in the manner prescribed by regulations under this Act, serve on the council of the . . . , London borough or county district in which the land is situated a notice requiring that council to purchase his interest in the land in accordance with Schedule 19 to this Act.

(2) Where, for the purpose of determining whether the conditions specified in subsection (1)(*a*) to (*c*) of this section are satisfied in relation to the land, any question arises as to what is or would in any particular circumstances be a reasonably beneficial use of that land, then in determining that question for that purpose, no account shall be taken of any prospective use of that land which would involve the carrying out of new development or of any works requiring listed building consent which might be executed to the building, other than works for which the local planning authority or the Secretary of State have undertaken to grant such consent.

(3) In this section and in Schedule 19 to this Act, "the land" means the building in respect of which listed building consent has been refused, or granted subject to conditions, or modified by the imposition of conditions, and in respect of which its owner serves a notice under this section, together with any land comprising the building, or contiguous or adjacent to it, and owned with it, being land as to which the owner claims that its use is substantially inseparable from that of the building and that it ought to be treated, together with the building, as a single holding.

(4) Subsections (5) and (6) of section 180 of this Act shall apply to a listed building purchase notice as they apply to a purchase notice under that section.

(5) A notice under this section is in this Act referred to as a "listed building purchase notice". **[225]**

NOTES
Commencement: 1 April 1972.
Words omitted repealed by the Statute Law (Repeals) Act 1975.

191. Purchase notices in other cases

(1) Sections 180 to 183, 186 and 187 of this Act are provisions falling within subsection (2) of section 60 of this Act; and subsection (1) of the said section 60 and subsection (2) of section 63 of this Act, shall have effect accordingly.

(2) Where, in the case of an application for planning permission, a notice under section 72(1) of this Act is served in respect of the whole or part of the land to which the application relates, the provisions of sections 180 to 183, 186 and 187 of this Act shall have effect as if the application had been an effective application for planning permission, and as if that permission had been refused in respect of that land or that part thereof, as the case may be. **[226]**

NOTES
Commencement: 1 April 1972.
Sub-s (2): repealed by the Housing and Planning Act 1986, s 49(2), Sch 12, Part III. See Appendix.

191A. Public telecommunications operators

[In the preceding provisions of this Part of this Act and in Schedule 19 to this Act the references to statutory undertakers shall be deemed to include references to a public telecommunications operator.] **[227]**

NOTES
Commencement: 5 August 1984.
Commencement order: SI 1984 No 876.
Added by the Telecommunications Act 1984, s 109, Sch 4, para 53.

Interests of owner-occupiers affected by planning proposals

192. Scope of these provisions

(1) The provisions of sections 193 to 207 of this Act shall have effect in relation to land which—

(a) is land indicated in a structure plan in force for the district in which it is situated either as land which may be required for the purposes of any [of the functions, that is to say, those of a government department, local authority or statutory undertakers, or of the National Coal Board or the establishment or running by a public telecommunications operator of a telecommunication system], or as land which may be included in an action area; or

(b) is land allocated for the purposes of any such functions by a local plan in force for the district or is land defined in such a plan as the site of proposed development for the purposes of any such functions; or

[(bb) is land indicated in a unitary development plan in force for the district in which it is situated either as land which may be required for the purpose of any such functions or as land which may be included in an action area; or

(bc) is land which by a unitary development plan is allocated for the purposes, or defined as the site, of proposed development for any such functions;]

(c) is land indicated in a development plan (otherwise than by being dealt with in a manner mentioned in the preceding paragraphs) as land on which a highway is proposed to be constructed or land to be included in a highway as proposed to be improved or altered; or

(d) is land on or adjacent to the line of a highway proposed to be constructed, improved or altered, as indicated in an order or scheme which has come into operation under the provisions of Part II of [the Highways Act 1980 relating to trunk roads, special roads or classified roads (or under the corresponding provisions of Part II of the Highways Act 1959 or section 1 of the Highways Act 1971) being land in relation to which a power of compulsory acquisition conferred by any of the provisions of Part XII of the said Act of 1980 (including a power compulsorily to acquire any right by virtue of section 250)] may become exercisable, as being land required for purposes of construction, improvement or alteration as indicated in the order or scheme; or

(e) is land shown on plans approved by a resolution of a local highway authority as land comprised in the site of a highway as proposed to be constructed, improved or altered by that authority; or

(f) is land on which the Secretary of State proposes to provide a trunk road or a special road and has given to the local planning authority written notice of his intention to provide the road, together with maps or plans sufficient to identify the proposed route of the road; or

(g) is land in the case of which—

(i) there is in force a compulsory purchase order [providing] for the acquisition of a right or rights over that land;

and

(ii) the [appropriate authority] have power to serve, but have not served, notice to treat in respect of the right or rights;

(*h*) is land indicated by information published in pursuance of [section 257 of the Housing Act 1985 as land which a local authority propose to acquire in the exercise of their powers under the provisions of Part VIII of that Act relating to general improvement areas]

(*i*) is land authorised by a special enactment to be compulsorily acquired, or land falling within the limits of deviation within which powers of compulsory acquisition conferred by a special enactment are exercisable; or

(*j*) is land in respect of which a compulsory purchase order is in force, where the appropriate authority have power to serve, but have not served, notice to treat in respect of the land.

(2) Paragraph (*a*) of subsection (1) of this section shall not apply to land situated in a district for which a local plan is in force, where that plan—

(*a*) allocates any land in the district for the purposes of such functions as are mentioned in that paragraph; or

(*b*) defines any land in the district as the site of proposed development for the purposes of any such functions.

(3) Interests qualifying for protection under these provisions are either—

(*a*) interests in hereditaments or parts of hereditaments; or

(*b*) interests in agricultural units or parts of agricultural units.

(4) An interest in the whole or part of a hereditament shall be taken to be an interest qualifying for protection under these provisions if, on the date of service of a notice under section 193 of this Act in respect thereof, either—

(*a*) the annual value of the hereditament does not exceed such amount as may be prescribed for the purposes of this paragraph by an order made by the Secretary of State, and the interest in question is the interest of an owner-occupier of the hereditament; or

(*b*) in a case not falling within the preceding paragraph, the interest in question is the interest of a resident owner-occupier of the hereditament.

(5) An interest in the whole or part of an agricultural unit shall be taken to be an interest qualifying for protection under these provisions if, on the date of service of a notice under section 193 of this Act in respect thereof, it is the interest of an owner-occupier of the unit.

(6) In this section and in the said sections 193 to 207 "these provisions" means the provisions of this section and of those sections, "the specified descriptions" means the descriptions contained in subsection (1)(*a*) to (*j*) of this section and "blight notice" means a notice served under section 193 or 201 of this Act [or section 78 of the Land Compensation Act 1973].   **[228]**

NOTES

Commencement: 1 April 1972.

This section derived from the Town and Country Planning Act 1962, s 138.

Sub-s (1): para (*a*) amended by the Telecommunications Act 1984, s 109, Sch 4, para 53; paras (*bb*), (*bc*) added by the Local Government Act 1985, s 4, Sch 1, para 16; para (*h*) amended by the Housing (Consequential Provisions) Act 1985, s 4, Sch 2, para 22; third amendment made by the Highways Act 1980, s 343, Sch 24; other amendments made by the Land Compensation Act 1973, s 75(1).

Sub-s (6): amended by the Land Compensation Act 1973, s 82(2).

193. Power to serve blight notice

(1) Where the whole or part of a hereditament or agricultural unit is comprised in land of any of the specified descriptions, and a person claims that—

(*a*) he is entitled to an interest in that hereditament or unit; and

(*b*) the interest is one which qualifies for protection under these provisions; and

(*c*) he has made reasonable endeavours to sell that interest; and

(*d*) [in consequence of the fact that the hereditament or unit or a part of it was, or was likely to be, comprised in land of any of the specified descriptions, he has been unable to sell that interest except at a price substantially lower than that for which it might reasonably have been expected to sell if no part of the hereditament or unit were, or were likely to be, comprised in such land],

he may serve on the appropriate authority a notice in the prescribed form requiring that authority to purchase that interest to the extent specified in, and otherwise in accordance with, these provisions.

(2) Subsection (1) of this section shall apply in relation to an interest in part of a hereditament or agricultural unit as it applies in relation to an interest in the entirety of a hereditament or agricultural unit:

Provided that this subsection shall not enable any person—

(*a*) if he is entitled to an interest in the entirety of a hereditament or agricultural unit, to make any claim or serve any notice under this section in respect of his interest in part of the hereditament or unit; or

(*b*) if he is entitled to an interest only in part of a hereditament or agricultural unit, to make or serve any such claim or notice in respect of his interest in less than the entirety of that part.

(3) . . .

(4) In these provisions "the claimant", in relation to a blight notice, means the person who served that notice, and any reference to the interest of the claimant, in relation to such a notice, is a reference to the interest which the notice requires the appropriate authority to purchase as mentioned in subsection (1) of this section.   [229]

NOTES

Commencement: 1 April 1971.

Amended by the Land Compensation Act 1973, ss 77, 86, Sch 3.

194. Objection to blight notice

(1) Where a blight notice has been served in respect of a hereditament or an agricultural unit, the appropriate authority, at any time before the end of the period of two months beginning with the date of service of that notice, may serve on the claimant a counter-notice in the prescribed form objecting to the notice.

(2) Subject to the following provisions of this section, the grounds on which objection may be made in a counter-notice to a notice served under section 193 of this Act are—

(*a*) that no part of the hereditament or agricultural unit to which the notice relates is comprised in land of any of the specified descriptions;

(*b*) that the appropriate authority (unless compelled to do so by virtue of these provisions) do not propose to acquire any part of the hereditament, or (in the case of an agricultural unit) any part of the affected areas in the exercise of any relevant powers;

(*c*) that the appropriate authority propose in the exercise of relevant powers to acquire a part of the hereditament or (in the case of an agricultural unit) a part of the affected area specified in the counter-notice, but (unless compelled to do so by virtue of these provisions) do not propose to acquire any other part of that hereditament or area in the exercise of any such powers;

(*d*) that [(in the case of land falling within paragraph (*a*) [or (*bb*)] or (*c*) but not (*d*), (*e*) or (*f*) of section 192(1) of this Act)] the appropriate authority (unless compelled to do so by virtue of these provisions) do not propose to acquire in the exercise of any relevant powers any part of the hereditament or (in the case of an agricultural unit) any part of the affected area during the period of [fifteen] years from the date of the counter-notice or such longer period from that date as may be specified in the counter-notice;

(*e*) that, on the date of service of the notice under section 193 of this Act, the claimant was not entitled to an interest in any part of the hereditament or agricultural unit to which the notice relates;

(*f*) that (for reasons specified in the counter-notice) the interest of the claimant is not an interest qualifying for protection under these provisions;

(*g*) that the conditions specified in paragraphs (*c*) and (*d*) of section 193(1) of this Act are not fulfilled.

(3) An objection may not be made on the grounds mentioned in paragraph (*d*) of subsection (2) of this section if it may be made on the grounds mentioned in paragraph (*b*) of that subsection.

(4) Where the appropriate enactment [confers power to acquire rights over land], subsection (2) of this section shall have effect as if—

(*a*) in paragraph (*b*) after the word "acquire" there were inserted the words "or to acquire any rights over";

(*b*) in paragraph (*c*) for the words "do not propose to acquire" there were substituted the words "propose neither to acquire, nor to acquire any right over";

(*c*) in paragraph (*d*) after the words "affected area" there were inserted "or to acquire any right over any part thereof".

(5) Any counter-notice served under this section in respect of a blight notice shall specify the grounds (being one or more of the grounds mentioned in the preceding provisions of this section or, as relevant, in section 201(6) of this Act [or section 78(3) or 80(1) of the Land Compensation Act 1973]) on which the appropriate authority object to the notice.

(6) In this section "relevant powers", in relation to any land falling within any of the specified descriptions, means any powers under which the appropriate authority are or could be authorised—

(*a*) to acquire [or to acquire any rights over] that land compulsorily as being land falling within that description; or

(*b*) to acquire [or to acquire any rights over] that land compulsorily for any of the relevant purposes;

. . . and "the relevant purposes", in relation to any such land, means the purposes for which, in accordance with the circumstances by virtue of which that land falls within the description in question, it is liable to be acquired or is indicated as being proposed to be acquired.   **[230]**

NOTES
Commencement: 1 April 1972.
This section derived from the Town and Country Planning Act 1962, s 140, the Town and Country Planning Act 1968, s 35(1), (2), (6), and the Highways Act 1971, Sch 7, paras 5-7.
Sub-s (2): first and third amendments in square brackets made by the Local Government, Planning and Land Act 1980, s 90, Sch 15; second words in square brackets prospectively added by the Local Government Act 1985, s 4, Sch 1, para 16, as from a day or days to be appointed.
Sub-ss (4)–(6): amended by the Land Compensation Act 1973, ss 75(3), 82(3).

195. Reference of objection to Lands Tribunal

(1) Where a counter-notice has been served under section 194 of this Act objecting to a blight notice, the claimant, at any time before the end of the period of two months beginning with the date of service of the counter-notice, may require the objection to be referred to the Lands Tribunal.

(2) On any such reference, if the objection is not withdrawn, the Lands Tribunal shall consider the matters set out in the notice served by the claimant and the grounds of the objection specified in the counter-notice; and, subject to subsection (3) of this section, unless it is shown to the satisfaction of the Tribunal that the objection is not well-founded, the Tribunal shall uphold the objecion.

(3) An objection on the grounds mentioned in section 194(2)(*b*), (*c*) or (*d*) of this Act shall not be upheld by the Tribunal unless it is shown to the satisfaction of the Tribunal that the objection is well-founded.

(4) If the Tribunal determines not to uphold the objection, the Tribunal shall declare that the notice to which the counter-notice relates is a valid notice.

(5) If the Tribunal upholds the objection, but only on the grounds mentioned in section 194(2)(*c*) of this Act, the Tribunal shall declare that the notice is a valid notice in relation to the part of the hereditament or (in the case of an agricultural unit) of the affected area specified in the counter-notice as being the part which the appropriate authority propose to acquire as therein mentioned, but not in relation to any other part of the hereditament of affected area.

(6) In any case falling within subsection (4) or subsection (5) of this section, the Tribunal shall give directions specifying the date on which notice to treat (as mentioned in section 196 of this Act) is to be deemed to have been served.
        [231]

NOTES
Commencement: 1 April 1972.

196. Effect of valid blight notice

(1) Where a blight notice has been served, and either—
  (*a*) no counter-notice objecting to that notice is served in accordance with these provisions; or
  (*b*) where such a counter-notice has been served, the objection is withdrawn, or, on a reference to the Lands Tribunal, is not upheld by the Tribunal,
the appropriate authority shall be deemed to be authorised to acquire compulsorily under the appropriate enactment the interest of the claimant in the hereditament, or (in the case of an agricultural unit) the interest of the

claimant in so far as it subsists in the affected area, and to have served a notice to treat in respect thereof on the date mentioned in subsection (2) of this section.

(2) The said date—

(*a*) in a case where, on a reference to the Lands Tribunal, the Tribunal determines not to uphold the objection, is the date specified in directions given by the Tribunal in accordance with section 195(6) of this Act;

(*b*) in any other case, is the date on which the period of two months beginning with the date of service of the blight notice comes to an end.

(3) Where the appropriate authority have served a counter-notice objecting to a blight notice on the grounds mentioned in section 194(2)(*c*) of this Act, then if either—

(*a*) the claimant, without referring that objection to the Lands Tribunal, and before the time for so referring it has expired, gives notice to the appropriate authority that he accepts the proposal of the authority to acquire the part of the hereditament or affected area specified in the counter-notice, and withdraws his claim as to the remainder of that hereditament or area; or

(*b*) on a reference to the Lands Tribunal, the Tribunal makes a declaration in accordance with section 195(5) of this Act in respect of that part of the hereditament or affected area,

the appropriate authority shall be deemed to be authorised to acquire compulsorily under the appropriate enactment the interest of the claimant in so far as it subsists in the part of the hereditament or affected area specified in the counter-notice (but not in so far as it subsists in any other part of that hereditament or area) and to have served a notice to treat in respect thereof on the date mentioned in subsection (4) of this section.

(4) The said date—

(*a*) in a case falling within paragraph (*a*) of subsection (3) of this section, is the date on which notice is given in accordance with that paragraph; and

(*b*) in a case falling within paragraph (*b*) of that subsection, is the date specified in directions given by the Lands Tribunal in accordance with section 195(6) of this Act. **[232]**

NOTES
Commencement: 1 April 1972.

197. Compensation for compulsory purchase of historic buildings and of land in clearance areas

Where an interest in land is acquired in pursuance of a blight notice and the interest is one—

(*a*) in respect of which a compulsory purchase order is in force under section 1 of the [Acquisition of Land Act 1981] (as applied by section 114 of this Act) containing a direction for minimum compensation under section 117 of this Act; or

(*b*) in respect of which a compulsory purchase order is in force under [section 290 of the Housing Act 1985 (acquisition of land for clearance)];

the compensation payable for the acquisition shall, in a case falling within paragraph (*a*) of this section, be assessed in accordance with the direction mentioned in that paragraph and, in a case falling within paragraph (*b*) of this section, be assessed in accordance with [the said Act of 1985], in either case as if the notice to treat deemed to have been served in respect of the interest under section 196 of this Act had been served in pursuance of the compulsory purchase order.   **[233]**

NOTES
Commencement: 1 April 1972.
This section derived from the Town and Country Planning Act 1968, s 36.
First amendment in square brackets made by the Acquisition of Land Act 1981, s 34(1), Sch 4; other amendments in square brackets made by the Housing (Consequential Provisions) Act 1985, s 4, Sch 2, para 22.

198. Withdrawal of blight notice

(1) Subject to subsection (2) of this section, the person by whom a blight notice has been served may withdraw the notice at any time before the compensation payable in respect of a compulsory acquisition in pursuance of the notice has been determined by the Lands Tribunal, or at any time before the end of the period of six weeks beginning with the date on which the compensation is so determined; and, where such a notice is withdrawn by virtue of this subsection, any notice to treat deemed to have been served in consequence thereof shall be deemed to have been withdrawn.

(2) A person shall not be entitled by virtue of subsection (1) of this section to withdraw a notice after the appropriate authority have exercised a right of entering and taking possession of land in pursuance of a notice to treat deemed to have been served in consequence of that notice.

(3) No compensation shall be payable in respect of the withdrawal of a notice to treat which is deemed to have been withdrawn by virtue of subsection (1) of this section.   **[234]**

NOTES
Commencement: 1 April 1972.

199. Effect on powers of compulsory acquisition of counter-notice disclaiming intention to acquire

(1) The provisions of subsection (2) of this section shall have effect where the grounds of objection specified in a counter-notice served under section 194 of this Act consist of or include the grounds mentioned in paragraph (*b*) or (*d*) of subsection (2) of that section, and either—

(*a*) the objection on the grounds mentioned in that paragraph is referred to and upheld by the Lands Tribunal; or
(*b*) the time for referring that objection to the Lands Tribunal expires without its having been so referred.

(2) If a compulsory purchase order has been made under the appropriate enactment in respect of land which consists of or includes the whole or part of the hereditament or agricultural unit to which the counter-notice relates, or if the land in question falls within section 192(1)(*i*) of this Act, any power conferred by that order, or by special enactment, as the case may be, for the compulsory acquisition of the interest of the claimant in the hereditament or agricultural unit or any part thereof shall cease to have effect.

(3) The provisions of subsection (4) of this section shall have effect where

the grounds of objection specified in a counter-notice under section 194 of this Act consist of or include the grounds mentioned in paragraph (*c*) of subsection (2) of that section, and either—

(*a*) the objection on the grounds mentioned in that paragraph is referred to and upheld by the Lands Tribunal; or

(*b*) the time for referring that objection to the Lands Tribunal expires without its having been so referred;

and in subsection (4) of this section any reference to "the part of the hereditament or affected area not required" is a reference to the whole of that hereditament or area except the part specified in the counter-notice as being the part which the appropriate authority propose to acquire as mentioned in the counter-notice.

(4) If a compulsory purchase order has been made under the appropriate enactment in respect of land which consists of or includes any of the part of the hereditament or affected area not required, or if the land in question falls within section 192(1)(*i*) of this Act, any power conferred by that order, or by the special enactment, as the case may be, for the compulsory acquisition of the interest of the claimant in any land comprised in the part of the hereditament or affected area not required shall cease to have effect. **[235]**

NOTES
Commencement: 1 April 1972.

200. Death of claimant after service of blight notice

(1) In relation to any time after the death of a person who has served a blight notice, the provisions mentioned in subsection (2) of this section shall apply as if any reference therein to the claimant were a reference to the claimant's personal representatives.

(2) The said provisions are sections 194(1), 195(1) and 196(3) of this Act.

[236]

NOTES
Commencement: 1 April 1972.

201. Power of mortgagee to serve blight notice

(1) Where the whole or part of a hereditament or agricultural unit is comprised in land falling within any of the specified descriptions and a person claims that—

(*a*) he is entitled as mortgagee (by virtue of a power which has become exercisable) to sell an interest in the hereditament or unit, giving immediate vacant possession of the land; and

(*b*) he has made reasonable endeavours to sell that interest; and

(*c*) [in consequence of the fact that the hereditament or unit or a part of it was, or was likely to be, comprised in land of any of the specified descriptions, he has been unable to sell that interest except at a price substantially lower than that for which it might reasonably have been expected to sell if no part of the hereditament or unit were, or were likely to be, comprised in such land],

then, subject to the provisions of this section, he may serve on the appropriate authority a notice in the prescribed form requiring that authority to purchase that interest to the extent specified in, and otherwise in accordance with, these provisions.

(2) Subsection (1) of this section shall apply in relation to an interest in part of a hereditament or agricultural unit as it applies in relation to an interest in the entirety of a hereditament or agricultural unit:

Provided that this subsection shall not enable a person—

(a) if his interest as mortgagee is in the entirety of a hereditament or agricultural unit, to make any claim or serve any notice under this section in respect of any interest in part of the hereditament or unit; or

(b) if his interest as mortgagee is only in part of a hereditament or agricultural unit, to make or serve any such notice or claim in respect of any interest in less than the entirety of that part.

(3) Notice under this section shall not be served unless one or other of the following conditions is satisfied with regard to the interest which the mortgagee claims he has the power to sell—

(a) the interest could be the subject of a notice under section 193 of this Act served by the person entitled thereto on the date of service of the notice under this section; or

(b) the interest could have been the subject of such a notice served by that person on a date not more than six months before the date of service of the notice under this section.

(4) No notice under this section shall be served in respect of a hereditament or agricultural unit, or any part of a hereditament or agricultural unit, at a time when a notice already served under section 193 of this Act is outstanding with respect to the hereditament, unit or part; and no notice shall be so served under that section at a time when a notice already served under this section is so outstanding.

(5) For the purposes of subsection (4) of this section, a notice served under this section or section 193 of this Act shall be treated as outstanding with respect to a hereditament or agricultural unit, or to part of a hereditament or agricultural unit, until—

(a) it is withdrawn in relation to the hereditament, unit or part; or

(b) an objection to the notice having been made by a counter-notice under section 194 of this Act, either—

    (i) the period of two months specified in section 195 of this Act elapses without the claimant having required the objection to be referred to the Lands Tribunal under that section; or

    (ii) the objection, having been so referred to the Lands Tribunal, is upheld by the Tribunal with respect to the hereditament, unit or part.

(6) The grounds on which objection may be made in a counter-notice under section 194 of this Act to a notice under this section are those specified in paragraphs (a) to (c) of subsection (2) of that section and, in a case to which it applies the grounds specified in paragraph (d) of that subsection and also the following grounds—

(a) that, on the date of service of the notice under this section, the claimant had no interest as mortgagee in any part of the hereditament or agricultural unit to which the notice relates;

(b) that (for reasons specified in the counter-notice) the claimant had not on that date the power referred to in subsection (1)(a) of this section;

(c) that the conditions specified in subsection (1)(*b*) and (*c*) of this section
are not fulfilled;

(*d*) that (for reasons specified in the counter-notice) neither of the
conditions specified in subsection (3) of this section was, on the date
of service of the notice under this section, satisfied with regard to the
interest referred to in that subsection.   **[237]**

NOTES
Commencement: 1 April 1972.
Amended by the Land Compensation Act 1973, s 77.

202. Saving for claimant's right to sell whole hereditament, etc

(1) The provisions of sections 194(2)(*c*), 195(5), 196(3) and 199(3) and (4) of this
Act relating to hereditaments shall not affect the right of a claimant under
section 92 of the Lands Clauses Consolidation Act 1845 to sell the whole of the
hereditament, or (in the case of an agricultural unit) the whole of the affected
area, which he has required the authority to purchase.

(2) The said provisions shall not affect the right of a claimant under section
8 of the Compulsory Purchase Act 1965 to sell (unless the Lands Tribunal
otherwise determines) the whole of the hereditament, or (in the case of an
agricultural unit) the whole of the affected area, which he has required the
authority to purchase; and accordingly in determining whether or not to uphold
an objection relating to a hereditament on the grounds mentioned in section
194(2)(*c*) of this Act the Tribunal shall consider (in addition to the other matters
which they are required to consider) whether—

(*a*) in the case of a house, building or manufactory, the part proposed to
be acquired can be taken without material detriment to the house,
building or manufactory; or

(*b*) in the case of a park or garden belonging to a house, the part proposed
to be acquired can be taken without seriously affecting the amenity or
convenience of the house.   **[238]**

NOTES
Commencement: 1 April 1972.

203. Meaning of "owner-occupier" and "resident owner-occupier"

(1) Subject to the following provisions of this section, in these provisions
"owner-occupier", in relation to a hereditament, means a person who—

(*a*) occupies the whole or a substantial part of the hereditament in right
of an owner's interest therein, and has so occupied the hereditament
or that part thereof during the whole of the period of six months
ending with the date of service; or

(*b*) occupied, in right of an owner's interest, the whole or a substantial
part of the hereditament during the whole of a period of six months
ending not more than twelve months before the date of service, the
hereditament, or that part thereof, as the case may be, having been
unoccupied since the end of that period.

(2) Subject to the following provisions of this section, in these provisions
"owner-occupier", in relation to an agricultural unit, means a person who—

(*a*) occupies the whole of that unit, and has occupied it during the whole
of the period of six months ending with the date of service; or

(*b*) occupied the whole of that unit during the whole of a period of six
months ending not more than twelve months before the date of
service,

and, at all times material for the purposes of paragraph (*a*) or paragraph (*b*) of
this subsection, as the case may be, has been entitled to an owner's interest in
the whole or part of that unit.

(3) In these provisions "resident owner-occupier", in relation to a
hereditament, means an individual who—

(*a*) occupies the whole or a substantial part of the hereditament as a
private dwelling in right of an owner's interest therein, and has so
occupied the hereditament or that part thereof, as the case may be,
during the whole of the period of six months ending with the date of
service; or

(*b*) occupied, in right of an owner's interest, the whole or a substantial
part of the hereditament as a private dwelling during the whole of a
period of six months ending not more than twelve months before the
date of service, the hereditament, or that part thereof, as the case may
be, having been unoccupied since the end of that period.

(4) In this section "owner's interest", in relation to a hereditament or
agricultural unit, means a freehold interest therein or a tenancy thereof granted
or extended for a term of years certain of which, on the date of service, not less
than three years remain unexpired; and "date of service", in relation to a
hereditament or agricultural unit, means the date of service of a notice in respect
thereof under section 193 of this Act.   **[239]**

NOTES
Commencement: 1 April 1972.

204. Special provisions as to partnerships

(1) The provisions of this section shall have effect for the purposes of the
application of these provisions to a hereditament or agricultural unit occupied
for the purposes of a partnership firm.

(2) Occupation for the purposes of the firm shall be treated as occupation
by the firm, and not as occupation by any one or more of the partners
individually, and the definitions of "owner-occupier" in section 203(1) and (2)
of this Act shall apply in relation to the firm accordingly.

(3) If, after the service by the firm of a blight notice, any change occurs
(whether by death or otherwise) in the constitution of the firm, any proceedings,
rights or obligations consequential upon that notice may be carried on or
exercised by or against, or (as the case may be) shall be incumbent upon, the
partners for the time being constituting the firm.

(4) Nothing in this section or elsewhere in these provisions shall be construed
as indicating an intention to exclude the operation of section 19 of the
Interpretation Act 1889 (whereby, unless the contrary intention appears,
"person" includes any body of persons corporate or unincorporate) in relation
to any of these provisions.

(5) Subsection (2) of this section shall not affect the definition of "resident
owner-occupier" in section 203(3) of this Act.   **[240]**

NOTES
Commencement: 1 April 1972.

205. "Appropriate authority" for purposes of these provisions

(1) Subject to the following provisions of this section, in these provisions "the appropriate authority", in relation to any land, means the government department, local authority or other body [or person] by whom, in accordance with the circumstances by virtue of which the land falls within any of the specified descriptions, the land is liable to be acquired or is indicated as being proposed to be acquired or, as the case may be any right over the land is proposed to be acquired.

(2) If any question arises—

    (*a*) whether the appropriate authority in relation to any land for the purpose of these provisions is the Secretary of State or a local highway authority; or

    (*b*) which of two or more local highway authorities is the appropriate authority in relation to any land for those purposes; or

    (*c*) which of two or more local authorities is the appropriate authority in relation to any land for those purposes,

that question shall be referred to the Secretary of State, whose decision shall be final.

(3) If any question arises which authority is the appropriate authority for the purposes of these provisions—

    (*a*) section 194(1) of this Act shall have effect as if the reference to the date of service of the blight notice were a reference to that date or the date on which that question is determined, whichever is the later;

    (*b*) section 201(3)(*b*) of this Act shall apply with the substitution for the period of six months of a reference to that period extended by so long as it takes to obtain a determination of the question; and

    (*c*) section 203(1)(*b*), (2)(*b*) and (3)(*b*) of this Act shall apply with the substitution for the reference to twelve months before the date of service of a reference to that period extended by so long as it takes to obtain a determination of the question. **[241]**

NOTES

Commencement: 1 April 1972.

This section derived from the Town and Country Planning Act 1962, s 147, and the Town and Country Planning Act 1968, ss 34(5), 37(5).

Sub-s (1): amended by the Telecommunications Act 1984, s 109, Sch 4, para 53.

206. "Appropriate enactment" for purposes of these provisions

(1) Subject to the following provisions of this section, in these provisions "the appropriate enactment", in relation to land falling within any of the specified descriptions, means the enactment which provides for the compulsory acquisition of land as being land falling within that description or, as respects the description contained in paragraph (*g*) of section 192(1) of this Act, the enactment under which the compulsory purchase order referred to in that paragraph was made.

(2) In relation to land falling within the description contained in section 192(1)(*b*) of this Act an enactment shall, for the purposes of subsection (1) of this section be taken to be an enactment which provides for the compulsory acquisition of land as being land falling within that description if—

    (*a*) the enactment provides for the compulsory acquisition of land for the purposes of the functions which are indicated in the development plan as being the functions for the purposes of which the land is allocated or is proposed to be developed; or

(b) where no particular functions are so indicated in the development plan, the enactment provides for the compulsory acquisition of land for the purposes of any of the functions of the government department, local authority or other body for the purposes of whose functions the land is allocated or is defined as the site of proposed development.

(3) Where, in accordance with the circumstances by virtue of which any land falls within any of the specified descriptions, it is indicated that the land is proposed to be acquired for highway purposes, any enactment under which a highway authority are or (subject to the fulfilment of the relevant conditions) could be authorised to acquire that land compulsorily for highway purposes shall, for the purposes of subsection (1) of this section, be taken to be an enactment providing for the compulsory acquisition of that land as being land falling within the description in question.

(4) In subsection (3) of this section the reference to the fulfilment of the relevant conditions is a reference to such one or more of the following as are applicable to the circumstances in question, that is to say—

(a) the coming into operation of any requisite order [made, or having effect as if made] under the provisions of Part II of [the Highways Act 1980] relating to trunk roads;

(b) the coming into operation of any requisite scheme or order [made, or having effect as if made] under the provisions of the said Part II relating to special roads;

(c) the coming into operation of the requisite scheme [made, or having effect as if made, under section 106(3) of the said Act];

(d) the coming into operation of the requisite order [relating to a classified road made, or having effect as if made, under section 14 of the said Act];

(e) the making or approval of any requisite plans.

(5) If, apart from this subsection, two or more enactments would be the appropriate enactment in relation to any land for the purposes of these provisions, the appropriate enactment for those purposes shall be taken to be that one of those enactments under which, in the circumstances in question, it is most likely that (apart from these provisions) the land would have been acquired by the appropriate authority.

(6) If any question arises as to which enactment is the appropriate enactment in relation to any land for the purposes of these provisions, that question shall be referred—

(a) where the appropriate authority are a government department, to the Minister or Board in charge of that department;

(b) where the appropriate authority are statutory undertakers, to the appropriate Minister; and

(c) in any other case, to the Secretary of State,

and the decision of the Minister, Secretary of State or Board to whom a question is referred under this subsection shall be final. **[242]**

NOTES

Commencement: 1 April 1972.

Amended by the Highways Act 1980, s 343, Sch 24.

207. General interpretation of these provisions

(1) Subject to the following provisions of this section, in these provisions the following expressions have the meanings hereby assigned to them respectively, that is to say:—

"the affected area", in relation to an agricultural unit, means so much of that unit as, on the date of service, consists of land falling within any of the specified descriptions;

"agricultural unit" means land which is occupied as a unit for agricultural purposes, including any dwellinghouse or other building occupied by the same person for the purpose of farming the land;

"annual value", in relation to a hereditament, means the value which, on the date of service, is shown in the valuation list as the rateable value of that hereditament, except that, where the rateable value differs from the net annual value, it means the value which on that date is shown in the valuation list as the net annual value thereof;

"the claimant" has the meaning assigned to it by section 193(4) of this Act;

"hereditament" means the aggregate of the land which forms the subject of a single entry in the valuation list for the time being in force for a rating area;

. . .

"special enactment" means a local enactment, or a provision contained in an Act other than a local or private Act, being a local enactment or provision authorising the compulsory acquisition of land specifically identified therein; and in this definition "local enactment" means a local or private Act, or an order confirmed by Parliament or brought into operation in accordance with special parliamentary procedure;

"these provisions", "the specified descriptions" and "blight notice" have the meanings assigned to them respectively in section 192(6) of this Act.

(2) Where any land is on the boundary between two or more rating areas, and accordingly—

(*a*) different parts of that land form the subject of single entries in the valuation lists for the time being in force for those areas respectively; but

(*b*) if the whole of that land had been in one of those areas, it would have formed the subject of a single entry in the valuation list for that area,

the whole of that land shall be treated, for the purposes of the definition of "hereditament" in subsection (1) of this section, as if it formed the subject of a single entry in the valuation list for a rating area.

(3) Land which forms the subject of an entry in the valuation list by reason only that it is land over which any shooting, fishing or other sporting rights are exercisable, or that it is land over which a right of exhibiting advertisements is let out or reserved, shall not be taken to be a hereditament within the said definition.

(4) Where, in accordance with subsection (2) of this section, land whereof different parts form the subject of single entries in the valuation lists for the time being in force for two or more rating areas is treated as if it formed the subject of a single entry in the valuation list for a rating area, the definition of "annual value" in subsection (1) of this section shall apply as if any reference therein to a value shown in the valuation list were a reference to the aggregate

of the values shown (as rateable values or as net annual values, as the case may be) in those valuation lists in relation to the different parts of that land.

(5) In this section "date of service" has the same meaning as in section 203 of this Act.   **[243]**

NOTES
Commencement: 1 April 1972.
Words omitted repealed by the Land Compensation Act 1973, s 86, Sch 3.

Supplementary provisions

208. No withdrawal of constructive notice to treat

Without prejudice to the provisions of section 198(1) of this Act, the power conferred by section 31 of the Land Compensation Act 1961 to withdraw a notice to treat shall not be exercisable in the case of a notice to treat which is deemed to have been served by virtue of any of the provisions of this Part of this Act.   **[244]**

NOTES
Commencement: 1 April 1972.

PART X

HIGHWAYS

Stopping up and diversion of highways

209. Highways affected by development: orders by Secretary of State

(1) The Secretary of State may by order authorise the stopping up or diversion of any highway if he is satisfied that it is necessary to do so in order to enable development to be carried out in accordance with planning permission granted under Part III of this Act [or by virtue of Schedule 32 to the Local Government, Planning and Land Act 1980], or to be carried out by a government department.

(2) Any order under this section may make such provision as appears to the Secretary of State to be necessary or expedient for the provision or improvement of any other highway, and may direct—

(a) that any highway so provided or improved shall for the purposes of [the Highways Act 1980] be a highway maintainable at the public expense;

(b) that the Secretary of State, or [any county council [, metropolitan district council] or London borough council specified in the order or, if it is so specified, . . . the Common Council of the City of London], shall be the highway authority for that highway;

(c) in the case of a highway for which the Secretary of State is to be the highway authority, that the highway shall, on such date as may be specified in the order, become a trunk road within the meaning of [the Highways Act 1980].

(3) Any order made under this section may contain such incidental and consequential provisions as appear to the Secretary of State to be necessary or expedient, including in particular—

(a) provision for authorising the Secretary of State, or requiring any other authority or person specified in the order—

       (i) to pay, or to make contributions in respect of, the cost of doing any work provided for by the order or any increased expenditure to be incurred which is attributable to the doing of any such work;

or

      (ii) to repay, or to make contributions in respect of, any compensation paid by the highway authority in respect of restrictions imposed under section 1 or 2 of the Restriction of Ribbon Development Act 1935 in relation to any highway stopped up or diverted under the order;

   (*b*) provision for the preservation of any rights of statutory undertakers in respect of any apparatus of theirs which immediately before the date of the order is under, in, on, over, along or across the highway to which the order relates.

(4) An order may be made under this section authorising the stopping up or diversion of any highway which is temporarily stopped up or diverted under any other enactment.

(5) The provisions of this section shall have effect without prejudice to—

   (*a*) any power conferred on the Secretary of State by any other enactment to authorise the stopping up or diversion of a highway;
   (*b*) the provisions of [Part VI of the Acquisition of Land Act 1981]; or
   (*c*) the provisions of section 214(1)(*a*) of this Act.   **[245]**

NOTES

Commencement: 1 April 1972.

This section derived from the Town and Country Planning Act 1962, s 153(1), (2), (4), (5), and the Town and Country Planning Act 1968, s 97(1).

Sub-s (1): amended by the Local Government,Planning and Land Act 1980, s 179, Sch 32.

Sub-s (2): paras (*a*), (*c*), amended by the Highways Act 1980, s 343, Sch 24; in para (*b*) first amendment made by the Local Government Act 1972,.s 182, Sch 16; second amendment made and words omitted repealed by the Local Government Act 1985, ss 8, 102, Sch 4, para 50(*a*), Sch 17.

Sub-s (5): amended by the Acquisition of Land Act 1981, s 34(1), Sch 4.

210. Footpaths and bridleways affected by development: orders by local planning authorities, etc

(1) Subject to section 217 of this Act, a competent authority may by order authorise the stopping up or diversion of any footpath or bridleway if they are satisfied as mentioned in section 209(1) of this Act.

(2) An order under this section may, if the competent authority are satisfied that it should do so, provide—

   (*a*) for the creation of an alternative highway for use as a replacement for the one authorised by the order to be stopped up or diverted, or for the improvement of an existing highway for such use;
   (*b*) for authorising or requiring works to be carried out in relation to any footpath or bridleway for whose stopping up or diversion, creation or improvement, provision is made by the order;
   (*c*) for the preservation of any rights of statutory undertakers in respect of apparatus of theirs which immediately before the date of the order is under, in, on, over, along or across any such footpath or bridleway;
   (*d*) for requiring any person named in the order to pay, or make contributions in respect of, the cost of carrying out any such works.

(3) An order may be made under this section authorising the stopping up or

diversion of a footpath or bridleway which is temporarily stopped up or diverted under any other enactment.

[(4) In this section "competent authority" means, in the case of development authorised by a planning permission, the local planning authority who granted the permission or, in the case of a permission granted by the Secretary of State, who would have had power to grant it and in the case of development carried out by a government department, the local planning authority who would have had power to grant planning permission on an application in respect of the development in question if such an application had fallen to be made.]

[(5) Where the planning permission relates to a transferred matter, as defined in section 86(11) of the Local Government, Planning and Land Act 1980, but was granted by a county planning authority before the transfer date, as so defined, this section shall have effect in relation to it as if—

        (i) the words "the district planning" were substituted for the words "a competent" in subsections (1) and (2);

and

        (ii) subsection (4) were omitted.]   **[246]**

NOTES

    Commencement: 12 January 1981 (sub-s (5)); 1 April 1974 (sub-s (4)); 1 April 1972 (remainder).
    This section derived from the Town and Country Planning Act 1968, s 94(1)-(4)
    Sub-s (4): substituted by the Local Government Act 1972, s 182, Sch 16.
    Sub-s (5): added by the Local Government, Planning and Land Act 1980, s 90, Sch 15.
    See further: SI 1986 No 452, art 6.

211. Highways crossing or entering route of proposed new highway, etc

(1) If planning permission is granted under Part III of this Act for constructing or improving, or the Secretary of State proposes to construct or improve, a highway (hereafter in this section referred to as "the main highway"), the Secretary of State may by order authorise the stopping up or diversion of any other highway which crosses or enters the route of the main highway or which is, or will be, otherwise affected by the construction or improvement of the main highway, if it appears to the Secretary of State expedient to do so—

        (*a*) in the interests of the safety of users of the main highway; or
        (*b*) to facilitate the movement of traffic on the main highway.

(2) Subsections (2) to (5) of section 209 of this Act shall apply to an order under this section as they apply to an order under that section.   **[247]**

NOTES

    Commencement: 1 April 1972.

Conversion of highway into footpath or bridleway

212. Order extinguishing right to use vehicles on highway

(1) The provisions of this section shall have effect where a local planning authority by resolution adopt a proposal for improving the amenity of part of their area, being a proposal which involves a highway in that area (being a highway over which the public have a right of way with vehicles, but not a trunk road or a road classified as a principal road ...) being changed to a footpath or bridleway.

(2) The Secretary of State may, on an application [by a local planning authority who have so resolved made after consultation with the highway

authority (if different) and any other authority who are a local planning authority for the area in question] by order provide for the extinguishment of any right which persons may have to use vehicles on that highway.

(3) An order made under subsection (2) of this section may include such provision as the Secretary of State (after consultation with [every authority who are a local planning authority for the area in question and] the highway authority) thinks fit for permitting the use on the highway of vehicles (whether mechanically propelled or not) in such cases as may be specified in the order, notwithstanding the extinguishment of any such right as is mentioned in that subsection; and any such provision may be framed by reference to particular descriptions of vehicles, or to particular persons by whom, or on whose authority, vehicles may be used, or to the circumstances in which, or the times at which, vehicles may be used for particular purposes.

(4) No provision contained in, or having effect under, any enactment, being a provision prohibiting or restricting the use of footpaths, footways or bridleways shall affect any use of a vehicle on a highway in relation to which an order made under subsection (2) of this section has effect, where the use is permitted in accordance with provisions of the order included by virtue of subsection (3) of this section.

(5) Any person who, at the time of an order under subsection (2) of this section coming into force, has an interest in land having lawful access to a highway to which the order relates shall be entitled to be compensated by the local planning authority [on whose application the order was made] in respect of any depreciation in the value of his interest which is directly attributable to the order and of any other loss or damage which is so attributable.

In this subsection "lawful access" means access authorised by planning permission granted under this Act, the Act of 1947 or the Act of 1962, or access in respect of which no such permission is necessary.

(6) A claim for compensation under subsection (5) of this section shall be made to the local planning authority [on whose application the order was made] within the time and in the manner prescribed by regulations under this Act.

(7) Sections 178 and 179 of this Act shall have effect in relation to compensation under subsection (5) of this section as they have effect in relation to compensation to which those sections apply.

(8) Without prejudice to section 287(3) of this Act, the Secretary of State may, on an application [by an authority who are a local planning authority for the area in question made after consultation with the highway authority (if different) and any other authority who are a local planning authority for that area] by order revoke an order made by him in relation to a highway under subsection (2) of this section; and the effect of the order shall be to reinstate any right to use vehicles on the highway, being a right which was extinguished by virtue of the order under that subsection.

[(8A) An order under subsection (8) of this section may make provision requiring the removal of any obstruction of a highway resulting from the exercise of powers under Part VIIA of the Highways Act 1980.]

(9) Subsections (2), (3) and (5) of section 209 of this Act shall apply to an order under this section as they apply to an order under that section.   **[248]**

NOTES
Commencement: 13 July 1982 (sub-s (8A)); 1 April 1972 (remainder).
Sub-s (1): words omitted repealed by the Local Government Act 1974, s 42, Sch 8.
Sub-ss (2), (3), (5): amended except as to Greater London, by the Local Government Act 1972, s 182, Sch 16,
Sub-s (8A): added by the Local Government (Miscellaneous Provisions) Act 1982, s 20, Sch 5, Part II.

Extinguishment of rights of way

214. Extinguishment of public rights of way over land held for planning purposes

(1) Where any land has been acquired or appropriated for planning purposes and is for the time being held by a local authority for the purposes for which it was acquired or appropriated—

 (a) the Secretary of State may by order extinguish any public right of way over the land if he is satisfied that an alternative right of way has been or will be provided or that the provision of any alternative right of way is not required;

 (b) subject to section 217 of this Act, the local authority may by order extinguish any such right over the land, being a footpath or bridleway, if they are satisfied as aforesaid.

(2) In this section any reference to the acquisition or appropriation of land for planning purposes shall be construed in accordance with section 133(1) of this Act as if this section were in Part VI of this Act.   **[249]**

NOTES
Commencement: 1 April 1972.

Procedure for making and confirming orders

215. Procedure for making of orders by Secretary of State

(1) Before making an order under section 209, 211, 212, or 214(1)(a) of this Act the Secretary of State shall publish in at least one local newspaper circulating in the relevant area, and in the London Gazette, a notice—

 (a) stating the general effect of the order;

 (b) specifying a place in the relevant area where a copy of the draft order and of any relevant map or plan may be inspected by any person free of charge at all reasonable hours during a period of twenty-eight days from the date of the publication of the notice; and

 (c) stating that, within that period, any person may by notice to the Secretary of State object to the making of the order.

(2) Not later than the date on which that notice is so published, the Secretary of State—

 (a) shall serve a copy of the notice, together with a copy of the draft order and of any relevant map or plan, on every local authority in whose area any highway or, as the case may be, any land to which the order relates is situated, and on any water, hydraulic power, gas or electricity undertakers having any cables, mains, pipes or wires laid along, across, under or over any highway to be stopped up or diverted or, as the case may be, any land over which a right of way is to be extinguished, under the order; and

 (b) shall cause a copy of the notice to be displayed in a prominent position at the ends of so much of any highway as is proposed to be stopped up or diverted or, as the case may be, of the right of way proposed to be extinguished under the order.

(3) If before the end of the said period of twenty-eight days an objection is received by the Secretary of State from any local authority or undertakers on whom a notice is required to be served under subsection (2) of this section, or from any other person appearing to him to be affected by the order, and the objection is not withdrawn, the Secretary of State shall cause a local inquiry to be held:

Provided that, if the objection is made by a person other than such a local authority or undertakers, the Secretary of State may dispense with such an inquiry if he is satisfied that in the special circumstances of the case the holding of such an inquiry is unnecessary.

(4) Subsections (2) to (5) of section 290 of the Local Government Act 1933 (evidence and costs at local inquiries) shall apply in relation to an inquiry caused to be held by the Secretary of State under subsection (3) of this section as they apply in relation to an inquiry caused to be held by a department under subsection (1) of the said section 290, with the substitution for the references to a department of references to the Secretary of State.

(5) After considering any objections to the order which are not withdrawn, and, where a local inquiry is held, the report of the person who held the inquiry, the Secretary of State (subject to subsection (6) of this section) may make the order either without modification or subject to such modifications as he thinks fit.

(6) Where the order contains a provision requiring any such payment, repayment or contribution as is mentioned in section 209(3)(a) of this Act, and objection to that provision is duly made, in accordance with subsection (3) of this section, by an authority or person who would be required thereby to make such a payment, repayment or contribution, and the objection is not withdrawn, the order shall be subject to special parliamentary procedure.

(7) Immediately after the order has been made, the Secretary of State shall publish, in the manner specified in subsection (1) of this section, a notice stating that the order has been made, and naming a place where a copy of the order may be seen at all reasonable hours; and the provisions of subsection (2) of this section shall have effect in relation to any such notice as they have effect in relation to a notice under subsection (1) of this section.

(8) In this section "the relevant area", in relation to an order, means the area in which any highway or land to which the order relates is situated, and "local authority" means the council of a county, . . . , county district or parish, . . . , . . . , the council of a London borough [the Inner London Education Authority, a joint authority established by Part IV of the Local Government Act 1985], and the parish meeting of a rural parish not having a separate parish council.   **[250]**

NOTES

Commencement: 1 April 1972.

This section derived from the Town and Country Planning Act 1962, s 154, the London Government Act 1963, s 29(4), and the Town and Country Planning Act 1968, s 97(3).

Sub-s (8): first words omitted repealed by the Local Government Act 1972, s 272, Sch 30; second words omitted repealed by the Local Government Act 1985, s 102, Sch 17; words in square brackets prospectively added by the Local Government Act 1985, s 84, Sch 14, para 48(a), as from a day or days to be appointed in accordance with s 84.

216. Procedure in anticipation of planning permission, etc

(1) Where the Secretary of State would, if planning permission for any development had been granted under Part III of this Act, have power to make an order under section 209 or 211 of this Act authorising the stopping-up or diversion of a highway in order to enable that development to be carried out, then, notwithstanding that such permission has not been granted, the Secretary of State may, in the circumstances specified in subsections (2) to (4) of this section, publish notice of the draft of such an order in accordance with section 215 of this Act.

(2) The Secretary of State may publish such a notice as aforesaid where the relevant development is the subject of an application for planning permission and either—

(a) that application is made by a local authority or statutory undertakers or the National Coal Board; or

(b) that application stands referred to the Secretary of State in pursuance of a direction under section 35 of this Act; or

(c) the applicant has appealed to the Secretary of State under section 36 of this Act against a refusal of planning permission or of approval required under a development order, or against a condition of any such permission or approval.

(3) The Secretary of State may publish such a notice as aforesaid where—

(a) the relevant development is to be carried out by a local authority, statutory undertakers or the National Coal Board and requires, by virtue of an enactment, the authorisation of a government department; and

(b) the developers have made application to the department for that authorisation and also requested a direction under section 40 of this Act or, in the case of the National Coal Board, under section 2 of the Opencast Coal Act 1958, that planning permission be deemed to be granted for that development.

(4) The Secretary of State may publish such a notice as aforesaid where the council of a county . . . , [metropolitan district or] London borough, a joint planning board, or the Inner London Education Authority certify that they have begun to take such steps, in accordance with regulations made by virtue of section 270 of this Act, as are requisite in order to enable them to obtain planning permission for the relevant development.

(5) Section 215(5) of this Act shall not be construed as authorising the Secretary of State to make an order under section 209 or 211 of this Act of which notice has been published by virtue of subsection (1) of this section until planning permission is granted for the development which occasions the making of the order.   **[251]**

NOTES

Commencement: 1 April 1972.

This section derived from the Town and Country Planning Act 1968, ss 90, 91(3).

Sub-s (4): words omitted repealed by the Local Government Act 1972, s 272, Sch 30; amendment in square brackets made by the Local Government Act 1985, s 8, Sch 4, para 50(*b*).

217. Confirmation of orders made by other authorities

(1) An order made under section 210 or 214(1)(*b*) of this Act shall not take effect unless confirmed by the Secretary of State, or unless confirmed, as an unopposed order, by the authority who made it.

(2) The Secretary of State shall not confirm any such order unless satisfied as to every matter of which the authority making the order are required under section 210 or 214(1)(*b*) (as the case may be) to be satisfied.

(3) The time specified—

(*a*) in an order under section 210 as the time from which a footpath or bridleway is to be stopped up or diverted; or

(*b*) in an order under section 214(1)(*b*) as the time from which a right of way is to be extinguished,

shall not be earlier than confirmation of the order.

(4) Schedule 20 to this Act shall have effect with respect to the confirmation of orders under section 210 or 214(1)(*b*) of this Act and the publicity for such orders after they are confirmed.   **[252]**

NOTES
Commencement: 1 April 1972.

Supplementary provisions

218. Compulsory acquisition of land in connection with highways

(1) The Secretary of State or a local highway authority may be authorised to acquire land compulsorily—

(*a*) for the purpose of providing or improving any highway which is to be provided or improved in pursuance of an order under section 209, 211 or 212 of this Act or for any other purpose for which land is required in connection with such an order; or

(*b*) for the purpose of providing any public right of way which is to be provided as an alternative to a right of way extinguished under section 214(1)(*a*) of this Act.

(2) The [Acquisition of Land Act 1981] shall apply to the acquisition of land under this section . . .   **[253]**

NOTES
Commencement: 1 April 1972.
Amended by the Acquisition of Land Act 1981, s 34, Schs 4, 6.

219. Concurrent proceedings in connection with highways

(1) In relation to orders under sections 209, 211 and 212 of this Act, regulations made under this Act may make provision for securing that any proceedings required to be taken for the purposes of the acquisition of land under section 218 of this Act (as mentioned in subsection (1)(*a*) of that section) may be taken concurrently with any proceedings required to be taken for the purposes of the order.

(2) In relation to orders under section 214(1)(*a*) of this Act, regulations made under this Act may make provision for securing—

(*a*) that any proceedings required to be taken for the purposes of such an order may be taken concurrently with any proceedings required to be taken for the purposes of the acquisition of the land over which the right of way is to be extinguished; or

(*b*) that any proceedings required to be taken for the purposes of the acquisition of any other land under section 218 of this Act (as mentioned in subsection (1)(*b*) of that section) may be taken concurrently with either or both of the proceedings referred to in the preceding paragraph.   **[254]**

NOTES
Commencement: 1 April 1972.

220. Provisions as to telegraphic lines

[(1) Where in pursuance of an order under section 209, 211 or 212 of this Act a highway is stopped up or diverted and immediately before the date on which the order became operative there was under, in, on, over, along or across the highway any telecommunication apparatus kept installed for the purposes of a telecommunications code system, the operator of that system shall have the same powers in respect of the telecommunication apparatus as if the order had not become operative; but any person entitled to land over which the highway subsisted shall be entitled to require the alteration of the apparatus.

(2) Where any such order provides for the improvement of a highway, other than a trunk road, and, immediately before the date on which the order became operative, there was under, in, over, along or across the highway any telecommunication apparatus kept installed for the purposes of a telecommunications code system, the local highway authority shall be entitled to require the alteration of the apparatus.

This subsection does not have effect so far as it relates to the alteration of any telecommunication apparatus for the purpose of authority's works as defined in Part II of the Public Utilities Street Works Act 1950.

(3) Where an order to which this subsection applies is made, and at the time of the publication of the notice required by section 215(1) of or, as the case may be, paragraph 1 of Schedule 20 to this Act any telecommunication apparatus was kept installed for the purposes of a telecommunications code system under, in, on, over, along or across the land over which the right of way subsisted—

(*a*) the power of the operator of the system to remove the apparatus shall, notwithstanding the making of the order, be exercisable at any time not later than the end of the period of three months from the date on which the right of way is extinguished or authorised to be stopped up or diverted and shall be exercisable in respect of the whole or any part of the apparatus after the end of that period if before the end of that period the operator of the system has given notice to the authority of his intention to remove the apparatus or that part of it, as the case may be;

(*b*) the operator of the system may by notice given in that behalf to the authority not later than the end of the said period of three months abandon the telecommunication apparatus or any part of it;

(*c*) subject to paragraph (*b*) of this subsection, the operator of the system shall be deemed at the end of that period to have abandoned any part of the apparatus which the operator has then neither removed nor given notice of his intention to remove;

(*d*) the operator of the system shall be entitled to recover from the authority the expense of providing, in substitution for the apparatus and any other telecommunication apparatus connected with it which is rendered useless in consequence of the removal or abandonment of the first-mentioned apparatus, any telecommunication apparatus in such other place as the operator may require;

(e) where under the preceding provisions of this subsection the operator
of the system has abandoned the whole or any part of any
telecommunication apparatus that apparatus or that part of it shall
vest in the authority and shall be deemed, with its abandonment, to
cease to be kept installed for the purposes of a telecommunications
code system.

(4) Subsection (3) of this section applies—

(a) to any order made by or on the application of a local authority under
section 214(1) of this Act extinguishing a public right of way; and

(b) to any order made by a competent authority under section 210 of this
Act authorising the stopping up or diverting of a footpath or
bridleway;

and in this subsection "competent authority" has the same meaning as in the
said section 210.

(5) As soon as reasonably practicable after the making of any such order as
is mentioned in subsection (4) above in circumstances in which subsection (3)
above applies in relation to the operator of any telecommunications code
system, the person by whom the order was made shall give notice to the operator
of the making of the order.

(6) Paragraph 1(2) of the telecommunications code (alteration of apparatus
to include moving, removal or replacement of apparatus) shall apply for the
purposes of the preceding provisions of this section as it applies for the purposes
of that code.

(7) Paragraph 21 of the telecommunications code (restriction on removal of
telecommunications apparatus) shall apply in relation to any entitlement
conferred by this section to require the alteration, moving or replacement of
any telecommunication apparatus as it applies in relation to an entitlement to
require the removal of any such apparatus.]   **[255]**

NOTES
Commencement: 5 August 1984.
Commencement order: SI 1984, No 876
Substituted by the Telecommunications Act 1984, s 109, Sch 4, para 53.

221. Application of s 32 of Mineral Workings Act 1951 to orders under Part X

(1) In subsections (1) and (2) of section 32 of the Mineral Workings Act 1951
(power of Ministers to make temporary order for stopping up or diversion of
highway in connection with working of surface minerals)—

(a) references to section 209 of this Act (except the reference to subsection
(3) of that section) shall include references to section 210 of this Act;

(b) the reference to the said subsection (3) shall include a reference to
subsection (2) of the said section 210; and

(c) references to the Secretary of State shall include references to a
competent authority for the purposes of the said section 210.

(2) In subsection (3) of the said section 32 (rights of statutory undertakers
in respect of their apparatus where order is made under section 209 of this Act)
the reference to section 209 of this Act shall include a reference to section 211
of this Act.

(3) This section has effect in lieu of the amendments of the said section 32
made by sections 91(4) and 94(5) of the Act of 1968.   **[256]**

NOTES
Commencement: 1 April 1972.

PART XI

STATUTORY UNDERTAKERS

Preliminary

222. Meaning of "operational land".

In this Act "operational land" means, in relation to statutory undertakers—

(*a*) land which is used for the purpose of carrying on their undertaking; and

(*b*) land in which an interest is held for that purpose,

not being land which, in respect of its nature and situation, is comparable rather with land in general than with land which is used, or in which interests are held, for the purpose of the carrying on of statutory undertakings.   **[257]**

NOTES
Commencement: 1 April 1972.

223. Cases in which land is to be treated as not being operational land

(1) Where an interest in land is held by statutory undertakers for the purpose of carrying on their undertaking and—

(*a*) the interest was acquired by them on or after 6th December 1968; or

(*b*) it was held by them immediately before that date but the circumstances were then such that the land did not fall to be treated as operational land for the purposes of the Act of 1962,

then subsection (2) of this section shall have effect for the purpose of determining whether the land is to be treated as operational land for the purposes of this Act and shall so have effect notwithstanding the definition of operational land in section 222 of this Act.

(2) The land shall not be treated as operational land for the purposes of this Act unless one or both of the following conditions are satisfied with respect to it, namely—

(*a*) there is, or at some time has been, in force with respect to the land a specific planning permission for its development and that development, if carried out, would involve or have involved the use of the land for the purpose of the carrying on of the statutory undertakers' undertaking; or

(*b*) the undertakers' interest in the land was acquired by them as the result of a transfer under the provisions of [the Gas Act 1972 or] the Transport Act 1968 [or the Transport (London) Act 1969] from other statutory undertakers and the land was, immediately before transfer, operational land of those other undertakers.

(3) A specific planning permission for the purpose of subsection (2)(*a*) of this section is a planning permission—

(*a*) granted on an application in that behalf under Part III of this Act or the enactments previously in force and replaced by that Part of this Act; or

(b) granted by provisions of a development order granting planning permission generally for development which has received specific parliamentary approval; or

(c) granted by a special development order in respect of development specifically described in the order; or

(d) deemed to be granted by virtue of a direction of a government department under section 40 of this Act, section 41 of the Act of 1962 or section 35 of the Act of 1947;

and the reference in paragraph (b) of this subsection to development which has received specific parliamentary approval shall be construed as referring to development authorised by a local or private Act of Parliament or by an order approved by both Houses of Parliament or by an order which has been brought into operation in accordance with the provisions of the Statutory Orders (Special Procedure) Act 1945, being an Act or order which designates specifically both the nature of the development thereby authorised and the land upon which it may be carried out.   **[258]**

NOTES

Commencement: 1 April 1972.

This section derived from the Town and Country Planning Act 1968, s 69.

Sub-s (2): first amendment made by the Gas Act 1972, s 40; second amendment made by the London Regional Transport Act 1984, s 71(3)(a), Sch 6, para 9.

224. Meaning of "the appropriate Minister"

[(1) In this Act "the appropriate Minister" means—

(a) in relation to statutory undertakers carrying on any railway, light railway, tramway, road transport, dock, harbour or pier undertaking, the Secretary of State for Transport;

(b) in relation to statutory undertakers carrying on an undertaking for the supply of electricity, gas or hydraulic power, the Secretary of State for Energy;

(c) in relation to the British Airports Authority or the Civil Aviation Authority or statutory undertakers carrying on any lighthouse undertaking, the Secretary of State for Trade;

(d) in relation to the Post Office, the Secretary of State for Industry;

[(dd) in relation to statutory undertakers carrying on an undertaking for the supply of water, in the application of this Act to England, the Secretary of State for the Environment;]

(e) in relation to statutory undertakers carrying on an undertaking for the supply of water, in the application of this Act to Wales, the Secretary of State for Wales; and

(f) in relation to any other statutory undertakers, the Secretary of State for the Environment.]

(2) This Act shall have effect as if references to the Secretary of State and the appropriate Minister—

(a) were references to the Secretary of State and the appropriate Minister, if the appropriate Minister is not the one concerned as the Secretary of State; and

(b) were references to the one concerned as the Secretary of State alone, if he is also the appropriate Minister;

and similarly with the references to a Minister and the appropriate Minister and with any provision requiring the Secretary of State to act jointly with the appropriate Minister.   **[259]**

NOTES
Commencement: 8 November 1976 (sub-s (1)); 1 April 1972 (sub-s (2)).
Sub-s (1): substituted by the Secretary of State for Transport Order 1976, SI 1976 No 1775; para
(*dd*) added by the Local Government, Planning and Land Act 1980, s 90, Sch 15.
The Post Office: this reference includes a reference to British Telecommunications by virtue of
the British Telecommunications Act 1981, s 87, Sch 3, para 11(2).

General provisions

225. Applications for planning permission by statutory undertakers

(1) Where—

> (*a*) an application for planning permission to develop land to which this subsection applies is made by statutory undertakers and is referred to the Secretary of State under Part III of this Act; or
>
> (*b*) an appeal is made to the Secretary of State under Part III of this Act from the decision on such an application; or
>
> (*c*) such an application is deemed to be made under subsection [(3) of section 88B] of this Act on an appeal under that section by statutory undertakers,

the application or appeal shall be dealt with by the Secretary of State and the appropriate Minister.

(2) Subsection (1) of this section applies—

> (*a*) to operational land; and
>
> (*b*) to land in which the statutory undertakers hold, or propose to acquire, an interest with a view to its being used for the purpose of carrying on their undertaking where the planning permission, if granted on the application or appeal, would be for development involving the use of the land for that purpose.

(3) An application for planning permission which is deemed to have been made by virtue of section 95(6) of this Act shall be determined by the Secretary of State and the appropriate Minister.

(4) Notwithstanding anything in Part III of this Act, planning permission to develop operational land of statutory undertakers shall not, except with their consent, be granted subject to conditions requiring that any buildings or works authorised by the permission shall be removed, or that any use of the land so authorised shall be discontinued, at the end of a specified period.

(5) Subject to the provisions of this Part of this Act as to compensation, the provisions of this Act shall apply to an application which is dealt with under this section by the Secretary of State and the appropriate Minister as if it had been dealt with by the Secretary of State.   **[260]**

NOTES
Commencement: 1 April 1972.
Sub-s (1): amended by the Local Government and Planning (Amendment) Act 1981, s 1,
Schedule.

226. Development requiring authorisation of government department

(1) Where the authorisation of a government department is required in respect of any development of operational land, then, except where that authorisation has been granted without any direction as to the grant of planning permission, the Secretary of State and the appropriate Minister shall not be required to deal with an application for planning permission under section 225(1) of this Act.

(2) The provisions of subsection (3) of section 40 of this Act shall have effect for the purposes of this section as they have effect for the purposes of that section.   **[261]**

NOTES
Commencement: 1 April 1972.

227. Revocation or modification of permission to develop operational land

In relation to any planning permission, granted on the application of statutory undertakers, for the development of operational land, the provisions of Part III of this Act with respect to the revocation and modification of planning permission shall have effect as if, for any reference therein to the Secretary of State, there were substituted a reference to the Secretary of State and the appropriate Minister.   **[262]**

NOTES
Commencement: 1 April 1972.

228. Order requiring discontinuance of use etc of operational land

The provisions of Part III of this Act with respect to the making of orders requiring the discontinuance of any use of land or imposing conditions on the continuance thereof, or requiring buildings or works on land to be altered or removed, shall have effect, in relation to operational land of statutory undertakers, as if, for any reference therein to the Secretary of State, there were substituted a reference to the Secretary of State and the appropriate Minister.
    [263]

NOTES
Commencement: 1 April 1972.

230. Extinguishment of rights of way, and rights as to apparatus, of statutory undertakers

(1) Where any land has been acquired by a Minister, a local authority or statutory undertakers under Part VI of this Act or compulsorily under any other enactment, or has been appropriated by a local authority for planning purposes, and—

(a) there subsists over that land a right vested in or belonging to statutory undertakers for the purpose of the carrying on of their undertaking, being a right of way or a right of laying down, erecting, continuing or maintaining apparatus on, under or over the land; or

(b) there is on, under or over the land apparatus vested in or belonging to statutory undertakers for the purpose of the carrying on of their undertaking,

the acquiring or appropriating authority, if satisfied that the extinguishment of the right or, as the case may be, the removal of the apparatus, is necessary for the purpose of carrying out any development with a view to which the land was acquired or appropriated, may serve on the statutory undertakers a notice stating that, at the end of the period of twenty-eight days from the date of service of the notice or such longer period as may be specified therein, the right will be extinguished or requiring that, before the end of such period as aforesaid, the apparatus shall be removed.

(2) The statutory undertakers on whom a notice is served under subsection (1) of this section may, before the end of the period of twenty-eight days from

the service of the notice, serve a counter-notice on the acquiring or appropriating authority stating that they object to all or any of the provisions of the notice and specifying the grounds of their objection.

(3) If no counter-notice is served under subsection (2) of this section—

(a) any right to which the notice relates shall be extinguished at the end of the period specified in that behalf in the notice; and

(b) if, at the end of the period so specified in relation to any apparatus, any requirement of the notice as to the removal of the apparatus has not been complied with, the acquiring or appropriating authority may remove the apparatus and dispose of it in any way the authority may think fit.

(4) If a counter-notice is served under subsection (2) of this section on a local authority or on statutory undertakers, the authority or undertakers may either withdraw the notice (without prejudice to the service of a further notice) or may apply to the Secretary of State and the appropriate Minister for an order under this section embodying the provisions of the notice, with or without modification.

(5) If a counter-notice is served under subsection (2) of this section on a Minister, he may withdraw the notice (without prejudice to the service of a further notice) or he and the appropriate Minister may make an order under this section embodying the provisions of the notice, with or without modification.

(6) In this section any reference to the appropriation of land for planning purposes shall be construed in accordance with section 133(1) of this Act as if this section were in Part VI of this Act.

[(7) In subsection (1) above—

(a) the reference in paragraph (a) to a right vested in or belonging to statutory undertakers for the purpose of the carrying on of their undertaking shall include a reference to a right conferred by or in accordance with the telecommunications code on the operator of a telecommunications code system; and

(b) the reference in paragraph (b) to apparatus vested in or belonging to statutory undertakers for the purpose of the carrying on of their undertaking shall include a reference to telecommunication apparatus kept installed for the purposes of any such system;

and for the purposes of this subsection, in this section (except, without prejudice to section 34(4) of the Telecommunications Act 1984, in those paragraphs and the words preceding them) and in sections 231, 237(2) and 238 of this Act references to statutory undertakers shall have effect as references to the operator of any such system, references, in relation to such an operator, to the carrying on of his undertaking shall have effect as references to the running of the telecommunications code system in question and references to the appropriate Minister shall have effect as references to the Secretary of State for Trade and Industry.]   **[264]**

NOTES

Commencement: 5 August 1984 (sub-s (7)); 1 April 1972 (sub-ss (1)-(6)).

Commencement order: SI 1984, No 876.

This section derived from the Town and Country Planning Act 1962, s 164, and the Town and Country Planning Act 1968, s 72.

Sub-s (7): added with savings by the Telecommunications Act 1984, s 109, Sch 4, para 53.

231. Orders under s 230

(1) Where a Minister and the appropriate Minister propose to make an order under section 230(5) of this Act, they shall prepare a draft of the order.

(2) Before making an order under subsection (4) or subsection (5) of section 230 of this Act, the Ministers proposing to make the order—

   (a) shall afford to the statutory undertakers on whom notice was served under subsection (1) of that section an opportunity of objecting to the application for, or proposal to make the order; and

   (b) if any objection is made, shall consider the objection and afford to those statutory undertakers (and, in a case falling within subsection (4) of that section, to the local authority or statutory undertakers on whom the counter-notice was served) an opportunity of appearing before, and being heard by, a person appointed by the Secretary of State and the appropriate Minister for the purpose,

and may then, if they think fit, make the order in accordance with the application or in accordance with the draft order, as the case may be, either with or without modification.

(3) Where an order is made under section 230 of this Act—

   (a) any right to which the order relates shall be extinguished at the end of the period specified in that behalf in the order; and

   (b) if, at the end of the period so specified in relation to any apparatus, any requirement of the order as to the removal of the apparatus has not been complied with, the acquiring or appropriating authority may remove the apparatus and dispose of it in any way the authority may think fit.   **[265]**

NOTES

Commencement: 1 April 1972.

232. Notice for same purposes as s 230 but given by statutory undertakers to developing authority

(1) Subject to the provisions of this section, where land has been acquired or appropriated as mentioned in section 230(1) of this Act, and—

   (a) there is on, under or over the land any apparatus vested in or belonging to statutory undertakers; and

   (b) the undertakers claim that development to be carried out on the land is such as to require, on technical or other grounds connected with the carrying on of their undertaking, the removal or re-siting of the apparatus affected by the development,

the undertakers may serve on the acquiring or appropriating authority a notice claiming the right to enter on the land and carry out such works for the removal or re-siting of the apparatus or any part of it as may be specified in the notice.

(2) Where, after the land has been acquired or appropriated as aforesaid, development of the land is begun to be carried out, no notice under this section shall be served later than twenty-one days after the beginning of the development.

(3) Where a notice is served under this section, the authority on whom it is served may, before the end of the period of twenty-eight days from the date of service, serve on the statutory undertakers a counter-notice stating that they object to all or any of the provisions of the notice and specifying the grounds of their objection.

(4) If no counter-notice is served under subsection (3) of this section, the statutory undertakers shall, after the end of the period of twenty-eight days therein mentioned, have the rights claimed in their notice.

(5) If a counter-notice is served under subsection (3) of this section, the statutory undertakers who served the notice under this section may either withdraw it or may apply to the Secretary of State and the appropriate Minister for an order under this section conferring on the undertakers the rights claimed in the notice or such modified rights as the Secretary of State and the appropriate Minister think it expedient to confer on them.

(6) Where, by virtue of this section or of an order of Ministers thereunder, statutory undertakers have the right to execute works for the removal or resisting of apparatus, they may arrange with the acquiring or appropriating authority for the works to be carried out by that authority, under the superintendence of the undertakers, instead of by the undertakers themselves.

[(7) In subsection (1)(*a*) above, the reference to apparatus vested in or belonging to statutory undertakers shall include a reference to telecommunication apparatus kept installed for the purposes of a telecommunications code system; and, for the purposes of this subsection, in this section references (except in the said subsection (1)(*a*) to statutory undertakers shall have effect as references to the operator of any such system and references to the appropriate Minister shall have effect as references to the Secretary of State for Trade and Industry.]   **[266]**

NOTES

    Commencement: 5 August 1984 (sub-s (7); 1 April 1972 (sub-ss (1)-(6)).
    Commencement order: SI 1984, No 876.
    This section derived from the Town and Country Planning Act 1968, s 73(1)-(6).
    Sub-s (7): added by the Telecommunications Act 1984, s 109, Sch 4, para 53.

233. Extension or modification of functions of statutory undertakers

(1) The powers conferred by this section shall be exercisable where, on a representation made by statutory undertakers, it appears to the Secretary of State and the appropriate Minister to be expedient that the powers and duties of those undertakers should be extended or modified, in order—

    (*a*) to secure the provision of services which would not otherwise be provided, or satisfactorily provided, for any purpose in connection with which a local authority or Minister may be authorised under Part VI of this Act to acquire land or in connection with which any such person may compulsorily acquire land under any other enactment; or

    (*b*) to facilitate an adjustment of the carrying on of the undertaking necessitated by any of the acts and events mentioned in subsection (2) of this section.

(2) The said acts and events are—

    (*a*) the acquisition under Part VI of this Act or compulsorily under any other enactment of any land in which an interest was held, or which was used, for the purpose of the carrying on of the undertaking of the statutory undertakers in question;

    (*b*) the extinguishment of a right or the imposition of any requirement by virtue of section 230 of this Act;

    (*c*) a decision on an application made by the statutory undertakers for planning permission to develop any such land as is mentioned in paragraph (*a*) of this subsection;

(*d*) the revocation or modification of planning permission granted on any such application;

(*e*) the making of an order under section 51 of this Act in relation to any such land.

(3) The powers conferred by this section shall also be exercisable where, on a representation made by a local authority or Minister, it appears to the Secretary of State and the appropriate Minister to be expedient that the powers and duties of statutory undertakers should be extended or modified, in order to secure the provision of new services, or the extension of existing services, for any purpose in connection with which the local authority or Minister making the representation may be authorised under Part VI of this Act to acquire land under any other enactment.

(4) Where the powers conferred by this section are exercisable, the Secretary of State and the appropriate Minister may, if they think fit, by order provide for such extension or modification of the powers and duties of the statutory undertakers as appears to them to be requisite in order to secure the services in question, as mentioned in subsection (1)(*a*) or (3) of this section, or to secure the adjustment in question, as mentioned in subsection (1)(*b*) of this section, as the case may be.

(5) Without prejudice to the generality of subsection (4) of this section, an order under this section may make provision—

(*a*) for empowering the statutory undertakers to acquire (whether compulsorily or by agreement) any land specified in the order, and to erect or construct any buildings or works so specified;

(*b*) for applying, in relation to the acquisition of any such land or the construction of any such works, enactments relating to the acquisition of land and the construction of works;

(*c*) where it has been represented that the making of the order is expedient for the purposes mentioned in subsection (1)(*a*) or (3) of this section, for giving effect to such financial arrangements between the local authority or Minister and the statutory undertakers as they may agree, or as, in default of agreement, may be determined to be equitable in such manner and by such tribunal as may be specified in the order;

(*d*) for such incidental and supplemental matters as appear to the Secretary of State and the appropriate Minister to be expedient for the purposes of the order.   **[267]**

NOTES
Commencement: 1 April 1972.

234. Procedure in relating to orders under s 233

(1) As soon as may be after making such a representation as is mentioned in subsection (1) or subsection (3) of section 233 of this Act—

(*a*) the statutory undertakers, in a case falling within subsection (1) of that section; or

(*b*) the local authority or Minister making the representation, in a case falling within subsection (3) thereof,

shall publish, in such form and manner as may be directed by the Secretary of State and the appropriate Minister, a notice giving such particulars as may be so directed of the matters to which the representation relates, and specifying the time within which, and the manner in which, objections to the making of an order on the representation may be made, and shall also, if it is so directed by the Secretary of State and the appropriate Minister, serve a like notice on such persons, or persons of such classes, as may be so directed.

(2) Orders under section 233 of this Act shall be subject to special parliamentary procedure.   **[268]**

NOTES
Commencement: 1 April 1972.

235. Relief of statutory undertakers from obligations rendered impracticable

(1) Where, on a representation made by statutory undertakers, the appropriate Minister is satisfied that the fulfilment of any obligation incurred by those undertakers in connection with the carrying on of their undertaking has been rendered impracticable by an act or event to which this subsection applies, the appropriate Minister may, if he thinks fit, by order direct that the statutory undertakers shall be relieved of the fulfilment of that obligation, either absolutely or to such extent as may be specified in the order.

(2) Subsection (1) of this section applies to the following acts and events, that is to say—

(a) the compulsory acquisition under Part VI of this Act or under any other enactment of any land in which an interest was held, or which was used, for the purpose of the carrying on of the undertaking of the statutory undertakers; and

(b) the acts and events specified in section 233(2)(b) to (e) of this Act.

(3) As soon as may be after making a representation to the appropriate Minister under subsection (1) of this section, the statutory undertakers shall, as may be directed by the appropriate Minister, either publish (in such form and manner as may be so directed) a notice giving such particulars as may be so directed of the matters to which the representation relates, and specifying the time within which, and the manner in which, objections to the making of an order on the representation may be made, or serve such a notice on such persons, or persons of such classes, as may be so directed, or both publish and serve such notices.

(4) If any objection to the making of an order under this section is duly made and is not withdrawn before the order is made, the order shall be subject to special parliamentary procedure.

(5) Immediately after an order is made under this section by the appropriate Minister, he shall publish a notice stating that the order has been made and naming a place where a copy of it may be seen at all reasonable hours, and shall serve a like notice—

(a) on any person who duly made an objection to the order and has sent to the appropriate Minister a request in writing to serve him with the notice required by this subsection, specifying an address for service; and

(b) on such other persons (if any) as the appropriate Minister thinks fit.

(6) Subject to subsection (7) of this section, and to the provisions of Part XII of this Act, an order under this section shall become operative on the date on which the notice required by subsection (5) of this section is first published.

(7) Where in accordance with subsection (4) of this section the order is subject to special parliamentary procedure, subsection (6) of this section shall not apply.   **[269]**

NOTES

Commencement: 1 April 1972.

236. Objections to orders under ss 233 and 235

(1) For the purposes of sections 233 and 235 of this Act, an objection to the making of an order thereunder shall not be treated as duly made unless—

    (*a*) the objection is made within the time and in the manner specified in the notice required by the section under which the order is proposed to be made; and

    (*b*) a statement in writing of the grounds of the objection is comprised in or submitted with the objection.

(2) Where an objection to the making of such an order is duly made in accordance with subsection (1) of this section and is not withdrawn, the following provisions of this section shall have effect in relation thereto:

Provided that, in the application of those provisions to an order under section 233 of this Act, any reference to the appropriate Minister shall be construed as a reference to the Secretary of State and the appropriate Minister.

(3) Unless the appropriate Minister decides apart from the objection not to make the order, or decides to make a modification which is agreed to by the objector as meeting the objection, the appropriate Minister, before making a final decision, shall consider the grounds of the objection as set out in the statement, and may, if he thinks fit, require the objector to submit within a specified period a further statement in writing as to any of the matters to which the objection relates.

(4) In so far as the appropriate Minister, after considering the grounds of the objection as set out in the original statement and in any such further statement, is satisfied that the objection relates to a matter which can be dealt with in the assessment of compensation, the appropriate Minister may treat the objection as irrelevant for the purpose of making a final decision.

(5) If, after considering the grounds of the objection as set out in the original statement and in any such further statement, the appropriate Minister is satisfied that, for the purpose of making a final decision, he is sufficiently informed as to the matters to which the objection relates, or if, where a further statement has been required, it is not submitted within the specified period, the appropriate Minister may make a final decision without further investigation as to those matters.

(6) Subject to subsections (4) and (5) of this section, the appropriate Minister, before making a final decision, shall afford to the objector an opportunity of appearing before, and being heard by, a person appointed for the purpose by the appropriate Minister; and if the objector avails himself of that opportunity, the appropriate Minister shall afford an opportunity of appearing and being heard on the same occasion to the statutory undertakers, local authority or Minister on whose representation the order is proposed to be made, and to any other persons to whom it appears to the appropriate Minister to be expedient to afford such an opportunity.

(7) Notwithstanding anything in the preceding provisions of this section, if

it appears to the appropriate Minister that the matters to which the objection relates are such as to require investigation by public local inquiry before he makes a final decision, he shall cause such an inquiry to be held; and where he determines to cause such an inquiry to be held, any of the requirements of those provisions to which effect has not been given at the time of that determination shall be dispensed with.

(8) In this section any reference to making a final decision, in relation to an order, is a reference to deciding whether to make the order or what modification (if any) ought to be made.   **[270]**

NOTES
Commencement: 1 April 1972.

Compensation

237. Right to compensation in respect of certain decisions and orders

(1) Statutory undertakers shall, subject to the following provisions of this Part of this Act, be entitled to compensation from the local planning authority—

    (*a*) in respect of any decision made in accordance with section 225 of this Act whereby planning permission to develop operational land of those undertakers is refused or is granted subject to conditions where—

        (i) planning permission for that development would have been granted by a development order but for a direction given under such an order that planning permission so granted should not apply to the development; and

        (ii) it is not development which has received specific parliamentary approval (within the meaning given to that expression by section 223(3) of this Act);

    (*b*) in respect of any order under section 45 of this Act as modified by section 227 thereof, whereby planning permission, granted on the application of those undertakers for the development of any such land, is revoked or modified.

(2) Where, by virtue of section 230 of this Act, any right vested in or belonging to statutory undertakers is extinguished, or any requirement is imposed on statutory undertakers, those undertakers shall be entitled to compensation from the acquiring or appropriating authority at whose instance the right was extinguished or the requirement imposed.

(3) Where works are carried out for the removal or re-siting of statutory undertakers' apparatus, being works which the undertakers have the right to carry out by virtue of section 232 of this Act or an order of Ministers thereunder, the undertakers shall be entitled to compensation from the acquiring or appropriating authority.

(4) Notwithstanding anything in subsection (1) of this section, if the decision or order in question relates to land acquired by the statutory undertakers after 7th January 1947, and the Secretary of State and the appropriate Minister are satisfied, having regard to the nature, situation and existing development of the land and of any neighbouring land, and to any other material considerations, that it is unreasonable that compensation should be recovered in respect of that decision or order, they may include therein a direction that subsection (1) of this section shall not apply to that decision or order.

(5) For the purposes of this section the conditions referred to in sections 41

and 42 of this Act shall be disregarded and no compensation shall be payable under this section in respect of the imposition of any condition to which section 71 or 82 of this Act applies. **[271]**

NOTES
Commencement: 1 April 1972.
Sub-s (5): repealed in part by the Housing and Planning Act 1986, s 49(2), Sch 12, Part III. See Appendix.

238. Measure of compensation to statutory undertakers

(1) Where statutory undertakers are entitled to compensation—

(*a*) as mentioned in subsection (1), (2) or (3) of section 237 of this Act; or

(*b*) under the provisions of section 170 in respect of an order made under section 51 [, 51A or 51B] of this Act as modified by section 228 thereof; or

(*c*) in respect of a compulsory acquisition of land which has been acquired by those undertakers for the purposes of their undertaking, where the first-mentioned acquisition is effected under a compulsory purchase order confirmed or made without the appropriate Minister's certificate;

the amount of the compensation shall (subject to section 239 of this Act) be an amount calculated in accordance with the following provisions of this section.

(2) The said amount, subject to subsections (3) and (4) of this section, shall be the aggregate of the following amounts, that is to say—

(*a*) the amount of any expenditure reasonably incurred in acquiring land, providing apparatus, erecting buildings or doing work for the purpose of any adjustment of the carrying on of the undertaking rendered necessary by the proceeding giving rise to compensation;

(*b*) whichever of the following is applicable, namely—

(i) where such an adjustment is made, the estimated amount of any decrease in net receipts from the carrying on of the undertaking pending the adjustment, in so far as the decrease is directly attributable to the proceeding giving rise to compensation, together with such amount as appears reasonable compensation for any estimated decrease in net receipts from the carrying on of the undertaking in the period after the adjustment has been completed, in so far as the decrease is directly attributable to the adjustment;

(ii) where no such adjustment is made, such amount as appears reasonable compensation for any estimated decrease in net receipts from the carrying on of the undertaking which is directly attributable to the proceeding giving rise to compensation;

(*c*) where the compensation is under section 237(2) of this Act, and is in respect of the imposition of a requirement to remove apparatus, the amount of any expenditure reasonably incurred by the statutory undertakers in complying with the requirement, reduced by the value after removal of the apparatus removed.

(3) Where any such adjustment as is mentioned in paragraph (*a*) of subsection (2) of this section is made, the aggregate amount mentioned in that subsection shall be reduced by such amount (if any) as appears to the Lands Tribunal to be appropriate to offset—

(*a*) the estimated value of any property (whether moveable or immoveable) belonging to the statutory undertakers and used for the carrying on of their undertaking which, in consequence of the adjustment, ceases to be so used, in so far as the value of the property has not been taken into account under paragraph (*c*) of that subsection; and

(*b*) the estimated amount of any increase in net receipts from the carrying on of the undertaking in the period after the adjustment has been completed, in so far as that amount has not been taken into account under paragraph (*b*) of that subsection and is directly attributable to the adjustment,

and by any further amount which appears to the Lands Tribunal to be appropriate, having regard to any increase in the capital value of immoveable property belonging to the statutory undertakers which is directly attributable to the adjustment, allowance being made for any reduction made under paragraph (*b*) of this subsection.

(4) Where the compensation is under section 237(3) of this Act and the acquiring or appropriating authority carry out the works, then, in addition to any reduction falling to be made under subsection (3) of this section, the aggregate amount mentioned in subsection (2) of this section shall be reduced by the actual cost to the authority of carrying out the works.

(5) References in this section to a decrease in net receipts shall be construed as references to the amount by which a balance of receipts over expenditure is decreased, or a balance of expenditure over receipts is increased, or, where a balance of receipts over expenditure is converted into a balance of expenditure over receipts, as references to the aggregate of the two balances; and references to an increase in net receipts shall be construed accordingly.

(6) In this section—

"proceeding giving rise to compensation" means—

(*a*) except in relation to compensation under section 237(3) of this Act, the particular action (that is to say, the decision, order, extinguishment of a right, imposition of a requirement, or acquisition) in respect of which compensation falls to be assessed, as distinct from any development or project in connection with which that action may have been taken;

(*b*) in relation to compensation under the said section 237(3), the circumstances making it necessary for the apparatus in question to be removed or re-sited;

"the appropriate Minister's certificate" [means such a certificate as is mentioned in section 16 of, or paragraph 3 of Schedule 3 to, the Acquisition of Land Act 1981]. **[272]**

NOTES
Commencement: 1 April 1972.
This section derived from the Town and Country Planning Act 1962, s 171, and the Town and Country Planning Act 1968, s 73(7), (8).
Sub-s (1): amended by the Town and Country Planning (Minerals) Act 1981, s 34, Sch 1.
Sub-s (6): amended by the Acquisition of Land Act 1981, s 34(1), Sch 4.

239. Exclusion of s 238 at option of statutory undertakers

(1) Where statutory undertakers are entitled to compensation in respect of such a compulsory acquisition as is mentioned in section 238(1)(*c*) of this Act, the statutory undertakers may by notice in writing under this section elect that the compensation shall be ascertained in accordance with the enactments (other than rule (5) of the rules set out in section 5 of the Land Compensation Act 1961) which would be applicable apart from section 238 of this Act; and if the undertakers so elect the compensation shall be ascertained accordingly.

(2) An election under this section may be made either in respect of the whole of the land comprised in the compulsory acquisition in question or in respect of part of that land.

(3) Any notice under this section shall be given to the acquiring authority before the end of the period of two months from the date of service of notice to treat in respect of the interest of the statutory undertakers. **[273]**

NOTES
Commencement: 1 April 1972.

240. Procedure for assessing compensation where s 238 applies

(1) Where the amount of any such compensation as is mentioned in subsection (1) of section 238 of this Act falls to be ascertained in accordance with the provisions of that section, the compensation shall, in default of agreement, be assessed by the Lands Tribunal, if apart from this section it would not fall to be so assessed.

(2) For the purposes of any proceedings arising before the Lands Tribunal in respect of compensation falling to be ascertained as mentioned in subsection (1) of this section, the provisions of sections 2 and 4 of the Land Compensation Act 1961 shall apply as they apply to proceedings on a question referred to the Tribunal under section 1 of that Act, but with the substitution in section 4 of that Act, for references to the acquiring authority, of references to the person from whom the compensation is claimed. **[274]**

NOTES
Commencement: 1 April 1972.

Supplementary provisions

241. Special provisions as to display of advertisements on operational land

(1) The provisions of this Part of this Act specified in subsection (2) of this section do not apply in relation to the display of advertisements on operational land of statutory undertakers.

(2) The said provisions are sections 225 to 228 and 237(1) and (4) of this Act. **[275]**

NOTES
Commencement: 1 April 1972.

PART XII

VALIDITY OF PLANNING INSTRUMENTS AND DECISIONS AND PROCEEDINGS RELATING THERETO

242. Validity of development plans and certain orders, decisions and directions

(1) Except as provided by the following provisions of this Part of this Act, the validity of—

> (a) a structure plan, *a local plan* [, local plan or unitary development plan] or any alteration, repeal or replacement of any such plan, whether before or after the plan, alteration, repeal or replacement has been approved or adopted; or

(b) an order under any provision of Part X of this Act except section 214(1)(a), whether before or after the order has been made; or

(c) an order under section 235 of this Act, whether before or after the order has been made; or

(d) any such order as is mentioned in subsection (2) of this section, whether before or after it has been confirmed; or

(e) any such action on the part of the Secretary of State as is mentioned in subsection (3) of this section,

shall not be questioned in any legal proceedings whatsoever.

(2) The orders referred to in subsection (1)(d) of this section are orders of any of the following descriptions, that is to say—

(a) any order under section 45 of this Act or under the provisions of that section as applied by or under any other provision of this Act;

(b) any order under section 51 of this Act;

[(ba) any order under section 51A of this Act;

(bb) any order under section 51B of this Act;]

(c) any tree preservation order;

(d) any order made in pursuance of section 63(4) of this Act;

(e) any order under Part II of Schedule 11 to this Act.

(3) The action referred to in subsection (1)(e) of this section is action on the part of the Secretary of State of any of the following descriptions, that is to say—

(a) any decision of the Secretary of State on an application for planning permission referred to him under section 35 of this Act;

(b) any decision of the Secretary of State on an appeal under section 36 of this Act;

(c) the giving by the Secretary of State of any direction under section 38 of this Act;

(d) any decision by the Secretary of State to confirm a completion notice under section 44 of this Act;

(e) any decision of the Secretary of State relating to an application for consent under a tree preservation order, or relating to an application for consent under any regulations made in accordance with section 63 of this Act, or relating to any certificate or direction under any such order or regulations, whether it is a decision of the Secretary of State on appeal or a decision on an application referred to him for determination in the first instance;

(f) any decision of the Secretary of State to grant planning permission under [paragraph (a) of section 88B(1) of this Act or to discharge a condition or limitation under paragraph (b) of that subsection];

(g) any decision of the Secretary of State on an application for an established use certificate referred to him under subsection (1) of section 95 of this Act or on an appeal under subsection (2) of that section;

(h) any decision of the Secretary of State [to grant listed building consent under paragraph (a) of section 97A(4) of this Act or to discharge a condition or limitation under paragraph (b) of that subsection];

(i) any decision of the Secretary of State to confirm a purchase notice or listed building purchase notice;

(j) any decision of the Secretary of State not to confirm a purchase notice or listed building purchase notice, including any decision not to confirm such a notice in respect of part of the land to which it relates, and including any decision to grant any permission, or give any direction, in lieu of confirming such a notice, either wholly or in part;

(k) any decision of the Secretary of State on an application referred to him under paragraph 4 of Schedule 11 to this Act (being an application for listed building consent for any works) or on an appeal under paragraph 8 of that Schedule.

(4) Nothing in this section shall affect the exercise of any jurisdiction of any court in respect of any refusal or failure on the part of the Secretary of State to take any such action as is mentioned in subsection (3) of this section.   **[276]**

NOTES

Commencement: 1 April 1972.

This section derived from the Town and Country Planning Act 1962, s 176, and the Town and Country Planning Act 1968, Sch 9, para 35.

Sub-s (1): in para (*a*) words in italics prospectively repealed and words in square brackets prospectively substituted by the Local Government Act 1985, s 4, Sch 1, para 16, as from a day or days to be appointed; prospectively amended by the Housing and Planning Act 1986, s 25(3), Sch 6, Part II, para 4. See Appendix.

Sub-s (2): amended by the Town and Country Planning (Minerals) Act 1981, s 34, Sch 1.

Sub-s (3): paras (*f*), (*h*) amended by the Local Government (Miscellaneous Provisions) Act 1982, s 47, Sch 6, para 7; prospectively amended by the Housing and Planning Act 1986, s 33, Sch 7, Part I, para 2. See Appendix.

243. Validity of enforcement notices and similar notices

(1) Subject to the provisions of this section—

(a) the validity of an enforcement notice shall not, except by way of an appeal under Part V of this Act, be questioned in any proceedings whatsoever on any of the grounds [on which such an appeal may be brought];

(b) the validity of a listed building enforcement notice shall not, except by way of an appeal under Part V of this Act, be questioned in any proceedings whatsoever on any of the grounds [on which such an appeal may be brought].

[(2) Subsection (1)(a) of this section shall not apply to proceedings brought under section 89(5) of this Act against a person who—

(a) has held an interest in the land since before the enforcement notice was issued under Part V of this Act; and

(b) did not have a copy of the enforcement notice served on him under that Part of this Act; and

(c) satisfies the court—

(i) that he did not know and could not reasonably have been expected to know that the enforcement notice had been issued; and

(ii) that his interests have been substantially prejudiced by the failure to serve him with a copy of it.

(2A) Where the enforcement notice was served before the passing of the Local Government and Planning (Amendment) Act 1981, subsection (2) of this section shall have effect as if—

(a) in paragraph (a), the word "served" were substituted for the word "issued";

(b) the following paragraph were substituted for paragraph (b):—

"(b) did not have the enforcement notice or a copy of it served on him under that Part of this Act; and"

(c) in paragraph (c)—

(i) in sub-paragraph (i) the word "served" were substituted for the word "issued"; and

(ii) the words "with a copy of it" were omitted from sub-paragraph (ii).]

(3) Subject to subsection (4) of this section, the validity of a notice which has been served under section 65 of this Act on the owner and occupier of the land shall not, except by way of an appeal under Part V of this Act, be questioned in any proceedings whatsoever on any of the grounds specified in section 105(1)(*a*) to (*c*) of this Act.

(4) Subsection (3) of this section shall not apply to proceedings brought under section 104 of this Act against a person on whom the notice referred to in that subsection was not served, but who has held an interest in the land since before that notice was served on the owner and occupier of the land, if he did not appeal against the notice under Part V of this Act.

(5) The validity of a notice purporting to be an enforcement notice shall not depend on whether any non-compliance to which the notice relates was a non-compliance with conditions, or with limitations, or with both; and any reference in such a notice to non-compliance with conditions or limitations (whether both expressions are used in the notice or only one of them) shall be construed as a reference to non-compliance with conditions, or with limitations, or both with conditions and limitations, as the case may require.   **[277]**

NOTES
Commencement: 1 April 1972.
Amended by the Local Government and Planning (Amendment) Act 1981, s 1, Schedule.

244. Proceedings for questioning validity of development plans and certain orders under Parts X and XI

(1) If any person aggrieved by a structure plan or local plan or by any alteration, repeal or replacement of any such plan desires to question the validity of the plan, alteration, repeal or replacement on the ground that it is not within the powers conferred by Part II of this Act, or that any requirement of the said Part II or of any regulations made thereunder has not been complied with in relation to the approval or adoption of the plan, alteration, repeal or replacement, he may, within six weeks from the date of the publication of the first notice of the approval or adoption of the plan, alteration, repeal or replacement required by regulations under section 18(1) of this Act, make an application to the High Court under this section.

(2) On any application under this section the High Court—

(*a*) may by interim order wholly or in part suspend the operation of the plan, alteration, repeal or replacement, either generally or in so far as it affects any property of the applicant, until the final determination of the proceedings;

(*b*) if satisfied that the plan, alteration, repeal or replacement is wholly or to any extent outside the powers conferred by Part II of this Act, or that the interests of the applicant have been substantially prejudiced by the failure to comply with any requirement of the said Part II or of any regulations made thereunder, may wholly or in part quash the plan, alteration, repeal or replacement, as the case may be, either generally or in so far as it affects any property of the applicant.

(3) The preceding provisions of this section shall apply, subject to any

necessary modifications, to an order under section 209, 211, 212 or 214(1)(*a*) of this Act as they apply to a structure plan, and as if, in subsection (1) of this section, for the reference to the notice therein mentioned, there were substituted a reference to the notice required by section 215(7) of this Act.

(4) The said provisions shall apply, subject to any necessary modifications, to an order under section 210 or 214(1)(*b*) of this Act as they apply to a structure plan, and as if, in subsection (1) of this section, for the reference to the date on which the notice therein mentioned is first published there were substituted a reference to the date on which the notice required by paragraph 6 of Schedule 20 to this Act is first published in accordance with that paragraph.

(5) Subsections (1) and (2) of this section shall apply, subject to any necessary modifications, to an order under section 235 of this Act as they apply to a structure plan.

[(6) Subsections (1) and (2) of this section shall apply to a unitary development plan as they apply to a structure plan or local plan as if references to Part II of this Act and section 18(1) of this Act were references to Part I of Schedule 1 to the Local Government Act 1985 and paragraph 14 of that Schedule.]   **[278]**

NOTES
  Commencement: 1 April 1972; to be appointed (sub-s (6)).
  This section derived from the Town and Country Planning Act 1962, s 178.
  Sub-s (6): prospectively added by the Local Government Act 1985, s 4, Sch 1, para 16, as from a day or days to be appointed.
  New sub-s (7) prospectively inserted by the Housing and Planning Act 1986, s 25(3), Sch 6, Part II, para 5. See Appendix.

245. Proceedings for questioning validity of other orders, decisions and directions

(1) If any person—

    (*a*) is aggrieved by any order to which this section applies and desires to question the validity of that order, on the grounds that the order is not within the powers of this Act, or that any of the relevant requirements have not been complied with in relation to that order; or

    (*b*) is aggrieved by any action on the part of the Secretary of State to which this section applies and desires to question the validity of that action, on the grounds that the action is not within the powers of this Act, or that any of the relevant requirements have not been complied with in relation to that action,

he may, within six weeks from the date on which the order is confirmed or the action is taken, as the case may be, make an application to the High Court under this section.

(2) Without prejudice to subsection (1) of this section, if the authority directly concerned with any order to which this section applies, or with any action on the part of the Secretary of State to which this section applies, desire to question the validity of that order or action on any of the grounds mentioned in subsection (1) of this section, the authority may, within six weeks from the date on which the order is confirmed or the action is taken, as the case may be, make an application to the High Court under this section.

(3) This section applies to any such order as is mentioned in subsection (2) of section 242 of this Act and to any such action on the part of the Secretary of State as is mentioned in subsection (3) of that section.

(4) On any application under this section the High Court—

(*a*) may by interim order suspend the operation of the order or action, the validity whereof is questioned by the application, until the final determination of the proceedings;

(*b*) if satisfied that the order or action in question is not within the powers of this Act, or that the interests of the applicant have been substantially prejudiced by a failure to comply with any of the relevant requirements in relation thereto, may quash that order or action:

Provided that paragraph (*a*) of this subsection shall not apply to applications questioning the validity of tree preservation orders.

(5) In relation to a tree preservation order, or to an order made in pursuance of section 63(4) of this Act, the powers conferred on the High Court by subsection (4) of this section shall be exercisable by way of quashing or (where applicable) suspending the operation of the order either in whole or in part, as the court may determine.

(6) References in this section to the confirmation of an order include the confirmation of an order subject to modifications as well as the confirmation of an order in the form in which it was made.

(7) In this section "the relevant requirements", in relation to any order or action to which this section applies, means any requirements of this Act or of the Tribunals and Inquiries Act 1971 (or any enactment replaced thereby), or of any order, regulations or rules made under this Act or under that Act (or any such enactment) which are applicable to that order or action, [and any reference to the authority directly concerned with any order or action to which this section applies—

(*a*) in relation to any such decision as is mentioned in section 242(3)(*i*) or (*j*) of this Act, is a reference to the council on whom the notice in question was served and, in a case where the Secretary of State has modified such a notice wholly or in part by substituting another local authority or statutory undertakers for that council, includes a reference to that local authority or statutory undertakers;

(*b*) in any other case in Greater London, is a reference to the local planning authority; and

(*c*) in any other case outside Greater London, is a reference to the local planning authority who made the order in question or made the decision or served the notice to which the proceedings in question relate, or who referred the matter to the Secretary of State, or, where the order or notice in question was made or served by him, the authority named in the order or notice.].   **[279]**

NOTES
Commencement: 1 April 1972.
Amended by the Local Government Act 1972, s 182, Sch 16.

246. Appeals to High Court relating to enforcement notices and smilar notices

[(1) Where the Secretary of State gives a decision in proceedings on an appeal under Part V of this Act against—

(*a*) an enforcement notice; or

(*b*) a listed building enforcement notice,

the appellant or the local planning authority or any other person having an interest in the land to which the notice relates may, according as rules of court may provide, either appeal to the High Court against the decision on a point of law or require the Secretary of State to state and sign a case for the opinion of the High Court.

(1A) Where the Secretary of State gives a decision in proceedings on an appeal under Part V of this Act against a notice under section 103 of this Act, the appellant or the local planning authority or any person (other than the appellant) on whom the notice was served may, according as rules of court may provide, either appeal to the High Court against the decision on a point of law or require the Secretary of State to state and sign a case for the opinion of the High Court.]

(2) At any stage of the proceedings on any such appeal as is mentioned in subsection (1) of this section, the Secretary of State may state any question of law arising in the course of the proceedings in the form of a special case for the decision of the High Court; and a decision of the High Court on a case stated by virtue of this subsection shall be deemed to be a judgment of the court within the meaning of [section 16 of the Supreme Court Act 1981] (jurisdiction of the Court of Appeal to hear and determine appeals from any judgment of the High Court).

(3) In relation to any proceedings in the High Court or the Court of Appeal brought by virtue of this section the power to make rules of court shall include power to make rules—

(a) prescribing the powers of the High Court or the Court of Appeal with respect to the remitting of the matter with the opinion or direction of the court for re-hearing and determination by the Secretary of State; and

(b) providing for the Secretary of State, either generally or in such circumstances as may be prescribed by the rules, to be treated as a party to any such proceedings and to be entitled to appear and to be heard accordingly.

(4) . . . no appeal to the Court of Appeal shall be brought by virtue of this section except with the leave of the High Court or the Court of Appeal.

(5) In this section "decision" includes a direction or order, and references to the giving of a decision shall be construed accordingly.

[(6) In the case of a listed building enforcement notice issued by the Historic Buildings and Monuments Commission for England subsection (1) above shall apply as if the reference to the local planning authority were a reference to the Commission.]   **[280]**

NOTES
   Commencement: 1 April 1986 (sub-s (6)); 27 August 1981 (sub-ss (1), (1A)); 1 April 1972 (remainder).
   This section derived from the Town and Country Planning Act 1962, s 180.
   Sub-ss (1), (1A): substituted for existing sub-s (1) by the Local Government and Planning (Amendment) Act 1981, s 1, Schedule.
   Sub-s (2): words in square brackets substituted by the Supreme Court Act 1981, s 152(1), Sch 5.
   Sub-s (4): words omitted repealed by the Administration of Justice Act 1977, s 32, Sch 5.
   Sub-s (6): added by the Local Government Act 1985, s 6, Sch 2, para 1.

247. Appeals to High Court against decisions under s 53

(1) If, in the case of any decision to which this section applies, the person who made the application to which the decision relates, or the local planning authority, is dissatisfied with the decision in point of law, that person or the local planning authority (as the case may be) may, according as rules of court

may provide, either appeal against the decision to the High Court or require the Secretary of State to state and sign a case for the opinion of the High Court.

(2) This section applies to any decision of the Secretary of State—

    (*a*) on an application under section 53 of this Act which is referred to the Secretary of State under the provisions of section 35 of this Act as applied by that section; or

    (*b*) on an appeal from a decision of the local planning authority under section 53 of this Act, being an appeal brought under the provisions of section 36 of this Act as so applied.

(3) Where an application under section 53 of this Act is made as part of an application for planning permission, the preceding provisions of this section shall have effect in relation to that application in so far as it is an application under the said section 53, but not in so far as it is an application for planning permission.

(4) In relation to proceedings in the High Court or the Court of Appeal brought by virtue of this section, the power to make rules of court shall include power to make rules prescribing the powers of the High Court or the Court of Appeal with respect to—

    (*a*) the giving of any decision which might have been given by the Secretary of State;

    (*b*) the remitting of the matter, with the opinion or direction of the court, for re-hearing and determination by the Secretary of State;

    (*c*) the giving of directions to the Secretary of State.

(5) . . . no appeal to the Court of Appeal shall be brought by virtue of this section except with the leave of the High Court or the Court of Appeal.

(6) Without prejudice to the preceding provisions of this section, the power to make rules of court in relation to proceedings in the High Court or the Court of Appeal brought by virtue of this section shall include power to make rules providing for the Secretary of State, either generally or in such circumstances as may be prescribed by the rules, to be treated as a party to any such proceedings and to be entitled to appear and to be heard accordingly. **[281]**

NOTES
Commencement: 1 April 1972.
Words omitted repealed by the Administration of Justice Act 1977, s 32, Sch 5.

248. Special provisions as to decisions relating to statutory undertakers

In relation to any action which—

    (*a*) apart from the provisions of Part XI of this Act, would fall to be taken by the Secretary of State, and, if so taken, would be action falling within section 242(3) of this Act; but

    (*b*) by virtue of Part XI of this Act, is required to be taken by the Secretary of State and the appropriate Minister,

the provisions of sections 242 and 245 of this Act shall have effect (subject to section 249 of this Act) as if any reference in those provisions to the Secretary of State were a reference to the Secretary of State and the appropriate Minister. **[282]**

NOTES
Commencement: 1 April 1972.

249. Special provisions as to orders subject to special parliamentary procedure

(1) Where an order under section 209, 211, 212 or 235 of this Act is subject to special parliamentary procedure, then—

    (*a*) if the order is confirmed by Act of Parliament under section 6 of the Statutory Orders (Special Procedure) Act 1945, the provisions of sections 242 and 244 of this Act shall not apply to the order;

    (*b*) in any other case, section 244 of this Act shall have effect in relation to the order as if, in subsection (1) of that section, for the reference to the date therein mentioned there were substituted a reference to the date on which the order becomes operative under section 6 of the said Act of 1945.

(2) Where by virtue of Part XI of this Act any such action as is mentioned in section 248 of this Act is required to be embodied in an order, and that order is subject to special parliamentary procedure, then—

    (*a*) if the order in which the action is embodied is confirmed by Act of Parliament under section 6 of the said Act of 1945, the provisions of sections 242 and 245 of this Act shall not apply;

    (*b*) in any other case, the provisions of section 245 of this Act shall apply with the substitution, for any reference to the date on which the action is taken, of a reference to the date on which the order becomes operative under section 6 of the said Act of 1945.   **[283]**

NOTES
Commencement: 1 April 1972.

PART XIII

FINANCIAL PROVISIONS

Grants for development etc

250. Grants for development etc

(1) The Secretary of State may with the consent of the Treasury and after consultation with such associations of local authorities as appear to the Secretary of State to be concerned and with any local authority with whom consultation appears to him to be desirable, make regulations providing for the payment to local authorities for any year of grants of such amounts, and payable over such periods and subject to such conditions, as may be determined by or under the regulations in respect of expenditure incurred by those authorities (whether before or after the passing of this Act) in or in connection with the acquisition of land approved for the purposes of the regulations, being land required for or in connection with—

    (*a*) the development or redevelopment as a whole of any area (whether or not defined in a development plan as an area of comprehensive development); or

    (*b*) the relocation of population or industry, or the replacement of open space, in the course or in consequence of such development or redevelopment,

or in respect of expenditure so incurred in or in connection with the clearing or preliminary development of such land.

(2) For the purposes of regulations under this section land appropriated by a local authority (whether before or after the passing of this Act) for use for purposes described in subsection (1) of this section may be treated as acquired

by that authority for those purposes at a cost of such amount, and defrayed in such manner, as may be determined by or under the regulations.

(3) Provision may be made by regulations under this section—

(a) for the inclusion, in the expenditure incurred by local authorities in the acquisition of land approved for the purposes of the regulations, of any sums or part of sums paid by those authorities in connection with any restriction imposed on the development or use of the land by or under any enactment (whether by way of compensation or by way of contribution towards damage or expense incurred in consequence of the restriction);

(b) for the calculation of grants payable under the regulations by reference to the amount of the annual costs incurred or treated as being incurred by local authorities in respect of the borrowing of money to defray the expenditure in respect of which the grants are made, or by reference to the excess of such annual costs over receipts of those authorities which are attributable to such expenditure, or over the annual value of such receipts, or by reference to such other considerations as may be prescribed by the regulations;

(c) for the payment of capital sums in substitution for any periodical grants payable under the regulations in respect of such annual costs;

and for the purposes of this section "clearing" and "preliminary development" means the carrying out of such works as may be prescribed by or determined under the regulations.

(4) In this section "year" means a period of twelve months beginning with the first day of April.   **[284]**

NOTES
Commencement: 1 April 1972.
This section and ss 251, 252 repealed by the Housing and Planning Act 1986, s 48(1)(c) and s 49(2), Sch 12, Part III. See Appendix. For a saving, see s 48(2)(b) of that Act. See Appendix.

251. Maximum amount of grants under s 250

(1) Subject to the following provisions of this section, the amount of any grant paid to a local authority in accordance with regulations made under section 250 of this Act—

(a) where that amount is calculated by reference to annual costs incurred or treated as incurred by the authority in respect of the borrowing of money to defray expenditure in respect of which the grant is made, or by reference to the excess of such annual costs over the receipts, or the annual value of receipts, mentioned in subsection (3)(b) of that section, shall not exceed an amount equal to fifty per cent. of those costs, or of that excess, as the case may be;

(b) in any other case, shall not exceed an amount equal to fifty per cent. of the amount of the expenditure in respect of which the grant is made.

(2) In respect of land of any of the following descriptions, that is to say—

(a) land comprised in a compulsory purchase order made by a local authority under the Act of 1944 or the Act of 1947, and confirmed before 26th February 1954, being land acquired for war-damage redevelopment;

(b) land acquired by agreement for war-damage redevelopment with the consent of the Minister of Housing and Local Government given before that date;

(c) land appropriated by a local authority for war-damage redevelopment before that date; and

(d) land acquired or appropriated for war-damage redevelopment (whether before or after that date), being land contiguous or adjacent to land falling within any of the preceding paragraphs,

subsection (1)(*a*) of this section shall apply (subject to subsection (3) of this section) as if for the words "fifty per cent." there were substituted the words "ninety per cent.".

(3) Subsection (2) of this section shall not authorise the payment, in the case of any land, of a grant at a higher rate in respect of a year or part of a year which, together with the preceding years or parts of years in respect of which grants at a higher rate have been paid in the case of that land, would extend beyond a total period of eight years.

(4) In this section "war-damage redevelopment" means the redevelopment as a whole of an area of extensive war damage, and includes the relocation of population or industry, or the replacement of open space, in the course of such redevelopment.

(5) In this section references to a grant at a higher rate are references to a grant of an amount which—

(*a*) was or would have been authorised by section 93 of the Act of 1947 as that section had effect or would have had effect apart from section 50 of the Act of 1954 and the Local Government Act 1958 and this Act; but

(*b*) otherwise than by virtue of the provisions of the Act of 1954 corresponding to subsections (2) and (3) of this section, was not or would not have been authorised by the provisions substituted by the Act of 1954 for the said section 93.   [285]

NOTES
Commencement: 1 April 1972.
Repealed as noted to s 250 above.

252. Supplementary provisions as to grants under s 250

(1) Any approval of the Secretary of State required for the purposes of the payment of grant under section 250 of this Act in connection with the acquisition of land may be given subject to compliance with requirements imposed by the Secretary of State for securing that any negotiations for the acquisition of the land by the local authority will be carried out by the Valuation Office, and that any valuation of the land for the purposes of the acquisition, or for any purposes of the regulations, will be made by that office.

(2) Subject to subsection (1) of this section, any regulations made for the purposes of section 250 of this Act may make provision whereby the payment of grants in pursuance of the regulations is dependent upon the fulfilment of such conditions as may be determined by or in accordance with the regulations, and may also make provision for requiring local authorities to whom grants have been so paid to comply with such requirements as may be so determined.
                                                                              [286]

NOTES
Commencement: 1 April 1972.
Repealed as noted to s 250 above.

Grants for research and education

253. Grants for research and education

The Secretary of State may, with the consent of the Treasury, make grants for assisting establishments engaged in promoting or assisting research relating to, and education with respect to, the planning and design of the physical environment. **[287]**

NOTES
Commencement: 1 April 1972.

Contributions to certain expenditure

254. Contributions by Ministers towards compensation paid by local authorities

Where compensation is payable by a local authority under this Act in consequence of any decision or order given or made under—

    (*a*) Part III or Part IV of this Act;
    (*b*) sections 87 to 100 of this Act;
    (*c*) the provisions of Part IX of this Act relating to purchase notices;
    (*d*) Schedule 9 to this Act,

then if that decision or order was given or made wholly or partly in the interest of a service which is provided by a government department and the cost of which is defrayed out of moneys provided by Parliament, the Minister responsible for the administration of that service may pay to that authority a contribution of such amount as he may with the consent of the Treasury determine. **[288]**

NOTES
Commencement: 1 April 1972.

255. Contributions by local authorities and statutory undertakers

(1) Without prejudice to the provisions of [section 274 of the Highways Act 1980 (contributions by local authorities towards expenses of highway authorities)], any local authority may contribute towards any expenses incurred by a local highway authority in the acquisition of land under Part VI of this Act, or in the construction or improvement of roads on land so acquired, or in connection with any development required in the interests of the proper planning of the area of the local authority.

(2) Any local authority and any statutory undertakers may contribute towards—

    (*a*) any expenses incurred by a local planning authority in or in connection with the carrying out of a survey or the preparation of a structure plan or local plan under Part II of this Act [or of a unitary development plan under Part I of Schedule 1 to the Local Government Act 1985];
    (*b*) any expenses incurred by a local planning authority, or by the council of a county district, in or in connection with the performance of any of their functions under Part III (except section 28), Part IV, Part V (except section 101 and 103) or Part VI (except section 126) of this Act, under the provisions of Part IX of this Act relating to purchase notices and listed building purchase notices or under Schedule 11 to this Act.

(3) Where any expenses are incurred by a local authority in the payment of compensation payable in consequence of anything done under—

(a) Part III or Part IV of this Act;
(b) sections 87 to 100 of this Act;
(c) the provisions of Part IX of this Act relating to purchase notices and listed building purchase notices;

the Secretary of State may, if it appears to him to be expedient to do so, require any other local authority to contribute towards those expenses such sum as appears to him to be reasonable, having regard to any benefit accruing to that authority by reason of the proceeding giving rise to the compensation.

(4) The provisions of subsection (3) of this section shall apply in relation to payments made by a local authority to any statutory undertakers in accordance with financial arrangements to which effect is given under section 233(5)(c) of this Act, as they apply in relation to compensation payable by such an authority in consequence of anything done under Part III or Part IV of this Act, and the reference in subsection (3) of this section to the proceeding giving rise to the compensation shall be construed accordingly.

(5) For the purposes of this section, contributions made by a local planning authority towards the expenditure of a joint advisory committee shall be deemed to be expenses incurred by that authority for the purposes for which that expenditure is incurred by the committee. **[289]**

NOTES
Commencement: 1 April 1972.
This section derived from the Town and Country Planning Act 1962, s 189.
Sub-s (1): amended by the Highways Act 1980, s 343, Sch 24.
Sub-s (2): in para (a) words in square brackets prospectively added by the Local Government Act 1985, s 4, Sch 1, para 16, as from a day or days to be appointed.

256. Assistance for acquisition of property where objection made to blight notice in certain cases

The council of a county, . . . , London borough or county district or the Greater London Council may, subject to such conditions [as the council may think fit], advance money to any person for the purposes of enabling him to acquire a hereditament or agricultural unit in respect of which a counter-notice has been served under section 194 of this Act specifying the grounds mentioned in subsection 2(d) of that section as, or as one of, the grounds of objection if, in the case of a hereditament, its annual value does not exceed such amount as may be prescribed for the purposes of section 192(4)(a) of this Act. **[290]**

NOTES
Commencement: 1 April 1972.
Words omitted repealed by the Local Government Act 1972, s 272, Sch 30; amendment in square brackets made by the Local Government, Planning and Land Act 1980, s 90, Sch 15.

Recovery of compensation etc

257. Recovery from acquiring authorities of sums paid by way of compensation

(1) Where an interest in land is compulsorily acquired, or is sold to an authority possessing compulsory purchase powers, and any of the land comprised in the acquisition or sale is land in respect of which a notice to which this section applies is registered (whether before or after the completion of the acquisition or sale) in respect of a planning decision or order made before the service of the notice to treat, or the making of the contract, in pursuance of which the

acquisition or sale is effected, the Secretary of State shall, subject to the following provisions of this section, be entitled to recover from the acquiring authority a sum equal to so much of the amount of the compensation specified in the notice as (in accordance with section 158(6) of this Act) is to be treated as attributable to that land.

(2) This section applies to notices registered under subsection (5) of section 158 of this Act and to notices registered under the provisions of that subsection as applied by section 166(5) of this Act.

(3) If, immediately after the completion of the acquisition or sale, there is outstanding some interest in the land comprised therein to which a person other than the acquiring authority is entitled, the sum referred to in subsection (1) of this section shall not accrue due until that interest either ceases to exist or becomes vested in the acquiring authority.

(4) No sum shall be recoverable under this section in the case of a compulsory acquisition or sale where the Secretary of State is satisfied that the interest in question is being acquired for the purposes of the use of the land as a public open space.

(5) Where by virtue of the preceding provisions of this section the Secretary of State recovers a sum in respect of any land, by reason that it is land in respect of which a notice is registered under the provisions of section 158(5) of this Act as applied by section 166 of this Act, section 168(2) and (3) of this Act shall have effect in relation to that sum as if it were a sum recovered as mentioned in section 168(2) of this Act.

(6) In this section and in section 258 of this Act "interest" (where the reference is to an interest in land) means the fee simple or a tenancy of the land, and does not include any other interest therein.   **[291]**

NOTES
Commencement: 1 April 1972.

258. Recovery from acquiring authorities of sums paid in respect of war-damaged land

(1) Where an interest in land is compulsorily acquired by, or sold to, an authority possessing compulsory purchase powers, and a payment exceeding £20 has become or becomes payable under section 59 of the Act of 1947 in respect of that interest, the Secretary of State shall, subject to the following provisions of this section, be entitled to recover the amount of the payment from the acquiring authority.

(2) If, before 18th November 1952, operations were begun in, on, over or under the land, or a use of the land was instituted, being operations or a use—

(a) in respect of which a development charge has at any time been determined to be payable, or it has at any time been determined that no development charge was payable; or

(b) comprised in a scheme of development exempt from development charge,

subsection (1) of this section shall not apply to so much of any payment referred to in that subsection as was attributable to any land in relation to which the determination was made or, as the case may be, which is included in that scheme of development.

(3) No amount shall be recoverable under this section in respect of any land

in relation to which an amount has become recoverable by the Secretary of State under the provisions of section 159 of this Act as applied by section 279 of this Act.

(4) If the acquisition or sale in question does not extend to the whole of the land to which the payment under the said section 59 related, the amount recoverable under this section shall be so much of that payment as, in accordance with subsection (5) of this section, is to be treated as apportioned to the land in which the interest acquired or sold subsists.

(5) For the purposes of this section a payment under section 59 of the Act of 1947 shall be treated as apportioned, as between different parts of the land to which it related, in the way in which it might reasonably be expected to have been so apportioned if, under the scheme made under that section, the authority determining the amount of the payment had been required (in accordance with the same principles as applied to the determination of that amount) to apportion it between different parts of that land.

(6) In this section references to a scheme of development exempt from development charge are references to a scheme of development such that, if the operations and uses of land comprised in the scheme had all been begun or instituted before 18th November 1952, all those operations and uses would have been exempt from the provisions of Part VII of the Act of 1947 by virtue of regulations made thereunder; and references to the amount of a payment shall be construed as including any interest payable on the principal amount of the payment. **[292]**

NOTES
Commencement: 1 April 1972.
Act of 1947: Town and Country Planning Act 1947.

259. Sums recoverable from acquiring authorities reckonable for purposes of grant

Where a sum is recoverable from an authority under section 257 or 258 of this Act by reference to an acquisition or purchase of an interest in land, and in respect thereof, or of a subsequent appropriation of the land, a grant became or becomes payable to that or some other authority under an enactment, the power conferred by that enactment to pay the grant shall include, and shall be deemed always to have included, power to pay a grant in respect of that sum as if it had been expenditure incurred by the acquiring authority in connection with the acquisition or purchase. **[293]**

NOTES
Commencement: 1 April 1972.

Expenses and receipts of Ministers

260. Expenses of government departments

(1) The following expenses of the Secretary of State shall be paid out of moneys provided by Parliament, that is to say—

> (a) any expenses incurred by the Secretary of State under subsection (2) of section 50 of this Act or under that subsection as applied by subsection (7) of section 63 of this Act, or in the payment of expenses of any committee established under the said section 63;

(*b*) any sums necessary to enable the Secretary of State to make any payments becoming payable by him under Part VII or Part VIII of this Act;

(*c*) any expenses incurred by the Secretary of State under Part X of this Act;

(*d*) any expenses incurred by the Secretary of State in the making of grants in accordance with regulations made under section 250 of this Act or grants under section 253 of this Act;

(*e*) subject to the provisions of subsection (4) of section 261 of this Act, any instalment payable by the Secretary of State under subsections (2) and (3) of that section;

(*f*) any administrative expenses incurred by the Secretary of State for the purposes of this Act.

(2) There shall be paid out of moneys provided by Parliament any expenses incurred by any government department (including the Secretary of State)—

(*a*) in the acquisition of land under Part VI of this Act;

(*b*) in the payment of compensation under section 118(4), 237(2) or 281 of this Act;

(*c*) under section 128(5)(*b*) of this Act; or

(*d*) under section 254 of this Act. **[294]**

NOTES

Commencement: 1 April 1972.

Sub-s (1)(*d*): repealed in part by the Housing and Planning Act 1986, s 49(2), Sch 12, Part III. See Appendix.

261. Payments under s 59 of Act of 1947 and Parts I and V of Act of 1954

(1) The Secretary of State shall pay out of moneys provided by Parliament any payments falling to be made by him on or after 1st April 1968 under—

(*a*) section 59 of the Act of 1947 (war-damaged land); or

(*b*) any provision of Part I or Part V of the Act of 1954.

(2) The aggregate of the sums issued to the Minister of Housing and Local Government or the Central Land Board out of the Consolidated Fund in any financial year ending before the said 1st April under section 64(1) of the Act of 1954 (sums required for making payments under Part I or Part V of the Act of 1954) shall be repaid by the Secretary of State into the National Loans Fund, as mentioned in subsection (3) of this section, with interest thereon at such rate as the Treasury may determine, such interest accruing, in respect of the whole aggregate, from such date in the financial year in which the sums were issued as the Treasury may determine.

(3) The said aggregate shall be repaid by twenty equal annual instalments, of principal and interest combined, falling due on the anniversary of the date determined under subsection (2) of this section, the first such instalment falling due in the financial year next following the financial year in which the sums in question were issued.

(4) Any sums received by the Secretary of State by virtue of—

(*a*) the provisions of section 159 of this Act, as applied by Schedule 24 to this Act to compensation paid under Part V of the Act of 1954; or

(*b*) the provisions of section 257 of this Act as so applied

shall be paid into the Consolidated Fund. **[295]**

NOTES

Commencement: 1 April 1972.

Act of 1947: Town and Country Planning Act 1947.

Act of 1954: Town and Country Planning Act 1954.

262. General provisions as to receipts of Secretary of State

Without prejudice to section 261 of this Act, and subject to the provisions of section 168 of this Act, any sums received by the Secretary of State under any provision of this Act shall be paid into the Consolidated Fund.   **[296]**

NOTES
Commencement: 1 April 1972.

Expenses of county councils and Greater London Council

263. Expenses of county councils and Greater London Council

(1) The council of a county may direct that any expenses incurred by them under the provisions of this Act specified in Parts I and II of Schedule 21 to this Act shall be treated as expenses for special county purposes chargeable upon such part of the county as may be specified in the directions.

(2) The Greater London Council may direct that any expenses incurred by them under—

    (*a*) Part II of this Act;
    (*b*) Schedule 3 to this Act;
    (*c*) Part II of Schedule 5 to this Act;
    (*d*) any of the provisions of this Act specified in Part I of Schedule 21 to this Act;
    (*e*) any other provision of this Act conferring functions on local authorities,

shall be treated as expenses for special London purposes chargeable upon such part of Greater London as may be specified in the directions.   **[297]**

NOTES
Commencement: 1 April 1972.

PART XIV

APPLICATION OF ACT TO SPECIAL CASES

Minerals

264. Power to modify Act in relation to minerals

(1) In relation to development consisting of the winning and working of minerals, the provisions of this Act specified in Parts I and II of Schedule 21 to this Act shall have effect subject to such adaptations and modifications as may be prescribed by regulations made under this Act with the consent of the Treasury.

    [(1A) In this Act—

      "development consisting of the winning and working of minerals" includes the extraction of minerals from a mineral-working deposit; and "mineral-working deposit" means any deposit of material remaining after minerals have been extracted from land or otherwise deriving from the carrying out of operations for the winning and working of minerals in, on or under land.]

    (2) In relation to interests in land consisting of or comprising minerals

(being either the fee simple or tenancies of such land) and in relation to claims established (as mentioned in section 135(2) of this Act) wholly or partly in respect of such land, the provisions of this Act specified in Part III of Schedule 21 to this Act shall have effect subject to such adaptations and modifications as may be prescribed by regulations made under this Act with the consent of the Treasury.

(3) Regulations made for the purposes of this section shall be of no effect unless they are approved by resolution of each House of Parliament.

(4) Any regulations made by virtue of subsection (1) of this section shall not apply—

> (*a*) to the winning and working, on land held or occupied with land used for the purposes of agriculture, of any minerals reasonably required for the purposes of that use, including the fertilisation of the land so used and the maintenance, improvement or alteration of buildings or works thereon which are occupied or used for those purposes; or
> (*b*) to development consisting of the winning and working of any minerals vested in the National Coal Board, being development to which any of the provisions of this Act relating to operational land of statutory undertakers apply by virtue of regulations made under section 273 of this Act;

and nothing in subsection (1) of this section or in this subsection shall be construed as affecting the prerogative right of Her Majesty (whether in right of the Crown or of the Duchy of Lancaster) or of the Duke of Cornwall to any gold or silver mine.   **[298]**

NOTES
   Commencement: 1 April 1972.
   Sub-s (1A): prospectively added by the Town and Country Planning (Minerals) Act 1981, s 1(2), as from a day to be appointed.

264A. Duty of planning authorities to review mineral workings

[(1) It shall be duty of every mineral planning authority—

> (*a*) to undertake at such intervals as they consider fit reviews of every site in their area in, on or under which operations for the winning and working of minerals—
>
>> (i)   are being carried out; or
>> (ii) have been carried out at any time during the relevant period; or
>> (iii) are authorised by planning permission but have not been begun; and
>
> (*b*) to make in respect of any such site any order under section 45, 51, 51A or 51B of this Act that they consider appropriate.

(2) In subsection (1) of this section "the relevant period", in relation to a review, means the period of five years preceding the date of the beginning of the review or such other period as may be prescribed.]   **[299]**

NOTES
   Commencement: 19 May 1986.
   Commencement order: SI 1986 No 760.
   Added by the Town and Country Planning (Minerals) Act 1981, s 3.

Crown land

266. Exercise of powers in relation to Crown land

(1) Notwithstanding any interest of the Crown in Crown land, but subject to the following provisions of this section—

(a) a plan approved, adopted or made under Part II of this Act [or Part I of Schedule 1 to the Local Government Act 1985] or the Greater London development plan may include proposals relating to the use of Crown land, and any power to acquire land compulsorily under Part VI of this Act may be exercised in relation to any interest therein which is for the time being held otherwise than by or on behalf of the Crown;

(b) any restrictions or powers imposed or conferred by Part III, Part IV or Part V of this Act, by the provisions of Part IX of this Act relating to purchase notices and listed building purchase notices, or by any of the provisions of sections 225 to 228 of this Act, shall apply and be exercisable in relation to Crown land, to the extent of any interest therein for the time being held otherwise than by or on behalf of the Crown;

(c) a building which for the time being is Crown land may be included in a list compiled or approved by the Secretary of State under section 54 of this Act.

(2) Except with the consent of the appropriate authority—

(a) no order or notice shall be made [, issued] or served under any of the provisions of sections 51, [51A, 51B,] 60, 65, 87 or 96 of this Act or under any of those provisions as applied by any order or regulations made under Part IV of this Act, in relation to land which for the time being is Crown land;

(b) no interest in land which for the time being is Crown land shall be acquired compulsorily under Part VI of this Act.

(3) No enforcement notice shall be [issued] under section 87 of this Act in respect of development carried out by or on behalf of the Crown after the appointed day on land which was Crown land at the time when the development was carried out.

(4) No listed building enforcement notice shall be [issued] in respect of works executed by or on behalf of the Crown in respect of a building which was Crown land at the time when the works were executed.

(5) No purchase notice or listed building purchase notice shall be served in relation to any interest in Crown land unless an offer has been previously made by the owner of that interest to dispose of it to the appropriate authority on terms that the price payable for it shall be equal to (and shall, in default of agreement, be determined in like manner as) the compensation which would be payable in respect of that interest if it were acquired in pursuance of a purchase notice, and that offer has been refused by the appropriate authority.

(6) The rights conferred by the provisions of sections 192 to 207 of this Act shall be exercisable by a person who (within the meaning of those provisions) is an owner-occupier of a hereditament or agricultural unit which is Crown land, or is a resident owner-occupier of a hereditament which is Crown land, in the same way as they are exercisable in respect of a hereditament or agricultural unit which is not Crown land, and those provisions shall apply accordingly.

(7) In this Part of this Act "Crown land" means land in which there is a Crown interest or a Duchy interest: "Crown interest" means an interest belonging to Her Majesty in right of the Crown, or belonging to a government department, or held in trust for Her Majesty for the purposes of a government department; "Duchy interest" means an interest belonging to Her Majesty in right of the Duchy of Lancaster, or belonging to the Duchy of Cornwall; and for the purposes of this section and section 267 of this Act "the appropriate authority" in relation to any land—

(a) in the case of land belonging to Her Majesty in right of the Crown and forming part of the Crown Estate, means the Crown Estate Commissioners, and, in relation to any other land belonging to Her Majesty in right of the Crown, means the government department having the management of that land;

(b) in relation to land belonging to Her Majesty in right of the Duchy of Lancaster, means the Chancellor of the Duchy;

(c) in relation to land belonging to the Duchy of Cornwall, means such person as the Duke of Cornwall, or the possessor for the time being of the Duchy of Cornwall, appoints;

(d) in the case of land belonging to a government department or held in trust for Her Majesty for the purposes of a government department, means that department;

and, if any question arises as to what authority is the appropriate authority in relation to any land, that question shall be referred to the Treasury, whose decision shall be final.   **[300]**

NOTES

Commencement: 1 April 1972.

This section derived from the Town and Country Planning Act 1962, s 199.

Sub-s (1): in para (a) words in square brackets prospectively added by the Local Government Act 1985, s 4, Sch 1, para 16, as from a day or days to be appointed.

Sub-s (2): first words in square brackets added by the Local Government and Planning (Amendment) Act 1981, s 1, Schedule; second words in square brackets added by the Town and Country Planning (Minerals) Act 1981, s 34, Sch 1; prospectively amended by the Housing and Planning Act 1986, s 33, Sch 7, Part I, para 3. See Appendix.

Sub-ss (3), (4): amended by the Local Government and Planning (Amendment) Act 1981, s 1, Schedule.

267. Agreements relating to Crown land

(1) The appropriate authority and the local planning authority for the area in which any Crown land is situated may make agreements for securing the use of the land, so far as may be prescribed by any such agreement, in conformity with the provisions of the development plan applicable thereto; and any such agreement may contain such consequential provisions, including provisions of a financial character, as may appear to be necessary or expedient having regard to the purposes of the agreement.

(2) An agreement made under this section by a government department shall not have effect unless it is approved by the Treasury.

(3) In considering whether to make or approve an agreement under this section relating to land belonging to a government department, or held in trust for Her Majesty for the purposes of a government department, the department and the Treasury shall have regard to the purposes for which the land is held by or for the department.   **[301]**

NOTES

Commencement: 1 April 1972.

268. Supplementary provisions as to Crown and Duchy interests

(1) Subject to the following provisions of this section—

    (*a*) where there is a Crown interest in any land, the provisions of Part VII of this Act and of sections 166 to 168 thereof, and the provisions of Schedules 15, 16 and 17 to this Act and the provisions of Schedule 24 to this Act in so far as they relate to Part VII or to sections 166 to 168 of this Act, shall have effect in relation to any private interest or Duchy interest as if the Crown interest were a private interest; and

    (*b*) where there is a Duchy interest in any land, those provisions shall have effect in relation to that interest, and to any private interest, as if the Duchy interest were a private interest.

(2) References in this Act to claims established under Part VI of the Act of 1947 include references to claims so established in accordance with arrangements made under section 88(2) of that Act (which provided for the application of Part VI of that Act to Duchy interests and for the payment of sums in lieu of development charges in respect of such interests); references to development charges include references to sums determined in accordance with such arrangements to be appropriate in substitution for development charges; and references to the amount of an established claim or of a development charge shall be construed accordingly.

(3) Where in accordance with an agreement under section 267 of this Act, the approval of a local planning authority is required in respect of any development of land in which there is a Duchy interest, the provisions of this Act referred to in subsection (1)(*a*) of this section shall have effect in relation to the withholding of that approval, or the giving thereof subject to conditions, as if it were a refusal of planning permission, or a grant of planning permission subject to conditions, as the case may be.

(4) In this section "private interest" means an interest which is neither a Crown interest nor a Duchy interest.   **[302]**

NOTES
    Commencement: 1 April 1972.
    Act of 1947: Town and Country Planning Act 1947.

Isles of Scilly

269. Application of Act to Isles of Scilly

(1) The Secretary of State shall, after consultation with the Council of the Isles of Scilly, by order provide for the application to those Isles of the provisions of this Act specified in Parts I and II of Schedule 21 to this Act as if those Isles were a separate county.

(2) In relation to land in the Isles of Scilly, the provisions of this Act specified in Part III of the said Schedule [and section 109A of this Act] shall have effect as if those Isles were a county district and the Council of the Isles were the council of that district.

(3) The Secretary of State may, after consultation with the Council of the Isles of Scilly, by order provide for the application to those Isles of the provisions of this Act specified in Part IV of the said Schedule as if those Isles were a separate county or county district.

(4) Any order under subsection (1) or (3) of this section may provide for the application of the provisions there mentioned to the Isles subject to such modifications as may be specified in the order.   **[303]**

NOTES
Commencement: 1 April 1972.
Sub-s (2): amended by the Local Government (Miscellaneous Provisions) Act 1982, s 36.
Prospectively amended by the Housing and Planning Act 1986, s 33, Sch 7, Part I, para 4. See Appendix.

Local planning authorities

270. Application to local planning authorities of provisions as to planning control and enforcement

(1) In relation to land of local planning authorities and to the development by local authorities of land in respect of which they are the local planning authorities, the provisions of this Act specified in Part V of Schedule 21 to this Act shall have effect subject to such exceptions and modifications as may be prescribed by regulations made under this Act.

(2) Subject to the provisions of section 40 of this Act, any such regulations may in particular provide for securing—

> (*a*) that any application by such an authority for planning permission to develop such land, or for any other consent required in relation to such land under the said provisions, shall be made to the Secretary of State and not to the local planning authority;
> (*b*) that any order or notice authorised to be made [, issued] or served under those provisions in relation to such land shall be made [, issued] or served by the Secretary of State and not by the local planning authority.

(3) Sections 26, 27 and 29(2) and (3) of this Act shall apply, with the necessary modifications, in relation to applications made to the Secretary of State in pursuance of regulations made for the purposes of subsection (1) of this section, as they apply in relation to applications for planning permission which fall to be determined by the local planning authority.   **[304]**

NOTES
Commencement: 1 April 1972.
Amended by the Local Government and Planning (Amendment) Act 1981, s 1, Schedule.

271. Application to local planning authorities of provisions as to listed buildings

[The provisions of this Act specified in Part VI of Schedule 21 to this Act shall have effect for the purpose of applications by local planning authorities relating to the execution of works for the demolition, alteration or extension of listed buildings, subject to such exceptions and modifications as may be prescribed by regulations; and the regulations may in particular provide for the making of applications for listed building consent to the Secretary of State and for [the issue or service] of notices under the said provisions by him.]   **[305]**

NOTES
Commencement: 31 August 1974.
Substituted by the Town and Country Amenities Act 1974, s 7; amended by the Local Government and Planning (Amendment) Act 1981, s 1, Schedule.

(New s 271A prospectively inserted by the Housing and Planning Act 1986, s 33, Sch 7, Part I, para 5. See Appendix.)

272. Special provisions as to statutory undertakers who are local planning authorities

In relation to statutory undertakers who are local planning authorities, section 241 of this Act and the provisions specified in subsection (2) of that section shall have effect subject to such exceptions and modifications as may be prescribed by regulations made under this Act.   **[306]**

NOTES
  Commencement: 1 April 1972.

Other special cases

273. National Coal Board

(1) Regulations made under this Act by the Secretary of State for the Environment and the Secretary of State for Trade and Industry with the consent of the Treasury may direct that any of the provisions of this Act specified in Part I of Schedule 21 to this Act or of section 223 of this Act, being provisions relating to statutory undertakers and to land of such undertakers, shall apply, subject to such adaptations, modifications and exceptions as may be specified in the regulations, in relation to the National Coal Board, and in relation to land (including mines) of that Board of any such class as may be specified in the regulations, as if the Board were statutory undertakers and as if land of any class so specified were operational land.

(2) Without prejudice to the generality of subsection (1) of this section, any regulations made thereunder may in particular provide that any compensation payable to the National Coal Board by virtue of any of the provisions applied by the regulations, being compensation which, in the case of statutory undertakers, would be assessable in accordance with the provisions of section 238 of this Act, shall, instead of being assessed in accordance with that section, be assessed in accordance with the provisions of the regulations.   **[307]**

NOTES
  Commencement: 1 April 1972.

274. Ecclesiastical property

(1) Without prejudice to the provisions of the [Acquisition of Land Act 1981] with respect to notices served under that Act, where under any of the provisions of this Act a notice [or copy of a notice] is required to be served on an owner of land, and the land is ecclesiastical property, a like notice [or copy] shall be served on the Church Commissioners.

(2) Where the fee simple of any ecclesiastical property is in abeyance—
  (a) if the property is situated elsewhere than in Wales, then for the purposes of the provisions of this Act specified in Part VII of Schedule 21 to this Act the fee simple shall be treated as being vested in the Church Commissioners;
  (b) in any case, the fee simple shall, for the purposes of a compulsory acquisition of the property under Part VI of this Act, be treated as being vested in the Church Commissioners, and any notice to treat shall be served, or be deemed to have been served, accordingly.

(3) Any compensation payable under Part VIII (except sections 171, 172 and 175) or section 212 of this Act in respect of land which is ecclesiastical property shall be paid to the Church Commissioners, to be applied for the

purposes for which the proceeds of a sale by agreement of the land would be applicable under enactment or Measure authorising, or disposing of the proceeds of, such a sale.

(4) Any sum which under any of the provisions of this Act specified in Part III of Schedule 21 to this Act is payable in relation to land which is, or on the appointed day was, ecclesiastical property, and apart from this subsection would be payable to an incumbent, shall be paid to the Church Commissioners, to be applied for the purposes mentioned in subsection (3) of this section; and where any sum is recoverable under section 159, 168 or 279 of this Act in respect of any such land, the Church Commissioners may apply any money or securities held by them in the payment of that sum.

(5) In this section "ecclesiastical property" means land belonging to an ecclesiastical benefice, or being or forming part of a church subject to the jurisdiction of a bishop of any diocese or the site of such a church, or being or forming part of a burial ground subject to such jurisdiction. **[308]**

NOTES
Commencement: 1 April 1972.
Sub-s (1): first amendment made by the Acquisition of Land Act 1981, s 34(1), Sch 4 and; second and third amendments made by the Local Government and Planning (Amendment) Act 1981, s 1, Schedule.

275. Settled land, and land of universities and colleges

(1) The purposes authorised for the application of capital moneys—

  (a) by section 73 of the Settled Land Act 1925 and by that section as applied by section 28 of the Law of Property Act 1925 in relation to trusts for sale; and
  (b) by section 26 of the Universities and College Estates Act 1925,

and the purposes authorised by section 71 of the Settled Land Act 1925, by that section as so applied, and by section 30 of the Universities and College Estates Act 1925 as purposes for which moneys may be raised by mortgage, shall include the payment of any sum recoverable under section 159, 168 or 279 of this Act.

(2) The classes of works specified in Part II of Schedule 3 to the Settled Land Act 1925 (which specifies improvements which may be paid for out of capital money, subject to provisions under which repayment out of income may be required to be made) shall include works specified by the Secretary of State as being required for properly maintaining a listed building which is settled land within the meaning of that Act. **[309]**

NOTES
Commencement: 1 April 1972.

PART XV

MISCELLANEOUS AND SUPPLEMENTARY PROVISIONS

276. Default powers of Secretary of State

(1) If it appears to the Secretary of State, after consultation with the local planning authority, to be expedient that any order to which this subsection applies should be made, he may . . . himself make such an order; and any order so made by the Secretary of State shall have the like effect as if it had been made by the local planning authority and confirmed by the Secretary of State under Part III or IV of this Act.

(2) Subsection (1) of this section applies to the following orders, that is to say—

> (*a*) orders under section 45 of this Act, or under the provisions of that section as applied by any order or regulations made under Part IV of this Act;
>
> (*b*) orders under section 51 of this Act;
>
> [(*ba*) orders under section 51A of this Act;
>
> (*bb*)orders under section 51B of this Act;]
>
> (*c*) tree preservation orders and orders amending or revoking them.

(3) The provisions of Part III or Part IV of this Act, and of any regulations made thereunder, with respect to the procedure to be followed in connection with the submission by the local planning authority of any order to which subsection (1) of this section applies, with respect to the confirmation of such an order by the Secretary of State, and with respect to the service of copies thereof as so confirmed, shall have effect, subject to any necessary modifications, in relation to any proposal by the Secretary of State to make such an order by virtue of subsection (1) of this section, in relation to the making thereof by the Secretary of State, and in relation to the service of copies thereof as so made.

(4) Without prejudice to subsection (3) of this section, where the Secretary of State proposes under subsection (1) of this section to make any such order as is mentioned in subsection (2)(*a*) or (*b*) of this section he shall serve a notice of the proposal on the local planning authority; and if within such period as may be specified in the notice (not being less than twenty-eight days from the date of service) the authority so require, the Secretary of State before making the order shall afford to the authority an opportunity of appearing before, and being heard by, a person appointed by him for the purpose.

[(5) If it appears to the Secretary of State, after consultation with the local planning authority, to be expedient that a completion notice under section 44 of this Act or a stop notice should be served in respect of any land, he may himself serve such a notice; and any notice so served shall have the like effect as a notice served by the local planning authority.

(5A) If it appears to the Secretary of State, after consultation with the local planning authority, to be expedient that—

> (*a*) an enforcement notice; or
>
> (*b*) a listed building enforcement notice,

should be issued in respect of any land, he may himself issue such a notice; and any notice so issued shall have the like effect as a notice issued by the local planning authority.

(5B) In relation to an enforcement notice or a listed building enforcement notice issued by the Secretary of State sections 89 and 91 to 93, or, as the case may be, sections 98 and 99 of this Act shall apply as if for any reference to the local planning authority there were substituted a reference to the Secretary of State.]

(6) If the Secretary of State is satisfied, after holding a local inquiry—

> (*a*) that the council of a county, county borough, London borough or county district have failed to take steps for the acquisition of any land which, in the opinion of the Secretary of State, ought to be acquired by that council under section 112 of this Act for a purpose which it is necessary to achieve in the interests of the proper planning of an area in which the land is situated; or

(*b*) that a local authority have failed to carry out, on land acquired by them under section 68 of the Act of 1962 or section 112 of this Act or appropriated by them under section 121 of this Act, any development which, in the opinion of the Secretary of State, ought to be carried out,

the Secretary of State may by order require the council or authority to take such steps as may be specified in the order for acquiring the land, or carrying out the development, as the case may be.

(7) Any order under subsection (6) of this section shall be enforceable, on the application of the Secretary of State, by mandamus.   **[310]**

NOTES
    Commencement: 27 August 1981 (sub-ss (5), (5A), (5B)); 1 April 1972 (remainder).
    This section derived from the Town and Country Planning Act 1962, s 207, and the Town and Country Planning Act 1968, s 82.
    Sub-s (1): words omitted repealed by the Local Government Act 1974, s 42, Sch 8.
    Sub-s (2): amended by the Town and Country Planning (Minerals) Act 1981, s 34, Sch 1.
    Sub-s (5): substituted by the Local Government and Planning (Amendment) Act 1981, s 1, Schedule.

277. Designation of conservation areas

[(1) Every local planning authority shall from time to time determine which parts of their area are areas of special architectural or historic interest the character or appearance of which it is desirable to preserve or enhance, and shall designate such areas as conservation areas.

(2) It shall be the duty of a local planning authority, [from time to time], to review the past exercise of functions under this section and to determine whether any parts or any further parts of their area should be designated as conservation areas; and, if they so determine, they shall designate those parts accordingly.

(3) . . .

(4) The Secretary of State may from time to time, after consultation with a local planning authority, determine that any part of the authority's area which is not for the time being designated as a conservation area is an area of special architectural or historic interest the character or appearance of which it is desirable to preserve or enhance; and, if he so determines, he may designate that part as a conservation area.

[(5) Before making a determination under this section the Historic Buildings and Monuments Commission for England and a county planning authority shall respectively consult the council of each London borough or district of which any part is included in the area to which the proposed determination relates; and before designating any area in Greater London as a conservation area the Commission shall obtain the consent of the Secretary of State.]

(6) A local planning authority shall give notice to the Secretary of State of the designation of any part of their area as a conservation area under subsection (1) or (2) above, and of any variation or cancellation of any such designation, and the Secretary of State shall give notice to a local planning authority of the designation of any part of their area as a conservation area under subsection (4) above, and of any variation or cancellation of any such designation: and a notice under this subsection shall contain sufficient particulars to identify the area affected.

[(6A) Where a designation under subsection (1) or (2) above, or a variation or cancellation of it, affects an area in England, subsection (6) above shall have effect as if the first reference to the Secretary of State were a reference to him and the Historic Buildings and Monuments Commission for England; and where a designation under subsection (4) above, or a variation or cancellation of it, affects an area in England, subsection (6) above shall have effect as if the second reference to a local planning authority were a reference to the authority and the Commission.]

(7) Notice of any such designation, variation or cancellation as is mentioned in subsection (6) above, with particulars of its effect, shall be published in the London Gazette and in at least one newspaper circulating in the area of the local planning authority, by that authority or, as the case may be, the Secretary of State.

(8) Where any area is for the time being designated as a conservation area special attention shall be paid to the desirability of preserving or enhancing its character or appearance in the exercise, with respect to any buildings or or other land in that area, of any powers under this Act, Part I of the Historic Buildings and Ancient Monuments Act 1953 or the Local Authorities (Historic Buildings) Act 1962.

(9) The designation of any area as a conservation area shall be [a local land charge].

(10) The functions of a local planning authority under this section shall be exercisable—

(a) in Greater London, by [the Historic Buildings and Monuments Commission for England] and also, in relation to a London borough, by the council of that borough;

[(aa) in a metropolitan county, by the local planning authority;]

(b) in [any part of a National Park outside a metropolitan county], by the county planning authority;

(c) elsewhere, by the district planning authority;

but outside a National Park a county planning authority shall also have power to make determinations and designations under this section.] **[311]**

NOTES
Commencement: 1 April 1986 (sub-s (5)); 1 April 1984 (sub-s (6A)); 31 August 1974 (remainder).
Commencement order: SI 1984 No 208.
Substituted by the Town and Country Amenities Act 1974, s 1.
Sub-s (2): amended by the Local Government, Planning and Land Act 1980, s 90, Sch 15.
Sub-s (3): repealed by the Local Government, Planning and Land Act 1980, s 194, Sch 34.
Sub-s (5): substituted by the Local Government Act 1985, s 6, Sch 2, para 1.
Sub-s (6A): added by the National Heritage Act 1983, s 33, Sch 4, para 21.
Sub-s (9): amended by the Local Land Charges Act 1975, s 17(2), Sch 1.
Sub-s (10): amended by the Local Government Act 1985, s 6, Sch 2, para 1.

277A. Control of demolition in conservation areas

[(1) This section applies to all buildings in conservation areas other than—

(a) listed buildings;

(b) excepted buildings within the meaning of section 58(2) above; and

(c) buildings in relation to which a direction under subsection (4) below is for the time being in force.

(2) A building to which this section applies shall not be demolished without the consent of the appropriate authority.

(3) . . .

(4) The Secretary of State may direct that this section shall not apply to a description of buildings specified in the direction . . .

(5) A direction under subsection (4) above relating to a description of buildings may be given either to an individual local planning authority or to local planning authorities generally.

(6) The Secretary of State may vary or revoke a direction under subsection (4) above by a further direction under that subsection.

(7) The appropriate authority for the purposes of this section is—

(a) in relation to applications for consent made by local planning authorities, the Secretary of State; and

(b) in relation to other applications for consent, the local planning authority or the Secretary of State.

(8) The following provisions of this Act, namely—

section 55,
section 56(3), (5) and (6),
sections 96 to 99,
section 172,
section 190,
section 266(1)(b),
paragraph 2 of Schedule 3,
Parts I and II of Schedule 11, and
Schedule 19,

shall have effect in relation to buildings to which this section applies as they have effect in relation to listed buildings; but regulations may provide that they shall have effect in relation to buildings to which this section applies subject to such exceptions and modifications as may be prescribed.

(9) Any such regulations may make different provision—

(a) in relation to applications made by local planning authorities, and

(b) in relation to other applications.

(10) Any proceedings on or arising out of an application for listed building consent made while this section applies to a building shall lapse when it ceases to apply to it, and any listed building consent granted with respect to the building shall also lapse; but the fact that this section has ceased to apply to a building shall not affect the liability of any person to be prosecuted and punished for an offence under section 55 or 98 of this Act committed by him with respect to the building while this section applied to it.

(11) The functions of a local planning authority under this section shall be exercisable—

(a) in Greater London [or a metropolitan county, by the local planning authority;]

(b) in [any part of a National Park outside a metropolitan county], by the county planning authority; and

(c) elsewhere, by the county planning authority and the district planning authority.] **[312]**

NOTES
Commencement: 31 August 1974.
Added by the Town and Country Amenities Act 1974, s 1; amended by the Local Government,
Planning and Land Act 1980, s 90, Sch 15.
Sub-s (8): new sub-s (8) substituted by the Housing and Planning Act 1986, s 40, Sch 9, Part I,
para 8(2). See Appendix.
Sub-s (11): amended by the Local Government Act 1985, s 6, Sch 2, para 1; amended by the
Housing and Planning Act 1986, s 40, Sch 9, Part I, para 8(3). See Appendix.

277B. Formulation and publication of proposals for preservation and enhancement of conservation areas

[(1) It shall be the duty of a local planning authority to formulate and publish, [from time to time], proposals for the preservation and enhancement of any parts of their area which are conservation areas.

(2) Proposals under this section shall be submitted for consideration to a public meeting in the area to which they relate; and the local planning authority shall have regard to any views concerning the proposals expressed by persons attending the meeting.

(3) . . .   **[313]**

NOTES
Commencement: 31 August 1974.
Added by the Town and Country Amenities Act 1974, s 1; amended by the Local Government,
Planning and Land Act 1980, ss 90, 194, Schs 15, 34.

278. Assumptions as to planning permission in determining value of interests in land

(1) In any case where the value or depreciation in value of an interest in land falls to be determined on the assumption that planning permission would be granted for development of any class specified in Schedule 8 to this Act, it shall be further assumed, as regards development of any class specified in paragraph 1 or 3 of that Schedule, that such permission would be granted subject to the condition set out in Schedule 18 to this Act.

(2) In the application of the said Schedule 8 for the purposes of any determination to which subsection (1) of this section applies—

   (a) paragraph 3 of that Schedule shall be construed as not extending to works involving any increase in the cubic content of a building erected after the appointed day (including any building resulting from the carrying out of such works as are described in paragraph 1 of that Schedule); and

   (b) paragraph 7 of that Schedule shall not apply to any such building.

(3) For the purposes of subsections (1) and (2) of this section, so far as applicable to any determination of existing use value as defined in section 187(5) of this Act, references to Schedule 8 to this Act, and to paragraphs 1, 3 and 7 of that Schedule, shall be construed as references to Schedule 3 to the Act of 1947 and to the corresponding paragraphs of that Schedule; and that Schedule shall have effect as if it contained a paragraph corresponding to paragraph 13 of Schedule 8 to this Act.

(4) Except as provided in section 168(4) of this Act, nothing in the preceding provisions of this section or in paragraph 13 of Schedule 8 affects the meaning of "new development" in this Act or any determination to be made for the purpose of Part VII of this Act.

(5) For the avoidance of doubt it is hereby declared that where, under any provision of this Act, the value of an interest in land is required to be assessed

on the assumption that planning permission would be granted for development of any class specified in Schedule 8 to this Act, that assumption is to be made on the footing that any such development must comply with the provisions of any enactment, other than this Act, which would be applicable to it.   **[314]**

NOTES
Commencement: 1 April 1972.
Act of 1947: Town and Country Planning Act 1947.

279. Recovery, on subsequent development, of payments in respect of war-damaged land

(1) In relation to notices registered under section 57 of the Act of 1954 (which provided for the registration of notices of payments made under section 59 of the Act of 1947) the provisions of sections 159 and 160 of this Act shall have effect (subject to the following provisions of this section) as they have effect in relation to notices registered under section 158 of this Act.

(2) The said provisions shall have effect as mentioned in subsection (1) of this section, but as if—

(a) any reference therein to the compensation specified in a notice were a reference to the payment so specified; and

(b) section 159 of this Act applied to every description of new development.

(3) No amount shall be recoverable by the Secretary of State by virtue of this section in respect of any land in relation to which an amount has become recoverable under section 258 of this Act.

(4) Subsection (5) of section 258 of this Act shall apply for the purposes of this section as it applies for the purposes of that section.   **[315]**

NOTES
Commencement: 1 April 1972.
Act of 1954: Town and Country Planning Act 1954.
Act of 1947: Town and Country Planning Act 1947.

280. Rights of entry

(1) Any person duly authorised in writing by the Secretary of State or by a local planning authority may at any reasonable time enter any land for the purpose of surveying it in connection with—

(a) the preparation, approval, adoption, making or amendment of a structure plan or local plan relating to the land under Part II of this Act [or a unitary development plan relating to the land under Part I of Schedule 1 to the Local Government Act 1985], including the carrying out of any survey under that Part;

(b) any application under Part III or sections 60 or 63 of this Act, or under any order or regulations made thereunder, for any permission, consent or determination to be given or made in connection with that land or any other land under Part III or either of those sections of this Act or under any such order or regulations;

(c) any proposal by the local planning authority or by the Secretary of State to make [, issue] or serve any order or notice under Part III (other than section 44), Part IV or Part V of this Act, or under any order or regulations made thereunder or any notice under section 115 of this Act.

(2) Any person duly authorised in writing by the Secretary of State may at any reasonable time enter any land for the purpose of surveying any building thereon in connection with a proposal to include the building in, or exclude it from, a list compiled or approved under section 54 of this Act.

(3) Any person duly authorised in writing by the Secretary of State or a local planning authority may at any reasonable time enter any land for the purpose of ascertaining whether, with respect to any building on the land, an offence has been, or is being, committed under section 55 or 98 of, or Schedule 11 to, this Act, or whether the building is being maintained in a proper state of repair.

(4) Any person duly authorised in writing by the Secretary of State or a local authority may at any reasonable time enter any land for the purpose of ascertaining whether—

(*a*) an offence appears to have been committed under section 57 of this Act; or

(*b*) any of the functions conferred by section 101 or 103 of this Act should or may be exercised in connection with the land,

or for the purpose of exercising any of those functions in connection with the land.

[(4A) Any person duly authorised in writing by the council of a district or a London borough may at any reasonable time enter any land for the purpose of exercising a power conferred on the council by section 109A above if—

(*a*) the land is unoccupied; and

(*b*) it would be impossible to exercise the power without entering the land.]

(5) Any person, being an officer of the Valuation Office or a person duly authorised in writing by the Secretary of State, may at any reasonable time enter any land for the purpose of surveying it, or estimating its value, in connection with a claim for compensation under Part VII of this Act in respect of that land or any other land.

(6) Any person, being an officer of the Valuation Office or a person duly authorised in writing by a local planning authority, may at any reasonable time enter any land for the purpose of surveying it, or estimating its value, in connection with a claim for compensation in respect of that land or any other land, being compensation payable by the local planning authority under Part VIII of this Act (other than section 175), under section 212(5) of this Act or under Part XI of this Act (other than section 237(2) or 238(1)(*c*)).

(7) Any person, being an officer of the Valuation Office or a person duly authorised in writing by a local authority or Minister authorised to acquire land under section 112 or 113 of this Act, and any person duly authorised in writing by local authority having power to acquire land under Part VI of this Act, may at any reasonable time enter any land for the purpose of surveying it, or estimating its value, in connection with any proposal to acquire that land or any other land, or in connection with any claim for compensation in respect of any such acquisition.

(8) Any person duly authorised in writing by the Secretary of State or by a local planning authority may at any reasonable time enter any land in respect of which an order or notice has been made or served as mentioned in subsection (1)(*c*) of this section, for the purpose of ascertaining whether the order or notice has been complied with.

(9) Subject to the provisions of section 281 of this Act, any power conferred by this section to survey land shall be construed as including power to search and bore for the purpose of ascertaining the nature of the subsoil or the presence of minerals therein.

[(10) In subsections (1)(*c*), (3), (4) and (8) above references to a local planning authority or local authority include, in relation to a building situated in Greater London, a reference to the Historic Buildings and Monuments Commission for England.]   [316]

NOTES
Commencement: 1 April 1986 (sub-s (10)); 13 July 1982 (sub-s (4A)); 1 April 1972 (remainder).
This section derived from the Town and Country Planning Act 1962, s 211, and the Civic Amenities Act 1967, s 28(1).
Sub-s (1): in para (*a*) words in square brackets prospectively added by the Local Government Act 1985, s 4, Sch 1, para 16(7) as from a day or days to be appointed; para (*c*) amended by the Local Government and Planning (Amendment) Act 1981, s 1, Schedule.
New sub-s (1A) prospectively inserted by the Housing and Planning Act 1986, s 33, Sch 7, Part I, para 6(*a*). See Appendix.
Sub-s (4): prospectively amended by the Housing and Planning Act 1986, s 33, Sch 7, Part I, para 6(*b*). See Appendix.
Sub-s (4A): added by the Local Government (Miscellaneous Provisions) Act 1982, s 36.
New sub-s (6A) prospectively inserted by the Housing and Planning Act 1986, s 33, Sch 7, Part I, para 6(*c*). See Appendix.
Sub-s (8): prospectively amended by the Housing and Planning Act 1986, s 33, Sch 7, Part I, para 6(*d*). See Appendix.
Sub-s (10): added by the Local Government Act 1985, s 6, Sch 2, para 1.

281. Supplementary provisions as to rights of entry

(1) A person authorised under section 280 of this Act to enter any land shall, if so required, produce evidence of his authority before so entering, and shall not demand admission as of right to any land which is occupied unless twenty-four hours' notice of the intended entry has been given to the occupier.

(2) Any person who wilfully obstructs a person acting in the exercise of his powers under section 280 of this Act shall be guilty of an offence and liable on summary conviction to a fine not exceeding [level 2 on the standard scale].

(3) If any person who, in compliance with the provisions of section 280 of this Act, is admitted into a factory, workshop or workplace discloses to any person any information obtained by him therein as to any manufacturing process or trade secret, he shall, unless the disclosure is made in the course of performing his duty in connection with the purpose for which he was authorised to enter the premises, be guilty of an offence and liable on summary conviction to a fine not exceeding [the prescribed sum] or on conviction on indictment to imprisonment for a term not exceeding two years or a fine, or both.

(4) Where any land is damaged in the exercise of a right of entry conferred under section 280 of this Act, or in the making of any survey for the purpose of which any such right of entry has been so conferred, compensation in respect of that damage may be recovered by any person interested in the land from the Secretary of State or authority on whose behalf the entry was effected.

(5) The provisions of section 179 of this Act shall apply in relation to compensation under subsection (4) of this section as they apply in relation to compensation under Part VIII of this Act.

(6) Where under section 280 of this Act a person proposes to carry out any works authorised by virtue of subsection (9) of that section—

(*a*) he shall not carry out those works unless notice of his intention to do so was included in the notice required by subsection (1) of this section; and

(*b*) if the land in question is held by statutory undertakers, and those undertakers object to the proposed works on the grounds that the carrying out thereof would be seriously detrimental to the carrying on of their undertaking, the works shall not be carried out except with the authority of the appropriate Minister.   **[317]**

NOTES

Commencement: 1 April 1972.

This section derived from the Town and Country Planning Act 1962, s 212.

Sub-s (2): maximum fine, as originally increased by the Criminal Law Act 1977, s 31(6), converted to a level on the standard scale by the Criminal Justice Act 1982, ss 37, 46.

Sub-s (3): amended by the Magistrates' Courts Act 1980, s 32(2).

282. Local inquiries

(1) The Secretary of State may cause a local inquiry to be held for the purposes of the exercise of any of his functions under any of the provisions of this Act.

(2) The provisions of subsections (2) to (5) of section 290 of the Local Government Act 1933 (which relate to the giving of evidence at, and defraying the cost of, local inquiries) shall have effect with respect to any inquiry held by virtue of this section as if the Secretary of State were a department for the purposes of that section.   **[318]**

NOTES

Commencement: 1 April 1972.

New sub-s (2) substituted by the Housing and Planning Act 1986, s 49(1), Sch 11, Part I, para 8(1). See Appendix.

(New s 282A prospectively inserted by the Housing and Planning Act 1986, s 49(1), Sch 11, Part I, para 9(1). See Appendix.)

(New s 282B inserted by the Housing and Planning Act 1986, s 49(1), Sch 11, Part I, para 10. See Appendix.)

283. Service of notices

(1) Subject to the provisions of this section, any notice or other document required or authorised to be served or given under this Act may be served or given either—

    (*a*) by delivering it to the person on whom it is to be served or to whom it is to be given; or

    (*b*) by leaving it at the usual or last known place of abode of that person, or, in a case where an address for service has been given by that person, at that address; or

    (*c*) by sending it in a prepaid registered letter, or by the recorded delivery service, addressed to that person at his usual or last known place of abode, or, in a case where an address for service has been given by that person, at that address; or

    (*d*) in the case of an incorporated company or body, by delivering it to the secretary or clerk of the company or body at their registered or principal office, or sending it in a prepaid registered letter, or by the recorded delivery service, addressed to the secretary or clerk of the company or body at that office.

(2) Where the notice or document is required or authorised to be served on any person as having an interest in premises, and the name of that person cannot be ascertained after reasonable inquiry, or where the notice or document is required or authorised to be served on any person as an occupier of premises, the notice or document shall be taken to be duly served if—

    (*a*) being addressed to him either by name or by the description of "the owner" or "the occupier", as the case may be, of the premises (describing them) it is delivered or sent in the manner specified in subsection (1)(*a*), (*b*) or (*c*) of this section; or

    (*b*) being so addressed, and marked in such manner as may be prescribed by regulations under this Act for securing that it shall be plainly identifiable as a communication of importance, it is sent to the premises in a prepaid registered letter or by the recorded delivery service and is not returned to the authority sending it, or is delivered to some person on those premises, or is affixed conspicuously to some object on those premises.

(3) Where the notice or other document is required to be served on or given to all persons having interests in, or being occupiers of, premises comprised in any land, and it appears to the authority required or authorised to serve or give the notice or other document that any part of that land is unoccupied, the notice or document shall be taken to be duly served on all persons having interests in, and on any occupiers of, premises comprised in that part of the land (other than a person who has given to that authority an address for the service of the notice or document on him) if it is addressed to "the owners and any occupiers" of that part of the land (describing it) and is affixed conspicuously to some object on the land.   **[319]**

NOTES
Commencement: 1 April 1972.

284. Power to require information as to interests in land

(1) For the purpose of enabling the Secretary of State or a local authority to make an order or [issue or] serve any notice or other document which, by any of the provisions of this Act, he or they are authorised or required to make [, issue] or serve, the Secretary of State or the local authority may [by notice in writing] require the occupier of any premises and any person who, either directly or indirectly, receives rent in respect of any premises [to give in writing within twenty-one days after the date on which the notice is served, or such longer time as may be specified in the notice, or as the Secretary of State or (as the case may be) the local authority may allow, such information as to the matters mentioned in subsection (1A) of this section as may be so specified.]

[(1A) The matters referred to in subsection (1) of this section are—

  (a) the nature of the interest in the premises of the person on whom the notice is served;
  (b) the name and address of any other person known to him as having an interest in the premises;
  (c) the purpose for which the premises are being used;
  (d) the time when that use began;
  (e) the name and address of any person known to the person on whom the notice is served as having used the premises for that purpose;
  (f) the time when any activities being carried out on the premises began.]

(2) Any person who, [without reasonable excuse, fails to comply with a notice served on him under subsection (1) of this section] shall be guilty of an offence and liable on summary conviction to a fine not exceeding [level 3 on the standard scale].

(3) Any person who, having been [required by a notice under subsection (1) of this section] to give any information, knowingly makes any misstatement in respect thereof shall be guilty of an offence and liable on summary conviction to a fine not exceeding [the prescribed sum] or on conviction on indictment to imprisonment for a term not exceeding two years or to a fine, or both.   **[320]**

NOTES
Commencement: 22 August 1977 (sub-s (1A)); 1 April 1972 (remainder).
This section derived from the Town and Country Planning Act 1962, s 215.
Sub-s (1): first and second amendments made by the Local Government and Planning

(Amendment) Act 1981, s 1, Schedule; third and fourth amendments made by the Town and Country Planning (Amendment) Act 1977, s 3.

Sub-s (1A): added by the Town and Country Planning (Amendment) Act 1977, s 3.

Sub-s (2): first amendment made by the Town and Country Planning (Amendment) Act 1977, s 3; maximum fine increased and converted to a level on the standard scale by the Criminal Justice Act 1982, ss 37, 38, 46.

Sub-s (3): first amendment made by the Town and Country Planning (Amendment) Act 1977, s 3; second amendment made by the Magistrates' Courts Act 1980, s 32(2).

285. Offences by corporations

(1) Where an offence under this Act (other than section 57 or paragraph 4 of Schedule 12) which has been committed by a body corporate is proved to have been committed with the consent or connivance of, or to be attributable to any neglect on the part of, a director, manager, secretary or other similar officer of the body corporate, or any person who was purporting to act in any such capacity, he, as well as the body corporate, shall be guilty of that offence and be liable to be proceeded against accordingly.

(2) In subsection (1) of this section the expression "director", in relation to any body corporate established by or under an enactment for the purpose of carrying on under national ownership an industry or part of an industry or undertaking, being a body corporate whose affairs are managed by the members thereof, means a member of that body corporate.   **[321]**

NOTES

Commencement: 1 April 1972.

286. Combined applications

(1) Regulations made under this Act may provide for the combination in a single document, made in such form and transmitted to such authority as may be prescribed by the regulations, of—

(*a*) an application for planning permission in respect of any development; and

(*b*) an application required, under any enactment specified in the regulations, to be made to a local authority in respect of that development.

(2) Before making any regulations under this section, the Secretary of State shall consult with such local authorities or associations of local authorities as appear to him to be concerned.

(3) Different provision may be made by any such regulations in relation to areas in which different enactments are in force.

(4) An application required to be made to a local authority under an enactment specified in any such regulations shall, if made in accordance with the provisions of the regulations, be valid notwithstanding anything in that enactment prescribing, or enabling any authority to prescribe, the form in which, or the manner in which, such an application is to be made.

(5) Subsection (4) of this section shall have effect without prejudice to—

(*a*) the validity of any application made in accordance with the enactment in question; or

(*b*) any provision of that enactment enabling a local authority to require further particulars of the matters to which the application relates.

(6) In this section "application" includes a submission.   **[322]**

NOTES
Commencement: 1 April 1972.

287. Regulations and orders

(1) The Secretary of State may make regulations under this Act—

> (a) for prescribing the form of any notice, order or other document authorised or required by any of the provisions of this Act to be served, made or issued by any local authority;
> (b) for any purpose for which regulations are authorised or required to be made under this Act, not being a purpose for which regulations are authorised or required to be made by another Minister.

(2) Any power conferred by this Act to make regulations shall be exercisable by statutory instrument; and any statutory instrument containing regulations made under this Act (except regulations which, by virtue of any provision of this Act, are of no effect unless approved by a resolution of each House of Parliament) shall be subject to annulment in pursuance of a resolution of either House of Parliament.

(3) Any power conferred by any of the provisions of this Act to make an order shall include power to vary or revoke any such order by a subsequent order.

(4) The power to make orders under sections 1(2), 21, 22(2)(*f*), 24, 55(3), 69, 73(6), [74(4)], 75(8), 192(4)(*a*) and 269 of this Act shall be exercisable by statutory instrument.

(5) Any statutory instrument—

> (a) which contains an order under subsection (2) of section 1 of this Act which has been made after a local inquiry has been held in accordance with the proviso to that subsection; or
> (b) which contains a development order or an order under section 69, 73(6), 75(8) or 192(4)(*a*) of this Act [or an order under section 74(4) not falling within subsection (7) of this section],

shall be subject to annulment in pursuance of a resolution of either House of Parliament.

(6) Without prejudice to subsection (5) of this section, where a development order makes provision for excluding or modifying any enactment contained in a public general Act (other than any of the enactments specified in Schedule 22 to this Act) the order shall not have effect until that provision is approved by a resolution of each House of Parliament.

(7) Any order under this Act which designates an area for the purposes of section 74(4)(*b*) of this Act shall cease to have effect at the end of the period of twenty-eight days beginning with the day on which the order is made (but without prejudice to anything previously done under the order or to the making of a new order) unless before the end of that period the order is approved by a resolution of each House of Parliament.

(8) In reckoning any period for the purposes of subsection (7) of this section, no account shall be taken of any time during which Parliament is dissolved or prorogued or during which both Houses are adjourned for more than four days.

(9) Any order under section 69, 73(6), [74(4)] or 75(8) of this Act may contain

such supplementary and incidental provisions as may appear to the Secretary of State to be appropriate.

(10) Any power (exercisable in accordance with section 294(2) of this Act) to make regulations or orders under this Act before the date of the commencement of this Act shall include power, by any regulations or order so made, to revoke any regulations or order made under any of the enactments which, as from that date, are repealed by this Act or having effect by virtue of any of those enactments as if made thereunder. **[323]**

NOTES
Commencement: 1 April 1972.
Amended by the Control of Office Development Act 1977, s 3.
Sub-s (4): prospectively amended by the Housing and Planning Act 1986, s 25(3), Sch 6, Part II, para 6(*a*); amended by the Housing and Planning Act 1986, s 40, Sch 9, Part I, para 5(2); repealed in part by the Housing and Planning Act 1986, s 49(2), Sch 12, Part III. See Appendix.
Sub-s (5): prospectively amended by the Housing and Planning Act 1986, s 25(3), Sch 6, Part II, para 6(*b*); amended by the Housing and Planning Act 1986, s 40, Sch 9, Part I, para 5(2); repealed in part by the Housing and Planning Act 1986, s 49(2), Sch 12, Part III. See Appendix.
Sub-s (7): repealed by the Housing and Planning Act 1986, s 49(2), Sch 12, Part III. See Appendix.
Sub-s (9): amended by the Housing and Planning Act 1986, s 40, Sch 9, Part I, para 5(2); prospectively repealed by the Housing and Planning Act 1986, s 49(2), Sch 12, Part III. See Appendix.

288. Licensing planning areas

(1) Where the united district for which, by an order under section 1 of this Act, a joint planning board is constituted comprises a licensing planning area, or the whole or part of such a united district is included in a licensing planning area, the Secretary of State may by order revoke or vary any order in force under Part VII of the Licensing Act 1964 so far as may be necessary or expedient in consequence of the order under section 1 of this Act.

(2) Subject to subsection (1) of this section, nothing in any order made under section 1 of this Act shall affect the validity of any order in force under Part VII of the Licensing Act 1964 if made before the date of the order under section 1 of this Act. **[324]**

NOTES
Commencement: 1 April 1972.

289. Act not excluded by special enactments

For the avoidance of doubt it is hereby declared that the provisions of this Act, and any restrictions or powers thereby imposed or conferred in relation to land, apply and may be exercised in relation to any land notwithstanding that provision is made by any enactment in force at the passing of the Act of 1947, or by any local Act passed at any time during the Session of Parliament held during the regnal years 10 & 11 Geo. 6, for authorising or regulating any development of the land. **[325]**

NOTES
Commencement: 1 April 1972.
Act of 1947: Town and Country Planning Act 1947.

290. Interpretation

(1) In this Act, except in so far as the context otherwise requires and subject to the transitional provisions hereinafter contained, the following expressions have the means hereby assigned to them respectively, that is to say:—

"acquiring authority", in relation to the acquisition of an interest in land (whether compulsorily or by agreement) or to a proposal so to acquire such an interest, means the government department, local authority or other body by whom the interest is, or is proposed to be, acquired;
"the Act of 1944" means the Town and Country Planning Act 1944;
"the Act of 1947" means the Town and Country Planning Act 1947;
"the Act of 1954" means the Town and Country Planning Act 1954;
"the Act of 1959" means the Town and Country Planning Act 1959;

"the Act of 1962" means the Town and Country Planning Act 1962;

"the Act of 1968" means the Town and Country Planning Act 1968;

"advertisement" means any word, letter, model, sign, placard, board, notice, device or representation, whether illuminated or not, in the nature of, and employed wholly or partly for the purposes of, advertisement, announcement or direction, and (without prejudice to the preceding provisions of this definition), includes any hoarding or similar structure used, or adapted for use, for the display of advertisements, and references to the display of advertisements shall be construed accordingly;

["aftercare condition" has the meaning assigned to it by section 30A(2) of this Act;]

"agriculture" includes horticulture, fruit growing, seed growing, dairy farming, the breeding and keeping of livestock (including any creature kept for the production of food, wool, skins or fur, or for the purpose of its use in the farming of land), the use of land as grazing land, meadow land, osier land, market gardens and nursery grounds, and the use of land for woodlands where that use is ancillary to the farming of land for other agricultural purposes, and "agricultural" shall be construed accordingly;

"the appointed day" means 1st July 1948;

"the appropriate Minister" has the meaning assigned to it by section 224 of this Act;

"area of extensive war damage" and "area of bad layout or obsolete development" mean respectively an area consisting of land shown to the satisfaction of the Secretary of State to have sustained war damage or, as the case may be, to be badly laid out or of obsolete development, or consisting of such land together with other land contiguous or adjacent thereto, being in each case land comprised in an area which is defined by a development plan as an area of comprehensive development;

"authority possessing compulsory purchase powers", in relation to the compulsory acquisition of an interest in land, means the person or body of persons effecting the acquisition, and, in relation to any other transaction relating to an interest in land, means any person or body of persons who could be or have been authorised to acquire that interest compulsorily for the purposes for which the transaction is or was effected, or a body (being a parish council [community council] or parish meeting . . .) on whose behalf a [district council or] county council could be or have been so authorised;

"authority to whom Part II of the Act of 1959 applies" means a body of any of the descriptions specified in Part I of Schedule 4 to the Act of 1959;

"bridleway" has the same meaning as in [the Highways Act 1980];

"building" (except in sections 73 to 86 of this Act and Schedule 12 thereto) includes any structure or erection, and any part of a building, as so defined, but does not include plant or machinery comprised in a building;

"buildings or works" includes waste materials, refuse and other matters deposited on land, and references to the erection or construction of buildings or works shall be construed accordingly;

"building operations" includes rebuilding operations, structural alterations of or additions to buildings, and other operations normally undertaken by a person carrying on business as a builder;

"caravan site" has the meaning assigned to it by section 1(4) of the Caravan Sites and Control of Development Act 1960;

"clearing", in relation to land, means the removal of buildings or materials from the land, the levelling of the surface of the land, and the carrying out of such other operations in relation thereto as may be prescribed;

"common" includes any land subject to be enclosed under the Inclosure Acts 1845 to 1882, and any town or village green;

"compulsory acquisition" does not include the vesting in a person by an Act of Parliament of property previously vested in some other person;

"conservation area" means an area designated under section 277 of this Act;

"development" has the meaning assigned to it by section 22 of this Act, and "develop" shall be construed accordingly;

["development consisting of the winning and working of minerals" shall be construed in accordance with section 264(1A) of this Act;]

"development order" has the meaning assigned to it by section 24 of this Act;

"development plan" (subject to section 21 of, and paragraphs 1 and 8 of Schedule 6 to, this Act) shall be construed in accordance with section 20 of this Act [and paragraph 15 of Schedule 1 to the Local Government Act 1985];

"disposal" means disposal by way of sale, exchange or lease, or by way of the creation of any easement, right or privilege, or in any other manner, except by way of appropriation, gift or mortgage, and "dispose of " shall be construed accordingly;

"enactment" includes an enactment in any local or private Act of Parliament, and an order, rule, regulation, bye-law or scheme made under an Act of Parliament;

"enforcement notice" means a notice under section 87 of this Act;

"engineering operations" includes the formation or laying out of means of access to highways;

["enterprise zone scheme" means a scheme or modified scheme having effect to grant planning permission by virtue of Schedule 32 to the Local Government, Planning and Land Act 1980;]

"erection", in relation to buildings as defined in this subsection, includes extension, alteration and re-erection;

"established use certificate" has the meaning assigned to it by section 94 of this Act;

"footpath" has the same meaning as in [the Highways Act 1980];

"fuel or field garden allotment" means any allotment set out as a fuel allotment, or a field garden allotment, under an Inclosure Act;

"functions" includes powers and duties;

"government department" includes any Minister of the Crown;

"the Greater London development plan" (except in Part II of Schedule 5 to this Act) means the development plan submitted to the Minister of Housing and Local Government under section 25 of the London Government Act 1963 and approved by the Secretary of State under section 5 of the Act of 1962 or the corresponding provision of this Act;

"highway" has the same meaning as in [the Highways Act 1980];

"improvement", in relation to a highway, has the same meaning as in [the Highways Act 1980]

"industrial development certificate" has the meaning assigned to it by section 67 of this Act;

"joint planning board" has the meaning assigned to it by section 1 of this Act;

"land" means any corporeal hereditament, including a building, and, in relation to the acquisition of land under Part VI of this Act, includes any interest in or right over land;

"lease" includes an underlease and an agreement for a lease or underlease, but does not include an option to take a lease or a mortgage, and "leasehold interest" means the interest of the tenant under a lease as so defined;

"listed building" has the meaning assigned to it by section 54(9) of this Act;

"listed building consent" has the meaning assigned to it by section 55(2) of this Act;

"listed building enforcement notice" has the meaning assigned to it by section 96 of this Act;

"listed building purchase notice" has the meaning assigned to it by section 190 of this Act;

"local authority" (except in section 215 of this Act) means the council of a county, . . . county district, . . . , the council of a London borough and any other authority (except the Receiver for the Metropolitan Police District) who are a local authority within the meaning of the Local Loans Act 1875 and includes any river authority, any drainage board and any joint board or joint committee if all the constituent authorities are local authorities within the meaning of that Act;

"local highway authority" means a highway authority other than the Secretary of State;

"local planning authority" has the meaning assigned to it by section 1 of, . . . , this Act;

"London borough" includes the City of London, references to the council of a London borough or the clerk to such a council being construed, in relation to the City, as references to the Common Council of the City and the town clerk of the City respectively;

"means of access" includes any means of access, whether private or public, for vehicles or for foot passengers, and includes a street;

["mineral compensation modifications" has the meaning assigned to it by section 178A(8) of this Act;

"mineral planning authority"—

(a) in respect of any site outside Greater London, has the meaning assigned to it by section 1(2B) of this Act; and

(b) in respect of any site in Greater London, has the meaning assigned to it by paragraph 4B of Schedule 3 to this Act;

"mineral-working deposit" has the meaning assigned to it by section 264(1A) of this Act;]

"minerals" includes all minerals and substances in or under land of a kind ordinarily worked for removal by underground or surface working, except that it does not include peat cut for purposes other than sale;

"Minister" means any Minister of the Crown or other government department;

"mortgage" includes any charge or lien on any property for securing money or money's worth;

"new development" has the meaning assigned to it by section 22(5) of this Act;

"open space" means any land laid out as a public garden, or used for the purposes of public recreation, or land which is a disused burial ground;

"operational land" has the meaning assigned to it by section 222 of this Act;

"owner", in relation to any land, means (except in sections 27 and 29 of this Act) a person, other than a mortgagee not in possession, who, whether in his own right or as trustee for any other person, is entitled to receive the rack rent of the land, or, where the land is not let at a rack rent, would be so entitled if it were so let;

"planning decision" means a decision made on an application under Part III of this Act;

"planning permission" means permission under Part III of this Act, and in construing references to planning permission to develop land or to carry out any development of land, or to applications for such permission, regard shall be had to section 32(2) of this Act;

"planning permission granted for a limited period" has the meaning assigned to it by section 30(2) of this Act;

"prescribed" (except in relation to matters expressly required or authorised by this Act to be prescribed in some other way) means prescribed by regulations under this Act;

"previous apportionment", in relation to an apportionment for any of the purposes of the relevant provisions, means an apportionment made before the apportionment in question, being—

(*a*) an apportionment for any of the purposes of the relevant provisions as made, confirmed or varied by the Lands Tribunal on a reference to that Tribunal; or

(*b*) an apportionment for any of those purposes which might have been referred to the Lands Tribunal by virtue of any of the relevant provisions, where the time for such a reference has expired without its being required to be so referred, or where, after it had been so referred, the reference was withdrawn before the Tribunal gave their decision thereon; or

(*c*) an apportionment made by or with the approval of the Central Land Board in connection with the approval by the Board, under section 2(2) of the Town and Country Planning Act 1953 of an assignment of part of the benefit of an established claim (as defined by section 135(4) of this Act),

and in this definition "the relevant provisions" means any of the provisions of Part VII of this Act or of Part VI of the Act of 1962, any of those provisions as applied by any other provision of this Act or that Act, and any of the provisions of the Act of 1954;

"purchase notice" has the meaning assigned to it by section 180 of this Act;

["relevant order" has the meaning assigned to it by section 178C(3) of this Act;]

"relocation of population or industry", in relation to any area, means the rendering available elsewhere than in that area (whether in an existing community or a community to be newly established) of accommodation for residential purposes or for the carrying on of business or other activities, together with all appropriate public services, facilities for public worship, recreation and amenity, and other requirements, being accommodation to be rendered available for persons or undertakings who are living or carrying on business or other activities in that area or who were doing so but by reason of war circumstances are no longer for the time being doing so, and whose continued or resumed location in that area would be inconsistent with the proper planning thereof;

"replacement of open space", in relation to any area, means the rendering of land available for use as an open space, or otherwise in an undeveloped state, in substitution for land in that area which is so used;

["restoration condition" has the meaning assigned to it by section 30A(2) of this Act;

"restriction on the winning and working of minerals" has the meaning assigned to it by section 178C(1) of this Act;

"special consultations" has the meaning assigned to it by section 178B of this Act;

"the statutory maximum" means the prescribed sum within the meaning of section 32 of the Magistrates' Courts Act 1980 (£1,000 or another sum fixed by order under section 143 of that Act to take account of changes in the value of money);]

"statutory undertakers" means persons authorised by any enactment, to carry on any railway, light railway, tramway, road transport, water transport, canal, inland navigation, dock, harbour, pier or lighthouse undertaking, or any undertaking for the supply of electricity, gas, hydraulic power or water, and "statutory undertaking" shall be construed accordingly;

["steps for the protection of the environment" has the meaning assigned to it by section 51B(3) of this Act;]

"stop notice" has the meaning assigned to it by section 90 of this Act;

["suspension order" and "supplementary suspension order" have the meanings assigned to them by section 51B of this Act;]

"tenancy" has the same meaning as in the Landlord and Tenant Act 1954;

"tree preservation order" has the meaning assigned to it by section 60 of this Act;

"use", in relation to land, does not include the use of land for the carrying out of any building or other operations thereon;

"Valuation Office" means the Valuation Office of the Inland Revenue Department;

"Wales" includes Monmouthshire and references to England shall be construed accordingly;

"war damage" has the same meaning as in the War Damage Act 1943.

(2) If, in relation to anything required or authorised to be done under this Act, any question arises as to which Minister is or was the appropriate Minister in relation to any statutory undertakers, that question shall be determined by the Treasury; and if any question so arises whether land of statutory undertakers is operational land, that question shall be determined by the Minister who is the appropriate Minister in relation to those undertakers.

(3) Words in this Act importing a reference to service of a notice to treat shall be construed as including a reference to the constructive service of such a notice which, by virtue of any enactment, is to be deemed to be served.

(4) With respect to reference in this Act to planning decisions—

(a) in relation to a decision altered on appeal by the reversal or variation of the whole or part thereof, such references shall be construed as references to the decision as so altered;

(b) in relation to a decision upheld on appeal, such references shall be construed as references to the decision of the local planning authority and not to the decision of the Secretary of State on the appeal;

(c) in relation to a decision given on an appeal in the circumstances mentioned in section 37 of this Act, such references shall be construed as references to the decision so given;

(d) the time of a planning decision, in a case where there is or was an appeal, shall be taken to be or have been the time of the decision as made by the local planning authority (whether or not that decision is or was altered on that appeal) or, in the case of a decision given on an appeal in the circumstances mentioned in section 37 of this Act, the time when in accordance with that section notification of a decision of the local planning authority is deemed to have been received.

(5) Subject to section 43(1) of this Act, for the purposes of this Act development of land shall be taken to be initiated—

    (*a*) if the development consists of the carrying out of operations, at the time when those operations are begun;

    (*b*) if the development consists of a change in use, at the time when the new use is instituted;

    (*c*) if the development consists both of the carrying out of operations and of a change in use, at the earlier of the times mentioned in the preceding paragraphs.

(6) In relation to the sale or acquisition of an interest in land, references in this Act to a contract are references to a contract in writing, or a contract attested by a memorandum or note thereof in writing signed by the parties thereto or by some other person or persons authorised by them in that behalf, and, where the interest is or was conveyed or assigned without a preliminary contract, are references to the conveyance or assignment; and references to the making of a contract are references to the execution thereof or (if it was not in writing) to the signature of the memorandum or note by which it was attested.

(7) In this Act—

    (*a*) references to a person from whom title is derived by another person include references to any predecessor in title of that other person;

    (*b*) references to a person deriving title from another person include references to any successor in title of that other person;

    (*c*) references to deriving title are references to deriving title either directly or indirectly.

(8) References in this Act to any of the provisions in Part V or VI of Schedule 21 to this Act include, except where the context otherwise requires, references to those provisions as modified under section 270 or 271 of this Act.

(9) References in this Act to any enactment shall, except where the context otherwise requires, be construed as references to that enactment as amended by or under any other enactment, including this Act. **[326]**

NOTES

Commencement: 1 April 1972.

Sub-s (1): prospectively amended by the Housing and Planning Act 1986, ss 25(3), 33, Sch 6, Part II, para 7, Sch 7, Part II, para 7; repealed in part by the Housing and Planning Act 1986, s 49(2), Sch 12, Part III. See Appendix.

Definition "authority possessing compulsory purchase powers": words omitted repealed by the local Government Act 1972, s 272, Sch 30; amendments in square brackets made by SI 1977 No 293.

Definitions "bridleway", "footpath", "highway", "improvement": amended by the Highways Act 1980, s 343, Sch 24.

Definition "development plan": words in square brackets prospectively added by the Local Government Act 1985, s 4, Sch 1, para 16, as from a day or days to be appointed.

  Definition "enterprise zone scheme": added by the Local Government, Planning and Land Act 1980, s 179, Sch 32.

Definitions "after care condition", "development consisting of winning and working of minerals", "mineral compensation modifications", "mineral planning authority", "mineral working deposit", "relevant order", "restoration condition", "restriction on the winning and working of minerals", "special consultations", "the statutory maximum", "steps for the protection of the environment", "suspension order": added by the Town and Country Planning (Minerals) Act 1981, s 34, Sch 1.

Definition "local authority": first words omitted repealed by the Local Government Act 1972, s 272, Sch 30; second words omitted repealed by the Local Government Act 1985, s 102, Sch 17.

Definition "local planning authority": words omitted repealed by the Local Government Act 1985, s 102, Sch 17.

293. Saving for Interpretation Act 1889 s 38

The inclusion in this Act of any express savings, transitional provision or amendment shall not be taken as prejudicing the operation of section 38 of the Interpretation Act 1889 (which relates to the effect of repeals). **[327]**

NOTES
Commencement: 1 April 1972.

294. Commencement

(1) Except as provided in section 21 of this Act and subject to the following provisions of this section, this Act shall come into operation on 1st April 1972 (in this section referred to as "the commencement date").

(2) This section, any provisions of this Act which confer any power to make regulations or orders, or which (whether expressly or as construed in accordance with section 32(3) of the Interpretation Act 1889) confer any power to revoke or vary any regulations or orders, and any provisions of this Act relating to the exercise of any such power, shall come into operation on the passing of this Act; but no regulations or order shall be made under this Act so as to come into operation before the commencement date.

(3) In subsection (2) of this section the reference to provisions of this Act relating to the exercise of any such power as is therein mentioned includes a reference to any provisions of this Act whereby statutory instruments containing regulations or an order are subject to annulment in pursuance of a resolution of either House of Parliament, or whereby any regulations or order or any provisions thereof require the approval of each of those Houses.

(4) Any reference in this Act to the commencement of this Act is a reference to the coming into operation of so much of this Act as comes into operation on the commencement date, and any reference to the date of the commencement of this Act is a reference to that date; and if any Act passed after the passing of this Act refers to the commencement of this Act, subsections (2) and (3) of this section and section 21 of this Act shall be disregarded for the purpose of construing that reference in accordance with section 36 of the Interpretation Act 1889 (which relates to the meaning of "commencement" with reference to an Act).

(5) The preceding provisions of this section shall have effect without prejudice to the generality of section 37 of the Interpretation Act 1889 (which relates to the exercise of statutory powers between the passing and the commencement of an Act). **[328]**

NOTES
Commencement: 28 October 1971.

295. Short title and extent

(1) This Act may be cited as the Town and Country Planning Act 1971.

(2) This Act, except so far as it . . . (by Schedule 23) amends any enactment which extends to Scotland or Northern Ireland, extends to England and Wales only. **[329]**

NOTES
Commencement: 1 April 1972.
Words omitted repealed by the House of Commons Disqualification Act 1975, s 10(2), Sch 3.

SCHEDULES
SCHEDULE 1
Section 1

JOINT PLANNING BOARDS

1. A joint planning board constituted by an order under section 1 of this Act shall consist of such number of members as may be determined by the order, to be appointed by the constituent councils.

2. A joint planning board so constituted shall be a body corporate, with perpetual succession and a common seal.

3. An order constituting a joint planning board and any order amending or revoking any order constituting a joint planning board—

    (*a*) may, without prejudice to the provisions of section 293 of the Local Government Act 1933 (which authorises the application of the provisions of that Act to joint boards), provide for regulating the appointment, tenure of office and vacation of office of members of the board, for regulating the meetings and proceedings of the board, and for the payment of the expenses of the board by the constituent councils;

    (*b*) may provide for the transfer and compensation of officers, the transfer of property and liabilities, and the adjustment of accounts and apportionment of liabilities;

    (*c*) may contain such other provisions as appear to the Secretary of State to be expedient for enabling the board to exercise their functions; and

    (*d*) may apply to the board, with any necessary modifications and adaptations, any of the provisions of [sections 102 and 103 of the Local Government Act 1972].

[330]

NOTES
    Commencement: 1 April 1972.
    Amended, except as to Greater London, by the Local Government Act 1972, s 182, Sch 16.

SCHEDULE 4
Section 19

SURVEYS AND DEVELOPMENT PLANS IN GREATER LONDON

1. . . .

Surveys by London borough councils

2. The matters to be so examined or kept under review by a London borough council shall be such of the matters mentioned in section 6 as have not been examined or kept under review by the Greater London Council, . . .

Joint surveys

3. . . .

4. . . .

The Greater London development plan as a structure plan

5.—(1) The Greater London development plan shall be a structure plan for Greater London approved under section 9 of this Act and may be altered under section 10 accordingly.

(2) . . .

(3) The Secretary of State may direct that any area or part of an area indicated by the development plan as an area intended for comprehensive development, redevelopment or improvement as a whole shall be treated as an action area, and references in this Schedule to an action area shall be construed accordingly.

Alteration of structure plan on proposal of London borough council

6. . . .

Exclusion of ss. 7 to 10 B, 11 and 12

7. Sections 7 to 10 of this Act do not apply to the London borough councils and sections 10B, [10C, 11, 12 and 14(5) to (7)] apply neither to those councils nor to the Greater London Council.

Local plans : who may prepare them

8.—(1) In the following provisions of this paragraph, and in paragraph 9 below, "G.L.C. action area" means an action area in whose case it is indicated in the Greater London development plan that it is for the Greater London Council, and not a London borough council, to prepare a local plan for that area.

(2) . . .

(3) At any time either before or after the Secretary of State's final approval of the Greater London development plan—

    (a) a London borough council may, if they think fit, prepare a local plan for the whole or any part of the borough;

    (b), (c) . . .

but this sub-paragraph shall not be taken to authorise the preparation of a local plan . . . for the whole or any part of a G.L.C. action area.

(4) . . .

(5) Different local plans (joint or other) may be prepared for different purposes for the same part of any area.

Duty of planning authorities to prepare local plans for action areas

9.—(1) As soon as practicable after the Secretary of State's final approval of the Greater London development plan—

    (a) the Greater London Council prepare a local plan for every G.L.C. action area; and

    (b) in the case of any other action area—

        (i) if it is wholly comprised within a London borough, the council of that borough shall prepare a local plan for the area, and

        (ii) if not, the council of every London borough in which any part of the action area falls shall prepare a local plan for that part;

but this sub-paragraph shall not be taken to require a council to do again any thing which they have already done.

(2) . . .

(3) Where a council are required by this paragraph to prepare a local plan, they shall take steps for the adoption of that plan.

Local plans by direction of Secretary of State

10.—(1) Without prejudice to the foregoing provisions, the Greater London Council or a London borough council shall, if the Secretary of State gives them (either before or after he finally approves the Greater London development plan) a direction in that behalf with respect to any area of Greater London, as soon as practicable prepare for that area a local plan of such a nature as may be specified in the direction, and take steps for the adoption of the plan; but no such directions shall require a council to take any steps to comply therewith until after the Secretary of State's final approval of the Greater London development plan.

(2) Before giving a direction to a council under this paragraph the Secretary of State shall consult the council with respect thereto and, in the case of a direction to be given to

a London borough council, he shall also, before giving it, consult the Greater London Council.

General provisions as to local plans

11.—(1) The following provisions of this paragraph shall apply with respect to any local plan prepared under this Schedule by the Greater London Council or a London borough council . . . and in those provisions "the council" means the council preparing the local plan . . .

(2) The plan shall consist of a map and a written statement and shall—

(*a*) formulate in such detail as the council think appropriate their proposals for the development and other use of land in the area for which the plan is prepared, or for any description of development and other use of such land (including in either case such measures as the council think fit for the improvement of the physical environment and the management of traffic); and

(*b*) contain such matters as may be prescribed, . . .

(3) The plan shall contain, or be accompanied by, such diagrams, illustrations and descriptive material as the council think appropriate for the purpose of explaining or illustrating the proposals in the plan, or as may be prescribed . . . ; and any such diagrams, illustrations and descriptive material shall be treated as forming part of the plan.

(4) In formulating their proposals in the plan the council shall—

(*a*) secure that the proposals conform generally to the Greater London development plan as it stands for the time being (whether or not the Secretary of State has finally approved the plan, but taking into account any feature or element of it in the case of which he has indicated his approval), and

(*b*) have regard to any information and any other considerations which appear to them to be relevant, or which may be prescribed, or which the Secretary of State may in any particular case direct them to take into account.

(5) Before giving a direction to the council under this paragraph the Secretary of State shall consult the council with respect thereto and, in the case of a direction to be given to a London borough council, he shall also, before giving it, consult the Greater London Council.

Publicity for local plan prepared by single council

12.—(1) Where the Greater London Council or a London borough council propose to prepare a local plan, the council shall take such steps as will in their opinion secure—

(*a*) that adequate publicity is given, in any London borough affected by the plan, to any relevant matter arising out of a survey under section 6 of this Act (including any joint survey) and to the matters proposed to be included in the plan;

(*b*) that persons who may be expected to desire an opportunity of making representations to the council with respect to those matters are made aware that they are entitled to an opportunity of doing so; and

(*c*) that such persons are given an adequate opportunity of making such representations;

and the council shall consider any representations made to them within the prescribed period.

(2) *After preparing a local plan* [subject to section [15A(6)] of this Act, when a local plan has been prepared and, in a case where the council preparing it are required to obtain a certificate under section 14 of this Act, they have obtained that certificate,] the council shall before adopting it or submitting it for approval under section 14 of this Act (but not before the Secretary of State has finally approved the Greater London development plan) make copies of the plan available for inspection at their office . . . and—

(a) in the case of a plan prepared by the Greater London Council, send a copy of the plan to the council of any London borough affected by the plan,

(b) in the case of a plan prepared by a London borough council, send a copy to the Greater London Council, and

(c) in any case send a copy to the Secretary of State.

(3) Each copy of a plan made available for inspection as required by sub-paragraph (2) above shall be accompanied by a statement of the time within which objections to the local plan may be made to the council who have prepared the plan; and the copy sent to the Secretary of State shall be accompanied by a statement containing ... particulars ...

(a) of the steps which the council preparing the plan have taken to comply with sub-paragraph (1) above, and

(b) of the council's consultations with, and their consideration of the views of, other persons.

Publicity for joint local plans

13. ...

Power of Secretary of State to suspend adoption

14.—(1) In relation to a local plan (joint or other) prepared under this Schedule, section 14(1) of this Act shall have effect as if the reference to section 12 were to the following provisions of this paragraph.

(2) If, on considering the statement submitted with, and the matters included in, a local plan so prepared and other information provided by the authority who prepared the plan (or as the case may be, the authorities who joined in its preparation) the Secretary of State is not satisfied that the purposes of paragraph 12(1)(a) to (c) above ... have been adequately achieved by the steps taken in that behalf by the authority or authorities, he may within twenty-one days of the receipt of the statement direct that no further steps for the adoption of the plan be taken without such further action as he may specify having been taken in order better to achieve those purposes and his being satisfied that such action has been taken.

(3) A planning authority who are given directions by the Secretary of State under this paragraph shall—

(a) forthwith withdraw copies of the local plan made available for inspection as required by paragraph 12 or 13 above, and

(b) in a case where objections to the plan have been made by any person, notify him that the Secretary of State has given such directions as aforesaid.

Other modifications of Part II in relation to preparation and adoption of joint local plans

15. ...

Alteration etc. of local plans

16.—(1) In relation to a local plan adopted for an area in Greater London ... section 15 of this Act shall apply as if the following were substituted for subsection (3)—

"(3) The provisions of paragraphs 11(4) and (5) and 12 of Schedule 4 to this Act, and of sections 13 and 14 of this Act, shall apply in relation to the making of proposals for the alteration, repeal or replacement of a local plan under this section, and to alterations to a local plan so proposed, as they apply in relation to the preparation of a local plan under that Schedule and to a local plan prepared thereunder.";

...

(2)–(4) ...

Consultation between planning authorities

17.—(1) A London borough council shall before preparing a local plan under this Schedule, or proposals for the alteration, repeal or replacement of such a plan, and before complying with paragraph 12(2) of this Schedule in relation to any such plan or proposals, consult the Greater London Council.

(2) . . .

(3) The Greater London Council shall, before preparing a local plan or proposals for the alteration, repeal or replacement of such a plan, consult the council of any London borough in which there is comprised any part of the area of the plan, and shall consult that council before complying with paragraph 12(2) of this Schedule in relation to any such plan or proposals.

(4) Where under this paragraph any local planning authority is required to consult another such authority with respect to any matter, they shall inform the other authority of their proposals in relation to that matter and consider any representations made to them by the other authority within such time as may be prescribed.]   [331]

NOTES
Commencement: To be appointed (paras 7A, 7B); 12 October 1973 (remainder); and see s 21 of this Act.
Substituted by the Town and Country Planning (Amendment) Act 1972, s 4(1), Sch 1.
Paras 1, 4: repealed by the Local Government Act 1985, s 102, Sch 17.
Para 2: words omitted repealed by the Local Government Act 1985, s 102, Sch 17.
Para 3: repealed by the Local Government Act 1972, s 272, Sch 30.
Para 5: words omitted repealed by the Local Government Act 1985, s 102, Sch 17.
Para 6: repealed by the Local Government, Planning and Land Act 1980, s 194, Sch 34.
Para 7: amended by the Local Government Act 1972, s 182, Sch 16.
Para 8: sub-para (2) repealed by the Local Government Act 1985, s 102, Sch 17; in sub-paras (3), (4) words omitted repealed by the Local Government Act 1972, s 272, Sch 30.
Paras 9: words omitted repealed by the Local Government Act 1972, s 272, Sch 30.
Para 11: first and second words omitted repealed by the Local Government Act 1972, s 272, Sch 30; third and fourth words omitted repealed by the Local Government, Planning and Land Act 1980, s 89, Sch 14.
Para 12: words in italics prospectively repealed and words in square brackets prospectively substituted by the Local Government, Planning and Land Act 1980, s 89, Sch 14, as from a day to be appointed; further amended by the Local Government (Miscellaneous Provisions) Act 1982, s 47, Sch 6, para 7; Words omitted repealed by the Local Government, Planning and Land Act 1980, s 194, Sch 34.
Paras 13–17: words omitted repealed by the Local Government Act 1972, s 272, Sch 30.

SCHEDULE 5

Section 21

DEVELOPMENT PLANS: PROVISIONS IN FORCE UNTIL SUPERSEDED BY PART II OF THIS ACT

PART I

GENERAL

Surveys of planning areas and preparation of development plans

1.—(1) Any local planning authority who have not submitted to the Secretary of State a development plan for their area shall carry out a survey of their area and shall, within such period as the Secretary of State may in any particular case allow, submit to the Secretary of State a report of the survey together with a development plan for their area.

(2) Subject to the following provisions of this Part of this Schedule, in this Act "development plan" means a plan indicating the manner in which a local planning authority propose that land in their area should be used, whether by the carrying out thereon of development or otherwise, and the stages by which any such development should be carried out.

(3) Subject to the provisions of any regulations made under this Act for regulating

the form and content of development plans, any such plan shall include such maps and such descriptive matter as may be necessary to illustrate the proposals in question with such degree of particularity as may be appropriate to different parts of the area; and any such plan may in particular define the sites of proposed roads, public and other buildings and works, airfields, parks, pleasure grounds, nature reserves and other open spaces, or allocate areas of land for use for agricultural, residential, industrial or other purposes of any class specified in the plan.

(4) For the purposes of this paragraph, a development plan may define as an area of comprehensive development any area which, in the opinion of the local planning authority, should be developed or redeveloped as a whole for any one or more of the following purposes, that is to say—

(a) for the purposes of dealing satisfactorily with extensive war damage or conditions of bad lay-out or obsolete development; or

(b) for the purpose of providing for the relocation of population or industry or the replacement of open space in the course of the development or redevelopment of any other area; or

(c) for any other purpose specified in the plan;

and land may be included in any area so defined whether or not provision is made by the plan for the development or redevelopment of that particular land.

(5) At any time before a development plan with respect to the whole of the area of a local planning authority has been approved by the Secretary of State, that authority may, with the consent of the Secretary of State, and shall, if so required by directions of the Secretary of State, prepare and submit to him a development plan relating to part of that area; and the preceding provisions of this paragraph shall apply in relation to any such plan as they apply in relation to a plan relating to the whole of the area of a local planning authority.

Approval of development plans

2. The Secretary of State may approve any development plan submitted to him under paragraph 1 of this Schedule, either without modification or subject to such modifications as he considers expedient.

Amendment of development plans

3.—(1) At least once in every five years after the date on which a development plan for any area was approved by the Secretary of State, the local planning authority shall carry out a fresh survey of that area, and (subject to paragraph 1 of Schedule 7 to this Act) submit to the Secretary of State a report of the survey, together with proposals for any alterations or additions to the plan which appear to them to be required having regard thereto.

(2) Without prejudice to the provisions of sub-paragraph (1) of this paragraph, any local planning authority may (subject to paragraph 1 of Schedule 7 to this Act) at any time, and shall if so required by directions of the Secretary of State, submit to the Secretary of State proposals for such alterations or additions to the development plan for their area or any part thereof as appear to them to be expedient, or as may be required by those directions, as the case may be.

(3) Where proposals for alterations or additions to a development plan are submitted to the Secretary of State under this paragraph, the Secretary of State may amend that plan to such extent as he considers expedient having regard to those proposals and to any other material considerations.

(4) Where in accordance with the provisions of paragraph 1(5) of this Schedule a development plan has been prepared for part of the area of a local planning authority, and has been approved by the Secretary of State, then (without prejudice to the provisions of sub-paragraph (2) of this paragraph) the periods of five years mentioned in sub-paragraph (1) of this paragraph shall run from the date on which development plans in respect of the whole of the area have been approved by the Secretary of State.

Additional powers of Secretary of State with respect to development plans

4.—(1) Where, by virtue of any of the preceding provisions of this Schedule or of any directions of the Secretary of State thereunder, any development plan, report or proposals for alterations or additions to a development plan are required to be submitted to the Secretary of State, then—

> (a) if within the period allowed in that behalf under those provisions or directions no such plan, report or proposals, or no such plan or proposals satisfactory to the Secretary of State, have been so submitted; or
> (b) if at any time the Secretary of State is satisfied, after holding a local inquiry, that the local planning authority are not taking the steps necessary to enable them to submit such a plan, report or proposals within that period,

the Secretary of State may, after carrying out any survey which appears to him to be expedient for the purpose, make such development plan, or, as the case may be, amend the development plan to such extent, as he considers expedient.

(2) Where, under sub-paragraph (1) of this paragraph, the Secretary of State has power to make or amend a development plan, he may, if he thinks fit, authorise the local planning authority for any neighbouring area, or any other local planning authority which appears to the Secretary of State to have an interest in the proper planning of the area concerned, to submit such a plan to him for his approval, or as the case may be, to submit to him proposals for the amendment of the plan, and to carry out any survey of the land which appears to him to be expedient for the purpose.

(3) The Secretary of State may approve any plan submitted to him under sub-paragraph (2) of this paragraph, either without modification or subject to such modifications as he considers expedient, or, as the case may be, may amend any development plan, with respect to which proposals for amendment have been submitted to him under that sub-paragraph to such extent as he considers expedient having regard to those proposals and to any other material considerations.

(4) The preceding provisions of this Schedule shall, so far as applicable, apply to the making, approval or amendment of development plans under this paragraph, and to plans so made, approved or amended, as they apply to the approval or amendment of development plans under those provisions, and to plans approved or amended thereunder.

(5) Where the Secretary of State incurs expenses under this paragraph in connection with the making or amendment of a plan with respect to the area, or any part of the area, of a local planning authority, so much of those expenses as may be certified by the Secretary of State to have been incurred in the performance of functions of that authority shall on demand be repaid by that authority to the Secretary of State.

(6) Where, under this paragraph, a plan, or proposals for the amendment of a plan, are authorised to be submitted to the Secretary of State by the local planning authority for any area other than the area in which the land is situated, any expenses reasonably incurred in that behalf by that authority, as certified by the Secretary of State, shall be repaid to that authority by the local planning authority for the area in which the land is situated.

Incorporation in development plans of orders and schemes relating to highways and new towns

5.—(1) Where the Secretary of State—

> (a) makes an order under [section 10 of the Highways Act 1980 (or has made an order under section 7 of the Highways Act 1959)] directing that a highway proposed to be constructed by him shall become a trunk road; or
> [(b) makes an order relating to a trunk road under section 14 of the Highways Act 1980 (or has made an order under section 9 of the Highways Act 1959) or makes or confirms a scheme or order under section 16 or 18 of the Highways Act 1980 (or has made or confirmed a scheme or order under section 11 or 13 of the Highways Act 1959)],

any development plan approved or made under this Schedule which relates to land on which a highway is to be constructed or altered in accordance with that order or scheme shall have effect as if the provisions of that order or scheme were included in the plan.

(2) Where an order is made by the Secretary of State under section 1 of the New Towns Act 1965 designating an area as the site of a new town under that Act, any development plan approved or made under this Schedule which relates to land in that area shall have effect as if the provisions of that order were included in the plan.

(3) Nothing in this paragraph shall be construed as prohibiting the inclusion in a development plan, as approved or made by the Secretary of State or as for the time being amended, of provisions—

(a) defining the line of a highway proposed to be constructed or altered in accordance with any such order or scheme as is mentioned in sub-paragraph (1) of this paragraph; or

(b) defining an area designated as the site of a new town by any such order as is mentioned in sub-paragraph (2) of this paragraph; or

(c) defining land as likely to be made the subject of any such order or scheme as is mentioned in either of those sub-paragraphs.

(4) Provision may be made by regulations under this Act for enabling any proceedings preliminary to the making of any such order as is mentioned in sub-paragraph (1)(a) or (2) of this paragraph, to be taken concurrently with proceedings required under this Schedule to be taken in connection with the approval or making of a development plan relating to land to which any such order applies, or in connection with any amendment of a development plan rendered necessary or desirable in consequence of any such order.

Supplementary provisions as to development plans

6.—(1) A local planning authority, before preparing a development plan relating to any land in a county district, or proposals for alterations or additions to any such plan, shall consult with the council of that district, and shall, before submitting any such plan or proposals to the Secretary of State, give to that council an opportunity to make representations with respect thereto and shall consider any representations so made.

(2) Provision may be made by regulations under this Act with respect to the form and content of development plans, and with respect to the procedure to be followed in connection with the preparation, submission, approval, making and amendment of such plans; and such regulations shall in particular make provision for securing—

(a) that notice shall be given by advertisement in the London Gazette, and in at least one newspaper circulating in the area concerned, of the submission to the Secretary of State of any such plan, or of proposals for the amendment of any such plan, and of any proposal by the Secretary of State to make or amend such a plan, and of the place or places where copies of the plan or proposals as so submitted, or of any such proposal of the Secretary of State, may be inspected;

(b) that objections and representations duly made in accordance with the regulations shall be considered; and that such local inquiries or other hearings as may be prescribed shall be held, before such a plan is approved, made or amended by the Secretary of State; and

(c) that copies of any such plan as approved or made by the Secretary of State, including any amendments thereof, shall be available for inspection by the public, and that copies thereof (including reproductions, on such scale as may be appropriate, of any relevant maps) shall be available for sale to the public at a reasonable cost.

(3) If, as the result of any objections or representations considered, or local inquiry or other hearing held, in connection with a development plan or proposals for amendment of such a plan submitted to or prepared by the Secretary of State under this Schedule, the Secretary of State is of opinion that the local planning authority, or any other authority or person, ought to be consulted before he decides whether to approve or make the plan, either with or without modifications, or to amend the plan, as the case may be, he shall consult that authority or person but shall not be under any obligation to consult any other authority or person, or to afford any opportunity for further objections or representations, or to cause any further local inquiry or other hearing to be held.

(4) Subject to the preceding provisions of this paragraph, the Secretary of State may give directions to any local planning authority, or to local planning authorities generally—

    (a) for formulating the procedure for the carrying out of their functions under the preceding provisions of this Schedule;

    (b) for requiring them to give him such information as he may require for the purpose of the exercise of any of his functions under those provisions.

Publication and date of operation of development plans

7.—(1) Immediately after a development plan has been approved or made or amended by the Secretary of State under this Schedule, the local planning authority shall publish, in such manner as may be prescribed, a notice stating that the plan has been approved, made or amended, as the case may be, and naming a place where a copy of the plan or of the plan as amended, may be seen at all reasonable hours, and shall serve a like notice—

    (a) on any person who duly made an objection to, or representation with respect to, the proposed plan or amendment, and has sent to the local planning authority a request in writing to serve him with the notice required by this subsection, specifying an address for service; and

    (b) on such other persons (if any) as may be required by general or special directions given by the Secretary of State.

(2) Subject to the provisions of Part XII of this Act as to the validity of development plans and of amendments of such plans, a development plan, or an amendment of a development plan, shall become operative on the date on which the notice required by sub-paragraph (1) of this paragraph is first published. **[332]**

NOTES
    Commencement: 1 April 1972.
    Repealed for certain purposes by SI 1975 Nos 782, 783, 1278, 1279; 1976 Nos 104, 814, 1162; 1977 Nos 469, 1364, 1768; 1978 Nos 556, 724, 726; 1979 Nos 139, 202, 203, 328, 890, 1042, 1189, 1486, 1623, 1625, 1627, 1629; 1980 Nos 3, 40, 66, 102, 175, 301, 459, 461, 493, 576, 578, 829, 933, 964, 1099, 1156, 1210, 1404, 1452, 1548, 1560, 1635.
    Amended by the Highways Act 1980, s 343, Sch 24.

SCHEDULE 6
Section 21

DEVELOPMENT PLANS: MODIFICATIONS OF THIS ACT PENDING REPEAL OF SCHEDULE 5

1. After section 147(5) there shall be inserted the following subsection:—

"(5A) Except in relation to Greater London, the reference in subsection (4) of this section to the development plan for the area in which the land is situated is a reference to the development plan for that area as approved by the Secretary of State or, if the plan so approved has been amended by the Secretary of State, to that plan as so amended."

2. For section 242(1)(a) there shall be substituted:—

"(a) a development plan or an amendment of a development plan, whether before or after it has been approved or made; or".

3. For subsections (1) and (2) of section 244 there shall be substituted:—

"(1) If any person aggrieved by a development plan, or by an amendment of a development plan, desires to question the validity thereof or of any provision contained therein on the grounds that it is not within the powers of this Act, or that any requirement of this Act or of any regulation made thereunder has not been complied with in relation to the approval or making of the plan, or, as the case may be, in relation to the making of the amendment, he may, within six weeks from the date on which the notice required by paragraph 7(1) of Schedule 5 to this Act is first published, make an application to the High Court under this section.

(2) On any application under this section the High Court—

(*a*) may by interim order suspend the operation of the plan or amendment, as the case may be, or of any provision contained therein, either generally or in so far as it affects any property of the applicant, until the final determination of the proceedings;

(*b*) if satisfied that the plan or amendment, or any provision contained therein, is not within the powers of this Act, or that the interests of the applicant have been substantially prejudiced by a failure to comply with any requirement of this Act or of any regulation made thereunder, may quash the plan or amendment or any provision contained therein, either generally or in so far as it affects any property of the applicant."

and in subsections (3), (4) and (5) of the said section 244 for the words " structure plan" there shall be substituted the words "development plan".

4. In section 255(2)(*a*) for the words "a structure plan or local plan under Part II of this Act" there shall be substituted the words "a development plan under Schedule 5 to this Act".

5. For section 266(1)(*a*) there shall be substituted:—

"(*a*) a development plan approved or made under Part I of Schedule 5 to this Act or the Greater London development plan may include proposals relating to the use of Crown land and any power to acquire land compulsorily under Part VI of this Act may be exercised in relation to any interest therein which is for the time being held otherwise than by or on behalf of the Crown;"

6. After section 279 there shall be inserted the following section:—

"279A. Where, in accordance with the provisions of Part III, Part IV or Part V of this Act, a local planning authority are required to have regard to the provisions of the development plan in relation to the exercise of any of their functions, then, in relation to the exercise of those functions during any period before such a plan has become operative with respect to the area of that authority, the authority—

(*a*) shall have regard to any directions which may be or have been given to them by the Secretary of State as to the provisions to be included in such a plan; and

(*b*) subject to any such directions, shall have regard to the provisions which in their opinion will be required to be so included for securing the proper planning of their area."

and section 3(6) of this Act shall have effect in relation to any reference to the local planning authority in the said section 279A.

7. For section 280(1)(*a*) there shall be substituted:—

"(*a*) the preparation, approval, making or amendment of a development plan relating to the land under Schedule 5 to this Act, including the carrying out of any survey under that Schedule;"

8. In section 290(1), for the definition of "development plan" there shall be substituted:—

" 'development plan' has the meaning assigned to it by paragraphs 1 and 8 of Schedule 5 to this Act, and includes a plan made in accordance with sub-paragraph (5) of the said paragraph 1;"

9. In Schedule 2, in paragraph 5, for the words "structure plans and local plans" there shall be substituted the words "development plans".

10. . . .

11. In Part I of Schedule 21 after the words "Schedules 1 and 2" there shall be inserted the words "Part I of Schedule 5".   **[333]**

NOTES

Commencement: See s 21 of this Act.

Repealed for certain purposes by SI 1975 Nos 782, 783, 1278, 1279; 1976 Nos 104, 814, 1162; 1977 Nos 469, 1364, 1768; 1978 Nos 556, 724, 726; 1979 Nos 139, 202, 203, 328, 890, 1042, 1189, 1486, 1623, 1625, 1627, 1629; 1980 Nos 3, 40, 66, 102, 175, 301, 459, 461, 493, 576, 578, 829, 933, 964, 1099, 1156, 1210, 1404, 1452, 1548, 1560, 1635.

Para 10: repealed by the Local Government Act 1985, s 102, Sch 17.

SCHEDULE 7
Section 21

DEVELOPMENT PLANS: TRANSITION FROM SCHEDULE 5 TO PART II OF THIS ACT

1. Until the repeal of Part I of Schedule 5 to this Act and, where applicable, paragraph 8 of that Schedule as respects any district (whether the whole or part of the area of a local planning authority), proposals for any alterations or additions to a development plan in force in the area consisting of or comprising that district shall not without the approval of the Secretary of State be submitted to him under paragraph 3 or 9 of that Schedule.

2. On the repeal of the said Part I and, where applicable, the said paragraph 8 as respects any district, the development plan which was in force in the area consisting of or comprising that district immediately before the repeal takes effect (hereafter in this Schedule referred to as "the old development plan") shall, subject to the following provisions of this Schedule, continue in force as respects that district and be treated for the purposes of this Act, any other enactment relating to town and country planning, the Land Compensation Act 1961, the Land Commission Act 1967 and [the Highways Act 1980] as being comprised in, or as being, the development plan therefor.

[3. Subject to the following provisions of this Schedule, where by virtue of paragraph 2 of this Schedule the old development plan for any district is treated as being comprised in a development plan for that district—

(a) if there is a conflict between any of its provisions and those of the structure plan for that district, the provisions of the structure plan shall be taken to prevail for the purposes of Parts III, IV, V, VI, VII and IX of this Act and Schedule 11 to this Act; and

(b) if there is a conflict between any of its provisions and those of a local plan, the provisions of the local plan shall be taken to prevail for the purposes of those Parts of this Act and that Schedule.]

4. Where a structure plan is in force in any district, but no local plan is in force in that district, a street authorisation map prepared in pursuance of the Town and Country Planning (Development Plans) Regulations 1965 or the Town and Country Planning (Development Plans for Greater London) Regulations 1966 for any area consisting of or comprising that district shall—

(a) if in force immediately before the structure plan comes into force be treated for the purposes of this Act as having been adopted as a local plan by the local planning authority;

(b) if immediately before the structure plan comes into force it was under consideration by the Secretary of State be treated for those purposes as having been so adopted on being approved by the Secretary of State.

5. Where a structure plan is in force in any district, but no local plan is in force in that district, then, for any of the purposes of the Land Compensation Act 1961—

(a) the development plan or current development plan shall as respects that district be taken as being whichever of the following plans gives rise to those assumptions as to the grant of planning permission which are more favourable to the owner of the land acquired, for that purpose, that is to say, the structure plan, so far as applicable to the district, and any alterations thereto, together with the Secretary of State's notice of approval of the plan and alterations, and the old development plan;

(b) land situated in an area defined in the current development plan as an area of comprehensive development shall be taken to be situated in whichever of the following areas leads to such assumptions as aforesaid, that is to say, any area wholly or partly within that district selected by the structure plan as an action area and the area so defined in the old development plan.

[5A. Subject to paragraph 5C of this Schedule, on the adoption or approval of a local plan under section 14 of this Act so much of any old development plan as relates to the area to which the local plan relates shall cease to have effect.

5B. The Secretary of State may by order direct that any of the provisions of the old development plan shall continue in force in relation to the area to which the local plan relates.

5C. If the Secretary of State makes an order under paragraph 5B of this Schedule, the provisions of the old development plan specified in the order shall continue in force to the extent so specified.]

6. Subject to paragraph 7 of this Schedule, the Secretary of State may by order wholly or partly revoke a development plan continued in force under this Schedule whether in its application to the whole of the area of a local planning authority or in its application to part of that area and make such consequential amendments to the plan as appear to him to be necessary or expedient.

7. Before making an order with respect to a development plan under paragraph [5B or] 6 of this Schedule, the Secretary of State shall consult with the local planning authority for the area to which the plan relates . . . .

8. Any reference in the preceding provisions of this Schedule to a development plan shall as respects any district in Greater London, be construed as a reference to the initial development plan within the meaning of paragraph 8 of Schedule 5 to this Act, the Greater London development plan and any development plan prepared for the area consisting of or comprising that district by the council of the relevant London borough.

9. Any reference in paragraphs 1 and 2 of this Schedule to the repeal of Part I of Schedule 5 to this Act or paragraph 8 of that Schedule shall, in a case where that repeal is brought into force by an order under section 21 of this Act on different days, be construed as a reference to a repeal of such of the provisions of the said Part I or the said paragraph 8 as may be specified in the order.

10. In relation to any development plan continued in force by virtue of this Schedule, sections 242 and 244 of this Act shall have effect with the same substitutions as are specified in paragraphs 2 and 3 of Schedule 6 to this Act.   **[334]**

NOTES
  Commencement: See s 21 of this Act.
  This Schedule derived from the Town and Country Planning Act 1968, Sch 10, paras 1-9.
  In para 2 amendment made by the Highways Act 1980, s 343, Sch 24; in para 7 words omitted repealed by the Local Government Act 1985, s 102, Sch 17; other amendments made by the Local Government, Planning and Land Act 1980, s 89, Sch 14.

SCHEDULE 8

Sections 22, 43, 164, 169, 180, 278

DEVELOPMENT NOT CONSTITUTING NEW DEVELOPMENT

PART I

DEVELOPMENT NOT RANKING FOR COMPENSATION UNDER S 169

1. The carrying out of any of the following works, that is to say—

  (*a*) the rebuilding, as often as occasion may require, of any building which was in existence on the appointed day, or of any building which was in existence before that day but was destroyed or demolished after 7th January 1937, including the making good of war damage sustained by any such building;

  (*b*) the rebuilding, as often as occasion may require, of any building erected after the appointed day which was in existence at a material date;

  (*c*) the carrying out of works for the maintenance, improvement or other alteration of any building, being works which affect only the interior of the building, or which do not materially affect the external appearance of the building and (in either case) are works for making good war damage,

so long as (in the case of works falling within any of the preceding sub-paragraphs) the cubic content of the original building is not exceeded—

(i) in the case of a dwellinghouse, by more than one-tenth or 1,750 cubic feet, whichever is the greater; and

(ii) in any other case, by more than one-tenth.

2. The use as two or more separate dwellinghouses of any building which at a material date was used as a single dwellinghouse.　　　**[335]**

NOTES

Commencement: 1 April 1972.

PART II

DEVELOPMENT RANKING FOR COMPENSATION UNDER S 169

3. The enlargement, improvement, or other alteration, as often as occasion may require, of any such building as is mentioned in paragraph 1(*a*) or (*b*) of this Schedule, or any building substituted for such a building by the carrying out of any such operations as are mentioned in that paragraph, so long as the cubic content of the original building is not increased or exceeded—

(*a*) in the case of a dwellinghouse by more than one-tenth or 1,750 cubic feet, whichever is the greater; and

(*b*) in any other case, by more than one-tenth.

4. The carrying out, on land which was used for the purposes of agriculture or forestry at a material date, of any building or other operations required for the purposes of that use, other than operations for the erection, enlargement, improvement or alteration of dwellinghouses or of buildings used for the purposes of market gardens, nursery grounds or timber yards or for other purposes not connected with general farming operations or with the cultivation or felling of trees.

5. The winning and working, on land held or occupied with land used for the purposes of agriculture, of any minerals reasonably required for the purposes of that use, including the fertilisation of the land so used and the maintenance, improvement or alteration of buildings or works thereon which are occupied or used for those purposes.

6. In the case of a building or other land which, at a material date, was used for a purpose falling within any general class specified in the Town and Country Planning (Use Classes for Third Schedule Purposes) Order 1948, or which having been unoccupied on and at all times since the appointed day, was last used (otherwise than before 7th January 1937) for any such purpose, the use of that building or land for any other purpose falling within the same general class.

7. In the case of any building or other land which, at a material date, was in the occupation of a person by whom it was used as to part only for a particular purpose, the use for that purpose of any additional part of the building or land not exceeding one-tenth of the cubic content of the part of the building used for that purpose on the appointed day, or on the day thereafter when the building began to be so used, or, as the case may be, one-tenth of the area of the land so used on that day.

8. The deposit of waste materials or refuse in connection with the working of minerals, on any land comprised in a site which at a material date was being used for that purpose, so far as may be reasonably required in connection with the working of those minerals.　　　**[336]**

NOTES

Commencement: 1 April 1972.

PART III

SUPPLEMENTARY PROVISIONS

9. Any reference in this Schedule to the cubic content of a building shall be construed as a reference to that content as ascertained by external measurement.

10. Where, after the appointed day, any buildings or works have been erected or constructed, or any use of land has been instituted, and any condition imposed under

Part III of this Act, limiting the period for which those buildings or works may be retained, or that use may be continued, has effect in relation thereto, this Schedule shall not operate except as respects the period specified in that condition.

11. For the purposes of paragraph 3 of this Schedule—

(a) the erection, on land within the curtilage of any such building as is mentioned in that paragraph, of an additional building to be used in connection with the original building shall be treated as the enlargement of the original building; and

(b) where any two or more buildings comprised in the same curtilage are used as one unit for the purposes of any institution or undertaking, the reference in that paragraph to the cubic content of the original building shall be construed as a reference to the aggregate cubic content of those buildings.

12. In this Schedule "at a material date" means at either of the following dates, that is to say—

(a) the appointed day; and

(b) the date by reference to which this Schedule falls to be applied in the particular case in question:

Provided that sub-paragraph (b) of this paragraph shall not apply in relation to any buildings, works or use of land in respect of which, whether before or after the date mentioned in that sub-paragraph, an enforcement notice served before that date has become or becomes effective.

13.—(1) In relation to a building erected after the appointed day, being a building resulting from the carrying out of any such works as are described in paragraph 1 of this Schedule, any reference in this Schedule to the original building is a reference to the building in relation to which those works were carried out and not to the building resulting from the carrying out of those works.

(2) This paragraph has effect subject to section 278(4) of this Act.   **[337]**

NOTES

Commencement: 1 April 1972.

(New Sch 8A prospectively inserted by the Housing and Planning Act 1986, s 25(2), Sch 6, Part I. See Appendix.)

SCHEDULE 9

Sections 36, 88, 95, 97, 103, Sch 11, para 8

DETERMINATION OF CERTAIN APPEALS BY PERSONS APPOINTED BY SECRETARY OF STATE

Determination of appeals by appointed person

1.—(1) An appeal to which this Schedule applies, being an appeal of a prescribed class, shall, except in such classes of case as may for the time being be prescribed or as may be specified in directions given by the Secretary of State, be determined by a person appointed by the Secretary of State for the purpose instead of by the Secretary of State.

(2) Regulations made for the purpose of this paragraph may provide for the giving of publicity to any directions given by the Secretary of State under this paragraph.

(3) This paragraph shall not affect any provision contained in this Act or any instrument thereunder that an appeal shall lie to, or a notice of appeal shall be served on, the Secretary of State.

Powers and duties of person determining appeal

2.—(1) A person appointed under this Schedule to determine an appeal shall have the like powers and duties in relation to the appeal as the Secretary of State under whichever are relevant of the following provisions, that is to say—

(a) in relation to appeals under section 36 subsections (3) and (5) of that section;

(b) in relation to appeals under section 88 [section 88A and section 88B(1) and (2) of this Act];

(c) in relation to appeals under section 95 subsections (2) and (3) of that section;

(*d*) in relation to appeals under section 97 [section 97A(1) to (4) of this Act];

(*e*) in relation to appeals under section 103 [subsections (3E) and (3F) of that section];

(*f*) in relation to appeals under paragraph 8 of Schedule 11 to this Act, sub-paragraph (3) of that paragraph.

(2) The provisions of section 36(4), [88(7)], 95(4), [97(6), 103(3C)] and paragraph 8(4) of Schedule 11 to this Act relating to the affording of an opportunity of appearing before, and being heard by, a person appointed by the Secretary of State, shall not apply to an appeal which falls to be determined by a person appointed under this Schedule but before the determination of any such appeal the Secretary of State shall, unless (in the case of an appeal under section 36) the appeal is referred to a Planning Inquiry Commission under section 48 of this Act, ask the applicant or appellant, as the case may require, and the local planning authority whether they wish to appear before and be heard by the person so appointed, and—

(*a*) the appeal may be determined without a hearing of the parties if both of them express a wish not to appear and be heard as aforesaid; and

(*b*) the person so appointed shall, if either of the parties expresses a wish to appear and be heard, afford to both of them an opportunity of so doing.

(3) Where an appeal to which this Schedule applies has been determined by a person appointed under this Schedule, his decision shall be treated as that of the Secretary of State and—

(*a*) except as provided by Part XII of this Act, the validity of his decision shall not be questioned in any proceedings whatsoever;

(*b*) it shall not be a ground of application to the High Court under section 245 of this Act, or of appeal to the High Court under section 246 or 247 thereof, that the appeal ought to have been determined by the Secretary of State and not by that person, unless the challenge to the person's power to determine the appeal was made (either by the appellant or the local planning authority) before his decision on the appeal was given.

(4) Where in any enactment (including this Act) there is a reference to the Secretary of State in a context relating or capable of relating to an appeal to which this Schedule applies, or to any thing done or authorised or required to be done by, to or before the Secretary of State on or in connection with any such appeal, then so far as the context permits it shall be construed, in relation to an appeal determined or falling to be determined by a person appointed under this Schedule, as a reference to that person.

Determination of appeals by Secretary of State

3.—(1) The Secretary of State may, if he thinks fit, direct that an appeal, which by virtue of paragraph 1 of this Schedule and apart from this sub-paragraph, falls to be determined by a person appointed by the Secretary of State shall instead be determined by the Secretary of State.

(2) A direction under this paragraph shall state the reasons for which it is given and shall be served on the person, if any, so appointed, the applicant or appellant, the local planning authority and any person who has made representations relating to the subject matter of the appeal which the authority are required to take into account under section 29(3)(*a*) of this Act.

(3) Where in consequence of a direction under this paragraph an appeal to which this Schedule applies falls to be determined by the Secretary of State, the provisions of this Act which are relevant to the appeal shall, subject to the following provisions of this paragraph, apply to the appeal as if this Schedule had never applied to it.

(4) Where in consequence of a direction under this paragraph the Secretary of State determines an appeal himself, he shall, unless (in the case of an appeal under section 36) the appeal is referred to a Planning Inquiry Commission under section 48 of this Act, afford to the applicant or appellant, the local planning authority and any person who has made any such representations as aforesaid an opportunity of appearing before and being heard by a person appointed by the Secretary of State for that purpose either—

(a) if the reasons for the direction raise matters with respect to which either the applicant or appellant, or the local planning authority or any such person, have not made representations; or

(b) if the applicant or appellant or the local planning authority had not been asked in pursuance of paragraph 2(2) of this Schedule whether they wished to appear before and be heard by a person appointed to hear the appeal, or had been asked that question and had expressed no wish in answer thereto, or had expressed a wish to appear and be heard as aforesaid, but had not been afforded an opportunity of doing so.

(5) Except as provided by sub-paragraph (4) of this paragraph, where the Secretary of State determines an appeal in consequence of a direction under this paragraph he shall not be obliged to afford any person an opportunity of appearing before and being heard by a person appointed for the purpose, or of making fresh representations or making or withdrawing any representations already made; and in determining the appeal the Secretary of State may take into account any report made to him by any person previously appointed to determine it.

Appointment of another person to determine appeal

4.—(1) Where the Secretary of State has appointed a person to determine an appeal under this Schedule the Secretary of State may, at any time before the determination of the appeal, appoint another person to determine it instead of the first-mentioned person.

(2) If before the appointment of a person under this paragraph to determine an appeal, the Secretary of State had with reference to the person previously appointed, asked the question referred to in paragraph 2(2) of this Schedule, the question need not be asked again with reference to the person appointed under this paragraph and any answers to the question shall be treated as given with reference to him, but—

(a) the consideration of the appeal or any inquiry or other hearing in connection therewith, if already begun, shall be begun afresh; and

(b) it shall not be necessary to afford any person an opportunity of making fresh representations or modifying or withdrawing any representations already made.

Local inquiries and hearings

5.—(1) A person appointed under this Schedule to determine an appeal may (whether or not the parties have asked for an opportunity to appear and be heard) hold a local inquiry in connection with the appeal and shall hold such an inquiry if the Secretary of State directs him to do so.

(2) Subject to sub-paragraph (3) of this paragraph, the costs—

(a) of any hearing held by virtue of paragraph 2(2)(b) of this Schedule; and

(b) of any inquiry held by virtue of this paragraph,

shall be defrayed by the Secretary of State.

(3) Subsections (2) to (5) of section 290 of the Local Government Act 1933 (evidence and costs at local inquiries) shall apply in relation to an inquiry held under this paragraph as they apply in relation to an inquiry caused to be held by a department under subsection (1) of that section, with the substitution for references to a department (other than the first reference in subsection (4)) of references to the Secretary of State.

Stopping of appeals

6. If before or during the determination of an appeal under section 36 of this Act which is to be or is being determined in accordance with paragraph 1 of this Schedule, the Secretary of State forms the opinion mentioned in subsection (7) of that section, he may direct that the determination shall not be begun or proceeded with.

Supplementary provisions

7.—(1) The Tribunals and Inquiries Act 1971 shall apply to a local inquiry or other hearing held in pursuance of this Schedule as it applies to a statutory inquiry held by the Secretary of State, but as if in section 12(1) of that Act (statement of reasons for decisions) the reference to any decision taken by the Secretary of State were a reference to a decision taken by a person appointed to determine the relevant appeal under this Schedule.

(2) The functions of determining an appeal and doing anything in connection therewith conferred by this Schedule on a person appointed to determine an appeal thereunder who is an officer of the Department of the Environment or the Welsh Office shall be treated for the purposes of the Parliamentary Commissioner Act 1967—

  (a) if he was appointed by the Secretary of State for the time being having general responsibility in planning matters in relation to England, as functions of that Department; and

  (b) if he was appointed by the Secretary of State for the time being having general responsibility in planning matters in relation to Wales, as functions of the Welsh Office. **[338]**

NOTES

Commencement: 1 April 1972.

Amended by the Local Government and Planning (Amendment) Act 1981, s 1, Schedule.

New para 3A inserted by the Housing and Planning Act 1986, s 49(1), Sch 11, Part I, para 11. See Appendix.

Para 5: new sub-para (1A) inserted subject to the saving contained in SI 1987 No 304, art 3, by the Housing and Planning Act 1986, s 49(1), Sch 11, Part I, para 12; new sub-para (3) substituted by the Housing and Planning Act 1986, s 49(1), Sch 11, Part I, para 8(2); new sub-para (4) inserted by the Housing and Planning Act 1986, s 49(1), Sch 11, Part I, para 9(2). See Appendix.

SCHEDULE 10

Section 48

CONSTRUCTION OF REFERENCES IN SECTIONS 48 AND 49 TO "THE RESPONSIBLE MINISTER OR MINISTERS"

1. In relation to matters specified in the first column of the Table below (being in each case a matter mentioned in subsection (1)(a), (b), (c) or (d) of section 48 of this Act as one which may be referred to a Planning Inquiry Commission under that section) "the responsible Minister or Ministers" for the purposes of sections 48 and 49 of this Act—

  (a) in the case of a matter affecting England only, are those specified opposite in the second column of the Table;

  (b) in the case of a matter affecting Wales only, are those specified opposite in the third column of the Table; and

  (c) in the case of a matter affecting both England and Wales, are those specified opposite in the fourth column of the Table.

2. Where an entry in the second, third or fourth columns of the Table specifies two or more Ministers, that entry shall be construed as referring to those Ministers acting jointly.

TABLE

Referred Matter	Affecting England only	Affecting Wales only	Affecting both England and Wales
1. Application for planning permission or appeal under section 36 of this Act—			
(a) relating to land to which section 225(1) of this Act applies;	The Secretary of State for the time being having general responsibility in planning matters in relation to England and the appropriate Minister (if different).	The Secretary of State for the time being having general responsibility in planning matters in relation to Wales and the appropriate Minister (if different).	The Secretaries of State for the time being having general responsibility in planning matters in relation to England and in relation to Wales and the appropriate Minister (if different).

Referred Matter	Affecting England only	Affecting Wales only	Affecting both England and Wales
(b) relating to other land.	The Secretary of State for the time being having general responsibility in planning matters in relation to England.	The Secretary of State for the time being having general responsibility in planning matters in relation to Wales.	The Secretaries of State for the time being having general responsibility in planning matters in relation to England and in relation to Wales.
2. Proposal that a government department should give a direction under section 40 of this Act or that development should be carried out by or on behalf of a government department.	The Secretary of State for the time being having general responsibility in planning matters in relation to England and the Minister (if different) in charge of the government department concerned.	The Secretary of State for the time being having general responsibility in planning matters in relation to Wales and the Minister (if different) in charge of the government department concerned.	The Secretaries of State for the time being having general responsibility in planning matters in relation to England and in relation to Wales and the Minister (if different) in charge of government department concerned.

[339]

NOTES
Commencement: 1 April 1972.

SCHEDULE 11

Sections 56, 58

Control of Works for Demolition, Alteration or Extension of Listed Buildings

Part I

Applications for Listed Building Consent

Form of application and effect of consent

1.—(1) Provision may be made by regulations under this Act with respect to the form and manner in which applications for listed building consent are to be made, the manner in which such applications are to be advertised and the time within which they are to be dealt with by local planning authorities or, as the case may be, by the Secretary of State.

(2) Any listed building consent shall (except in so far as it otherwise provides) enure for the benefit of the building and of all persons for the time being interested therein.

2.—(1) Regulations under this Act may provide that an application for listed building consent, or an appeal against the refusal of such an application, shall not be entertained unless it is accompanied by a certificate in the prescribed form and corresponding to one or other of those described in section 27(1)(a) to (d) of this Act and any such regulations may—

(a) include requirements corresponding to sections 27(2) and (4) and 29(3) of this Act; and

(b) make provision as to who, in the case of any building, is to be treated as the owner for the purposes of any provision of the regulations made by virtue of this sub-paragraph.

(2) If any person issues a certificate which purports to comply with the requirements of regulations made by virtue of this paragraph and which contains a statement which he knows to be false or misleading in a material particular, or recklessly issues a certificate which purports to comply with those requirements and which contains a statement which is false or misleading in a material particular, he shall be guilty of an offence and liable on summary conviction to a fine not exceeding [level 3 on the standard scale].

Directions as to manner of dealing with applications

3. ...

Reference of applications to Secretary of State or Greater London Council

4.—(1) The Secretary of State may give directions requiring applications for listed building consent to be referred to him instead of being dealt with by the local planning authority.

(2) A direction under this paragraph may relate either to a particular application, or to applications in respect of such buildings as may be specified in the direction.

(3) An application in respect of which a direction under this paragraph has effect shall be referred to the Secretary of State accordingly.

(4) Before determining an application referred to him under this paragraph, the Secretary of State shall, if either the applicant or the authority so desire, afford to each of them an opportunity of appearing before, and being heard by, a person appointed by the Secretary of State.

(5) The decision of the Secretary of State on any application referred to him under this paragraph shall be final.

5.—(1) Subject to the following provisions of this paragraph, a local planning authority ... to whom application is made for listed building consent shall not grant such consent, unless they have notified the Secretary of State of the application (giving particulars of the works for which the consent is required) and either—

(*a*) a period of twenty-eight days has expired, beginning with the date of the notification, without the Secretary of State having directed the reference of the application to him; or

(*b*) the Secretary of State has notified the authority that he does not intend to require the reference of the application.

(2) The Secretary of State may at any time before the said period expires give notice to the authority that he requires further time in which to consider whether to require the reference of the application to him and sub-paragraph (1) of this paragraph shall then have effect with the substitution for a period of twenty-eight days of such longer period as may be specified in the Secretary of State's notice.

[(3) Sub-paragraph (1) above shall not apply where the local planning authority to whom application is made is a London borough council, unless the application is made by the Historic Buildings and Monuments Commission for England.]

6.—(1) Subject to the following provisions of this paragraph, where application for listed building consent is made to a local planning authority, being a London borough council, and the authority do not determine to refuse it, they shall notify *the Greater London Council* [the Historic Buildings and Monuments Commission for England (in this paragraph referred to as "the Commission")] of the application (giving particulars of the works for which the consent is required) and shall not grant such consent unless authorised or directed to do so under sub-paragraph (2) of this paragraph.

(2) On receipt of notification under sub-paragraph (1) of this paragraph *the Greater London Council* [the Commission] may either—

(*a*) authorise the local planning authority to grant or refuse the application, as they think fit; or

(*b*) give them directions as to how they are to determine it.

(3) *The Greater London Council* [The Commission] shall not authorise the local planning authority as mentioned in sub-paragraph (2)(*a*) of this paragraph, nor under sub-paragraph (2)(*b*) of this paragraph direct them to grant listed building consent, unless the *Council* [Commission] have notified the Secretary of State of the application made to the local planning authority (giving particulars of the works for which the consent is required) and either—

(*a*) a period of twenty-eight days has expired, beginning with the date of the notification, without the Secretary of State having directed the reference of the application to him; or

(*b*) the Secretary of State has notified the *Council* [Commission] that he does not intend to require the reference of the application.

(4) The Secretary of State may at any time before the said period of twenty-eight days expires give notice to the *Council* [Commission] that he requires further time in which to consider whether to require the reference of the application to him and sub-paragraph (3) of this paragraph shall then have effect with the substitution for the period of twenty-eight days of such longer period as may be specified in the Secretary of State's notice.

[(5) Where the Commission direct the local planning authority under sub-paragraph (2)(*b*) of this paragraph to refuse listed building consent, the authority may, within twenty-eight days from the date of the direction, notify the Secretary of State of the application made to them (giving particulars of the works for which the consent is required); and if the authority do so notify the Secretary of State, they shall not give effect to the Commission's direction unless either—

(*a*) a period of twenty-eight days has expired, beginning with the date of the notification, without the Secretary of State having directed the reference of the application to him; or

(*b*) the Secretary of State has notified the authority that he does not intend to require the reference of the application.

(6) The Secretary of State may at any time before the said period of twenty-eight days expires give notice to the local planning authority that he requires further time in which to consider whether to require the reference of the application to him and sub-paragraph (5)(*a*) of this paragraph shall then have effect with the substitution for the period of twenty-eight days of such longer period as may be specified in the Secretary of State's notice.

(7) Where after receiving notification under sub-paragraph (5) of this paragraph the Secretary of State directs the reference of the application to him, paragraph 4(4) of this Schedule shall apply as if the reference to the authority were a reference to the authority or the Commission.

(8) Sub-paragraph (1) of this paragraph shall not apply where the application for listed building consent is made by the Commission.]

7.—(1) The Secretary of State may give directions that, in the case of such descriptions of applications for listed building consent as he may specify, other than such consent for the demolition of a building, paragraphs 5 and 6 of this Schedule shall not apply; and accordingly, so long as the directions are in force local planning authorities may determine applications of such descriptions in any manner they think fit, without notifying the Secretary of State or, as the case may be, [the Historic Buildings and Monuments Commission for England].

[(1A) Where directions are in force under sub-paragraph (1) of this paragraph, the Secretary of State may give to any local planning authority a direction that, in the case of such descriptions of applications for listed building consent as are specified in the direction, paragraph 5 or (as the case may be) paragraph 6 of this Schedule shall apply in relation to the authority.

(1B) So long as the direction is in force, paragraph 5 or 6 (as the case may be) shall apply in the case of any application of any description so specified—

(*a*) made to the authority after the coming into force the direction, or

(*b*) made to them (but not disposed of by their granting or refusing consent) before the coming into force of the direction.

notwithstanding sub-paragraph (1) of this paragraph.]

(2) Without prejudice to the preceding provisions of this Schedule, the Secretary of State may give directions to local planning authorities requiring them, in such cases or classes of case as may be specified in the directions, to notify to him and to such other

persons as may be so specified any applications made to them for listed building consent, and the decisions taken by the authorities thereon.

Appeal against decision

8.—(1) Where an application is made to the local planning authority for listed building consent and the consent is refused by the authority or is granted by them subject to conditions, the applicant, if he is aggrieved by the decision, may by notice served in the prescribed manner within such period as may be prescribed, not being less than twenty-eight days from the receipt by him of notification of the decision, appeal to the Secretary of State.

(2) A person appealing under this paragraph may include in his notice thereunder, as the ground or one of the grounds of his appeal, a claim that the building is not of special architectural or historic interest and ought to be removed from any list compiled or approved by the Secretary of State under section 54 of this Act, or—

    (*a*) in the case of a building to which subsection (10) of that section applies, that the Secretary of State should give a direction under that subsection with respect to the building; or

    (*b*) in the case of a building subject to a building preservation notice under section 58 of this Act, that the building should not be included in a list compiled or approved under the said section 54.

(3) Subject to the following provisions of this paragraph, the Secretary of State may allow or dismiss an appeal thereunder, or may reverse or vary any part of the decision of the authority, whether the appeal relates to that part thereof or not, and—

    (*a*) may deal with the application as if it had been made to him in the first instance; and

    (*b*) may, if he thinks fit, exercise his power under section 54 of this Act to amend any list compiled or approved thereunder by removing from it the building to which the appeal relates or his power under subsection (10) of that section to direct that that subsection shall no longer apply to the building.

(4) Before determining an appeal under this paragraph, the Secretary of State shall, if either the applicant or the local planning authority so desire, afford to each of them an opportunity of appearing before, and being heard by, a person appointed by the Secretary of State for the purpose.

(5) The decision of the Secretary of State on any appeal under this paragraph shall be final.

(6) Schedule 9 to this Act applies to appeals under this paragraph.

Appeal in default of decision

9. Where an application is made to the local planning authority for listed building consent, then unless within the prescribed period from the date of the receipt of the application, or within such extended period as may at any time be agreed upon in writing between the applicant and the authority, the authority either—

    (*a*) give notice to the applicant of their decision on the application; or

    (*b*) give notice to him that the application has been referred to the Secretary of State in accordance with directions given under paragraph 4 of this Schedule,

the provisions of paragraph 8 of this Schedule shall apply in relation to the application as if listed building consent had been refused by the authority and as if notification of their decision had been received by the applicant at the end of the prescribed period or at the end of the said extended period, as the case may be.   **[340]**

NOTES

    Commencement: 1 April 1972.

    This Part derived from the Town and Country Planning Act 1968, s 56, Sch 5, Part I.

    Para 1: new sub-para (1) substituted and new sub-para (1A) inserted by the Housing and Planning Act 1986, s 40, Sch 9, Part I, para 9. See Appendix.

    Para 2: maximum fine increased and converted to a level on the standard scale by the Criminal Justice Act 1982, ss 37, 38, 46.

    Para 3: repealed by the Local Government, Planning and Land Act 1980, s 194, Sch 34.

    Para 5: amended by the Local Government Act 1985, ss 6, 102, Sch 2, para 1, Sch 17; sub-para (2) amended except in relation to any notice given by the Secretary of State before 1 April 1987 by the Housing and Planning Act 1986, s 40, Sch 9, Part I, para 10(1). See Appendix.

Para 6: words in italics repealed and words in square brackets substituted or added with savings by the Local Government Act 1985, ss 6, 102, Sch 2, para 1, Sch 17 and SI 1985 No 1781; sub-para (4) amended except in relation to any notice given by the Secretary of State before 1 April 1987 by the Housing and Planning Act 1986, s 40, Sch 9, Part I, para 10(2); sub-para (6) except in relation to any notice given by the Secretary of State before 1 April 1987 amended by the Housing and Planning Act 1986, s 40, Sch 9, Part I, para 10(3). See Appendix.

Para 7: sub-para (1) amended by the Local Government Act 1985, ss 6, Sch 2, para 1, and by the Housing and Planning Act 1986, s 40, Sch 9, Part I, para 11(2); sub-paras (1A), (1B) added by the National Heritage Act 1983, s 40, Sch 5, para 6; new sub-para (1A) inserted by the Housing and Planning Act 1986, s 40, Sch 9, Part I, para 11(2); new sub-para (1B) substituted by the Housing and Planning Act 1986, s 40, Sch 9, Part I, para 11(3); new sub-para (3) inserted by the Housing and Planning Act 1986, s 40, Sch 9, Part I, para 11(4). See Appendix.

Para 8: sub-para (1) amended by the Housing and Planning Act 1986, s 40, Sch 9, Part I, para 3(2). See Appendix.

Para 9: amended by the Housing and Planning Act 1986, s 40, Sch 9, Part I, para 3(3); new sub-para (2) inserted by the Housing and Planning Act 1986, s 40, Sch 9, Part I, para 3(3). See Appendix.

PART II

REVOCATION OF LISTED BUILDING CONSENT

10.—(1) If it appears to the local planning authority, having regard to the development plan and to any other material considerations, that it is expedient to revoke or modify listed building consent in respect of any works to a building, being consent granted on an application made under Part I of this Schedule, the authority, subject to the following provisions of this paragraph, may by order revoke or modify the consent to such extent as (having regard to those matters), they consider expedient.

(2) Except as provided in paragraph 12 of this Schedule, an order under this paragraph shall not take effect unless it is confirmed by the Secretary of State; and the Secretary of State may confirm any such order submitted to him either without modification or subject to such modifications as he considers expedient.

(3) Where a local planning authority submit an order to the Secretary of State for confirmation under this paragraph, the authority shall serve notice on the owner and on the occupier of the building affected and on any other person who in their opinion will be affected by the order; and if within such period as may be specified in that notice (not being less than twenty-eight days after the service thereof) any person on whom the notice is served so requires, the Secretary of State, before confirming the order, shall afford to that person and to the local planning authority an opportunity of appearing before, and being heard by, a person appointed by the Secretary of State for the purpose.

(4) The power conferred by this paragraph to revoke or modify listed building consent in respect of any works may be exercised at any time before those works have been completed, but the revocation or modification shall not affect so much of those works as has been previously carried out.

11.—(1) If it appears to the Secretary of State, after consultation with the local planning authority, to be expedient that an order under paragraph 10 of this Schedule should be made, he may . . . himself make such an order, and any order so made by the Secretary of State shall have the like effect as if it had been made by the authority and confirmed by the Secretary of State under that paragraph.

(2) The provisions of paragraph 10 of this Schedule shall have effect, subject to any necessary modifications, in relation to any proposal by the Secretary of State to make such an order by virtue of this paragraph, in relation to the making thereof by the Secretary of State and in relation to the service of copies thereof as so made.

12.—(1) The following provisions shall have effect where the local planning authority have made an order under paragraph 10 of this Schedule but have not submitted the order to the Secretary of State for confirmation by him, and—

> (a) the owner and occupier of the land and all persons who in the authority's opinion will be affected by the order have notified the authority in writing that they do not object to the order; . . .

(2) The authority shall advertise in the prescribed manner the fact that the order has been made, and the advertisement shall specify—

> (a) the period (not being less than twenty-eight days from the date on which the advertisement first appears) within which persons affected by the order may give notice to the Secretary of State that they wish for an opportunity of appearing before, and being heard by, a person appointed by the Secretary of State for the purpose; and
>
> (b) the period (not being less than fourteen days from the expiration of the period referred to in paragraph (a) of this sub-paragraph) at the expiration of which,

if no such notice is given to the Secretary of State, the order may take effect by virtue of this paragraph and without being confirmed by the Secretary of State.

(3) The authority shall also serve notice to the same effect on the persons mentioned in sub-paragraph (1)(a) of this paragraph, . . .

(4) The authority shall send a copy of any advertisement published under sub-paragraph (2) of this paragraph to the Secretary of State, not more than three days after the publication.

(5) If within the period referred to in sub-paragraph (2)(a) of this paragraph no person claiming to be affected by the order has given notice to the Secretary of State as aforesaid and the Secretary of State has not directed that the order be submitted to him for confirmation, the order shall, at the expiration of the period referred to in sub-paragraph (2)(b) of this paragraph, take effect by virtue of this paragraph and without being confirmed by the Secretary of State as required by paragraph 10(2) of this Schedule.

(6) This paragraph does not apply to an order revoking or modifying a listed building consent granted by the Secretary of State. **[341]**

NOTES
Commencement: 1 April 1972.
First words omitted repealed by the Local Government Act 1974, s 42, Sch 8; second and third words omitted repealed by the Local Government, Planning and Land Act 1980, ss 90, 194, Schs 15, 34.

PART III

PROVISIONS APPLICABLE ON LAPSE OF BUILDING PRESERVATION NOTICE

13. The provisions of this Part of this Schedule apply where a building preservation notice ceases to be in force by virtue of section 58(3) of this Act, otherwise than by reason of the building to which it relates being included in a list compiled or approved under section 54 of this Act.

14. The fact that the building preservation notice has ceased to be in force shall not affect the liability of any person to be prosecuted and punished for an offence under section 55 or 98 of this Act committed by him with respect to the said building while the notice was in force.

15. Any proceedings on or arising out of an application for listed building consent made while the building preservation notice was in force shall lapse and any listed building consent granted with respect to the building, while the notice was in force, shall also lapse.

16. Any listed building enforcement notice served by the local planning authority while the building preservation notice was in force shall cease to have effect and any proceedings thereon under sections 96 and 97 of this Act shall lapse, but section 99(1) and (2) of this Act shall continue to have effect as respects any expenses incurred by the local authority, owner or occupier as therein mentioned and with respect to any sums paid on account of such expenses. **[342]**

NOTES
Commencement: 1 April 1972.

SCHEDULE 14
Section 94

PROVISIONS AS TO ESTABLISHED USE CERTIFICATES

Application for certificate and appeal against refusal thereof

1. An application for an established use certificate shall be made in such manner as may be prescribed by a development order, and shall include such particulars, and be verified by such evidence, as may be required by such an order or by any directions given thereunder, or by the local planning authority or, in the case of an application referred to the Secretary of State, by him.

2. Provision may be made by a development order for regulating the manner in which applications for established use certificates are to be dealt with by local planning authorities, and, in particular—

(a) for requiring the authority to give to any applicant for such a certificate, within such time as may be prescribed by the order, such notice as may be so prescribed as to the manner in which his application has been dealt with;

(b) for requiring the authority to give to the Secretary of State and to such other persons as may be prescribed by or under the order, such information as may be so prescribed with respect to applications for such certificates made to the authority, including information as to the manner in which any such application has been dealt with.

3.—(1) A development order may provide that an application for an established use certificate, or an appeal against the refusal of such an application, shall not be entertained unless it is accompanied by a certificate in such form as may be prescribed by the order and corresponding to one or other of those described in section 27(1)(*a*) to (*d*) of this Act; and any such order may—

(a) include requirements corresponding to section 27(2), (3) and (4), and section 29(3) of this Act; and

(b) make provision as to who, in the case of any land, is to be treated as the owner for the purposes of any provision of the order made by virtue of this sub-paragraph.

(2) If any person issues a certificate which purports to comply with any provision of a development order made by virtue of sub-paragraph (1) above and which contains a statement which he knows to be false or misleading in a material particular, or recklessly issues a certificate which purports to comply with those requirements and which contains a statement which is false or misleading in a material particular, he shall be guilty of an offence and liable on summary conviction to a fine not exceeding [level 3 on the standard scale].

Provisions with respect to grant of certificate

4. An established use certificate shall be in such form as may be prescribed by a development order and shall specify—

(a) the land to which the certificate relates and any use thereof which is certified by the certificate as established;

(b) by reference to the paragraphs of section 94(1) of this Act, the grounds on which that use is so certified; and

(c) the date on which the application for the certificate was made, which shall be the date at which the use is certified as established.

5. Where the Secretary of State grants an established use certificate, he shall give notice to the local planning authority of that fact.

6. In section 34 of this Act references to applications for planning permission shall include references to applications for established use certificates; and the information which may be prescribed as being required to be contained in a register kept under that section shall include information with respect to established use certificates granted by the Secretary of State.   **[343]**

NOTES
Commencement: 1 April 1972.
Para 3: maximum fine increased and converted to a level on the standard scale by the Criminal Justice Act 1982, ss 37, 38, 46.

SCHEDULE 15

Section 138

ADJUSTMENT OF CLAIM HOLDINGS

PART I

ADJUSTMENT OF CLAIM HOLDINGS PLEDGED TO CENTRAL LAND BOARD AS SECURITY FOR DEVELOPMENT CHARGES

1.—(1) In this Part of this Schedule references to the pledging of a claim holding to the Central Land Board are references to any transaction whereby—

(a) the holder of the claim holding mortgaged it to the Central Land Board as security, or part of the security, for one or more development charges determined, or thereafter to be determined, by the Board; or

(b) the holder and the Central Land Board agreed that a development charge determined by the Board should be set off against any payment which might thereafter become payable to the holder by reference to that holding; or

(c) the Central Land Board refrained from determining a development charge, which would otherwise have fallen to be determined by them, in consideration of a mortgage of the holding, with or without other claim holdings.

(2) All pledges of claim holdings to the Central Land Board made by the same person, whether or not made at the same time, other than any pledge to which paragraph 2(1) of this Schedule applies, shall for the purposes of this Part of this Schedule be treated collectively as a single pledge made at the time when the last of those pledges was made.

(3) Where a development charge covered by a pledge to the Central Land Board was determined in respect of land consisting of, or forming part of, the area of a claim holding—

(a) which was not comprised in the pledge; but

(b) whose holder immediately before the time of completion was the person who would, apart from the pledge, have been liable to pay the unpaid balance of the development charge,

then, for the purposes of this Part of this Schedule, that claim holding shall be deemed to have been comprised in the pledge.

(4) In this Part of this Schedule references to the determination of a development charge in respect of any land are references to a determination of the Central Land Board that the charge was payable in respect of the carrying out of operations in, on, over or under that land, or in respect of the use of that land.

(5) For the purposes of this Part of this Schedule the amount of a development charge—

(a) in a case where the Central Land Board determined that amount as a single capital payment, shall be taken to have been the amount of that payment; and

(b) in a case where the Board determined that amount otherwise than as a single capital payment, shall be taken to have been the amount of the single capital payment which would have been payable if the Board had determined the amount as such a payment;

and references in this Part of this Schedule to the unpaid balance of a development charge are references to the amount of the charge, if no sum was actually paid to the Board on account of the charge, or if any sum was so paid, are references to the amount of the charge reduced by the amount or aggregate amount of the sum or sums so paid, other than any sum paid by way of interest.

(6) In relation to the pledging of a claim holding to the Central Land Board, references in this Part of this Schedule to a development charge covered by the pledge are references to a development charge the payment of which was secured, or partly secured by, the pledge, or, as the case may be, which was agreed to be set off against any payment which might become payable by reference to that claim holding.

(7) References in this Part of this Schedule to a mortgage of a claim holding do not include a mortgage which was subsequently discharged.

2.—(1) Where a claim holding was pledged to the Central Land Board in accordance with the special arrangements relating to owners of single house plots, that claim holding shall, subject to sub-paragraph (2) of this paragraph, be deemed to have been extinguished as from the time when it was pledged to the Board.

(2) Where a claim holding (in this sub-paragraph referred to as "the original holding") was pledged as mentioned in sub-paragraph (1) of this paragraph but was so pledged by reference to a plot of land which did not extend to the whole of the area of the original holding, that sub-paragraph shall not apply, but there shall be deemed to have been substituted for the original holding, as from the time of the pledge, a claim holding with an area consisting of so much of the area of the original holding as was not comprised in that plot of land, and with a value equal to that fraction of the value of the original holding which then attached to so much of the area of the original holding as was not comprised in that plot.

3. Without prejudice to paragraph 2 of this Schedule, where a pledge to the Central Land Board comprised one or more claim holdings, and the unpaid balance of the development charge covered by the pledge, or (if more than one) the aggregate of the unpaid balances of the development charges so covered, was equal to or greater than the value of the claim holding, or the aggregate value of the claim holdings, as the case may be, the holding or holdings shall be deemed to have been extinguished as from the time of the pledge.

4. Where a pledge to the Central Land Board comprised only a single claim holding with an area of which every part either consisted of, or formed part of, the land in respect of which some development charge covered by the pledge was determined, and paragraph 3 of this Schedule does not apply, the value of that claim holding shall be deemed to have been reduced, as from the time of the pledge, by the unpaid balance of the development charge covered by the pledge, or (if more than one) by the aggregate of the unpaid balances of all the development charges covered by the pledge.

5.—(1) The provisions of this paragraph shall have effect in the case of a pledge of one or more claim holdings to the Central Land Board to which neither paragraph 3 nor paragraph 4 of this Schedule applies.

(2) Any claim holding comprised in the pledge with an area of which every part either consisted of, or formed part of, the land in respect of which some development charge covered by the pledge was determined shall be allocated to the development charge in question, or (if more than one) to those development charges collectively.

(3) Any claim holding comprised in the pledge with an area part of which did, and part of which did not, consist of, or form part of, such land as is mentioned in sub-paragraph (2) of this paragraph shall be treated as if, at the time of the pledge, the claim holding (in this sub-paragraph referred to as "the parent holding") had been divided into two separate claim holdings, that is to say—

   (a) a claim holding with an area consisting of so much of the area of the parent holding as consisted of, or formed part of, such land as is mentioned in sub-paragraph (2) of this paragraph, and with a value equal to that fraction of the value of the parent holding which then attached to that part of the area of the parent holding; and

   (b) a claim holding with an area consisting of the residue of the area of the parent holding, and with a value equal to that fraction of the value of the parent holding which then attached to the residue of the area of the parent holding,

and the claim holding referred to in head (a) of this sub-paragraph shall be allocated to the development charge in question, or (if more than one) to those development charges collectively.

(4) Paragraph 3 or paragraph 4 of this Schedule shall then apply in relation to each claim holding (if any) allocated in accordance with sub-paragraph (2) or sub-paragraph (3) of this paragraph to any development charge, or to any development charges collectively, as if the pledge had comprised only that claim holding and had covered only that development charge or those development charges.

(5) If, after the application of the preceding provisions of this paragraph, there remains outstanding any claim holding not allocated in accordance with those provisions, or any claim holding which (having been so allocated) is deemed to have been reduced in value but not extinguished, an amount equal to the aggregate of—

(*a*) the unpaid balance of any development charge covered by the pledge to which no claim holding was so allocated; and

(*b*) the amount (if any) by which the value of any claim holding so allocated which is deemed to have been extinguished falls short of the unpaid balance of the development charge, or the aggregate of the unpaid balances of the development charges, to which it was so allocated,

shall be treated as having been deducted from the value of the claim holding so remaining outstanding, or (if more than one) as having been deducted rateably from the respective values of those claim holdings, and the value of any such holding shall be deemed to have been reduced accordingly as from the time of the pledge. **[344]**

NOTES
Commencement: 1 April 1972.

PART II

ADJUSTMENT BY REFERENCE TO PAYMENTS IN RESPECT OF WAR-DAMAGED LAND

6.—(1) The provisions of this Part of this Schedule shall have effect where a payment under the scheme has become, or becomes payable in respect of an interest in land, and a claim holding related (or would, apart from this Part of this Schedule, have related) to the like interest in the whole or part of that land, with or without any other land.

(2) In this Part of this Schedule "the scheme" means the scheme made under section 59 of the Act of 1947, "the date of the scheme" means 12th December 1949, and "payment under the scheme" means a payment which has become, or becomes, payable by virtue of the scheme.

(3) In relation to any payment under the scheme "the payment area", in this Part of this Schedule, means the land in respect of which the payment became or becomes payable, and references to the amount of the payment shall be construed as references to the principal amount thereof, excluding any interest payable thereon in accordance with section 65(3) of the Act of 1947.

7. If the payment area is identical with the area of the claim holding, then—

(*a*) in the case of a payment of an amount equal to the value of the claim holding, the claim holding shall be deemed to have been extinguished as from the date of the scheme;

(*b*) in the case of a payment of an amount less than the value of the claim holding, the value of the claim holding shall be deemed to have been reduced, as from the date of the scheme, by the amount of the payment.

8.—(1) If the payment area forms part of the area of the claim holding, the holding (in this paragraph referred to as "the parent holding") shall be treated, as from the date of the scheme, as having been divided into two claim holdings, that is to say—

(*a*) a claim holding with an area consisting of that part of the area of the parent holding which constituted the payment area, and with a value equal to that fraction of the value of the parent holding which attached to that part of the area of the parent holding; and

(*b*) a claim holding with an area consisting of the residue of the area of the parent holding, and with a value equal to that fraction of the value of the parent holding which attached to the residue of the area of the parent holding.

(2) Where sub-paragraph (1) of this paragraph applies, paragraph 7 of this Schedule shall have effect in relation to the claim holding referred to in sub-paragraph (1)(*a*) of this paragraph as if it were the parent holding.

9. If the payment area includes the area of the claim holding together with other land, paragraph 7 of this Schedule shall apply as if—

(*a*) the payment area had been identical with the area of the claim holding; but

(b) the amount of the payment had been so much of the actual amount thereof, as might reasonably be expected to have been attributed to the area of the claim holding if, under the scheme, the authority determining the amount of the payment had been required (in accordance with the same principles as applied to the determination of that amount) to apportion it between the area of the claim holding and the rest of the payment area.

10. If the payment area includes part of the area of the claim holding together with other land not comprised in the area of the claim holding—

    (a) paragraph 8 of this Schedule shall apply as if the part of the payment area area comprised in the area of the claim holding had been the whole of the payment area; and

    (b) paragraph 9 of this Schedule shall apply as if the part of the area of the claim holding comprised in the payment area had been the whole of the area of the claim holding. **[345]**

NOTES
    Commencement: 1 April 1972.
    Act of 1947: Town and Country Planning Act 1947.

PART III

ADJUSTMENT IN CASES OF PARTIAL DISPOSITION OF CLAIM HOLDINGS

11. The provisions of this Part of this Schedule shall have effect where, by virtue of a disposition of part of the benefit of an established claim, not being a mortgage made otherwise than by way of assignment (in this Part of this Schedule referred to as "the relevant disposition"), different persons became entitled to different parts of the benefit of that established claim.

12. As from the date of the relevant disposition, each of those different parts shall be treated as having constituted a separate claim holding.

13. The area and value of any such separate claim holding at any time after the relevant disposition shall be taken to have been such as may, in the requisite manner, be or have been determined to be just and appropriate in all the circumstances.

14. In paragraph 13 of this Schedule the reference to determination in the requisite manner of the area and value of a claim holding is a reference to the determination thereof on the occasion of an apportionment affecting that holding which fell or falls to be made for any of the purposes of the Act of 1954, of Part VI of the Act of 1962 or Schedule 5 thereto, of Part VII of this Act or of this Schedule, being a determination made—

    (a) by the authority making that apportionment; or
    (b) where, under the Act of 1954, Part VI of the Act of 1962 or Part VII of this Act, that authority's findings were or are referred to the Lands Tribunal, by that Tribunal,

having regard in particular to the principles mentioned in paragraph 15 of this Schedule.

15.—(1) The said principles are those set out in the following provisions of this paragraph.

(2) The aggregate of the values of all claim holdings representing parts of the benefit of the same established claim must not exceed the amount of the established claim.

(3) Subject to sub-paragraph (2) of this paragraph, where a claim holding representing part only of the benefit of an established claim was pledged to the Central Land Board, otherwise than as mentioned in paragraph 2 of this Schedule, and by virtue of Part I of this Schedule the value of that claim holding is deemed to have been reduced by reference to an amount due by way of development charge, the value of that holding at the time of the pledge is not to be taken to have been less than the amount credited for the purposes of the pledge by reference to the holding.

(4) In the case of the claim holding representing the part of the benefit of an

established claim which was the subject of the relevant disposition, if it was not a claim holding to which sub-paragraph (5) of this paragraph applies—

    (a) the area of that claim holding is to be taken to be the claim area of that established claim, less the area of any claim holding to which the said sub-paragraph (5) applies which represents part of the benefit of the same established claim; and

    (b) the value of the claim holding immediately after the relevant disposition is, subject to sub-paragraphs (2) and (3) of this paragraph, to be taken to have been that part of the amount of the established claim to which the holder purported to become entitled under the terms of the relevant disposition.

(5) Where any person who was entitled to a claim holding representing part only of the benefit of an established claim—

    (a) at any time while so entitled was also entitled to the interest in land to which the established claim related in so far as that interest subsisted in part only of the claim area; and

    (b) became entitled to both that holding and that interest in such circumstances that the authority making the apportionment in question or the Lands Tribunal, as the case may be, were or are satisfied that the holding and the interest were intended to relate to one another,

the area of that claim holding is to be taken to be that part of the claim area, and the value of the holding immediately after the relevant disposition (however that or any other disposition affecting the holding was expressed, but subject to sub-paragraphs (2) to (4) of this paragraph) is to be taken to have been an amount equal to so much of the amount of the established claim as might reasonably be expected to have been attributed to that part of the claim area if the authority determining the amount of that established claim had been required to apportion it, in accordance with the same principles as applied to its determination, between that part and the residue of the claim area.

16. Paragraph 1 of this Schedule shall apply for the purposes of this Part of this Schedule as it applies for the purposes of Part I thereof.   **[346]**

NOTES
    Commencement: 1 April 1972.
    Act of 1954: Town and Country Planning Act 1954.
    Act of 1962: Town and Country Planning Act 1962.

PART IV

ADJUSTMENT IN RESPECT OF PAYMENTS UNDER PART I OF ACT 1954

17. The provisions of this Part of this Schedule shall have effect where, by virtue of Part I of the Act of 1954, a payment became or becomes payable in respect of a claim holding.

18. Subject to the following provisions of this Part of this Schedule, if either—

    (a) the principal amount of the payment was or is not less than the value of the claim holding; or

    (b) the payment (whatever its amount) became or becomes payable under Case D (that is to say, by virtue of section 8 of the Act of 1954, which related to cases where a claim holding had been disposed of for valuable consideration),

the claim holding shall be deemed to have been extinguished; and if the principal amount of the payment (not being a payment under Case D) was or is less than the value of the claim holding, the value of that holding shall be deemed to have been reduced by the principal amount of the payment.

19. Paragraph 18 of this Schedule shall apply where two or more payments under Part I of the Act of 1954 were or are payable in respect of the same claim holding, with the substitution, for references to the principal amount of the payment, of references to the aggregate of the principal amounts of the payments.

20.—(1) Where one or more relevant acts or events have occurred in relation to a claim holding (in this paragraph referred to as "the parent holding") and any such act or event did not extend to the whole of the area of the parent holding, then, for the purposes of the preceding provisions of this Part of this Schedule, and for the purposes of Part V of this Schedule and of Part VII of this Act—

(a) the parent holding shall be treated as having been divided immediately before the time of completion, into as many separate claim holdings, with such areas, as may be necessary to ensure that, in the case of each holding, either any relevant act or event extending to the area of that holding extended to the whole thereof or no relevant act or event extended to the area of that holding;

(b) the value of each of the separate holdings respectively shall be taken to have been that fraction of the value of the parent holding which then attached to the part of the area of the parent holding constituting the area of the separate holding; and

(c) the portion of the amount of any payment under Part I of the Act of 1954 which, by the authority determining that amount, was or is apportioned to the area of any of the separate claim holdings shall be taken to have been a payment payable under the said Part I in respect of that claim holding.

(2) In this paragraph "relevant act or event", in relation to a claim holding, means an act or event whereby, in accordance with the provisions of Part I of the Act of 1954, one or more payments became or become payable in respect of that claim holding.

21. For the purposes of this Part of this Schedule—

(a) a payment shall be treated as having become payable notwithstanding that the right to receive the payment was extinguished by section 14(2) of the Act of 1954 (which enabled the Central Land Board to set off payments against liabilities in respect of development charges);

(b) any reduction of the principal amount of a payment by virtue of that subsection shall be disregarded; and

(c) where in accordance with subsection (3) of section 14 or subsection (6) of section 58 of the Act of 1954 (which provided for cases of failure to apply for a payment within the appropriate period) an amount was determined as being the principal amount of a payment to which a person would have been entitled as mentioned in those subsections respectively, that payment shall be treated as if it had become due and as if the principal amount thereof had been the amount so determined.

22.—(1) Where in accordance with the preceding provisions of this Part of this Schedule a claim holding is deemed to have been extinguished or the value of a claim holding is deemed to have been reduced, the extinguishment or reduction, as the case may be, shall be deemed to have had effect immediately before the time of completion.

(2) References in this Part of this Schedule to the value of a claim holding are references to the value thereof immediately before the time of completion. **[347]**

NOTES
Commencement: 1 April 1972.
Act of 1954: Town and Country Planning Act 1954.

PART V

ADJUSTMENT IN RESPECT OF COMPENSATION UNDER PART V OF ACT OF 1954

23. Where compensation under Part V of the Act of 1954 became or becomes payable by reference to a claim holding, then (subject to the following provisions of this Part of this Schedule) for the purposes of Part VII of this Act—

(a) if the principal amount of the compensation was or is equal to the value of the claim holding at the time of completion (ascertained apart from this Part of this Schedule) the claim holding shall be deemed to have been extinguished immediately before that time;

(b) if the principal amount of the compensation was or is less than the value of the claim holding at that time (ascertained apart from this Part of this Schedule) the value of the claim holding shall be deemed to have been reduced immediately before that time by the principal amount of the compensation.

24. Where compensation became or becomes payable as mentioned in paragraph 23 of this Schedule, and at any time an amount became or becomes recoverable in respect thereof under section 29 of the Act of 1954, as applied by section 46 of that Act, or under section 159 of this Act as applied by Schedule 24 to this Act to compensation under Part V of the Act of 1954, then, for the purposes of Part VII of this Act, paragraph 23 of this Schedule shall have effect as from that time as if the principal amount of that compensation had been reduced by a sum equal to seven-eighths of the amount which so became or becomes recoverable.

25. Where, in the case of a claim holding (in this paragraph referred to as "the parent holding"), compensation under Part V of the Act 1954 became or becomes payable in respect of depreciation of the value of an interest in land by one or more planning decisions or orders, and any such decision or order did not extend to the whole of the area of the parent holding, then, both for the purposes of the preceding provisions of this Part of this Schedule and for the purposes of Part VII of this Act—

(a) the parent holding shall be treated as having been divided immediately before the time of completion into as many separate claim holdings, with such areas, as may be necessary to ensure that, in the case of each holding, either any such decision or order extending to the area of that holding extended to the whole thereof or no such decision or order extended to the area of that holding;

(b) the value of each of the separate holdings respectively shall be taken to have been that fraction of the value of the parent holding which then attached to the part of the area of the parent holding constituting the area of the separate holding; and

(c) the portion of the amount of any such compensation which, by the authority determining that amount, was or is apportioned to the area of any of the separate claim holdings shall be taken to have been compensation payable under Part V of the Act of 1954 in respect of that claim holding.   **[348]**

NOTES
Commencement: 1 April 1972.
Act of 1954: Town and Country Planning Act 1954.

Part VI

Supplementary Provisions

26. Where in accordance with any of the provisions of this Schedule a part of the benefit of an established claim constituted a separate claim holding, the interest in land to which that claim holding related—

(a) if the established claim related to the fee simple of the claim area, shall be taken to have been the fee simple of the area of the claim holding;

(b) if the established claim related to a leasehold interest, shall be taken to have been that leasehold interest in so far as it subsisted in the area of the claim holding.

27. Where in accordance with any of the provisions of this Schedule a claim holding (in this paragraph referred to as "the parent holding") is to be treated as divided into two or more claim holdings, a person who was the holder of one of those holdings shall be treated as having been the holder thereof at any time when he was the holder of the parent holding.

28. Expressions used in this Schedule and in Part VII of this Act have the same meanings in this Schedule as in that Part of this Act.

29. In this Schedule "the holder", in relation to a claim holding, means the person for the time being entitled to the holding, or, in the case of a holding subject to a mortgage made otherwise than by way of assignment, means the person who would for the time being have been entitled to the holding if it had not been mortgaged, and "the time of completion" means the time when, in accordance with section 138 of this Act, the adjustment of claim holdings is deemed to have been completed.   **[349]**

NOTES
Commencement: 1 April 1972.

SCHEDULE 16

Section 141

CALCULATION OF VALUE OF PREVIOUS DEVELOPMENT OF LAND

1. Where for the purposes of section 141 of this Act the value of any development initiated before a time referred to in that section has to be ascertained with reference to that time, the value of the development shall be calculated in accordance with the provisions of this Schedule.

2. Subject to the following provisions of this Schedule, the value shall be calculated by reference to prices current at the time in question—

    (*a*) as if the development had not been initiated, but the land had remained in the state in which it was immediately before the development was initiated; and

    (*b*) on the assumption that (apart from the provisions of Part III of this Act, the provisions of Part III of the Act of 1962 or the provisions of the Act of 1947, as the case may be) the development could at that time lawfully be carried out,

and shall be taken to be the difference between the value which in those circumstances the land would have had at that time if planning permission for that development had been granted unconditionally immediately before that time and the value which in those circumstances the land would have had at that time if planning permission for that development had been applied for and refused immediately before that time, and it could be assumed that planning permission for that development, and any other new development of that land, would be refused on any subsequent application.

3. If the development involved the clearing of any land, the reference in paragraph (2)(*a*) of this Schedule to the state to the land immediately before the development shall be construed as a reference to the state of the land immediately after the clearing thereof but before the carrying out of any other operations.

4.—(1) If the development was initiated in pursuance of planning permission granted subject to conditions, paragraph 2 of this Schedule shall apply as if the reference to the granting of permission unconditionally were a reference to the granting of permission subject to the like conditions.

(2) If the permission referred to in sub-paragraph (1) of this paragraph was granted subject to conditions which consisted of, or included, a requirement expressed by reference to a specified period, the reference in that sub-paragraph to the like conditions shall be construed, in relation to the condition imposing that requirement, as a reference to a condition imposing the like requirement in respect of a period of like duration beginning at the time in question.

5. In the application of the preceding provisions of this Schedule to development initiated, but not completed, before the time in question, references to permission for that development shall be construed as references to permission for so much of that development as had been carried out before that time.   **[350]**

NOTES
Commencement: 1 April 1972.
Act of 1962: Town and Country Planning Act 1962.
Act of 1947: Town and Country Planning Act 1947.

SCHEDULE 17

Section 142

APPORTIONMENT OF UNEXPENDED BALANCE OF ESTABLISHED DEVELOPMENT VALUE

Determination of relevant area

1.—(1) Where, in the case of a compulsory acquisition to which section 142 of this Act applies, any area of the relevant land which, immediately before the relevant date, has an unexpended balance of established development value does not satisfy the conditions set out in sub-paragraph (2) of this paragraph, that area shall be treated as divided into as many separate areas as may be requisite to ensure that each of those separate areas satisfies those conditions.

(2) The conditions referred to in sub-paragraph (1) of this paragraph are—

(a) that all the interests (other than excepted interests) subsisting in the area in question subsist in the whole of that area; and

(b) that any rentcharge charged on that area is charged on the whole of it.

(3) Any area of the relevant land which has an unexpended balance of established development value and which complies with the conditions set out in sub-paragraph (2) of this paragraph is in this Schedule referred to, in relation to the interests subsisting therein, as "the relevant area", and the subsequent provisions of this Schedule shall have effect separately in relation to each relevant area.

Preliminary calculations

2. There shall be calculated the amount referable to the relevant area of the rent which might reasonably be expected to be reserved if the relevant land where to be let on terms prohibiting the carrying out of any new development but permitting the carrying out of any other development; and the amount so calculated is in this Schedule referred to as "the existing use rent".

3.—(1) If, in the case of an interest in fee simple which is subject to a rentcharge or in the case of a tenancy, so much of the rent reserved under the rentcharge or tenancy as is referable to the relevant area exceeds the existing use rent, there shall be calculated the capital value of the right to receive, for the period of the remainder of the term of the rentcharge or tenancy, an annual payment equal to the excess; and any amount so calculated in the case of any interest is in this Schedule referred to as "the rental liability" of that interest.

(2) Where the interest in fee simple is subject to more than one rentcharge, then, for the purposes of sub-paragraph (1) of this paragraph, in relation to any period included in the term of two or more of those rentcharges, those two or more rentcharges shall be treated as a single rentcharge charged on the relevant area for the duration of that period, with a rent reserved thereunder of an amount equal to the aggregate of so much of their respective rents as is referable to the relevant area.

4. In the case of any interest in reversion—

(a) there shall be calculated the capital value, as at the time immediately before the relevant date, of the right to receive a sum equal to the unexpended balance of established development value of the relevant area at that time, but payable at the end of the tenancy upon the termination of which the interest in question is immediately expectant; and the amount so calculated in the case of any interest is in this Schedule referred to as "the reversionary development value" of that interest;

(b) if so much of the rent reserved under the said tenancy as is referable to the relevant area exceeds the existing use rent, there shall also be calculated the capital value as at the said time of the right to receive, for the period of the remainder of the term of that tenancy, an annual payment equal to the excess; and any amount so determined in the case of any interest is in this Schedule referred to as "the rental increment" of that interest.

Apportionment of unexpended balance between interests

5. Where two or more interests (other than excepted interests) subsist in the relevant area, the portion of the unexpended balance of established development value of the relevant area attributable to each of those interests respectively shall be taken to be the following, that is to say—

(a) in the case of the interest in fee simple, an amount equal to the reversionary development value of that interest, less the amount (if any) by which any rental liability of that interest exceeds any rental increment thereof;

(b) in the case of tenancy in reversion, an amount equal to the reversionary development value of that tenancy, less the aggregate of—

   (i) the reversionary development value of the interest in reversion immediately expectant upon the termination of that tenancy; and
   (ii) the amount (if any) by which any rental liability of that tenancy exceeds any rental increment thereof;

(c) in the case of a tenancy other than a tenancy in reversion, the remainder (if any) of the said balance after the deduction of the aggregate of—

   (i) the reversionary development value of the interest in reversion immediately expectant upon the termination of that tenancy; and
   (ii) any rental liability of that tenancy.

Application of Schedule to past acquisitions

6. In relation to any compulsory acquisition to which section 142 of this Act applies, where the relevant date was a date before the commencement of this Act, the preceding provisions of this Schedule shall have effect with the necessary modifications.

Interpretation

7. In this Schedule—

(a) "the relevant land", in relation to a compulsory acquisition to which section 142 of this Act applies, means the land in which the interest acquired subsisted or subsists;
(b) "tenancy" does not include an excepted interest;
(c) any reference to an interest or tenancy in reversion does not include an interest or tenancy in reversion immediately expectant upon the termination of an excepted interest;
(d) "the relevant date" and "excepted interest" have the same meanings as in section 142 of this Act; and
(e) other expressions have the same meanings as in Part VII of this Act.   **[351]**

NOTES
Commencement: 1 April 1972.

SCHEDULE 18

Sections 168, 169, 180, 278

CONDITION TREATED AS APPLICABLE TO REBUILDING AND ALTERATIONS

1. Where the building to be rebuilt or altered is the original building, the amount of gross floor space in the building as rebuilt or altered which may be used for any purpose shall not exceed by more than ten per cent. the amount of gross floor space which was last used for that purpose in the original building.

2. Where the building to be rebuilt or altered is not the original building, the amount of gross floor space in the building as rebuilt or altered which may be used for any purpose shall not exceed the amount of gross floor space which was last used for that purpose in the building before the rebuilding or alteration.

3. In determining under this Schedule the purpose for which floor space was last used in any building, no account shall be taken of any use in respect of which an effective enforcement notice has been or could be served or, in the case of a use which has been discontinued, could have been served immediately before the discontinuance.

4. For the purposes of this Schedule gross floor space shall be ascertained by external measurement; and where different parts of a building are used for different purposes, floor space common to those purposes shall be apportioned rateably.

5. In relation to a building erected after the appointed day, being a building resulting from the carrying out of any such works as are described in paragraph 1 of Schedule 8 to

this Act, any reference in this Schedule to the original building is a reference to the building in relation to which those works were carried out and not to the building resulting from the carrying out of those works.   **[352]**

NOTES
    Commencement: 1 April 1972.

SCHEDULE 19

Section 190

PROCEEDINGS ON LISTED BUILDING PURCHASE NOTICE

Action by council on whom listed building purchase notice is served

1.—(1) The council on whom a listed building purchase notice is served, shall, before the end of the period of three months beginning with the date of service of that notice, serve on the owner by whom the purchase notice was served a notice stating either—

  (*a*) that the council are willing to comply with the purchase notice; or
  (*b*) that another local authority or statutory undertakers specified in the notice under this sub-paragraph have agreed to comply with it in their place; or
  (*c*) that for reasons specified in the notice under this sub-paragraph, the council are not willing to comply with the purchase notice and have not found any other local authority or statutory undertakers who will agree to comply with it in their place and that they have transmitted a copy of the purchase notice to the Secretary of State, on a date specified in the notice under this sub-paragraph, together with a statement of the reasons so specified.

(2) Where the council on whom a listed building purchase notice is served by an owner have served on him a notice in accordance with sub-paragraph (1)(*a*) or (*b*) of this paragraph the council, or the other local authority or statutory undertakers specified in the notice, as the case may be, shall be deemed to be authorised to acquire the interest of the owner compulsorily in accordance with the provisions of section 114 of this Act, and to have served a notice to treat in respect thereof on the date of service of the notice under sub-paragraph (1) of this paragraph.

(3) Where the council on whom a listed building purchase notice is served by an owner propose to serve on him a notice in accordance with sub-paragraph (1)(*c*) of this paragraph they shall transmit a copy of the purchase notice to the Secretary of State together with a statement of their reasons; and section 182 of this Act shall then apply in relation to the purchase notice as it applies in relation to a purchase notice under section 180 of this Act with the substitution for references therein to the Secretary of State taking action under section 183 of this Act of references to his taking action under paragraph 2 of this Schedule.

Action by Secretary of State in relation to listed building purchase notice

2.—(1) Subject to the following provisions of this paragraph, if the Secretary of State is satisfied that the conditions specified in section 190(1)(*a*) to (*c*) of this Act are fulfilled in relation to a listed building purchase notice, he shall confirm the notice:

    Provided that, if he is satisfied that the said conditions are fulfilled only in respect of part of the land, he shall confirm the notice only in respect of that part and the notice shall have effect accordingly.

(2) The Secretary of State shall not confirm the purchase notice unless he is satisfied that the land comprises such land contiguous or adjacent to the building as is in his opinion required for preserving the building or its amenities, or for affording access to it, or for its proper control or management.

(3) If it appears to the Secretary of State to be expedient to do so in the case of a listed building purchase notice served on account of listed building consent being refused or granted subject to conditions, he may, in lieu of confirming the purchase notice, grant listed building consent for the works in respect of which the application was made or, where such consent for those works was granted subject to conditions, revoke or amend

those conditions so far as it appears to him to be required in order to enable the land to be rendered capable of reasonably beneficial use by the carrying out of those works.

(4) If it appears to the Secretary of State to be expedient to do so, in the case of a listed building purchase notice served on account of listed building consent being revoked or modified by an order under Part II of Schedule 11 to this Act he may, in lieu of confirming the notice, cancel the order revoking the consent or, where the order modified the consent by the imposition of conditions, revoke or amend those conditions so far as appears to him to be required in order to enable the land to be rendered capable of reasonably beneficial use by the carrying out of the works in respect of which the consent was granted.

(5) If it appears to the Secretary of State that the land, or any part of it, could be rendered capable of reasonably beneficial use within a reasonable time by the carrying out of any other works for which listed building consent ought to be granted, he may in lieu of confirming the listed building purchase notice or in lieu of confirming it so far as it relates to that part of the land, as the case may be, direct that listed building consent for those works shall be granted in the event of an application being made in that behalf.

(6) If it appears to the Secretary of State that the land, or any part of the land, could be rendered capable of reasonably beneficial use within a reasonable time by the carrying out of any development for which planning permission ought to be granted, he may, in lieu of confirming the listed building purchase notice, or in lieu of confirming it so far as it relates to that part of the land, as the case may be, direct that planning permission for that development shall be granted in the event of an application being made in that behalf.

(7) If it appears to the Secretary of State, having regard to the probable ultimate use of the building or the site thereof, that it is expedient to do so, he may, if he confirms the notice, modify it either in relation to the whole or in relation to any part of the land, by substituting another local authority or statutory undertakers for the council on whom the notice was served.

(8) In section 182 of this Act as applied by paragraph 1(3) of this Schedule, any reference to the taking of action by the Secretary of State under this paragraph is a reference to the taking by him of any such action as is mentioned in sub-paragraphs (1) or (3) to (7) of this paragraph, or to the taking by him of a decision not to confirm the purchase notice on the grounds that any of the conditions referred to in sub-paragraph (1) of this paragraph are not fulfilled.

Effect of Secretary of State's action in relation to listed building purchase notice

3.—(1) Where the Secretary of State confirms a listed building purchase notice, the council on whom the notice was served (or, if under paragraph 2(7) of this Schedule the Secretary of State modified the notice by substituting another local authority or statutory undertakers for that council, that other local authority or those statutory undertakers) shall be deemed to be authorised to acquire the relevant interest compulsorily in accordance with the provisions of section 114 of this Act and to have served a notice to treat in respect thereof on such date as the Secretary of State may direct.

(2) If, before the end of the relevant period, the Secretary of State has neither confirmed the purchase notice nor taken any such action in respect thereof as is mentioned in sub-paragraphs (3) to (6) of paragraph 2 of this Schedule, and has not notified the owner by whom the notice was served that he does not propose to confirm the notice, the notice shall be deemed to be confirmed at the end of that period and the council on whom the notice was served shall be deemed to have been authorised to acquire the relevant interest compulsorily in accordance with the provisions of section 114 of this Act and to have served a notice to treat in respect thereof at the end of that period.

(3) In this paragraph—

(a) "the relevant interest" means the owner's interest in the land or, if the purchase notice is confirmed by the Secretary of State in respect of only part of the land, the owner's interest in that part;

(b) "the relevant period" is whichever of the following periods first expires, that is to say—
  (i) the period of nine months beginning with the date of the service of the purchase notice; and
  (ii) the period of six months beginning with the date on which a copy of the purchase notice was transmitted to the Secretary of State.

(4) Where the Secretary of State has notified the owner by whom a listed building purchase notice has been served of a decision on his part to confirm, or not to confirm, the notice (including any decision to confirm the notice only in respect of part of the land, or to give any direction as to the granting of listed building consent), and that decision of the Secretary of State is quashed under the provisions of Part XII of this Act, the purchase notice shall be treated as cancelled, but the owner may serve a further listed building purchase notice in its place.

(5) For the purposes of any regulations made under this Act as to the time within which a listed building purchase notice may be served, the service of a listed building purchase notice under sub-paragraph (4) of this paragraph shall not be treated as out of time if the notice is served within the period which would be applicable in accordance with those regulations if the decision to refuse listed building consent or to grant it subject to conditions (being the decision in consequence of which the notice is served) had been made on the date on which the decision of the Secretary of State was quashed as mentioned in sub-paragraph (4) of this paragraph.

Special provision as to compensation where listed building purchase notice served

4. Where in consequence of listed building consent being revoked or modified by an order under Part II of Schedule 11 to this Act, compensation is payable by virtue of section 172 of this Act in respect of expenditure incurred in carrying out any works to the building in respect of which the consent was granted, then if a listed building purchase notice is served in respect of an interest in the land, any compensation payable in respect of the acquisition of that interest in pursuance of the notice shall be reduced by an amount equal to the value of the works in respect of which compensation is payable by virtue of that section. **[353]**

NOTES
  Commencement: 1 April 1972.
  Para 1: sub-para (1)(c) amended by the Housing and Planning Act 1986, s 49(1), Sch 11, Part I, para 5(2)(a); sub-para (3) amended by the Housing and Planning Act 1986, s 49(1), Sch 11, Part I, para 5(2)(b). See Appendix.
  Para 3: sub-para (3)(b) amended by and new sub-para (3A) inserted by the Housing and Planning Act 1986, s 49(1), Sch 11, Part I, para 7(2). See Appendix.

SCHEDULE 20
Section 217

PROCEDURE IN CONNECTION WITH ORDERS RELATING TO FOOTPATHS AND BRIDLEWAYS

PART I

CONFIRMATION OF ORDERS

1.—(1) Before an order under section 210 or 214(1)(b) of this Act is submitted to the Secretary of State for confirmation or confirmed as an unopposed order, the authority by whom the order was made shall give notice in the prescribed form—
  (a) stating the general effect of the order and that it has been made and is about to be submitted for confirmation or to be confirmed as an unopposed order;
  (b) naming a place in the area in which the land to which the order relates is situated where a copy of the order may be inspected free of charge [and copies thereof may be obtained at a reasonable charge] at all reasonable hours; and
  (c) specifying the time (not being less than twenty-eight days from the date of the first publication of the notice) within which, and the manner in which, representations or objections with respect to the order may be made.

(2) Subject to sub-paragraph (4) of this paragraph, the notice to be given under sub-paragraph (1) of this paragraph shall be given—
  (a) by publication . . . in at least one local newspaper circulating in the area in which the land to which the order relates is situated; and

(*b*) by serving a like notice on—

    (i) every owner, occupier and lessee (except tenants for a month or a period less than a month and statutory tenants within the meaning of the Rent Act 1968) of any of that land;

    (ii) every council, the council of every rural parish and the parish meeting of every rural parish not having a separate parish council, being a council or parish whose area includes any of that land; and

    (iii) any statutory undertakers to whom there belongs, or by whom there is used, for the purposes of their undertaking, any apparatus under, in, on, over, along or across that land; and

    [(iv) every person on whom notice is required to be served in pursuance of sub-paragraph (2A) of this paragraph; and

    (v) such other persons as may be prescribed in relation to the area in which that land is situated or as the authority may consider appropriate; and]

[(*c*) by causing a copy of the notice to be displayed in a prominent position—

    (i) at the ends of so much of any footpath or bridleway as is to be stopped up, diverted or extinguished by the order;

    (ii) at council offices in the locality of the land to which the order relates; and

    (iii) at such other places as the authority may consider appropriate.]

[(2A) Any person may, on payment of such reasonable charge as the authority may consider appropriate, require an authority to give him notice of all such orders under section 210 or 214(1)(*b*) of this Act as are made by the authority during a specified period, are of a specified description and relate to land comprised in a specified area; and in this sub-paragraph "specified" means specified in the requirement.]

(3) In sub-paragraph (2) of this paragraph "council" means a county council, a ... district council, ... *or a London borough council* [a London borough council, the Inner London Education Authority or a joint authority established by Part IV of the Local Government Act 1985] [and "council offices" means offices or buildings acquired or provided by a council or by the council of a parish or community or the parish meeting of a parish not having a separate parish council].

(4) Except in the case of an owner, occupier or lessee being a local authority or statutory undertakers, the Secretary of State may in any particular case direct that it shall not be necessary to comply with sub-paragraph (2)(*b*)(i) of this paragraph; but if he so directs in the case of any land, then in addition to publication the notice shall be addressed to "the owners and any occupiers" of the land (describing it) and a copy or copies of the notice shall be affixed to some conspicuous object or objects on the land.

[(5) Sub-paragraph (2)(*b*) and (*c*) and, where applicable, sub-paragraph (4) of this paragraph shall be complied with not less than 28 days before the expiration of the time specified in the notice.

(6) A notice required to be served by sub-paragraph (2)(*b*)(i), (ii), (iii) or (v) of this paragraph shall be accompanied by a copy of the order.

(7) A notice required to be displayed by sub-paragraph (2)(*c*)(i) of this paragraph at the ends of so much of any way as is affected by the order shall be accompanied by a plan showing the general effect of the order so far as it relates to that way.]

2. If no representations or objections are duly made, or if any so made are withdrawn, the authority by whom the order was made may, instead of submitting the order to the Secretary of State, themselves confirm the order (but without any modification).

3.—(1) If any representation or objection duly made is not withdrawn, the Secretary of State shall, before confirming the order, if the objection is made by a local authority cause a local inquiry to be held, and in any other case either—

    (*a*) cause a local inquiry to be held; or

    (*b*) afford to any person by whom any representation or objection has been duly made and not withdrawn an opportunity of being heard by a person appointed by the Secretary of State for the purpose, and, after considering the report of the person appointed to hold the inquiry or to hear representations or objections, may confirm the order, with or without modifications:

Provided that in the case of an order under section 210 of this Act, if objection is made by statutory undertakers on the ground that the order provides for the creation of a public right of way over land covered by works used for the purpose of their undertaking, or over the curtilage of such land, and the objection is not withdrawn, the order shall be subject to special parliamentary procedure.

(2) Notwithstanding anything in the preceding provisions of this paragraph, the Secretary of State shall not confirm an order so as to affect land not affected by the order as submitted to him, except after—

(a) giving such notice as appears to him requisite of his proposal so to modify the order, specifying the time (not being less than twenty-eight days from the date of the first publication of the notice) within which, and the manner in which, representations or objections with respect to the proposal may be made;

(b) holding a local inquiry or affording to any person by whom any representation or objection has been duly made and not withdrawn an opportunity of being heard by a person appointed by the Secretary of State for the purpose; and

(c) considering the report of the person appointed to hold the inquiry or to hear representations or objections as the case may be;

and, in the case of an order under section 210 of this Act, if objection is made by statutory undertakers on the ground that the order as modified would provide for the creation of a public right of way over land covered by works used for the purposes of their undertaking, or over the curtilage of such land, and the objection is not withdrawn, the order shall be subject to special parliamentary procedure.

[3A.—(1) A decision of the Secretary of State under paragraph 3 of this Schedule shall, except in such classes of case as may for the time being be prescribed or as may be specified in directions given by the Secretary of State, be made by a person appointed by the Secretary of State for the purpose instead of by the Secretary of State; and a decision made by a person so appointed shall be treated as a decision of the Secretary of State.

(2) The Secretary of State may, if he thinks fit, direct that a decision which, by virtue of sub-paragraph (1) of this paragraph and apart from this sub-paragraph, falls to be made by a person appointed by the Secretary of State shall instead be made by the Secretary of State; and a direction under this sub-paragraph shall state the reasons for which it is given and shall be served on the person, if any, so appointed, the authority and any person by whom a representation or objection has been duly made and not withdrawn.

(3) Where the Secretary of State has appointed a person to make a decision under paragraph 3 of this Schedule the Secretary of State may, at any time before the making of the decision, appoint another person to make it instead of the person first appointed to make it.

(4) Where by virtue of sub-paragraph (2) or (3) of this paragraph a particular decision falls to be made by the Secretary of State or any other person instead of the person first appointed to make it, anything done by or in relation to the latter shall be treated as having been done by or in relation to the former.

(5) Regulations under this Act may provide for the giving of publicity to any directions given by the Secretary of State under this paragraph.]

4.—(1) The Secretary of State shall not confirm an order under section 210 of this Act which extinguishes a right of way over land under, in, on, over, along or across which there is any apparatus belonging to or used by statutory undertakers for the purposes of their undertaking, unless the undertakers have consented to the confirmation of the order; and any such consent may be given subject to the condition that there are included in the order such provisions for the protection of the undertakers as they may reasonably require.

(2) The consent of statutory undertakers to any such order shall not be unreasonably withheld; and any question arising under this paragraph whether the withholding of

consent is unreasonable, or whether any requirement is reasonable, shall be determined by whichever Minister is the appropriate Minister in relation to the statutory undertakers concerned.

5. Regulations under this Act may, subject to this Part of this Schedule, make such provision as the Secretary of State thinks expedient as to the procedure on the making, submission and confirmation of orders under sections 210 and 214(1)(*b*) of this Act. **[354]**

NOTES

Commencement: 28 February 1983 (para 3A); 1 April 1972 (remainder).
This Part derived from the Town and Country Planning Act 1968, Sch 7, Part I.
Para 1: in sub-para (3) words omitted repealed by the Local Government Act 1972, s 272, Sch 30, second words repealed by the Local Government Act 1985, s 102, Sch 17, second words in italics prospectively repealed and subsequent words in square brackets prospectively substituted by the Local Government Act 1985, s 84, Sch 14, para 48(*b*), as from a day or days to be appointed in accordance with s 84; other amendments made by the Wildlife and Countryside Act 1981, s 63, Sch 16.
Para 3A: added by the Wildlife and Countryside Act 1981, s 63, Sch 16.

PART II
PUBLICITY FOR ORDERS AFTER CONFIRMATION

6. [(1)] As soon as may be after an order under section 210 or 214(1)(*b*) of this Act has been confirmed by the Secretary of State or confirmed as an unopposed order, the authority by whom the order was made shall publish, in the manner required by paragraph 1(2) of this Schedule, a notice in the prescribed form, describing the general effect of the order, stating that it has been confirmed, and naming a place where [a copy of the order] as confirmed may be inspected free of charge [and copies thereof may be obtained at a reasonable charge] at all reasonable hours, and shall—

[(*a*) serve a like notice on any persons on whom notices were required to be served under paragraph 1(2)(*b*) or (4) of this Schedule; and
(*b*) cause like notices to be displayed in the like manner as the notices required to be displayed under paragraph 1(2)(*c*) of this Schedule:]

Provided that no such notice or copy need be served on a person unless he has sent to the authority a request in that behalf, specifying an address for service.

[(2) A notice required to be served by sub-paragraph (1)(*a*) of this paragraph on—

(*a*) a person on whom notice was required to be served by paragraph 1(2)(*b*)(i), (ii), or (iii) of this Schedule; or
(*b*) in the case of an order which has been confirmed with modifications, a person on whom notice was required to be served by paragraph 1(2)(*b*)(v) of this Schedule,

shall be accompanied by a copy of the order as confirmed.

(3) As soon as may be after a decision not to confirm an order under the said section 210 or 214(1)(*b*), the authority by whom the order was made shall give notice of the decision by serving a copy of it on any persons on whom notices were required to be served under paragraph 1(2)(*b*) or (4) of this Schedule.]

[7. As soon as may be after an order under section 210 or 214(1)(*b*) of this Act has come into operation otherwise than—

(*a*) on the date on which it was confirmed by the Secretary of State or confirmed as an unopposed order; or
(*b*) at the expiration of a specified period beginning with that date,

the authority by whom the order was made shall give notice of its coming into operation by publication in at least one local newspaper circulating in the area in which the land to which the order relates is situated.]   **[355]**

NOTES

Commencement: 28 February 1983 (para 7); 1 April 1972 (remainder).
Amended by the Wildlife and Countryside Act 1981, s 63, Sch 16.

SCHEDULE 21

Part I

Sections 1 to 3.

Section 22.

Section 23 except subsection (7).

Section 24 except subsection (6).

Section 25.

Section 29(1).

Section 30.

Section 31(1).

Sections 32 and 33.

Section 34(1) and (3).

Section 35 with the omission in subsection (4) of the reference to sections 26 and 27.

Section 36(1) to (6) with the omission in subsection (5) of the reference to section 27.

Section 37.

Section 40.

Section 45.

Sections 50 to 53.

Section 54 except subsections (8), (10) and (11).

Section 60.

Sections 63 to 68.

Section 89.

Sections 91 to 93.

Section 102.

[Sections 104 to 109.

Sections 110 and 111.]

Sections 118 to 125.

Sections 127 to 133.

Section 164.

Section 165 with the omission in subsection (2) of the references to sections 166 to 168.

Section 169 except subsection (5).

Section 170.

Section 174.

Section 176.

Sections 178 and 179.

Section 180(1) to (4).

Sections 181 to 183.

Sections 186 to 189.

Section 191(1).

Section 209.

Section 214 except subsection (1)(*b*).

Section 215.

Sections 218 and 219.

Section 220.

Section 222.

Sections 224 to 231.

Sections 233 to 236.

Section 237 except subsection (3).

Section 238 except subsections (4) and (6)(*b*).

Sections 239 to 241.

Section 242(1) except paragraphs (*d*) and (*e*).

Section 243 except subsection (5).

Section 244.

Section 246.

Section 249 with the omission in subsection (2) of the references to section 245.

Section 250.

Section 251(1).

Section 252.

Sections 254 and 255.

Section 263(1).

Sections 264 and 265.

Section 266(1) (the reference, in paragraph (*b*), to Part III being construed as not referring to sections 26 and 27 and the reference, in that paragraph, to Part IV being construed as not referring to sections 73 to 86) and section 266(2) to (5) and (7).

Section 267.

Section 270.

Section 272

Section 274 except subsections (2)(*a*) and (4).

Section 275(2).

Section 276.

Section 280 except subsections (4) and (5).

Section 281.

Section 284.

Section 288.

Schedules 1 and 2.

Schedule 8.

Schedule 22.

Any other provisions of this Act in so far as they apply, or have effect for the purposes of, any of the provisions specified above.   **[356]**

NOTES

Commencement: 1 April 1972.

Amended by the Local Government (Miscellaneous Provisions) Act 1982, s 36, and by the Housing and Planning Act 1986, s 49(1), Sch 11, Part I, para 21. See Appendix.

Repealed in part by the Housing and Planning Act 1986, s 49(2), Sch 12, Part III. See Appendix.

PART II

Section 4.

Sections 6 to 21.

Section 26(2) to (6) except subsection (2)(*a*) and the reference to it in subsection (6), and subsection (8).

Section 28(2)(*b*) and (3).

Section 29(4).

Section 31(2) and (3).

Section 34(2).

Section 36(7) and (8).

Sections 41 to 44.

Sections 46 to 49.

Section 54(10) and (11).

Sections 55 and 56.

Section 58.

Sections 79 to 81.

Sections 87 and 88.

Section 90.

Sections 94 to 100.

Section 103(4).

Sections 112 to 117.

Sections 171 to 173.

Section 177.

Section 180(5) and (6).

Section 184.

Section 190.

Section 197.

Sections 201 and 202.

Sections 210 to [212].

Section 214(1)(*b*).

Sections 216 and 217.

Section 221.

Section 223.

Section 232.

Section 237(3).

Section 238(4) and (6)(*b*).

Section 253.

Section 256.

Section 271.

Section 285.

Schedules 4, 7, 9, 10, 11, 14, 19 and 20.

[357]

NOTES
Commencement: 1 April 1972.
Amended by the Local Government (Miscellaneous Provisions) Act 1982, s 20, Sch 5, Part II.
Repealed in part by the Housing and Planning Act 1986, s 49(2), Sch 12, Part III. See Appendix.

PART III

Sections 38 and 39.

Section 72.

Sections 134 to 163.

Sections 166 to 168.

Section 169(5).

Section 191(2).

Section 251(2) to (5).

Sections 257 to 259.

Section 261(2) to (4).

Section 268.

Section 274(4).

Section 275(1).

Section 279.

Section 280(5).

Schedules 15 and 16.

Any other provisions of this Act in so far as they apply, or have effect for the purposes of, any of the provisions specified above.   **[358]**

NOTES
Commencement: 1 April 1972.
Repealed in part by the Housing and Planning Act 1986, s 49(2), Sch 12, Part III. See Appendix.

PART IV

Section 28.

Section 54(8).

Section 57.

Section 59.

Sections 61 and 62.

Section 101.

Section 102(1).

Section 103.

Section 126.

Section 277.

Section 280(4).   **[359]**

NOTES
Commencement: 1 April 1972.

PART V

Sections 22 to 25.

Section 29(1), (5) and (6).

Section 30.

Section 31(1).

Sections 32 and 33.

Section 34 except subsection (2).

Sections 35 to 37.

Section 40.

Section 45.

Sections 50 to 53.

Section 54 except subsections (2) and (9) to (11).

Section 60.

Sections 63 to 68.

Section 72.

[Sections 73 to 86.]

Sections 87 to 95.

Section 102.

Sections 104 to 111.

Section 177.   **[360]**

NOTES
    Commencement: 1 April 1972.
    Amended by the Control of Office Development Act 1977, s 4, and by the Housing and Planning
Act 1986, s 49(1), Sch 11, Part I, para 21.See Appendix.
    Repealed in part by the Housing and Planning Act 1986, s 49(2), Sch 12, Part III. See Appendix.

PART VI

Section 28(2)(*b*) and (3).

Section 29(4).

Section 31(2) and (3).

Section 54(2) and (9) to (11).

Section 55.

Section 56.

Section 58.

Sections 96 to 100.

Sections 114 to 117.

Sections 171 to 173.

Section 180(5) and (6).

Section 190.

Schedules 11 and 19.   **[361]**

NOTES
Commencement: 1 April 1972.
Amended by the Housing and Planning Act 1986, s 40, Sch 9, Part I, para 12. See Appendix.

PART VII

Section 24(6).

Section 26 except subsections (2)(*b*) and (3) to (9).

Section 27.

Section 29(2) and (3).

Section 142 except subsections (2)(*b*) and (6)(*b*).

Section 143 (construed as if in section 142 the said subsections were omitted).

Sections 192 to 196.

Sections 198 to 200.

Sections 203 to 207.

Section 242 except subsection (1)(*a*) to (*c*).

Section 243(5).

Section 245.

Sections 247 and 248.

Section 249(2).

Section 266(1) (construed as if the reference to Part III were a reference only to sections 26 and 27) and (6).

Section 274(2) except paragraph (*b*).

Schedule 17.

Any other provisions of this Act in so far as they apply, or have effect for the purposes of, any of the provisions specified above.   **[362]**

NOTES
Commencement: 1 April 1972.

SCHEDULE 22

Section 287(6)

ENACTMENTS EXEMPTED FROM SECTION 287(6) OF THIS ACT

1. Section 107 of the Public Health Act 1936.

[2. The following provisions of the Highways Act 1980:—
section 73(1) to (3), (6) and (9) to (11).
section 74 except subsection (6).
sections 188, 193 and 196.
section 200(2) and (4).
section 241.
section 261(5) and, so far as it relates to (5), (6).
section 307(5) and (7).
Schedule 9.]

[3. The following further provisions of the Highways Act 1980:—

(*a*) sections 187 and 200(1) so far as applicable for the purposes of section 188 of that Act;

(*b*) section 247(6) so far as applicable for the purposes of section 241 of that Act;

(*c*) in section 307—

(i) subsections (1) to (3) so far as applicable for the purposes of section 73 of that Act;

(ii) subsections (1), (3) and (6) so far as applicable for the purposes of section 74 of that Act;
(iii) subsections (1) and (3) so far as applicable for the purposes of sections 193 and 200(2) of that Act;

(*d*) section 311 so far as applicable for the purposes of section 74 of that Act.]

[4. Section 279 of the Highways Act 1980 so far as the purposes in question are the purposes of the exercise—

(*a*) by a county council [or metropolitan district council] in relation to roads maintained by that council; . . .

(*b*) . . .

of their powers under section 73(1) to (3), (6) and (9) to (11) or section 241 of that Act.]

5. Any enactment making such provision as might by virtue of any Act of Parliament have been made in relation to the area to which the order applies by means of a byelaw, order or regulation not requiring confirmation by Parliament.

6. Any enactment which has been previously excluded or modified by a development order, and any enactment having substantially the same effect as any such enactment.
[363]

NOTES
Commencement: 1 January 1981 (paras 2-4); 1 April 1972 (remainder).
This Schedule derived from the Town and Country Planning Act 1962, Sch 11.
Paras 2, 3: substituted by the Highways Act 1980, s 343, Sch 24.
Para 4: substituted by the Highways Act 1980, s 343, Sch 24; words omitted repealed by the Local Government Act 1985, ss 8, 102, Sch 4, para 50(*c*), Sch 17.

LOCAL GOVERNMENT ACT 1972
(c 70)

An Act to make provision with respect to local government and the functions of local authorities in England and Wales; to amend Part II of the Transport Act 1968; to confer rights of appeal in respect of decisions relating to licences under the Home Counties (Music and Dancing) Licensing Act 1926; to make further provision with respect to magistrates' courts committees; to abolish certain inferior courts of record; and for connected purposes   [26 October 1972]

PART IX

FUNCTIONS

The environment

182. Town and country planning

(1) . . .

(2) In England (exclusive of [the metropolitan counties,] Greater London and the Isles of Scilly) and in Wales all functions conferred on local planning authorities by or under the Town and Country Planning Act 1971 shall, subject to subsection (4) and section 183 below and to Part I of Schedule 16 to this Act, be exercisable both by county planning authorities and by district planning authorities.

(3) In that Schedule—

(*a*) Part I shall have effect with respect to the exercise by such authorities of functions under that Act and for making minor amendments and modifications of that Act;

(b) Part II shall have effect with respect to the exercise by such authorities of functions under other enactments relating to town and country planning and for making minor amendments and modifications of such other enactments; and

(c) Part III shall have effect with respect to arrangements for obtaining advice in connection with certain of those functions.

(4) As respects an area in a National Park [outside a metropolitan county] all functions conferred by or under the Town and Country Planning Act 1971 on a local planning authority or district planning authority shall, subject to the provisions of subsections (5) and (6) below, be functions of the county planning authority and no other authority, and references in that Act, in its application to a National Park [outside a metropolitan county], to a local planning authority or district planning authority shall be construed accordingly.

(5) The functions conferred on a local planning authority by the following provisions of that Act, that is to say, sections 60, 61, 62 and 103 (tree preservation and replacement), and section 65 (waste land) shall, as respects any part of a National Park [outside a metropolitan county], be exercisable concurrently with the county planning authority by the district planning authority whose area includes that part of the Park.

(6) Where an order is made under section 7 of the National Parks and Access to the Countryside Act 1949 designating, or extending the area of, a National Park, the functions exercisable by a local planning authority immediately before the coming into force of the order for any area which under the order becomes part of the Park shall continue to be exercisable by that authority as respects that area unless and until a joint planning board is constituted under section 1 of the Town and Country Planning Act 1971 or a National Park Committee is appointed under Part I of Schedule 17 to this Act for an area co-terminous with or including that area or, as the case may be, is authorised to exercise those functions. [364]

NOTES

Commencement: 26 October 1972 (certain purposes); 1 April 1974 (remainder).

Sub-s (1): amends the Town and Country Planning Act 1971, s 1(1), (2); repealed in part by the Housing and Planning Act 1986, s 49(2), Sch 12, Part III. See Appendix.

Sub-ss (2), (4), (5): amended by the Local Government Act 1985, ss 3(5), 7, Sch 3, para 3.

Sub-s (5): amended by the Housing and Planning Act 1986, s 49(1), Sch 11, Part I, para 22. See Appendix.

183. Discharge of functions of planning authorities

(1) The functions of a local planning authority under sections 6 to 10 of the Town and Country Planning Act 1971 (surveys and structure plans) shall be exercisable by the county planning authority and references in those sections to a local planning authority shall be construed accordingly.

(2), (3) . . . [365]

NOTES

Commencement: 26 October 1972 (certain purposes); 1 April 1974 (remainder).

Sub-s (2): amends the Town and Country Planning Act 1971; prospectively repealed by the Housing and Planning Act 1986, s 49(2), Sch 12, Part III. See Appendix.

Sub-s (3): repealed by the Local Government, Planning and Land Act 1980, s 89, Sch 14, para 16.

184. National Park and countryside functions

(1) The functions conferred on a local planning authority by or under the National Parks and Access to the Countryside Act 1949 and the Countryside Act 1968 shall, as respects England elsewhere than [in the metropolitan

counties,] Greater London and the Isles of Scilly and as respects Wales, be exercisable in accordance with the following provisions of this section.

(2) The following of the said functions, that is to say those conferred by—

(a) Part II and sections 61, 62, 63, 78, 90(5), 92 (so far as relating to parking places in a National Park), 99(3) and 101(3) of the said Act of 1949; and

(b) sections 12(5), 13 and 14 of the said Act of 1968;

shall, subject to subsection (3) below and Schedule 17 to this Act, be functions of the county planning authority.

(3) The functions of a local planning authority under sections 9 and 11 of the said Act of 1949 shall as respects any area outside a National Park be exercisable both by county planning authorities and district planning authorities.

(4) All other functions conferred by or under any other provision of the said Acts of 1949 and 1968 on a local planning authority shall, subject to Schedule 17 of this Act, be exercisable both by county planning authorities and district planning authorities.

(5) References in the said Acts of 1949 and 1968 to a local planning authority shall be construed accordingly.

(6) Part I of Schedule 17 to this Act shall have effect instead of section 8 of the said Act of 1949 (which, as amended by Schedule 4 to the said Act of 1968, provides for the administration of local authorities' planning and countryside functions in National Parks).

(7) Sections 27 to 38 of the said Act of 1949 and Parts II to IV of Schedule 3 to the said Act of 1968 (survey of public paths, etc.) shall have effect subject to the modifications specified in Part II of the said Schedule 17 and those Acts shall have effect subject to the further modifications specified in Part III of that Schedule.

(8) In that Schedule "the 1949 Act" and "the 1968 Act" mean the said Acts of 1949 and 1968 respectively.   **[366]**

NOTES
Commencement: 1 April 1974.
Sub-s (1): amended by the Local Government Act 1985, s 7, Sch 3, para 3.

SCHEDULES
SCHEDULE 16

Section 182

FUNCTIONS UNDER, AND AMENDMENT AND MODIFICATION OF, ENACTMENTS RELATING
TO TOWN AND COUNTRY PLANNING

PART I

TOWN AND COUNTRY PLANNING ACT 1971

Structure and local plans

1–5 . . .

6. In Part I of Schedule 5 in its application outside Greater London for references to the local planning authority there shall be substituted references to th county planning authority.

7. The local planning authority who are to be treated by paragraph 4 of Schedule 7

as having adopted any street authorisation map mentioned in that paragraph shall be the county planning authority.

Joint plans

8.—(1) The following provisions of this paragraph shall have effect where two or more county planning authorities prepare a structure plan jointly.

(2) The county planning authorities shall take such steps as will in their opinion secure—

(a) that persons who may be expected to desire an opportunity of making representations to any of the authorities are made aware that they are entitled to an opportunity of doing so;

(b) that such persons are given an adequate opportunity of making such representations.

(3) Section 8(1)(b) and (c) shall not apply in relation to a joint structure plan and references in section 8 to subsection (1) of that section and the purposes of paragraphs (a) to (c) thereof shall include references respectively to sub-paragraph (2) above and the purposes of paragraphs (a) and (b) thereof.

(4) Each of the county planning authorities by whom a joint structure plan has been prepared shall have the duty imposed by section 8(2) of making copies of the plan available for inspection.

9.[(1) Where a structure plan has been prepared jointly, the power of making proposals under section 10 for the alteration or for the repeal and replacement of the plan may be exercised as respects their respective areas by any of the authorities by whom it was prepared, and the Secretary of State may under that section direct any of them to submit such proposals as respects their respective areas.]

(2) . . .

10.—(1) The following provisions of this paragraph shall have effect where two or more local planning authorities prepare a local plan jointly.

[(2) The local planning authorities shall jointly take such steps as will in their opinion secure—

(a) that adequate publicity is given in their areas to the matters proposed to be inclined in the plan;

(b) that persons who may be expected to desire an opportunity of making representations to any of the authorities are made aware that they are entitled to an opportunity of doing so; and

(c) that such persons are given an adequate opportunity of making such representations.

(3) The local planning authorities shall consider any representations made to them within the prescribed period.

(3A) Subsection (1) of section 12 shall not apply in relation to joint local plans.

(3B) References in subsections (3) and (4) of that section to subsection (1) of that section and to the purposes of paragraphs (a) to (c) of that subsection shall include references respectively to sub-paragraph (2) above and the purposes of paragraphs (a) to (c) of that sub-paragraph.]

(4) Each of the local planning authorities by whom a joint local plan has been prepared shall have the duty imposed by section 12(2) of making copies of the plan available for inspection, and objections to the plan may be made to any of those authorities and the statement required by section 12(2) to accompany copies of the plan made available for inspection shall state that objections may be so made.

11.—(1) It shall fall to each of the local planning authorities by whom a joint local plan was prepared to adopt the plan under section 14(1) and they may do so as respects any part of their area to which the plan relates, but any modifications subject to which it is adopted must be agreed between all those authorities.

(2) Where a structure plan has been jointly prepared by two or more county planning authorities or a local plan has been jointly prepared by two or more district planning authorities, a request for a certificate under section 14(5) that the local plan conforms generally to the structure plan shall be made by each district planning authority to the county planning authority for the area comprising the district planning authority's area and it shall fall to that county planning authority to deal with the request.

12.—(1) Where a local plan has been prepared jointly, the power of [making] proposals under section 15(1) for the alteration, repeal or replacement of the plan may be exercised as respects their respective areas by any of the authorities by whom it was prepared and the Secretary of State may under that subsection direct any of them to [make] such proposals as respects their respective areas.

(2) In relation to the joint [making] of such proposals the reference in section 15(3) (as it has effect outside Greater London) to section 12 shall include a reference to paragraph 10 above.

13. The date appointed under section 18(4) for the coming into operation of a local plan prepared jointly by two or more local planning authorities or for the alteration, repeal or replacement of a local plan in pursuance of proposals so prepared shall be one jointly agreed by those authorities and be specified in their respective resolutions adopting the plan.

14.—(1) Paragraph 10(3) and (4) above shall not, and the following provisions of this paragraph shall, apply in Greater London.

(2) . . .

(3) Sub-paragraph (1)(*b*) and (*c*) of paragraph 12 of that Schedule shall not apply in relation to joint local plans and the reference in sub-paragraph (3) of that paragraph to sub-paragraph (1) of that paragraph, and the reference in paragraph 14(2) to sub-paragraph (1)(*a*) to (*c*) of the said paragraph 12, shall both include a reference to paragraph 10(2) above.

(4) . . .

(5) Each of the local planning authorities by whom a joint local plan has been prepared for any part of Greater London shall have the duty imposed by sub-paragraph (2) of the said paragraph 12 of making copies of the plan available for inspection, and objections to the plan may be made to any of those authorities and the statement required by sub-paragraph (3) of that paragraph to accompany copies of the plan made available for inspection shall state that objections may be so made.

(6) In relation to the joint submission of proposals under section 15(1) for the alteration, repeal or replacement of a local plan the reference in section 15(3) (as it has effect in Greater London) to the said paragraph 12 shall include a reference to paragraph 10 above and the foregoing provisions of this paragraph.

Planning and special control

15.—(1) The functions of a local planning authority of determining—

    (*a*) applications for planning permission under Part III;
    (*b*) applications for determining under section 53 whether an application for such permission is required;
    (*c*) applications for an established use certificate under section 94;

shall, subject to sub-paragraph (2) below be exercised by the district planning authority.

(2) The functions of a local planning authority of determining any such application as aforesaid which appears to the district planning authority to relate to a county matter shall be exercised by the county planning authority . . .

[(3) Every application mentioned in sub-paragraph (1) above shall be made to the district planning authority.

(3A) The district planning authority shall send to the county planning authority, as soon as may be and in any case not later than seven days after they have received it, a copy of any application for planning permission which appears to them to relate to a county matter.

(3B) Subject to sub-paragraph (3C) below, the district planning authority shall send to the local highway authority, as soon as may be after they have received it, a copy of any application for planning permission which does not appear to them to relate to a county matter.

(3C) If the local highway authority specifies any case or class of case in which a copy of such an application as is mentioned in sub-paragraph (3B) above need not be sent to them, the duty imposed on the district planning authority by that sub-paragraph shall not extend to any application to which the direction relates.]

(4) The foregoing provisions of this paragraph shall not apply to applications relating to land in a National Park, but paragraph 16 below shall apply to such applications instead.

16.—(1) Each of the following applications under the Town and Country Planning Act 1971, that is to say—

(a) applications for planning permission;
(b) applications for determining under section 53 whether an application for such permission is required;
(c) applications for listed building consent under section 55;
(d) applications for consent to the display of advertisements under section 63; and
(e) applications for an established use certificate under section 94;

shall, if relating to land in a National Park, be made to the district planning authority who shall, unless it falls to be determined by them, send it on to the county planning authority and, in the case of an application for planning permission, shall send a copy to the local highway authority, except where the local highway authority are a local planning authority and except in any case or class of case with respect to which the local highway authority otherwise direct.

(2) Where any such application relating to land in a National Park or an application so relating for approval of a matter reserved under an outline planning permission within the meaning of section 42 falls to be determined by a county planning authority, that authority shall before determining it consult with the district planning authority for the area in which the land to which the application relates is situated.

17. The Secretary of State shall include in a development order under section 24 provision enabling a local highway authority to impose restrictions on the grant by the local planning authority of planning permission for the following descriptions of development relating to land in the area of the local highway authority, that is to say—

(a) the formation, laying out or alteration of any means of access to a road classified under [section 12(3) of the Highways Act 1980 or] section 27 of the Local Government Act 1966 or to a proposed road the route of which has been adopted by resolution of the local highway authority and notified as such to the local planning authority;
(b) any other operations or use of land which appear to the local highway authority to be likely to result in a material increase in the volume of traffic entering or leaving such a classified or proposed road, to prejudice the improvement or construction of such a road or to result in a material change in the character of traffic entering, leaving or using such a road.

18. The provisions which may be contained in any such order shall include provision—

(a) requiring a county planning authority who are determining any application mentioned in paragraph 15 above and relating to a county matter, or an application for approval of a matter reserved under an outline planning permission within the meaning of section 42 and so relating, to afford the district planning authority for the area in which the land to which the application relates is situated an opportunity to make recommendations to the county planning authority as to the manner in which the application shall be determined, and to take into account any such recommendations;

(b) requiring a county or district planning authority who have received any application so mentioned or any application for such approval (including any such application relating to land in a National Park) to notify the district or county planning authority, as the case may be, of the terms of their decision, or, where the application is referred to the Secretary of State, the date when it was so referred and, when notified to them, the terms of his decision.

[19.—(1) Subject to sub-paragraph (3) below, the district planning authority shall consult the county planning authority for their area before determining any application to which this sub-paragraph applies.

(2) Sub-paragraph (1) above applies to any application for planning permission for the carrying out—

(a) of any development of land which would materially conflict with or prejudice the implementation—

(i) of any policy or general proposal contained in a structure plan which has been approved by the Secretary of State;
(ii) of any policy or general proposal contained in a structure plan which has been submitted to the Secretary of State for approval;
(iii) of any proposal to include in a structure plan any matter to which the county planning authority have given publicity under section 8 (publicity in connection with preparation of structure plans) or under that section as applied by section 10 (alteration of structure plans);
(iv) of a fundamental provision of a development plan which has been approved by the Secretary of State (whether under Part I of Schedule 5 or under any enactment replaced by that Part of that Schedule) so far as the development plan is in force in the district planning authority's area;
(v) of any proposal contained in a local plan which has been prepared by the county planning authority (whether or not the plan has been adopted by the authority or approved by the Secretary of State);
(vi) of any proposal to include in a local plan which the county planning authority are preparing any matter to which they have given publicity under section 12 (publicity in connection with preparation of local plans);
(vii) of any proposal to include in alterations which the county planning authority are proposing for a local plan any matter to which they have given publicity under the said section 12 as applied by section 15 (publicity in connection with alteration of local plans);

(b) of any development of land which would, by reason of its scale or nature the location of the land, be of major importance for the implementation of a structure plan which has been approved by the Secretary of State;
(c) of any development of land in an area which the county planning authority have notified to the district planning authority, in writing, as an area in which development is likely to affect or be affected by the winning and working of minerals, other than coal;
(d) of any development of land which the county planning authority have notified the district planning authority, in writing, that they themselves propose to develop;
(e) of any development of land which would prejudice the carrying out of development proposed by the county planning authority and notified to the district planning authority under paragraph (d) above;
(f) of any development of land in England in respect of which the county planning authority have notified the district planning authority, in writing, that it is proposed that it shall be used for waste disposal;
(g) of any development of land which would prejudice a proposed use of land for waste disposal notified to the district planning authority under paragraph (f) above.

(3) The district planning authority may determine an application to which sub-paragraph (1) above applies without the consultation required by that sub-paragraph if the county planning authority have given them directions authorising them to do so.

(4) A direction under sub-paragraph (3) above may relate to a class of applications or to a particular application.

(5) Subject to sub-paragraph (6) below, where the district planning authority are required to consult the county planning authority before determining an application for planning permission—

(a) they shall give the county planning authority notice that they propose to consider the application and send them a copy of it; and

(b) they shall not determine it until the expiration of such period from the date of the notice as a development order may provide.

(6) A district planning authority may determine an application for planning permission before the expiration of such a period as is mentioned in sub-paragraph (5)(*b*) above—

(a) if they have received representations concerning the application from the county planning authority before the expiration of that period; or

(b) if the county planning authority have notified them that they do not wish to make representations.

(7) Where a district planning authority are required to consult the county planning authority before determining an application for planning permission, they shall in determining it take into account any representations relating to it which they have received from the county planning authority before the expiration of the period mentioned in sub-paragraph (5)(*b*) above.

(8) In this paragraph "development order" has the meaning assigned to it by section 24 of the Town and Country Planning Act 1971.]

20.—(1) Where a district planning authority [or, in a metropolitan county, a local planning authority] have been notified in writing by the council of a parish or community wholly or partly situated in the area of that authority that the council wish to be informed of every application for planning permission relating to land in the parish or community or of every application so relating for approval of a matter reserved under an outline planning permission within the meaning of section 42, or of any description of such applications, and receive any such application or, as the case may be, an application of any such description, they shall inform the council in writing of the application, indicating the nature of the development to which the application relates and identifying the land to which it relates.

(2) The provisions which may be contained in a development order under section 24 shall include provision requiring—

(a) a local planning authority, who are determining any application of which the council of a parish or community are entitled to be informed, to afford that council an opportunity to make representations to the local planning authority as to the manner in which the application should be determined and to take into account any such representations;

(b) the district planning authority [or, in a metropolitan county, a local planning authority] to notify that council of the terms of their or [, in a non-metropolitan county,] the county planning authority's decision on any such application or, where the application is referred to the Secretary of State, the date when it was so referred and, when notified to them, the terms of his decision.

21.—(1) In section 28(2) (publicity for applications affecting conservation areas), for the words "The local planning authority" there shall be substituted the words "In Greater London the local planning authority, in a National Park the county planning authority and elsewhere the district planning authority".

(2) Where it is the duty of the district planning authority to take the steps required by section 28(2) in relation to an application which falls to be determined by the county planning authority, the district planning authority shall as soon as may be after taking those steps notify the county planning authority of the steps which they have taken and the date on which they took them.

22 . . .

23. Elsewhere than in a National Park the functions of a local planning authority under section 44 (completion notices) shall be exercisable by the district planning authority, except that where the relevant planning permission was granted by the county planning authority, those functions, so far as relating to that permission, shall be exercisable by the county planning authority and also by the district planning authority after consulting the county planning authority.

24.—(1) The functions of a local planning authority of—

(a) making orders under section 45 revoking or modifying planning permission, or under section 51 requiring discontinuance of use, or imposing conditions on continuance of use, or requiring the alteration or removal of buildings or works, or

[(b) issuing enforcement notices under section 87 or serving stop notices under section 90,]

shall, subject to [sub-paragraphs (2) to (4)] below, be exercisable by the district planning authority.

(2) In a case where it appears to the district planning authority that the functions mentioned in sub-paragraph (1) above relate to county matters they shall not exercise those functions without first consulting the county planning authority.

(3) [Subject to sub-paragraph (4) below, those] functions shall also be exercisable by a county planning authority in a case where it appears to that authority that they relate to a matter which should properly be considered a county matter.

[(4) In relation to a matter which is a county matter by virtue of any of the provisions of paragraph 32(a) to (cd) below the functions of a local planning authority specified in sub-paragraph (1)(b) above shall only be exercisable by the county planning authority in their capacity as mineral planning authority.]

25.—(1) . . . the functions of a local planning authority under sections 34 (registers of applications and decisions), sections 55, 56, 96, 99 and Schedule 11 (listed buildings) and sections 63 and 109 (control of advertisements) shall be exercised by the district planning authority.

(2) . . .

26.—(1) Sections 48 and 49 (planning inquiry commissions) shall be amended in accordance with sub-paragraphs (2) and (3) below.

(2) The copy of the notice required to be served by section 49(2) on a local planning authority shall, in the case of a proposal that a government department should give a direction under section 40 or that development should be carried out by or on behalf of a government department, be served on the local planning authority who, in the opinion of the Secretary of State, would have been responsible for dealing with an application for planning permission for the development in question if such an application had fallen to be made.

(3) References in sections 48(6)(b) and 49(3) to the local planning authority shall be construed as references to the local planning authority on whom the said copy is required to be served.

27. Where a county planning authority or district planning authority have made a tree preservation order under section 60 or the Secretary of State has made such an order by virtue of section 276 (default powers), the power of varying and revoking the order and the powers of dispensing with section 62, or serving, or appearing on an appeal relating to, a notice under section 103 (enforcement of duties as to replacement of trees) shall be exercisable only by the authority who made the order or, in the case of an order made by the Secretary of State, the authority named in the order.

28 . . .

29. In sections 91(1) and 93(4)(b) (enforcement notices) and section 108(2) (enforcement of orders under s. 51 requiring discontinuance of use, etc.) any reference to the local planning authority shall be construed as a reference to the authority who [issued]

the notice or made the order in question or, in the case of a notice [issued] or an order made by the Secretary of State, the authority named in the notice or order.

30 . . .

31. The powers of local authorities under sections 114, 115 and 126 (compulsory acquisition and management of listed buildings) and 119 (acquisition of land by agreement) shall be exercisable by joint planning boards as well as by the local authorities mentioned in those sections.

32. In the foregoing provisions of this Schedule "county matter" means in relation to any application, order or notice—

    (a) the winning and working of minerals in, on or under land (whether by surface or underground working) or the erection of any building, plant or machinery—

        (i) which it is proposed to use in connection with the winning and working of minerals or with their treatment or disposal in or on land adjoining the site of the working; or

        (ii) which a person engaged in mining operations proposes to use in connection with the grading, washing, grinding or crushing of minerals;

    [(aa) the use of land, or the erection of any building, plant or machinery on land, for the carrying out of any process for the preparation or adaptation for sale of any mineral or the manufacture of any article from a mineral where—

        (i) the land forms part of or adjoins a site used or proposed to be used for the winning and working of minerals; or

        (ii) the mineral is, or is proposed to be, brought to the land from a site used, or proposed to be used, for the winning and working of minerals by means of a pipeline, conveyor belt, aerial ropeway, or similar plant or machinery, or by private road, private waterway or private railway;]

    (b) the carrying out of searches and tests of mineral deposits or the erection of any building, plant or machinery which it is proposed to use in connection therewith;

    (c) the disposal of mineral waste;

    [(ca) the use of land for any purpose required in connection with the transport by rail or water of aggregates (that is to say, any of the following, namely—

        (i) sand and gravel;

        (ii) crushed rock;

        (iii) artificial materials of appearance similar to sand, gravel or crushed rock and manufactured or otherwise derived from iron or steel slags, pulverised fuel ash, clay or mineral waste),

or the erection of any building, plant or machinery which it is proposed to use in connection therewith;

    (cb) the erection of any building, plant or machinery which it is proposed to use for the coating of roadstone or the production of concrete or of concrete products or artificial aggregates, where the building, plant or machinery is to be erected in or on land which forms part of or adjoins a site used or proposed to be used—

        (i) for the winning and working or minerals; or

        (ii) for any of the purposes mentioned in sub-paragraph (ca) above;

    (cc) the erection of any building, plant or machinery which it is proposed to use for the manufacture of cement;

    (cd) the carrying out of operations in, on, over or under land, or a use of land, where the land is or forms part of a site used or formerly used for the winning and working of minerals and where the operations or use would conflict with or prejudice compliance with [a restoration condition or an aftercare condition];]

    (d) . . .

    (e) the carrying out of operations, in, on, over or under land, or any use of land, which is situated partly in and partly outside a National Park;

    (f) the carrying out of any operation which is, as respects the area in question, a prescribed operation or an operation of a prescribed class or any use which is, as respects that area, a prescribed use or use of a prescribed class.

[32A. In paragraph 32 above "the winning and working of minerals" includes the extraction of minerals from a mineral-working deposit, as defined in section 264(1A).]

33. . . . .

Compensation

34.—(1) Claims for payment of compensation under the following provisions, that is to say, section 164 (compensation where planning permission is revoked or modified), including that section as applied by section 165, and sections 169, 170, 171, 172, 173, 176 and 177 (compensation in connection with other restrictions) shall, subject to sub-paragraph (3) below, be made to and paid by the local planning authority who took the action by virtue of which the claim arose or, where that action was taken by the Secretary of State, the local planning authority from whom the appeal was made to him or who referred the matter to him, or, in the case of an order made or notice served by him by virtue of section 276 (default powers) the appropriate authority, and references in those sections to a local planning authority shall be construed accordingly.

(2) In this paragraph "appropriate authority" means—

- (a) in the case of a claim for compensation under section 164, 165 or 172, the local planning authority who granted, or are to be treated for the purposes of section 164 as having granted, the planning permission or listed building consent the revocation or modification of which gave rise to the claim;
- (b) in the case of a claim for compensation under section 173 or 176, the district planning authority;
- (c) in the case of a claim for compensation under section 170 or 177, the local planning authority named in the relevant order or stop notice of the Secretary of State.

(3) The Secretary of State may after consultation with all the authorities concerned direct that where a local planning authority is liable to pay compensation under any of the provisions mentioned in sub-paragraph (1) above in any particular case or class of case they shall be entitled to be reimbursed the whole of the compensation or such proportion of it as he may direct from one or more authorities specified in the direction.

35. Claims for payment of compensation under a tree preservation order by virtue of section 174, and claims for payment of compensation under section 175 by virtue of directions given in pursuance of such an order, shall be made to and paid by the local planning authority who made the order or, in the case of an order made by the Secretary of State, the authority named in the order.

36. The local planning authority by whom compensation is to be paid under section 237(1)(a) to statutory undertakers shall be the authority who referred the application for planning permission to the Secretary of State and the appropriate Minister, or from whose decision the appeal was made to them or who served the enforcement notice appealed against, as the case may be.

Purchase notices

37. The duty of the Secretary of State to give a notice under section 182(2)(c) (procedure on purchase notices) to the local planning authority shall be a duty to give it—

- (a) to the county planning authority and also, where that authority is a joint planning board, to the county council; and
- (b) to the district council on whom the purchase notice in question was served and also, where that council is a constituent member of a joint planning board, to that board.

38. The local planning authority by whom compensation is to be paid and on whom a claim for compensation is to be served under section 187(2) (compensation where purchase notice served) shall be the district planning authority.

39–42 . . .

Miscellaneous

43 . . .

45. In section 192(1) (scope of blight provisions), the reference in paragraph (*f*) to the local planning authority shall be construed, in relation to land in a National Park, as a reference to the county planning authority and, in relation to land elsewhere, as a reference to the district planning authority.

46 . . .

47.—(1) The local planning authority to whom the Secretary of State may give directions under section 276(1) (default powers) and whom he is required to consult under that subsection or serve with a notice of his proposals under section 276(4) shall be the county planning authority or the district planning authority, as he thinks appropriate, and references in those subsections to the local planning authority shall be construed accordingly.

(2) In section 276(5) any reference to the local planning authority shall be construed—

(*a*) in relation to a listed building enforcement notice, as a reference to the district planning authority; and

(*b*) in any other case, as a reference to the county planning authority or the district planning authority, as the Secretary of State thinks appropriate

48–50 . . .

51.—(1) The validity of any permission, determination or certificate granted, made or issued or purporting to have been granted, made or issued by a local planning authority in respect of an application mentioned in paragraph 15 or 16 above shall not be called in question in any legal proceedings, or in any proceedings under the Town and Country Planning Act 1971 which are not legal proceedings, on the ground that the permission, determination or certificate should have been granted, made or given by some other local planning authority.

(2) The validity of any order or notice mentioned in paragraph 24 above and purporting to have been made[, issued] or served by a local planning authority shall not be called in question in any such proceedings on the ground—

(*a*) in the case of an order or notice purporting to have been made[, issued] or served by a district planning authority, that they failed to comply with paragraph 24(2) above;

(*b*) in the case of an order or notice purporting to have been made[, issued] or served by a county planning authority, that they had no power to make[, issue] or serve it because it did not relate to a county matter.

52. The foregoing provisions of this Schedule, except paragraphs 10 to 14, 21, 22, 28, 33, 39, 40, 43, 46, . . . and 51, shall not apply to Greater London.

53. In this Part of this Schedule a reference made to any enactment without specifying the Act in which it is contained shall be construed as a reference to a provision of the Town and Country Planning Act 1971.   **[367]**

NOTES

Commencement: 1 April 1974.

Paras 1–5, 21, 22, 28, 33, 39–44, 46, 49: words omitted amend the Town and Country Planning Act 1971; paras 1–3 prospectively repealed by the Housing and Planning Act 1986, s 49(2), Sch 12, Part III. See Appendix.

Para 9: sub-para (1) substituted by the Local Government, Planning and Land Act 1980, s 89, Sch 14, para 17; sub-para (2) repealed by the Local Government (Miscellaneous Provisions) Act 1982, s 47, Sch 7, Part XVI.

Paras 10, 12, 15, 25: amended by the Local Government, Planning and Land Act 1980, ss 86, 89, 90, 194, Sch 14, paras 19, 20, Sch 15, para 15, Sch 34, Part X.

Paras 10–12: new paras 10–12 prospectively substituted except as respects Greater London by the Housing and Planning Act 1986, s 49(1), Sch 11, Part I, para 23(2). See Appendix.

Para 14: sub-paras (2), (4) repealed by the Local Government Act 1985, s 102, Sch 17.

Para 17: amended by the Highways Act 1980, s 343(2), Sch 24, para 22, and by the Housing and Planning Act 1986, s 49(1), Sch 11, Part I, para 2(2). See Appendix.

Para 19: substituted by the Local Government, Planning and Land Act 1980, s 86(2); sub-para (2) prospectively amended by the Housing and Planning Act 1986, s 49(1), Sch 11, Part I, para 23(3). See Appendix.

Para 20: amended by SI 1986 No 452, art 5.

Para 24: first amendment made by the Local Government and Planning (Amendment) Act 1981, s 1, Schedule, para 28; other amendments made by the Town and Country Planning (Minerals) Act 1981, s 2(4).

Paras 29, 51: amended by the Local Government and Planning (Amendment) Act 1981, s 1, Schedule, para 28.

Para 30: repealed by the Local Government and Planning (Amendment) Act 1981, s 1, Schedule, para 28.

Para 32: sub-paras (*aa*), (*ca*) to (*cd*) added and para (*d*) repealed by the Local Government, Planning and Land Act 1980, s 86; para (*cd*) amended by the Town and Country Planning (Minerals) Act 1981, s 34, Sch 1, para 12.

Para 32A: prospectively added by the Town and Country Planning (Minerals) Act 1981, s 2(1), as from a day to be appointed.

Para 48: repealed by the Town and Country Amenities Act 1974, s 13(2), Schedule.

Para 50: repealed by the Local Government Act 1985, s 102, Sch 17.

Para 52: amended by Local Government Act 1985, s 102, Sch 17.

PART II
OTHER ENACTMENTS

The Building Restrictions (War-time Contraventions) Act 1946

54.—(1) Elsewhere than in Greater London [, a metropolitan county] or a National Park the functions conferred by section 2 of the Building Restrictions (War-Time Contraventions) Act 1946 (power to sanction war-time non-compliance with building laws or planning control) on the authority responsible for enforcing planning control shall, subject to sub-paragraph (3) below—

(*a*) in the case of works on, or a use of, land which in the opinion of the district planning authority relates to a county matter as defined by paragraph 32 of this Schedule, be exercised by the county planning authority;

(*b*) in any other case, be exercised by the district planning authority.

(2) [As respects an area in a National Park outside a metropolitan county] the said functions shall be exercised by the county planning authority.

(3) Every application made under section 2(1) of the said Act of 1946 to an authority responsible for enforcing planning control shall be made to the district planning authority who, in the case of an application falling to be determined by the county planning authority, shall send it on to the latter.

(4) A county planning authority determining any such application shall afford the district planning authority for the area in which the land to which the application relates is situated an opportunity to make recommendations to the county planning authority as to the manner in which the application should be determined and shall take any such recommendations into account.

(5) A county or district planning authority who have dealt with any such application shall notify the district or county planning authority, as the case may be, of the terms of their determination or, in a case where the application has been referred to the Secretary of State, the date when it was so referred.

(6) The validity of any determination made by a local planning authority under section 2 of the said Act of 1946 shall not be called in question in any legal proceedings, or in any proceedings under that section which are not legal proceedings, on the ground that the determination should have been made by some other local planning authority.

The Land Compensation Act 1961

55.—(1) Elsewhere than in Greater London [, a metropolitan county] or a National Park the functions of a local planning authority of determining applications and issuing certificates under section 17 of the Land Compensation Act 1961 shall—

(*a*) in the case of an application specifying only a class of development which appears, or classes of development each of which appear, to the district planning authority to relate to a county matter, be exercised by the county planning authority;

(*b*) in any other case, be exercised by the district planning authority.

(2) [As respects an area in a National Park outside a metropolitan county] the said functions shall be exercised by the county planning authority.

(3) Every application mentioned in sub-paragraph (1) above shall be made to the district planning authority who, in the case of an application falling to be determined by the county planning authority, shall send it on to the latter.

(4) A county planning authority determining any such application shall consult with the district planning authority on the question whether planning permission for development of any class which appears to the former not to relate to a county matter [would have been granted if the land in question were not proposed to be acquired by any authority possessing compulsory purchase powers.]

(5) A district planning authority determining any such application shall consult with the county planning authority on the question whether planning permission for development of any class which appears to the former to relate to a county matter [would have been granted if the land in question were not proposed to be acquired by any authority possessing compulsory purchase powers.]

(6) A county planning authority by whom a certificate is issued under section 17 of the Land Compensation Act 1961 shall notify the district planning authority of the terms of the certificate and the district planning authority by whom a certificate is so issued shall, if it specifies development relating to a county matter, notify the county planning authority of the terms of the certificate.

(7) In this paragraph "county matter" has the meaning ascribed to it by paragraph 32 of this Schedule.

56, 57 . . .   **[368]**

NOTES
  Commencement: 1 April 1974.
  Para 54: amended by the Local Government Act 1985, ss 3(5), 7, Sch 3, para 4.
  Para 55: sub-paras (1), (2) amended by the Local Government Act 1985, ss 3(5), 7, Sch 3, para 4; sub-paras (4), (5) amended with savings by the Local Government, Planning and Land Act 1980 s 193, Sch 33, para 13.
  Para 56: repealed by the New Towns Act 1981, s 81, Sch 13.
  Para 57: repealed by the Town and Country Amenities Act 1974, s 13(2), Schedule.

PART III

ARRANGEMENTS FOR OBTAINING ADVICE

58. The Secretary of State may from time to time direct a district planning authority to submit to him for his approval within a period specified in the direction the arrangements which the authority propose to make to obtain specialist advice in connection with their functions—

(*a*) under section 55, 56, 58, 96 or 99 of, or Schedule 11 to, the Town and Country Planning Act 1971;
(*b*) under section 277 of that Act; or
(*c*) under section 8 of the Town and Country Planning (Amendment) Act 1972.

59. If the Secretary of State is not satisfied about any arrangements mentioned in paragraph 58 above, he may after consultation with the district planning authority and the other authority concerned—

(*a*) direct the district planning authority and another local planning authority specified in the direction to enter into an agreement under section 113 above for the placing at the disposal of the former, for the purpose of giving them any such specialist advice as in mentioned in that paragraph, of the services of officers employed by the latter who are qualified to give such advice; or

(b) direct the district planning authority and another local planning authority so specified to enter into arrangements for the discharge by the latter of any of the functions mentioned in that paragraph and also direct that the arrangements shall contain terms so specified or terms on lines laid down by him. **[369]**

NOTES
Commencement: 1 April 1974.

LAND COMPENSATION ACT 1973
(c 26)

ARRANGEMENT OF SECTIONS

PART V
PLANNING BLIGHT

Extension of classes of blighted land

An Act to confer a new right to compensation for depreciation of the value of interests in land caused by the use of highways, aerodromes and other public works; to confer powers for mitigating the injurious effect of such works on their surroundings; to make new provision for the benefit of persons displaced from land by public authorities; to amend the law relating to compulsory purchase and planning blight; to amend section 35 of the Roads (Scotland) Act 1970; and for purposes connected with those matters [23 May 1973]

PART V

PLANNING BLIGHT

Extension of classes of blighted land

68. Land affected by proposed structure

(1) In paragraph (*a*) of section 192(1) of the Act of 1971 (land indicated in a structure plan in force for the relevant district as land which may be required for the purposes of functions of public authorities or as land which may be included in an action area) the reference to a structure plan in force shall include a reference to—

    (*a*) a structure plan which has been submitted to the Secretary of State under section 7 of that Act;

    (*b*) proposals for alterations to a structure plan which have been submitted to the Secretary of State under section 10 of that Act;

    (*c*) modifications proposed to be made by the Secretary of State in any such plan or proposals as are mentioned in the preceding paragraphs, being modifications of which he has given notice in accordance with regulations under Part II of that Act.

(2) In paragraph (*b*) of the said section 192(1) (land allocated for the purposes of functions of public authorities by a local plan in force for the relevant district and land defined in such a plan as the site of proposed development for the purposes of any such functions) the references to a local plan in force shall include a reference to—

    (*a*) a local plan of which copies have been made available for inspection under section 12(2) of the Act of 1971;

    (*b*) proposals for alterations to a local plan of which copies have been made available for inspection under section 15(3) of that Act;

    (*c*) modifications proposed to be made by the local planning authority or the Secretary of State in any such plan or proposals as are mentioned in the preceding paragraphs, being modifications of which notice has been given by the authority or the Secretary of State in accordance with regulations under Part II of that Act.

(3) In section 138(1)(*b*) of the town and Country Planning Act 1962 as it has effect by virtue of paragraph 58 of Schedule 24 to the Act of 1971 (provisions corresponding to section 192(1)(*b*) of the Act of 1971 pending coming into force of local plans) the reference to a development plan shall include a reference to—

    (*a*) proposals for alterations to a development plan submitted to the Secretary of State under paragraph 3 or 9 of Schedule 5 to the Act of 1971;

    (*b*) modifications proposed to be made by the Secretary of State in any such proposals, being modifications of which notice has been given by the Secretary of State by advertisement.

(4) No blight notice shall be served by virtue of subsection (1) or (2) above at any time after the copies of the plan or proposals made available for inspection have been withdrawn under—

    (*a*) section 8(6) or 12(5) of the Act of 1971 (directions by Secretary of State requiring further publicity); or

    (*b*) section 10B of that Act (withdrawal of structure plans);

but so much of the said section 10B as provides that a structure plan which has been withdrawn shall be treated as never having been submitted shall not invalidate any blight notice served by virtue of subsection (1)(*a*) above before the withdrawal of the structure plan.

(5) No blight notice shall be served by virtue of this section after the relevant plan or alterations have come into force (whether in their original form or with modifications) or the Secretary of State has decided to reject or, in the case of a local plan, the local planning authority have decided to abandon the plan or alterations and notice of the decision has been given by advertisement.

(6) Where an appropriate authority have served a counter-notice objecting to a blight notice served by virtue of this section, then, if the relevant plan or alterations come into force (whether in their original form or with modifications) the appropriate authority may serve on the claimant, in substitution for the counter-notice already served, a further counter-notice specifying different grounds of objection, and section 195 of the Act of 1971 (reference of objections to Lands Tribunal) shall have effect in relation to the further counter-notice as it has effect in relation to the counter-notice already served;

Provided that a further counter-notice under this subsection shall not be served—

    (*a*) at any time after the end of the period of two months beginning with the date on which the relevant plan or alterations come into force; or
    (*b*) if the objection in the counter-notice already served has been withdrawn or the Lands Tribunal has already determined whether or not to uphold that objection.

(7) References in subsections (1) to (3) above to anything done under any of the provisions there mentioned include references to anything done under those provisions as they apply by virtue of section 17 of, or paragraph 4 of of the provisions there mentioned include references to anything done under those provisions as they apply by virtue of section 17 of, or paragraph 4 of Schedule 5 to, the Act of 1971 (default powers of Secretary of State).

(8) In the application of this section to Greater London—

    (*a*) the reference to section 10 of the Act of 1971 shall include a reference to paragraph 6 of Schedule 4 to that Act;
    (*b*) for the reference to section 12(2) of that Act there shall be substituted a reference to paragraphs 12(2) and 13(2) of that Schedule;
    (*c*) for the reference to section 12(5) of that Act there shall be substituted a reference to paragraph 14(3) of that Schedule;
    (*d*) for the reference to section 15(3) of that Act there shall be substituted a reference to the said section 15(3) as substituted by paragraph 16(1), and to paragraph 16(4), of that Schedule.

(9) In this section references to alterations to a local plan include references to its replacement, and references to alterations to a development plan include references to additions to it.

(10) In relation to land falling within section 192(1)(*b*) of the Act of 1971 or section 138(1)(*b*) of the Town and Country Planning Act 1962, as extended by this section, "the appropriate enactment" for the purposes of sections 192 to 207 of the Act of 1971 shall be determined in accordance with section 206(2) of that Act as if references therein to the development plan were references to any such plan, proposed or modifications as are mentioned in subsection (2)(*a*), (*b*) or (*c*) and subsection (3)(*a*) or (*b*) above.   **[370]**

NOTES

Commencement: 23 May 1973.

Act of 1971: Town and Country Planning Act 1971.

69. Land affected by proposed highway orders

[(1) In section 192(1)(*d*) of the Act of 1971 (land on or adjacent to line of highway proposed to be constructed etc. as indicated in an order or scheme which has come into operation under the provisions of Part II of the Highways Act 1980 relating to trunk roads, special roads or classified roads, or under the corresponding provisions of Part II of the Highways Act 1959 or section 1 of the Highways Act 1971) the reference to an order or scheme which has come into operation as aforesaid shall include a reference to—

 (*a*) an order or scheme which has been submitted for confirmation to, or prepared in draft by, the Minister of Transport or the Secretary of State under the provisions of Part II of the said Act of 1980 relating to trunk roads, special roads or classified roads and in respect of which a notice has been published under paragraph 1, 2 or 10 of Schedule 1 to that Act;

 (*b*) an order or scheme under Part II of the Highways Act 1959 or section 1 of the Highways Act Highways Act 1959 or section 1 of the Highways Act 1971, being an order or scheme which corresponds to any such order or scheme as is mentioned in paragraph (*a*) above and which has been submitted for confirmation to, or been prepared in draft by, the Minister of Transport or the Secretary of State and in respect of which a notice has been published under paragraph 1, 2 or 7 of Schedule 1 to the said Act of 1959.]

(2) No blight notice shall be served by virtue of this section at any time after the relevant order or scheme has come into operation (whether in its original form or with modifications) or the Secretary of State has decided not to confirm or make the order or scheme.

(3) Subsection (6) of section 68 above shall have effect in relation to a blight notice served by virtue of this section as it has effect in relation to a blight notice served by virtue of that section taking references to the relevant plan or alterations as references to the relevant order or scheme.   **[371]**

NOTES

 Commencement: 1 January 1981 (sub-s (1)); 23 May 1973 (remainder).
 Sub-s (1): substituted by the Highways Act 1980, s 343(2), Sch 24, para 23.
 Act of 1971: Town and Country Planning Act 1971.

70. Land affected by proposed compulsory purchase orders

(1) Section 192(1)(*g*) and (*j*) of the Act of 1971 (land in respect of which a compulsory purchase order is in force where a notice to treat has not been served) shall apply also to land in respect of which a compulsory purchase order has been submitted for confirmation to, or been prepared in draft by, a Minister and in respect of which a notice has been published under paragraph 3(1)(*a*) of Schedule 1 to the Acquisition of Land (Authorisation Procedure) Act 1946 or under any corresponding enactment applicable thereto.

(2) No blight notice shall be served by virtue of this section at any time after the relevant compulsory purchase order has come into force (whether in its original form or with modifications) or the Minister concerned has decided not to confirm or make the order.

(3) In relation to land falling within the said section 192(1)(*g*) or (*j*) by virtue of this section "the appropriate enactment" for the purposes of sections

192 to 207 of the Act of 1971 shall be the enactment which would provide for the compulsory acquisition of the land or of the rights over the land if the relevant compulsory purchase order were confirmed or made. **[372]**

NOTES
Commencement: 23 May 1973.
Act of 1971: Town and Country Planning Act 1971.

71. Land affected by resolution of planning authority or directions of Secretary of State

(1) Section 192(1) of the Act of 1971 shall have effect as if the land specified therein included land which—

(*a*) is land indicated in a plan (not being a development plan) approved by a resolution passed by a local planning authority for the purpose of the exercise of their powers under Part III of that Act as land which may be required for the purposes of any functions of a government department, local authority or statutory undertakers; or

(*b*) is land in respect of which a local planning authority have resolved to take action to safeguard it for development for the purposes of any such functions or been directed by the Secretary of State to restrict the grant of planning permission in order to safeguard it for such development.

(2) Paragraph (*a*) of the said section 192(1) shall not apply to land within subsection (1) above.

(3) In relation to land falling within subsection (1) above "the appropriate enactment" for the purposes of sections 192 to 207 of the Act of 1971 shall be determined in accordance with section 206(2) of that Act as if references therein to the development plan were references to the resolution or direction in question. **[373]**

NOTES
Commencement: 23 May 1973.
Act of 1971: Town and Country Planning Act 1971.

72. Land affected by orders relating to new towns

(1) Section 192(1) of the Act of 1971 shall have effect as if the land specified therein included land which—

(*a*) is land within an area described as the site of a proposed new town in the draft of an order in respect of which a notice has been published under paragraph 2 of Schedule 1 to the [New Towns Act 1981]; or

(*b*) is land within an area designated as the site of a proposed new town by an order which has come into operation under section 1 of the said [Act of 1981].

(2) No blight notice shall be served by virtue of subsection (1) (*a*) above at any time after the order there mentioned has come into operation (whether in the form of the draft or with modifications) or the Secretary of State has decided not to make the order.

(3) Until such time as a development corporation is established for the new town, sections 192 to 207 of the Act of 1971 shall have effect in relation to land within subsection (1) above as if "the appropriate authority" and "the appropriate enactment" were the Secretary of State and subsection (4) below respectively.

(4) Until such time as aforesaid the Secretary of State shall have power to acquire compulsorily any interest in land in pursuance of a blight notice served by virtue of subsection (1) above; and where he acquires an interest as aforesaid, then—

    (*a*) if the land is or becomes land within subsection (1) (*b*) above, the interest shall be transferred by him to the development corporation established for the new town; and

    (*b*) in any other case, the interest may be disposed of by him in such manner as he thinks fit.

(5) The Land Compensation Act 1961 shall have effect in relation to the compensation payable in respect of the acquisition of an interest by the Secretary of State under subsection (4) above as if the acquisition were by a development corporation under the [New Towns Act 1981] and as if, in the case of land within subsection (1) (*a*) above, the land formed part of an area designated as the site of a new town by an order which has come into operation under section 1 of the said [Act of 1981].

(6) . . .   [374]

NOTES
    Commencement: 23 May 1973.
    Sub-ss (1), (5): amended by the New Towns Act 1981, s 81, Sch 12.
    Sub-s (6): repealed by the New Towns Act 1982, s 81, Sch 13.
    Act of 1971: Town and Country Planning Act 1971.

73. Land affected by slum clearance resolution

(1) Section 192(1) of the Act of 1971 shall have effect as if the land specified therein included land which—

    (*a*) is land within an area declared to be a clearance area by a resolution under [section 289 of the Housing Act 1985]; or

    (*b*) is land surrounded by or adjoining an area declared as aforesaid to be a clearance area, being land which a local authority have determined to purchase under [section 290 of that Act].

(2) . . .

(3) In relation to land within subsection (1) above "the appropriate enactment" for the purposes of sections 192 to 207 of the Act of 1971 shall be [section 290 of the Housing Act 1985].

(4) Where an interest in land is acquired in pursuance of a blight notice served by virtue of subsection (1) (*a*) above the compensation payable for the acquisition shall be assessed in accordance with [section 585 of the Housing Act 1985] (site value) and Schedule 2 to the Land Compensation Act 1961 shall not apply.

(5) Where the land in which an interest is acquired as aforesaid comprises a house—

    (*a*) [Part I of Schedule 24 to the Housing Act 1985] (payments in respect of well-maintained houses) shall have effect as if the house had been made the subject of a compulsory purchase order under [section 290] of that Act as being unfit for human habitation;

    (*b*) [Part II of that Schedule] (payments to owner-occupiers) shall have effect as if the house had been purchased at site value in pursuance of a compulsory purchase order made by virtue of the said [section 290];

and references in [that Schedule] to the date of the making of the compulsory purchase order and the date when the house was purchased compulsorily shall be respectively construed as references to the date of service of the blight notice and the date of acquisition in pursuance of that notice. **[375]**

NOTES
Commencement: 23 May 1973.
Amended by the Housing (Consequential Provisions) Act 1985, ss 3, 4, Sch 1, Part I, Sch 2, para 24.
Sub-s (2): repealed by the Housing Act 1974, s 130, Sch 15.
Act of 1971: Town and Country Planning Act 1971.

74. Land affected by proposed exercise of powers under section 22

(1) In section 192(1)(*d*) of the Act of 1971—

(*a*) . . .
(*b*) the reference to land required for purposes of construction, improvement or alteration as indicated in an order or scheme there mentioned shall include a reference to land required for the purposes of [section 246(1) of the Highways Act 1980].

(2) Section 192(1) of the Act of 1971 shall have effect as if the land specified therein included land which—

(*a*) is land shown on plans approved by a resolution of a local highway authority as land propsoed to be acquired by them for the purposes of [the said section 246(1)]; or
(*b*) is land shown in a written notice given by the Secretary of State to the local planning authority as land proposed to be acquired by him for those purposes in connection with a trunk road or special road which he proposes to provide. **[376]**

NOTES
Commencement: 23 May 1973.
Amended by the Highways Act 1980, s 343(2), (3), Sch 24, para 23, Sch 25.
Act of 1971: Town and Country Planning Act 1971.

75. Land affected by compulsory purchase orders providing for acquisition of rights over land

(1) Section 192(1)(*g*) of the Act of 1971 (land in respect of which there is in force a compulsory purchase order made by a highway authority in the exercise of highway land acquisition powers and providing for the acquisition of rights over land) shall apply generally to land in respect of which there is in force a compulsory purchase order providing for the acquisition of a right or rights over that land, and the provisions of that Act mentioned in subsections (2) and (3) below shall accordingly be amended in accordance with those subsections.

(2), (3) . . . **[377]**

NOTES
Commencement: 23 May 1973.
Sub-ss (2), (3): amend the Town and Country Planning Act 1971, ss 192, 194.
Act of 1971: Town and Country Planning Act 1971.

76. Land affected by new street orders

(1) Section 192(1) of the Act of 1971 shall have effect as if the land specified therein included land which—

(*a*) either—

(i) is within the outer lines prescribed by an order under [section 188 of the Highways Act 1980 (or its predecessor, section 159 of the Highways Act 1959)] (orders prescribing minimum width of new streets); or

(ii) has a frontage to a highway declared to be a new street by an order under section 30 of the Public Health Act 1925 and lies within the minimum width of the street prescribed by any byelaws or local Act applicable by virtue of the order; and

(*b*) is, or is part of—

(i) a dwelling erected before, or under construction on, the date on which the order is made; or

(ii) the curtilage of any such dwelling.

(2) The grounds on which objection may be made in a counter-notice to a blight notice served by virtue of subsection (1) above shall not include those specified in section 194(2)(*b*) or (*c*) of the Act of 1971.

(3) In relation to land within subsection (1) above "the appropriate authority" and "the appropriate enactment" for the purposes of sections 192 to 207 of the Act of 1971 shall be the highway authority for the highway in relation to which the order mentioned in that subsection was made and [section 239(6) of the said Act of 1980] respectively.

(4) This section shall not enable a blight notice to be served in respect of any land in which the appropriate authority have previously acquired an interest either in pursuance of a blight notice served by virtue of this section or by agreement in circumstances such that they could have been required to acquire it in pursuance of such a notice.   **[378]**

NOTES
Commencement: 23 May 1973.
Sub-ss (1), (3): amended by the Highways Act 1980, s 343(2), Sch 24, para 23.
Act of 1971: Town and Country Planning Act 1971.

Attempts to sell blighted property

77. Amended requirements about attempts to sell blighted property

(1), (2) . . .

(3) This section does not affect any blight notice served before the passing of this Act.   **[379]**

NOTES
Commencement: 23 May 1973.
Sub-ss (1), (2): amend the Town and Country Planning Act 1971, ss 193, 201.

Blight notices by personal representatives

78. Power of personal representative to serve blight notice

(1) Where the whole or part of a hereditament or agricultural unit is comprised in land of any of the specified descriptions, and a person claims that—

(*a*) he is the personal representative of a person ("the deceased") who at the date of his death was entitled to an interest in that hereditament or unit; and

(b) the interest was one which would have qualified for protection under sections 192 to 207 of the Act of 1971 if a notice under section 193 of that Act had been served in respect thereof on that date; and

(c) he has made reasonable endeavours to sell that interest; and

(d) in consequence of the fact that the hereditament or unit or a part of it was, or was likely to be, comprised in land of any of the specified descriptions, he has been unable to sell that interest except at a price substantially lower than that for which it might reasonably have been expected to sell if no part of the hereditament or unit were, or were likely to be, comprised in such land; and

(e) one or more individuals are (to the exclusion of any body corporate) beneficially entitled to that interest,

he may serve on the appropriate authority a notice in the prescribed form requiring that authority to purchase that interest to the extent specified in, and otherwise in accordance with, the said sections 192 to 207.

(2) Subsection (1) above shall apply in relation to an interest in part of a hereditament or agricultural unit as it applies in relation to an interest in the entirety of a hereditament or agricultural unit:

Provided that this subsection shall not enable any person—

(a) if the deceased was entitled to an interest in the entirety of a hereditament or agricultural unit, to make any claim or serve any notice under this section in respect of the deceased's interest in part of the hereditament or unit; or

(b) if the deceased was entitled to an interest only in part of the hereditament or agricultural unit, to make or serve any such claim or notice in respect of that deceased's interest in less than the entirety of that part.

(3) Subject to sections 73(2) and 76(2) above and 80(2) below, the grounds on which objection may be made in a counter-notice under section 194 of the Act of 1971 to a notice under this section are those specified in paragraphs (a) to (c) of subsection (2) of that section and, in a case to which it applies, the grounds specified in paragraph (d) of that subsection and also the following grounds—

(a) that the claimant is not the personal representative of the deceased or that, on the date of the deceased's death, the deceased was not entitled to an interest in any part of the hereditament or agricultural unit to which the notice relates;

(b) that (for reasons specified in the counter-notice) the interest of the deceased is not such as is specified in subsection (1) (b) above;

(c) that the conditions specified in subsection (1) (c), (d) or (e) above are not fulfilled.

(4) For the purpose of section 201(4) and (5) of the Act of 1971 (which prevent the service of concurrent blight notices under sections 193 and 201 of that Act) a notice served under this section shall be treated as a notice served under the said section 193.

(5) ...

[380]

NOTES

Commencement: 23 May 1973.

Sub-s (5): repealed by the Highways Act 1980, s 343 (3), Sch 25.

Act of 1971: Town and Country Planning Act 1971.

Blight notices in respect of agricultural units

79. Blight notice requiring purchase of whole agricultural unit

(1) Where a blight notice is served in respect of an interest in the whole or part of an agricultural unit and on the date of service that unit or part contains land (hereafter referred to as "the unaffected area") which does not fall within any of the specified descriptions as well as land (hereafter referred to as "the affected area") which does so, the claimant may include in the notice—

(*a*) a claim that the unaffected area is not reasonably capable of being farmed, either by itself or in conjuction with other relevant land, as a separate agricultural unit; and

(*b*) a requirement that the appropriate authority shall purchase his interest in the whole of the unit or, as the case may be, in the whole of the part of it to which the notice relates.

(2) Subect to section 80(3) below, "other relevant land" in subsection (1) above means—

(*a*) land comprised in the remainder of the agricultural unit if the blight notice is served only in respect of part of it;

(*b*) land comprised in any other agricultural unit occupied by the claimant on the date of service, being land in respect of which he is then entitled to an owner's interest as defined in section 203(4) of the Act of 1971.   **[381]**

NOTES
Commencement: 23 May 1973.
Act of 1971: Town and Country Planning Act 1971.

80. Objection to blight notice requiring purchase of whole agricultural unit

(1) The grounds on which objection may be made in a counter-notice to a blight notice served by virtue of section 79 above shall include the grounds that the claim made in the notice is not justified.

(2) Objection shall not be made to a blight notice served by virtue of section 79 above on the grounds mentioned in section 194(2)(*c*) of the Act of 1971 (part only of affected area proposed to be acquired) unless it is also made on the grounds mentioned in subsection (1) above; and the Lands Tribunal shall not uphold an objection to any such notice on the grounds mentioned in the said section 194(2)(*c*) unless it also upholds the objection on the grounds mentioned in subsection (1) above.

(3) Where objection is made to a blight notice served by virtue of section 79 above on the grounds mentioned in subsection (1) above and also on those mentioned in the said section 194(2)(*c*), the Lands Tribunal, in determining whether or not to uphold the objection, shall treat that part of the affected area which is not specified in the counter-notice as included in "other relevant land" as defined in section 79(2) above.

(4) If the Lands Tribunal upholds an objection but only on the grounds mentioned in subsection (1) above, the Tribunal shall declare that the blight notice is a valid notice in relation to the affected area but not in relation to the unaffected area.

(5) If the Tribunal upholds an objection both on the grounds mentioned in subsection (1) above and on the grounds mentioned in the said section 194(2)(*c*) (but not on any other grounds) the Tribunal shall declare that the blight notice

is a valid notice in relation to the part of the affected area specified in the counter-notice as being the part which the appropriate authority propose to acquire as therein mentioned but not in relation to any other part of the affected area or in relation to the unaffected area.

(6) In a case falling within subsection (4) or (5) above, the Tribunal shall give directions specifying a date on which notice to treat (as mentioned in section 81 below and section 196 of the Act of 1971) is to be deemed to have been served.

(7) Section 195(5) of the Act of 1971 shall not apply to any blight notice served by virtue of section 79 above. **[382]**

NOTES
Commencement: 23 May 1973.
Act of 1971: Town and Country Planning Act 1971.

81. Effect of blight notice requiring purchase of whole agricultural unit

(1) In relation to a blight notice served by virtue of section 79 above, subsection (1) of section 196 of the Act of 1971 shall have effect as if for the words "or (in the case of an agricultural unit) the interest of the claimant in so far as it subsists in the affected area" there were substituted the words "or agricultural unit" and subsection (3) of that section shall not apply to any such blight notice.

(2) Where the appropriate authority have served a counter-notice objecting to a blight notice on the grounds mentioned in section 80(1) above, then if either—

(a) the claimant, without referring that objection to the Lands Tribunal, and before the time for so referring it has expired, gives notice to the appropriate authority that he withdraws his claim as to the unaffected area; or

(b) on a reference to the Tribunal, the Tribunal makes a declaration in accordance with section 80(4) above,

the appropriate authority shall be deemed to be authorised to acquire compulsorily under the appropriate enactment the interest of the claimant in so far as it subsists in the affected area (but not in so far as it subsists in the unaffected area) and to have served a notice to treat in respect thereof on the date mentioned in subsection (3) below.

(3) The said date—

(a) in a case falling within paragraph (a) of subsection (2) above, is the date on which notice is given in accordance with that paragraph; and

(b) in a case falling within paragraph (b) of that subsection, is the date specified in directions given by the Tribunal in accordance with section 80(6) above.

(4) Where the appropriate authority have served a counter-notice objecting to a blight notice on the grounds mentioned in section 80(1) above and also on the grounds mentioned in section 194(2)(c) of the Act of 1971 then if either—

(a) the claimant, without referring that objection to the Lands Tribunal, and before the time for so referring it has expired, gives notice to the appropriate authority that he accepts the proposal of the authority to acquire the part of the affected area specified in the counter-notice, and withdraws his claim as to the remainder of that area and as to the unaffected area; or (*b*) on a reference to the Tribunal, the Tribunal makes a declaration in accordance with section 80(5) above in respect of that part of the affected area,

the appropriate authority shall be deemed to be authorised to acquire compulsorily under the appropriate enactment the interest of the claimant in so far as it subsists in the part of the affected area specified in the counter-notice (but not in so far as it subsists in any other part of that area or in the unaffected area) and to have served a notice to treat in respect thereof on the date mentioned in subsection (5) below.

(5) The said date—

(*a*) in a case falling within paragraph (*a*) of subsection (4) above, is the date on which notice is given in accordance with that paragraph; and

(*b*) in a case falling within paragraph (*b*) of that subsection, is the date specified in directions given by the Tribunal in accordance with section 80(6) above.

(6) The compensation payable in respect of the acquisition by virtue of this section of an interest in land comprised in—

(*a*) the unaffected area of an agricultural unit; or

(*b*) if the appropriate authority have served a counter-notice objecting to the blight notice on the grounds mentioned in the said section 194(2)(*c*), so much of the affected area of the unit as is not specified in the counter-notice,

shall be assessed on the assumptions mentioned in section 5(2), (3) and (4) above.

(7) In relation to a blight notice served by virtue of section 79 above references to "the appropriate authority" and "the appropriate enactment" shall be construed as if the unaffected area of an agricultural unit were part of the affected area.

(8) The provisions in section 200(2) of the Act of 1971 (operation of blight provisions where claimant dies after serving blight notice) shall include subsections (2) and (4) above. **[383]**

NOTES
Commencement: 23 May 1973.
Act of 1971: Town and Country Planning Act 1971.

Supplementary

82. Supplementary provisions for Part V

(1) In this Part of this Act "the Act of 1971" means the Town and Country Planning Act 1971.

(2), (3) . . .

(4) In sections 192 to 207 of the Act of 1971 references to "these provisions" shall include references to this Part of this Act, and references to "the specified descriptions" shall include references to the descriptions contained in section 192(1) (*a*), (*b*), (*d*), (*g*) and (*j*) of that Act as extended by this Part of this Act and to the descriptions contained in sections 71, 72, 73, 74(2) and 76 above.

(5) The Act of 1971 shall have effect as if this Part of this Act were included in the said sections 192 to 207. **[384]**

NOTES
Commencement: 23 May 1973.
Sub-ss (2), (3): amend the Town and Country Planning Act 1971, ss 192, 194.

LOCAL GOVERNMENT, PLANNING AND LAND ACT 1980
(c 65)

ARRANGEMENT OF SECTIONS

*An Act to relax controls over local and certain other authorities; to amend the law
relating to the publication of information, the undertaking of works and the
payment of allowances by local authorities and other bodies; to make further
provision with respect to rates and to grants for local authorities and other
persons and for controlling the expenditure of local authorities; to amend the
law relating to planning; to make provision for a register of public land and the
disposal of land on it; to repeal the Community Land Act 1975; to continue the
Land Authority for Wales; to make further provision in relation to land
compensation, development land, derelict land and public bodies' acquisitions
and disposals of land; to amend the law relating to town development and new
towns; to provide for the establishment of corporations to regenerate urban
areas; to make further provision in relation to gipsies and their caravan sites;
to abolish the Clean Air Councils and certain restrictions on the Greater London
Council; to empower certain further authorities to confer honorary distinctions;
and for connected purposes.* [13 November 1980]

PART IX

TOWN AND COUNTRY PLANNING

Allocation of planning functions

86. Distribution of planning functions between planning authorities

(1), (2) . . .

(3) It shall be the duty of a local planning authority when exercising their
functions under section 29 of the Town and Country Planning Act 1971
(determination of applications) to seek the achievement of the general objectives
of the structure plan for the time being in force for their area.

(4) . . .

(5) Nothing in the general transfer provisions shall prevent a county
planning authority determining an application to which this subsection applies
after the commencement date if it was made before that date.

(6) Subsection (5) above applies to any application which relates to a
transferred matter and which is of a description mentioned in paragraph
15(1)(*a*), (*b*) or (*c*) of Schedule 16 to the Local Government Act 1972.

(7) . . .

(8) Subject to subsection (10) below, the provisions to which this subsection applies shall come into operation on the commencement date.

(9) The provisions to which subsection (8) above applies are—

(*a*) the general transfer provisions;

(*b*) ...

(10) A development order required to be made for the purposes of any of the provisions to which subsection (8) above applies may be made before the commencement date.

(11) In this section—

"the commencement date" means the date on which there expires the period of two months beginning with the day on which this Act is passed; "the general transfer provisions" means—

(*a*) subsections (1) to (4) above;

...

"transferred matter" means a matter which before the commencement date is a county matter, as defined in paragraph 32 of Schedule 16 to the Local Government Act 1972, but which ceases to be a county matter in consequence of the provisions of this Part of this Act. **[385]**

NOTES

Commencement: 13 November 1980 (sub-ss (5), (6), (8)–(11)); 13 January 1981 (remainder).
Sub-ss (1), (2), (4): amend the Local Government Act 1972, Sch 16.
Sub-s (7): repealed by the Local Government Act 1985, s 102, Sch 17.
Sub-ss (9), (11): words omitted repealed by the Local Government Act 1985, s 102, Sch 17.

Planning fees

87. Fees for planning applications etc

(1) The Secretary of State may by regulations make such provision as he thinks fit for the payment of a fee of the prescribed amount to a local planning authority in England or Wales or a planning authority in Scotland in respect of an application made to them under the planning enactments for any permission, consent, approval, determination or certificate.

(2) Regulations under subsection (1) above may provide for the transfer—

(*a*) of prescribed fees received in respect of any description of application by an authority in England or Wales to whom applications fall to be made to any other authority by whom applications of that description fall to be dealt with;

(*b*) of prescribed fees received in respect of any application or class of applications by a district planning authority in Scotland to a regional planning authority where the regional planning authority have exercised the powers conferred upon them by section 179(1) of the Local Government (Scotland) Act 1973.

(3) The Secretary of State may by regulations make such provision as he thinks fit for the payment to him of a fee of the prescribed amount in respect of an application for planning permission which is deemed to be made to him under the planning enactments.

(4) Regulations under subsection (1) or (3) above may provide for the remission or refunding of a prescribed fee (in whole or in part) in prescribed circumstances.

(5) Regulations under subsection (1) or (3) of this section shall be made by statutory instrument.

(6) No such regulations shall be made unless a draft of the regulations has been laid before and approved by resolution of each House of Parliament.

(7) Any sum paid to the Secretary of State under this section shall be paid into the Consolidated Fund.

(8) In this section "the planning enactments" means—

(a) in England and Wales, the Town and Country Planning Act 1971 and orders and regulations made under it; and

(b) in Scotland, the Town and Country Planning (Scotland) Act 1972 and orders and regulations made under it,

and "prescribed" means prescribed by regulations under subsection (1) or (3) of this section.   **[386]**

NOTES
Commencement: 13 November 1980.

PART XIV

LAND—MISCELLANEOUS

Development Land

116. Assessment of development land

(1) If the Secretary of State directs an authority to do so, it shall make an assessment of land which is in its area and which is in its opinion available and suitable for development for residential purposes.

(2) In connection with any assessment under subsection (1) above, the authority shall comply with such directions as the Secretary of State may give.

(3) In particular, he may give directions about any consultations to be made prior to the assessment (whether with other authorities or with builders or developers or other persons), about the way any consultation is to be made, and about producing reports of assessments and making copies of the reports available to the public, and directions that an authority is to make the assessment alone or jointly with another authority or authorities.

(4) The following are authorities for the purposes of this section, namely—

(a) (in the application of the section to England and Wales) the councils of counties, districts and London boroughs . . . ;

(b) (in the application of the section to Scotland) regional, general and district planning authorities.   **[387]**

NOTES
Commencement: 13 November 1980.
Sub-s (4): words omitted repealed by the Local Government Act 1985, s 102, Sch 17.

Miscellaneous provisions about land

119. Planning Boards: Land acquisition

(1) [A board constituted in pursuance of section 1 of the Town and Country Planning Act 1971 or reconstituted in pursuance of Schedule 17 to the Local Government Act 1972] shall, on being authorised to do so by the Secretary of

State, have the same power to acquire land compulsorily as the local authorities to whom section 112 of the Town and Country Planning Act 1971 applies have under that section.

(2) [Any such board] shall have the same power to acquire land by agreement as the local authorities mentioned in subsection (1) of section 119 of that Act have under subsection (1)(*a*) of that section.

(3) The following sections of that Act shall apply (with the necessary modifications) as if [any such board were a local authority]:—

> 112(1) and (4) (compulsory acquisition)
> 118 (extinguishment of rights)
> 119(1)(*a*) and (3) (acquisition by agreement)
> 120 (acquisition for purposes of exchange)
> 121 (appropriation of land forming part of common etc)
> 122 (appropriation of land held for planning purposes)
> 123 (disposal of land held for planning purposes)
> 124 (development of land held for planning purposes)
> 125 (buildings of architectural interest etc)
> 127 (power to override easements etc)
> 128 (consecrated land etc)
> 129 (open spaces)
> 130(3) (displacement of persons).

[(4) On being authorised to do so by the Secretary of State any such board shall have, for any purpose for which by virtue of this section they may acquire land compulsorily, the power to purchase compulsorily rights over land not in existence when their compulsory purchase is authorised which section 13 of the Local Government (Miscellaneous Provisions) Act 1976 confers on the local authorities to whom subsection (1) of that section applies, and subsections (2) to (5) of that section shall accordingly apply to the purchase of rights under this subsection as they apply to the purchase of rights under the said subsection (1).

[388]

NOTES
    Commencement: 13 July 1982 (sub-s (4)); 13 November 1980 (remainder).
    Amended by the Local Government (Miscellaneous Provisions) Act 1982, s 35.

122. Acquisition and disposal of land by the Crown

(1) Where, in exercise of the power conferred by section 2 of the Commissioners of Works Act 1852, section 113 of the Town and Country Planning Act 1971 or section 103 of the Town and Country Planning (Scotland) Act 1972 (acquisition of land necessary for the public service) the Secretary of State has acquired, or proposes to acquire, any land (the "public service land") and in his opinion other land ought to be acquired together with the public service land—

> (*a*) in the interests of the proper planning of the area concerned; or
> (*b*) for the purpose of ensuring that the public service land can be used, or developed and used, (together with that other land) in what appears to the Secretary of State to be the best, or most economic, way; or
> (*c*) where the public service land or any land acquired, or which the Secretary of State proposes to acquire, by virtue of paragraph (*a*) or (*b*) above, forms part of a common or open space or fuel or field garden allotment, for the purpose of being given in exchange therefor,

the said sections 2 and 113, or as the case may be 103, shall apply to that other land as if its acquisition were necessary for the public service.

In the application of this subsection to Scotland the words "or fuel or field garden allotment" shall be omitted.

(2) The said sections 2, 113 and 103 shall be construed and have effect as if references to land necessary for the public service included land which it is proposed to use not only for the public service but also—

(*a*) to meet the interests of proper planning of the area, or

(*b*) to secure the best, or most economic, development or use of the land,

for other purposes.

(3) The said sections 2, 113 and 103 shall be construed and have effect as if references to the public service included the service in the United Kingdom—

(*a*) of any international organisation or institution whether or not the United Kingdom or Her Majesty's Government in the United Kingdom is or is to become a member;

(*b*) of any office or agency established by such an organisation or institution or for its purposes, or established in pursuance of a treaty (whether or not the United Kingdom is or is to become a party to the treaty);

(*c*) of a foreign sovereign Power or the Government of such a Power;

and for the purposes of paragraph (*b*) above "treaty" includes any international agreement, and any protocol or annex to a treaty or international agreement.

(4) Where the Secretary of State proposes to dispose of any of his land and is of the opinion that it is necessary, in order to facilitate that disposal, to acquire adjoining land, then, notwithstanding that the acquisition of that adjoining land is not necessary for the public service, the said section 2 shall apply as if it were necessary for the public service.

(5) Where the Secretary of State is authorised by the said section 2 to acquire land by agreement for a particular purpose, he may acquire that land notwithstanding that it is not immediately required for that purpose; and any land acquired by virtue of this subsection may, until required for the purpose for which it was acquired, be used for such purpose as the Secretary of State may determine.

(6) The Secretary of State may dispose of land held by him and acquired by him or any other Minister under the said sections 2, 113 or 103 to such person, in such manner and subject to such conditions as may appear to the Secretary of State to be expedient, and in particular may under this subsection dispose of land held by him for any purpose in order to secure the use of the land for that purpose.

(7) Any expenditure of the Secretary of State attributable to this section shall be paid out of money provided by Parliament.

(8) This section (which re-enacts section 37 of the Community Land Act 1975 with modifications) shall be taken to have come into force on 12 December 1975 but, in relation to the period before the passing of this Act, shall have effect as if for subsection (3) there were substituted:—

(3) The said sections 2, 113 and 103 shall be construed and have effect as if references to the public service included the service in the United Kingdom—

(*a*) of any international organisation or institution of which the United Kingdom, or Her Majesty's Government in the United Kingdom, is, or is to become, a member;

(*b*) of any office or agency established by such an organisation or institution or for its purposes, or established in pursuance of a treaty to which the United Kingdom is, or is to become, a party;

and for the purposes of paragraph (*b*) above "treaty" includes any international agreement, and any protocol or annex to a treaty or international agreement.

[389]

NOTES
Commencement: 12 December 1975.

PART XVI
URBAN DEVELOPMENT
Urban development areas

134. Urban development areas

(1) Subject to subsection (2) below, if the Secretary of State is of opinion that it is expedient in the national interest to do so, he may by order made by statutory instrument designate any area of land as an urban development area.

(2) An area of land in England may only be so designated if—

(*a*) it is in a metropolitan district; or
(*b*) it is in an inner London borough or partly in an inner London borough and partly in an outer London borough which has a boundary in common with that inner London borough.

(3) Separate parcels of land may be designated as one urban development area.

(4) No order under this section shall have effect until approved by a resolution of each House of Parliament. **[390]**

NOTES
Sub-s (1): repealed in part by the Housing and Planning Act 1986, s 49(2), Sch 12, Part III. See Appendix.
Sub-s (2): repealed by the Housing and Planning Act 1986, s 47 and s 49(2), Sch 12, Part III. See Appendix.

Urban development corporations

135. Urban development corporations

(1) For the purposes of regenerating an urban development area, the Secretary of State shall by order made by statutory instrument establish a corporation (an urban development corporation) for the area.

(2) An order under this section may be made at the same time as an order under section 134 above.

(3) No order under this section shall have effect until approved by a resolution of each House of Parliament.

(4) An urban development corporation shall be a body corporate by such name as may be prescribed by the order establishing it.

(5) Schedule 26 below shall have effect with respect to urban development corporations.

(6) It is hereby declared that an urban development corporation is not to be regarded as the servant or agent of the Crown or as enjoying any status, immunity or privilege of the Crown and that the corporation's property is not to be regarded as the property of, or property held on behalf of, the Crown.

[391]

136. Objects and general powers

(1) The object of an urban development corporation shall be to secure the regeneration of its area.

(2) The object is to be achieved in particular by the following means (or by such of them as seem to the corporation to be appropriate in the case of its area), namely, by bringing land and buildings into effective use, encouraging the development of existing and new industry and commerce, creating an attractive environment and ensuring that housing and social facilities are available to encourage people to live and work in the area.

(3) Subject to sections 137 and 138 below, for the purpose of achieving the object an urban development corporation may—

(*a*) acquire, hold, manage, reclaim and dispose of land and other property;
(*b*) carry out building and other operations;
(*c*) seek to ensure the provision of water, electricity, gas, sewerage and other services;
(*d*) carry on any business or undertaking for the purposes of the object; and
(*e*) generally do anything necessary or expedient for the purposes of the object or for purposes incidental to those purposes.

(4) No provision of this Part of this Act by virtue of which any power is exercisable by an urban development corporation shall be construed as limiting the effect of subsection (3) above.

(5) Without prejudice to the generality of the powers conferred on urban development corporations by this Act, such a corporation, for the purpose of achieving the object,—

(*a*) may, with the consent of the Secretary of State, contribute such sums as he with the Treasury's concurrence may determine towards expenditure incurred or to be incurred by any local authority or statutory undertakers in the performance of any statutory functions of the authority or undertakers, including expenditure so incurred in the acquisition of land; and
(*b*) may, with the like consent, contribute such sums as the Secretary of State with the like concurrence may determine by way of assistance towards the provision of amenities.

(6) To avoid doubt it is declared that subsection (3) above relates only to the capacity of an urban development corporation as a statutory corporation; and nothing in this section authorises such a corporation to disregard any enactment or rule of law.

(7) A transaction between a person and an urban development corporation shall not be invalidated by reason of any failure by the corporation to observe the object in subsection (1) above or the requirement in subsection (3) above that the corporation shall exercise the powers conferred by that subsection for the purpose of achieving that object.   [392]

137. Exclusion of functions

(1) An order under section 135 above may provide that any functions which may be exercisable by an urban development corporation by virtue of this Part of this Act and which are specified in the order are not to be exercised by the corporation established by the order, either as regards the whole of its area or

as regards a portion of that area; and this Part of this Act shall apply to the corporation accordingly.

(2) An order under section 135 above may amend any provision of a previous order under that section which was included in that order by virtue of subsection (1) above.

(3) Nothing in subsection (2) above shall prejudice the operation of section 145 of the Interpretation Act 1978 (power to amend orders etc).   [393]

138. Restrictions on powers

(1) Without prejudice to any provision of this Act requiring the consent of the Secretary of State to be obtained for anything to be done by an urban development corporation, he may give directions to such a corporation for restricting the exercise by it of any of its powers under this Act or for requiring it to exercise those powers in any manner specified in the directions.

(2) Before giving a direction under subsection (1) above, the Secretary of State shall consult the corporation, unless he is satisfied that because of urgency consultation is impracticable.

(3) A transaction between a person and an urban development corporation acting in purported exercise of its powers under this Act shall not be void by reason only that it was carried out in contravention of a direction given under subsection (1) above, and such a person shall not be concerned to see or enquire whether a direction under that subsection has been given or complied with.

[394]

139. Allocation or transfer of functions

(1) If it appears to the Secretary of State, in the case of an urban development area, that there are exceptional circumstances which render it expedient that the functions of an urban development corporation under this Part of this Act should be performed by the urban development corporation established for the purposes of any other area instead of by a separate corporation established for the purpose, he may, instead of establishing such a separate corporation, by order direct that those functions shall be performed by the urban development corporation established for the other area.

(2) If it appears to the Secretary of State that there are exceptional circumstances which render it expedient that the functions of an urban development corporation established for one area should be transferred to the urban development corporation established for the purposes of another area, or to a new urban development corporation to be established for the first-mentioned area, he may, by order, provide for the dissolution of the first-mentioned corporation and for the transfer of its functions, property, rights and liabilities to the urban development corporation established for the purposes of the other area or (as the case may be) to a new corporation established for the purposes of the first-mentioned area by the order.

(3) Without prejudice to section 14 of the Interpretation Act 1978, an order under this section providing for the exercise of functions in relation to an area by the urban development corporation established for the purposes of another area, or for the transfer of such functions to such a corporation, may modify the name and constitution of that corporation in such manner as appears to the Secretary of State to be expedient, and for the purposes of this Act that

corporation shall be treated as having been established for the purposes of each of those areas.

(4) Before making an order under this section providing for the transfer of functions from or to an urban development corporation or for the exercise of any functions by such a corporation, the Secretary of State shall consult that corporation.

(5) An order under this section shall make, with regard to a corporation on which functions are conferred by the order, the same provision as that which may be made with regard to a corporation under section 137 above.

(6) An order under this section shall be made by statutory instrument.

(7) No order under this section shall have effect until approved by a resolution of each House of Parliament.   **[395]**

140. Consultation with local authorities

(1) An urban development corporation shall prepare a code of practice as to consultation with the relevant local authorities about the exercise of its powers.

(2) In this section "the relevant local authorities" means local authorities the whole or any part of whose area is included in the urban development area.

(3) Preparation of the code shall be completed not later than the expiration of the period of 12 months from the date of the establishment of the corporation.

(4) A corporation may from time to time revise the whole or any part of its code.

(5) A corporation shall prepare and revise its code in consultation with the relevant local authorities.   **[396]**

Planning blight

147. Planning blight

(1) Section 192(1) of the 1971 Act (scope of provisions about blight) and section 181(1) of the 1972 Act (which makes similar provisions for Scotland) shall have effect as if the land specified in them included land which—

> (*a*) is land within an area intended to be designated as an urban development area by an order which has been made under section 134 above but which has not come into effect; or
> (*b*) is land within an area which has been so designated by an order under that section which has come into effect.

(2) No blight notice shall be served by virtue of subsection (1)(*a*) above at any time after the order has come into effect.

(3) Until such time as an urban development corporation is established for the urban development area, sections 192 to 207 of the 1971 Act and sections 181 to 196 of the 1972 Act shall have effect in relation to land within subsection (1) above as if "the appropriate authority" and "the appropriate enactment" were the Secretary of State and subsection (4) below respectively.

(4) Until such time as aforesaid the Secretary of State shall have power to acquire compulsorily any interest in land in pursuance of a blight notice served by virtue of subsection (1) above; and where he acquires an interest as aforesaid, then—

(*a*) if the land is or becomes land within subsection (1)(*b*) above, the interest shall be transferred by him to the urban development corporation established for the urban development area; and

(*b*) in any other case, the interest may be disposed of by him in such manner as he thinks fit.

(5) The Land Compensation Act 1961 and, in relation to Scotland, the Land Compensation (Scotland) Act 1963 shall have effect in relation to the compensation payable in respect of the acquisition of an interest by the Secretary of State under subsection (4) above as if the acquisition were by an urban development corporation under this Part of this Act and as if, in the case of land within subsection (1)(*a*) above, the land formed part of the area designated as an urban development area by an order under section 134 above which has come into effect. **[397]**

Planning functions

148. Planning control

(1) An urban development corporation may submit to the Secretary of State proposals for the development of land within the urban development area, and the Secretary of State, after consultation with the local planning authority within whose area (or in Scotland the regional, general and district planning authorities within whose areas) the land is situated and with any other local authority which appears to him to be concerned, may approve any such proposals either with or without modification.

(2) Without prejudice to the generality of the powers conferred by section 24 of the 1971 Act or section 21 of the 1972 Act, a special development order made by the Secretary of State under that section with respect to an urban development area may grant permission for any development of land in accordance with proposals approved under subsection (1) above, subject to such conditions, if any (including conditions requiring details of any proposed development to be submitted to the local planning authority, or in Scotland the planning authority exercising district planning functions within the meaning of section 172 of the Local Government (Scotland) Act 1973), as may be specified in the order.

(3) The Secretary of State shall give to an urban development corporation such directions with respect to the disposal of land vested in or acquired by it under this Act and with respect to the development by it of such land, as appear to him to be necessary or expedient for securing, so far as practicable, the preservation of any features of special architectural or historic interest, and in particular of buildings included in any list compiled or approved or having effect as if compiled or approved under section 54(1) of the 1971 Act (which relates to the compilation or approval by the Secretary of State of lists of buildings of special architectural or historic interest) or under section 52(1) of the 1972 Act (which makes similar provision for Scotland).

(4) References in this section to the local planning authority are—

(*a*) in relation to land outside Greater London, references to the district planning authority and also (in relation to proposals for any development which is a county matter, as defined in paragraph 32 of Schedule 16 to the Local Government Act 1972) to the county planning authority; and

(b) in relation to land in Greater London, references to the authority which is the local planning authority as ascertained in accordance with Schedule 3 to the Town and Country Planning Act 1971.   **[398]**

149. Corporation as planning authority

(1) If the Secretary of State so provides by order, an urban development corporation shall be the local planning authority for the whole or any portion of its area in place of any authority which would otherwise be the local planning authority for such purposes of Part III of the 1971 Act, and in relation to such kinds of development, as may be prescribed.

(2) The order may provide—

(a) that any enactment relating to local planning authorities shall not apply to the corporation; and

(b) that any such enactment which applies to the corporation shall apply to it subject to such modifications as may be specified in the order.

(3) If the Secretary of State so provides by order—

(a) an urban development corporation specified in the order shall have, in the whole or any portion of its area and in place of any authority (except the Secretary of State) which would otherwise have them, the functions conferred by such of the provisions of the 1971 Act mentioned in Part I of Schedule 29 to this Act as are specified in the order;

(b) such of the provisions of the 1971 Act specified in Part II of that Schedule as are mentioned in the order shall have effect, in relation to an urban development corporation specified in the order and to land in that corporation's area, subject to the modifications there specified.

(4) An order under subsection (3) above may provide—

(a) that any enactment relating to local planning authorities shall apply to the urban development corporation specified in the order for the purposes of any of the provisions specified in Schedule 29 to this Act which relate to land in the urban development area by virtue of the order; and

(b) that any such enactment which so applies to the corporation shall apply to it subject to such modifications as may be specified in the order.

(5) In relation to an urban development corporation which is the local planning authority by virtue of an order under subsection (1) above, section 270 of the 1971 Act (application to local planning authorities of provisions as to planning control and enforcement) shall have effect for the purposes of Part III of the 1971 Act prescribed by that order, and in relation to the kinds of development so prescribed, as if—

(a) in subsection (1), the reference to the development by local authorities of land in respect of which they are the local planning authorities included a reference to the development by the corporation of land in respect of which it is the local planning authority;

(b) in subsection (2)—

(i) in paragraph (a) the words "the corporation" were substituted for the words "such an authority" and the word "corporation" were substituted for the words "local planning authority"; and

(ii) in paragraph (*b*) the word "corporation" were substituted for the words "local planning authority".

(6)–(10) (*Apply to Scotland.*)

(11) An order under this section shall have effect subject to such savings and transitional and supplementary provisions as may be specified in the order.

(12) The power to make an order under this section shall be exercisable by statutory instrument subject to annulment in pursuance of a resolution of either House of Parliament.

(13) In this section "prescribed" means prescribed by an order under this section. **[399]**

150. Planning: corporation and local highway authority

(1) The reference to the local planning authority in paragraph 17 of Schedule 16 to the Local Government Act 1972 (duty to include in a development order under section 24 of the 1971 Act provisions enabling a local highway authority to impose restrictions on the grant by the local planning authority of planning permission for certain descriptions of development) shall not be construed as including a reference to an urban development corporation who are the local planning authority by virtue of an order under section 149 above, and no provision of a development order which is included in it by virtue of that paragraph is to be construed as applying to such a corporation.

(2) The Secretary of State may include in a development order under section 24 of the 1971 Act provision enabling a local highway authority to impose restrictions on the grant by an urban development corporation who are the local planning authority of planning permission under the 1971 Act for such descriptions of development as may be specified in the order. **[400]**

PART XVIII

ENTERPRISE ZONES

179. Enterprise zones

Schedule 32 below (which makes special provision about planning and rates in zones designated under the Schedule) shall have effect. **[401]**

SCHEDULE 26

Section 135

URBAN DEVELOPMENT CORPORATIONS

Members

1. An urban development corporation (in this Schedule referred to as a "corporation") shall consist of a chairman, a deputy chairman and such number of other members (not less than five but not exceeding 11) as the Secretary of State may by order under section 135 above prescribe.

2.—(1) The members of a corporation shall be appointed by the Secretary of State.

(2) In appointing members of the corporation the Secretary of State shall have regard to the desirability of securing the services of people having special knowledge of the locality in which the urban development area is or will be situated.

(3) In relation to the possible appointment of people falling within sub-paragraph (2)

above, the Secretary of State shall consult such local authorities as appear to him to be concerned with the regeneration of the urban development area.

(4) The Secretary of State shall appoint two of the members to be respectively chairman and deputy chairman of the corporation.

3. Subject to the following provisions of this Schedule, a member of the corporation, and the chairman and deputy chairman of the corporation, shall hold and vacate office as such in accordance with the terms of the instrument by which they are respectively appointed.

4. If the chairman or deputy chairman ceases to be a member of the corporation, he shall also cease to be chairman or deputy chairman, as the case may be.

5. Any member of the corporation may, by notice in writing addressed to the Secretary of State, resign his membership; and the chairman or deputy chairman may, by the like notice, resign his office as such.

6. If the Secretary of State is satisfied that a member of the corporation (including the chairman or deputy chairman)—

    (*a*) has become bankrupt or made an arrangement with his creditors (or in Scotland has had his estate sequestrated or has made a trust deed for the behoof of his creditors or a composition contract), or

    (*b*) is incapacitated by physical or mental illness, or

    (*c*) has been absent from meetings of the corporation for a period longer than 3 consecutive months without the permission of the corporation, or

    (*d*) is otherwise unable or unfit to discharge the functions of a member, or is unsuitable to continue as a member,

the Secretary of State may remove him from his office.

7. A member of the corporation who ceases to be a member or ceases to be chairman or deputy chairman shall be eligible for reappointment.

Remuneration

8. The corporation may pay to each member such remuneration and allowances as the Secretary of State may determine with the consent of the Minister for the Civil Service.

9. The corporation may pay or make provision for paying, to or in respect of any member, such sums by way of pensions, allowances and gratuities as the Secretary of State may determine with the consent of the Minister for the Civil Service.

10. Where a person ceases to be a member otherwise than on the expiry of his term of office and it appears to the Secretary of State that there are special circumstances which make it right for him to receive compensation, the corporation may make to him payment of such amount as the Secretary of State may determine with the consent of the Minister for the Civil Service.

Staff

11.—(1) A corporation may, with the approval of the Secretary of State, appoint such officers and servants as the corporation may determine.

(2) References in paragraph 12 below to employees of a corporation are to persons appointed in pursuance of this paragraph.

12.—(1) Employees of a corporation shall be appointed at such remuneration and on such other terms and conditions as the corporation may determine.

(2) A corporation may pay such pensions, allowances or gratuities as it may determine to or in respect of any of its employees, make such payments as it may determine towards the provision of pensions, allowances or gratuities to or in respect of any of its employees or provide and maintain such schemes as it may determine (whether contributory or not) for the payment of pensions, allowances or gratuities to or in respect of any of its employees.

(3) The reference in sub-paragraph (2) above to pensions, allowances or gratuities to or in respect of any of a corporation's employees includes a reference to pensions, allowances to gratuities by way of compensation to or in respect of any of the corporation's employees who suffer loss of office or employment or loss or diminution of emoluments.

(4) If an employee of a corporation becomes a member and was by reference to his employment by the corporation a participant in a pension scheme maintained by the corporation for the benefit of any of its employees, the corporation may determine that his service as a member shall be treated for the purposes of the scheme as service as an employee of the corporation whether or not any benefits are to be payable to or in respect of him by virtue of paragraph 9 above.

(5) A determination of the corporation for the purposes of this paragraph is ineffective unless made with the approval of the Secretary of State given with the consent of the Minister for the Civil Service.

Meetings and proceedings

13. The quorum of the corporation and the arrangements relating to its meetings shall, subject to any directions given by the Secretary of State, be such as the corporation may determine.

14. The validity of any proceedings of the corporation shall not be affected by any vacancy among its members or by any defect in the appointment of any of its members.

Instruments, etc

15. The fixing of the seal of the corporation shall be authenticated by the signature of the chairman or of some other member authorised either generally or specially by the corporation to act for that purpose.

16. Any contract or instrument which, if made or executed by a person not being a body corporate, would not be required to be under seal may be made or executed on behalf of the corporation by any person generally or specially authorised by it to act for that purpose.

17. Any document purporting to be a document duly executed under the seal of the corporation shall be received in evidence and shall, unless the contrary is proved, be deemed to be so executed.

House of Commons disqualification

18. In Part III of Schedule 1 to the House of Commons Disqualification Act 1975 (disqualifying offices), there shall be inserted at the appropriate place in alphabetical order—

"Any member, in receipt of remuneration, of an urban development corporation (within the meaning of Part XVI of the Local Government, Planning and Land Act 1980)".   **[402]**

SCHEDULE 29

Section 149

PLANNING FUNCTIONS OF URBAN DEVELOPMENT CORPORATIONS—ENGLAND AND WALES

PART I

ENACTMENTS REFERRED TO IN SECTION 149(3)(*a*)

Section 55 (control of works of demolition, alteration or extension of listed buildings).
Section 58 (building preservation notice in respect of building not listed).
Section 59 (planning permission to include appropriate provision for preservation and planting of trees).
Section 60 (tree preservation orders).
Section 61 (provisional tree preservation orders).
Section 61A (trees in conservation areas).

Section 62 (replacement of trees).
Section 63 (control of advertisements).
Section 65 (proper maintenance of waste land).
Section 87 (power to serve enforcement notice).
Section 90 (stop notices).
Section 91 (execution and cost of works required by enforcement notice).
Section 96 (power to serve listed building enforcement notice).
Section 99 (execution and cost of works required by listed building enforcement notice).
Section 101 (urgent works for preservation of certain unoccupied buildings).
Section 103 (enforcement of duties as to replacement of trees).
Section 107 (execution and cost of works required by notice as to waste land).
Section 109 (enforcement of control as to advertisements).
Section 114 (compulsory acquisition of listed building in need of repair).
Section 115 (repairs notice as preliminary to compulsory acquisition under s 114).
Section 117 (minimum compensation in case of listed building deliberately left derelict).
Section 126 (management etc. of listed buildings acquired by local authority or Secretary of State).
Section 271 (application to local planning authorities of provisions as to listed buildings).
Section 277 (designation of conservation area).
Section 277A (control of demolition in conservation area).
Section 277B (formulation and publication of proposals for preservation and enhancement of conservation area).
Schedule 11 (control of works for demolition, alteration or extension of listed buildings). **[403]**

NOTES
Repealed in part by the Housing and Planning Act 1986, s 49(2), Sch 12, Part III. See Appendix.

PART II

ENACTMENTS REFERRED TO IN SECTION 149(3)(*b*)

An order made by virtue of section 149(3)(*b*) may make the following modifications in relation to the urban development corporation specified in the order and to land in that corporation's area:—

1. Section 181 (action by council on whom purchase notice is served) shall have effect as if—

(*a*) after "undertakers" there were inserted—

(i) in paragraph (*b*) of subsection (1), "or an urban development corporation";
(ii) in paragraph (*c*) of that subsection, "or any urban development corporation"; and
(iii) in subsection (2), "or urban development corporation"; and

(*b*) at the end of subsection (4), there were added "or, in the case of an urban development corporation, section 142 of the Local Government, Planning and Land Act 1980, and "urban development corporation" means a corporation established by an order under section 135 of that Act".

2. Section 182 (procedure on reference of purchase notice to Secretary of State) shall have effect as if—

(*a*) in subsection (2)(*d*)—

(i) after "undertakers", in the first place where it occurs, there were inserted "or an urban development corporation"; and
(ii) after that word, in the second place where it occurs, there were inserted "or that corporation"; and

(*b*) there were added after subsection (4)—

"(5) In subsection (3) and (4) of this section any reference to persons, authorities or statutory undertakers includes a reference to an urban development corporation established by an order under section 135 of the Local Government, Planning and Land Act 1980.".

3. Section 183 (action by Secretary of State in relation to purchase notice) shall have effect as if after "undertakers", in subsection (4), there were inserted "or an urban development corporation established by an order under section 135 of the Local Government Planning and Land Act 1980.".

4. Section 186 (effect of Secretary of State's action in relation to purchase notice) shall have effect as if—

   (*a*) in subsection (1)—

   > (i) after "undertakers", in the first place where it occurs, there were inserted "or an urban development corporation"; and
   > (ii) after that word, in the second place where it occurs, there were inserted "or that corporation"; and

   (*b*) the following subsection were inserted after that subsection—

   > "(1A) In subsection (1) of this section 'urban development corporation' means an urban development corporation established by an order under section 135 of the Local Government, Planning and Land Act 1980.".

5. Section 212 (order extinguishing right to use vehicles on highway) shall have effect as if—

   (*a*) in subsection (1), for "The provisions" there were substituted "Subject to subsection (1A) of this section, the provision"; and

   (*b*) the following subsection were inserted after that subsection—

   > "(1A) Any reference in this section to a local planning authority is to be construed as a reference to an urban development corporation established by an order under section 135 of the Local Government, Planning and Land Act 1980.".

6. Section 213 (provision of amenity for highway reserved to pedestrians) shall have effect as if after "boroughs" in subsection (5)(*b*) there were inserted "and

   (*c*) in an area designated as an urban development area by an order under section 134 of the Local Government, Planning and Land Act 1980, the urban development corporation established for that area by an order under section 135 of that Act;".

7. Section 214 (extinguishment of public rights of way over land held for planning purposes) shall have effect as if—

   (*a*) in subsection (1), for "Where" there were substituted "Subject to subsection (1A) of this section, where"; and

   (*b*) the following subsection were inserted after that subsection—

   > "(1A) Where any land has been acquired by an urban development corporation or has vested in such a corporation and is for the time being held by them for the purpose of regenerating their area—
   >
   > (*a*) the Secretary of State may by order extinguish any public right of way over the land if he is satisfied that an alternative right of way has been or will be provided or that the provision of an alternative right of way is not required;
   > (*b*) subject to section 217 of this Act, the urban development corporation may by order extinguish any such right over the land being a footpath or bridleway, if they are satisfied as aforesaid."; and

   (*c*) at the end of subsection (2) there were added "and any reference to an urban development corporation is a reference to an urban development corporation established by an order under section 135 of the Local Government, Planning and Land Act 1980.".

8. Section 284 (power to require information as to interests in land) shall have effect as if in subsection (1)—

(a) after the words "local authority", in the first place where they occur, there were inserted "or an urban development corporation established by an order under section 135 of the Local Government, Planning and Land Act 1980"; and

(b) after those words, in the second and third places where they occur, there were inserted "or corporation".

9. Schedule 19 (proceedings on listed building purchase notice) shall have effect as if—

  (a) in paragraph 1—

    (i) in sub-paragraph (1)(b), after "undertakers" there were inserted "or an urban development corporation established by an order under section 135 of the Local Government, Planning and Land Act 1980";

    (ii) in sub-paragraph (1)(c), after "undertakers" there were inserted "or an urban development corporation";

    (iii) in sub-paragraph (2), after "undertakers", there were inserted "or corporation";

  (b) in paragraph 2(7), after "undertakers" there were inserted "or an urban development corporation"; and

  (c) in paragraph 3(1)—

    (i) after "undertakers", in the first place where it occurs, there were inserted "or an urban development corporation";

    (ii) after that word, in the second place where it occurs, there were inserted "or that corporation".   **[404]**

SCHEDULE 32

Section 179

ENTERPRISE ZONES

PART I

DESIGNATION OF ZONES

Invitation to prepare scheme

1.—(1) The bodies which may be invited to prepare a scheme under this Schedule are, in relation to England and Wales—

  (a) a district council;
  (b) a London borough council;
  (c) a new town corporation;
  (d) an urban development corporation.

(2) (*Applies to Scotland.*)

(3) The Secretary of State may invite any of the bodies to prepare a scheme relating to the development of an area falling within the district, borough, district or general planning authority area, new town area or urban development area (as the case may be) and send the scheme to him in accordance with this Schedule.

(4) The invitation shall be made with a view to the designation as an enterprise zone of the area for which the scheme may be prepared.

(5) The invitation—

  (a) shall specify the area for which the scheme may be prepared;
  (b) may contain directions as to the drawing up of the scheme (in particular, as to its form or content or any consultations to be made).

(6) The invitation may specify an area in which publicity is to be given under paragraph 2(2)(b) below.

(7) In this paragraph—

"new town area" means an area designated as the site of a new town by an order under section 1 of the New Towns Act 1965 or section 1 of the New Towns (Scotland) Act 1968;

"new town corporation" means a development corporation established under either of those Acts;

"urban development area" means an area designated as such under this Act;

"urban development corporation" means a corporation established as such under this Act.

Preparation of draft scheme

2.—(1) A body which receives an invitation may prepare a scheme in draft in accordance with the terms of the invitation.

(2) If it prepares a scheme under sub-paragraph (1) above, it shall take such steps as will in its opinion secure—

    (*a*) that—

        (i) if the area for which the scheme is to be prepared is within Greater London, adequate publicity is given to its provisions in Greater London;

        (ii) if the area for which the scheme is to be prepared is in England or Wales but outside Greater London, adequate publicity is given to its provisions in the county in which the area is situated; and

        (iii) (*applies to Scotland*); and

    (*b*) that adequate publicity is also given to the provisions of the scheme in any area specified under paragraph 1(6) above;

    (*c*) that persons who may be expected to want to make representations to the body with respect to the provisions are made aware that they are entitled to do so; and

    (*d*) that such persons are given an adequate opportunity of making such representations within a period specified by the body (the specified period).

(3) The body shall consider any representation—

    (*a*) which is made to it within the specified period, and

    (*b*) which is made on the ground that all or part of the development specified in the scheme should not be granted planning permission in accordance with the terms of the scheme.

Adoption of scheme

3.—(1) After the expiry of the specified period or, if any representations falling within paragraph 2(3) above have been made, after considering them, the body may adopt the scheme by resolution.

(2) The scheme adopted may be the scheme prepared in draft or, subject to sub-paragraph (3) below, that scheme as modified to take account of any such representation or any matter arising out of the representation.

(3) A scheme may not be modified in any way inconsistent with the Secretary of State's invitation under paragraph 1 above.

(4) As soon as practicable after adopting a scheme under this Schedule, the body shall—

    (*a*) send a copy of the scheme to the Secretary of State,

    (*b*) deposit a copy of the scheme at its principal office, and

    (*c*) publish an advertisement in accordance with sub-paragraphs (7) and (8) below.

(5) Any member of the public may inspect the copy so deposited, and make copies of or extracts from it, at any reasonable time without payment.

(6) The body shall make available copies of the scheme, at a reasonable cost, to any member of the public.

(7) The advertisement shall contain—

(*a*) a statement that the scheme has been adopted;
(*b*) a statement that a copy of the scheme can be inspected without payment;
(*c*) a statement of the address where and times when it can be inspected; and
(*d*) a statement that, if the Secretary of State makes an order designating the area to which the scheme relates as an enterprise zone, the order will have effect to grant planning permission in accordance with the scheme.

(8) The advertisement shall be published—

(*a*) in the London Gazette or, if the scheme relates to an area in Scotland, the Edinburgh Gazette; and
(*b*) on at least two occasions, in a newspaper circulating in the area to which the scheme relates.

Questioning scheme's validity

4.—(1) If a person is aggrieved by a scheme adopted by a body under this Schedule and he wishes to question its validity on the ground that it is not within the powers conferred by this Schedule, or that any requirement of this Schedule has not been complied with, he may within the period of six weeks commencing with the first publication (whether in the London or Edinburgh Gazette or otherwise) under paragraph 3(8) above make an application under this paragraph to the High Court or, if the scheme relates to an area in Scotland, the Court of Session.

(2) On such an application the High Court or the Court of Session, if satisfied—

(*a*) that the scheme is wholly or to any extent outside the powers conferred by this Schedule, or
(*b*) that the interests of the applicant would be substantially prejudiced by the failure to comply with any requirement of this Schedule if an order were made under this Schedule designating the area to which the scheme relates as an enterprise zone,

may order that the Secretary of State shall not make an order under this Schedule designating the area as an enterprise zone in pursuance of the scheme, but (in a case where sub-paragraph (*b*) above applies) may further order that, if steps are taken to comply with the requirement concerned, an order may be made designating the area.

(3) No order made by the Court under sub-paragraph (2) above prejudices the making of an order under this Schedule designating the area as an enterprise zone in pursuance of another scheme (so long as this Schedule is complied with).

(4) Except as provided by this paragraph, the validity of a scheme adopted under this Schedule shall not be questioned in any legal proceedings whatsoever.

Designation of enterprise zone

5.—(1) If a body adopts a scheme under this Schedule, the Secretary of State may (if he thinks it expedient to do so) by order designate the area to which the scheme relates as an enterprise zone.

(2) No order may be made until—

(*a*) the expiry of the period of six weeks commencing with the first publication (whether in the London or Edinburgh Gazette or otherwise) under paragraph 3(8) above, or
(*b*) if an application in relation to the scheme is made under paragraph 4(1) above, the time at which any proceedings arising out of the application are disposed of,

whichever is the later.

(3) The power to make the order shall be exercisable—

(*a*) by statutory instrument subject to annulment in pursuance of a resolution of either House of Parliament, and
(*b*) only with the Treasury's consent.

(4) The order shall—

(*a*) specify the date of the designation taking effect (the effective date);
(*b*) specify the period for which the area is to remain an enterprise zone;
(*c*) define the boundaries of the zone by means of a plan or map;
(*d*) designate as the enterprise zone authority the body which was invited to prepare the scheme.

(5) The power to amend orders conferred by section 14 of the Interpretation Act 1978 does not include power to amend an order made under this paragraph.

(6) The power to revoke orders conferred by that section does not include power to revoke an order made under this paragraph before the expiry of the period mentioned in sub-paragraph (4)(*b*) above.

(7) In relation to England and Wales, the order may provide that the enterprise zone authority shall be the local planning authority for the zone for such purposes of the 1971 Act, and in relation to such kinds of development, as may be prescribed in the order.

(8) (*Applies to Scotland.*)

(9) In the following provisions of this Schedule references to a scheme are, in relation to an area designated as an enterprise zone under this paragraph, to the scheme adopted for the area under paragraph 3(1) above.

Publicity of designation

6.—(1) As soon as practicable after the making of an order under paragraph 5 above, the body which adopted the scheme shall publish an advertisement in accordance with sub-paragraphs (2) and (3) below.

(2) The advertisement shall contain—

(*a*) a statement that the order has been made and will have effect to make the area an enterprise zone; and
(*b*) a statement that a copy of the scheme can be inspected without payment and a statement of the address where and times when it can be inspected.

(3) The advertisement shall be published—

(*a*) in the London Gazette or, if the scheme relates to an area in Scotland, the Edinburgh Gazette; and
(*b*) on at least two occasions, in a newspaper circulating in the area to which the scheme relates.

Right of entry

7.—(1) Any person duly authorised in writing by a body which has been invited to prepare a scheme under this Schedule may at any reasonable time enter any land in the area to which the scheme relates (or could relate) for the purpose of surveying the land in connection with the preparation or adoption of a scheme under this Schedule.

(2) In relation to England and Wales, subsection (9) of section 280 and subsections (1) to (6) of section 281 of the 1971 Act (giving of notice, compensation for damage, etc) shall apply in relation to sub-paragraph (1) above as they apply in relation to section 280.

(3) (*Applies to Scotland.*)

Acts referred to in Part I

8. In this Part of this Schedule—

"1971 Act" means the Town and Country Planning Act 1971.   **[405]**

PART II
MODIFICATION OF SCHEME, ETC

Modification of scheme

9.—(1) Where an order has been made under paragraph 5 above, the Secretary of State may invite the enterprise zone authority to prepare modifications to the scheme.

(2) The invitation may contain directions as to the drawing up of the modifications (in particular, as to their form or content or any consultation to be made).

10.—(1) The enterprise zone authority may prepare modifications to a scheme in draft in accordance with the terms of the invitation.

(2) Paragraphs 2(2) and (3), 3 and 4 above shall apply in relation to modifications to a scheme as they apply in relation to a scheme.

11.—(1) If an enterprise zone authority adopts modifications to a scheme, the Secretary of State may (if he thinks it expedient to do so) notify the authority of his approval of them.

(2) No such modification may be given until—

    (*a*) the expiry of the period of six weeks commencing with the first publication (whether in the London or Edinburgh Gazette or otherwise) under paragraph 3(8) above (as applied by paragraph 10 above); or

    (*b*) if an application in relation to the scheme is made under paragraph 4(1) above (as so applied), the time at which any proceedings arising out of the application are disposed of,

whichever is the later.

(3) The notification shall specify the date of the modifications taking effect (the effective date of modification).

12.—(1) As soon as practicable after the date of the notification, the enterprise zone authority shall publish an advertisement in accordance with sub-paragraphs (2) and (3) below.

(2) The advertisement shall contain—

    (*a*) a statement that the Secretary of State has notified the authority of his approval of the modifications; and

    (*b*) a statement that a copy of the modifications can be inspected without payment; and

    (*c*) a statement of the address where and times when they can be inspected.

(3) The advertisement shall be published—

    (*a*) in the London Gazette or, if the scheme relates to an enterprise zone in Scotland, the Edinburgh Gazette; and

    (*b*) on at least two occasions, in a newspaper circulating in the enterprise zone.

13. The power to modify a scheme under the preceding provisions of this Part of this Schedule includes power wholly to replace a scheme.

14. In the following provisions of this Schedule references to a modified scheme are references to a scheme modified under this Part of this Schedule.

Modification of orders by Secretary of State

15.—(1) Subject to sub-paragraph (3) below, the Secretary of State may (if he thinks it expedient to do so) by order modify any order made under paragraph 5 above.

(2) Without prejudice to the generality of sub-paragraph (1) above, an order under this paragraph—

    (*a*) may extend the period for which the zone is to remain an enterprise zone; and (*b*) may provide—

> (i) if the enterprise zone is in England or Wales, that the enterprise zone authority shall be the local planning authority for the zone for different purposes of the 1971 Act, or in relation to different kinds of development; and
>
> (ii) (*applies to Scotland*).

(3) The power conferred by sub-paragraph (1) above does not include—

> (*a*) power to alter the boundaries of an enterprise zone;
> (*b*) power to designate a different enterprise zone authority for the zone; or
> (*c*) power to reduce the period for which the zone is to remain an enterprise zone.

(4) The power to make an order under this paragraph shall be exercisable—

> (*a*) by statutory instrument subject to annulment in pursuance of a resolution of either House of Parliament, and
> (*b*) only with the Treasury's consent.

(5) The power to amend orders conferred by section 14 of the Interpretation Act 1978 does not include power to amend an order made under this paragraph.

(6) The power to revoke orders conferred by that section does not include power to revoke any order made under this paragraph which extends the period for which a zone is to remain an enterprise zone before the expiry of the extended period.

Change of enterprise zone authority

16.—(1) This paragraph applies where—

> (*a*) the body designated as an enterprise zone authority is a new town corporation or an urban development corporation; and
> (*b*) the Secretary of State intends to make an order dissolving that body under section 41 of the New Towns Act 1965 or section 36 of the New Towns (Scotland) Act 1968 or under section 166 above.

(2) Where this paragraph applies, the Secretary of State may by order made by statutory instrument designate as the enterprise zone authority for the zone any body which he could have invited to prepare a scheme for the area comprised in the zone under paragraph 1 above.

(3) An order under this paragraph shall specify the date on which the body is to become the enterprise zone authority.   **[406]**

Part III
Planning

General

17.—(1) An order designating an enterprise zone under this Schedule shall (without more) have effect on the effective date to grant planning permission for development specified in the scheme or for development of any class so specified.

(2) The approval of a modified scheme under paragraph 11 above shall (without more) have effect on the effective date of modification to grant planning permission for development specified in the modified scheme or for development of any class so specified.

(3) Planning permission so granted shall be subject to such conditions or limitations as may be specified in the scheme or modified scheme or (if none are specified) unconditional.

(4) Subject to sub-paragraph (5) below, where planning permission is so granted for any development or class of development, the enterprise zone authority may direct that the permission shall not apply in relation—

> (*a*) to a specified development; or

(*b*) to a specified class of development; or

(*c*) to a specified class of development in a specified area within the enterprise zone.

(5) An enterprise zone authority shall not give a direction under sub-paragraph (4) above unless they have submitted it to the Secretary of State and he has notified them that he approves of their giving it.

(6) If the scheme or the modified scheme specifies matters, in relation to any development it permits, which will require approval by the enterprise zone authority, the permission shall have effect accordingly.

(7) Notwithstanding sub-paragraphs (1) to (6) above, planning permission may be granted under the 1971 Act or the 1972 Act in relation to land in an enterprise zone (whether the permission is granted in pursuance of an application made under Part III of the 1971 Act or Part III of the 1972 Act or by a development order).

(8) Nothing in this Part of this Schedule prejudices the right of any person to carry out development apart from this Part.

Amendments of 1971 Act

18.—(1) This paragraph amends the 1971 Act in consequence of paragraph 17 above.

(2) In section 41(3) (exceptions to provisions about limit of duration of planning permission) insert after paragraph (*a*)—

"(*aa*) to any planning permission granted by an enterprise zone scheme;".

(3) In section 53(1) (application to determine whether planning permission required, having regard to development order) after "development order" insert "and of any enterprise zone scheme".

(4) In section 209(1) (stopping up or diversion of highway) insert after "Part III of this Act" the words "or by virtue of Schedule 32 to the Local Government, Planning and Land Act 1980".

(5) In section 290(1) (interpretation) insert at the appropriate place in alphabetical order—

"enterprise zone scheme" means a scheme or modified scheme having effect to grant planning permission by virtue of Schedule 32 to the Local Government, Planning and Land Act 1980;".

19. (*Applies to Scotland.*)

Enterprise zone authority as planning authority

20.—(1) Where under paragraph 5(7) above an order designating an enterprise zone provides that the enterprise zone authority shall be the local planning authority for the zone, then while the zone subsists, the enterprise zone authority shall be, to the extent mentioned in the order and to the extent that it is not already, the local planning authority for the zone in place of any authority which would otherwise be the local planning authority for the zone.

(2) (*Applies to Scotland.*)

Saving where scheme is modified

21. Nothing in a modified scheme shall prevent the carrying on of operations started before the effective date of modification in accordance with the scheme as it had effect before that date.

Termination of enterprise zone

22.—(1) This paragraph has effect where an area ceases to be an enterprise zone, and in this paragraph a reference to the termination date is to the date when the area so ceases.

(2) The scheme does not authorise the carrying out of operations after the termination date, even if they started to be carried out before that date in accordance with the scheme.

Structure and local plans

23.—(1) As soon as practicable after an order has been made under paragraph 5 above or a notification has been given under paragraph 11 above—

(a) any county planning authority for an area in which the enterprise zone is wholly or partly situated shall review any structure plan for their area or for part of it which relates to the whole or part of the zone in the light of the provisions of the scheme or modified scheme; and

(b) any local planning authority for an area in which the enterprise zone is wholly or partly situated shall review any local plan prepared by it which relates to any land in the zone.

(2) A county planning authority shall submit to the Secretary of State proposals for any alterations to a structure plan which they consider necessary to take account of the scheme or the modified scheme.

(3) Where an enterprise zone is wholly or partly situated in Greater London, sub-paragraphs (1) and (2) above shall have effect as if the references to the county planning authority were references to the Greater London Council and the references to the structure plan were accordingly references to the Greater London development plan.

(4) A local planning authority shall make prosposals for any alterations to such a local plan as is mentioned in sub-paragraph (1)(b) above which they consider necessary to take account of the scheme or the modified scheme, or for the repeal or replacement of any of those plans whose repeal or replacement they consider necessary for that purpose.

(5) This paragraph shall apply only to England and Wales.

24. (*Applies to Scotland.*)

Regulations

25.—(1) The Secretary of State may by regulations made by statutory instrument—

(a) make provision as to the procedure for giving a direction under paragraph 17(4) above;

(b) make provision as to the method and procedure relating to the approval of matters specified in a scheme or modified scheme as mentioned in paragraph 17(6) above;

(c) make transitional and supplementary provision in relation to any provision mentioned in paragraph 20 above of an order designating an enterprise zone.

(2) Regulations under sub-paragraph (1) above may modify any planning enactment or may apply any planning enactment (with or without modification) in making any provision mentioned in that sub-paragraph.

Interpretation

26.—(1) In this Part of this Schedule—

"planning enactment" means any provision of the 1971 Act or of the 1972 Act or of any instrument made under either of them;
"the 1971 Act" means the Town and Country Planning Act 1971;
"the 1972 Act" means the Town and Country Planning (Scotland) Act 1972.

(2) Any expression used in this Part of this Schedule and to which a meaning is assigned—

(a) in relation to England and Wales, by the 1971 Act; or

(b) (*applies to Scotland*),

has, in relation to England and Wales or, as the case may be, in relation to Scotland, the meaning so assigned to it. **[407]**

NOTES
New paras 21 and 22 substituted by the Housing and Planning Act 1986, s 54(1). See Appendix.
Para 26: new sub-para (1A) inserted by the Housing and Planning Act 1986, s 54(2). See Appendix.

PLANNING INQUIRIES (ATTENDANCE OF PUBLIC) ACT 1982
(c 21)

An Act to require that evidence at planning inquiries held under the Town and Country Planning Act 1971 be given in public, subject to certain exceptions.

[28 June 1982]

1. Planning inquiries to be held in public, subject to certain exceptions

(1) Subject to subsection (2) below, at any planning inquiry oral evidence shall be heard in public and documentary evidence shall be open to public inspection.

(2) Subject to subsection (3) below, the Secretary of State may, in the case of any planning inquiry, direct that evidence of any description indicated in the direction shall not be heard or (as the case may be) open to inspection at that inquiry by anyone other than such persons or persons of such descriptions as he may specify in that direction.

(3) The Secretary of State may give a direction under subsection (2) above only if he is satisfied—

(a) that giving evidence of the description indicated or (as the case may be) making it available for inspection would be likely to result in the disclosure of information as to any of the matters mentioned in subsection (4) below; and
(b) that the public disclosure of that information would be contrary to the national interest.

(4) The matters referred to in subsection (3)(a) above are—

(a) national security; and
(b) the measures taken or to be taken to ensure the security of any premises or property.

(5) In this section "planning inquiry" means any local inquiry held under—

(a) section 49(3) of the Town and Country Planning Act 1971 (inquiry held by a Planning Inquiry Commission);
(b) section 282(1) of that Act (inquiry held for purpose of discharging functions of Secretary of State); or
(c) paragraph 5 of Schedule 9 to that Act (inquiry held by person appointed by Secretary of State to determine appeal).   **[408]**

NOTES
Commencement: 28 June 1982.

2. Short title and extent

(1) This Act may be cited as the Planning Inquiries (Attendance of Public) Act 1982.

(2) This Act extends to England and Wales only.   **[409]**

NOTES
Commencement: 28 June 1982.

TOWN AND COUNTRY PLANNING ACT 1984
(c 10)

ARRANGEMENT OF SECTIONS

An Act to make further provision with respect to the application to Crown land of the enactments relating to town and country planning; and to enable persons in occupation of land by virtue of a licence in writing to appeal against certain enforcement notices issued under those enactments [12 April 1984]

1. Application for planning permission etc in anticipation of disposal of Crown land

(1) This section has effect for the purpose of enabling Crown land, or an interest in Crown land, to be disposed of with the benefit of—

(a) planning permission, listed building consent or conservation area consent; or

(b) a determination under section 53 of the Act of 1971 or section 51 of the Act of 1972 (determination whether planning permission is required).

(2) Notwithstanding the interest of the Crown in the land in question, an application for any such permission, consent or determination as is mentioned in subsection (1) above may be made by—

(a) the appropriate authority; or

(b) any person authorised by that authority in writing;

and, subject to subsections (3) to (5) below, all the statutory provisions relating to the making and determination of any such application shall accordingly apply as if the land were not Crown land.

(3) Any planning permission granted by virtue of this section shall apply only—

(a) to development carried out after the land in question has ceased to be Crown land; and

(b) so long as that land continues to be Crown land, to development carried out by virtue of a private interest in the land;

and any listed building consent or conservation area consent granted by virtue of this section shall apply only to works carried out as aforesaid.

(4) In relation to any application made by virtue of this section for any such determination as is mentioned in subsection (1)(b) above, subsection (1) of each of the sections there mentioned shall have effect as if for the reference to an application for planning permission being required there were substituted a reference to such an application being required in the event of the proposed operations or change of use being carried out or made otherwise than by or on behalf of the Crown.

(5) The Secretary of State may by regulations—

  (a) modify or exclude any of the statutory provisions referred to in subsection (2) above in their application by virtue of that subsection and any other statutory provisions in their application to permissions, consents or determinations granted or made by virtue of this section;

  (b) make provision for requiring a local planning authority or, in Scotland, a planning authority to be notified of any disposal of, or of an interest in, any Crown land in respect of which an application has been made by virtue of this section; and

  (c) make such other provision in relation to the making and determination of applications by virtue of this section as he thinks necessary or expedient.

(6) In this section "conservation area consent" means consent under section 277A of the Act of 1971 or section 262A of the Act of 1972 (demolition of buildings in conservation areas), "statutory provisions" means provisions contained in or having effect under any enactment and references to the disposal of an interest in Crown land include references to the grant of an interest in such land.

(7) This section shall not be construed as affecting any right to apply for any such permission, consent or determination as is mentioned in subsection (1) above in respect of Crown land in a case in which such an application can be made by virtue of a private interest in the land.

(8) Any permission or consent granted before the date on which this section comes into force which would have been a valid planning permission, listed building consent or conservation area consent but for the fact that—

  (a) the land in respect of which it was granted was Crown land; and

  (b) no interest in the land was for the time being held otherwise than by or on behalf of the Crown,

shall be deemed to have been a valid planning permission, listed building consent or conservation area consent, as the case may be; but any permission or consent validated by this subsection shall have effect (and be deemed always to have had effect) as provided in subsection (3) above.   **[410]**

NOTES

  Commencement: 12 August 1984.

  Act of 1971: Town and Country Planning Act 1971.

  Act of 1972: Town and Country Planning (Scotland) Act 1972.

  Sub-s (1): prospectively amended by the Housing and Planning Act 1986, s 33, Sch 7, Part I, para 8(a). See Appendix.

  New sub-s (3A) prospectively inserted by the Housing and Planning Act 1986, s 33, Sch 7, Part I, para 8(b). See Appendix.

2. Tree preservation orders in anticipation of disposal of Crown land

(1) A local planning authority or, in Scotland, a planning authority may make a tree preservation order in respect of Crown land in which no interest is for the time being held otherwise than by or on behalf of the Crown if they consider it expedient to do so for the purpose of preserving trees or woodlands on the land in the event of its ceasing to be Crown land or becoming subject to a private interest.

(2) No tree preservation order shall be made by virtue of this section except with the consent of the appropriate authority.

(3) A tree preservation order made by virtue of this section shall not take effect until the land in question ceases to be Crown land or becomes subject to a private interest, whichever first occurs.

(4) A tree preservation order made by virtue of this section shall not require confirmation under section 60 of the Act of 1971 or section 58 of the Act of 1972 until after the occurrence of the event by virtue of which it takes effect in accordance with subsection (3) above; and any such order shall by virtue of this subsection continue in force until—

    (*a*) the expiration of the period of six months beginning with the occurrence of that event; or

    (*b*) the date on which the order is confirmed,

whichever first occurs.

(5) On the occurrence of any event by virtue of which a tree preservation order takes effect in accordance with subsection (3) above the appropriate authority shall as soon as practicable give to the authority that made the order a notice in writing of the name and address of the person who has become entitled to the land in question or to a private interest in it; and the procedure prescribed under the provisions mentioned in subsection (4) above in connection with the confirmation of the order shall apply as if the order had been made on the date on which that notice is received by the authority.

(6) . . .

(7) Any order made before the date on which this section comes into force which would have been a valid tree preservation order but for the fact that—

    (*a*) the land in respect of which it was made was Crown land; and

    (*b*) no interest in the land was for the time being held otherwise than by or on behalf of the Crown,

shall be deemed to have been a valid tree preservation order; but any order validated by this subsection shall have effect (and be deemed always to have had effect) as provided in subsection (3) above.   **[411]**

NOTES
    Commencement: 12 August 1984.
    Sub-s (6): amends the Town and Country Planning (Scotland) Act 1972, s 58(4).
    Act of 1971: Town and Country Planning Act 1971.
    Act of 1972: Town and Country Planning (Scotland) Act 1972.

3. Control of development on Crown land

(1) This section applies to development of Crown land carried out otherwise than by or on behalf of the Crown at a time when no person is entitled to occupy it by virtue of a private interest.

(2) Where it appears to a local planning authority or, in Scotland, a planning authority that development to which this section applies has taken place in their area they may, if they consider it expedient to do so having regard to the provisions of the development plan and to any other material considerations, issue a notice under this section (a "special enforcement notice") and serve copies of it in accordance with subsection (6) below.

(3) No special enforcement notice shall be issued except with the consent of the appropriate authority.

(4) A special enforcement notice shall specify—

    (*a*) the matters alleged to constitute development to which this section applies; and

    (*b*) the steps which the authority issuing the notice require to be taken for restoring the land to its condition before the development took place or for discontinuing any use of the land which has been instituted by the development.

(5) A special enforcement notice shall also specify the date on which it is to take effect and the period within which any such steps as are mentioned in subsection (4)(*b*) above are to be taken and may specify different periods for the taking of different steps.

(6) A copy of a special enforcement notice shall be served, not later than twenty-eight days after the date of its issue and not later than twenty-eight days before the date specified in the notice as the date on which it is to take effect—

(*a*) on the person who carried out the development alleged in the notice;
(*b*) on any person who is occupying the land on the date on which the notice is issued; and
(*c*) on the appropriate authority;

but paragraph (*a*) above shall not apply if the authority issuing the notice are unable after reasonable enquiry to identify or trace the person mentioned in that paragraph.

(7) Any such person as is mentioned in subsection (6)(*a*) or (*b*) above (whether or not served with a copy of the special enforcement notice) may, at any time before the date specified in the notice as the date on which it is to take effect, appeal against the notice to the Secretary of State on the ground that the matters alleged in the notice have not taken place or do not constitute development to which this section applies.

(8) The provisions contained in or having effect under sections 88(3) to (10) and 88A(1) and (2) of the Act of 1971 (supplementary provisions relating to appeals against enforcement notices) shall apply to special enforcement notices issued by local planning authorities and to appeals against such notices under subsection (7) above as they apply to enforcement notices and to appeals under section 88; and the Secretary of State may by regulations apply to such special enforcement notices and appeals under that subsection such other provisions of that Act (with such modifications as he thinks fit) as he thinks necessary or expedient.

(9) The provisions contained in or having effect under subsections (2) to (5) of section 85 of the Act of 1972 (supplementary provisions relating to appeals against enforcement notices in Scotland) shall apply to special enforcement notices issued by planning authorities and to appeals against such notices under subsection (7) above as they apply to enforcement notices and to appeals under that section; and the Secretary of State may by regulations apply to such special enforcement notices and appeals under that subsection such other provisions of that Act (with such modifications as he thinks fit) as he thinks necessary or expedient.   **[412]**

NOTES
  Commencement: 12 August 1984 (for effect, see s 7).
  Act of 1971: Town and Country Planning Act 1971.
  Act of 1972: Town and Country Planning (Scotland) Act 1972.

4. Persons in occupation of land by virtue of a licence or contract

(1) A person who is entitled to occupy Crown land by virtue of a licence in writing or, in Scotland, a contract in writing shall be treated for the purposes of—

(*a*) section 266(1)(*b*) of the Act of 1971 so far as applicable to Parts III to V of that Act or, as the case may be, section 253(1)(*b*) of the Act of 1972 so far as applicable to Parts III to V of that Act (planning control etc. in relation to Crown land where there is a private interest); and

(*b*) sections 1, 2 and 3 above,

as having an interest in land, and references in section 1 above to the disposal or grant of an interest in Crown land, and in that section and sections 2 and 3 above to a private interest in such land, shall be construed accordingly.

(2) The persons entitled to appeal under section 88 or 97 of the Act of 1971 against an enforcement notice or listed building enforcement notice (whether or not in respect of Crown land) shall include any person who—

(*a*) on the date on which the notice is issued occupies the land or building to which the notice relates by virtue of a licence in writing; and

(*b*) continues to occupy the land or building as aforesaid when the appeal is brought.

(3) The references in subsection (2) above to section 97 of the Act of 1971 and a listed building enforcement notice include references to that section as applied by section 277A of that Act (buildings in conservation areas) and to a notice under section 97 as so applied. **[413]**

NOTES

Commencement: 12 August 1984 (for effect, see s 7).
Act of 1971: Town and Country Planning Act 1971.
Act of 1972: Town and Country Planning (Scotland) Act 1972.

5. Requirement of planning permission for continuance of use instituted by the Crown

(1) A local planning authority or, in Scotland, a planning authority in whose area any Crown land is situated may agree with the appropriate authority that subsection (2) below shall apply to such use of land by the Crown as is specified in the agreement, being a use resulting from a material change made or proposed to be made by the Crown in the use of the land.

(2) Where an agreement is made under subsection (1) above in respect of any Crown land, then, if at any time the land ceases to be used by the Crown for the purpose specified in the agreement, the Act of 1971 or, as the case may be, the Act of 1972 shall have effect in relation to any subsequent private use of the land as if the specified use by the Crown had required planning permission and been authorised by planning permission granted subject to a condition requiring its discontinuance at that time.

(3) The condition referred to in subsection (2) above shall not be enforceable against any person who had a private interest in the land at the time when the agreement was made unless the local planning authority or planning authority by whom the agreement was made have notified him of the making of the agreement and of the effect of that subsection.

(4) An agreement made under section (1) above by a local planning authority shall be a local land charge, and for the purposes of the Local Land Charges Act 1975 the local planning authority by whom an agreement is made under that subsection shall be treated as the originating authority as respects the charge constituted by the agreement.

(5) An agreement made under subsection (1) above by a planning authority shall be recorded in the appropriate Register of Sasines or, as appropriate,

registered in accordance with the Land Registration (Scotland) Act 1979, and the condition referred to in subsection (2) above shall not be enforceable against any person acquiring title to the land after the agreement is made unless the agreement has been so recorded or registered before he acquired title.

(6) References in this section to the use of land by the Crown include references to its use on behalf of the Crown, and "private use" means use otherwise than by or on behalf the Crown. **[414]**

NOTES
Commencement: 12 August 1984.
Act of 1971: Town and Country Planning Act 1971.
Act of 1972: Town and Country Planning (Scotland) Act 1972.

6. Interpretation and supplementary provisions

(1) In this Act—

"the Act of 1971" means the Town and Country Planning Act 1971;
"the Act of 1972" means the Town and Country Planning (Scotland) Act 1972;
"the appropriate authority", "Crown land" and "Crown interest" have the meaning given in section 266(7) of the Act of 1971 or, as respects Scotland, section 253(7) of the Act of 1972 and "Duchy interest" has the meaning given in the said section 266(7);
"private interest" means an interest which is neither a Crown interest nor a Duchy interest.

(2) The Act of 1971 and the provisions of this Act so far as applicable to England and Wales shall have effect as if those provisions were included in that Act.

(3) Section 269 of the Act of 1971 (application of provisions of that Act to Isles of Scilly) shall have effect as if the provisions of this Act, so far as applicable to England and Wales, were included among the provisions specified in Part I of Schedule 21 to that Act (provisions that may be applied to the Isles as if they were a separate county).

(4) The Act of 1972 and the provisions of this Act so far as applicable to Scotland shall have effect as if those provisions were included in that Act. **[415]**

NOTES
Commencement: 12 August 1984.

7. Short title, commencement and extent

(1) This Act may be cited as the Town and Country Planning Act 1984.

(2) This Act shall not come into force until the end of the period of four months beginning with the day on which it is passed; but—

(*a*) section 3 above shall apply to any development carried out after the passing of this Act; and
(*b*) section 4(2) and (3) above shall apply to any notice (whenever issued) which is expressed to take effect after the end of that period.

(3) This Act does not extend to Northern Ireland. **[416]**

NOTES
Commencement: 12 August 1984.

TOWN AND COUNTRY PLANNING (COMPENSATION) ACT 1985
(c 19)

An Act to restrict the circumstances in which compensation is payable under sections 165 and 169 of the Town and Country Planning Act 1971 and sections 154 and 158 of the Town and Country Planning (Scotland) Act 1972. [9 May 1985]

1. Restriction on compensation: England and Wales

. . .   **[417]**

NOTES

Commencement: 9 May 1985 (for effect, see s 3).

This section amends the Town and Country Planning Act 1971, ss 165, 169.

2. Restriction on compensation: Scotland

. . .   **[418]**

NOTES

Commencement: 9 May 1985 (for effect, see s 3).

This section applies to Scotland only.

3. Short title and commencement

(1) This Act may be cited as the Town and Country Planning (Compensation) Act 1985.

(2) Sections 1(1) and 2(1) above have effect in relation to the refusal or conditional grant of planning permission on any application made on or after the day on which this Act is passed; but where the period mentioned in the subsections inserted by those provisions begins before that day it shall not expire until the end of the period of twelve months beginning with that day.

(3) Sections 1(2) and 2(2) above have effect in relation to the refusal or conditional grant of planning permission on any application made after 23rd January 1985.   **[419]**

NOTES

Commencement: 9 May 1985 (for effect, see s 3).

PART II
SECONDARY LEGISLATION

TOWN AND COUNTRY PLANNING (USE CLASSES FOR THIRD SCHEDULE PURPOSES) ORDER 1948
(SI 1948 NO 955)

NOTES
Made: 5 May 1948
Authority: Town and Country Planning Act 1971, Sch 8, para 6

ARRANGEMENT OF ARTICLES

1. Citation

This Order may be cited as the Town and Country Planning (Use Classes for Third Schedule Purposes) Order 1948.   **[420]**

2. Interpretation

(1) The Interpretation Act 1889, shall apply to the interpretation of this Order as it applies to the interpretation of an Act of Parliament.

(2) In this Order, unless the context otherwise requires, the following expressions have the meanings respectively assigned to them, namely:—

"the Act" means the Town and Country Planning Act 1947;

"shop" means a building used for the carrying on of any retail trade or retail business wherein the primary purpose is the selling of goods (excluding refreshments other than light refreshments) by retail, and without prejudice to the generality of the foregoing includes a building used for the purposes of a hairdresser, undertaker, ticket agency or receiving office for goods to be washed, cleaned or repaired, or for other purposes appropriate to a shopping area, but does not include a building used as an amusement arcade, pin-table saloon, funfair, garage, petrol filling station, hotel or premises licensed for the sale of intoxicating liquors for consumption on the premises;

"light refreshments" means eatables not cooked on the premises, and beverages;

"building" includes part of a building;

"office" includes a bank;

"industrial building" means a building (other than a building in or adjacent to and belonging to a quarry or mine and other than a shop) used for the carrying on of any process for or incidental to any of the following purposes, namely,—

(a) the making of any article or of part of any article, or

(b) the altering, repairing, ornamenting, finishing, cleaning, washing, packing or canning, or adapting for sale, or breaking up or demolition of any article, or

(c) without prejudice to the foregoing paragraphs, the getting, dressing or treatment of minerals, being a process carried on in the course of trade or business other than agriculture, and for the purposes of this definition the expression "article" means an article of any description, including a ship or vessel;

> "light industrial building" means an industrial building (not being a special industrial building) in which the processes carried on or the machinery installed are such as could be carried on or installed in any residential area without detriment to the amenity of that area by reason of noise, vibration, smell, fumes, smoke, soot, ash, dust or grit;
> "general industrial building" means an industrial building other than a light industrial building or a special industrial building;
> "special industrial building" means an industrial building used for one or more of the purposes specified in Classes V, VI, VII, VIII and IX referred to in the Schedule to this Order;
> "wholesale warehouse" means a building where business, principally of a wholesale nature, is transacted and goods are stored or displayed, but only incidentally to the transaction of that business;
> "repository" means a building (excluding any land occupied therewith) where storage is the principal use and where no business is transacted other than incidentally to such storage;

and references to a building may, except where otherwise provided, include references to land occupied therewith and used for the same purposes.   **[421]**

NOTES
    The Act: see now Town and Country Planning Act 1971.

3. Use Classes

(1) The classes specified in the Schedule to this Order, shall be the general classes for the purposes of paragraph 6 of the Third Schedule to the Act.

(2) Where a group of contiguous or adjacent buildings used as parts of a single undertaking includes industrial buildings used for purposes falling within two or more of the classes specified in the Schedule to this Order as Classes III to IX inclusive, those particular two or more classes may, in relation to that group of buildings, and so long as the area occupied in that group by either general or special industrial buildings is not substantially increased thereby be treated as a single class for the purposes of this Order.

(3) A use which is ordinarily incidental to and included in any use specified in the Schedule to this Order is not excluded from that use as an incident thereto merely by reason of its specification in the said Schedule as a separate use. **[422]**

NOTES
    Sch 3, para 6, to the Act: see now Town and Country Planning Act 1971, Sch 8, para 6.

SCHEDULE

Class I.—Use as a shop for any purpose except as:—

> (i) a fried fish shop;
> (ii) a tripe shop;
> (iii) a shop for the sale of pet animals or birds;
> (iv) a cats-meat shop.

Class II.—Use as an office for any purpose.

Class III.—Use as a light industrial building for any purpose.

Class IV.—Use as a general industrial building for any purpose.

Class V.—Use for any work which is registerable under the Alkali, &c. Works Regulation Act 1906, as extended by the Alkali, &c. Works Orders 1928 to 1939, except a process ancillary to the getting, dressing or treatment of minerals, carried on in or adjacent to a quarry or mine.

Use for any of the following processes, except as aforesaid, so far as not registerable under the above Act:—

    (i) smelting, calcining, sintering or other reduction of ores or minerals;
    (ii) converting, re-heating, annealing, hardening or carburising, forging or casting, of iron or other metals;
    (iii) galvanising;
    (iv) recovering of metal from scrap;
    (v) pickling or treatment of metal in acid;
    (vi) chromium plating.

(Special Industrial Group A)

Class VI.—Use for any of the following processes so far as not included in Class V and except a process ancillary to the getting, dressing or treatment of minerals, carried on in or adjacent to a quarry or mine:—

    (i) burning of building bricks;
    (ii) lime and dolomite burning;
    (iii) carbonisation of coal in coke ovens;
    (iv) production of calcium carbide, lampblack or zinc oxide;
    (v) crushing or screening of stone or slag.

(Special Industrial Group B)

Class VII.—Use for any of the following purposes so far as not included in Class V:—

The production or employment of

    (i) cyanogen or its compounds;
    (ii) liquid or gaseous sulphur dioxide;
    (iii) sulphur chlorides.

Salt glazing.
Sintering of sulphur bearing materials.
The manufacture of glass, where the sodium sulphate used exceeds 1.5 per cent. of the total weight of the melt.
The production of ultramarine or zinc chloride.

(Special Industrial Group C)

Class VIII.—Use for any of the following purposes, so far as not included in Class V:—

The distilling, refining or blending of oils, the production or employment of cellulose lacquers (except their employment in garages in connection with minor repairs), hot pitch or bitumen, or pyridine; the stoving of enamelled ware; the production of amyl acetate, aromatic esters, butyric acid, caramel, hexamine, iodoform, B-naphthol, resin products (except synthetic resins, plastic moulding or extrusion compositions and plastic sheets, rods, tubes, filaments, fibres or optical components produced by casting, calendering, moulding, shaping or extrusion), salicylic acid, or sulphonated organic compounds; paint and varnish manufacture (excluding mixing, milling and grinding); the production of rubber from scrap; or the manufacture of acetylene from calcium carbide, for sale or for use in a further chemical process.

(Special Industrial Group D)

Class IX.—Use for carrying on any of the following industries, businesses or trades so far as not included in Class V:—

Animal charcoal manufacturer.
Blood albumen maker.
Blood boiler.
Bone boiler or steamer.

Bone burner.
Bone grinder.
Breeder of maggots from putrescible animal matter.
Candle maker.
Catgut manufacturer.
Chitterling or nettlings boiler.
Dealer in rags or bones (including receiving, storing, sorting or manipulating rags in or likely to become in an offensive condition, or any bones, rabbit-skins, fat or putrescible animal products of a like nature).
Fat melter or fat extractor.
Fellmonger.
Fish curer.
Fish oil manufacturer.
Fish skin dresser or scraper.
Glue maker.
Gut scraper or gut cleaner.
Leather dresser.
Maker of meal for feeding poultry, dogs, cattle, or other animals from any fish, blood, bone, fat or animal offal, either in an offensive condition or subjected to any process causing noxious or injurious effluvia.
Manufacturer of manure from bones, fish, fish offal, blood, spent hops, beans or other putrescible animal or vegetable matter.
Parchment maker.
Size maker.
Skin drier.
Soap boiler.
Tallow melter or refiner.
Tanner.
Tripe boiler or cleaner.

(Special Industrial Group E)

Class X.—Use as a wholesale warehouse for any purpose, except storage of offensive or dangerous goods.

Class XI.—Use as a repository for any purpose except storage of offensive or dangerous goods.

Class XII.—Use as a building for public worship or religious instruction or for the social or recreational activities of the religious body using the building.

Class XIII.—Use as a residential or boarding school, a residential college, an orphanage or a home or institution providing for the boarding, care and maintenance of children (other than a hospital, home, hostel, or institution included in Class XVII or Class XVIII).

Class XIV.—Use as a boarding or guest house, a residential club, a hostel or a hotel providing sleeping accommodation.

Class XV.—Use (other than for persons of unsound mind, mental defectives or epileptic persons) as a convalescent home, a nursing home, a sanatorium or a hospital.

Class XVI.—Use (other than residentially) as a health centre, a school treatment centre, a clinic, a creche, a day nursery or a dispensary, or use as a consulting room or surgery unattached to the residence of the consultant or practitioner.

Class XVII.—Use as a hospital, home or institution for persons of unsound mind, mental defectives, or epileptic persons.

Class XVIII.—Use as a home, hostel or institution in which persons may be detained by order of a court or which is approved by one of His Majesty's Principal Secretaries of State for persons required to reside there as a condition of a probation or a supervision order.

Class XIX.—Use as a theatre, a cinema or a music hall.

Class XX.—Use as an art gallery (other than for business purposes), a museum, a public library or a public reading room.

Class XXI.—Use as a dance hall, a skating rink, a swimming bath, a turkish or other vapour or foam bath or a gymnasium, or for indoor games.

Class XXII.—Use as a public hall, a concert hall, an exhibition hall, a social centre, a community centre or a non-residential club.   **[423]**

TOWN AND COUNTRY PLANNING (TREE PRESERV-ATION ORDER) REGULATIONS 1969
(SI 1969 NO 17)

NOTES
   Made: 7 January 1969
   Amended by Town and Country Planning (Tree Preservation Order) (Amendment) Regulations 1981, SI 1981 No 14.
   Authority: Town and Country Planning Act 1971, ss 60, 61, 287, Sch 24, para 1

ARRANGEMENT OF REGULATIONS

1. Citation and commencement

These regulations may be cited as the Town and Country Planning (Tree Preservation Order) Regulations 1969 and shall come into operation on 10th February 1969.   **[424]**

2. Interpretation

(1) In these regulations, unless the context otherwise requires—

"the Act" means the Town and Country Planning Act 1962;

"the Act of 1967" means the Civic Amenities Act 1967;

"authority" includes a local planning authority making an order as hereinafter defined, and a local authority making such an order under powers delegated by a local planning authority;

"The Conservator of Forests" means in relation to an order the Forestry Commissioners' Conservator of Forests for the conservancy in which the trees included in the order are situated;

"District Valuer" means in relation to an order the officer of the Commissioners of Inland Revenue for the time being appointed to be District Valuer and Valuation Officer for the area in which the trees included in the order are situated;

"the Minister" means, except as respects Wales, the Minister of Housing and Local Government and as respects Wales the Secretary of State;

"order" means a tree preservation order made under section 29 of the Act and includes an order amending or revoking such an order;

"Wales" includes Monmouthshire.

(2) The Interpretation Act 1889 shall apply to the interpretation of these regulations as it applies to the interpretation of an Act of Parliament.   **[425]**

NOTES

S 29 of the Act of 1962: see now Town and Country Planning Act 1971, s 60.

4. Form and contents of order

(1) An order shall be in the form (or substantially in the form) set out in the Schedule hereto.

(2) The order shall define the position of the trees, groups of trees, or woodlands to which it relates, and for that purpose shall include a map.   **[426]**

5. Procedure

An authority shall, on making an order—

> (a) place on deposit for inspection at a place or places convenient to the locality in which the trees, or groups of trees, or woodlands are situated a certified copy or copies of the order and of the map;
>
> (b) send a copy of the order and the map to the Conservator of Forests and the District Valuer together with a list of all the persons served under (c) of this regulation;
>
> (c) serve on the owners and occupiers of the land affected by the order, and on any other person then known to them to be entitled to work by surface working any minerals in that land or to fell any of the trees affected by the order, a copy of the order and the map together with a notice stating—
>
>> (i) the grounds for making the order;
>>
>> (ii) the address or addresses of the place or places where a certified copy or copies of the order and map have been deposited for inspection, and the hours during which they may be inspected;
>>
>> (iii) that objections and representations with respect to the order may be made to [the authority] in accordance with regulation 7 hereof, a copy of which regulation shall be included in or appended to the notice;
>>
>> (iv) . . .
>>
>> (v) where the order contains a direction under section 16 of the Act of 1967, the effect of the direction.   **[427]**

NOTES

Amended by SI 1981 No 14.

S 16 of the Act of 1967: see now Town and Country Planning Act 1971, s 61.

7. Objections and representations

(1) Every objection or representation with respect to an order shall be made in writing to [the authority, and shall state the grounds thereof], and specify the particular trees, groups of trees, or woodlands in respect of which it is made.

(2) An objection or representation shall be duly made if it complies with paragraph (1) of this regulation and is received by [the authority] within 28 days from the date of the service of the notice of the making of the order.   **[428]**

NOTES

Amended by SI 1981 No 14.

8. Consideration by the Minister

(1) ...

(2) [The authority] shall, before deciding whether to confirm the order, take into consideration any objections and representations duly made in accordance with regulation 7 hereof, and, if a local inquiry is held, the report of that inquiry.   **[429]**

NOTES
    Amended by SI 1981 No 14.

9. Action on receipt of Minister's decision

[The authority shall, as soon as practicable after reaching a decision on the order, inform the owners and occupiers of the land to which the order relates, the Conservator of Forests, the District Valuer and any other person on whom notice has been served in accordance with the provisions of regulation 5 hereof, of their decision; and, in addition, where the order has been confirmed subject to modifications, the authority shall serve on every such person a copy of the order and the map as confirmed.]   **[430]**

NOTES
    Commencement: 13 January 1981.
    Substituted by SI 1981 No 14.

SCHEDULE

FORM OF TREE PRESERVATION ORDER

TOWN AND COUNTRY PLANNING ACTS 1962 AND 1968

[CIVIC AMENITIES ACT 1967][1]

([2])

[The   Council[3]] [The

Council,[4] on behalf of   Council[3]] in

this order called " the authority ", in pursuance of the powers conferred in that behalf by section 29 of the Town and Country Planning Act 1962 [and section 16 of the Civic Amenities Act 1967],[1] and subject to the provisions of the Forestry Act 1967, hereby makes the following order : —

1. In this Order—

" the Act " means the Town and Country Planning Act 1962 ;

" owner " means the owner in fee simple, either in possession or who has granted a lease or tenancy of which the unexpired portion is less than three years ; lessee (including a sub-lessee) or tenant in possession, the unexpired portion of whose lease or tenancy is three years or more ; and a mortgagee in possession ; and " the Minister " means the [Minister of Housing and Local Government] [Secretary of State for Wales].

2. Subject to the provisions of this Order and to the exemptions specified in the Second Schedule hereto, no person shall, except with the consent of the authority and in accordance with the conditions, if any, imposed on such consent, cut down, top, lop or wilfully destroy or cause or permit the cutting down, topping, lopping or wilful destruction of any tree specified in the First Schedule hereto or comprised in a group of trees or in a woodland therein specified, the position of which trees, groups of trees and woodlands is defined in the manner indicated in the said First Schedule on the map annexed hereto[5] which map shall, for the purpose of such definition as aforesaid, prevail where any ambiguity arises between it and the specification in the said First Schedule.

3. An application for consent made to the authority[6] under Article 2 of this Order shall be in writing stating the reasons for making the application, and shall by reference if necessary to a plan specify the trees to which the application relates, and the operations for the carrying out of which consent is required.

4.—(1) Where an application for consent is made to the authority[6] under this Order, the authority may grant such consent either unconditionally, on subject to such conditions (including conditions requiring the replacement of any tree by one or more trees on the site or in the immediate vicinity thereof), as the authority may think fit, or may refuse consent :

Provided that where the application relates to any woodland specified in the First Schedule to this Order the authority shall grant consent so far as accords with the principles of good forestry, except where, in the opinion

NOTE : If it is desired to fell any of the trees included in this Order whether included as trees, groups of trees or woodlands, and the trees are trees for the felling of which a licence is required under the Forestry Act 1967, application should be made *not* to the authority for consent under this Order but to the Conservator of Forests for a licence under that Act (section 15(5)).

Margin notes:

[1] Include only where order contains a direction under section 16 of the Civic Amenities Act 1967.

[2] Insert title of Order.

[3] Insert name of local planning authority.

[4] Insert name.

[5] Map to be to a scale of not less than 25 inches to one mile, except in the case of large woodlands when the scale shall be 6 inches to one mile.

[6] When Tree Preservation Order is made by a District Council on behalf of a County Council an application for consent should be made to the District Council. See also note at foot of this page.

of the authority, it is necessary in the interests of amenity to maintain the special character of the woodland or the woodland character of the area, and shall not impose conditions on such consent requiring replacement or replanting.

(2) The authority shall keep a register of all applications for consent under this Order containing information as to the nature of the application, the decision of the authority thereon, any compensation awarded in consequence of such decision and any directions as to replanting of woodlands ; and every such register shall be available for inspection by the public at all reasonable hours.

5. Where the authority refuse consent under this Order or grant such consent subject to conditions they may when refusing or granting consent certify in respect of any trees for which they are so refusing or granting consent that they are satisfied—

(a) that the refusal or condition is in the interests of good forestry ; or

(b) in the case of trees other than trees comprised in woodlands, that the trees have an outstanding or special amenity value.

6.—(1) Where consent is granted under this Order to fell any part of a woodland other than consent for silvicultural thinning then unless—

(a) such consent is granted for the purpose of enabling development to be carried out in accordance with a permission to develop land under Part III of the Act, or

(b) the authority with the approval of the Minister dispense with replanting,

the authority shall give to the owner of the land on which that part of the woodland is situated a direction in writing specifying the manner in which and the time within which he shall replant such land and where such a direction is given and the part is felled the owner shall, subject to the provision of this Order and section 25 of the Countryside Act 1968, replant the said land in accordance with the direction.

(2) Any direction given under paragraph (1) of this Article may include requirements as to—

(a) species ;

(b) number of trees per acre ;

(c) the erection and maintenance of fencing necessary for protection of the replanting ;

(d) the preparation of ground, draining, removal of brushwood, lop and top ; and

(e) protective measures against fire.

7. On imposing any condition requiring the replacement of any tree under Article 4 of the Order, or on giving a direction under Article 6 of this Order with respect to the replanting of woodlands, the authority shall if such condition or direction relates to land in respect of which byelaws made by a river authority, a drainage board, the Conservators of the River Thames or the Lee Conservancy Catchment Board restrict or regulate the planting of trees, notify the applicant or the 'owner of the land, as the case may be, of the existence of such byelaws and that any such condition or direction has effect subject to the requirements of the river authority, drainage board, the Conservators of the River Thames or the Lee Conservancy Catchment Board under those byelaws and the condition or direction shall have effect accordingly.

8. The provisions set out in the Third Schedule to this Order, being provisions of Part III of the Act and of section 80 of the Town and Country Planning Act 1968 adapted and modified for the purposes of this Order, shall apply in relation thereto.

9. Subject to the provisions of this Order, any person who has suffered loss or damage in consequence of any refusal (including revocation or modification) of consent under this Order or of any grant of any such consent subject to conditions, shall, if he makes a claim on the authority within the time and in the manner prescribed by this Order, be entitled to recover from the authority compensation in respect of such loss or damage :

Provided that no compensation shall be payable in respect of loss or damage suffered by reason of such refusal or grant of consent in the case of any trees the subject of a certificate in accordance with Article 5 of this Order.

10. In assessing compensation payable under the last preceding Article account shall be taken of :

(a) any compensation or contribution which has been paid whether to the claimant or any other person, in respect of the same trees under the terms of this or any other Tree Preservation Order under section 29 of the Act or under the terms of any Interim Preservation Order made under section 8 of the Town and Country Planning (Interim Development) Act 1943, or any compensation which has been paid or which could have been claimed under any provision relating to the preservation of trees or protection of woodlands contained in an operative scheme under the Town and Country Planning Act 1932, and

(b) any injurious affection to any land of the owner which would result from the felling of the trees the subject of the claim.

11.—(1) A claim for compensation under this Order shall be in writing and shall be made by serving it on the authority, such service to be effected by delivering the claim at the offices of the authority addressed to the Clerk thereof or by sending it by prepaid post so addressed.

(2) The time within which any such claim shall be made as aforesaid shall be a period of twelve months from the date of the decision of the authority, or of the Minister, as the case may be, or where an appeal has been made to the Minister against the decision of the authority, from the date of the decision of the Minister on the appeal.

12. Any question of disputed compensation shall be determined in accordance with the provisions of section 128 of the Act.

7 This provision is not to be included unless it appears to the authority that the Order should take effect immediately.

13.—[(1) The provisions of section 16 of the Civic Amenities Act 1967 shall apply to this Order and the Order shall take effect on]⁷

[(2) This order shall apply to any tree specified in the First Schedule hereto, which is to be planted as mentioned therein, as from the time when that tree is planted]⁸

8 This provision may be included in relation to trees to be planted pursuant to a condition imposed under Section 12(1) of the Civic Amenities Act 1967.

NOTE : Any person contravening the provisions of this Order is guilty of an offence under subsection (1) of section 62 of the Act and liable on summary conviction to a fine not exceeding fifty pounds ; and if in the case of a continuing offence the contravention is continued after conviction he is guilty of a further offence thereunder and liable on summary conviction to an additional fine not exceeding forty shillings for every day on which the contravention is so continued. Under sections 13, 14 and 15 of the Civic Amenities Act 1967 if a tree is wilfully cut down or destroyed, or if topping or lopping is carried out in such a way as to be likely to destroy the tree the fine is £250 or twice the value of the tree whichever is the greater. If a tree other than one which is part of woodland is removed or destroyed in contravention of the Order it is the duty of the owner of the land, unless on his application the local authority dispense with the requirement, to plant another tree of appropriate size and species, at the same place as soon as he reasonably can.

FIRST SCHEDULE*

Trees Specified Individually

(encircled in black on the map)

No. on Map	Description	Situation
[T1]	[Oak]	
[T2]	[Ash]	

Trees Specified by References to an Area

(within a dotted black line on the map)

No. on Map	Description	Situation
[A1]	[The several trees of whatever species standing in the area numbered A1 on the map]	
[A2]	[The several oak, beech, and larch trees standing in the area numbered A2 on the map]	

Groups of Trees

(within a broken black line on the map)

No. on Map	Description	Situation
[G1]	[Group consisting of 3 oak, 2 ash and 3 elm]	
[G2]	[Group consisting of 10 beech]	

Woodlands

(within a continuous black line on the map)

No. on Map	Description	Situation
[W1]	[Mixed hardwoods consisting mainly of]	
[W2]	[Mixed conifers and deciduous trees consisting mainly of]	

SECOND SCHEDULE

This Order shall not apply so as to require the consent of the authority to

(1) the cutting down of any tree on land which is subject to a forestry dedication convenant where

(a) any positive covenants on the part of the owner of the land contained in the same deed as the forestry dedication covenant and at the time of the cutting down binding on the then owner of the land are fulfilled ;

(b) the cutting down is in accordance with a plan of operations approved by the Forestry Commission under such deed.

---

* Every heading should be included in the Schedule, and the word "NONE" written in where necessary. The entries above are shown as examples in each category.

(2) the cutting down of any tree which is in accordance with a plan of operations approved by the Forestry Commission under the approved woodlands scheme.

*(3) The cutting down, topping or lopping of a tree exempted from the provisions of this Order by section 29(7) of the Act namely a tree which is dying or dead or has become dangerous, or the cutting down, topping or lopping of which is in compliance with obligations imposed by or under an Act of Parliament or so far as may be necessary for the prevention or abatement of a nuisance.

(4) the cutting down, topping or lopping of a tree

(a) in pursuance of the power conferred on the Postmaster General by virtue of section 5 of the Telegraph (Construction) Act 1908 ;

(b) by or at the request of

(i) a statutory undertaker where the land on which the tree is situated is operational land as defined by the Act and either works on such land cannot otherwise be carried out or the cutting down, topping or lopping is for the purpose of securing safety in the operation of the undertaking ;

(ii) an electricity board within the meaning of the Electricity Act 1947, where such tree obstructs the construction by the board of any main transmission line or other electric line within the meaning respectively of the Electricity (Supply) Act 1919 and the Electric Lighting Act 1882 or interferes or would interfere with the maintenance or working of any such line ;

(iii) a river authority established under the Water Resources Act 1963, a drainage board constituted or treated as having been constituted under the Land Drainage Act 1930, the Conservators of the River Thames, or the Lee Conservancy Catchment Board, where the tree interferes or would interfere with the exercise of any of the functions of such river authority, drainage board, Conservators of the River Thames or Lee Conservancy Catchment Board in relation to the maintenance, improvement or construction of water courses or of drainage works ; or

(iv) the Minister of Defence for the Royal Air Force, the Minister of Technology or the Board of Trade where in the opinion of such Minister or Board the tree obstructs the approach of aircraft to. or their departure from, any aerodrome or hinders the safe and efficient use of aviation or defence technical installations ;

(c) where immediately required for the purpose of carrying out development authorised by the planning permission granted on an application made under Part III of the Act, or deemed to have been so granted for any of the purposes of that Part ;

(d) which is a fruit tree cultivated for fruit production growing or standing on land comprised in an orchard or garden ;

[Where the trees are within the area administered by the Conservators of the River Thames]

[(e) in pursuance of the powers conferred on the Conservators of the River Thames by virtue of section 105 of the Thames Conservancy Act 1932].

* NOTE: Section 13(1) of the Civic Amenities Act 1967 requires, unless on the application of the owner the local authority dispense with the requirement, that any tree removed or destroyed under section 29(7) of the Town and Country Planning Act 1962, shall be replaced by another tree of appropriate size and species. In order to enable the local planning authority to come to a decision, on whether or not to dispense with the requirement, notice of the proposed action should be given to the local planning authority which except in a case of emergency shall be of not less than five days.

THIRD SCHEDULE

Provisions of the following parts of (*a*) Part III of the Town and Country Planning Act 1962 and (*b*) section 80 of the Town and Country Planning Act 1968 as adapted and modified to apply to this Order.

(a) Part III of the Town and Country Planning Act 1962

21.—(1) Without prejudice to the following provisions as to the revocation or modification of consents, any consent under the Order, including any direction as to replanting given by the authority on the granting of such consent, shall (except in so far as the consent otherwise provides), enure for the benefit of the land and of all persons for the time being interested therein.

22.—(1) The Minister may give directions to the authority requiring applications for consent under the Order to be referred to him instead of being dealt with by the authority. *Reference of applications to the Minister.*

22.—(2) A direction under this section may relate either to a particular application or to applications of a class specified in the direction.

22.—(3) Any application in respect of which a direction under this section has effect shall be referred to the Minister accordingly.

22.—(4) Where an application for consent under the Order is referred to the Minister under this section, the provisions of Articles 4 and 5 of the Order shall apply as they apply to an application which falls to be determined by the authority.

22.—(5) Before determining an application referred to him under this section the Minister shall, if either the applicant or the authority so desire, afford to each of them an opportunity of appearing before, and being heard by, a person appointed by the Minister for the purpose.

22.—(6) The decision of the Minister on any application referred to him under this section shall be final.

23.—(1) Where an application is made to the authority[17] for consent under the Order and that consent is refused by that authority or is granted by them subject to conditions, or where any certificate or direction is given by the authority, the applicant, if he is aggrieved by their decision on the application, or by any such certificate, or the person directed if he is aggrieved by the direction, may by notice under this section appeal to the Minister. *Appeals against decisions. 17 See Note 6*

23.—(2) A notice under this section shall be served in writing within twenty-eight days from the receipt of notification of the decision, certificate or direction, as the case may be, or such longer period as the Minister may allow.

23.—(4) Where an appeal is brought under this section from a decision, certificate or direction of the authority, the Minister, subject to the following provisions of this section, may allow or dismiss the appeal, or may reverse or vary any part of the decision of the authority, whether the appeal relates to that part thereof or not, or may cancel any certificate or cancel or vary any direction, and may deal with the application as if it had been made to him in the first instance.

23.—(5) Before determining an appeal under this section, the Minister shall, if either the appellant or the authority so desire, afford to each of them an opportunity of appearing before, and being heard by, a person appointed by the Minister for the purpose.

23.—(7) The decision of the Minister on any appeal under this section shall be final.

24. Where an application for consent under the Order is made to the authority, then unless within two months from the date of receipt of the *Appeal in default of decision.*

application, or within such extended period as may at any time be agreed upon in writing between the applicant and the authority, the authority either—

(a) give notice to the applicant of their decision on the application ; oi

(b) give notice to him that the application has been referred to the Minister in accordance with directions given under section 22 above

the provisions of the last preceding section shall apply in relation to the application as if the consent to which it relates had been refused by the authority, and as if notification of their decision had been received by the applicant at the end of the said period of two months, or at the end of the said extended period, as the case may be.

Power to revoke or modify the consent under the Order.

27.—(1) If it appears to the authority that it is expedient to revoke or modify any consent under the Order granted on an application made under Article 3 of the Order, the authority may by Order revoke or modify the consent to such extent as they consider expedient.

27.—(2) (Subject to the provisions of section 16 of the Civic Amenities Act 1967 and section 80 of the Town and Country Planning Act 1968) an Order under this section shall not take effect unless it is confirmed by the Minister ; and the Minister may confirm any such Order submitted to him either without modification or subject to such modifications as he considers expedient.

27.—(3) Where an authority submit an Order to the Minister for his confirmation under this section, the authority shall furnish the Minister with a statement of their reason for making the Order and shall serve notice together with a copy of the aforesaid statement on the owner and on the occupier of the land affected, and on any other person who in their opinion will be affected by the Order, and if within the period of twenty-eight days from the service thereof any person on whom the notice is served so requires, the Minister, before confirming the Order, shall afford to that person, and to the authority, an opportunity of appearing before, and being heard by, a person appointed by the Minister for the purpose.

27.—(4) The power conferred by this section to revoke or modify a consent may be exercised at any time before the operations for which consent has been given have been completed :

Provided that the revocation or modification of consent shall not affect so much of those operations as has been previously carried out.

27.—(5) Where a notice has been served in accordance with the provisions of subsection (3) of this section, no operations or further operations as the case may be, in pursuance of the consent granted, shall be carried out pending the decision of the Minister under subsection (2) of this section.

(b) Town and Country Planning Act 1968

Unopposed revocation or modification of consent.

80.—(1) The following provisions shall have effect where the local planning authority have made an Order (hereinafter called " such Order " under section 27 above revoking or modifying any consent granted on an application made under a tree preservation order but have not submitted such Order to the Minister for confirmation by him and the owner and the occupier of the land and all persons who in the authority's opinion will be affected by such Order have notified the authority in writing that they do not object to such Order.

80.—(2) The authority shall advertise the fact that such Order has been made and the advertisement shall specify (a) the period (not less than twenty-eight days from the date on which the advertisement first appears within which persons affected by such Order may give notice to the Minister that they wish for an opportunity of appearing before, and being heard by, a person appointed by the Minister for the purpose and (*b*) the period (not less than 14 days from .the expiration of the period referred to in paragraph (*a*) above) at the expiration of which, if no such notice is given to the Minister, such Order may take effect by virtue of this section and without being confirmed by the Minister.

80.—(3) The authority shall also serve notices to the same effect on the persons mentioned in subsection (1) above.

80.—(4) The authority shall send a copy of any advertisement published under subsection (2) above to the Minister, not more than three days after the publication.

80.—(5) If within the period referred to in subsection (2)(*a*) above no person claiming to be affected by such Order has given notice to the Minister as aforesaid and the Minister has not directed that such Order be submitted to him for confirmation, such Order shall at the expiration of the period referred to in subsection (2)(*b*) of this section take effect by virtue of this section and without being confirmed by the Minister as required by section 27(2) of the Town and Country Planning Act 1962.

80.—(6) This section does not apply to such Order revoking or modifying a consent granted or deemed to have been granted by the Minister under Part III or Part IV of the Town and Country Planning Act 1962 or under Part II or Part V of the Town and Country Planning Act 1968.

Given under the official seal of the Minister of Housing and Local Government on 6th January 1969.

(L.S.)   *Anthony Greenwood,*
                Minister of Housing and Local Government.

George Thomas,
One of Her Majesty's Principal Secretaries of State,
Welsh Office,

7th January 1969.

[431]

NOTES
Amended by SI 1975 No 148.

TOWN AND COUNTRY PLANNING (USE CLASSES) ORDER 1972
(SI 1972 NO 1385)

NOTES
Made: 11 September 1972
Authority: Town and Country Planning Act 1971, s 22

(Revoked and replaced by SI 1987 No 764.)

ARRANGEMENT OF ARTICLES

1. Citation and commencement

This order may be cited as the Town and Country Planning (Use Classes) Order 1972 and shall come into operation on 23rd October 1972. **[432]**

NOTES
Commencement: 23 October 1972.

2. Interpretation

(1) The Interpretation Act 1889 shall apply to the interpretation of this order as it applies to the interpretation of an Act of Parliament.

(2) In this order—

"the Act" means the Town and Country Planning Act 1971;

"shop" means a building used for the carrying on of any retail trade or retail business wherein the primary purpose is the selling of goods by retail, and includes a building used for the purposes of a hairdresser, undertaker, travel agency, ticket agency or post office or for the reception of goods to be washed, cleaned or repaired, or for any other purpose appropriate to a shopping area, but does not include a building used as a funfair, amusement arcade, pin-table saloon, garage, launderette, petrol filling station, office, betting office, hotel, restaurant, snackbar or cafe or premises licensed for the sale of intoxicating liquors for consumption on the premises;

"office" includes a bank and premises occupied by an estate agency, building society or employment agency, or (for office purposes only) for the business of car hire or driving instruction but does not include a post office or betting office;

"post office" does not include any building used primarily for the sorting or preparation for delivery of mail or for the purposes of Post Office administration;

"betting office" means any building in respect of which there is for the time being in force a betting office licence pursuant to the provisions of the Betting and Gaming Act 1960;

"launderette" includes any building used for the purpose of washing or cleaning clothes or fabrics in coin-operated machines;

"industrial building" means a building (other than a building in or adjacent to and belonging to a quarry or mine and other than a shop) used for the carrying on of any process for or incidental to any of the following purposes, namely:—

(*a*) the making of any article or of part of any article, or

(*b*) the altering, repairing, ornamenting, finishing, cleaning, washing, packing or canning, or adapting for sale, or breaking up or demolition of any article, or

(*c*) without prejudice to the foregoing paragraphs, the getting, dressing or treatment of minerals,

being a process carried on in the course of trade or business other than agriculture, and for the purposes of this definition the expression "article" means an article of any description, including a ship or vessel;

"light industrial building" means an industrial building (not being a special industrial building) in which the processes carried on or the machinery installed are such as could be carried on or installed in any residential area without detriment to the amenity of that area by reason of noise, vibration, smell, fumes, smoke, soot, ash, dust or grit;

"general industrial building" means an industrial building other than a light industrial building or a special industrial building;

"special industrial building" means an industrial building used for one or more of the purposes specified in Classes V, VI, VII, VIII and IX referred to in the Schedule to this order;

"motor vehicle" means any motor vehicle for the purposes of the Road Traffic Act 1960

["hazardous substance" and "notifiable quantity" have the meanings assigned to those terms by the Notification of Installations Handling Hazardous Substances Regulations 1982;

"site" means the whole of the area of land within a single unit of occupation;].

(3) References in this order to a building may, except where otherwise provided, include references to land occupied therewith and used for the same purposes.   **[433]**

NOTES

Commencement: 23 October 1972.

Para (2): definitions "hazardous substance", "notifiable quantity" and "site" added by SI 1983 No 1614.

3. Use Classes

(1) Where a building or other land is used for a purpose of any class specified in the Schedule to this order, the use of such building or other land for any other purpose of the same class shall not be deemed for the purposes of the Act to involve development of the land.

[(1A) The classes specified in the Schedule to this order shall not include any use of a building or other land for any purpose which involves the manufacture, processing, keeping or use of a hazardous substance in such circumstances as will result in there being at any one time a notifiable quantity of such substance in, on, over or under that building or land, or any site of which that building or land forms part.]

(2) Where a group of contiguous or adjacent buildings used as parts of a single undertaking includes industrial buildings used for purposes falling within two or more of the classes specified in the Schedule to this order as Classes III to IX inclusive, those particular two or more classes may, in relation to that

group of buildings, and so long as the area occupied in that group by either general or special industrial buildings is not substantially increased thereby, be treated as a single class for the purposes of this order.

(3) A use which is ordinarily incidental to and included in any use specified in the Schedule to this order is not excluded from that use as an incident thereto merely by reason of its specification in the said Schedule as a separate use. **[434]**

NOTES
Commencement: 1 May 1984 (para (1A)); 23 October 1972 (remainder).
Para (1A): added by SI 1983 No 1614.

SCHEDULE

Class I.—Use as a shop for any purpose except as:—

    (i) a shop for the sale of hot food;
    (ii) a tripe shop;
    (iii) a shop for the sale of pet animals or birds;
    (iv) a cats-meat shop;
    (v) a shop for the sale of motor vehicles.

Class II.—Use as an office for any purpose.

Class III.—Use as a light industrial building for any purpose.

Class IV.—Use as a general industrial building for any purpose.

Class V. (*Special Industrial Group A*)—Use for any work which is registrable under the Alkali &c Works Regulation Act 1906, as extended by the Alkali &c Works Orders' 1966 and 1971 and which is not included in any of Classes VI, VII, VIII or IX of this Schedule.

Class VI. (*Special Industrial Group B*)—Use for any of the following processes, except a process ancillary to the getting, dressing or treatment of minerals which is carried on in or adjacent to a quarry or mine:—

    (i) smelting, calcining, sintering or reduction of ores, minerals, concentrates or mattes;
    (ii) converting, refining, re-heating, annealing, hardening, melting, carburising, forging or casting of metals or alloys, other than pressure die-casting;
    (iii) recovery of metal from scrap or drosses or ashes;
    (iv) galvanizing;
    (v) pickling or treatment of metal in acid;
    (vi) chromium plating.

Class VII. (*Special Industrial Group C*)—Use for any of the following processes except a process ancillary to the getting, dressing or treatment of minerals which is carried on in or adjacent to a quarry or mine:—

    (i) burning of bricks or pipes;
    (ii) lime or dolomite burning;
    (iii) production of zinc oxide, cement or alumina;
    (iv) foaming, crushing, screening or heating of minerals or slag;
    (v) processing by heat of pulverized fuel ash;
    (vi) production of carbonate of lime and hydrated lime;
    (vii) production of inorganic pigments by calcining, roasting or grinding.

Class VIII. (*Special Industrial Group D*)—Use for any of the following purposes:—

    (i) distilling, refining or blending of oils (other than petroleum or petroleum products);
    (ii) production or employment of cellulose and employment of other pressure sprayed metal finishes (other than the employment of any such finishes in vehicle repair workshops in connection with minor repairs, and the

application of plastic powder by the use of fluidised bed and electrostatic spray techniques);
  (iii) boiling of linseed oil and the running of gum;
  (iv) processes involving the use of hot pitch or bitumen (except the use of bitumen in the manufacture of roofing felt at temperatures not exceeding 220/C and also the manufacture of coated roadstone);
   (v) stoving of enamelled ware;
  (vi) production of aliphatic esters of the lower fatty acids, butyric acid, caramel, hexamine, iodoform,napthols, resin products (excluding plastic moulding or extrusion operations and production of plastic sheets, rods, tubes, filaments, fibres or optical components produced by casting, calendering, moulding, shaping or extrusion), salicylic acid or sulphonated organic compounds;
 (vii) production of rubber from scrap;
(viii) chemical processes in which chlorphenols or chlorcresols are used as intermediates;
  (ix) manufacture of acetylene from calcium carbide;
   (x) manufacture, recovery or use of pyridine or picolines, any methyl or ethyl amine or acrylates.

Class IX. (*Special Industrial Group E*)—Use for carrying on any of the following industries, businesses or trades:—

Animal charcoal manufacturer.
Animal hair cleanser, adapter or treater.
Blood albumen maker.
Blood boiler.
Bone boiler or steamer.
Bone burner.
Bone grinder.
Breeder of maggots from putrescible animal matter.
Candle maker.
Catgut manufacturer.
Chitterling or nettlings boiler.
Dealer in rags or bones (including receiving, storing, sorting or manipulating rags in or likely to become in an offensive condition, or any bones, rabbit-skins, fat or putrescible animal products of a like nature).
Fat melter or fat extractor.
Fellmonger.
Fish curer.
Fish oil manufacturer.
Fish skin dresser or scraper.
Glue maker.
Gut scraper or gut cleaner.
Maker of feeding stuff for animals or poultry from any meat, fish, blood, bone, feathers, fat or animal offal, either in an offensive condition or subjected to any process causing noxious or injurious effluvia.
Manufacture of manure from bones, fish, offal, blood, spent hops, beans or other putrescible animal or vegetable matter.
Size maker.
Skin drier.
Soap boiler.
Tallow melter or refiner.
Tripe boiler or cleaner.

Class X.—Use as a wholesale warehouse or repository for any purpose.

Class XI.—Use as a boarding or guest house, or an hotel providing sleeping accommodation.

Class XII.—Use as a residential or boarding school or a residential college.

Class XIII.—Use as a building for public worship or religious instruction or for the social or recreational activities of the religious body using the building.

Class XIV.—Use as a home or institution providing for the boarding, care and maintenance of children, old people or persons under disability, a convalescent home, a nursing home, a sanatorium or a hospital.

Class XV.—Use (other than residentially) as a health centre, a school treatment centre, a clinic, a creche, a day nursery or a dispensary, or use as a consulting room or surgery unattached to the residence of the consultant or practitioner.

Class XVI.—Use as an art gallery (other than for business purposes), a museum, a public library or reading room, a public hall, or an exhibition hall.

Class XVII.—Use as a theatre, cinema, music hall or concert hall.

Class XVIII.—Use as a dance hall, skating rink, swimming bath, Turkish or other vapour or foam bath, or as a gymnasium or sports hall. **[435]**

NOTES
Commencement: 23 October 1972.

TOWN AND COUNTRY PLANNING (LIMIT OF ANNUAL VALUE) ORDER 1973
(SI 1973 NO 425)

NOTES
Made: 12 March 1973
Authority: Town and Country Planning Act 1971, ss 192(4)(*a*), 287

1. (1) This order may be cited as the Town and Country Planning (Limit of Annual Value) Order 1973, and shall come into operation on 1st April 1973.

(2) The Interpretation Act 1889 shall apply for the interpretation of this order as it applies for the interpretation of an Act of Parliament. **[436]**

NOTES
Commencement: 1 April 1973.

2. The amount prescribed for the purposes of section 192(4)(*a*) of the Town and Country Planning Act 1971 shall be two thousand two hundred and fifty pounds. **[437]**

NOTES
Commencement: 1 April 1973.

TOWN AND COUNTRY PLANNING (INQUIRIES PROCEDURE) RULES 1974
(SI 1974 NO 419)

NOTES
Made: 11 March 1974
Authority: Tribunals and Inquiries Act 1971, s 11

ARRANGEMENT OF RULES

1. Citation and commencement

(1) These Rules may be cited as the Town and Country Planning (Inquiries Procedure) Rules 1974.

(2) These Rules shall come into operation on 1st April 1974 but, save as provided in rule 17, shall not affect any application referred to the Secretary of State or appeal brought before that date. **[438]**

NOTES
_____
Commencement: 1 April 1974.

2. Application of Rules

(1) These Rules do not, except to the extent provided by paragraph (3) of this rule, apply to inquiries held under the provisions of Schedule 9 to the Town and Country Planning Act 1971, but save as aforesaid apply—

> (*a*) to local inquiries caused by the Secretary of State to be held for the purpose of applications for planning permission referred to him under section 35 of the Town and Country Planning Act 1971 and appeals to him under section 36 of that Act and (to the extent provided in rule 15) to hearings before a person appointed by the Secretary of State for the purpose of any such application or appeal;

> (*b*) to local inquiries caused by the Secretary of State to be held for the purpose of applications for consent referred to him under a tree preservation order and appeals to him under such an order and (to the extent provided in rule 15) to hearings before a person appointed by the Secretary of State for the purpose of any such application or appeal, subject to the following modifications—

>> (i) rule 4 shall not apply and the references in these Rules to section 29 parties shall be omitted;

>> (ii) references to development shall be construed as references to the cutting down, topping or lopping of trees;

>> (iii) references to permission shall be construed as references to consent;

> (*c*) to local inquiries caused by the Secretary of State to be held for the purposes of applications referred to him and appeals to him under Part I of Schedule 11 to the Town and Country Planning Act 1971 (including applications and appeals under that part of that Schedule as applied by [section 277A of that Act] and (to the extent provided in rule 15) to hearings before a person appointed by the Secretary of State for the purpose of any such application or appeal, subject to the following modifications—

(i) references to development shall be construed as references to works for the demolition, alteration or extension of a listed building or to works for the demolition of a building in a conservation area as the case may be;

(ii) references to permission shall be construed as references to listed building consent;

(*d*) to local inquiries caused by the Secretary of State to be held for the purpose of applications for consent referred to him under the Town and Country Planning (Control of Advertisements) Regulations 1969 to 1974 and appeals to him under those Regulations and (to the extent provided in rule 15) to hearings before a person appointed by the Secretary of State for the purpose of any such application or appeal, subject to the following modifications—

(i) rule 4 shall not apply and the references in these Rules to section 29 parties shall be omitted;

(ii) references to development shall be construed as references to the display of advertisements;

(iii) references to permission shall be construed as references to consent.

(2) . . .

(3) Where the Secretary of State in exercise of his powers under paragraph 3(1) of Schedule 9 to the Town and Country Planning Act 1971, directs that an appeal (which, by virtue of paragraph 1(1) of that Schedule and the regulations made thereunder, falls to be determined by a person appointed by the Secretary of State) shall, instead of being determined by that person, be determined by the Secretary of State, these Rules apply in relation to any step taken or thing done after the giving of the said direction, but do not affect any step taken or thing done before the giving of such direction. **[439]**

NOTES
Commencement: 1 April 1974.
Amended by SI 1986 No 420, Sch 1.

3. Interpretation

(1) In these Rules, unless the context otherwise requires—

"the Act" means the Towns and Country Planning Act 1971;

"the Act of 1972" means the Local Government Act 1972;

"applicant" in the case of an appeal means the appellant;

"appointed person" means the person appointed by the Secretary of State to hold the inquiry;

["the Commission" means the Historic Buildings and Monuments Commission for England;]

"conservation area" means an area designated under section 277 of the Act;

. . .

"inquiry" means a local inquiry to which these Rules apply;

"the land" means the land (inluding trees and buildings) to which the inquiry relates;

"listed buildings" has the meaning assigned to it by section 54 of the Act;

"listed building consent" means required by section 55(2) of the Act in respect of works for the demolition, extension or alteration of a listed building and the consent required by that subsection as applied by [section 277A of that Act] for works for the demolition of a building in a conservation area;

"local authority" has the meaning assigned to it by section 290(1) of the Act;

["local planning authority" means—

    (i) in relation to an application referred to the Secretary of State, the local planning authority, or any local authority or committee acting pursuant to section 101 of the Act of 1972, who would otherwise have dealt with the application; and

    (ii) in relation to an appeal, the local planning authority, or any such local authority or committee, who were responsible for dealing with the application.]

"National Park Committee" has the meaning assigned to it by paragraph 5 of Schedule 17 to the Act of 1972;

"referred application" means an application referred to the Secretary of State under section 35 of the Act, or that section as applied by a tree preservation order, or under regulation 28 of the Town and Country Planning (Control of Advertisements) Regulations 1969 or under paragraph 4 of Schedule 11 to the Act;

"section 29 parties" means—

    (i) in relation to referred application, persons from whom representations are received within the time prescribed—

        (a) in pursuance of section 29(2) or (3) of the Act, as applied by section 35(4), or

        (b) in the case of applications referred under paragraph 4 of Schedule 11 to the Act, in pursuance of regulations made under paragraph 2 of the said Schedule; and

    (ii) in relation to appeals, persons from whom representations are received within the time prescribed—

        (a) by the local planning authority in pursuance of section 29(3) of the Act, or by the Secretary of State in pursuance of section 29(3) as applied by section 36(5), or

        (b) in the case of appeals brought under paragraph 8 of Schedule 11 to the Act, in pursuance of regulations made under paragraph 2 of the said Schedule.

"tree preservation order" means an order under section 60 of the Act;

"trees" includes groups of trees and woodlands.

(2) References in these Rules to section 29 of the Act shall be construed as including where appropriate references to regulations made under paragraph 2 of Schedule 11 to the Act.

(3) The Interpretation Act 1889 shall apply to the interpretation of these Rules as it applies to the interpretation of an Act of Parliament.   **[440]**

NOTES

Commencement: 1 April 1974.

Amended by SI 1986 No 420, Sch 1.

---

4. Preliminary information to be supplied by local planning authority

(1) The local planning authority, on being notified of the Secretary of State's intention to proceed with the consideration of an application or appeal to which

these Rules apply and of the name and address of any person who, pursuant to the provisions of section 29 of the Act, has made representations to the Secretary of State shall forthwith inform the applicant in writing of the name and address of every section 29 party and the Secretary of State of all such persons who have made representations to the local planning authority.

(2) Where the Secretary of State or any local authority has given to the local planning authority a direction restricting the grant of permission for the development for which application was made or a direction as to how an application for planning permission is to be determined and where any government department or local authority has expressed in writing to the local planning authority the view that the application should not be granted either wholly or in part, or should be granted only subject to conditions, or, in the case of an application for consent under a tree preservation order, should be granted together with a direction requiring the replanting of trees, the local planning authority shall inform the Secretary of State, government department or authority concerned, as the case may be, that such direction or expression of view is relevant to the application or appeal and the Secretary of State, government department or authority, as the case may be, shall (except where such action has already been taken) forthwith furnish to the local planning authority a statement in writing of the reasons for the direction or expression of view.

[(3) Where, in a case relating to listed building consent, the Commission has given a direction to the local planning authority pursuant to paragraph 6(2)(*b*) of Schedule 11 to the Act as to how the application is to be determined, the Commission shall at the request of that authority forthwith provide them with a statement in writing of the reasons for the direction.] **[441]**

NOTES
  Commencement: 1 April 1986 (para (3)); 1 April 1974 (remainder).
  Para (3): added by SI 1986 No 420, Sch 1.
  The Act: Town and Country Planning Act 1971.

5. Notification of inquiry

(1) A date, time and place for the holding of the inquiry shall be fixed and may be varied by the Secretary of State who shall give not less than 42 days' notice in writing of such date, time and place to the applicant and to the local planning authority and to all section 29 parties at the addresses furnished by them:

Provided that—

  (i) with the consent of the applicant and of the local planning authority, the Secretary of State may give such lesser period of notice as shall be agreed with the applicant and the local planning authority and in that event he may specify a date for service of the statements referred to in paragraphs (1) and (2) of rule 6 later than the date therein prescribed;

  (ii) where it becomes necessary or advisable to vary the time or place fixed for the inquiry, the Secretary of State shall give such notice of the variation as may appear to him to be reasonable in the circumstances.

(2) Without prejudice to the foregoing provisions of this rule, the Secretary of State may require the local planning authority to take one or more of the following steps—

(*a*) to publish in one or more newspapers circulating in the locality in which land is situated such notices of the inquiry as he may direct;

(*b*) to serve notice of the inquiry in such form and on such persons or classes of persons as he may specify;

(*c*) to post such notices of the inquiry as he may direct in a conspicuous place or places near to the land;

but the requirements as to the period of notice contained in paragraph (1) of this rule shall not apply to any such notices.

(3) Where the land is under the control of the applicant, he shall, if so required by the Secretary of State, affix firmly to some object on the land, in such a manner as to be readily visible to and legible by the public, such notice of the inquiry as the Secretary of State may specify, and thereafter for such period before the inquiry as the Secretary of State may specify, the applicant shall not remove the notice, or cause or permit it to be removed.   **[442]**

NOTES
Commencement: 1 April 1974.

6. Statement to be served before inquiry

(1) In the case of a referred application, the Secretary of State shall (where this has not already been done), not later than 28 days before the date of the inquiry (or such later date as he may specify under proviso (i) to paragraph (1) of rule 5), serve or cause to be served on the applicant, on the local planning authority and on the section 29 parties a written statement of the reasons for his direction that the application be referred to him and of any points which seem to him to be likely to be relevant to his consideration of the application; and where a government department has expressed in writing to the Secretary of State the view that the application should not be granted either wholly or in part, or should be granted only subject to conditions, or, in the case of an application for consent under a tree preservation order, should be granted together with a direction requiring the replanting of trees, the Secretary of State shall include this expression of view in his statement and shall supply a copy of the statement to the government department concerned.

(2) Not later than 28 days before the date of the inquiry (or such later date as the Secretary of State may specify under proviso (i) to paragraph (1) of rule 5), the local planning authority shall—

(*a*) serve on the applicant and on the section 29 parties a written statement of any submission which the local planning authority propose to put forward at the inquiry, and

(*b*) supply a copy of the statement to the Secretary of State.

(3) Where the Secretary of State or a local authority has given a direction restricting the grant of permission for the development for which application was made or a direction as to how the application was to be determined, the local planning authority shall mention this in their statement and shall include in the statement a copy of the direction and the reasons given for it and shall, within the period specified in paragraph (2) above, supply a copy of the statement to the Secretary of State or local authority concerned; and where a government department or a local authority has expressed in writing to the local planning authority the view that the application should not be granted either wholly or in part, or should be granted only subject to conditions, or, in the case of an application for consent under a tree preservation order, should be granted together with a direction requiring the replanting of trees, and the local planning

authority propose to rely on such expression of view in their submissions at the inquiry, they shall include it in their statement and shall, within the period specified in paragraph (2) above, supply a copy of the statement to the government department or local authority concerned.

[(3A) In a case where any such direction as is mentioned in rule 4(3) has been given, the local planning authority shall include in their statement the terms of the direction and of any statement of reasons for the direction provided by the Commission.]

(4) Where the local planning authority intend to refer to, or put in evidence, at the inquiry documents (including maps and plans), the authority's statement shall be accompanied by a list of such documents, together with a notice stating the times and place at which the documents may be inspected by the applicant and the section 29 parties; and the local planning authority shall afford them a reasonable opportunity to inspect and, where practicable, to take copies of the documents.

(5) The local planning authority shall afford any other person interested a reasonable opportunity to inspect and, where practicable, to take copies of any statement served by the Secretary of State under paragraph (1) or by the authority under paragraph (2) and of the other documents referred to in paragraph (4) as well as of any statement served on the authority by the applicant under paragraph (6) of this rule.

(6) The applicant shall, if so required by the Secretary of State, serve on the local planning authority, on the section 29 parties and on the Secretary of State, within such time before the inquiry as the Secretary of State may specify, a written statement of the submissions which he proposes to put forward at the inquiry; and such statement shall be accompanied by a list of any documents (including maps and plans) which the applicant intends to refer to or put in evidence at the inquiry, and he shall, if so required by the Secretary of State, afford the local planning authority and the section 29 parties a reasonable opportunity to inspect and, where practicable, to take copies of such documents. **[443]**

NOTES
  Commencement: 1 April 1986 (para (3A)); 1 April 1974 (remainder).
  Para (3A): added by SI 1986 No 420, Sch 1.

7. Appearances at inquiry

(1) The persons entitled to appear at the inquiry shall be—

  (a) the applicant;
  (b) the local planning authority;
  (c) where the land is not in Greater London [or a metropolitan county], the council of the administrative county in which the land is situated, if not the local planning authority;
  (d) where the land is not in Greater London, the council of the district in which the land is situated (or the Council of the Isles of Scilly, as the case may be), if not the local planning authority;
  (e) where the land is in a National Park, the National Park Committee (if any), if not the local planning authority;
  (f) any joint planning board constituted under section 1 of the Act (or any joint planning board or special planning board reconstituted under Part I of Schedule 17 to the Act of 1972), where that board is not the local planning authority;

(g) where the land is in an area desigated as the site of a new town, the development corporation of the new town;

(h) section 29 parties;

(i) the council of the parish or community in which the land is situated, if that council has made representations to the local planning authority in respect of the application in pursuance of a provision of a development order made under section 24 of the Act;

(j) any persons on whom the Secretary of State has required notice to be served under rule 5(2) (b).

[(k) where the application was required to be notified to the Commission under paragraph 6 of Schedule 11 to the Act (listed building consent in Greater London), the Commission.]

(2) Any other person may appear at the inquiry at the discretion of the appointed person.

(3) A local authority may appear by their clerk or by any other officer appointed for the purpose by the local authority, or by counsel or solicitor; and any other person may appear on his own behalf or be represented by counsel, solicitor or any other person.

(4) Where there are two or more persons having a similar interest in the matter under inquiry, the appointed person may allow one or more persons to appear for the benefit of some or all persons so interested.   **[444]**

NOTES
Commencement: 1 April 1974.
Amended by SI 1986 No 420, Sch 1.
The Act: Town and Country Planning Act 1971.

8. Representatives of government departments at inquiry

(1) Where either—

(a) the Secretary of State has given a direction restricting the grant of permission for the development for which application was made, or

(b) a government department has expressed in writing the view that the application should not be granted either wholly or in part or should be granted only subject to conditions or, in the case of an application under a tree preservation order, should be granted together with a direction requiring the replanting of trees, and the Secretary of State or the local planning authority have included this view in their statement as required by paragraph (1) or (3) of rule 6,

the applicant may, not later than 14 days before the date of the inquiry apply in writing to the Secretary of State for a representative of his department or of the other government department concerned to be made available at the inquiry.

(2) Where an application is made to the Secretary of State under the last foregoing paragraph he shall make a representative of his department available to attend the inquiry or, as the case may be, transmit the application to the other government department concerned, who shall make a representative of that department available to attend the inquiry.

(3) A representative of a government department who, in pursuance of this rule, attends an inquiry into a referred application shall state the reasons for the Secretary of State's direction restricting the grant of permission or, as the case may be, the reasons for the view expressed by his department and included in the Secretary of State's statement under rule 6(1) or the local planning authority's

statement under rule 6(3) and shall give evidence and be subject to cross-examination to the same extent as any other witness.

(4) A representative of a government department who, in pursuance of this rule, attends an inquiry on an appeal, shall be called as a witness by the local planning authority and shall state the reasons for the Secretary of State's direction or, as the case may be, the reasons for the view expressed by his department and included in the authority's statement under rule 6 (3), and shall give evidence and be subject to cross-examination to the same extent as any other witness.

(5) Nothing in either of the last two foregoing paragraphs shall require a representative of a government department to answer any question which in the opinion of the appointed person is directed to the merits of government policy and the appointed person shall disallow any such question. **[445]**

NOTES
  Commencement: 1 April 1974.

9. Representatives of local authorities at inquiry

(1) Where any local authority has—

  (a) given to the local planning authority a direction restricting the grant of planning permission or a direction as to how an application for planning permission was to be determined; or
  (b) expressed in writing the view that an application for planning permission should not be granted wholly or in part or should be granted only subject to conditions, and the local planning authority have included this view in their statement, as required under rule 6(3),

the applicant may, not later than 14 days before the date of the inquiry, apply in writing to the Secretary of State for a representative of the authority concerned to be made available to attend the inquiry.

(2) Where an application is made to the Secretary of State under the last foregoing paragraph he shall transmit the application to the authority concerned, who shall make a representative of the authority available to attend the inquiry.

(3) A representative of a local authority who, in pursuance of this rule, attends an inquiry shall be called as a witness by the local planning authority and shall state the reasons for the authority's direction or, as the case may be, the reasons for the view expressed by them and included in the local planning authority's statement under rule 6(3) and shall give evidence and be subject to cross-examination to the same extent as any other witness. **[446]**

NOTES
  Commencement: 1 April 1974.

9A. Representatives of the Commission at inquiry

[(1) In a case falling within rule 4(3), the applicant or the local planning authority may, not later than 14 days before the date of the inquiry, apply in writing to the Secretary of State for a representative of the Commission to be made available at the inquiry.

(2) The Secretary of State shall transmit any application made under paragraph (1) to the Commission who shall make a representative available to attend the inquiry.

(3) A representative of the Commission who, in pursuance of paragraph (2), attends the inquiry shall be called as a witness by the local planning authority and shall give evidence and be subject to cross-examination to the same extent as any other witness.] **[447]**

NOTES
Commencement: 1 April 1986.
Added by SI 1986 No 420, Sch 1.

10. Procedure at inquiry

(1) Except as otherwise provided in these Rules, the procedure at the inquiry shall be such as the appointed person shall in his discretion determine.

(2) Unless in any particular case the appointed person with the consent of the applicant otherwise determines, the applicant shall begin and shall have the right of final reply; and the other persons entitled or permitted to appear shall be heard in such order as the appointed person may determine.

(3) The applicant, the local planning authority and the section 29 parties shall be entitled to call evidence and cross-examine persons giving evidence, but any other person appearing at the inquiry may do so only to the extent permitted by the appointed person.

(4) The appointed person shall not require or permit the giving or production of any evidence, whether written or oral, which would be contrary to the public interest; but save as aforesaid and without prejudice to the provisions of rule 8(5) any evidence may be admitted at the discretion of the appointed person, who may direct that documents tendered in evidence may be inspected by any person entitled or permitted to appear at the inquiry and that facilities be afforded him to take or obtain copies thereof.

(5) The appointed person may allow the local planning authority or the applicant, or both of them, to alter or add to the submissions contained in any statement served under paragraph (2) or (6) of rule 6, or any list of documents which accompanied such statement, so far as may be necessary for the purpose of determining the questions in controversy between the parties, but shall (if necessary by adjourning the inquiry) give the applicant or the local planning authority, as the case may be, and the section 29 parties an adequate opportunity of considering any such fresh submission or document; and the appointed person may make in his report a recommendation as to the payment of any additional costs occasioned by any such adjournment.

(6) If any person entitled to appear at the inquiry fails to do so, the appointed person may proceed with the inquiry at his discretion.

(7) The appointed person shall be entitled (subject to disclosure thereof at the inquiry) to take into account any written representations or statements received by him before the inquiry from any person.

(8) The appointed person may from time to time adjourn the inquiry and, if the date, time and place of the adjourned inquiry are announced before the adjournment, no further notice shall be required. **[448]**

NOTES
Commencement: 1 April 1974.

11. Site inspections

(1) The appointed person may make an unaccompanied inspection of the land before or during the inquiry without giving notice of his intention to the persons entitled to appear at the inquiry.

(2) The appointed person may, and shall if so requested by the applicant or the local planning authority before or during the inquiry, inspect the land after the close of the inquiry and shall, in all cases where he intends to make such an inspection, announce during the inquiry the date and time at which he proposes to do so.

(3) The applicant, the local planning authority and the section 29 parties shall be entitled to accompany the appointed person on any inspection after the close of the inquiry; but the appointed person shall not be bound to defer his inspection if any person entitled to accompany him is not present at the time appointed. **[449]**

NOTES
Commencement: 1 April 1974.

12. Procedure after inquiry

(1) The appointed person shall after the close of the inquiry make a report in writing to the Secretary of State which shall include the appointed person's findings of fact and his recommendations, if any, or his reason for not making any recommendations.

(2) Where the Secretary of State—

    (*a*) differs from the appointed person on a finding of fact, or

    (*b*) after the close of the inquiry takes into consideration any new evidence (including expert opinion on a matter of fact) or any new issue of fact (not being a matter of government policy) which was not raised at the inquiry,

and by reason thereof is disposed to disagree with a recommendation made by the appointed person, he shall not come to a decision which is at variance with any such recommendation without first notifying the applicant, the local planning authority and any section 29 party who appeared at the inquiry of his disagreement and the reasons for it and affording them an opportunity of making representations in writing within 21 days or (if the Secretary of State has taken into consideration any new evidence or any new issue of fact, not being a matter of government policy) of asking within 21 days for the re-opening of the inquiry.

(3) The Secretary of State may in any case if he thinks fit cause the inquiry to be re-opened, and shall cause it to be re-opened if asked to do so in accordance with the last foregoing paragraph; and, if the inquiry is re-opened, paragraphs (1) and (2) of rule 5 shall apply as they applied to the original inquiry, with the substitution in paragraph (1) of "28" for "42". **[450]**

NOTES
Commencement: 1 April 1974.

13. Notification of decision

(1) The Secretary of State shall notify his decision, and his reasons therefor, in writing to the applicant, the local planning authority and the section 29 parties

and to any person who, having appeared at the inquiry, has asked to be notified of the decision.

(2) Where a copy of the appointed person's report is not sent with the notification of the decision, the notification shall be accompanied by a summary of the appointed person's conclusions and recommendations; and if any person entitled to be notified of the Secretary of State's decision under the last foregoing paragraph has not received a copy of the appointed person's report, he shall be supplied with a copy thereof on written application made to the Secretary of State within one month from the date of his decision.

(3) For the purpose of this rule "report" does not include documents, photographs or plans appended to the report but any person entitled to be supplied with a copy of the report under paragraph (2) of this rule may apply to the Secretary of State in writing within six weeks of the notification to him of the decision or the supply to him of the report, whichever is the later, for an opportunity of inspecting such documents, photographs and plans and the Secretary of State shall afford him an opportunity accordingly.   [451]

NOTES
Commencement: 1 April 1974.

14. Service of notices by post

Notices or documents required or authorised to be served or sent under the provisions of any of these Rules may be sent by post.   [452]

NOTES
Commencement: 1 April 1974.

15. Hearings

These Rules, except paragraphs (2) and (3) of rule 5 and rule 7(1)(*j*) shall apply to any such hearing as is mentioned in rule 2 and for that purpose references in these Rules to an inquiry shall be construed as references to such a hearing.
          [453]

NOTES
Commencement: 1 April 1974.

TOWN AND COUNTRY PLANNING APPEALS (DETER-MINATION BY APPOINTED PERSONS) (INQUIRIES PRO-CEDURE) RULES 1974
(SI 1974 NO 420)

NOTES
Made: 11 March 1974
Authority: Tribunals and Inquiries Act 1971, s 11

ARRANGEMENT OF RULES

1. Citation and commencement

(1) These Rules may be cited as the Town and Country Planning Appeals (Determination by Appointed Persons) (Inquiries Procedure) Rules 1974.

(2) These Rules shall come into operation on 1st April 1974 but, save as provided in rule 20, shall not affect any appeal brought before that date. **[454]**

NOTES

    Commencement: 1 April 1974.

2. Application of Rules

(1) These Rules apply—

    (*a*) to local inquiries held by a person appointed by the Secretary of State for the purpose of appeals to the said Secretary of State under section 36 of the Town and Country Planning Act 1971, where such appeals fall to be determined by the said person instead of by the said Secretary of State by virtue of the powers contained in Schedule 9 to that Act and of regulations made thereunder and (to the extent provided in rule 18) to hearings before such a person for the purposes of any such appeal;

    (*b*) to local inquiries held by a person appointed by the said Secretary of State for the purpose of appeals to the said Secretary of State under a tree preservation order, where such appeals fall to be determined as aforesaid, and (to the extent provided in rule 18) to hearings before such a person for the purpose of any such appeal, subject to the following modifications—

        (i) rule 4 shall not apply and the references in these Rules to section 29 parties shall be omitted;

        (ii) references to development shall be construed as references to the cutting down, topping or lopping of trees;

        (iii) references to permission shall be construed as references to consent;

    (*c*) to local inquiries held by a person appointed by the said Secretary of State for the purpose of appeals to the said Secretary of State under paragraph 8 of Schedule 11 to the Town and Country Planning Act 1971 (including appeals under that paragraph of that Schedule as applied by [section 277A of that Act)] where such appeals fall to be determined as aforesaid, and (to the extent provided in rule 18) to hearings before such a person for the purpose of any such appeal, subject to the following modifications—

    (i) references to development shall be construed as references to works for the demolition, alteration or extension of a listed building or to works for the demolition of a building in a conservation area as the case may be;

    (ii) references to permission shall be construed as references to listed building consent;

   (*d*) to local inquiries held by a person appointed by the said Secretary of State for the purpose of appeals to the said Secretary of State under the Town and Country Planning (Control of Advertisements) Regulations 1969 to 1974, where such appeals fall to be determined as aforesaid, and (to the extent provided in rule 18) to hearings before such a person for the purpose of any such appeal, subject to the following modifications—

    (i) rule 4 shall not apply and the references in these Rules to section 29 parties shall be omitted;

    (ii) references to development shall be construed as references to the display of advertisements;

    (iii) references to permission shall be construed as references to consent.

(2) ...   **[455]**

NOTES
Commencement: 1 April 1974.
Amended by SI 1986 No 420, Sch 2.

3. Interpretation

(1) In these Rules, unless the context otherwise requires—

"the Act" means the Town and Country Planning Act 1971;

"the Act of 1972" means the Local Government Act 1972;

"appointed person" means the person appointed by the Secretary of State to determine the appeal;

["the Commission" means the Historic Buildings and Monuments Commission for England;]

"conservation area" means an area designated under section 277 of the Act;

   ...

"inquiry" means a local inquiry to which these Rules apply;

"the land" means the land (including trees and buildings) to which the inquiry relates;

"listed building" has the meaning assigned to it by section 54 of the Act;

"listed building consent" means consent required by section 55(2) of the Act in respect of works for the demolition, extension or alteration of a listed building and the consent required by that subsection as applied by [section 277A of the Act] for works for the demolition of a building in a conservation area;

"local authority" has the meaning assigned to it by section 290(1) of the Act;

["local planning authority" means the local planning authority, or any local authority or committee acting pursuant to section 101 of the Act of 1972, who were responsible for dealing with the application.]

"National Park Committee" has the meaning assigned to it by paragraph 5 of Schedule 17 to the Act of 1972;

"section 29 parties" means persons from whom representations are received by the local planning authority in pursuance of section 29(3) of the Act, or by the Secretary of State in pursuance of section 29(3) as applied by section 36(5) of the Act, within the time prescribed and, in relation to appeals brought under paragraph 8 of Schedule 11 to the Act, persons from whom representations are received, in pursuance of regulations made under paragraph 2 of the said Schedule, within the time prescribed;

"tree preservation order" means an order under section 60 of the Act;

"trees" includes groups of trees and woodlands.

(2) References in these Rules to section 29 of the Act shall be construed as including where appropriate references to regulations made under paragraph 2 of Schedule 11 to the Act.

(3) The Interpretation Act 1889 shall apply to the interpretation of these Rules as it applies to the interpretation of an Act of Parliament.   [456]

NOTES
 Commencement: 1 April 1974.
 Amended by SI 1986 No 420, Sch 2.

4. Preliminary information to be supplied by local planning authority

(1) The local planning authority, on being notified by the Secretary of State of the intention to proceed with the consideration of an appeal to which these Rules apply and of the name and address of any person who, pursuant to the provisions of section 29 of the Act, has made representations to the Secretary of State, shall forthwith inform the appellant in writing of the name and address of every section 29 party and the Secretary of State of all such persons who have made representations to the local planning authority.

(2) Where any local authority has given to the local planning authority a direction restricting the grant of permission for the development for which application was made or a direction as to how an application for planning permission is to be determined and where any government department or local authority has expressed in writing to the local planning authority the view that the application should not be granted either wholly or in part, or should be granted only subject to conditions, or, in the case of an application for consent under a tree preservation order, should be granted together with a direction requiring the replanting of trees, the local planning authority shall inform the government department or authority concerned, as the case may be, that such direction or expression of view is relevant to the application or appeal and the government department or authority, as the case may be, shall (except where such action has already been taken) forthwith furnish to the local planning authority a statement in writing of the reasons for the direction or expression of view.

[(3) Where, in a case relating to listed building consent, the Commission has given a direction to the local planning authority pursuant to paragraph 6(2)(*b*)

of Schedule 11 to the Act as to how the application is to be determined, the
Commission shall at the request of that authority forthwith provide them with
a statement in writing of the reasons for the direction.]   **[457]**

NOTES
  Commencement: 1 April 1986 (para (3)); 1 April 1974 (remainder).
  Para (3): added by SI 1986 No 420, Sch 2.
  The Act: Town and Country Planning Act 1971.

5. Notification of inquiry

(1) A date, time and place for the holding of the inquiry shall be fixed and may
be varied by the Secretary of State, who shall give not less 42 days, notice in
writing of such date, time and place to the appellant and to the local planning
authority and to all section 29 parties at the addresses furnished by them:

  Provided that—

  (i) with the consent of the appellant and of the local planning
      authority, the Secretary of State may give such lesser period of
      notice as shall be agreed with the appellant and the local planning
      authority and in that event he may specify a date for service of
      the statements referred to in rule 7(1) later than the date therein
      prescribed;

  (ii) where it becomes necessary or advisable to vary the time or place
       fixed for the inquiry, the Secretary of State shall give such notice
       of the variation as may appear to him to be reasonable in the
       circumstances.

(2) Without prejudice to the foregoing provisions of this rule, the Secretary
of State may require the local planning authority to take one or more of the
following steps—

  (a) to publish in one or more newspapers circulating in the locality in
      which the land is situated such notices of the inquiry as he may direct;

  (b) to serve notice of the inquiry in such form, and on such persons or
      classes of persons as he may specify;

  (c) to post such notices of the inquiry as he may direct in a conspicuous
      place or places near to the land;

but the requirements as to the period of notice contained in paragraph (1) of
this rule shall not apply to any such notices.

(3) Where the land is under the control of the appellant he shall, if so
required by the Secretary of State, affix firmly to some object on the land, in
such a manner as to be readily visible to and legible by the public, such notice
of the inquiry as the Secretary of State may specify, and thereafter for such
period before the inquiry as the Secretary of State may specify, the appellant
shall not remove the notice or cause or permit it to be removed.   **[458]**

NOTES
  Commencement: 1 April 1974.

6. Notification of identity of appointed person

The Secretary of State shall give to the appellant, to the local planning authority
and to all section 29 parties written notice informing them of the name of the
appointed person:

  Provided that, where, in exercise of his powers under paragraph 4 of

Schedule 9 to the Act, the Secretary of State has appointed another person to determine the appeal in the place of a person previously appointed for that purpose and it is not practicable to give written notice of the new appointment before the inquiry is held, in lieu of the Secretary of State's giving such notice the person holding the inquiry shall, at the commencement thereof, announce his own name and the fact of his appointment. **[459]**

NOTES
Commencement: 1 April 1974.
The Act: Town and Country Planning Act 1971.

7. Statements to be served before inquiry

(1) Not later than 28 days before the date of the inquiry (or such later date as the Secretary of State may specify under proviso (i) to paragraph (1) of rule 5), the local planning authority shall—

(a) serve on the appellant and on the section 29 parties a written statement of any submission which the local planning authority propose to put forward at the inquiry, and

(b) supply a copy of the statement to the Secretary of State for transmission to the appointed person.

(2) Where a local authority has given a direction restricting the grant of permission for the development for which application was made or a direction as to how the application was to be determined, the local planning authority shall mention this in their statement and shall include in the statement a copy of the direction and the reasons given for it and shall, within the period specified in paragraph (1) above, supply a copy of the statement to the local authority concerned; and where a government department or a local authority has expressed in writing to the local planning authority the view that the application should not be granted, either wholly or in part, or should be granted only subject to conditions or, in the case of an appeal under a tree preservation order, should be granted together with a direction requiring the replanting of trees and the local planning authority propose to rely on such expression of view in their submissions at the inquiry they shall include it in their statement and shall within the period specified in paragraph (1) above, supply a copy of the statement to the government department or local authority concerned.

[(2A) In a case where any such direction as is mentioned in rule 4(3) has been given, the local planning authority shall include in their statement the terms of the direction and of any statement of reasons for the direction provided by the Commission.]

(3) Where the local planning authority intend to refer to, or put in evidence at the inquiry, documents (including maps and plans), the authority's statement shall be accompanied by a list of such documents, together with a notice stating the times and place at which the documents may be inspected by the appellant and the section 29 parties; and the local planning authority shall afford them a reasonably opportunity to inspect and, where practicable, to take copies of the documents.

(4) The local planning authority shall afford any other person interested a reasonable opportunity to inspect and, where practicable, to take copies of any document referred to in the preceding paragraph of this rule, as well as of any statement served on the authority by the appellant under paragraph (5) of this rule.

(5) The appellant shall, if so required by the Secretary of State, serve on the local planning authority, on the section 29 parties and on the Secretary of State for transmission to the appointed person, within such time before the inquiry as the Secretary of State may specify, a written statement of the submissions which he proposes to put forward at the inquiry; and such statement shall be accompanied by a list of any documents (including maps and plans) which the appellant intends to refer to or put in evidence at the inquiry and he shall, if so required by the Secretary of State, afford the local planning authority and the section 29 parties a reasonable opportunity to inspect and, where practicable, to take copies of such documents.   **[460]**

NOTES
    Commencement: 1 April 1986 (para (2A)); 1 April 1974 (remainder).
    Para (2A): added by SI 1986 No 420, Sch 2.

8. Appointed person may act in place of the Secretary of State

The appointed person may himself in place of the Secretary of State take such steps as the Secretary of State is required or enabled to take under or by virtue of rule 5, rule 7(1) or (5), rule 10(1) or (2), rule 11(1) or (2), or rule 11A(1) or (2) (as provided by rule 19 of these Rules).   **[461]**

NOTES
    Commencement: 1 April 1974.

9. Appearances at inquiry

(1) The persons who are entitled to appear at the inquiry shall be—

   (*a*) the appellant;
   (*b*) the local planning authority;
   (*c*) where the land is not in Greater London [or a metropolitan county] the council of the administrative county in which the land is situated, if not the local planning authority;
   (*d*) where the land is not in Greater London, the council of the district in which the land is situated (or the Council of the Isles of Scilly, as the case may be) if not the local planning authority;
   (*e*) where the land is in a National Park, the National Park Committee (if any), if not the local planning authority;
   (*f*) any joint planning board constituted under section 1 of the Act (or any joint planning board or special planning board reconstituted under Part I of Schedule 17 to the Act of 1972), where that board is not the local planning authority;
   (*g*) where the land is in an area designated as the site of a new town, the development corporation of the new town;
   (*h*) section 29 parties;
   (*i*) the council of the parish or community in which the land is situated, if that council has made representations to the local planning authority in respect of the application in pursuance of a provision of a development order made under section 24 of the Act;
   (*j*) any persons on whom the Secretary of State or the appointed person has required notice to be served under rule 5(2)(*b*).
   [(*k*) where the application was required to be notified to the Commission under paragraph 6 of Schedule 11 to the Act (listed building consent in Greater London), the Commission.]

(2) Any other person may appear at the inquiry at the discretion of the appointed person.

(3) A local authority may appear by their clerk or by any other officer appointed for the purpose by the local authority, or by counsel or solicitor; and any other person may appear on his own behalf or be represented by counsel, solicitor or any other person.

(4) Where there are two or more persons having a similar interest in the matter under inquiry, the appointed person may allow one or more persons to appear for the benefit of some or all of the persons so interested. **[462]**

NOTES
Commencement: 1 April 1974.
Amended by SI 1986 No 420, Sch 2.
The Act: Town and Country Planning Act 1971.
Act of 1972: Local Government Act 1972.

10. Representatives of government departments at inquiry

(1) Where a government department has expressed in writing the view that the application should not be granted, either wholly or in part, or should be granted only subject to conditions or, in the case of an appeal under a tree preservation order, should be granted together with a direction requiring the replanting of trees and the local planning authority have included this view in their statement as required by rule 7(2), the appellant may, not later than 14 days before the date of the inquiry, apply in writing to the Secretary of State for a representative of the government department concerned to be made available at the inquiry.

(2) The Secretary of State shall transmit any application made to him under the last foregoing paragraph to the government department concerned, who shall make a representative of the department available to attend the inquiry.

(3) A representative of a government department who, in pursuance of this rule, attends an inquiry or an appeal, shall be called as a witness by the local planning authority and shall state the reasons for the view expressed by his department and included in the authority's statement under rule 7(2), and shall give evidence and be subject to cross-examination to the same extent as any other witness.

(4) Nothing in the last foregoing paragraph shall require a representative of a government department to answer any question which in the opinion of the appointed person is directed to the merits of government policy and the appointed person shall disallow any such question. **[463]**

NOTES
Commencement: 1 April 1974.

11. Representatives of local authorities at inquiry

(1) Where any local authority has—

  (a) given to the local planning authority a direction restricting the grant of planning permission or a direction as to how an application for planning permission was to be determined; or

  (b) expressed in writing the view that an application for planning permission should not be granted wholly or in part or should be granted only subject to conditions, and the local planning authority have included this view in their statement, as required under rule 7(2),

the applicant may, not later than 14 days before the date of the inquiry, apply in writing to the Secretary of State for a representative of the authority concerned to be made available to attend the inquiry.

(2) Where an application is made to the Secretary of State under the last foregoing paragraph he shall transmit the application to the authority concerned, who shall make a representative of the authority available to attend the inquiry.

(3) A representative of a local authority who, in pursuance of this rule, attends an inquiry shall be called as a witness by the local planning authority and shall state the reasons for the authority's direction or, as the case may be, the reasons for the view expressed by them and included in the local planning authority's statement under rule 7(2) and shall give evidence and be subject to cross-examination to the same extent as any other witness. **[464]**

NOTES
Commencement: 1 April 1974.

11A. Representatives of the Commission at inquiry

[(1) In a case falling within rule 4(3), the applicant or the local planning authority may, not later than 14 days before the date of the inquiry, apply in writing to the Secretary of State for a representative of the Commission to be made available at the inquiry.

(2) The Secretary of State shall transmit any application made under paragraph (1) to the Commission who shall make a representative available to attend the inquiry.

(3) A representative of the Commission who, in pursuance of paragraph (2), attends the inquiry shall be called as a witness by the local planning authority and shall give evidence and be subject to cross-examination to the same extent as any other witness.] **[465]**

NOTES
Commencement: 1 April 1986.
Added by SI 1986 No 420, Sch 2.

12. Procedure at inquiry

(1) Except as otherwise provided in these Rules, the procedure at the inquiry shall be such as the appointed person shall in his discretion determine.

(2) Unless in any particular case the appointed person with the consent of the appellant otherwise determines, the appellant shall begin and shall have the right of final reply; and the other persons entitled or permitted to appear shall be heard in such order as the appointed person may determine.

(3) The appellant, the local planning authority and the section 29 parties shall be entitled to call evidence and cross-examine persons giving evidence, but any other person appearing at the inquiry may do so only to the extent permitted by the appointed person.

(4) The appointed person shall not require or permit the giving or production of any evidence, whether written or oral, which would be contrary to the public interest; but, save as aforesaid and without prejudice to the provisions of rule 10(4), any evidence may be admitted at the discretion of the appointed person, who may direct that documents tendered in evidence may be inspected by any person entitled or permitted to appear at the inquiry and that facilities be afforded him to take or obtain copies thereof.

(5) The appointed person may allow the local planning authority or the appellant, or both of them, to alter or add to the submissions contained in any

statement served under paragraph (1) or (5) of rule 7, or to any list of documents which accompanies such statement, so far as may be necessary for the purpose of determining the questions in controversy between the parties, but shall (if necessary by adjourning the inquiry) give the appellant or the local planning authority, as the case may be, and the section 29 parties an adequate opportunity of considering any such fresh submission or document; and the appointed person may make to the Secretary of State a recommendation as to the payment of any additional costs occasioned by any such adjournment.

(6) If any person entitled to appear at the inquiry fails to do so, the appointed person may proceed with the inquiry at his discretion.

(7) The appointed person shall be entitled (subject to disclosure thereof at the inquiry) to take into account any written representations or statements received by him before the inquiry from any person.

(8) The appointed person may from time to time adjourn the inquiry and, if the date, time and place of the adjourned inquiry are announced before the adjournment, no further notice shall be required. **[466]**

NOTES
Commencement: 1 April 1974.

13. Site inspections

(1) The appointed person may make an unaccompanied inspection of the land before or during the inquiry without giving notice of his intention to the persons entitled to appear at the inquiry.

(2) The appointed person may, and shall if so requested by the appellant or the local planning authority before or during the inquiry, inspect the land after the close of the inquiry and shall, in all cases where he intends to make such an inspection, announce during the inquiry the date and time at which he proposes to do so.

(3) The appellant, the local planning authority and the section 29 parties shall be entitled to accompany the appointed person on any inspection after the close of the inquiry; but the appointed person shall not be bound to defer his inspection if any person entitled to accompany him is not present at the time appointed. **[467]**

NOTES
Commencement: 1 April 1974.

14. Procedure after inquiry

(1) If, after the close of the inquiry, the appointed person proposes to take into consideration any new evidence (including expert opinion on a matter of fact) or any new issue of fact (not being a matter of government policy) which was not raised at the inquiry and which he considers to be material to his decision, he shall not come to a decision without first notifying the appellant, the local planning authority and any section 29 party who appeared at the inquiry of the substance of the new evidence or of the new issue of fact and affording them an opportunity of making representations thereon in writing within 21 days or of asking within that time for the re-opening of the inquiry.

(2) The appointed person may, in any case if he thinks fit, cause the inquiry to be re-opened and shall cause it to be re-opened if asked to do so in accordance with the foregoing paragraph; and if the inquiry is re-opened, paragraphs (1)

and (2) of rule 5 shall apply as they applied to the original inquiry, with the modifications that, for the figure "42" in paragraph (1), there shall be substituted the figure "28" and, for references to the Secretary State, wherever they occur, there shall be substituted references to the appointed person. **[468]**

NOTES
Commencement: 1 April 1974.

15. Costs

Where any person makes application at any inquiry for an award of costs, the appointed person shall report in writing the proceedings on such application to the Secretary of State, and may in such report draw attention to any considerations which appear to him to be relevant to the Secretary of State's decision on the matter. **[469]**

NOTES
Commencement: 1 April 1974.

16. Notification of decision

(1) Unless the Secretary of State has, under paragraph 3 of Schedule 9 to the Act, directed that the appeal shall be determined by the Secretary of State, the appointed person shall notify his decision and his reasons therefor in writing to the appellant, the local planning authority and the section 29 parties and to any person who, having appeared at the inquiry, has asked to be notified of the decision.

(2) Any person entitled to be notified of the decision of the appointed person under paragraph (1) of this rule may apply to the Secretary of State in writing within six weeks of the notification to him of the decision for an opportunity of inspecting any documents, photographs or plans listed in the notification and the Secretary of State shall afford him an opportunity accordingly. **[470]**

NOTES
Commencement: 1 April 1974.

17. Service of notices by post

Notices or documents required or authorised to be served or sent under the provisions of any of these Rules may be sent by post. **[471]**

NOTES
Commencement: 1 April 1974.

18. Hearings

These Rules, except paragraphs (2) and (3) of rule 5 and rule 9(1)(*j*), shall apply to any such hearing as is mentioned in rule 2, and for that purpose references in these Rules to an inquiry shall be construed as references to such a hearing.

[472]

NOTES
Commencement: 1 April 1974.

20. Revocation of previous Rules

Town and Country Planning Appeals (Determination by Appointed Persons) (Inquiries Procedure) Rules 1968 are hereby revoked, and any appeal to which those Rules applied and which has not been determined when these Rules come into operation shall be continued under these Rules. **[473]**

NOTES
Commencement: 1 April 1974.

TOWN AND COUNTRY PLANNING (DEVELOPMENT PLANS) ORDER 1974
(SI 1974 NO 460)

NOTES
Made: 13 March 1974
Authority: Local Government Act 1972, s 254(1), (2)(*a*), (*h*)

ARRANGEMENT OF ARTICLES

1. Title, application and commencement

(1) This order may be cited as the Town and Country Planning (Development Plans) Order 1974, and shall come into operation on 1st April 1974.

(2) This order shall apply to England (excluding Greater London) and Wales. **[474]**

NOTES
Commencement: 1 April 1974.

2. Interpretation

(1) The Interpretation Act 1889 shall apply for the interpretation of this order as it applies for the interpretation of an Act of Parliament.

(2) In this order—

"the Act" means the Town and Country Planning Act 1971;
"county planning authority" means a county planning authority as defined in section 1 of the Act;
"development plan" means a development plan as defined in Schedule 5 to the Act;
"district planning authority" means a district planning authority as defined in section 1 of the Act;

"existing authority" means the council of a county or county borough in existence immediately before 1st April 1974;

"structure plan" means a structure plan as defined in section 7 of the Act;

"Wales" means the area consisting of the counties established by section 20 of the Local Government Act 1972 (new local government areas in Wales), and "England" does not include any area included in any of those counties.

(3) References in this order to any enactment or instrument shall, unless the context otherwise requires, be construed as references to that enactment or instrument as amended by any subsequent enactment or instrument. **[475]**

NOTES
Commencement: 1 April 1974.

DEVELOPMENT PLANS OPERATIVE ON 1ST APRIL 1974

3. As from 1st April 1974 the development plan for the area of a county or district planning authority shall consist of such parts of any development plan operative immediately before 1st April 1974 as relate to the area of that authority. **[476]**

NOTES
Commencement: 1 April 1974.

4. Any proposals under Schedule 5 to the Act for the amendment of a development plan, which have been submitted to the Secretary of State before 1st April 1974 by an existing authority, shall be deemed to have been submitted by the county planning authority for the area to which the proposals for amendment relate, and where such proposals relate to an area which falls within the areas of two or more county planning authorities, each such county planning authority shall be deemed to have submitted the proposals for amendment in so far as they relate to land within their area. **[477]**

NOTES
Commencement: 1 April 1974.
The Act: Town and Country Planning Act 1971.

5. (1) Any sealed copy of the development plan for the area of an existing authority which is, immediately before 1st April 1974, in their custody or control shall, on 1st April 1974, be delivered to the county planning authority for the area to which the plan relates, or where the plan relates to land any part of which falls within the areas of two or more county planning authorities, to that county planning authority whose area includes the greatest part thereof.

(2) A county planning authority receiving a development plan under the provisions of paragraph (1) above shall, within one month of the date of receipt, deliver a copy of that plan, or any relevant parts thereof, to each other county or district planning authority whose area includes any part of the land to which the plan relates. **[478]**

NOTES
Commencement: 1 April 1974.

6. Structure plans submitted to the Secretary of State

Any structure plan submitted to the Secretary of State for approval under Part II of the Act, before 1st April 1974, by an existing authority, shall be deemed to have been submitted by the county planning authority for the area to which the plan relates or, where the area of the existing authority is, on 1st April 1974, included within the areas of two or more county planning authorities, by those authorities jointly. **[479]**

NOTES
  Commencement: 1 April 1974.
  The Act: Town and Country Planning Act 1971.

7. Structure and local plans register

(1) Any register maintained by an existing authority in accordance with regulation 42 of the Town and Country Planning (Structure and Local Plans) Regulations 1972 shall, on 1st April 1974, be delivered to the county planning authority for the area to which the register relates, or where the register relates to land any part of which falls within the areas of two or more county planning authorities, to that county planning authority whose area includes the greatest part thereof.

(2) A county planning authority receiving a register under the provisions of paragraph (1) above shall, within one month of the date of receipt of such register, deliver a copy of the register, or any relevant parts thereof, to each other county or district planning authority whose area includes all or any part of the land to which the register relates. **[480]**

NOTES
  Commencement: 1 April 1974.

8. Availability of documents

A county planning authority shall be entitled, at all reasonable times, to inspect and take copies of all plans and documents to which they reasonably require access in connection with their functions under Part II of the Act and which are, on 1st April 1974, in the possession or under the control of any other county or district planning authority and relate to, or form part of—

  (a) any development plan for their area, or proposals for amendment thereto which have been submitted to the Secretary of State; or
  (b) a structure plan for their area which has been submitted to the Secretary of State. **[481]**

NOTES
  Commencement: 1 April 1974.
  The Act: Town and Country Planning Act 1971.

TOWN AND COUNTRY PLANNING (COMPENSATION AND CERTIFICATES) REGULATIONS 1974
(SI 1974 NO 1242)

NOTES
  Made: 16 July 1974
  Authority: Town and Country Planning Act 1971, ss 145, 154, 156, 167, 287

ARRANGEMENT OF REGULATIONS

PART I

GENERAL

PART II

CLAIMS FOR COMPENSATION UNDER PART VII OF THE ACT

PART III

CLAIMS BY MORTGAGEES

PART IV

CLAIMS BY RENTCHARGE OWNERS

PART V

CLAIMS IN RESPECT OF SETTLED LAND

PART VI

CONTRIBUTIONS BY SECRETARY OF STATE UNDER PART VIII OF THE ACT TOWARDS COMPENSATION PAYABLE BY AUTHORITIES FOR REVOCATION OR MODIFICATION OF PLANNING PERMISSION

PART VII

APPLICATIONS FOR CERTIFICATES UNDER SECTION 145 OF THE ACT

SCHEDULES

PART I
GENERAL

1. Citation and commencement

These regulations may be cited as the Town and Country Planning (Compensation and Certificates) Regulations 1974 and shall come into operation on 1st September 1974. **[482]**

NOTES
Commencement: 1 September 1974.

2. Interpretation

(1) The Interpretation Act 1889 shall apply for the interpretation of these regulations as it applies for the interpretation of an Act of Parliament.

(2) In these regulations, unless the context otherwise requires—

"the Act" means the Town and Country Planning Act 1971;
"the Act of 1954" means the Town and Country Planning Act 1954;
"the Act of 1962" means the Town and Country Planning Act 1962;
"the claimant" means the person by or on whose behalf a claim for compensation is made under Part VII of the Act;
"new apportionment" means an apportionment which relates wholly or partly to any matter to which no previous apportionment as defined by section 290(1) of the Act, related;
"original applicant" means a person entitled to exercise the right to claim compensation under Part VII of the Act, apart from these regulations;
"rentcharge payment" and "rentcharge claim" mean respectively a sum payable by the Secretary of State out of compensation under Part VII of the Act to which a rentcharge owner is entitled, if he makes a claim in that behalf under Schedule 2 to these regulations and a claim for a rentcharge payment. **[483]**

NOTES
Commencement: 1 September 1974.

PART II
CLAIMS FOR COMPENSATION UNDER PART VII OF THE ACT

3. Form and delivery of claim

A claim for compensation under Part VII of the Act shall be made in the form, or substantially in the form, prescribed by Schedule 1 to these regulations and shall be sent to the local planning authority making the decision or order in respect of which the claim is made. **[484]**

NOTES
Commencement: 1 September 1974.

4. Action by local planning authorities

(1) The local planning authority shall in transmitting the claim to the Secretary of State furnish to the Secretary of State—

(a) any evidence and other information provided by the claimant in relation to the claim;

(b) where the claim relates to a planning decision of the authority, particulars of the application for planning permission and a copy of the planning decision;

(c) where the planning decision to which the claim relates was determined by the Secretary of State on a reference under section 35 of the Act, or on an appeal under section 36 of the Act, brief particulars of such decision and the Secretary of State's reference number, if known.

(2) The local planning authority shall as soon as may be after the receipt of the claim or notice thereof furnish to the Secretary of State a statement as to the provisions of the development plan so far as material thereto and as to any more favourable decision or permission for alternative development which could in their opinion be given pursuant to section 38 of the Act, and shall also furnish from time to time such other information as the Secretary of State may require for the exercise of his powers under that section.   [485]

NOTES
Commencement: 1 September 1974.

5. Supporting material

If required by the Secretary of State by a direction in writing—

(a) to provide evidence (which may include a statutory declaration) in connection with any particulars required to be supplied by the form prescribed by regulation 3 of these regulations;

(b) to provide further information as to his interest in the land to which the claim relates; or

(c) to provide further information as to the interests of any other persons,

the claimant shall furnish to the Secretary of State such evidence or information as is available to him within such period (not being less than 30 days) as the Secretary of State may specify in the direction.   [486]

NOTES
Commencement: 1 September 1974.

6. Determination of compensation

(1) Unless the claim is withdrawn, and subject to any modification made or having effect under section 155 of the Act, the Secretary of State shall cause such investigations to be made and such steps to be taken as he may deem requisite for a proper determination of the claim.

(2) The Secretary of State shall as soon as practicable thereafter cause to be prepared findings as to the amount (if any) which he determines as the amount of the compensation to be paid under the Act in respect of the said claim, and (except in a case where he determines that no compensation shall be paid in respect of the said claim, in which case the findings shall state such determination and the reason therefor) such findings shall state the depreciation in value of the claimant's interest and the amounts of the unexpended balances of established development value by reference to which the Secretary of State

determines the amount of the compensation to be paid in respect of the said claim.

(3) Where the claimant has failed to furnish any particulars or evidence required by the Secretary of State under regulation 5 of these regulations, the Secretary of State may defer the determination of the claim until after such particulars and evidence have been duly furnished, or if he at any time thinks fit may determine the claim notwithstanding such failure, and in so doing may disregard any particulars already supplied by the claimant to which such requirement had reference.

(4) The Secretary of State shall give notice of his findings to the claimant, and to every other person (if any) who has made and not withdrawn a claim for compensation in respect of the same planning decision, and, in a case where the findings include an apportionment, the Secretary of State shall give particulars of such apportionment to any other person entitled to an interest in land which it appears to the Secretary of State is substantially affected by the apportionment. **[487]**

NOTES
Commencement: 1 September 1974.

7. Disputes

(1) Subject to the provisions of paragraph (2) of this regulation, if the claimant or any other person to whom notice of the Secretary of State's findings has been given, wishes to dispute the findings, or any other person, to whom particulars of an apportionment included in those findings have been given or who claims that he is entitled to an interest in land which is substantially affected by such apportionment, wishes to dispute the apportionment, he may within 30 days of the issue of the Secretary of State's findings, give notice in writing to the Lands Tribunal that he disputes the findings, or as the case may be, the apportionment, and thereupon the dispute shall be referred to the Tribunal, and the Secretary of State shall notify accordingly all other persons to whom notices were given under the last preceding regulation.

(2) Where after receipt of a notice under the last preceding regulation any person signifies in writing to the Secretary of State his agreement to the findings or, as the case may be, to the apportionment, he shall not thereafter be entitled to give the notice referred to in the preceding paragraph.

(3) The claimant and any other person to whom notice of the findings has been given and, so far as the dispute relates to an apportionment, any other person to whom particulars of that apportionment have been given or who establishes that he is entitled to an interest in land which is substantially affected by that apportionment shall, on compliance with the rules of the Lands Tribunal for the time being in force, be afforded an opportunity to be heard in any dispute before the Lands Tribunal under this regulation.

(4) The Lands Tribunal shall by their decision either confirm or vary the Secretary of State's findings, or, as the case may be, the apportionment, and shall notify the parties of their decision. **[488]**

NOTES
Commencement: 1 September 1974.

8. Revision of findings by agreement

(1) If at any time after notice of a dispute has been given under the last preceding regulation the Secretary of State, the claimant and every other person to whom notice of the findings has been given and, so far as the reference relates to an apportionment, all other persons to whom particulars of that apportionment have been given or who are parties to the reference shall in writing agree the amount and distribution of the compensation to be paid under the Act, or, as the case may be, particulars of the apportionment, then on withdrawal of the reference the Secretary of State may revise the findings in accordance with such agreement and shall give notice of such revised findings in the manner prescribed by paragraph (4) of regulation 6 of these regulations.

(2) Where no notice of a dispute in respect of any findings of the Secretary of State is given under the last preceding regulation within the time limited in that behalf or where all references relating to such findings are withdrawn, then the findings or, in a case falling within paragraph (1) of this regulation, the revised findings shall be treated as conclusive for the purposes of section 156 and section 157 of the Act.   [489]

NOTES
Commencement: 1 September 1974.

PART III

CLAIMS BY MORTGAGEES

9. (1) This regulation applies to any compensation payable under Part VII of the Act, where, at the time when the right to claim the compensation has become exercisable, the said right is exercisable by reference to an interest in land, as defined in section 134(4) of the Act, which is subject to a mortgage created before 1st July 1948 or on or after 1st January 1955 and the moneys secured thereby have not been paid in full or charged exclusively on other land:

Provided that this regulation shall have effect, as regards any mortgage created on or after 1st January 1955, subject to any provision to the contrary in that mortgage.

(2) Where the Secretary of State has received from an original applicant a claim for any compensation to which this regulation applies and it appears to the Secretary of State that a mortgagee would be entitled on compliance with paragraph (3) of this regulation to receive the compensation or part of the compensation under paragraph (5) hereof the Secretary of State shall give notice to that mortgagee that such a claim has been made, and shall send a copy of the notice to any other mortgagee who might in his opinion be so entitled if he had priority and any such notice or copy may be sent to the last known address of any such mortgagee or his agent.

(3) Any mortgagee who has received a notice or copy under the last preceding paragraph and who may be entitled to receive in accordance with paragraph (5) of this regulation any compensation or part of any compensation to which this regulation applies, shall if he wishes to receive such payment or part notify the Secretary of State in writing within thirty days of the date of the notice, declaring that the moneys secured by the mortgage have not been paid in full or charged exclusively on other land, stating whether any other mortgagee has priority to him, and giving particulars of the interest to which the mortgage relates or related.

(4) Where an original applicant has failed to claim any compensation to which this regulation applies within the period prescribed in that behalf by the Act, the right to claim shall, in so far as it is exercisable by reference to any interest in land which is, or was, subject to a mortgage and subject to the allowing of an extended or further extended period by the Secretary of State, be exercisable by a mortgagee of the said interest, and where such right is so exercised paragraphs (2) and (3) of this regulation shall apply as if that mortgagee were an original applicant as well as a mortgagee and the original applicant shall be entitled, subject as aforesaid, to claim compensation only in respect of his interest in the part of the land (if any) not subject to the mortgage.

(5) Subject to the foregoing provisions of this regulation and to paragraph (7) hereof where any compensation to which this regulation applies falls to be paid and the moneys secured by the mortgage have not been paid in full or charged exclusively on other land comprised in the mortgage, the compensation shall be paid to the mortgagee who has given notice to the Secretary of State under paragraph (3) of this regulation, or where there is more than one such mortgagee, to the mortgagee having priority, and in either case the mortgagee shall be liable to account therefor as if such compensation had been proceeds of sale of the interest in land subject to the mortgage, or which was so subject, arising under a power of sale exercised by that mortgagee on the date when the compensation is paid:

Provided that where the rights of the mortgagee extend or extended only to part of the land by reference to which the compensation falls to be paid, this paragraph shall have effect in relation only to so much of the compensation as is attributable to the land subject to the mortgage, or which was so subject.

(6) Notwithstanding anything contained in the last preceding paragraph, where no mortgagee has notified the Secretary of State in accordance with paragraph (3) of this regulation that he wishes to receive any compensation the Secretary of State may pay the compensation to the person otherwise entitled thereto.

(7) The Secretary of State may require any mortgagee, empowered by these regulations or by regulations revoked by these regulations to give any notice or claim any compensation, to provide further particulars or evidence in support of his notice or claim (including further information as to any relevant interest in land and as to any other persons interested in such land) and the mortgagee shall furnish any particulars or evidence available to him within thirty days of any such requirement.   [490]

NOTES
Commencement: 1 September 1974.

PART IV

CLAIMS BY RENTCHARGE OWNERS

10. Rentcharge claims

(1) Where the Secretary of State receives from an original applicant a claim for any compensation payable under Part VII of the Act and that compensation is claimed by reference to an interest in land which is subject to a rentcharge created either before 1st July 1948, or on or after 1st January 1955, the Secretary of State shall give to any rentcharge owner appearing to him to be entitled to a rentcharge payment notice of the fact that such a claim has been made, and

such notice may be sent to the last known address of any such rentcharge owner or his agent.

(2) Any rentcharge owner who has received a notice under the last preceding paragraph and who is entitled to receive any rentcharge payment shall make a rentcharge claim to the Secretary of State within thirty days of the date of the said notice.

(3) Any rentcharge claim shall be in writing and shall state—

(*a*) the name and address of any agent whom the rentcharge owner appoints to act for him in connection with the payment of a rentcharge payment;

(*b*) the names and addresses of the owner of the charged land and the rentcharge owner;

(*c*) the amount of the rentcharge;

(*d*) the date when the rentcharge was created;

(*e*) particulars of the charged land, including if necessary such a plan of suitable size as may be requisite to identify the land; and

(*f*) particulars of any other rentcharge affecting the charged land known to the rentcharge owner.

(4) Where an original applicant has failed to claim any such compensation within the period prescribed in that behalf, the right to claim compensation shall, subject to the allowing of an extended or further extended period by the Secretary of State, be exercisable by any rentcharge owner, in so far as it is necessary to enable a rentcharge payment to be made to him or any other rentcharge owner, as if he were an original applicant, and such rentcharge owner shall with his claim under Part VII of the Act furnish to the Secretary of State a rentcharge claim; and where such right is so exercised, the original applicant shall be entitled to any compensation found to be payable in respect of the charged land in excess of any rentcharge payments, and subject as aforesaid may claim compensation only in respect of his interest in the part of the land (if any) not subject to the rentcharge.

(5) The Secretary of State may require any rentcharge owner, empowered by these regulations or by regulations revoked by these regulations to make a rentcharge claim, to provide further particulars or evidence in support of his claim (including further information as to any relevant interest in land and as to any other persons interested in such land) and the rentcharge owner shall furnish any particulars or evidence available to him within thirty days of any such requirement.   **[491]**

NOTES
Commencement: 1 September 1974.

11. Determination of payments

The provisions of Schedule 2 to these regulations (being provisions substantially corresponding, subject to the necessary modifications, with those of section 25 of the War Damage Act 1943, and of Part I of Schedule 4 to that Act) shall have effect for the purpose of determining whether a rentcharge payment is payable in respect of a rentcharge claim, and the amount of any such payment.   **[492]**

NOTES
Commencement: 1 September 1974.

12. Disputes

(1) Where a rentcharge claim has been duly made under paragraph (2) or paragraph (4) of regulation 10 in respect of a rentcharge (in this regulation referred to as "the rentcharge in question") the Secretary of State shall, on giving notice of his findings as to the amount of compensation, send a notice (in this regulation referred to as "a rentcharge notice") to the original applicant and the owner of the rentcharge in question.

(2) A rentcharge notice shall specify—

    (*a*) the amount of the rentcharge payment which the Secretary of State has determined to be payable in respect of the rentcharge in question, the annual equivalent of the rentcharge payment and the manner in which such amount and value have been ascertained under Schedule 2 to these regulations; and

    (*b*) the amount of any rentcharge payment which the Secretary of State has determined to be payable in respect of any prior rentcharge or would have so determined on a rentcharge claim by that rentcharge owner:

Provided that where no rentcharge payment is payable, the notice shall specify that fact as if an amount were determined to be payable.

(3) Subject to paragraph (5) of this regulation, if any person to whom a rentcharge notice has been sent wishes to dispute any part of that notice, he may, within thirty days of the issue of the rentcharge notice, give in writing to the Lands Tribunal a notice of dispute specifying the part or parts of the rentcharge notice to which the dispute relates, and thereupon the dispute shall be referred to the Lands Tribunal.

(4) Where a notice of dispute has been given under the last preceding paragraph, the Secretary of State shall notify the other person to whom the rentcharge notice was sent, and, where the dispute relates to or affects a rentcharge payment in respect of a rentcharge other than the rentcharge in question, shall notify the owner of that rentcharge.

(5) Where after receipt of a rentcharge notice any person signifies in writing to the Secretary of State his agreement to that notice, he shall not thereafter be entitled to give a notice of dispute under paragraph (3) of this regulation.

(6) The original applicant and the owner of the rentcharge in question and, so far as the dispute relates to or may affect the amount of a rentcharge payment in respect of a rentcharge other than the rentcharge in question, the owner of that rentcharge, shall, on compliance with the rules of the Lands Tribunal for the time being in force, be afforded an opportunity to be heard in any dispute before the Lands Tribunal under this regulation.

(7) The Lands Tribunal shall by their decision either confirm or vary the rentcharge notice relating to the rentcharge in question and shall notify the parties of their decision:

Provided that where on a reference of the Secretary of State's findings as to the compensation payable under Part VII of the Act the amount of such compensation has been varied by the Lands Tribunal, that variation shall be taken into account, but, save as aforesaid, the Tribunal shall not by their decision vary such amount.

(8) Where the Lands Tribunal vary a rentcharge notice under the last preceding paragraph, effect shall be given by the Secretary of State to such

variation in making any rentcharge payment out of the said compensation whether or not the rentcharge notice relating to that payment has been varied by the Tribunal.　　　　　　　　　　　　　　　　　　**[493]**

NOTES
　Commencement: 1 September 1974.

PART V

CLAIMS IN RESPECT OF SETTLED LAND

13. Where the right to claim any compensation under Part VII of the Act becomes exercisable by reference to an interest in land which is, at the time when the said right is exercisable, subject to a settlement, then—

(a) the right to claim compensation shall be exercisable by the trustees of the settlement;

(b) where a claim has been made by reference to such an interest as aforesaid and compensation falls to be paid, the compensation shall be paid to the trustees of the settlement, and to the extent that, as between the persons beneficially interested under the trusts of the settlement, any moneys so received by the said trustees ought to be treated as capital, such moneys shall be applicable as capital money under the Settled Land Act 1925, or as proceeds of sale arising under the trust for sale, as the case may be.　　　　　　　　　**[494]**

NOTES
　Commencement: 1 September 1974.

PART VI

CONTRIBUTIONS BY SECRETARY OF STATE UNDER PART VIII OF THE ACT TOWARDS COMPENSATION PAYABLE BY AUTHORITIES FOR REVOCATION OR MODIFICATION OF PLANNING PERMISSION

14. Proposal for contribution

(1) Where the Secretary of State proposes to pay a contribution under section 167 of the Act, he shall prepare a statement of the amount of the contribution showing the manner in which such amount has been ascertained.

(2) The Secretary of State shall send a copy of the said statement to any person appearing to him to have an interest in land to which the proposal relates or an interest which is substantially affected by an apportionment involved in the proposal.

(3) The Secretary of State shall also send a copy of the said statement to every other person who appears to him to be substantially affected by the reduction or extinguishment, as the case may be, of the unexpended balance of established development value of that land.

(4) Any person to whom a copy of the said statement has been sent may within 30 days thereafter give notice in writing to the Secretary of State that he objects to the proposal and shall specify whether his objection is made on the grounds—

(a) that compensation would not have been payable under Part VII of the Act or Part II or Part V of the Act of 1954 or Part VI of the Act of 1962, as the case may be; or

(b) that the amount of the compensation would have been less than the amount of the proposed contribution;

and the Secretary of State shall consider such objection.

(5) As soon as may be after giving effect to the preceding provisions of this regulation, the Secretary of State shall determine the amount of the contribution (if any) to be made, and shall serve notice in writing upon every person to whom a copy of the said statement was sent.   **[495]**

NOTES
Commencement: 1 September 1974.
The Act: Town and Country Planning Act 1971.
Act of 1954: Town and Country Planning Act 1954.
Act of 1962: Town and Country Planning Act 1962.

15. Disputes

(1) If any person who objected to the Secretary of State's proposal and did not withdraw his objection wishes to dispute the determination of the Secretary of State under the last preceding regulation, he may within 30 days of the Secretary of State's determination give notice in writing to the Lands Tribunal that he disputes the findings and shall specify whether he objects on the grounds—

(a) that compensation would not have been payable under Part VII of the Act or Part II or Part V of the Act of 1954 or Part VI of the Act of 1962, as the case may be; or

(b) that the amount of the compensation would have been less than the amount of the proposed contribution;

and thereupon the dispute shall be referred to the Lands Tribunal for determination and the Secretary of State shall notify accordingly all other persons to whom notices were given under the last preceding regulation.

(2) All persons to whom notices of any findings have been given shall be entitled to be heard in any dispute before the Lands Tribunal under paragraph (1) of this regulation.

(3) The Lands Tribunal shall by their decision either confirm or vary the Secretary of State's findings, or, as the case may be, the apportionment, and shall notify the parties of their decision.   **[496]**

NOTES
Commencement: 1 September 1974.
The Act: Town and Country Planning Act 1971.
Act of 1954: Town and Country Planning Act 1954.
Act of 1962: Town and Country Planning Act 1962.

16. Application of provisions of the Act

(1) The provisions of section 140(1) of the Act as to the reduction or extinguishment of the unexpended balance of established development value shall apply in a case where a contribution is paid under section 167 of the Act as they apply where compensation under Part VII of the Act becomes payable in respect of the depreciation of the value of an interest in land by a planning decision and as if the revocation or modification were such a decision.

(2) Where an amount becomes recoverable under section 160(6) as applied by section 168 of the Act, section 161 shall apply as if—

(a) the reference to compensation specified in a compensation notice were a reference to compensation for depreciation specified in the notice under section 166;

(b) the reference to section 160 were a reference to subsection (2) of that section as applied by section 168; and

(c) the reference to the compensation attributable to the land were a reference to the Secretary of State's contribution attributable to the land.   **[497]**

NOTES
Commencement: 1 September 1974.

PART VII

APPLICATIONS FOR CERTIFICATES UNDER SECTION 145 OF THE ACT

17. Applications for certificates under section 145(1)

(1) An application for a certificate under section 145(1) of the Act shall be in the form prescribed in Schedule 3 to these regulations, or a form substantially to the like effect, and shall be made by sending the application to the District Valuer of the Board of Inland Revenue.

(2) A separate application shall be made in respect of each parcel of land which is in separate occupation or separately rated at the time of the application, except where a certificate is required in respect of two or more contiguous parcels of land by a person entitled to an interest (including a mortgage or rentcharge) in such parcels or for the purposes of a transaction relating thereto.

(3) A certificate issued under the said section 145(1) shall be in the form prescribed in Schedule 4 to these regulations or a form substantially to the like effect.   **[498]**

NOTES
Commencement: 1 September 1974.

18. Applications for certificates under section 145(3)

An application for a certificate under section 145(3) of the Act shall be in the form prescribed in Schedule 5 to these regulations, or a form substantially to the like effect, and shall be made by sending the application to the District Valuer of the Board of Inland Revenue.   **[499]**

NOTES
Commencement: 1 September 1974.

19. Payment of fees

(1) Subject to the following paragraph of this regulation, the fee of twenty-five new pence payable on an application for a certificate under section 145(1) of the Act shall be paid by attaching to the application form adhesive postage stamps to the value of twenty-five new pence.

(2) Where an application involves a new apportionment the further fee of seventy-five new pence shall be sent to the Department of the Environment or the Welsh Office before the certificate is issued, or such further fee may be paid

with the initial fee of twenty-five new pence by sending with the application a
cheque or a money or postal order for the sum of one pound payable to the
Department and crossed.   **[500]**

NOTES
    Commencement: 1 September 1974.

SCHEDULES

SCHEDULE 1

Regulation 3

FORM OF CLAIM FOR THE PAYMENT OF COMPENSATION UNDER PART VII

Name and address of claimant (in BLOCK LETTERS)

*Surname...................................... Other Names...................................
(State whether Mr., Mrs. or Miss)

Address ....

            ....

If you have a professional adviser or agent to whom you wish communications regarding your claim to be sent, give his name and address here.

1. (i) Address and description of land with reference to which your claim is made. (You should enclose a map sufficient to identify the boundaries of the land).
   (ii) What is your interest in this land? (State whether freehold or leasehold, and if the latter give short particulars of the lease, including the rent payable).
   (iii) Date of acquisition.
   (iv) In what capacity do you claim, e.g., as beneficial owner, personal representatives, trustees, mortgagee or rentcharge owner?	

2. (i) Do you know of any other person who is interested in or has rights over the land, e.g., lessee, mortgagee, agricultural tenant, tenant (1 year or more) rentcharge owner? If so, give
   (a) name and address of such person and nature of interest or rights;
   (b) date of creation of interest or rights;
   (c) period of lease if applicable.
   (ii) Give details of any outgoings affecting the land, other than ordinary rates and taxes.	

3. Has any interest in the land been held by a public authority at any time since 1st July 1948?	

*Note: If the claim is made by personal representatives or by trustees, the full names of
the personal representatives/trustees must be given.

4. Give such particulars as you can (including reference number and date) of the planning decision which gives rise to your claim for compensation.	
5. Give particulars of any development of the land which has taken place since 1st July 1948 and the date of its commencement.	
6. (i) Do you know whether a claim for a payment out of the £300 million fund under Part VI of the Town and Country Planing Act 1947(a) was established with the Central Land Board in respect of the land to which the present application relates, or part of it? If so, give brief particulars, including the Board's reference number. (ii) Do you know of any application under Part I of the Town and Country Planning Act 1954 made, or pending, in respect of land included in your present claim or in respect of other land comprised in the claim referred to at (i) above? If so, give brief particulars.	
7. State what amount you claim as the depreciation in value caused by the planning decision. (Note.—Only land in respect of which a claim was established under Part VI of the Town and Country Planning Act 1947, is eligible for compensation).	

I declare that all the statements made on this form are true to the best of my knowledge and belief and I hereby claim the payment of such compensation as may be determined to be due to me.

Signature... Date...

Note: This form, when completed, should be sent to the Local Planning Authority by whom the planning decision was issued.

[501]

NOTES

Commencement: 1 September 1974.

SCHEDULE 2

Regulation 11

PROVISIONS FOR DETERMINING RENTCHARGE PAYMENTS

Definitions

1. In this Schedule—

"the relevant decision" means the planning decision in respect of which the right to claim compensation under Part VII of the Act becomes exercisable; and

"the material time" means the date of the relevant planning decision determined in accordance with the provisions of section 290(4) of the Act.

Entitlement to rentcharge payment

2.—(1) Where the right to claim any compensation under Part VII of the Act is exercisable by reference to an interest in land (being either a fee simple or a tenancy granted for a term of one hundred years or more) and—

(a) there was subsisting at the material time a rentcharge created either before 1st July 1948, or on or after 1st January 1955 and created out of part or the whole of the area of land by reference to which the said right is exercisable, or out of that land together with other land; and

(b) the amount of the rentcharge so far as attributable to the land subject thereto by reference to which the said right is exercisable (in this Schedule referred to as "the charged land") exceeds the available annual limited value of the charged land ascertained in accordance with paragraph 6 of this Schedule,

then, subject to paragraph 4 of this Schedule, that rentcharge owner shall be entitled, if he makes a rentcharge claim, to receive from the Secretary of State, out of the compensation which falls to be paid under Part VII of the Act, a sum equal to the capital equivalent of the excess:

Provided that the said sum shall not exceed the amount of the said compensation.

(2) Where the interest in land by reference to which the right to claim compensation is exercisable was subject at the material time to more than one such rentcharge as is mentioned in the preceding sub-paragraph, then—

(a) where more than one rentcharge owner has made a rentcharge claim the rentcharge payment to each of them who has so claimed shall be so paid out of the compensation that each rentcharge owner receives the payment to which he is entitled, or so much thereof as can be satisfied out of the compensation after rentcharge payments have been made to owners of any rentcharge having priority;

(b) where a rentcharge owner fails to make a rentcharge claim he shall not be entitled to the payment of any sum under this Schedule but the foregoing provisions of this paragraph shall have effect to enable such rentcharge payments to be made to other rentcharge owners as would have been payable if he had made such a claim.

Extinguishment of part of rentcharge

3. Where a rentcharge owner receives any sum under paragraph 2 of this Schedule, so much of the rentcharge as is equal to the annual equivalent of the said sum shall be extinguished on the date on which the said sum is paid, and as between the persons interested in the charged land on the one hand and any other land subject to the rentcharge on the other hand, the proper share of the persons interested in the charged land of the liability for the residue of the rentcharge in respect of any period after the extinguishment shall be treated as being the rentcharge attributable to the charged land, less the annual equivalent of the sum so paid.

Priority between rentcharges and mortgages

4. Where a rentcharge owner makes a rentcharge claim and the right to receive the compensation in respect of the interest in land out of which (or out of which together with any other interest) the rentcharge was created is vested by virtue of the provisions of regulation 9 of these regulations in a mortgagee of that interest, then—

(a) if the rentcharge had priority to the mortgage, the sum payable to the mortgagee under regulation 9 shall be reduced by the amount required for giving effect to the right conferred upon the rentcharge owner under paragraph 2 of this Schedule; and

(b) if the mortgage had priority to the rentcharge, the Secretary of State shall, when making the payment of any compensation to a mortgagee in pursuance of regulation 9, give to that mortgagee notice of—

    (i) the name and address of the rentcharge owner who has claimed the rentcharge payment, or, if that owner has appointed any agent to act for him in connection with the payment of such a sum, the name and address of that agent; and

    (ii) the amount of the rentcharge payment which the Secretary of State, or the Lands Tribunal if any dispute has been referred to them, has determined to be payable to the rentcharge owner out of compensation,

and the mortgagee to whom the compensation is paid under regulation 9 shall give effect to the right conferred by paragraph 2 of this Schedule on the rentcharge owner out of the sum to which the person who would have been entitled to the compensation apart from regulation 9 will become entitled under the provisions of paragraph (5) of regulation 9 relating to a mortgagee accounting for any compensation as if it were proceeds of a sale.

Provisions as to registered land

5. In cases in which the title to a rentcharge or to land subject thereto is registered under the Land Registration Act 1925, such provision may, without prejudice to the generality of section 144 of that Act, be made by rules under that section as may be expedient in consequence of the provisions of this Schedule, and in particular for securing (by the imposition of conditions as to the exercise of the right thereby conferred or otherwise) that the extinguishment of any part of a rentcharge by virtue of this Schedule shall not take effect without notice thereof being entered in the register.

Computation of rentcharge payment

6. The following provisions of this paragraph shall have effect for the purpose of ascertaining the amounts and values mentioned in the foregoing paragraphs of this Schedule, that is to say—

(a) the annual limited value of the charged land shall—

    (i) if the charged land is co-terminous with or greater in area than the land by reference to which compensation under Part VII of the Act falls to be paid, be taken to be five per cent. of the value of that land after the relevant decision;

    (ii) if the charged land is part of the land by reference to which the said compensation falls to be paid, be determined by apportioning to the charged land the appropriate part of the said percentage of the said value, and, in either case, the charged land shall be treated as if it were free from incumbrances, but subject to any easement or other restriction affecting the land at the material time;

(b) the available annual limited value of the charged land shall be taken to be the annual limited value thereof less the amount so far as attributable to any of the charged land, of—

    (i) any rentcharge having priority to the rentcharge in question to which the fee simple in the charged land was subject at the material time, or, where that rentcharge was created out of a tenancy of the land, to which either the fee simple therein or that tenancy or any superior tenancy thereof was subject at that time; and

    (ii) where that rentcharge was created out of a tenancy of the charged land, the rent reserved by the lease for the year current at the material time:

Provided that in ascertaining the available annual limited value of the charged land no deduction shall be made from the annual limited value therof in respect of any such amount as aforesaid, in so far as the owner of the rentcharge in question is liable for the payment of that amount as between himself and the owner of the interest out of which the rentcharge was created;

(*c*) the amount attributable to any land of a rentcharge, or of rent reserved by a lease, shall, where at the material time that land was the only land subject to the rentcharge, or out of which the rent issued, be taken to be the whole amount of the rentcharge payable or of the rent reserved for the year current at the said time, and where the charged land was not the only land subject to the rentcharge, shall be determined by apportioning or allocating to that land so much (if any) of the whole amount as may be appropriate having regard—

  (i) primarily to any apportionment or allocation of that rentcharge or rent which may have been made otherwise than so as to be binding on the owner of that rentcharge or on the landlord, as the case may be, before the material time; and

  (ii) subject as aforesaid, to the proportion borne by the annual value of that land immediately before the relevant decision to the annual value of the other land subject to the rentcharge or rent immediately before that decision;

(*d*) the capital equivalent of the excess of the amount of the rentcharge so far as attributable to the charged land over the available annual limited value of that land shall be taken to be that excess multiplied by the number of years purchase which the rentcharge might have been expected to realise on a sale thereof made in the open market immediately after the relevant decision if at that time the relevant decision had been a decision to the contrary effect.   **[502]**

NOTES
Commencement: 1 September 1974.

SCHEDULE 3

Regulation 17(1)

FORM OF APPLICATION FOR A CERTIFICATE UNDER SECTION 145(1)

Application No........................

Claim File No......./....../S.........

TOWN AND COUNTRY PLANNING ACT 1971

Original Unexpended Balance of Established Development Value
APPLICATION FOR A CERTIFICATE UNDER SECTION 145(1)

1. Name(s) and Address(es) of Applicant(s) (in block capitals)
   (*a*) Surname(s) (State whether Mr., Mrs., Miss) ....

   ....

   Other name(s)..

   (*b*) Present postal address(es)...

   ....

   ....

   Note: In the case of a joint application the names of each applicant should be given, but the Department or Welsh Office will send all communications to the first named applicant unless a written request to the contrary is made.

2. Particulars of Agent (if any) to whom the applicant wishes any communications about this application to be sent.

   Name ....

   Postal address..

   ....

   Telephone number... Profession...........................

3. Particulars of Land to which the application relates:—
   (i) Description, situation and extent of land (see note 1)..............................

   ....

   ....

   (ii) Nature of the applicant's present interest in the land, if freehold or leasehold, (if neither, state "none") (see note 2)...

   ....

   (iii) Give particulars of any other freehold or leasehold interest in the land with names and addresses of the persons entitled, so far as known (see note 3)

   ....

   ....

   ....

   Note 1. If a map is necessary to enable the land to be identified an accurate map of sufficiently large scale and with sufficient detail for this purpose must accompany this application.

   Note 2. Only a person who has an interest in the land to which this application relates is entitled under section 145(1) of the Act to a certificate if a new apportionment will be required before the certificate can be issued. If therefore on examination of this application it is found that the applicant has no interest in the land and that a new apportionment is involved, no certificate will be issued and he will be informed accordingly. In such cases the application fee of 25p will not be refunded.

   Note 3. Question (iii) need not be answered by applicants who have stated "none" in answer to question (ii).

4. Particulars of claim established under Part VI of the Town and Country Planning Act 1947 (if known).

    (i) Claim file number (as shown on the determination of development value) ....../....../S.........

    (ii) Name(s) and address(es) of the person(s) who owned the land, or interests in the land, on 1st July 1948...

....

....

    Note: The completion of this section is optional but it will assist the Department/Welsh Office if the information is provided.

5. Application Fee

    Under section 145(9) of the Act a fee of twenty-five new pence is payable in respect of this application. This fee must be paid by attaching to this form of application in the space provided below postage stamps to this value. If a new apportionment is necessary to enable the certificate to be given in respect of land to which the application relates, a further fee of seventy-five new pence will be payable before the certificate is issued. The Department, or Welsh Office, after examining the application will inform the applicant whether this further fee is payable.

6. Office for Receipt of Applications
This application form when duly completed and stamped should be sent by post or handed to the District Valuer of the Valuation District within which the land to which this application relates is situated.

7. Formal Application (to be signed by the applicant(s) whose name(s) is/are shown in paragraph 1 above).

    I/We hereby request the Secretary of State to issue to me/us a certificate in accordance with the provisions of section 145(1) of the Town and Country Planning Act 1971, and of the Town and Country Planning (Compensation and Certificates) Regulations 1974.

                    Signature..

                          ....

Date...

    A postage stamp or stamps to the value of twenty-five new pence should be attached to this form in the space below.

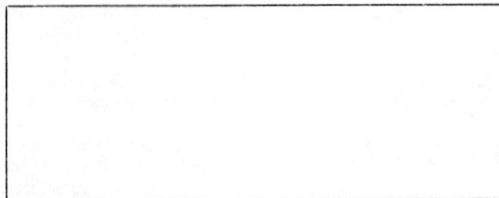

[503]

NOTES   ·
    Commencement: 1 September 1974.

SCHEDULE 4

Regulation 17(3)

FORM OF CERTIFICATE ISSUED UNDER SECTION 145(1)
ORIGINAL UNEXPENDED BALANCE OF ESTABLISHED DEVELOPMENT VALUE

CERTIFICATE issued under Section 145(1) of the Town and Country
Planning Act 1971

DESCRIPTION OF LAND...

....

....

Department's reference number..

Date of issue of certificate...

The Secretary of State for the Environment/Secretary of State for Wales hereby
certifies as follows:—

(i) the part(s) of the above described land [as] indicated in the Schedule hereto
*$\frac{\text{has/have severally}}{\text{has (have) not}}$ an original unexpended balance of established development
value within the meaning of section 136 of the Town and Country Planning
Act 1971;

(ii) on 1st July 1948, the state of the said part(s) was taken for the purposes of
Part VI of the Town and Country Planning Act 1947, to be

....

....

(iii) the following is the amount of the said original unexpended balance (i.e. the
unexpended balance as at 1st January 1955).

†(iv)

SCHEDULE

Signed...
Authorised by the Secretary of
State to sign in that behalf.

----

*Delete as appropriate.
†Additional information if any, to be inserted here.

[504]

NOTES
   Commencement: 1 September 1974.

SCHEDULE 5

Regulation 18

FORM OF APPLICATION FOR A CERTIFICATE UNDER SECTION 145(3)

Application No.........................

Claim File No......./....../S.........

TOWN AND COUNTRY PLANNING ACT 1971

Unexpended Balance of Established Development Value
Application for a Certificate under section 145(3)

1. Name and Address of Public Authority (in block capitals)

   (*a*) Name of Public Authority...

   (*b*) Postal Address..

   ....

2. PARTICULARS OF LAND to which the application relates

   (i) Description, situation and extent of land..

   ....

   (ii) Description of interest(s) being acquired..

   ....

   (iii) Details of the powers under which the acquisition is being effected. (It should
   be stated whether minerals are excluded from the acquisition)....................

   ....

   (iv) The date on which a notice to treat was served, or was deemed to have been
   served, with a view to the compulsory acquisition of an interest in the land

   ....

   ....

   (v) Is there more than one interest (i.e. freehold or leasehold) in the land? (Answer
   "Yes" or "No")..

   (vi) If the answer to (v) above is "Yes" give (if known) the names and addresses
   of the owners of other interests and the nature of their interests.

   ....

   ....

   ....

   ....

   ....

*3. PARTICULARS OF CLAIM ESTABLISHED UNDER PART VI OF THE TOWN AND COUNTRY PLANNING ACT 1947 (if known).

(i) Claim file number (as shown on the determination of development value) ..../......................./S.................

(ii) Name(s) and address(es) of the person(s) who owned the land, or an interest in the land on 1st July 1948...

....

....

Note—Question 3(ii) need be answered only if the Central Land Board's claim file number is not known.

*4. NEW DEVELOPMENT

Has any new development, within the meaning of section 22(5) of the Town and Country Planning Act 1971 been carried out on the land since 1st July 1948? If so, give details, including date of commencement...

....

....

*5. PREVIOUS ACQUISITIONS

Has any interest in the land previously been compulsorily acquired by a public authority or acquired by agreement by a public authority possessing compulsory purchase powers? If the answer is "Yes" give details.......................................

....

....

6. FORMAL APPLICATION

I/We hereby request the Secretary of State for the Environment/Secretary of State for Wales to issue to...(name of authority) a certificate in accordance with the provisions of section 145(3) of the Town and Country Planning Act 1971 showing the unexpended balance of established development value, if any, of the land described in paragraph 2 above immediately before the service of the notice mentioned in that paragraph.

Signature ....

(Rank of Signatory)..
For and on behalf of the above authority.

Date ....

*The completion of these sections is optional but it will assist the Department if the information is provided.

[505]

NOTES
Commencement: 1 September 1974.

TOWN AND COUNTRY PLANNING (TREE PRESERVATION ORDER) (AMENDMENT) AND (TREES IN CONSERVATION AREAS) (EXEMPTED CASES) REGULATIONS 1975
(SI 1975 NO 148)

NOTES
Made: 11 February 1975
Authority: Town and Country Planning Act 1971, ss 60, 61A, 287

1. Citation, commencement and interpretation

(1) These regulations may be cited as the Town and Country Planning (Tree Preservation Order) (Amendment) and (Trees in Conservation Areas) (Exempted Cases) Regulations 1975 and shall come into operation on 12th March 1975.

(2) The Interpretation Act 1889 shall apply for the interpretation of these regulations as it applies for the interpretation of an Act of Parliament.   **[506]**

NOTES
Commencement: 12 March 1975.

3. Trees in conservation areas—exempted cases

Section 61A of the Town and Country Planning Act 1971 shall not apply where the act is—

    (i) the cutting down, uprooting, topping or lopping of a tree in the curcumstances mentioned in sub-section (6) of section 60 of that Act;

    (ii) the cutting down of a tree in the circumstances mentioned in paragraph (1) or (2), or the cutting down, uprooting, topping or lopping of a tree in the circumstances mentioned in paragraph (3), of the Second Schedule to the Form of Tree Preservation Order contained in the Schedule to the Town and Country Planning (Tree Preservation Order) Regulations 1969 (as amended by these regulations);

    (iii) the cutting down of a tree in accordance with a felling licence granted by the Forestry Commissioners;

    (iv) the cutting down, uprooting, topping or lopping of a tree on land in the occupation of a local planning authority and the act is done by or with the consent of that authority;

    (v) the cutting down, uprooting, topping or lopping of a tree having a diameter not exceeding 75 millimetres, or the cutting down or uprooting of a tree having a diameter not exceeding 100 millimetres where the act is carried out to improve the growth of the other trees, the reference to "diameter" herein being construed as a reference to the diameter, measured over the bark, at a point 1.5 metres above the ground level.   **[507]**

NOTES
Commencement: 12 March 1975.

TOWN AND COUNTRY PLANNING GENERAL REGULATIONS 1976
(SI 1976 NO 1419)

NOTES
Made: 1 September 1976
Authority: Town and Country Planning Act 1971, ss 46, 91, 164, 169, 170, 177, 180, 187, 188, 189, 193, 194, 201, 212, 219, 270, 283, 287, 290; Land Compensation Act 1973, s 78

ARRANGEMENT OF REGULATIONS

PART I

TITLE, COMMENCEMENT AND INTERPRETATION

PART II

OBTAINING OF PLANNING PERMISSION BY LOCAL AUTHORITIES

Development Permissions

PART III

GENERAL

SCHEDULES

PART I

TITLE, COMMENCEMENT AND INTERPRETATION

1. Citation and commencement

These regulations may be cited as the Town and Country Planning General
Regulations 1976 and shall come into operation on 1st October 1976.   **[508]**

NOTES
Commencement: 1 October 1976.

2. Interpretation

(1) In these regulations, except so far as the context otherwise requires—

"the Act" means the Town and Country Planning Act 1971;
"the Common Council" means the Common Council of the City of
London;
"listed building" has the same meaning as in Part IV of the Act;
"local authority" means the council of a county or district, the Common
Council, . . . the council of a London borough and any other authority
(except the Receiver for the Metropolitan Police District) who are a
local authority within the meaning of the Local Loans Act 1875, and
includes any drainage board, any joint board or joint committee and any
special planning board established under paragraph 3 of Schedule 17 to
the Local Government Act 1972, if all the constituent authorities are
local authorities within the meaning of the said Act of 1875;
["local planning authority" includes an urban development corporation
where it is a local planning authority by virtue of an order made under
section 149 of the Local Government, Planning and Land Act 1980;]
["urban development area" means an area of land for the time being so
designated by an order made under section 134 of the Local Government,
Planning and Land Act 1980;
"urban development corporation" means a corporation established by an
order made under section 135 of the Local Government, Planning and
Land Act 1980.]

[(1A) Except so far as the context otherwise requires, "authority", except in
regulation 6, shall be construed as including an urban development corporation
where it is the local planning authority.]

(2) References in these regulations to the register of planning applications
are to be interpreted as references to the register kept, pursuant to section 34 of
the Act, by the local planning authority (as defined by article 17(1) of the Town
and Country Planning General Development Order 1973 (as amended) for the
area in which the land to which a resolution referred to in regulation 4(1) or
regulation 5(2) relates is situated.

(3) A regulation referred to in these regulations only by number means the
regulation so numbered in these regulations.

(4) The Interpretation Act 1889 shall apply for the interpretation of these
regulations as it applies for the interpretation of an Act of Parliament.   **[509]**

NOTES
Commencement: 1 October 1976.
Words omitted revoked and definition "local planning authority" substituted by SI 1986 No
443, reg 2, Sch 1, para 1; other amendments made by SI 1981 No 558.

PART II

OBTAINING OF PLANNING PERMISSION BY LOCAL AUTHORITIES

Development Permissions

3. Application of Part III of the Act

[In relation to —

(*a*) development by a local authority or an urban development corporation of land in respect of which they are a local planning authority, other than—

(i) development by a non-metropolitan district council of land and any part of which is in a National Park, and

(ii) development by another local planning authority of land in respect of which an urban development corporation is a local planning authority; and

(*b*) development of land vested in a local planning authority for the area in which the land is situated, other than—

(i) development of land any part of which is within a National Park and which is vested in a non-metropolitan district council, and

(ii) development of land in respect of which an urban development corporation is a local planning authority and which is vested in another local planning authority,

the provisions of Part III of the Act specified in Part V of Schedule 21 to the Act shall have effect subject to the exceptions and modifications prescribed in regulations 4 to 12.]   **[510]**

NOTES
    Commencement: 1 April 1986.
    Substituted by SI 1986 No 443, reg 2, Sch 1, para 2.

4. Deemed permission for development by a local authority

(1) The provisions of this regulation apply where the authority require a permission for development which they propose to carry out and which is not granted by a development order (other than a permission for development which consists in or includes works for the alteration or extension of a listed building) and where they resolve to seek permission for the carrying out of that development.

(2) The authority shall, after passing the resolution referred to in paragraph (1) of this regulation—

(*a*) give notice in writing—

(i) to all persons who at the date of the said resolution were entitled to a material interest (within the meaning of section 6(1) and (2) of the Community Land Act 1975) in any of the land on which the authority propose to carry out the development; and

(ii) where any of the said land constitutes or forms part of an agricultural holding (within the meaning of the Agricultural Holdings Act 1948), on every person who was at the date of the resolution a tenant of such a holding,

that they are seeking permission to carry out of the development, describing both the development and the land on which it is to be carried out;

(*b*) where the development consists of or includes development of any class which is prescribed for the purposes of section 26 of the Act, publish a notice of their proposal to seek permission for the development in a local newspaper circulating in the locality in which the land on which the authority proposes to carry out the development is situated, describing the development and the land on which it is to be carried out;

(*c*) where the development consists of or includes development within any of the descriptions set out in section 28(1) of the Act, publish in a local newspaper circulating in the locality in which the land is situated, and display (for not less than 7 days) on or near the land, notices describing the development;

and in each case such notice shall state that any objection to the proposal should be made to the authority in writing within such period (not being less than 21 days) as may be specified in the notice.

(3) After passing the resolution referred to in paragraph (1) of this regulation, the authority shall take steps to secure that a copy of it is placed in Part I of the register of planning applications, together with a plan indicating the land on which it is proposed to carry out the proposed development; and if the proposed development consists of or includes the carrying out of operations on the land and the resolution refers to plans showing details of those operations, those plans shall also be placed in Part I of the said register.

(4) The authority shall comply with the requirements of any development order and of any direction given by the Secretary of State thereunder as though the resolution to seek permission to carry out the development were an application for planning permission made to a local planning authority.

(5) On the expiry of—

(*a*) the period specified in the notice given pursuant to paragraph (2)(*a*) of this regulation; or

(*b*) the period specified in any notice given pursuant to paragraph (2)(*b*) of this regulation; or

(*c*) the period specified in any notice published or displayed pursuant to paragraph (2)(*c*) of this regulation; or

(*d*) the period specified in any development order or direction made thereunder (being a period during which a local planning authority is prohibited from granting planning permission on an application or from determining an application for planning permission); or

(*e*) the period of 21 days from the date when a copy of the resolution referred to in paragraph (1) of this regulation was placed in Part I of the register of planning applications,

whichever period last expires, the authority may, unless the Secretary of State has required them to make an application to him for permission for the development described in the resolution referred to in paragraph (1) of this regulation, resolve, by a resolution which is expressed to be passed for the purposes of this paragraph, to carry out that development; and, subject to the provisions of regulations 8 to 11, on the passing of such resolution permission shall be deemed to be granted by the Secretary of State for that development.

(6) After passing a resolution expressed to be passed for the purposes of paragraph (5) of this regulation the authority shall take steps to secure that particulars of the development concerned and of the land on which it is to be carried out, and the date of the authority's resolution, are placed in the register

of planning applications; and the provisions of section 34 of the Act shall apply as if the resolution were a decision on an application for planning permission made to the local planning authority.

(7) A permission deemed to be granted by virtue of paragraph (5) of this regulation shall ensure only for the benefit of the authority passing the resolution under that paragraph and not for the benefit of the land; but it shall be treated for all purposes of the Act as a permission granted by a planning decision given on an application, and as if it had been granted on the date of the authority's resolution under paragraph (5) of this regulation.

(8) Where the development authorised by a permission deemed to be granted by virtue of paragraph (5) of this regulation includes the erection of a building or the carrying out of any other operation, and plans showing details of the development have not been placed in Part I of the register of planning applications (pursuant to paragraph (3) of this regulation) before the passing of the resolution referred to in paragraph (5) of this regulation, the authority shall take steps to secure that as soon as practicable after the passing of the resolution under paragraph (5) of this regulation plans showing the details of the work authorised by the permission (including, in the case of a planning permission which authorises the erection of a building, details of the siting, design and external appearance of the building, the means of access of the building and (where appropriate), the landscaping of the site on which the building is to be erected) are placed in that Part of the said register.

(9) No plans relating to development authorised by a permission deemed to be granted by virtue of paragraph (5) of this regulation which have been placed in Part I of the register of planning applications pursuant to paragraph (3) or paragraph (7) of this regulation shall be removed from the said register until the development is completed.   **[511]**

NOTES
Commencement: 1 October 1976.

5. Deemed permission for development of land vested in a local authority which it does not itself propose to carry out

(1) The provisions of this regulation shall apply where the authority seek to obtain permission for development (other than a permission for development which consists of or includes works for the alteration or extension of a listed building) of land in their area which is vested in them but where they do not themselves propose to carry out such development.

(2) The authority shall pass a resolution, expressed to be passed for the purposes of this regulation, to seek permission for the development, and the provisions of paragraphs (2) to (4) of regulation 4 shall apply to such resolution as though it were a resolution of the kind referred to in paragraph (1) of that regulation.

(3) Where the development for which the authority seek to obtain permission consists of or includes the carrying out of operations, the resolution passed for the purposes of this regulation may state either—

    (a) that permission is to be sought for the carrying out of the development in accordance with such plans, showing details of the operations concerned, as may be specified in the resolution; or

    (b) that details of the operations are to be reserved for the approval of the local planning authority in the event of permission being obtained;

and where the resolution is in the form indicated at (*a*) above, the authority shall comply with the requirements of paragraph (3) of regulation 4 by taking steps to secure that copies of the plans specified in the resolution are placed in Part I of the register of planning applications, together with a copy of their resolution, before any of the notices referred to in paragraph (2) of regulation 4 is given or published (as the case may be).

(4) Paragraph (5) of regulation 4 shall apply with the following modifications:—

(*a*) for the reference to a resolution to carry out the development, there shall be substituted a reference to a resolution authorising the carrying out of the development pursuant to the provisions of this regulation;

(*b*) the resolution authorising the carrying out of the development may include such conditions as the authority think fit, and where such conditions are imposed the planning permission which is deemed, by virtue of the said paragraph (5), to be granted for the development shall be deemed to be granted subject to such conditions; and

(*c*) where the development includes the erection of a building, and the resolution passed for the purposes of this regulation is in the terms indicated at (*b*) of paragraph (3) of this regulation, the resolution authorising the carrying out of the development shall include conditions requiring the approval of the local planning authority to be obtained to the siting, design and external appearance of the building, the means of access to the building and (where appropriate) the landscaping of the site on which the building is to be erected.

(5) After passing a resolution authorising the carrying out of development pursuant to the provisions of this regulation, the authority shall—

(*a*) prepare a statement, in the form of a notice of the granting of planning permission under section 29 of the Act, describing the development authorised and the land on which it is authorised to be carried out, setting out the terms of the conditions (if any) included in the authority's resolution and giving the date of that resolution; and

(*b*) take steps to secure that particulars of the permission, as set out in the statement required under (*a*) above, are placed in the register of planning applications;

and the provisions of section 34 of the Act shall apply as if the resolution were a decision on an application for planning permission made to the local planning authority.

(6) Where a permission is deemed to be granted by virtue of paragraph (5) of regulation 4 as applied by paragraph (4) of this regulation, that deemed permission shall be treated for all purposes of the Act as a permission granted by a planning decision given on an application, and as if it had been granted on the date of the authority's resolution under paragraph (5) of regulation 4, as applied by paragraph (4) of this regulation.   [512]

NOTES
Commencement: 1 October 1976.

6. Exercise of powers by officers

(1) Where an authority proposing to seek permission for the carrying out of development under regulation 4 have made arrangements under section 101 of the Local Government Act 1972 for the discharge of the relevant functions by an officer of the authority, the provisions of the regulation 4 shall apply as

though references to the passing of a resolution by the authority to seek permission were references to the giving of written notice to the authority by that officer that he proposes to seek permission and references to a resolution to carry out the development were references to written notice given to the authority by that officer that the development is authorised pursuant to regulation 4(5).

(2) Where an authority proposing to seek permission for development under regulation 5 have made arrangements under section 101 of the Local Government Act 1972 for the discharge of the relevant functions by an officer of the authority, the provisions of regulation 5 shall apply as though references to the passing of a resolution by the authority to seek permission for the development were references to the giving of written notice to the authority by that officer that he proposes to seek permission under that regulation and references to a resolution authorising the carrying out of the development pursuant to the provisions of that regulation were references to the issuing by that officer of written notice, in the form of a notice of the granting of planning permission under section 29 of the Act, authorising the carrying out of development.   **[513]**

NOTES
Commencement: 1 October 1976.

7. Applications to the Secretary of State

(1) Where—

   (a) the authority require a permission for development which consists of or includes works for the alteration or extension of a listed building; or

   (b) the Secretary of State requires the authority to make an application to him for permission for any particular development,

the authority shall make application for permission for such development in the form of an application to the local planning authority and shall lodge the application with the Secretary of State; and such application shall be deemed to have been referred to the Secretary of State under section 35 of the Act, and the provisions of that section shall apply to the determination of the application by the Secretary of State.

(2) Where, in respect of any development to which regulation 4 or regulation 5 applies, the authority are required by the provisions of paragraph (4) of regulation 4 or the provisions of that paragraph as applied by paragraph (2) of regulation 5 (as the case may be) to comply with the requirements of any direction made under a development order which prohibits or restricts the granting of planning permission, the authority may make an application for permission for such development in the form set out in paragraph (1) of this regulation; and the provisions of that paragraph shall apply to such application as if it had been made pursuant to the requirements of that paragraph.

(3) Where an application is made under the provisions of this regulation section 34 of the Act shall apply to that application as though it had been made to the local planning authority.   **[514]**

NOTES
Commencement: 1 October 1976.

8. Industrial development

(1) No permission shall be deemed to be granted by virtue of paragraph (5) of regulation 4 (or by virtue of that paragraph as applied by paragraph (4) of

regulation 5) in a case where an industrial development certificate issued under section 67 of the Act would be required if an application had to be made under sections 25 and 31 of the Act, unless prior to the date of the authority's resolution to carry out the development, or the authority's resolution authorising the carrying out of the development (as the case may be), the Secretary of State has issued an industrial development certificate in respect of such development; and any planning permission deemed to be granted under the said paragraph (5) of regulation 4 (or that paragraph as applied) in respect of such development shall be deemed to have been granted subject to any conditions which may have been attached to such certificate.

(2) Where an application is made under the provisions of regulation 7 the application shall be accompanied by an industrial development certificate issued under section 67 of the Act in any case where such a certificate would have been required if the application had been made to the local planning authority under sections 25 and 31 of the Act. **[515]**

NOTES
Commencement: 1 October 1976.

10. Consultation and furnishing of information

(1) The authority shall notify the terms of any permission deemed to be granted under paragraph (5) of regulation 4 (or that paragraph as applied by paragraph (4) of regulation 5) to any other authority or person in any case where they would have been required to do so had the permission been granted on an application in respect of the development made to them under Part III of the Act.

(2) A county planning authority or district planning authority shall in every case before passing a resolution under paragraph (5) of regulation 4 (or that paragraph as applied by paragraph (4) of regulation 5) or making an application under regulation 7 consult with any other local planning authority for the area in which the land or any part thereof is situated.

[(3) An urban development corporation in Greater London shall not pass a resolution under regulation 4(5) (or under that regulation as applied by regulation 5(4)) or make an application under regulation 7 without first consulting the council of the London borough for the area in which the land or any part of it is situated.

(4) Paragraph (3) does not apply where the council has notified the corporation that they do not wish to be consulted pursuant to paragraph (3) about the development or a class of development which comprises the development.]

(5) Where under this regulation the authority are required to consult with any other authority, they shall give notice to that authority that they propose to pass a resolution to carry out the development, or authorising the carrying out of the development (as the case may be), and shall not pass such a resolution except after 21 days from the giving of the notice and after taking into account any representations received from that authority. **[516]**

NOTES
Commencement: 1 April 1986 (paras (3), (4)); 1 October 1976 (remainder).
Paras (3), (4): substituted for existing paras (3), (4), (4A) by SI 1986 No 443, reg 2, Sch 1, para 3.

11. Development affecting highways

(1) Where the authority seek to obtain permission under regulation 4 or regulation 5 for development which consists of or includes:—

(a) the formation, laying out or alteration of any means of access to a highway to which this regulation applies; or

(b) any other development of land within 67 metres (or such other distance as may be specified in a direction given by the Secretary of State under any development order) from the middle of a highway or proposed highway to which this regulation applies,

the authority shall notify the Secretary of State in writing of their proposal, and shall not pass a resolution for the purposes of paragraph (5) of regulation 4 or for the purposes of that paragraph as applied by paragraph (4) of regulation 5, as the case may be, for a period of 21 days from the date when such notification is given.

(2) This regulation applies to the following highways and proposed highways:—

(i) trunk roads;

(ii) any highway which is comprised in the route of special road to be provided by the Secretary of State in pursuance of a scheme under the provisions of Part II of the Highways Act 1959 and which has not for the time being been transferred to him;

(iii) any highway which has been or is to be provided by the Secretary of State in pursuance of an order under the provisions of Part II of the said Act relating to trunk roads and special roads and has not for the time being been transferred to any other highway authority;

(iv) any highway which the Secretary of State proposes to improve in pursuance of an order under the provisions of Part II of the said Act;

[(v) any highway which the Secretary of State proposes to construct or improve, being a highway the route of which is shown as such in the development plan, or in respect of which the Secretary of State has given notice in writing (a) in Greater London [or a metropolitan county], to the local planning authority, (b) elsewhere than in Greater London [or a metropolitan county], to the district planning authority or, in relation to an urban development area where the urban development corporation is the local planning authority, to the urban development corporation, together with maps or plans sufficient to identify the route of the highway to be constructed or the length of the highway to be improved.]   **[517]**

NOTES

Commencement: 1 October 1976.

Para (2)(v) added by SI 1981 No 558, amended by SI 1986 No 443, reg 2, Sch 1, para 4.

Para (2): first amendment in square brackets made by SI 1981 No 558; second and final amendments in square brackets made by SI 1986 No 443, reg 2, Sch 1, para 4.

12. Other consents

Where an authority require any consent or approval of a local planning authority under any provisions of the Act specified in Part V of Schedule 21 to the Act, other than a permission for development, and that authority are themselves the local planning authority by whom such consent or approval would be given, the application shall be made to the Secretary of State and his decision thereon shall be final and shall take the place of the decision of the local planning authority.

[518]

NOTES
Commencement: 1 October 1976.

13. Savings

Any application, reference, representation or notice made or given or any action taken under Part III of the Town and Country Planning General Regulations 1974 which at the coming into operation of these regulations is outstanding shall have effect as if made, given or taken under and in accordance with this Part of these regulations.

[519]

NOTES
Commencement: 1 October 1976.

PART III

GENERAL

14. Claims for compensation and purchase notices

(1) A claim for compensation made to a local planning authority under section 164, 165, 169, 170, 177, 187 or 212 of the Act, or a purchase notice served on the council of a district or London borough or on the Common Council under section 180, 188, 189 or 191 of the Act, shall be in writing and shall be served on that authority or council by delivering it at the offices of the authority or council, or by sending it by pre-paid post.

(2) The time within which any such claim or notice as is mentioned in paragraph (1) of this regulation shall be served shall be—

(*a*) in the case of a claim for compensation, 6 months; and
(*b*) in the case of a purchase notice, 12 months;

from the date of the decision in respect of which the claim or notice is made or given:

Provided that the period may be extended by the Secretary of State in any particular case.

[520]

NOTES
Commencement: 1 October 1976.

15. Marking of certain notices and documents

The manner in which a notice or document such as is referred to in subsection (2) of section 283 of the Act shall be marked in order that it shall be deemed to be duly served under head (*b*) of that subsection shall be by inscribing clearly and legibly upon the notice or document, and upon the envelope containing it, the words "Important—This Communication affects your Property".

[521]

NOTES
Commencement: 1 October 1976.

16. Application of the Public Health Act 1936 to enforcement notices

The provisions of sections 276, 289 and 294 of the Public Health Act 1936 shall apply in relation to steps required to be taken by an enforcement notice, or by a notice under section 65 of the Act, as if—

(a) references to a local authority were references to a local planning authority;

(b) references (in whatever form) to the execution of works under the said Act of 1936 were references to the taking of steps required to be taken under the notice;

(c) references in the said section 289 to the occupier were references to a person having an interest in the premises other than the owner; and

(d) the reference in the said section 294 to "expenses under this Act" were a reference to expenses incurred in the taking of such steps as aforesaid.   **[522]**

NOTES

Commencement: 1 October 1976.

17. Concurrent procedure for acquisition of land and extinguishment of rights of way

(1) Where under section 112 of the Act a compulsory purchase order for the acquisition of any land has been made by a local authority and submitted to the Secretary of State in accordance with the provisions of the Acquisition of Land (Authorisation Procedure) Act 1946, or where any land has been acquired by a local authority under section 119 of the Act, the succeeding provisions of this regulation shall apply in relation to the extinguishment of public rights of way over such land and the acquisition of land for the provision of alternative rights of way.

(2) The Secretary of State may on or after any such submission or acquisition publish in accordance with the provisions of section 215(1) of the Act notice of an order proposed to be made under section 214 of the Act relating to the extinguishment of any such right of way.

(3) On or after the publication of any such notice, the Secretary of State may prepare in draft or a local highway authority may make a compulsory purchase order under section 218(1) of the Act for the acquisition of land for providing an alternative right of way.

(4) Any other proceedings required to be taken in connection with the making of an order under section 214 of the Act may be taken concurrently with the proceedings required to be taken in connection with such an order as is mentioned in paragraph (1) of this regulation and any other proceedings for the making or confirmation of such a compulsory purchase order as is referred to in paragraph (3) of this regulation may be taken concurrently with either or both of the said proceedings:

Provided that—

(a) no such order under section 214 shall be made until the land over which the right of way subsists has been acquired by the local authority; and

(b) no such compulsory purchase order as is referred to in paragraph (3) of this regulation shall be made by the Secretary of State confirmed, until the original right of way has been extinguished by an order under section 214.   **[523]**

NOTES
Commencement: 1 October 1976.

18. Notices and counter-notices relating to planning blight

The forms set out in Schedule 1 hereto or forms substantially to the like effect
are the prescribed forms of blight notice for the purposes of sections 193 and
201 of the Act and section 78 of the Land Compensation Act 1973 and of
counter-notice for the purposes of section 194 of the Act. **[524]**

NOTES
Commencement: 1 October 1976.

19. Advertisement and notice of unopposed order revoking or modifying planning permission

The advertisement, for the purposes of section 46(2) of the Act, of an order
made under section 45 of the Act shall be in the form set out in Form 1 of
Schedule 2 to these regulations or a form substantially to the like effect; and the
notice required to be served by section 46(3) of the Act shall be in the form set
out in Form 2 of that Schedule or a form substantially to the like effect. **[525]**

NOTES
Commencement: 1 October 1976.

SCHEDULES

SCHEDULE 1

Regulation 18

FORM 1

Blight Notice

To   (a)

at   (b)

[I] [We]*   (c)
pursuant to the provisions of section 193(1) of the Town and Country Planning Act
1971 (hereinafter called "the Act of 1971") HEREBY GIVE YOU NOTICE:—

1. [I am] [We are]* entitled to the interest set out in the First Schedule hereto in
the [hereditament] [agricultural unit]* described in the Second Schedule hereto.

2. [[The] [Part of the]* [hereditament] [agricultural unit]* has been included in
land falling within paragraph (d) of section 192(1) of the Act of 1971 [as that paragraph
is amended or extended by section   (e) of the Land Compensation Act 1973 (hereinafter
called "the Act of 1973")].]

OR

[[The] [Part of the]* [hereditament] [agricultural unit]* has been included in land
falling within section 192(1) of the Act of 1971 [by virtue of section   (e) of the
Community Land Act 1975]*.]

3. [I] [We]* have made reasonable endeavours to sell [my] [our]* interest and in
consequence of the fact that [the] [part of the]* [hereditament] [agricultural unit]*
was or was likely to be comprised in land in one of the descriptions set out in section
192(1) of the Act of 1971 (as amended) [I] [we]* have been unable to sell that interest
except at a price substantially lower than that for which it might reasonably have been
expected to sell if no part of the [hereditament] [agricultural unit]* were, or were
likely to be, comprised in such land. Particulars of those endeavours are set out
[below] [in the letter accompanying this notice]*(f).

4. [My] [Our]* interest qualifies for protection under sections 192 to 207 of the Act
of 1971 because(g)

EITHER

[the annual value of the hereditament does not exceed the prescribed limit of annual
value and [my] [our]* interest is that of owner-occupier(s) of the hereditament within
the meaning of section 203(1) of the Act of 1971.]*

OR

[[my] [our]* interest is that of resident owner-occupier(s) of the hereditament within
the meaning of section 203(3) of the Act of 1971.]*

OR

[[my] [our]* interest is that of owner-occupier(s) of the agricultural unit within the
meaning of section 203(2) of the Act of 1971.]*

[5. [The] [The part of the] agricultural unit in which [I am] [we are]* entitled
to an interest contains land which does not fall within any of the descriptions set out
in section 192(1) of the Act of 1971 (as amended) as well as land which does so and
that area which is unaffected is not reasonably capable of being farmed either by itself
or in conjunction with other relevant land (within the meaning of section 79(2) of
the Act of 1973), as a separate agricultural unit.]

6. [[I] [We]* therefore require you to purchase [my] [our]* interest in the
[hereditament] [agricultural unit]*.]

OR

[[I] [We]* therefore require you to purchase [my] [our]* interest in [the whole of the
agricultural unit] [the whole of that part of the agricultural unit to which this notice
relates]*.]*(h)

First Schedule

Particulars of interest in land together with the names and addresses of any mortgagees thereof and a note of any other encumbrances thereon

Second Schedule

Particulars of the [hereditament] [agricultural unit]*(j)

Dated   19   Signed

[On behalf of   ]*

* Delete where inappropriate.

[526]

NOTES

Commencement: 1 October 1976.

FORM 2

Mortgagee's Blight Notice

To   (a)

at   (b)

[I] [We]*   (c)

pursuant to the provisions of section 201(1) of the Town and Country Planning Act
1971 (hereinafter called "the Act of 1971") HEREBY GIVE YOU NOTICE:—

1. [I am] [We are]* entitled as mortgagee(s) (by virtue of a power which has become
exercisable) to sell the interest (hereinafter called "the said interest") set out in the
First Schedule hereto in the [hereditament] [agricultural unit]* described in the
Second Schedule hereto, giving immediate vacant possession of the land.

2. [[The] [Part of the]* [hereditament] [agricultural unit]* has been included in
land falling within paragraph   (d) of section 192(1) of the Act of 1971 [as that paragraph is amended or extended by section   (e) of the Land Compensation Act 1973
(hereinafter called "the Act of 1973")]*.]*

OR

[[The] [Part of the]* [hereditament] [agricultural unit]* has been included in land
falling within section 192(1) of the Act of 1971 by virtue of section   (e) of the
Community Land Act 1975.]*

3. [I] [We]* have made reasonable endeavours to sell the said interest and in
consequence of the fact that [the] [part of the]* [hereditament] [agricultural unit]*
was or was likely to be comprised in land in one of the descriptions set out in section
192(1) of the Act of 1971 (as amended) [I] [we]* have been unable to sell that interest
except at a price substantially lower than that for which it might reasonably have
been expected to sell if no part of the [hereditament] [agricultural unit]* were, or
were likely to be, comprised in such land. Particulars of those endeavours are set out
[below] [in the letter accompanying this notice]*.(f)

4. [I am] [We are]* entitled to take advantage of the provisions of sections 192 to
207 of the Act of 1971 because (g)

EITHER

[the annual value of the hereditament does not exceed the prescribed limit of annual
value and the person entitled (otherwise than as mortgagee) to the said interest *either*
is an owner-occupier of the hereditament within the meaning of section 203(1) of the
Act of 1971 *or* was such an owner-occupier on an earlier date not more than six months
before the service of this notice, on which earlier date, namely   19 ,
the particulars in paragraph 2 above were correct in relation to the hereditament. (h)]*

OR

[the person entitled (otherwise than as mortgagee) to the said interest *either* is a
resident owner-occupier of the hereditament within the meaning of section 203(3) of
the Act of 1971 *or* was such a resident owner-occupier on an earlier date not more than
six months before the service of this notice, on which earlier date, namely
19 , the particulars in paragraph 2 above were correct in relation to the
hereditament. (h)]*

OR

[the person entitled (otherwise than as mortgagee) to the said interest *either* is an
owner-occupier of the agricultural unit within the meaning of section 203(2) of the
Act of 1971 *or* was such an owner-occupier on an earlier date, not more than six months
before the service of this notice, on which earlier date, namely   19 ,
the particulars in paragraph 2 above were correct in relation to the agricultural
unit. (h)]*

[5. [The] [Part of the] agricultural unit in which the said interest is held contains
land which does not fall within any of the descriptions set out in section 192(1) of
the Act of 1971 (as amended) as well as land which does so and that area which is
unaffected is not reasonably capable of being farmed, either by itself or in conjunction

with other relevant land (within the meaning of section 79(2) of the Act of 1973), as a separate agricultural unit.]

6. [[I] [We]* therefore require you to purchase the said interest in the [hereditament] [agricultural unit]*.]*

OR

[[I] [We]* therefore require you to purchase the said interest in [the whole of the agricultural unit] [the whole of that part of the agricultural unit to which this notice relates.]*]* (*i*).

FIRST SCHEDULE

Particulars of interest in land, together with the names and addresses of any other known mortgagees thereof and a note of any other encumbrances thereon known to the claimant

SECOND SCHEDULE

Particulars of the [hereditament] [agricultural unit](j)*

Dated   19

Signed

[On behalf of   ]*

*Delete where inappropriate.

[527]

NOTES

Commencement: 1 October 1976.

FORM 3
Personal Representative's Blight Notice

To   (a)

at   (b)

[I] [We]*   (c)

pursuant to the provisions of section 78(1) of the Land Compensation Act 1973 (hereinafter called "the Act of 1973") HEREBY GIVE YOU NOTICE:—

1. [I am] [We are]* the personal representative(s) of a person (hereinafter called "the deceased") who at the date of [his] [her]* death was entitled to the interest set out in the First Schedule hereto in the [hereditament] [agricultural unit]* described in the Second Schedule hereto.

2. [[The] [Part of the]* [hereditament] [agricultural unit]* has been included in land falling within paragraph   (d) of section 192(1) of the Town and Country Planning Act 1971 (hereinafter called "the Act of 1971") [as that paragraph is amended or extended by section   (e) of the Act of 1973]* and was so included on the date of death of the deceased.]*

OR

[[The] [Part of the]* [hereditament] [agricultural unit]* has been included in land falling within section 192(1) of the Act of 1971 by virtue of section   (e) of the Community Land Act 1975, and was so included on the date of the death of the deceased.]*

3. Since the date of death of the deceased [I] [We]* have made reasonable endeavours to sell [his] [her]* interest and in consequence of the fact that [the] [part of the]* [hereditament] [agricultural unit]* was or was likely to be comprised in land in one of the descriptions set out in section 192(1) of the Act of 1971 (as amended) [I] [we]* have been unable to sell that interest except at a price substantially lower than that for which it might reasonably have been expected to sell if no part of the [hereditament] [agricultural unit]* were, or were likely to be, comprised in such land. Particulars of those endeavours are set out [below] [in the letter accompanying this notice]*.(f).

4. The deceased's interest qualified for protection under sections 192 to 207 of the Act of 1971 because(g)

EITHER

[the annual value of the hereditament does not exceed the prescribed limit of annual value and [his] [her]* interest was that of owner-occupier of the hereditament within the meaning of section 203(1) of the Act of 1971.]*

OR

[[his] [her]* interest was that of resident owner-occupier of the hereditament within the meaning of section 203(3) of the Act of 1971.]*

OR

[[his] [her]* interest was that of owner-occupier of the agricultural unit within the meaning of section 203(2) of the Act of 1971.]*

5. One or more individuals are (to the exclusion of any body corporate) beneficially entitled to the deceased's interest in the [hereditament] [agricultural unit]*.

[6. [The] [The part of the] agricultural unit in which the deceased was entitled to an interest contains land which does not fall within any of the descriptions set out in section 192(1) of the Act of 1971 (as amended) as well as land which does so and that area which is unaffected is not reasonably capable of being farmed, either by itself or in conjunction with other relevant land (within the meaning of section 79(2) of the Act of 1973), as a separate agricultural unit.]

7. [[I] [We]* therefore require you to purchase the deceased's interest in the [hereditament] [agricultural unit]*.]*

OR

[[I] [We]* therefore require you to purchase the deceased's interest in [the whole of the agricultural unit] [the whole of that part of the agricultural unit to which this notice relates]*.]*(i)

FIRST SCHEDULE

Particulars of deceased's interest in land, together with the names and addresses of any mortgagees thereof and a note of any other encumbrances thereon

SECOND SCHEDULE

Particulars of the [hereditament] [agricultural unit]*(j)

Dated   19   .   Signed
                                    [On behalf of   ]*

* Delete where inappropriate.

Notes to Forms 1, 2 *and* 3

(a) Insert name of authority to be served.
(b) Insert address of authority.
(c) Insert full name(s) and address(es) of person(s) serving this notice.
(d) Insert letter of the paragraph of the subsection which is applicable.
(e) Insert (if appropriate) number of the section (and sub-section) of the Act of 1973 and/or 1975 which is applicable.
(f) Particulars of the steps taken to sell the land should be given here or in an accompanying letter, and should include dates, price asked and any offers received.
(g) The claimant should choose which paragraph is to form part of the notice and delete the others.
(h) Within the paragraph chosen, underline those words after "either" which are appropriate to the case.
(i) The second alternative paragraph applies only to agricultural units coming within the description set out in the preceding paragraph of the notice (where appropriate). The claimant should choose which alternative is to form part of the notice and delete the other.
(j) A plan should be attached to identify the land, if this is necessary.

[528]

NOTES
Commencement: 1 October 1976.

FORM 4

Counter-Notice Objecting to Blight Notice

To   (*a*)

THE   (*b*)

HEREBY GIVE YOU NOTICE under section 194(1) of the Town and Country
Planning Act 1971 that they OBJECT to the Blight Notice served by you on
                      19   under [section 193(1) of that Act] [section 201(1) of that
Act] [section 78(1) of the Land Compensation Act 1973]* in respect of the
[hereditament] [agricultural unit]* described as(*c*).

The grounds on which objection is taken are(*d*)—

Dated   19

                                                On behalf of the(*b*).

*   Delete where inappropriate.

NOTE: If you do not accept this objection, you may require the objection to be
referred to the Lands Tribunal, under the provisions of section 195 of the Town and
Country Planning Act 1971. In that case you should notify the Registrar, The Lands
Tribunal, 5 Chancery Lane, London WC2A 1LX within 2 months of the date of
service of this notice.

Notes to Form 4

(*a*)   Insert name and address of addressee.
(*b*)   Insert name of authority.
(*c*)   Insert particulars.
(*d*)   These must specify the grounds on which the authority object to the notice (being one or
        more of the grounds specified in section 194(2) of the Town and Country Planning Act
        1971 (as amended by paragraph 6(3) of Schedule 10 to the Community Land Act 1975)
        or, where relevant, in section 80 of the Land Compensation Act 1973). Regard should be
        had to the restrictions imposed by section 194(3) of the Town and Country Planning
        Act 1971 on the grounds on which objections may be made to a blight notice and (where
        appropriate) to the restrictions imposed by section 76 of the Land Compensation Act
        1973 on the grounds on which objections may be made to a blight notice served by virtue
        of one of those sections.

                                                                          [529]

NOTES
    Commencement: 1 October 1976.

SCHEDULE 2

Regulation 19

FORM 1

Advertisement under section 46(2) of the Making of a Revocation Order or Modification Order

Planning permission for   *(a)*
at   *(b)*.
NOTICE IS HEREBY GIVEN THAT THE   *(c)* council have made an order under section 45 of the Town and Country Planning Act 1971 to [revoke the above planning permission] [to the following extent   *(d)*]
[modify the above planning permission as follows   *(e)*].*

The council have been notified in writing by the owner and the occupier of the land [and by all other persons who in the council's opinion will be affected by the order]* that they do not object to the order.

Any person who will be affected by the order and who wishes for an opportunity of appearing before, and being heard by, a person appointed by the [Secretary of State for the Environment] [Secretary of State for Wales]* must give notice in writing to that effect to the [Secretary, Department of the Environment, 2 Marsham Street, London SW1P 3EB] [Secretary, Welsh Office, Summit House, Windsor Place, Cardiff CF1 3BX]* not later than   19   *(f)*.

If no such notice has been given by that date, the order will take effect, by virtue of the provisions of section 46 of the Town and Country Planning Act 1971, on 19   *(g)* without being confirmed by the Secretary of State.

* Delete where inappropriate.

[530]

NOTES
Commencement: 1 October 1976.

FORM 2

Notice under section 46(3) *of the Making of a Revocation Order or Modification Order*

Planning permission for   *(a)*
at   *(b)*.
TAKE NOTICE THAT THE   (*c*) council have made an order under
section 45 of the Town and Country Planning Act 1971 to [revoke the above planning
permission] [to the following extent   *(d)*]
[modify the above planning permission as follows   *(e)*]*.

The council have been notified in writing by the owner and the occupier of the land
[and by all other persons who in the council's opinion will be affected by the order]*
that they do not object to the order.

If you will be affected by the order and wish for an opportunity of appearing before,
and being heard by, a person appointed by the [Secretary of State for the Environment]
[Secretary of State for Wales]* you should give notice in writing to that effect to the
[Secretary, Department of the Environment, 2 Marsham Street, London SW1P 3EB]
[Secretary, Welsh Office, Summit House, Windsor Place, Cardiff CF1 3BX]* not later
than   19 (*f*).

If no such notice has been given by that date, the order will take effect, by virtue of
the provisions of section 46 of the Town and Country Planning Act 1971, on
                    19 (*g*) without being confirmed by the Secretary of State.

* Delete where inappropriate.

Notes to Forms 1 *and* 2

(*a*) Insert description of the development for which permission has been granted.
(*b*) Insert site or locality of development.
(*c*) Insert name of council.
(*d*) Insert particulars of extent of revocation.
(*e*) Insert particulars of modification.
(*f*) Insert a date not less than 28 days later than the date on which the relevant advertisement
       first appears.
(*g*) Insert a date not less than 14 days later than the date to which note (*g*) relates.

[531]

NOTES
   Commencement: 1 October 1976.

TOWN AND COUNTRY PLANNING (LISTED BUILDINGS AND BUILDINGS IN CONSERVATION AREAS) REGULATIONS 1977
(SI 1977 NO 228)

NOTES

Made: 14 February 1977

Authority: Town and Country Planning Act 1971, ss 54, 91, 99, 171, 172, 173, 190, 271, 277A, 290, Sch 11

(Revoked and replaced by SI 1987 No 349. See Appendix.)

ARRANGEMENT OF REGULATIONS

1. Citation and commencement

These regulations may be cited as the Town and Country Planning (Listed Buildings and Buildings in Conservation Areas) Regulations 1977 and shall come into operation on 1st April 1977.   **[532]**

NOTES

Commencement: 1 April 1977.

2. Interpretation

(1) In these regulations, unless the context otherwise requires—

"the Act" means the Town and Country Planning Act 1971;

"the Common Council" means the Common Council of the City of London;

"listed building consent" means consent required by section 55(2) of the Act in respect of works for the demolition, extension or alteration of a listed building and the consent required by that subsection (as applied by section 277A(8) of the Act and regulation 10 of and Schedule 3 to these regulations) for works for the demolition of a building in a conservation area;

["local planning authority" means—

(a) in regulation 9, the council of a district, the Common Council, the council of a London borough or (as respects Greater London) the Historic Buildings and Monuments Commission for England;

(b) in regulation 11, the council of a district or county, the Common Council or the council of a London borough; and

(c) elsewhere in these regulations, the council of a district, the Common Council or the council of a London borough.]

(2) The Interpretation Act 1889 shall apply for the interpretation of these regulations as it applies for the interpretation of an Act of Parliament.   **[533]**

NOTES
Commencement: 1 April 1977.
Amended by SI 1986 No 443, reg 2, Sch 1, para 5.

3. Applications for listed building consent

(1) An application to a local planning authority for listed building consent shall be made on a form issued by the local planning authority and obtainable from that authority, shall include the particulars required by that form to be supplied, and be accompanied by a plan sufficient to identify the building to which it relates and such other plans and drawings as are necessary to describe the works which are the subject of the application, together with two further copies of the form and plans and drawings, and shall be lodged with the local planning authority.

(2) On receipt of any such application together with a certificate under regulation 5 below the local planning authority shall send to the applicant an acknowledgement thereof in the terms (or substantially in the terms) set out in Part I of Schedule 1 hereto.

(3) Where, after the sending of an acknowledgement as required by paragraph (2) above, the local planning authority form the opinion that the application is invalid by reason of failure to comply with the requirements of paragraph (1) above or with any other statutory requirement, they shall as soon as may be notify the applicant that his application is invalid.

(4) Where a valid application under paragraph (1) above has been received by a local planning authority, the period within which the authority shall give notice to an applicant of their decision or of the reference of an application to the Secretary of State shall be 8 weeks from the date when the form of application and the certificate under regulation 5 below were lodged as required by paragraph (1) above or (except where the applicant has already given notice of appeal to the Secretary of State) such extended period as may at any time be agreed upon in writing between the applicant and the local planning authority.

(5) Every such notice of decision or reference to the Secretary of State shall be in writing and where the local planning authority decide to grant listed building consent subject to conditions or to refuse it, the notice shall state the reasons for the decision and shall be accompanied by a notification in the terms (or substantially in the terms) set out in Part II of Schedule 1 hereto.   **[534]**

NOTES
Commencement: 1 April 1977.

4. Advertisement of applications

(1) Subject to the provisions of this regulation, where an application for listed building consent is made to a local planning authority in respect of any building the authority shall—

  (*a*) publish in a local newspaper circulating in the locality in which the building is situated a notice indicating the nature of the works which are the subject of the application and naming a place within the locality where a copy of the application, and of all plans and other documents submitted with it, will be open to inspection by the public at all reasonable hours during the period of 21 days beginning with the date of publication of the notice; and

  (*b*) for not less than 7 days display on or near the said building a notice containing the same particulars as are required to contained in the notice to be published in accordance with sub-paragraph (*a*) above.

(2) An application for listed building consent shall not be determined by the local planning authority before both of the following periods have elapsed, namely—

  (*a*) the period of 21 days referred to in sub-paragraph (*a*) of paragraph (1) above; and

  (*b*) the period of 21 days beginning with the date on which the notice required by sub-paragraph (*b*) of the said paragraph (1) was first displayed;

and in determining the application the authority shall take into account any representations relating to the application which are received by them before both those periods have elapsed.

(3) The preceding paragraphs of this regulation shall not apply to any application for consent to carry out works affecting only the interior of a Grade II-listed building namely a building which when last notified to the authority by the Secretary of State as a building of special architectural or historic interest was classified as a building of Grade II and not of Grade II*.   **[535]**

NOTES
 Commencement: 1 April 1977.

5. Certificates to accompany applications and appeals

(1) A local planning authority shall not entertain any application for listed building consent unless it is accompanied by one or other of the following certificates signed by or on behalf of the applicant, that is to say—

  (*a*) a certificate stating that at the beginning of the period of 21 days ending with the date of the application, no person (other than the applicant) was the owner of the building to which the application relates;

  (*b*) a certificate stating that the applicant has given the requisite notice of the application to all the persons (other than the applicant) who, at the beginning of the period of 21 days ending with the date of the application, were owners of the building to which the application relates, and setting out the names of those persons, the addresses at which notice of the application was given to them respectively, and the date of service of each such notice;

  (*c*) a certificate stating that the applicant is unable to issue a certificate in accordance with either of the preceding sub-paragraphs, that he has given the requisite notice of the application to such one or more of the persons mentioned in the last preceding sub-paragraph as are specified in the certificate (setting out their names, the addresses at which notice of the application was given to them respectively, and the date of service of each such notice) that he has taken such steps as are reasonably open to him (specifying them) to ascertain the names and addresses of the remainder of those persons and that he has been unable to do so;

(*d*) a certificate stating that the applicant is unable to issue a certificate in accordance with sub-paragraph (*a*) above, that he has taken such steps as are reasonably open to him (specifying them) to ascertain the names and addresses of the persons mentioned in sub-paragraph (*b*) of this paragraph and that he has been unable to do so.

(2) Any such certificate as is mentioned in sub-paragraph (*c*) or sub-paragraph (*d*) of paragraph (1) above shall also contain a statement that the requisite notice of the application, as set out in the certificate, has on a date specified in the certificate (being a date not earlier than the beginning of the period mentioned in sub-paragraph (*b*) of paragraph (1) above) been published in a local newspaper circulating in the locality in which the building is situated.

(3) Where an application for listed building consent is accompanied by such a certificate as is mentioned in sub-paragraph (*b*), sub-paragraph (*c*), or sub-paragraph (*d*) of paragraph (1) above, the local planning authority shall not determine the application before the end of the period of 21 days beginning with the date appearing from the certificate to be the latest of the dates of service of notices as mentioned in the certificate, or the date of publication of a notice as therein mentioned, whichever is the later.

(4) Where an application for listed building consent is accompanied by such a certificate as is mentioned in sub-paragraph (*b*), sub-paragraph (*c*), or sub-paragraph (*d*) of paragraph (1) above, the local planning authority—

(*a*) in determining the application, shall take into account any representations relating thereto which are made to them, before the end of the period mentioned in paragraph (3) above, by any person who satisfies them that he is an owner of the building to which the application relates, and

(*b*) shall give notice of their decision to every person who has made representations which they were required to take into account in accordance with the preceding sub-paragraph.

(5) For the purposes of this regulation a person is to be treated as an owner of the building to which the application relates if he is entitled to any material interest (within the meaning of section 6(1) and (2) of the Community Land Act 1975) in any part of the land comprising that building.

(6) The provisions of this regulation shall apply, with any necessary modifications, where an application for listed building consent is referred (or is deemed to have been referred) to the Secretary of State under paragraph 4 of Schedule 11 to the Act or in relation to an appeal to the Secretary of State under paragraph 8 or paragraph 9 of that Schedule as they apply in relation to an application for listed building consent which falls to be determined by the local planning authority.

(7) Certificates issued for the purposes of this regulation shall be in the forms set out in Part I of Schedule 2 hereto.

(8) The requisite notices for the purposes of the provisions of this regulation in relation to applications shall be in the forms set out in Part II of Schedule 2 hereto.

(9) The requisite notices for the purposes of the provisions of this regulation in relation to appeals shall be in the forms set out in Part III of Schedule 2 hereto. **[536]**

NOTES
Commencement: 1 April 1977.

6. Appeals

(1) An applicant who desires to appeal—

> (*a*) against a decision of a local planning authority refusing listed building consent or granting consent subject to conditions; or
> (*b*) on the failure of a local planning authority to give notice of their decision or of the reference of the application to the Secretary of State,

shall give notice of appeal to the Secretary of State (on a form obtained from the Secretary of State) within six months of notice of the decision or of the expiry of the appropriate period allowed under regulation 3(4) above, as the case may be, or such longer period as the Secretary of State may at any time allow.

(2) Such a person shall also furnish to the Secretary of State a copy of each of the following documents—

> (i) the application;
> (ii) all relevant plans, drawings, particulars and documents submitted with the application, including a copy of the certificate given in accordance with regulation 5;
> (iii) the notice of the decision, if any;
> (iv) all other relevant correspondence with the local planning authority. **[537]**

NOTES
Commencement: 1 April 1977.

7. Claims for compensation and listed building purchase notices

(1) A claim for compensation made to a local planning authority under section 171(2), 172(1) or 173(3) of the Act, or a listed building purchase notice served on the council of a district, on the Common Council or on the Council of a London borough under section 190 of the Act, shall be in writing and shall be served on that authority or council by delivering it at the offices of the authority or council addressed to the clerk thereof, or by sending it so addressed by prepaid post.

(2) The time within which any such claim or notice as is mentioned in paragraph (1) above shall be served shall be—

> (*a*) in the case of a claim for compensation, 6 months; and
> (*b*) in the case of a listed building purchase notice, 12 months

from the date of the decision in respect of which the claim or notice is made or given, or such longer period as the Secretary of State may allow in any particular case. **[538]**

NOTES
Commencement: 1 April 1977.

8. Advertisement of unopposed revocation or modification order

Where by virtue of the provisions of paragraph 12(2) of Schedule 11 to the Act the making of an order under paragraph 10 of that Schedule in respect of works to a building is required to be advertised, the local planning authority shall publish in a local newspaper circulating in the area in which the building is situated an advertisement stating that the order has been made and specifying the periods required by the said paragraph 12(2) to be specified.   **[539]**

NOTES
Commencement: 1 April 1977.

9. Application of the Public Health Act 1936 to listed building enforcement notices

The provisions of sections 276, 289 and 294 of the Public Health Act 1936 shall apply in relation to steps required to be taken by a listed building enforcement notice, as if—

- (a) references to a local authority were references to a local planning authority;
- (b) references (in whatever form) to the execution of works under the said Act of 1936 were references to the taking of steps required to be taken under the notice;
- (c) references in the said section 289 to the occupier were references to a person having an interest in the premises other than the owner; and
- (d) the reference in the said section 294 to "expenses under this Act" were a reference to expenses incurred in the taking of such steps as aforesaid.   **[540]**

NOTES
Commencement: 1 April 1977.

10. Demolition of unlisted buildings in conservation areas

In their application to buildings to which section 277A of the Act applies, the provisions of the Act which are set out in column (1) of Schedule 3 to these regulations shall have effect as they have effect in relation to listed buildings, subject to the exceptions and modifications set out opposite such provisions in column (2) of the said Schedule 3.   **[541]**

NOTES
Commencement: 1 April 1977.

11. Applications by local planning authorities

(1) In relation to applications by local planning authorities relating to the execution of works for the demolition, alteration or extension of listed buildings, the provisions of the Act shall have effect subject to the exceptions and modifications prescribed in this regulation.

(2) Where a local planning authority require listed building consent for the demolition, alteration or extension of any listed building in their area, the authority shall make application to the Secretary of State for that consent.

(3) Any such application shall be in the form of an application to the local planning authority, and shall be deemed to have been referred to the Secretary of State under paragraph 4 of Schedule 11 to the Act and the provisions of the

said paragraph shall apply to the determination of the application by the Secretary of State.

(4) Where a local planning authority have made an application for listed building consent under paragraph (2) of this regulation they shall, before sending it to the Secretary of State—

    (*a*) publish in a local newspaper circulating in the locality in which the building is situated a notice indicating the nature of the works which are the subject of the application and naming a place within the locality where a copy of the application, and of all plans and other documents which it is intended to submit to the Secretary of State with it, will be open to inspection by the public at all reasonable hours during the period of 21 days beginning with the date of publication of the notice; and

    (*b*) for not less than 7 days display on or near the said building a notice containing the same particulars as are required to be contained in the notice to be published in accordance with sub-paragraph (*a*) above.

(5) In relation to a listed building belonging to a local planning authority, the Secretary of State may serve any notice authorised to be served by a local planning authority in relation to a listed building.   [542]

NOTES
    Commencement: 1 April 1977.

12. Form of notice that a building has become, or ceased to be, listed

The forms set out in Schedule 4 hereto (or forms substantially to the like effect) are the prescribed forms of notice for the purposes of section 54(7) of the Act.

[543]

NOTES
    Commencement: 1 April 1977.

SCHEDULES

SCHEDULE 1

Regulation 3

PART I

Notification to be sent to applicant on receipt of application

Your application dated   was received on   (*a*).

*[Examination of the form of application and accompanying plans and documents to ascertain whether your application complies with the statutory requirements has not been completed.

If on further examination it is found that the application is invalid for failure to comply with such requirements (or for any other reason) a further communication will be sent to you as soon as possible.]

If by   (b) *[you have not received notification that your application is invalid and] this authority have not given you notice of their decision (and you have not agreed with them in writing that the period within which their decision shall be given may be extended) you may appeal to the Secretary of State in accordance with paragraphs 8 and 9 of Schedule 11 to the Town and Country Planning Act 1971 by notice sent within six months from that date (unless the application has already been referred by this authority to the [Secretary of State for the Environment] [Secretary of State for Wales]). Appeals must be made on a form which is obtainable from the [Department of the Environment] (Welsh Office].

(a) Insert date when relevant document(s) referred to in regulation 3(1) were received.

(b) Insert date 8 weeks from date of receipt of application (as given at (a)).

*Delete where inappropriate.   **[544]**

NOTES
Commencement: 1 April 1977.

PART II

Notification to be sent to applicant on refusal of listed building consent or grant of consent subject to conditions (to be endorsed on notices of decision)

(1) If the applicant is aggrieved by the decision of the local planning authority to refuse listed building consent for the proposed works, or to grant consent subject to conditions, he may appeal to the [Secretary of State for the Environment] [Secretary of State for Wales] in accordance with paragraph 8 of Schedule 11 to the Town and Country Planning Act 1971 within six months of receipt of this notice. (Appeals must be made on a form which is obtainable from the [Department of the Environment] [Welsh Office]).
The Secretary of State has power to allow a longer period for the giving of a notice of appeal but he will not normally be prepared to exercise this power unless there are special circumstances which excuse the delay in giving notice of appeal.

(2) If listed building consent is refused, or granted subject to conditions, whether by the local planning authority or by the [Secretary of State for the Environment] [Secretary of State for Wales], and the owner of the land claims that the land has become incapable of reasonably beneficial use in its existing state and cannot be rendered capable of reasonably beneficial use by the carrying out of any works which have been or would be permitted, he may serve on the council of the district, or London borough in which the land is situated (or, where appropriate, on the Common Council of the City of London) a listed building purchase notice requiring that council to purchase his interest in the land in accordance with the provisions of section 190 of the Town and Country Planning Act 1971.

(3) In certain circumstances, a claim may be made against the local planning authority for compensation, where permission is refused or granted subject to conditions by the Secretary of State on appeal or on a reference of the application to him. The circumstances in which such compensation is payable are set out in section 171 of the Town and Country Planning Act 1971.   **[545]**

NOTES
Commencement: 1 April 1977.

SCHEDULE 2

Regulation 5

PART I

TOWN AND COUNTRY PLANNING ACT 1971

Certificate A*

I hereby certify that no person other than [myself] [the applicant] [the appellant]* was an owner (a) of the building to which the [application] [appeal]* relates at the beginning of the period of 20 days before the date of the accompanying [application] [appeal]*.

or

Certificate B*

I hereby certify that:

[I have] [The applicant has] [The appellant has]* given the requisite notice to all the persons other than [myself] [the applicant] [the appellant]* who, 20 days before the date of the accompanying [application] [appeal]*, were owners (a) of the building to which the [application] [appeal]* relates, viz:—

Name of owner
  Address
Date of service of
notice

or

Certificate C*

I hereby certify that:

1. [I am] [The applicant is] [The appellant is]* unable to issue a certificate in accordance with either sub-paragraph (a) or sub-paragraph (b) of regulation 5(1) of the Town and Country Planning (Listed Buildings and Buildings in Conservation Areas) Regulations 1977 in respect of the accompanying [application] [appeal]* dated

2. [I have] [The applicant has] [The appellant has]* given the requisite notice to the following persons other than [myself] [the applicant] the appellant]* who, 20 days before the date of the [application] [appeal]*, were owners (a) of the building to which the [application] [appeal]* relates, viz:—

Name of the owner
  Address
Date of service of
notice

3. [I have] [The applicant has] [The appellant has]* taken the steps listed below, being steps reasonably open to [me] [him]*, to ascertain the names and addresses of the other owners(a) of the building and [have] [has]* been unable to do so: (b)

4. Notice of the [application] [appeal]* as set out below has been published in the

(c) on   (d)

Copy of notice as published

or

Certificate D*

I hereby certify that:

1. [I am] [The applicant is] [The appellant is]* unable to issue a certificate in accordance with sub-paragraph (a) of regulation 5(1) of the Town and Country Planning (Listed Buildings and Buildings in Conservation Areas) Regulations 1977 in respect of the Accompanying [application] [appeal]* dated   and [have] [has]* taken the steps listed below, being steps reasonably open to [me] [him]*, to ascertain the names

and addresses of all the persons other than [myself] [himself]*, who, 20 days before the date of the [application] [appeal]* were owners(*a*) of the building to which the [application] [appeal]* relates and [have] [has]* been unable to do so:

  (*b*)

  2. Notice of the [application] [appeal]* as set out below has been published in the

(*c*) on   (*d*).

Copy of notice as published

Signed ... ...
....
[On behalf of ...
............]*
Date............
......

**Delete where inap-
  propriate.*

  Notes

  (*a*) "owner" means a person having a freehold interest or a leasehold interest the unexpired term of which was not less than 7 years.
  (*b*) Insert description of steps taken.
  (*c*) Insert name of a local newspaper circulating in the locality in which the land is situated.
  (*d*) Insert date of publication (which must not be earlier than 20 days before the application or appeal).   **[546]**

NOTES
  Commencement: 1 April 1977.

PART II
TOWN AND COUNTRY PLANNING ACT 1971
[Notice for service on individuals]
Proposal to carry out works for [demolishing] [altering] [extending]*

(*a*).

TAKE NOTICE that application is being made to the   (*b*) council by
                  (*c*) for listed building consent to   (*d*).

  If you should wish to make representations about the application, you should make them in writing, not later than   (*e*) to the Council at   (*f*).

Signed ... ...
....
[On behalf of ...
............]*
Date............
......

TOWN AND COUNTRY PLANNING ACT 1971
[Notice for publication in local newspapers]

Proposal to carry out works for [demolishing] [altering] [extending]*
(*a*).

Notice is hereby given that application is being made to the   (*b*) council by
(*c*)

for listed building consent to   (*d*).

Any owner of the building (namely a freeholder or a person entitled to an unexpired term of at least seven years under a lease of any part of the land comprising the building) who wishes to make representations to the above-mentioned council about the application should make them in writing not later than   (e) to the Council at
(f).

Signed . . . .
. . . .
[On behalf of . . .
. . . .]*
Date . . . .
. . . . . .

*Delete where in-
appropriate.

Notes

(a) Insert name, address or location of building with sufficient precision to ensure identification of it.
(b) Insert name of council.
(c) Insert name of applicant.
(d) Insert description of proposed works and name, address or location of building.
(e) Insert date not less than 20 days later than the date on which the notice is served or published.
(f) Insert address of council.   [547]

NOTES
Commencement: 1 April 1977.

PART III

TOWN AND COUNTRY PLANNING ACT 1971
[Notice for service on individuals]
Proposal to carry out works for [demolishing] [altering] [extending]*
(a).

TAKE NOTICE that an appeal is being made to [the Secretary of State for the Environment] [the Secretary of State for Wales]* by   (b) [against the decision of (c) council]* [on the failure of the   (c) council to give notice of a decision]* on an application to   (d).

If you should wish to make representations to the Secretary of State about the appeal you should make them not later than   (e), to the Secretary [Department of the Environment] [Welsh Office]* at

Signed . . . .
. . . .
[On behalf of . . .
. . . .]*
Date . . . .
. . . .

TOWN AND COUNTRY PLANNING ACT 1974
[Notice for publication in local newspapers]
Proposal to carry out works for [demolishing] [altering] [extending]*
(a).

Notice is hereby given that an appeal is being made to [the Secretary of State for the Environment] [the Secretary of State for Wales.]* by   (b) [against the decision of the (c) council]* [on the failure of the   (c) council to give notice of a decision]* on an application to   (d).

Any owner of the building (namely, a freeholder or a person entitled to an unexpired term of at least seven years under a lease of any land comprising the building who wishes to make representations to the Secretary of State about the appeal should make them in writing, not later than   (e), to the Secretary, [Department of the Environment] [Welsh Office]* at

Signed . . . .
. . . .
[On Behalf of . . .
. . . .]*
Date . . . .
. . . .

*Delete where in-
appropriate.

   (*a*) Insert name, address or location of building with sufficient precision to ensure identification of it.

   (*b*) Insert name of appellant.

   (*c*) Insert name of council.

   (*d*) Insert description of proposed works and name, address or location of building.

   (*e*) Insert date not less than 20 days later than the date on which the notice is served or published. **[548]**

NOTES
  Commencement: 1 April 1977.

Regulation 10   **SCHEDULE 3**

Column (1) Provisions of the Act relating to listed building control	Column (2) Exceptions and modifications

Section 55	1. In subsection (1), omit the words "or for its alteration or extension in any manner which would affect its character as a building of special architectural or historic interest".
	2. In subsection (2)—
	    (i) omit the words "or for its alteration or extension";
	    (ii) omit paragraph (b).
	3. Omit subsection (3).

Section 56(3), (5) and (6)	Omit subsection (3)
Section 96	In subsection (1), for the words "the character of the building as one of special architectural or historic interest", substitute the words "the character or appearance of the conservation area in which the building is situated".

Section 97	1. In subsection (1)—
	    (i) substitute the following paragraph for paragraph (a)—
	        "(a) that retention of the building is not necessary in the interests of preserving or enhancing the character or appearance of the conservation area in which it is situated;";
	    (ii) omit paragraph (h).
	2. In subsection (5), omit paragraphs (b) and (c).

Sections 98 and 99	None.
Section 172	None.
Section 190	None.
Section 266(1)(b)	None.
Schedule 3, paragraph 2	None.
Schedule 11, Parts I and II	1. In Part I, omit paragraphs 5, 7(1), 8(2) and (3)(b), and substitute the following paragraph for paragraph 6— "6. Where application for listed building consent is made to a local planning authority, being the council of a London borough, that authority shall notify the Greater London Council of that application, shall not determine such application until the expiry of a period of 21 days from such notification, shall take into account any representations made by the Greater London Council within such period in respect of that application, and shall notify the Greater London Council of their decision on that application."; 2. In Part II, omit paragraph 11.
Schedule 19	None. **[549]**

NOTES

    Commencement: 1 April 1977.

    Amended by SI 1986 No 443, reg 2, Sch 1, para 5.

SCHEDULE 4

Notice that a building has become listed

IMPORTANT—THIS COMMUNICATION AFFECTS YOUR PROPERTY

TOWN AND COUNTRY PLANNING ACT 1971

BUILDINGS OF SPECIAL ARCHITECTURAL OR HISTORIC INTEREST

To:

NOTICE IS HEREBY GIVEN that the building known as . . . .   situated in
. . . .   has been included in a list of buildings of special
architectural or historic interest compiled by the [Secretary of State for the Environ-
ment] (Secretary of State for Wales] under section 54 of the Town and Country Planning
Act 1971 on   19 .

Dated   19

[Town Clerk]
[Clerk of the Coun-
    cil]
[Chief Executive]

Note

Listing of Buildings of Special Architectural or Historic Interest

The above notice is addressed to you as owner or occupier of the building named,
which has been included in one of the lists of buildings of special architectural or historic
interest prepared under section 54 of the Town and Country Planning Act 1971 by the
[Secretary of State for the Environment] (Secretary of State for Wales]. The lists are
compiled by the Secretary of State as a statutory duty, on the advice of an expert
committee of architects and historians which advises him on these matters.

This notice does not call for any action on your part unless you propose at any time to
demolish the building or to do any works (either to the exterior or to the interior) which
would affect its character. In that event you will need to seek "listed building consent",
that is to say, the consent of the local planning authority (the Council) to the work you
wish to do.

Certain buildings are exempt from this requirement, notably ecclesiastical buildings
in use for the time being for ecclesiastical purposes.

Works which are urgently necessary in the interests of safety or of health, or to
preserve the building, may be carried out at any time without prior consent provided
that you notify the local planning authority in writing, as soon as reasonably practicable,
of the need for the works.

There is no right of appeal as such against the listing of a building but if the local
planning authority should refuse consent for the carrying out of any proposed works,
section 56(6) of the Town and Country Planning Act 1971 provides a right of appeal
against the refusal to the [Secretary of State for the Environment] [Secretary of State for
Wales]. You are not precluded at any time from writing to the Secretary of State
claiming that the building should cease to be listed, on the ground that it is not in fact of
special architectural or historic interest; and any such claim, with the evidence supporting
it, will be carefully considered.

A fuller explanation of the consequences of the listing of a building is enclosed with
this notice. If at any time you propose to take any action which may affect the character
of your building, you would be well advised to refer to the provisions of the Town and
Country Planning Act 1971, Part IV and Schedule 11, and of the Town and Country
Planning (Listed Buildings and Buildings in Conservation Areas) Regulations 1977 (S.I.
1977/228).

Notice that a building has ceased to be listed

IMPORTANT—THIS COMMUNICATION AFFECTS YOUR PROPERTY

TOWN AND COUNTRY PLANNING ACT 1971

BUILDINGS OF SPECIAL ARCHITECTURAL OR HISTORIC INTEREST

To:

NOTICE IS HEREBY GIVEN that the building known as

situated in   has, by an amendment made by the [Secretary of State for the Environment] [Secretary of State for Wales] under section 54(1) of the Town and Country Planning Act 1971 on   19 , been excluded from the list of buildings of special architectural or historic interest compiled by the Secretary of State.

Date:

[Town Clerk]
[Clerk of the Coun-
cil]
[Chief Executive]

Note

The building referred to in the above notice has been excluded from the list because*

*Insert reason for exclusion.   **[550]**

NOTES
    Commencement: 1 April 1977.

TOWN AND COUNTRY PLANNING GENERAL DEVELOPMENT ORDER 1977
(SI 1977 NO 289)

NOTES
    Made: 22 February 1977
    Authority: Town and Country Planning Act 1971, ss 24, 25, 26, 27, 31, 34, 36, 37, 42, 53, 287, Sch 14; Local Government Act 1972, s 182(3), Sch 16

ARRANGEMENT OF ARTICLES

1. Application, citation and commencement

(1) This order shall apply to all land in England and Wales:

Provided that if a special development order is made or has before the coming into operation of this order been made as to any land this order shall apply thereto to such extent only and subject to such modifications as may be specified in the special order.

(2) Nothing in this order shall apply to any permission which is deemed to be granted under section 64 of the Act.

(3) This order may be cited as the Town and Country Planning General Development Order 1977 and shall come into operation on 29th March 1977.

[551]

NOTES
Commencement: 29 March 1977.

2. Interpretation

(1) In this order, unless the context otherwise requires—

"the Act" means the Town and Country Planning Act 1971;
["the 1981 Act" means the Town and Country Planning (Minerals) Act 1981;]
["the 1984 Act" means the Telecommunications Act 1984;]
["aerodrome" means an aerodrome as defined in article 96 of the Air Navigation Order 1985 which is—

(*a*) licensed under that order,

(*b*) a Government aerodrome,

(*c*) one at which the manufacture, repair or maintenance of aircraft is carried out by a person carrying on business as a manufacturer or repairer of aircraft,

(*d*) one used by aircraft engaged in the public transport of passengers or cargo or aerial work; or

(*e*) one identified to the Civil Aviation Authority before 1st March 1986 for inclusion in the U.K. Aerodrome Index;

and for the purposes of this definition, the terms "aerial work", "Government aerodrome" and "public transport" have the meanings given in article 96;]

"agricultural land" and "agricultural unit" have the meanings respectively assigned to those expressions in the Agriculture Act 1947;

["amusement park" means an enclosed area of open land, or any part of a seaside pier, which is principally used (other than by way of a temporary use) as a funfair or otherwise for the purposes of providing public entertainment by means of mechanical amusements and side-shows; and, where part only of an enclosed area is commonly so used as a funfair or for such public entertainment, only the part so used shall be regarded as an amusement park;]

"aqueduct" does not include an underground conduit;

["area of outstanding natural beauty" means an area designated as such by an order made by the Countryside Commission under section 87 of the National Parks and Access to the Countryside Act 1949 and confirmed by the Secretary of State;]

"betting office" means any building in respect of which there is for the time being in force a betting office licence pursuant to the provisions of the Betting and Gaming Act 1963;

"building" does not include plant or machinery or a structure or erection of the nature of plant or machinery, and in Schedule 1 to this order does not include any gate, fence, wall or other means of enclosure, but except as aforesaid includes any structure or erection and any part of a building as so defined;

"caravan" has the same meaning as for the purposes of Part I of the Caravan Sites and Control of Development Act 1960 (as amended by the Caravan Sites Act 1968;

"caravan site" means land on which a caravan is stationed for the purpose of human habitation and land which is used in conjunction with land on which a caravan is so stationed;

"cemetery" includes a burial ground or any other place of interment for the dead;

"classified road" means a highway or proposed highway which for the time being:—

(i) is classified under section 27(2) of the Local Government Act 1966 as a principal road for the purposes of any enactment or instrument which refers to highways classified as principal roads; or

(ii) is classified under section 27(2) of the said Act of 1966 as a classified road for the purposes of this order or of any order revoked by this order or of any previous general development order made under the Act or under the Town and Country Planning Act 1962, or for the purposes of enactments and instruments which include this order or any such order as aforesaid; or

    (iii) continues by virtue of section 40(1) of the Local Government Act 1974 to be treated as a principal road or a classified road for the purposes mentioned in that subsection; or

    (iv) continues by virtue of section 27(4) of the Local Government Act 1966 to be treated as a classified road for the purpose of every existing enactment or instrument as defined in section 27(3) of that Act.

"the Common Council" means the Common Council of the City of London;

"contravention of previous planning control", in relation to any development, has the same meaning as for the purposes of section 23 of the Act;

"dwelling-house" does not include a building containing one or more flats, or a flat contained within such a building;

["existing", in relation to any building or other structure or any plant or machinery, means (except in the definition of "original") existing immediately before the carrying out of development described in this order;]

["fish pond" means a pond, tank, reservoir, stew or other structure to be used for the keeping of live fish or the cultivation or propagation of shellfish;]

"flat" means a separate and self-contained set of premises constructed for use for the purpose of a dwelling and forming part of a building from some other part of which it is divided horizontally;

["hazardous substance" and "notifiable quantity" have the meanings assigned to those terms by the Notification of Installations Handling Hazardous Substances Regulations 1982;]

"highway" has the meaning assigned to that term by section 294 of the Highways Act 1959;

"industrial process" means any process for or incidental to any of the following purposes, namely:—

(*a*) the making of any article or of part of any article, or

(*b*) the altering, repairing, ornamenting, finishing, cleaning, washing, packing or canning, or adapting for sale, or breaking up, or demolition, of any article, or

(*c*) without prejudice to the foregoing paragraphs, the getting, dressing or treatment of minerals,

being a process carried on in the course of trade or business, and for the purposes of this definition the expression "article" means an article of any description, including a ship or vessel;

"industrial undertakers" means undertakers by whom an industrial process is carried on, and "industrial undertaking" shall be construed accordingly;

"landscaping" means the treatment of land (other than buildings) being the site or part of the site in respect of which an outline planning permission is granted, for the purpose of enhancing or protecting the amenities of the site and the area in which it is situated and includes screening by fences, walls or other means, planting of trees, hedges, shrubs or grass, formation of banks, terraces or other earthworks, laying out of gardens or courts, and other amenity features;

"launderette" includes any building for the purpose of washing or cleaning clothes or fabrics in coin-operated machines;

["lawfully used" means used otherwise than—

(*a*) in contravention of previous planning control; or

(*b*) without planning permission granted or deemed to be granted under Part III of the Act;]

"listed building" means a building which is for the time being included in a list compiled or approved by the Secretary of State under section 54 of the Act;

"local authority" means the council of a county or district, the Common Council, ... the Council of a London borough and any other authority (except the Receiver for the Metropolitan Police District) who are a local authority within the meaning of the Local Loans Act 1875, and includes any drainage board, any joint board or joint committee and any special planning board established under paragraph 3 of Schedule 17 to the Local Government Act 1972, if all the constituent authorities are local authorities within the meaning of the said Act of 1875;

"local highway authority" means a highway authority other than the Secretary of State;

. . .

["microwave" means that part of the radio spectrum above 1000 MHz; "microwave antenna" means a satellite antenna or a terrestrial microwave antenna;]

"mine" includes any site on which mining operations are carried out;

"mineral undertakers" means undertakers engaged in mining operations and includes undertakers licensed under the Petroleum (Production) Act 1934 to search and bore for and get petroleum; and for the purposes of this order any land in respect of which a licence is in force under the said Act authorising any undertakers to search and bore for and get petroleum shall be deemed to be comprised in their undertaking;

"mining operations" means the winning and working of minerals in on or under land, whether by surface or underground working;

["notifiable pipeline" means a pipeline (as that term is defined in section 65 of the Pipelines Act 1962) which contains or is intended to contain a hazardous substance, but does not include a pipeline which has been authorised under section 1 of the Pipelines Act 1962, nor a pipeline which contains, or is intended to contain, no hazardous substance other than a substance within one of the following classes, namely:—

(*a*) a flammable gas (as specified in item 1 of Part II of Schedule 1 to the Notification of Installations Handling Hazardous Substances Regulations 1982) at a pressure of less than 8 bars absolute; or

(*b*) a flammable liquid, as specified in item 4 of Part II of the said Schedule;]

"office" includes a bank and premises occupied by an estate agency, building society or employment agency, or (for office purposes only) for the business of car hire or driving instruction but does not include a post office or betting office;

"original" means, in relation to a building existing on 1st July 1948, as existing on that date; and in relation to a building built on or after 1st July 1948, as so built;

"outline planning permission" means a planning permission for the erection of a building which is granted subject to a condition (in addition to any other conditions) which may be imposed requiring subsequent approval to be obtained from the local planning authority with respect to one or more reserved matters;

"painting" includes any application of colour;

"post office" does not include any building used primarily for the sorting or preparation for delivery of mail or for the purposes of Post Office administration;

"private way" means a highway or footpath which is not a highway maintainable at the public expense;

"proposed highway" has the meaning assigned to that term by section 295(1) of the Highways Act 1959;

["public call box" means any kiosk, booth, acoustic hood, shelter or similar structure which is erected or installed for the purpose of housing or supporting a public telephone and at which call box services are provided (or are to be provided) by a telecommunications code system operator;]

"public vehicle" means a public service vehicle, tramcar or trolley vehicle within the meaning of those expressions in the Road Traffic Act 1960;

"reserved matters" in relation to an outline permission, or an application for such permission, means any of the following matters relating to the building to which the planning permission or the application relates which are relevant to the proposal and in respect of which details have not been given in the application namely:

(a) siting, (b) design, (c) external appearance, (d) means of access, (e) the landscaping of the site;

["satellite antenna" means apparatus designed for transmitting microwave radio energy to satellites or receiving it from them, and includes any mountings or brackets attached to such apparatus;]

"shop" means a building used for the carrying on of any retail trade or retail business wherein the primary purpose is the selling of goods by retail, and includes a building used for the purposes of a hairdresser, undertaker, travel agency, ticket agency or post office or for the reception of goods to be washed, cleaned or repaired, or for any other purpose appropriate to a shopping area, but does not include a building used as a funfair, amusement arcade, pin-table saloon, garage, launderette, petrol filling station, office, betting office, hotel, restaurant, snackbar or cafe or premises licensed for sale of intoxicating liquors for consumption on the premises;

["site of archeological interest" means land which is included in the schedule of monuments compiled by the Secretary of State under section 1 of the Ancient Monuments and Archeological Areas Act 1979, or is within an area of land which before 1st March 1986 was designated as an area of archaeological importance under section 33 of that Act, or which is within a site registered in the County Sites and Monuments Record before that date;

"site of special scientific interest" means land to which section 28(1) of the Wildlife and Countryside Act 1981 applies;]

"special road" means a highway provided or to be provided in pursuance of a scheme under section 11 of the Highways Act 1959;

["stockpile" means a mineral-working deposit consisting primarily of minerals which have been deposited for the purposes of their processing or sale;]

["telecommunication apparatus" means any apparatus falling within the definition of that term in paragraph 1 of Schedule 2 to the 1984 Act;

"the telecommunications code" means the code contained in Schedule 2 to the 1984 Act;

"telecommunications code system operator" means a person who has been granted a licence under section 7 of the 1984 Act which applies the telecommunications code to him in pursuance of section 10 of that Act;

"telecommunication system" has the meaning assigned to that term by section 4(1) of the 1984 Act;]

["terrace house" means a dwellinghouse—

    (i) situated in a row of three or more buildings used, or designed for use, as single dwellinghouses; and

    (ii) sharing a party wall with, or having a main wall adjoining the main wall of, the dwellinghouse (or building designed for use as a dwellinghouse) on either side of it,

but includes the dwellinghouses at each end of such a row of buildings as is referred to;

["terrestrial microwave antenna" means apparatus designed for transmitting or receiving terrestrial microwave radio energy between two or more fixed points;]

"the Use Classes Order" means the Town and Country Planning (Use Classes) Order 1972;]

"trunk road" means a highway or proposed highway which, by virtue of section 7(1) or section 14 of the Highways Act 1959 or by virtue of an order or direction made or given under the said Act or any other Act is a trunk road;

"unadopted street" means a street as defined by the Public Health Act 1936 not being a highway maintainable at the public expense.

["urban development corporation" has the same meaning as in Part XVI of the Local Government, Planning and Land Act 1980; and

"warehouse" means a building used for any purpose within Class X of the Schedule to the Town and Country Planning (Use Classes) Order 1972;]

[(1A) Any reference in this order to the height of a building shall be construed as a reference to the height of that building when measured from ground level.

(1B) For the purposes of paragraph (1A) of this article, "ground level" means the level of the surface of the ground immediately adjacent to the building in question or, where the level of the surface of the ground on which the building is erected or is to be erected, as the case may be, is not uniform, the level of the highest part of the surface of the ground adjacent to the building.]

(2) The Interpretation Act 1889 shall apply for the interpretation of this order as it applies for the interpretation of an Act of Parliament.

(3) References in this order to the Secretary of State shall, in relation to Wales, be construed as references to the Secretary of State for Wales.

(4) In this order, unless the context otherwise requires references to any enactment or instrument shall be construed as references to that enactment or instrument as amended, extended or applied by or under any other enactment or instrument. [552]

NOTES
Commencement: 29 March 1977.
    Para (1): definitions 'the 1984 Act", "existing", "microwave", "microwave antenna", "public call box", "satellite antenna", "telecommunications apparatus", "the telecommunications code", "telecommunications code system operator", "telecommunication system", "terrestrial microwave antenna" added by SI 1985 No 1011, reg 2(*a*); definitions "hazardous substance", "notifiable quantity" and "notifiable pipeline" added by SI 1983 No 1615; definitions "terrace house" and "the Use Classes Order" added by SI 1981 No 245; definitions "the 1981 Act", "amusement park", "area of outstanding natural beauty", "fish pond", "lawfully used", "site of archaeological interest", "site of special scientific interest", "stockpile", "urban development corporation" and "warehouse" added and definition "aerodrome" substituted by SI 1985 No 1981, art 2; words omitted revoked by SI 1986 No 435, art 2, Sch 1, para 1.
    Paras (1A), (1B): added by SI 1981 No 245.

3. Permitted development

[(1) Subject to the subsequent provisions of this order, development of any class specified in Schedule 1 to this order is permitted by this order and may be undertaken upon land to which this order applies, without the permission of the local planning authority or of the Secretary of State:

Provided that—

(a) the permission granted by this order in respect of any such class of development shall be defined by any limitation and be subject to any condition imposed in the said Schedule in relation to that class; and

(b) the permission granted by this order in respect of any such class of development shall be subject to the condition that no building, plant or machinery, or structure or erection in the nature of plant or machinery (other than a mains, pipe or other apparatus belonging to a gas undertaker), authorised by the permission, and no floor space created by development authorised by the permission, shall be used for any purpose which involves the manufacture, processing, keeping or use of a hazardous substance in such circumstances as will result in there being at any one time a notifiable quantity of such substance in, on, over or under the land on which the building, plant or machinery, structure or erection or floorspace is situated, or any site of which that land forms part.]

(2) Nothing in this article or in Schedule 1 to this Order shall operate so as to permit any development contrary to a condition imposed in any permission granted or deemed to be granted under Part III of the Act otherwise than by this order.

[(2A) The permission granted by this article and Schedule 1 to this order shall not operate so as to permit the carrying out of any development for a purpose which involves, or is likely to involve, either the laying or construction of a notifiable pipeline or the manufacture, processing, keeping or use of a hazardous substance in such circumstances (in any of those cases) as will result in there being at any one time a notifiable quantity of a hazardous substance in, on, over or under the land on which the development would be carried out, or any site of which that land forms part, except in the following cases:—

(i) where the development is to be carried out in, on, over or under land which constitutes or forms part of a site in respect of which notification has been given to the Health and Safety Executive in pursuance of the requirements of the Notification of Installations Handling Hazardous Substances Regulations 1982 and the carrying out of the development is not likely to result in an increase in the quantity of such substance present at any one time in, on, over or under the land to a quantity which exceeds three times the quantity in respect of which such notification was last given;

(ii) where there is already a notifiable quantity of a hazardous substance present on the land in, on, over or under which the development is to be carried out but that land is excepted from the requirements of the Regulations referred to in subparagraph (i) above, and the carrying out of the development is not likely to result in an increase in the quantity of such substance present at any one time in, on, over or under that land to a quantity which exceeds three times the quantity present immediately before the development is begun;

(iii) where the development is to be carried out by a gas undertaker and consists of the laying of mains, pipes or other apparatus;

(iv) where the development is for the purpose of inspecting, repairing or renewing mains, pipes or other apparatus.

(2B) For the purposes of paragraphs (1) and (2A) above, "site" means the whole of the area of land within a single unit of occupation.]

(3) The permission granted by this article and Schedule 1 to this order shall not, except in relation to development permitted by classes IX, XII or XIV in the said Schedule, authorise any development which requires or involves the formation, laying out or material widening of a means of access to an existing highway which is a trunk or classified road, or creates an obstruction to the view of persons using any highway used by vehicular traffic at or near any bend, corner, junction or intersection so as to be likely to cause danger to such persons.

(4) Any development of class XII authorised by an Act or order subject to the grant of any consent or approval shall not be deemed for the purposes of this order to be so authorised unless and until that consent or approval is obtained; and in relation to any development of class XII authorised by any Act passed or order made after 1st July 1948 the foregoing provisions of this article shall have effect subject to any provision to the contrary contained in the Act or order.

[553]

NOTES
Commencement: 1 May 1984 (paras (1), (2A), (2B)); 29 March 1977 (remainder).
Para (1): substituted by SI 1983 No 1615.
Paras (2A), (2B): added by SI 1983 No 1615.

4. Directions restricting permitted development

(1) If either the Secretary of State or the appropriate local planning authority is satisfied that it is expedient that development of any of the classes specified in Schedule 1 to this order [(other than classes XXVI.2 and XXVII. 2)] should not be carried out in any particular area, or that any particular development of any of those classes should not be carried out, unless permission is granted on an application in that behalf, the Secretary of State or the appropriate local planning authority may direct that the permission granted by article 3 of this order shall not apply to:—

(a) all or any development of all or any of those classes in any particular area specified in the direction, or

(b) any particular development, specified in the direction, falling within any of those classes:

Provided that, in the case of development of class XII, no such direction shall have effect in relation to development authorised by any Act passed after 1st July 1948, or by any order requiring the approval of both Houses of Parliament approved after that date.

(2) Except in the cases specified in the next succeeding paragraph a direction by a local planning authority under this article shall require the approval of the Secretary of State and the Secretary of State may approve the direction with or without modifications.

(3) The approval of the Secretary of State shall not be required in the following cases:—

[(a) a direction relating to—

(i) a building which is included in a list compiled or approved under section 54 of the Act or in respect of which the Secretary of State

has given notice in writing to the authority making the direction that it is a building of architectural or historic interest; or
(ii) development within the curtilage of a listed building,
and to no other description of land or development, where the direction does not affect the carrying out of any of the operations referred to in paragraph (9) of this article;]

(b) a direction relating only to development in any particular area of any classes I to IV specified in Schedule 1 to this order if in the opinion of the appropriate local planning authority the development would be prejudicial to the proper planning of their area or constitute a threat to the amenities of their area:

Provided that—

(i) any direction made in pursuance of sub-paragraph (b) hereof shall remain in force for six months from the date on which it was made and shall then expire unless it has before the termination of the said six months been approved by the Secretary of State; and
(ii) any second or subsequent direction made in pursuance of sub-paragraph (b) which relates to the same development or to development of the same class or classes or any of them in the same area or part of the same area shall require the approval of the Secretary of State.

(4) A copy of any direction made in pursuance of paragraph (3)(b) of this article shall be sent by the local planning authority to the Secretary of State not later than the date on which notice is given as provided by paragraphs (5) or (6) of this article; and the Secretary of State may at any time during the period of six months referred to in paragraph (3)(b) hereof disallow the direction which shall thereupon cease to have effect. Notice of disallowance shall be given as soon as possible by the local planning authority in the same manner as notice of the direction was originally given.

(5) [Subject to the provisions of paragraphs (6) and (6A) of this article], notice of any direction made under this article shall as soon as may be after it has been approved by the Secretary of State (or, in the case of a direction to which paragraph (3) of this article applies, as soon as may be after it has been made) be served by the appropriate local planning authority on the owner and occupier of every part of the land affected, and such direction shall come into force in respect of any part of the land on the date on which notice thereof is served on the occupier of that part, or if there is no occupier, on the owner thereof.

[(5A) In the case of a direction to which paragraph (3)(b) of this article applies, if the direction is approved by the Secretary of State within the period of six months referred to in that sub-paragraph, then (subject to the provisions of paragraph (6) of this article) the authority who made the direction shall, as soon as may be, serve notice of such approval on the owner and occupier of every part of the land affected by the direction; and, where the Secretary of State has approved the direction with modifications, the notice shall indicate the effect of such modifications.]

[(6) Where, in the case of any direction given under paragraph (1)(a) of this article which specifies a particular area of land, the authority who made the direction are of the opinion that individual service in accordance with the provisions of paragraph (5) or (5A) above is impracticable because of the number of owners and occupiers of the land to which the direction relates, or the difficulty of identifying or locating such owners and occupiers (or any of them), they shall publish notice of the direction, or of approval of the direction by the Secretary of State (as the case may be), in at least one newspaper circulating in the locality in which the land is situated; and such notice shall contain a statement of the effect of the direction (and, where appropriate, the effect of any modifications to the direction made by the Secretary of State) and shall name a place or places where a copy of the direction, and of a map defining the area to which it relates, may be seen at all reasonable hours.

(6A) Where notice of a direction, or notice of approval of a direction (other than approval of a direction to which paragraph (5A) of this article applies) has been published in accordance with the provisions of paragraph (6) above, the direction shall come into force on the date on which such notice is first published.]

[(7) Any direction made by a local planning authority may be cancelled by a subsequent direction by that authority or by a direction made by the Secretary of State, and a cancelling direction given by the authority, if it contains no provisions other than the cancellation of the original direction, shall not require the approval of the Secretary of State; notice of a local authority's cancelling direction shall be given under paragraph (5) or (6) of this article as though it were a direction made under paragraph (1) of this article.]

(8) Any direction in force immediately before the coming into operation of this order under article 4 of the Town and Country Planning General Development Order 1973 shall, in so far as it relates to development permitted by this order, continue in force and have effect as if it were a direction given under this article, of which notice has been duly published or served, as the case may be.

(9) [No direction given or having effect under this article shall have effect in relation to:—

(i) the carrying out in the case of emergency of any development specified in Schedule 1 to this order;
(ii) the carrying out of any development under class XXIV, unless the direction specifically so provides; or
(iii) the carrying out of any of the following operations by a statutory undertaker, unless the direction specifically so provides:—]

(a) maintenance of bridges, buildings and railway stations;
(b) alteration and maintenance of railway track, and provision and maintenance of track equipment, including signal boxes, , signalling apparatus and other appliances and works required in connection with the movement of traffic by rail;
(c) maintenance of docks, harbours, quays, wharves, canals and towing paths;
(d) provision and maintenance of mechanical apparatus or appliances (including signalling equipment) required for the purposes of shipping or in connection with the embarking, disembarking, loading, discharging or transport of passengers, livestock or goods at a dock, quay, harbour, bank, wharf or basin;
(e) any development required in connection with the improvement, maintenance or repair of watercourses or drainage works;
(f) maintenance of buildings, runways, taxiways or aprons at an aerodrome;

(g) provision, alteration and maintenance of equipment, apparatus and works at an aerodrome, required in connection with the movement of traffic by air (but excepting buildings, the construction, erection, reconstruction or alteration of which is permitted by paragraph H of Class XVIII of Schedule 1 to this order).

[(10) In this article "appropriate local planning authority" means—

(a) in relation to a conservation area in a non-metropolitan county, either the county planning authority or the district planning authority; and

(b) in relation to any other area, the local planning authority whose function it would be to determine an application for planning permission for the development to which the direction under this article relates or is proposed to relate.

(11) On making a direction under this article or submitting such a direction to the Secretary of State for approval—

(a) a county planning authority shall give notice thereof to the district planning authority in whose area the land to which the direction relates is situated; and

(b) a district planning authority shall give notice thereof to the county planning authority.] |554|

NOTES
Commencement: 1 April 1986 (paras (10), (11)); 1 March 1986 (paras (5A), (6), (7)); 29 March 1977 (remainder).
Para (1): amended by SI 1985 No 1981, art 2.
Paras (3), (5), (9): amended by SI 1985 No 1981, art 2.
Para (5A): added by SI 1985 No 1981, art 2.
Paras (6), (7): substituted by SI 1985 No 1981, art 2.
Paras (10), (11): substituted by SI 1986 No 435, art 2, Sch 1, para 2.

4A. Directions restricting development under Class XXVI.2 or XXVII.2

[(1) If, on receipt of a notification from any person that he proposes to carry out development within class XXVI.2 or XXVII.2, a mineral planning authority are satisfied as mentioned in paragraph (2) below they may, within 21 days of receipt of the notification, direct that the permission granted by article 3 of this order shall not apply to the development, or to such part of the development as is specified in the direction.

(2) The mineral planning authority may make a direction under this article if they are satisfied that it is expedient that the development, or any part of it, should not be carried out unless permission for it is granted on an application because:—

(a) the land on which the development is to be carried out is within—

(i) a National Park,
(ii) an area of outstanding natural beauty,
(iii) a site of archaeological interest, unless the operation to be carried out is one described in the Schedule to the Areas of Archaeological Importance (Notification of Operations) (Exemption) Order 1984, or
(iv) a site of special scientific interest; or

(b) the development, either taken by itself or taken in conjunction with other development which is already being carried out in the area or in respect of which notification has been given in pursuance of the provisions of class XXVI.2 or XXVII.2, would cause serious detriment

to the amenity of the area in which it is to be carried out or would
adversely affect the setting of a building shown as grade 1 in the list
of buildings of special architectural or historic interest compiled by
the Secretary of State under section 54 of the Act; or

(c) the development would constitute a serious nuisance to the inhabitants
of a nearby residential building, hospital or school; or

(d) the development would endanger aircraft using a nearby aerodrome.

(3) A direction made under this article shall contain a statement as to the
day on which, if it is not disallowed under paragraph (5) below, it will come into
force, which shall be 29 days from the date on which notice of it is sent to the
Secretary of State in accordance with paragraph (4) below.

(4) As soon as may be a copy of a direction under this article shall be sent
by the mineral planning authority to the Secretary of State and to the person
who gave notice of the proposal to carry out development.

(5) The Secretary of State may, at any time within a period of 28 days
beginning on the day on which the direction is made, disallow the direction;
and immediately upon receipt of notice in writing from the Secretary of State
that he has disallowed the direction, the mineral planning authority shall give
notice in writing to the person who gave notice of the proposal that he is
authorised to proceed with the development.]   [555]

NOTES
Commencement: 1 March 1986.
Added by SI 1985 No 1981, art 2.

5. Applications for planning permission

(1) Subject to the following paragraphs of this article, an application to a local
planning authority for planning permission shall be made on a form issued by
the local planning authority and obtainable from that authority or from the
council with whom the application is to be lodged and shall include the
particulars required by such form to be supplied and be accompanied by a plan
sufficient to identify the land to which it relates and such other plans and
drawings as are necessary to describe the development which is the subject of
the application, together with such additional number of copies, not exceeding
three, of the form and plans and drawings as may be required by the local
planning authority; and a local planning authority may by a direction in writing
addressed to the applicant require such further information as may be specified
in the direction to be given to them in respect of an application for permission
made to them under this paragraph, to enable them to determine that
application.

(2) Where an applicant so desires, an application may be made for outline
planning permission for the erection of a building and, where such permission
is granted, the subsequent approval of the local planning authority shall be
required to such matters (being reserved matters as defined) as may be reserved
by condition.   The application shall be made on a form, as required by the
preceding paragraph, shall describe the development to which it relates, shall
be accompanied by a plan sufficient to identify the land to which it relates
(together with such additional copies, not exceeding three, of the form and plan
as may be required by the local planning authority) and may contain such
further information (if any) as to the proposal as the applicant desires:

[Provided that where—

(a) the local planning authority, or

(*b*) where the application is made to one authority but falls to be determined by another, either of those authorities,

are of the opinion] that in the circumstances of the case the application ought not to be considered separately from the siting or the design or external appearance of the building, or the means of access thereto or the landscaping of the site, they shall within the period of one month from the receipt of the application notify the applicant that they are unable to entertain it unless further details are submitted, specifying the matters as to which they require further information for the purpose of arriving at a decision in respect of the proposed development; and the applicant may either furnish the information so required or appeal to the Secretary of State within six months of receiving such notice, or such longer period as the Secretary of State may at any time allow, as if his application had been refused by the authority.

(3) Where a planning permission has previously been granted for development and that development has not yet been commenced, and where a time limit imposed by or under section 41 or section 42 of the Act (that is to say, a time limit on the commencement of the development or, in the case of an outline planning permission, on the submission of an application for the approval of reserved matters) has not yet expired, an application may be made for planning permission for the same development without complying with paragraphs (1) and (2) of this article; but such application shall be in writing and shall give sufficient information to enable the authority to identify the previous grant of planning permission. Where the local planning authority are of the opinion that further information is necessary to enable them to deal with the application, they may by a direction in writing addressed to the applicant require the submission of information, plans or drawings on such matters as may be specified in the direction.

(4) A local planning authority may by a direction in writing addressed to the applicant require to be produced to an officer of the authority such evidence in respect of an application for permission made to them as they may reasonably call for to verify any particulars of information given to them.

(5) This article shall be the regulations to be made for the purposes of section 25 of the Act.   **[556]**

NOTES
Commencement: 29 March 1977.
Amended by SI 1986 No 435, art 2, Sch 1, para 3.

6. Other forms of application

(1) An application to a local planning authority for approval of reserved matters shall be in writing, shall give particulars sufficient to identify the outline planning permission in respect of which it is made and shall include such particulars and be accompanied by such plans and drawings as are necessary to deal with the matters reserved in the outline planning permission together with such additional number of copies of the   application and plans and drawings as were required by the authority in relation to the application for outline planning permission.

(2) An application to a local planning authority for a determination under section 53 of the Act shall be in writing and shall contain a description of the operations or change of use proposed and be accompanied by a plan sufficient to identify the land to which the application relates. Where the proposal relates to the carrying out of operations, the application shall in addition be

accompanied by such plans or drawings as are necessary to show the nature of the operations which are covered by the proposal. Where the proposal relates to a change of use, full descriptions shall be given of the proposed use and of the use of the land at the date when the application is made (or, where the land is not in active use at that date, the purpose for which it was last used). The local planning authority may by a direction in writing require the applicant to furnish such further information as may be specified in the direction, to enable the application to be dealt with.   [557]

NOTES
Commencement: 29 March 1977.

7. General provisions relating to applications

[(1) Any application made under article 5 or 6 shall—

(a) where the land is in Greater London or a metropolitan county, be made to the local planning authority;
(b) where the land is situated elsewhere, be made to the district planning authority.]

(2) ...

[(3) When the local planning authority with whom an application has to be lodged receive—

(a) in the case of an application made under paragraph (1) or (2) of article 5, the form of application required by article 5(1), together with a certificate under section 27 of the Act;
(b) in the case of an application made under article 5(3), sufficient information to enable the authority to identify the previous grant of planning permission, together with a certificate under section 27 of the Act;
(c) in the case of an application made under article 6, the documents and information required by paragraph (1) or paragraph (2) of that article, as the case may be,

and the fee (if any) required to be paid in respect of that application (by virtue of the provisions of regulations made under section 87 of the Local Government, Planning and Land Act 1980) that authority shall as soon as may be send to the applicant an acknowledgment of the application in the terms (or substantially in the terms) set out in Part I of Schedule 2 hereto.]

(4) In the case of an application which falls to be determined by the county planning authority the district planning authority shall as soon as may be notify the applicant that the application will be so determined and shall transmit to the county planning authority all relevant plans, drawings, particulars and documents submitted with or in support of the application and notify the county planning authority of all action taken by the district planning authority in relation to the application.

(5) Where, after the sending of an acknowledgment as required by paragraph (3) of this article, the local planning authority, county planning authority or district planning authority (as the case may be) form the opinion that the application is invalid by reason of failure to comply with the requirements of article 5 or 6 or with any other statutory requirement they shall as soon as may be notify the applicant that his application is invalid.

[(6) Where a valid application under article 5 or 6 has been received by a local planning authority, the period within which the authority shall give notice to the applicant of their decision or determination, or of the reference of the application to the Secretary of State, shall (subject to the provisions of paragraph (6C) below) be eight weeks from the date when the application was received or (except where the applicant has already given notice of appeal to the Secretary of State) such extended period as may be agreed upon in writing between the applicant and the local planning authority by whom the application falls to be determined.

(6A) For the purposes of this article, the date when the application was received shall be taken to be—

   (*a*) in a case where a fee was required to be paid in respect of the application, the date when the form of application or the application in writing (as the case may be) and any certificates required by the Act were lodged with the authority mentioned in paragraph (1) of this article and the appropriate fee was paid to that authority or, where these events did not all occur on the same day, the date when the last such event occurred; or

   (*b*) in any other case, the date when the form of application or the application in writing (as the case may be) and any certificates required by the Act were lodged with the authority mentioned in paragraph (1) of this article.

(6B) Subject to the provisions of paragraph (6C) below, where an applicant sends to the local planning authority with whom his application has to be lodged a cheque for the amount of any fee due in respect of his application, the fee shall be taken as being paid on the date when the cheque is received by the authority.

(6C) Where a fee due in respect of an application has been paid in the manner described in paragraph (6B) above and the cheque received by the local planning authority is subsequently dishonoured, the period referred to in paragraph (6) above shall be calculated without regard to any time between the date when the authority send to the applicant written notice of the dishonouring of the cheque and the date when the authority are satisfied that they have received in full the amount of the fee due.]

(7) Every such notice shall be in writing and—

   (*a*) in the case of an application for planning permission or for approval of reserved matters, where the local planning authority decide to grant permission or approval subject to conditions or to refuse it, the notice shall—

      (i) state the reasons for the decision; and

      (ii) where the Secretary of State has given a direction restricting the grant of permission for the development referred to in the application or where he or a government department has expressed the view that the permission should not be granted (either wholly or in part) or should be granted subject to conditions, give details of the direction or of the view expressed, and

      (iii) where a local highway authority has given a direction restricting the grant of planning permission for the development referred to in the application or a county planning authority have given a direction as to how the application is to be determined, give details of the direction,

and shall be accompanied by a notification in the terms (or substantially in the terms) set out in Part II of Schedule 2 hereto;

(*b*) in the case of an application for a determination under section 53 of the Act (whether forming part of an application for planning permission or not), the local planning authority shall (except where they determine that the carrying out of operations or the making of a change in the use of land would not constitute or involve development of the land) state in such notice the grounds for their determination and include a statement to the effect that if the applicant is aggrieved by their decision he may appeal to the Secretary of State under section 36 of the Act (as applied by section 53 of the Act) within six months of receipt thereof or such longer period as the Secretary of State may at any time allow.

(8) A local planning authority shall furnish to such persons as may be prescribed by directions given by the Secretary of State under this order such information as may be so prescribed with respect to applications made to them under article 5 or 6 of this order including information as to the manner in which any such application has been dealt with.   **[558]**

NOTES
    Commencement: 1 April 1986 (para (1)); 29 March 1977 (remainder).
    Para (1): substituted for existing paras (1), (2) by SI 1986 No 435, art 2, Sch 1, para 4.
    Other amendments made by SI 1980 No 1946.

7A. [Where application has been made to a local planning authority for any consent, agreement or approval required by a condition imposed on a grant of planning permission (other than an application for approval of reserved matters) the authority shall give notice to the applicant of their decision on the application within a period of eight weeks from the date when the application was received by the authority.]   **[559]**

NOTES
    Commencement: 13 January 1981.
    Added by SI 1980 No 1946.

8. Notice under section 26

(1) The following classes of development are designated for the purposes of section 26 of the Act:—

(*a*) construction of buildings for use as public conveniences;

(*b*) construction of buildings or other operations, or use of land, for the disposal of refuse or waste materials or as a scrap yard or coal yard or for the winning or working of minerals;

(*c*) construction of buildings or other operations (other than the laying of sewers, the construction of pumphouses in a line of sewers, the construction of septic tanks and cesspools serving single dwelling-houses or single buildings in which not more than ten people will normally reside, work or congregate, and works ancillary thereto) or use of land, for the purpose of the retention, treatment or disposal of sewage, trade waste or sludge;

(*d*) construction of buildings to a height exceeding 20 metres;

(*e*) construction of buildings or use of land for the purposes of a slaughterhouse or knacker's yard; or for killing or plucking poultry;

(*f*) construction of buildings and use of buildings for any of the following purposes, namely, as a casino, a funfair or a bingo hall, a theatre, a cinema, a music hall, a dance hall, a skating rink, a swimming bath or gymnasium (not forming part of a school, college or university), or a Turkish or other vapour or foam bath;

(*g*) construction of buildings and use of buildings or land as a zoo or for the business of boarding or breeding cats or dogs;

(*h*) construction of buildings and use of land for motor car or motorcycle racing;

(*i*) use of land as a cemetery.

(2) The form of notice required to be published under section 26(2) of the Act shall be that set out in Part I of Schedule 3 hereto, and the copy of the notice accompanying the application shall be certified by or on behalf of the applicant as having been published in a named newspaper on a date specified in the certificate.

(3) Certificates issued for the purposes of section 26(2) of the Act shall be in the forms set out in Part II of Schedule 3 hereto.

(4) The form of notice required by section 26(3) of the Act to be posted on the land shall be that set out in Part III of Schedule 3 hereto.   **[560]**

NOTES
Commencement: 29 March 1977.

9. Certificates and notices under section 27

(1) Certificates issued for the purposes of section 27 of the Act shall be in the forms set out in Part I of Schedule 4 hereto.

(2) The requisite notices for the purposes of the provisions of the said section 27 in relation to applications shall be in the forms set out in Part II of Schedule 4 hereto.

(3) The requisite notices for the purposes of the provisions of the said section 27 in relation to appeals under section 36 of the Act shall be in the forms set out in Part III of Schedule 4 hereto.   **[561]**

NOTES
Commencement: 29 March 1977.

10. Directions restricting the grant of permission

(1) The Secretary of State may give directions restricting the grant of permission by a local planning authority, either indefinitely or during such period as may be specified in the directions, in respect of any such development or in respect of development of any such class as may be so specified.

(2) A local planning authority to which a direction has been given under this article shall deal with applications for permission for development to which such direction relates in such manner as to give effect to the terms of the direction.   **[562]**

NOTES
Commencement: 29 March 1977.

11. Special provisions as to permission for development affecting certain existing and proposed highways

(1) This article applies to the following highways and proposed highways:—

    (i) trunk roads;

    (ii) any highway which is comprised in the route of a special road to be provided by the Secretary of State in pursuance of a scheme under the provisions of Part II of the Highways Act 1959 and which has not for the time being been transferred to him;

(iii) any highway which has been or is to be provided by the Secretary of State in pursuance of an order under the provisions of Part II of the said Act relating to trunk roads and special roads and has not for the time being been transferred to any other highway authority;

(iv) any highway which the Secretary of State proposes to improve in pursuance of an order under the provisions of Part II of the said Act;

(v) any highway which the Secretary of State proposes to construct or improve, being a highway the route of which is shown as such in the development plan, or in respect of which the Secretary of State has given notice in writing to (*a*) in Greater London [or a metropolitan county], the local planning authority, or (*b*) elsewhere than in Greater London [or a metropolitan county], the district planning authority, together with maps or plans sufficient to identify the route of the highway to be constructed or the length of the highway to be improved.

[(2) On receipt of an application for planning permission for development which consists of or includes:—

(*a*) the formation, laying out or alteration or a means of access to any part of a trunk road which is subject to a speed limit exceeding 40 miles per hour or to a special road; or

(*b*) any development (other than development within the descriptions in sub-paragraph (*a*) above) of land within 67 metres (or such other distance as may be specified in a direction given by the Secretary of State under article 15(4) of this order) from the middle of—

(i) any highway which is to be provided by the Secretary of State and is within the description in paragraph (1)(iii) of this article; or

(ii) any highway within the descriptions in subparagraphs (iv) and (v) of paragraph (1) of this article,

the relevant local planning authority shall notify the Secretary of State and, in the case of an application which falls to be determined by the county planning authority, the county planning authority.

(2A) Such application as is referred to in paragraph (2) above shall not be determined unless:—

(*a*) the relevant local planning authority receive a direction given under article 10 of this order; or

(*b*) they receive notification, given by or on behalf of the Secretary of State, that he does not propose to give any such direction in respect of the development to which the application relates; or

(*c*) a period of 28 days (or such longer period as may be agreed in writing between the relevant local planning authority and the Secretary of State) from the date when notification was given to the Secretary of State has elapsed without receipt of such a direction or such notification.

(2B) In this article, "the relevant local planning authority" means—

(*a*) in relation to land in Greater London [or a metropolitan county], the local planning authority;

(b) in relation to land in an urban development area in respect of which the urban development corporation is the local planning authority, the urban development corporation; and

(c) in relation to any other land, the district planning authority.]

(3) Where under this article a local planning authority are required to notify the Secretary of State or the county planning authority of an application for planning permission they shall send to the Secretary of State at such office or address as he may appoint and to the county planning authority a copy of the relevant application and of every plan submitted therewith.   **[563]**

NOTES

Commencement: 1 March 1986 (para (2)); 29 March 1977 (remainder).
Para (1): amended by SI 1986 No 435, art 2, Sch 1, para 5.
Paras (2), (2A): substituted for existing para (2) by SI 1985 No 1981, art 2.
Para (2B): substituted for existing para (2) by SI 1985 No 1981, art 2; amended by SI 1986 No 435, art 2, Sch 1, para 5.

12. Power of local highway authority to issue directions restricting the grant of planning permission

(1) A local highway authority may give directions restricting the grant of planning permission by a local planning authority for the following descriptions of development relating to land in the area of the local highway authority:—

(a) the formation, laying out or alteration of any means of access to a classified road or to a proposed road the route of which has been adopted by resolution of the local highway authority and notified as such to the local planning authority;

(b) any other operations or use of land which appear to the local highway authority to be likely to result in a material increase in the volume of traffic entering or leaving such a classified or proposed road, to prejudice the improvement or construction of such a road or to result in a material change in the character of traffic entering, leaving or using such a road.

[(2) A local planning authority shall not determine an application for planning permission for development to which paragraph (1) of this article applies unless—

(a) they receive a direction given under paragraph (1) of this article;

(b) they receive notification from the local highway authority that that authority does not propose to give such a direction; or

(c) a period of 28 days from the date when a copy of the application was sent to the local highway authority in accordance with the requirements of paragraph 15(3B) of Schedule 16 to the Local Government Act 1972 (or such longer period as may be agreed in writing with the local highway authority) has elapsed without receipt of such a direction or such notification.]

(3) A local planning authority to which a direction has been given under this article shall deal with the application for permission for development to which such direction relates in such a manner as to give effect to the terms of the direction.

(4) This article does not apply to Greater London [or (except within a National Park) to a metropolitan county].   **[564]**

NOTES
Commencement: 1 March 1986 (para (2)); 29 March 1977 (remainder).
Para (2): substituted by SI 1985 No 1981, art 2.
Para (4): amended by SI 1986 No 435, art 2, Sch 1.

13. Application of bye-laws in relation to the construction of new streets

(1) Where permission is granted under Part III of the Act for development which consists of or includes the laying out or construction of a new street the bye-laws to which this article applies (except in so far as any such bye-law, by virtue of section 50 of the Public Health Act 1961 requires any person constructing a new street to provide separate sewers for foul water drainage and surface water drainage respectively) shall not apply to such development.

Before granting permission for such development, whether unconditionally or subject to conditions, a local planning authority who are not also the local highway authority shall consult with the local highway authority.

(2) This article applies to the following bye-laws:—

    (i) the bye-law made by the Metropolitan Board of Works on 17th March 1857 and confirmed by them on 3rd April 1857 under the Metropolis Management Act 1855;

    (ii) any bye-law made under section 157 of the Highways Act 1959 and any bye-law made under an enactment corresponding to the provisions of that section (being an enactment repealed by virtue of section 312 of the Highways Act 1959, or being an enactment so repealed as amended or extended by a local Act) which is for the time being in force by virtue of an order made by the Secretary of State under the said section 312 extending the period during which such bye-law is to remain in force. **[565]**

NOTES
Commencement: 29 March 1977.

14. Development not in accordance with the development plan

A local planning authority may in such cases and subject to such conditions as may be prescribed by directions given by the Secretary of State under this order grant permission for development which does not accord with the provisions of the development plan. **[566]**

NOTES
Commencement: 29 March 1977.

15. Consultations before the grant of permission

(1) Before permission is granted by a local planning authority for development in any of the following cases, whether unconditionally or subject to conditions, a local planning authority shall consult with the following authorities or persons, namely:—

    [(a) where it appears to that authority that the development is likely to affect land outside their area—

        (i) where that land is outside Greater London or a National Park, with the district council;

        (ii) where that land is in Greater London, with the Common Council or the council of the London borough, as the case may be;

(iii) where that land is in a National Park, with the county planning authority or, in a metropolitan county, with the local planning authority;]

[(*aa*) where it appears to the local planning authority that the development will involve the manufacture, processing, keeping or use of a hazardous substance in such circumstances that there will at any one time be, or is likely to be, a notifiable quantity of such substance in, on, over or under any land, with the Health and Safety Executive;]

(*b*) where it appears to the local planning authority that the development is likely to create or attract traffic which will result in a material increase in the volume of traffic entering or leaving a trunk road or using a level crossing over a railway, with the Secretary of State at such office or address as he may appoint;

(*c*) where the development involves the formation, laying out or alteration of any means of access to a highway (other than a trunk road) and the local highway authority concerned are not the authority making the decision, with the local highway authority concerned;

(*d*) where the development consists of the erection of a building (other than an alteration, extension or re-erection of an existing building or the erection of a building of a temporary character) in an area of coal working notified by the National Coal Board to the local planning authority, with the National Coal Board;

(*e*) where the development is of land which is situate within three kilometres from Windsor Castle, Windsor Great Park, or Windsor Home Park, or which is within 800 metres from any other royal palace or park, and might affect the amenities of that palace or park, with the Secretary of State at such office or address as he may appoint;

(*f*) where the development consists of or includes—

(i) the carrying out of works or operations in the bed of or on the banks of a river or stream;

(ii) the carrying out of building or other operations or use of land for the purpose of refining or storing mineral oils and their derivatives;

(iii) the use of land for the deposit of any kind of refuse or waste;

(iv) the carrying out of building or other operations (other than the laying of sewers, the construction of pumphouses in a line of sewers, the construction of septic tanks and cesspools serving single dwelling-houses or single buildings in which not more than ten people will normally reside, work or congregate, and works ancillary thereto) on land or use of land for the retention treatment or disposal of sewage, trade-waste or sludge;

(v) the use of land as a cemetery;

with the water authority exercising functions in the area in which the development is to take place;

(*g*) where the development is of land in an area of special interest notified to the local planning authority by the Nature Conservancy Council in accordance with section 23 of the National Parks and Access to the Countryside Act 1949, with the Nature Conservancy Council; except where the Council dispense with this requirement;

(*h*) where the development is of any land on which there is a theatre, as defined in the Theatres Trust Act 1976, with the Theatres Trust;

(*i*) where the development is not development for agricultural purposes and is not in accordance with the provisions of a development plan and—

(i) it would, in the opinion of the local planning authority, involve the loss of not less than 10 acres of land which is for the time being used (or was last used) for agricultural purposes; or

(ii) it would, in the opinion of the local planning authority, involve the loss of less than 10 acres of land which is for the time being used (or was last used) for agricultural purposes, but the circumstances are such that the development of that land is likely to lead to further loss of agricultural land,

with the Minister of Agriculture, Fisheries and Food.

[(*j*) where the development is of land in Greater London and would, in the opinion of the local planning authority, involve the demolition, in whole or in part, or the material alteration, of a building which is on a list of buildings of special architectural or historic interest compiled in pursuance of section 54 of the Act, with the Historic Buildings and Monuments Commission for England.]

(2) For the purposes of paragraph (1)(*i*) of this article, development is to be treated as not being in accordance with the provisions of a development plan if it would be inconsistent in any respect with the provisions of—

(i) a local plan adopted or approved in accordance with the provisions of section 14 of the Act; or

(ii) a development plan approved under Part I of Schedule 5 to the Act, or any other enactment which is re-enacted in that Schedule, which is in force in the area in which the land is situated; or

(iii) an old development plan within the meaning of paragraph 2 of Schedule 7 to the Act.

(3) ...

(4) The Secretary of State may give directions to a local planning authority requiring that authority to consult with the authorities, persons or bodies named in such directions in any case or class of case which may be specified in such directions and, before granting permission in any such case or class of case, the local planning authority shall enter into consultation accordingly.

(5) Where under this article a local planning authority are required to consult with any authority, person or body as to any application, they shall give not less than 14 days' notice to such authority, person or body that such application is to be taken into consideration, shall not determine the application until after the expiration of the period of such notice, and shall, in determining the application, take into account any representations received from such authority, person or body. **[567]**

NOTES

Commencement: 29 March 1977.

Para (1): sub-para (*aa*) added by SI 1983 No 1615; sub-para (*a*) substituted and sub-para (*j*) added by SI 1986 No 435, art 2, Sch 1, para 7.

Para (3): revoked by SI 1986 No 435, art 2, Sch 1, para 7.

15A. [Where a district planning authority are required by paragraph 19 of Schedule 16 to the Local Government Act 1972 to consult the county planning authority before determining an application for planning permission, they shall not determine the application until the expiration of a period of 28 days from the date of the notice which was given to the county planning authority under sub-paragraph (5)(*a*) of the said paragraph, or such longer period as may at any time be agreed in writing by the district planning authority.] **[568]**

NOTES
Commencement: 13 January 1981.
Added by SI 1980 No 1946.

16. Applications relating to county matters

(1) A county planning authority, before determining any of the following matters relating to a county matter, namely:—

(a) an application for planning permission under Part III of the Act;

(b) an application for determining under section 53 of the Act whether an application for such permission is required;

(c) an application for an established use certificate under section 94 of the Act;

(d) an application for approval of reserved matters;

shall afford the district planning authority for the area in which the land to which the application relates is situated an opportunity to make recommendations to the county planning authority as to the manner in which the application shall be determined and shall take any such recommendations into account.

(2) A county planning authority or a district planning authority who determine an application of any of the descriptions referred to in paragraph (1) of this article relating to a county matter (including any such application relating to land in a National Park) shall immediately notify the district planning authority or the county planning authority, as the case may be, of the terms of their decision, or, where such application is referred to the Secretary of State, the date when it was so referred and, when notified to them, the terms of the decision.

(3) In this article "county matter" has the meaning in relation to all matters which is assigned to that term in relation to certain matters in paragraph 32 of Schedule 16 to the Local Government Act 1972. **[569]**

NOTES
Commencement: 29 March 1977.

17. Notice to parish and community councils

[(1) A district planning authority or, in a metropolitan county, a local planning authority, on receiving any application of which the council of a parish or community are entitled to be informed, shall as soon as practicable notify that council of the application. In the case of a district planning authority, that authority shall at the same time notify that council of the name of the local planning authority who will determine the application and shall notify that authority, if not the district planning authority, of the date on which they give such notification.]

(2) On being notified of any such application the council of the parish or community shall as soon as practicable notify the local planning authority by whom the application will be determined whether they propose to make any representations as to the manner in which the application should be determined, and shall deliver any such representations to that authority within 14 days of the notification to them of the application.

(3) The local planning authority shall not determine any such application before—

(i) notification by the council of the parish or community that they do not propose to make any representations; or

(ii) receipt of representations from the council of the parish or community; or

(iii) the expiration of 14 days from the date when the council of the parish or community are notified,

whichever shall first occur, and in determining the application the local planning authority shall take into account any representations received from the council of the parish or community.

(4) The district planning authority [or, in a metropolitan county, the local planning authority] shall notify the council of the parish or community of the terms of the decision on any such application or, where the application is referred to the Secretary of State, the date when it was so referred and, when notified to them, the terms of his decision. **[570]**

NOTES
  Commencement: 1 April 1986 (para (1)); 29 March 1977 (remainder).
  Amended by SI 1986 No 435, art 2, Sch 1, para 8.

19. Notice of reference of applications to the Secretary of State

On referring any application to the Secretary of State under section 35 of the Act, pursuant to a direction in that behalf, a local planning authority shall serve on the applicant notice of the terms of the direction and of any reasons given by the Secretary of State for issuing the direction, and such notice shall inform the applicant that the application has been referred to the Secretary of State, and shall contain a statement that the Secretary of State will, if the applicant so desires, afford to the applicant an opportunity of appearing before and being heard by a person appointed by the Secretary of State for the purpose, and that the decision of the Secretary of State on the application will be final. **[571]**

NOTES
  Commencement: 29 March 1977.

20. Appeals

[(1) An applicant who desires to appeal—

(a) against a decision of a local planning authority refusing to grant—

(i) permission to develop land; or

(ii) any consent, agreement or approval of that authority required by a condition imposed on a grant of planning permission; or

(iii) any approval required under this order,

or granting any such permission, consent, agreement or approval subject to conditions; or

(b) against a determination of a local planning authority under section 53 of the Act; or

(c) on the failure of a local planning authority to give notice of their decision or determination, or of the reference of the application to the Secretary of State,

shall give notice of appeal to the Secretary of State within six months of notice of the decision or determination or of the expiry of the appropriate period allowed under article 7(6) or 7A of this order (as the case may be) or such longer period as the Secretary of State may at any time allow.

(1A) In the case of any appeal under paragraph (1) of this article in respect of—

(*a*) an application for any consent, agreement or approval required by a condition imposed on a grant of planning permission (other than an application for approval of a reserved matter); or

(*b*) an application for a determination under section 53 of the Act,

the applicant shall give notice of his appeal in writing, and in every other case the applicant shall give notice of his appeal on a form obtained from the Secretary of State.]

(2) Such person shall also furnish to the Secretary of State a copy of each of the following documents—

(i) the application;

(ii) all relevant plans, drawings, particulars and documents submitted with the application (including, in the case of an application for planning permission, a copy of any notice provided in accordance with section 26 of the Act and of the relevant certificate under that section and a copy of the certificate given in accordance with section 27 of the Act);

(iii) the notice of the decision or determination, if any;

(iv) all other relevant correspondence with the local planning authority.   **[572]**

NOTES

Commencement: 29 March 1977.

Amended by SI 1980 No 1946.

New art 20 substituted for art 20 above by SI 1987 No 702, art 2. See Appendix.

21. Register of applications

(1) In this article—

[(*a*) "the local planning register authority" means—

(i) the district planning authority (except in Greater London, a metropolitan county or a National Park);

(ii) in Greater London or a metropolitan county, the local planning authority; and

(iii) in a National Park (except in a metropolitan county), the county planning authority;]

(*b*) references to the Secretary of State shall be construed as including references to a person appointed by the Secretary of State under Schedule 9 to the Act to determine an appeal.

(2) The register of applications for planning permission which every local planning authority is required to keep under the provisions of section 34 of the Act shall be kept in two parts. Part I shall contain a copy of every application for planning permission and of any application for approval of reserved matters submitted to the local planning authority and not finally disposed of, together with copies of plans and drawings submitted in relation thereto. Part II shall contain the following copies and information in respect of every application for planning permission—

(*a*) a copy (which may be a photographic or other image or copy) of the application and of plans and drawings submitted in relation thereto;

(*b*) particulars of any direction given under the Act or this order in respect of the application;

(*c*) the decision (if any) of the local planning authority in respect of the application, the date of such decision and the name of the local planning authority;

(*d*) the date and effect of any decision of the Secretary of State in respect of the application, whether on appeal or on a reference under section 35 of the Act;

(*e*) the date of any subsequent approval (whether approval of reserved matters or any other approval required) given in relation to the application.

(3) Where, on an appeal to the Secretary of State under section 88 (enforcement notices) or 95 (applications for established use certificates) of the Act, the appellant is deemed to have made an application for planning permission for any development to which the appeal relates and the Secretary of State has granted permission for such development, the local planning register authority shall, on receipt of notification of the Secretary of State's decision, enter into Part II of the register referred to in the last preceding paragraph particulars of the development concerned and of the land on which it was carried out, and the date and effect of the Secretary of State's decision.

(4) The register of applications for a determination under section 53 of the Act which every local planning authority is required to keep under the provisions of section 34(1) of the Act (as applied by section 53(2) of the Act) shall contain the following information in respect of all applications relating to land within their area, namely—

(*a*) particulars of the application, including the name and address of the applicant, the date of the application and brief particulars of the proposal forming the subject of the application;

(*b*) the decision (if any) of the local planning authority in respect of the application, the date of such decision and the name of the local planning authority;

(*c*) the date and effect of any decision of the Secretary of State in respect of the application, whether on appeal or on a reference under section 35 of the Act.

(5) In the case of a register kept by the Common Council or by a London borough council, the register shall contain the same particulars (including, where appropriate, copies of applications, plans and drawings) in respect of applications made to the Greater London Council which relate to land in the area of the council keeping the register as are required by paragraph (2), paragraph (3) or paragraph (4) of this article, as the case may be, in respect of applications made to the local planning authority.

(6) Every register shall include an index for enabling a person to trace any entry in the register.

(7) Every entry in a register (including, in the case of a register of applications for planning permission, the placing in Part I of the register of the copies of the application, plans and drawings required by paragraph (2) of this article) shall be made within 14 days of the receipt of an application, or of the giving or making of the relevant direction, decision or approval as the case may be.

(8) Registers shall be kept at the office of the local planning register authority:

Provided that so much of any register as relates to land in a part of the area of that authority may be kept at a place within or convenient to that part.

(9) For the purposes of paragraph (2) of this article, an application shall not be treated as finally disposed of unless—

(a) if it has been decided by the authority (or the appropriate period allowed under article 7(6) of this order has expired without their giving a decision) and the period of six months specified in article 20 of this order has expired without any appeal having been made to the Secretary of State; or

(b) it has been referred to the Secretary of State under section 35 of the Act or an appeal has been made to the Secretary of State under section 36 of the Act, the Secretary of State has issued his decision and the period of six weeks specified in section 245 of the Act has expired without any application having been made to the High Court under that section; or

(c) an application has been made to the High Court under section 245 of the Act and the matter has been finally determined, either by final dismissal of the application by a Court or by the quashing of the Secretary of State's decision and the issue of a fresh decision (without a further application under the said section 245);

(d) it has been withdrawn by the applicant before being decided by the authority, or an appeal has been withdrawn by the applicant before the Secretary of State has issued his decision.   **[573]**

NOTES
Commencement: 29 March 1977.
Para (1): amended by SI 1986 No 435, art 2, Sch 1, para 9.

21A. Register of Enforcement and Stop Notices

[(1) Subject to paragraph (2) of this article the register which every district planning authority and every council of [a metropolitan district or] a London borough is required to keep under the provisions of section 92A of the Act shall contain the following information with respect to every enforcement notice issued in relation to land in their area:—

(a) the address of the land to which the notice relates or a plan by reference to which its situation can be ascertained;

(b) the name of the issuing authority;

(c) the date of issue of the notice;

(d) the date of service of copies of the notice;

(e) a statement or summary of the breach of planning control alleged and the requirements of the notice, including the period within which any required steps are to be taken;

(f) the date specified in the notice as the date on which it is to take effect;

(g) information on any postponement of the date specified as the date on which the notice will take effect by reason of section 88(10) of the Act (appeal to Secretary of State) and the date of the final determination or withdrawal of any appeal;

(h) the date of service and, if applicable, of withdrawal of any stop notice referring to the enforcement notice, together with a statement or summary of the activity prohibited by any such stop notice;

(i) the date, if any, on which the local planning authority are satisfied that steps required by the notice for a purpose mentioned in section 87(10)(b) of the Act (removal or alleviation of injury to amenity) have been taken.

(2) The entry relating to any enforcement notice or stop notice and everything relating to any such notice shall be removed from the register when the enforcement notice is quashed by the Secretary of State or withdrawn.

(3) Every register shall inlude an index for enabling a person to trace any entry in the register by reference to the address of the land to which the notice relates.

(4) Where a county planning authority issue an enforcement notice or serve a stop notice, they shall supply the information specified in paragraph (1) of this article to the district planning authority in whose area the land to which the notice relates is situated and shall inform the district planning authority of the withdrawal or quashing of any enforcement notice.

(5) ...

(6) The information prescribed in paragraph (1) of this article shall be entered in the register as soon as practicable and in any event within 14 days of the occurrence to which it relates, and information shall be so supplied under paragraphs (4) or (5) that entries may made within the said period of 14 days.

(7) Registers shall be kept at the office of the district or London borough council:

Provided that so much of the register as relates to land in a part of the area of that authority may be kept at a place within or convenient to that part.

(8) References to the Secrectary of State shall be construed as including references to a person appointed by the Secretary of State under Schedule 9 to the Act to determine an appeal.]   [574]

NOTES
Commencement: 27 November 1981.
Added by SI 1981 No 1569.
Para (1): amended by SI 1986 No 435, art 2, Sch 1, para 10.
Para (5): revoked by SI 1986 No 435, art 2, Sch 1, para 10.
The Act: Town and Country Planning Act 1971.

22. Established use certificate

(1) An application to a local planning authority for an established use certificate shall be in writing, shall be accompanied by such plans as are sufficient to identify clearly the land to which the application relates and shall give the following particulars:—

    (*a*) the address or location of the land to which the application relates;

    (*b*) a description of the use in respect of which a certificate is sought (being a use subsisting on the date when the application is made);

    (*c*) if there is more than one use of the land at the date when the application is made, a full description of all uses of the land at the relevant date and, where appropriate, an indication of the part of the land to which each of the uses relates;

    (*d*) whether the use referred to in sub-paragraph (*b*) above was begun before 1st January 1964 and, if not, the date when it was begun;

    (*e*) if the use referred to in sub-paragraph (*b*) above was begun on 1st January 1964 or a later date, particulars of the use of the land at 31st December 1963 and all subsequent uses, including the date when each such use began and ended;

    (*f*) the nature of the applicant's interest in the land;

    (*g*) a statement of the grounds (as set out in section 94(1) of the Act) upon which a certificate is sought;

    (*h*) such other information as the applicant considers necessary to substantiate or make good his claim.

The application shall be accompanied by such documentary evidence as the applicant is able to furnish in proof of his statements and, in a case where a certificate is being sought on ground (*b*) of section 94(1) of the Act (that is, that the use was begun before the beginning of 1964 under a planning permission granted subject to conditions or limitations, which either have never been complied with or have not been complied with since the end of 1963), a copy of the relevant planning permission or, where it is not possible to supply a copy, details of the condition in question and such particulars as the applicant is able to furnish in order that the permission may be identified.   The local planning authority may by a direction in writing require the applicant to furnish such further information as may be specified in the direction, to enable them to deal with the application.

(2) An application for an established use certificate shall not be entertained by the local planning authority unless it is accompanied by one or other of the following certificates signed by or on behalf of the applicant, that is to say:—

(*a*) a certificate stating that at the beginning of the period of twenty-one days ending with the date of the application, no person (other than the applicant) was the owner of any of the land to which the application relates;

(*b*) a certificate stating that the applicant has given the requisite notice of the application to all the persons (other than the applicant) who, at the beginning of the period of twenty-one days ending with the date of the application, were owners of any of the land to which the application relates, and setting out the names of those persons, the addresses at which notice of the application was given to them respectively, and the date of service of each such notice;

(*c*) a certificate stating that the applicant is unable to issue a certificate in accordance with either of the preceding sub-paragraphs, that he has given the requisite notice of the application to such one or more of the persons mentioned in the last preceding sub-paragraph as are specified in the certificate (setting out their names, the addresses at which notice of the application was given to them respectively and the date of the service of each such notice), that he has taken such steps as are reasonably open to him (specifying them) to ascertain the names and addresses of the remainder of those persons and that he has been unable to do so;

(*d*) a certificate stating that the applicant is unable to issue a certificate in accordance with sub-paragraph (*a*) of this paragraph, that he has taken such steps as are reasonably open to him (specifying them) to ascertain the names and addresses of the persons mentioned in sub-paragraph (*b*) of this paragraph and that he has been unable to do so.

For the purposes of this paragraph the persons who are to be treated as owners of the land to which application for an established use certificate relates are:—

(i) a person who, in respect of any part of the land, is entitled to the freehold or a lease the unexpired term of which at the relevant time is not less than 7 years; and

(ii) any other person who is the occupier of any part of the said land.

(3) Any such certificate as is mentioned in sub-paragraph (*c*) or sub-paragraph (*d*) of the last preceding paragraph shall also contain a statement that the requisite notice of the application, as set out in the certificate, has on a date specified in the certificate (being a date not earlier than the beginning of the period mentioned in sub-paragraph (*b*) of the said paragraph) been published

in a local newspaper circulating in the locality in which the land in question is situated.

(4) In addition to any other matters required to be contained in a certificate issued for the purposes of paragraph (2) of this article, every such certificate shall contain one or other of the following statements, that is to say:—

(*a*) a statement that none of the land to which the application relates constitutes or forms part of an agricultural holding;

(*b*) a statement that the applicant has given the requisite notice of the application to every person (other than the applicant) who, at the beginning of the period of 21 days ending with the date of the application, was a tenant of any agricultural holding any part of which was comprised in the land to which the application relates, and setting out the name of each such person, the address at which notice of the application was given to him, and the date of service of that notice.

(5) Where an application for an established use certificate is accompanied by such a certificate as is mentioned in sub-paragraph (*b*), sub-paragraph (*c*) or sub-paragraph (*d*) of paragraph (2) of this article, or by a certificate containing a statement in accordance with sub-paragraph (*b*) of paragraph (4) of this article, the local planning authority:—

(*a*) shall not determine the application before the end of the period of 21 days beginning with the date appearing from the certificate to be the latest of the dates of service of notices as mentioned in the certificate, or the date of publication of a notice as therein mentioned, whichever is the later;

(*b*) in determining the application, shall take into account any representations relating thereto which are made to them, before the end of the period mentioned in the preceding sub-paragraph, by any person who satisfies them that he is an owner (within the meaning of that term as defined in paragraph (2) of this article) of any land to which the application relates or that he is the tenant of an agricultural holding any part of which is comprised in that land; and

(*c*) shall give notice of their decision to every person who has made representations which they were required to take into account in accordance with the last preceding sub-paragraph.

(6) The provisions of paragraphs (1), (3) and (8) of article 7 of this order shall apply to an application for an established use certificate as they apply to an application for planning permission, with the modification that the form of the notice of receipt of the application which is to be sent to the applicant shall be as set out in Part I of Schedule 6 to this order. In the case of an application relating to land outside Greater London [or a metropolitan county] which falls to be determined by the county planning authority, the district planning authority shall as soon as may be notify the applicant that the application will be so determined and transmit to the county planning authority the application, all relevant plans, drawings, statements, particulars, certificates and correspondence and a statement of any action taken by the district planning authority in relation to the application.

(7) The local planning authority shall give notice to the applicant of their decision (or of the reference of the application to the Secretary of State, as the case may be) within a period of eight weeks from the date of receipt of the application, or (except where the applicant has already given notice of appeal to the Secretary of State) such extended period as may be agreed upon in writing between the applicant and (*a*) in Greater London [or a metropolitan county],

the local planning authority, (*b*) elsewhere, the district planning authority or, in the case of an application which falls to be determined by the county planning authority, either the district planning authority or the county planning authority.

(8) Where an established use certificate is not granted by the local planning authority on an application, the notice of their decision to refuse the application shall be given in writing, and state the grounds for their decision and include a statement to the effect that if the applicant is aggrieved by the decision he may appeal to the Secretary of State under section 95(2) of the Act.

(9) An applicant who desires to appeal against a decision of a local planning authority refusing an established use certificate, or refusing it in part, or against a deemed refusal of such a certificate, shall give notice of appeal in writing to the Secretary of State within six months of receipt of notice of the decision or of the expiry of the period allowed under paragraph (7) of this article, as the case may be, or such longer period as the Secretary of State may at any time allow. Such person shall also furnish to the Secretary of State copies of each of the following documents:—

    (i) the application;
   (ii) all relevant plans, drawings, statements and particulars submitted to them (including the certificate given under paragraph (2) of this article);
  (iii) the notice of the decision, if any;
  (iv) all other relevant documents and correspondence with the local planning authority.

(10) The provisions of paragraphs (2) to (4) of this article shall apply in relation to an appeal to the Secretary of State as they apply in relation to an application to the local planning authority for an established use certificate.

(11) The provisions of article 21 of this order relating to the register kept by the local planning authority in pursuance of section 34(1) of the Act shall apply in relation to applications for established use certificates as they apply in relation to applications for a determination under section 53 of the Act, with the modification that for the reference in paragraph (4)(*a*) to the proposal forming the subject of the application there shall be substituted a reference to the use in respect of which a certificate is sought.

(12) Certificate issued for the purposes of paragraph (2) of this article shall be in the form set out in Part I of Schedule 5 hereto. The requisite notices for the purposes of the provisions of the said paragraph in relation to applications for established use certificates shall be in the form set out in Part II of the said Schedule 5, and the requisite notices for the purposes of the provisions of paragraphs (9) and (10) of this article (that is, notices in relation to appeals against refusal of an established use certificate) shall be in the forms set out in Part III of the said Schedule.

(13) Established use certificates shall be issued in the form set out in Part II of Schedule 6 to this order adapted as may be necessary in the case of certificates granted on the grounds referred to in paragraph (*b*) of section 94(1) of the Act.

[575]

NOTES
  Commencement: 29 March 1977.
  Paras (6), (7): amended by SI 1986 No 435, art 2, Sch 1, para 11.

23. Directions and notices

(1) Any power conferred by this order to give a direction shall be construed as including power to cancel or vary the direction by a subsequent direction.

(2) Any notice or other document to be served or given under this order may be served or given in the manner prescribed by section 283 of the Act and by any regulations made under that section.   **[576]**

NOTES
Commencement: 29 March 1977.

24. Revocations and savings

(1) The statutory instruments specified in Schedule 7 hereto are hereby revoked, but without prejudice to any permission granted or determination made or certificate issued thereunder; and any application for planning permission or for a determination or for an established use certificate which at the coming into operation of this order is outstanding shall have effect as if made and be determined under and in accordance with the provisions of this order.

(2) Any directions in force immediately before the coming into operation of this order under articles 4, 5, 6, 7, 10, 11, 12, 14, 15, 18, 19, 22 or 23, of the Town and Country Planning General Development Orders 1973 to 1976 shall continue in force and have effect as if given under this order.   **[577]**

NOTES
Commencement: 29 March 1977.

SCHEDULES

SCHEDULE 1

The following development is permitted under article 3 of this order subject to the limitations contained in the description of that development in column (1) and subject to the conditions set out opposite that description in column (2).

Column (1)

Description of Development

Class 1.—Development within the curtilage of a dwellinghouse

[1. The enlargement, improvement or other alteration of a dwellinghouse [(other than by the carrying out of operations within paragraph 2A of this class)] so long as:

(*a*) the cubic content of the original dwellinghouse (as ascertained by external measurement) is not exceeded by more than—

  (i) in the case of a terrace house, 50 cubic metres or ten per cent, whichever is the greater; or
  (ii) in any other case, 70 cubic metres or fifteen per cent, whichever is the greater,
  subject (in either case) to a maximum of 115 cubic metres;

(*b*) the height of the buiding as so enlarged, improved or altered does not exceed the height of the highest part of the roof of the original dwellinghouse;

(*c*) no part of the building as so enlarged, improved or altered projects beyond the forwardmost part of any wall of the original dwellinghouse which fronts on a highway;

(*d*) no part of the building (as to enlarged, improved or altered) which lies within a distance of two metres from any boundary of the curtilage of the dwellinghouse has, as a result of the development, a height exceeding four metres;

(*e*) the area of ground covered by buildings within the curtilage (other than the original dwellinghouse) does not thereby exceed fifty per cent of the total area of the curtilage excluding the ground area of the original dwellinghouse:

Provided that:—

(*a*) the erection of a garage or coachhouse within the curtilage of the dwellinghouse shall be treated as the enlargement of the dwellinghouse for all purposes of this permission (including the calculation of cubic content) if any part of that building lies within a distance of five metres from any part of the dwellinghouse;

(*b*) the erection of a stable or loose-box anywhere within the curtilage of the dwellinghouse shall be treated as the enlargement of the dwellinghouse for all purposes of this permission (including the calculation of cubic content);

(*c*) for the purposes of this permission the extent to which the cubic content of the original dwellinghouse is exceeded shall be ascertained by deducting the amount of the cubic content of the original dwellinghouse from the amount of the cubic content of the dwellinghouse as enlarged, improved or altered (whether such enlargement, improvement or alteration was carried out in pursuance of this permission or otherwise);

(*d*) where any part of the dwellinghouse will, as a result of the development, lie within a distance of five metres from an existing garage or coachhouse, that building shall (for the purpose of the calculation of cubic content) be treated as forming part of the dwellinghouse as enlarged, improved or altered; and

(*e*) the limitation contained in subparagraph (*d*) above shall not apply to development consisting of:—

  (i) the insertion of a window (including a dormer window) into a wall or the roof of the original dwellinghouse, or the alteration or enlargement of an existing window; or

  (ii) any other alterations to any part of the roof of the original dwellinghouse.]

2. The erection or construction of a porch outside any external door of a dwellinghouse so long as:

(*a*) the floor area does not exceed 2 square metres;

(*b*) no part of the structure is more than 3 metres above the level of the ground;

(*c*) no part of the structure is less than 2 metres from any boundary of the curtilage which fronts on a highway.

[2A. The installation, alteration or replacement of a satellite antenna on a dwellinghouse or within the curtilage of a dwellinghouse, so long as:—

(*a*) the size of the antenna (excluding any projecting feed element) does not, when measured in any dimension, exceed 90 centimetres;

(*b*) there is no other satellite antenna installed on the dwellinghouse or anywhere else within the curtilage of the dwellinghouse;

(*c*) in the case of an antenna installed on a dwelling-house the highest part of the antenna is not higher than the highest part of the roof of the building on which it is installed.]

[3. The erection, construction or placing, and the maintenance, improvement or other alteration, within the curtilage of a dwellinghouse, of any building or enclosure (other than a dwelling, stable [, satellite antenna] or loose-box) required for a purpose incidental to the enjoyment of the dwellinghouse as such, including the keeping of poultry, bees, pet animals, birds or other livestock for the domestic needs or personal enjoyment of the occupants of the dwellinghouse, so long as:

(*a*) no part of such building or enclosure projects beyond the forwardmost part of any wall of the original dwellinghouse which fronts on a highway;

(*b*) in the case of a garage or coachhouse, no part of the building is within a distance of five metres from any part of the dwellinghouse;

(*c*) the height does not exceed, in the case of a building with a ridged roof, four metres or, in any other case, three metres;

(*d*) the area of ground covered by buildings within the curtilage (other than the original dwellinghouse) does not thereby exceed fifty per cent of the total area of the curtilage excluding the ground area of the original dwellinghouse.]

4. The construction within the curtilage of a dwellinghouse of a hardstanding for vehicles for a purpose incidental to the enjoyment of the dwellinghouse as such.

5. The erection or placing within the curtilage of a dwellinghouse of a tank for the storage of oil for domestic heating so long as:

    (*a*) the capacity of the tank does not exceed 3500 litres;

    (*b*) no part of the tank is more than 3 metres above the level of the ground;

    (*c*) no part of the tank projects beyond the forwardmost part of any wall of the original dwellinghouse which fronts on a highway.

Column (2)

Conditions

Column (1)

Description of Development

Class II.—Sundry minor operations

1. The erection or construction of gates, fences, walls or other means of enclosure not exceeding 1 metre in height where abutting on a highway used by vehicular traffic or 2 metres in height in any other case, and the maintenance, improvement or other alteration of any gates, fences, walls or other means of enclosure: so long as such improvement or alteration does not increase the height above the height appropriate for a new means of enclosure.

2. The formation, laying out and construction of a means of access to a highway not being a trunk or classified road, where required in connection with development permitted by article 3 of and Schedule 1 to this order (other than under this class).

3. The painting of the exterior of any building or work otherwise than for the purpose of advertisement, announcement or direction.

Column (2)

Conditions

Column (1)

Description of Development

[*Class III—Changes of use*

Development consisting of a change of use:—

    (*a*) to use as a light industrial building as defined by the Use Classes Order from use as a general industrial building as so defined;

    (*b*) to use as a light industrial building as defined by the Use Classes Order from use for any purpose included in class X referred to in the Schedule to the Use Classes Order;

    (*c*) to use for any purpose included in class X referred to in the Schedule to the Use Classes Order from use as a light industrial building or from use as a general industrial building (as defined respectively by the Use Classes Order);

    (*d*) to use as a shop for any purpose included in class I referred to in the Schedule to the Use Classes Order from use as:—

        (i) a shop for the sale of hot food;

        (ii) a tripe shop;

        (iii) a shop for the sale of pet animals or birds;

        (iv) a cats' meat shop; or

        (v) a shop for the sale of motor vehicles:

Provided that paragraphs (*b*) and (*c*) above apply only where the total amount of floor space in the building used for the purposes of the undertaking does not exceed 235 square metres.]

Column (2)

Conditions

Column (1)

Description of Development

Class IV.—Temporary buildings and uses

1. The erection or construction on land in, on, over or under which operations other than mining operations are being or are about to be carried out (being operations for which planning permission has been granted or is deemed to have been granted under Part III of the Act, or for which planning permission is not required), or on land adjoining such land, of buildings, works, plant or machinery needed temporarily in connection with the said operations, for the period of such operations.

Column (2)

Conditions

Such buildings, works, plant or machinery shall be removed at the expiration of the period of such operations and where they were sited on any such adjoining land, that land shall be forthwith reinstated.

Column (1)

Description of Development

2. The use of land (other than a building or the curtilage of a building) for any purpose or purposes except as a caravan site on not more than 28 days in total in any calendar year (of which not more than 14 days in total may be devoted to use for the purpose of motor car or motor-cycle racing or for the purpose of the holding of markets), and the erection or placing of moveable structures on the land for the purposes of that use:

Provided that for the purpose of the limitation imposed on the number of days on which land may be used for motor car or motor-cycle racing, account shall be taken only of those days on which races are held or practising takes place.

Column (2)

Conditions

Column (1)

Description of Development

Class V.—Uses by members of recreational organisations

The use of land, other than buildings and not within the curtilage of a dwellinghouse, for the purposes of recreation or instruction by members of an organisation which holds a certificate of exemption granted under section 269 of the Public Health Act 1936, and the erection or placing of tents on the land for the purposes of that use.

Column (2)

Conditions

Column (1)

Description of Development

Class VI.—Argicultural buildings, works and uses

1. The carrying out on agricultural land having an area of more than one acre and comprised in an agricultural unit of building or engineering operations [(other than engineering operations to which paragraph 4 below applies)] requisite for the use of that land for the purposes of agriculture (other than the placing on land of structures not designed for those purposes or the provision and alteration of dwellings), so long as:—

    (a) the ground area covered by a building erected pursuant to this permission does not, either by itself or after the addition thereto of the ground area covered by any existing building or buildings (other than a dwellinghouse) within the same unit erected or in course of erection within the preceding two years and wholly or partly within 90 metres of the nearest part of the said building, exceed 465 square metres;

    (b) the height of any buildings or works does not exceed 3 metres in the case of a building or works within 3 kilometres of the perimeter of an aerodrome, nor 12 metres in any other case;

    (c) no part of any buildings (other than moveable structures) or works is within 25 metres of the metalled portion of a trunk or classified road.

2. The erection or construction and the maintenance, improvement or other alteration of roadside stands for milk churns, except where they would abut on any trunk or classified road.

3. The winning and working, on land held or occupied with land used for the purposes of agriculture, of any minerals reasonably required for the purposes of that use, including—

    (i) the fertilisation of the land so used, and

    (ii) the maintenance, improvement or alteration of buildings or works thereon which are occupied or used for the purposes aforesaid,

so long as no excavation is made within 25 metres of the metalled portion of a trunk or classified road.

[4. The carrying out of operations for the construction of fishponds (including the excavation of land and the winning and working of minerals) and other engineering operations on agricultural land used for the purposes of any business of fish farming or of shellfish farming which is registered in a register kept by the Minister of Agriculture Fisheries and Food or the Secretary of State (as the case may be) for the purposes of an order made under section 7 of the Diseases of Fish Act 1983 where—

    (a) the area of the site within which the operations are carried out does not exceed 2 hectares;

    (b) no operations are carried out within 25 metres of the metalled portion of a trunk or classified road;

    (c) in a case where the operations involve the winning or working of minerals, they comply with both of the following limitations:—

        (i) that no excavation exceeds a depth of 2.5 metres; and

        (ii) that the area of excavation (taken together with any other excavations carried out on the land within the preceding two years) does not exceed 0.2 hectares.]

Column (2)

Conditions

[1. In the case of operations which involve the deposit on or under the land of refuse or waste materials no such material shall be brought onto the land from elsewhere.

2. Where an operation involves the extraction of any mineral from the land, or from any disused railway embankment on the land, or the removal of any mineral from a mineral-

working deposit on the land, and no planning permission has been granted (on an application made to the local planning authority under Part III of the Act) for the winning and working of that mineral, the mineral shall not be moved off the land.]

[No minerals extracted during the course of the operations shall be moved to any place outside the land from which they were extracted, except to the land which is held or occupied with that land and is used for agricultural purposes.]

Column (1)

Description of Development

Class VII.—Forestry buildings and works

The carrying out on land used for the purposes of forestry (including afforestation) of building and other operations (other than the provision or alteration of dwellings) requisite for the carrying on of those purposes, and the formation, alteration and maintenance of private ways on such land, so long as:—

(a) the height of any buildings or works within 3 kilometres of the perimeter of an aerodrome does not exceed 3 metres;

(b) no part of any buildings (other than moveable structures) or works is within 25 metres of the metalled portion of a trunk or classified road.

Column (2)

Conditions

Column (1)

Description of Development

Class VIII.—Development for industrial purposes

[1. Development of the following descriptions, carried out by an industrial undertaker on land used (otherwise than (i) in contravention of previous planning control or (ii) without planning permission granted or deemed to be granted under Part III of the Act) for the carrying out of any industrial process, and for the purposes of such process, or on land used (otherwise than as aforesaid) as a dock, harbour or quay for the purposes of an industrial undertaking:—

(i) the provision, rearrangement or replacement of private ways or private railways, sidings or conveyors;

(ii) the provision or rearrangement of sewers, mains, pipes, cables or other apparatus;

(iii) the installation or erection, by way of addition or replacement, of plant or machinery, or structures or erections of the nature of plant or machinery, not exceeding 15 metres in height or the height of the plant, machinery, structure or erection so replaced, whichever is the greater;

[(iv) the extension or alteration of buildings (whether erected before or after 1st July 1948), so long as the height of the original building is not exceeded, the cubic content of the original building (as ascertained by external measurement) is not increased by more than 25%, and its aggregate floor space is not increased by more than 1000 square metres.]

so long as:—

(a) in the case of operations carried out under subparagraph (iii) or (iv), the external appearance of the premises of the undertaking is not materially affected;

(b) in the case of operations carried out under subparagraph (iv), no part of the building is, as a result of the development, within a distance of five metres from any boundary of the curtilage of the premises; and

(c) in the case of operations carried out under subparagraph (iv), no certificate would be required under section 67 of the Act if an application for planning permission for the development in question were made:

Provided that the erection on land within the curtilage of any such building of an additional building to be used in connection with the original building shall be treated as an extension of the original building, and where any two or more original buildings comprised in the same curtilage are used as one unit for the purposes of the undertaking, the reference in this permission to the cubic content shall be construed as a reference to the aggregate cubic content of those buildings, and the reference to the aggregate floor space as a reference to the total floor space of those buildings.]

2. The deposit by an industrial undertaker of waste material or refuse resulting from an industrial process on any land comprised in a site which was used for such deposit on 1st July 1948, whether or not the superficial area or the height of the deposit is thereby extended.

Column (2)

Conditions

Column (1)

Description of Development

Class IX.—Repairs to unadopted streets and private ways

The carrying out of works required for the maintenance or improvement of an unadopted street or private way, being works carried out on land within the boundaries of the street or way.

Column (2)

Conditions

Column (1)

Description of Development

Class X.—Repairs to services

The carrying out of any works for the purpose of inspecting, repairing or renewing sewers, mains, pipes, cables, or other apparatus, including the breaking open of any land for that purpose.

Column (2)

Conditions

Column (1)

Description of Development

Class XI.—War damaged buildings, works and plant

The rebuilding, restoration or replacement of buildings, works or plant which have sustained war damage, so long as:—

   (a) the cubic content of the building or of the works or plant immediately before the occurrence of such damage is not increased by more than such amount (if any) as is permitted under Class I or Class VIII;
   (b) there is no material alteration from the external appearance immediately before the occurrence of such damage except with the approval of the local planning authority.

Column (2)

Conditions

Column (1)

Description of Development

Class XII.—Development under local or private Acts, or orders

Development authorised (i) by any local or private Act of Parliament or (ii) by any order approved by both Houses of Parliament or (iii) by any order made under section 14 or section 16 of the Harbours Act 1964 being, in any such case, a local or private Act, or an order, which designates specifically both the nature of the development thereby authorised and the land upon which it may be carried out:

Provided that where the development consists of or includes the erection, construction, alteration or extension of any building (which expression shall include any bridge, aqueduct, pier or dam, but not any other structure or erection), or the formation laying out or alteration of a means of access to any highway used by vehicular traffic this permission shall be exercisable in respect of such building or access as the case may be only if the prior approval of (*a*) the district planning authority (except in Greater London [, a metropolitan county] or a National Park); (*b*) in Greater London [or a metropolitan county], the local planning authority, or (*c*) in a National Park [outside a metropolitan county], the county planning authority is obtained for the detailed plans and specifications thereof; but that authority shall not refuse to grant approval, or impose conditions on the grant thereof, unless they are satisfied that it is expedient so to do on the ground that:—

> (*a*) the design, or external appearance of such building, bridge, aqueduct, pier or dam would injure the amenity of the neighbourhood and is reasonably capable of modification so as to conform with such amenity; or
>
> (*b*) in the case of a building, bridge, aqueduct, pier or means of access, the erection, construction, formation, laying out, alteration or extension, ought to be and could reasonably be carried out elsewhere on the land.

Column (2)

Conditions

Column (1)

Description of Development

Class XIII.—Development by local authorities

1. The erection or construction and the maintenance, improvement or other alteration by a local authority [or by an urban development corporation] of:—

> (i) such small ancillary buildings, works and equipment as are required on land belonging to or maintained by them, for the purposes of any functions exercised by them on that land otherwise than as statutory undertakers;.
>
> (ii) lamp standards, information kiosks, passenger shelters, public shelters and seats, telephone boxes, fire alarms, public drinking fountains, horse-troughs, refuse bins or baskets, barriers for the control of persons waiting to enter public vehicles, and such smimilar structures or works as may be required in connection with the operation of any public service administered by them.

2. The deposit by a local authority of waste material or refuse on any land comprised in a site which was used for that purpose on 1st July 1948, whether or not the superficial area or the height of the deposit is thereby extended.

Column (2)

Conditions

Column (1)

Description of Development

Class XIV.—Development by local highway authorities . . .

The carrying out by a local highway authority . . . of any works required for or incidental to the maintenance or improvement of existing highways being works carried out on land outside but abutting on the boundary of the highway.

Column (2)

Conditions

Column (1)

Description of Development

Class XV.—Development by drainage authorities

Any development by a drainage authority within the meaning of the Land Drainage Act 1930, in, on or under any watercourse or drainage works, in connection with the improvement or maintenance of such watercourse or drainage works.

Column (2)

Conditions

Column (1)

Description of Development

Class XVI.Development by water authorities

Development of any of the following descriptions by a water authority established under the Water Act 1973:—

    (*a*)   the laying underground of mains, pipes or other apparatus;

    (*b*)   the improvement, maintenance or repair of watercourses or land drainage works;

Column (2)

Conditions

Column (1)

Description of Development

    (*c*)   the erection, construction or placing of buildings, plants, or apparatus on land or the carrying out of engineering operations in, on, over or under land, for the purpose of surveys or investigations.

Column (2)

Conditions

On completion of the survey or investigation, or at the end of 6 months from the commencement of the development permitted by this class, whichever is the sooner, all such operations shall cease and all such buildings, plant or apparatus shall be removed and the land restored to its former condition.

Column (1)

Description of Development

Class XVII.—Development for sewerage and sewage disposal

Any development by or on behalf of a water authority (established under the Water Act 1973), or by a Development Corporation authorised under section 34 of the New Towns Act 1965 to exercise powers relating to sewerage or sewage disposal, being development not above ground level required in connection with the provision, improvement or maintenance of sewers.

Column (2)

Conditions

Column (1)

Description of Development

Class XVIII.—Development by statutory undertakers

A. Railway or light railway undertakings.

Development by the undertakers of operational land of the undertaking, being development which is required in connection with the movement of traffic by rail, other than:

    (i) the construction of railways;

    (ii) the construction or erection, or the reconstruction or alteration so as materially to affect the design or external appearance thereof, of—

        (*a*) any railway station or bridge;

        (*b*) any hotel;

        (*c*) any residential or educational building, office, or building to be used for manufacturing or repairing work which is not situate wholly within the interior of a railway station;

        (*d*) any car park, shop, restaurant, garage, petrol filling station or other building or structure provided in pursuance of the powers contained in section 14 (1) (*d*) of the Transport Act 1962 or section 10 (1) (*x*) of the Transport Act 1968 which is not situate wholly within the interior of a railway station.

B. Dock, pier, harbour, water transport, canal or inland navigation undertakings.

    1. Development by the undertakers or their lessees of operational land of the undertaking, being development which is required for the purpose of shipping, or in connection with the embarking, disembarking, loading, discharging or transport of passengers, livestock or goods at a dock, pier or harbour, or the movement of traffic by canal or inland navigation, or by any railway forming part of the undertaking, other than the construction or erection, or the reconstruction or alteration so as materially to affect the design or external appearance thereof, of:—

        (*a*) any bridge or other building not required in connection with the handling of traffic;

        (*b*) any hotel;

        (*c*) any educational building not situate wholly within the limits of a dock, pier or harbour;

        (*d*) any car park, shop, restaurant, garage, petrol filling station or other building not situate wholly within the limits of a dock, pier or harbour, provided in pursuance of the powers contained in any of the following enactments:—

the Transport Act 1962 section 14(1)(*d*);

the Transport Act 1968 section 10(1)(*x*);

the Transport Act 1968 section 50(6).

2. The improvement, maintenance or repair of any inland waterway to which section 104 of the Transport Act 1968 applies which is not a commercial waterway or a cruising waterway, and the repair or maintenance of culverts, weirs, locks, aqueducts, sluices, reservoirs, let-off valves or other works used in connection with the control and operation of such waterways.

3. The use of any land for the spreading of dredgings.

C. Water or hydraulic power undertakings.

Development required for the purposes of the undertakings of any of the following descriptions, that is to say:—

(i) the laying underground of mains, pipes, or other apparatus;

(ii) the improvement, maintenance or repair of watercourses or land drainage works;

(iii) the maintenance or repair of works for measuring the flow in any watercourse or channel or the improvement of any such works (otherwise than by the erection or installation, by way of addition or replacement, of any structures of the nature of buildings or of any plant or machinery);

(iv) the installation in a water distribution system of booster stations, meter or switch gear houses, not exceeding (except where constructed underground elsewhere than under a highway) 29 cubic meters in capacity;

Column (2)

Conditions

Column (1)

Description of Development

(v) the erection, construction or placing of buildings, plant or apparatus on land, or the carrying out of engineering operations, in, on, over or under land, for the purpose of surveys or investigations.

Column (2)

Conditions

On completion of the survey or investigation or at the expiration of six months from the commencement of the development the subject of this permission, whichever is the sooner, all such operations shall cease and all such buildings, plant or apparatus shall be removed and the land restored to its former condition.

Column (1)

Description of Development

(vi) any other development carried out in, on, over or under the operational land of the undertaking except:—

(a) the erection, or the reconstruction or alteration so as materially to affect the design or external appearance thereof, of buildings;
(b) the installation or erection, by way of addition or replacement, of any plant or machinery, or structure or erections of the nature of plant or machinery, exceeding 15 metres in height or the height of the plant, machinery, structure or erection so replaced, whichever is the greater.

Column (1)

Description of Development

D. Gas undertakings.

Development required for the purposes of the undertaking of any of the following descriptions, that is to say:—

(i) the laying underground of mains, pipes, or other apparatus;

(ii) the installation in a gas distribution system of apparatus for measuring, recording, controlling or varying the pressure flow or volume of gas, and structures for housing such apparatus not exceeding (except where constructed underground elsewhere than under a highway) 29 cubic metres in capacity;

(iii) the construction, in any storage area or protective area specified in an order made under section 4 of the Gas Act 1965 of boreholes, other than those shown in the order as approved by the Secretary of State for Energy for the purpose of subsection (6) of the said section 4, and the erection or construction, in any such area, of any plant or machinery, or structure or erections in the nature of plant or machinery, not exceeding 6 metres in height which is required in connection with the construction of any such borehole;

(iv) the placing and storage on land of pipe and other apparatus needed for inclusion in a main or pipe which is being or is about to be laid or constructed in pursuance of a planning permission granted or deemed to be granted under Part III of the Act;

Column (2)

Conditions

On completion of the laying or construction of the main or pipe, or at the expiration of nine months from the commencement of the development, the subject of this permission, whichever is the sooner, such pipe and apparatus shall be removed and the land shall be restored to its condition before the development took place.

Approval of the details of the design and external appearance of the buildings shall be obtained from (a) the district planning authority (except in Greater London or a National Park), (b) in Greater London, the local planning authority, or (c) in a National Park, the county planning authority before the erection of the building has begun.

Column (1)

Description of development

(v) the erection on operational land of the undertaking, solely for the protection of plant or machinery, or structures or erections of the nature of plant or machinery, of buildings not exceeding 15 metres in height;

(vi) any other development carried out in, on, over or under operational land of the undertaking except:—

(a) the erection, or the reconstruction or alteration so as materially to affect the design or external appearance thereof, of buildings;

(b) the installation of any plant or machinery, or structures or erections of the nature of plant or machinery, exceeding 15 metres in height, or capable, without addition, of being extended to a height exceeding 15 metres;

(c) the replacement of any plant or machinery, or structures or erections of the nature of plant or machinery, to a height exceeding 15 metres or the height of the plant, machinery, structure or erection so replaced, whichever is the greater.

E. Electricity undertakings.

Development required for the purpose of the undertaking of any of the following descriptions, that is to say:—

(i) the laying underground of pipes, cables of any other apparatus, and the construction of such shafts and tunnels as may be necessary in connection therewith;

(ii) the installation in an electric line of feeder or service pillars, or transforming or switching stations or chambers not exceeding (except when constructed underground elsewhere than under a highway [used by vehicular traffic]) 29 cubic metres in capacity;

(iii) the installation of service lines to individual consumers from an electric line;

[(iv) the extension or alteration of buildings on operational land, so long as the height of the original building is not exceeded, the cubic content of the original building (as ascertained by external measurement) is not increased by more than 25%, and its aggregate floor space is not increased by more than 1000 square metres.]

Column (2)

Conditions

Column (1)

Description of Development

(v) the sinking of any boreholes for the purpose of ascertaining the nature of the sub-soil, and the installation of any plant or machinery, or structures or erections of the nature of plant or machinery, as may be necessary in connection therewith;

Column (2)

Conditions

On completion of the development or at the expiration of six months from the commencement of the development the subject of this permission, whichever is the sooner, such plant or machinery or structures or erections shall be removed and the land shall be restored to its condition before the development took place.

Column (1)

Description of Development

(vi) the erection on operational land of the undertaking, solely for the protection of plant or machinery, or structures or erections, of the nature of plant or machinery, of buildings not exceeding 15 metres in height;

Column (2)

Conditions

Approval of the details of the design and external appearance of the buildings shall be obtained from (*a*) the district planning authority (except in Greater London [, a metropolitan county] or a National Park), (*b*) in Greater London [or a metropolitan county], the local planning authority, or (*c*) in a National Park [outside a metropolitan county], the county planning authority, before the erection of the building has begun.

Column (1)

Description of Development

(vii) any other development carried out on, in or under the operational land of the undertaking except:—

    (*a*) the erection, or the reconstruction so as materially to affect the design or external appearance thereof, of buildings; or

    (*b*) the installation or erection, by way of addition or replacement, of any plant or machinery, or structures or erections of the nature of plant or machinery, exceeding 15 metres in height or the height of the plant, machinery, structure or erection so replaced, whichever is the greater.

F. Tramway or road transport undertakings.

Development required for the purposes of the undertaking of any of the following descriptions, that is to say:—

(i) the installation of posts, overhead wires, underground cables, feeder pillars, or transformer boxes not exceeding 17 cubic metres in capacity in, on, over or adjacent to a highway for the purpose of supplying current to public vehicles;

(ii) the installation of tramway tracks; conduits and drains and pipes in connection therewith for the working of tramways;

(iii) the installation of telephone cables and apparatus, huts, step posts and signs required in connection with the operation of public vehicles;

(iv) the erection or construction, and the maintenance, improvement or other alteration of passenger shelters and barriers for the control of persons waiting to enter public vehicles;

(v) any other development of operational land of the undertaking, other than:—

    (*a*) the erection, or the reconstruction or alteration so as materially to affect the design or external appearance thereof, of buildings;

    (*b*) the installation or erection, by way of addition or replacement, of any plant or machinery, or structures or erections of the nature of plant or machinery, exceeding 15 metres in height, or the height of the plant, machinery, structure or erection so replaced, whichever is the greater;

    (*c*) development, not wholly within the interior of an omnibus or tramway station, in pursuance of the powers contained in section 14 (1) (i) (*d*) of the Transport Act 1962 or section 10 (1) (*x*) of the Transport Act 1968.

G. Lighthouse Undertakings.

Development required for the purposes of the functions of a general or local lighthouse authority under the Merchant Shipping Act 1894 and any other statutory provisions made with respect to a local lighthouse authority, or in the exercise by a local lighthouse authority of rights, powers or duties acquired by usage prior to the Merchant Shipping Act 1894, except the erection, or the reconstruction or alternaton so as materially to affect the design or external appearance thereof, of offices.

H. The British Airports Authority.

Development by the Authority of operational land of the undertaking, being development which is required in connection with the provision by the Authority of services and facilties necessary or desirable for the operation of an aerodrome, other than:—

(i) the construction or erection, or the reconstruction or alteration so as materially to affect the design or external appearance thereof, of:—

    (*a*) any hotel;

    (*b*) any building (not being a building required in connection with the movement or maintenance of aircraft or with the embarking, disembarking, loading, discharge or transport of passengers, livestock or goods at an aerodrome); and

(ii) the construction or extension of runways.

[I. Post Office.

Development required for the purposes of the undertaking of any of the following descriptions:

(1) the installation of posting boxes or self-service machines;

(2) any other development carried out in, on, over or under the operational land of the undertaking except:—

    (*a*) the erection or reconstruction of buildings or the alteration of buildings so as materially to affect the design or external appearance thereof:

    (*b*) the installation or erection, by way of addition or replacement, of any plant or machinery, or structure or erection of the nature of plant or machinery, which exceeds 15 metres in height, or the height of the existing plant, machinery or structure or erection, whichever is the greater.]

[J. Civil Aviation Authority.

1. The carrying out within the perimeter of an aerodrome at which the Civil Aviation Authority provide air traffic control services of development required in connection with the provision of services and facilities which are necessary or desirable either for

providing air traffic control services or for assisting the navigation of aircraft using the aerodrome.

2. The carrying out, on any operational land of the Authority which is outside but within 8 kilometres of the perimeter of an aerodrome at which the Authority provide air traffic control services, of development required in connection with the provision of services and facilities which are necessary or desirable either for providing such air traffic control services or for assisting the navigation of aircraft using the aerodrome, with the exception of:—

    (a) the erection of buildings to be used for purposes other than housing equipment used in connection with the provision of air traffic control services or in connection with assisting the navigation of aircraft;

    (b) the erection of any building exceeding a height of 4 metres;

    (c) the installation or erection, by way of addition or replacement, of any radio mast, radar mast, antenna or other apparatus which exceeds the height of the mast, antenna or apparatus which is being replaced, or a height of 15 metres, whichever is the greater.

3. The carrying out, on land which was operational land of the Authority on 1st March 1986 and remains operational land, of development required in connection with the provision by the Authority of services and facilities necessary or desirable for assisting the navigation of aircraft, except—

    (a) the erection of buildings to be used for purposes other than housing equipment used in connection with assisting the navigation of aircraft;

    (b) the erection of any building exceeding a height of 4 metres;

    (c) the installation or erection of any radio mast, radar mast, antenna or other apparatus, save by way of replacement or substitution for an existing mast or antenna or existing apparatus by one which does not exceed the height of the mast, antenna or apparatus which is being replaced, or a height of 15 metres, whichever is the greater.

4. The use of land by or on behalf of the Civil Aviation Authority in case of emergency, for a period not exceeding six months, for the stationing of moveable apparatus required for the replacement of unserviceable apparatus.

5. The use of land by or on behalf of the Civil Aviation Authority, for a period not exceeding six months, for the purpose of providing services and facilities in connection with air traffic control services or assistance in the navigation of aircraft, and the erection or placing of moveable structures on the land for the purposes of such use.

6. The use of land by or on behalf of the Civil Aviation Authority, for a period not exceeding six months, for the stationing and operation of apparatus in connection with the carrying out of surveys or investigations.]

Column (2)

Conditions

[On or before the expiry of any period of six months referred to in paragraphs 4 to 6, all such uses shall cease and any apparatus or structure shall be removed, and the land shall be restored to its condition before the development took place.]

Column (1)

Description of Development

Class XIX.—Development by mineral undertakers

1. Where mining operations have been carried out in any land at any time on or after 1st January 1946 and before 1st July 1948,

    (a) in conformity with the provisions of a planning scheme or of permission granted thereunder or in accordance with permission granted at any time before 22nd July 1943 by or under an interim development order and in force immediately before 1st July 1948, or (*b*) under article 4 of the Town and Country Planning (General Interim Development) Order 1946,

and an application for permission to continue those mining operations in adjoining land was made during the period of six months from 1st July 1948 or was treated by virtue of paragraph 1 of Schedule 10 to the Town and Country Planning Act 1947 as having been made under that Act, the continuation of those operations until the application (or any appeal in respect thereof) has been dealt with.

2. The erection, alteration or extension by mineral undertakers on land in or adjacent to and belonging to a quarry or mine comprised in their undertaking of any building, plant or machinery, or structure or erection of the nature of plant or machinery, which is required in connection with the winning or working of minerals, including coal won or worked by virtue of section 36(1) of the Coal Industry Nationalisation Act 1946, but not any other coal, in pursuance of permission granted or deemed to be granted under Part III of the Act, or which is required in connection with the treatment or disposal of such minerals:

Provided that where the development consists of or includes the erection, alteration or extension of a building, this permission shall be exercisable in respect of such building only if the prior approval of the [minerals planning authority] is obtained for the detailed plans and specifications of the building; but that authority shall not refuse to grant approval, or impose conditions on the grant thereof, unless they are satisfied that it is expedient so to do on the ground that:—

(*a*) the erection, alteration or extension of such building would injure the amenity of the neighbourhood and modifications can reasonably be made or conditions can reasonably be imposed in order to avoid or reduce the injury; or
(*b*) the proposed building or extension ought to be, and can reasonably be, sited elsewhere.

3. The deposit of refuse or waste materials by, or by licence of, a mineral undertaker in excavations made by such undertaker and already lawfully used for that purpose so long as the height of such deposit does not exceed the level of the land adjoining any such excavation.

Column (2)

Conditions

Column (1)

Description of Development

Class XX.—Development by the National Coal Board

Development of any of the following descriptions carried out by the National Coal Board, or their lessees or licensees, that is to say:—

(i) the winning and working underground, in a mine commenced before 1st July 1948, of coal or other minerals mentioned in paragraph 1 of Schedule 1 to the Coal Industry Nationalisation Act 1946, and any underground development incidental thereto;

(ii) any development required in connection with coal industry activities as defined in section 63 of the Coal Industry Nationalisation Act 1946 and carried out in the immediate vicinity of a pithead:

Provided that where the development consists of or includes the erection, alteration or extension of a building this permission shall be exercisable in respect of such building only if the prior approval of the [minerals planning authority] is obtained for the detailed plans and specifications of the building, but the [minerals planning authority] shall not refuse to grant approval, or impose conditions on the grant thereof unless they are satisfied that it is expedient so to do on the ground that:—

(*a*) the erection, alteration or extension of such building would injure the amenity of the neighbourhood and modifications can reasonably be made or conditions can reasonably be imposed in order to avoid or reduce the injury; or

(*b*) the proposed building or extension ought to be, and can reasonably be, sited elsewhere;

Column (2)

Conditions

Column (1)

Description of Development

(iii) the deposit of waste materials or refuse resulting from colliery production activities as defined by paragraph 2 of Schedule 1 to the Coal Industry Nationalisation Act 1946 on land comprised in a site used for the deposit of waste materials or refuse on 1st July 1948, whether or not the superficial or the height of the deposit is thereby extended;

Column 2

Conditions

1. If the [minerals planning authority] so require, the Board shall, within such period as the authority may specify (not being less than three months from the date when the requirement is made) submit to them for approval a scheme making provision for the manner in which the depositing of waste materials or refuse is to be carried out and for the carrying out of operations in relation thereto (including, where appropriate, the stripping and storage of surface soil and the after-treatment of the deposit) for the preservation of amenity, such scheme to relate only to the depositing and after-treatment of waste materials or refuse deposited after 1st April 1974.

2. Where a scheme submitted in accordance with condition 1 has been approved the depositing of waste materials or refuse and their after-treatment shall be carried out in accordance with the scheme, or in accordance with the scheme as modified by conditions imposed on the grant of approval, as the case may be.

Column (1)

Description of Development

(iv) development by the National Coal Board consisting of the temporary use of land for the purpose of prospecting for coal workable by opencast methods and carrying out of any operations requisite for that purpose.

Column (2)

Conditions

1. No development shall be begun until after the expiration of 42 days from the date of service of notice in writing on the [minerals planning authority], indicating the nature, extent and probable duration of the prospecting.

2. At the expiration of the period of prospecting, any buildings, plant or machinery and any waste materials shall be removed and any boreholes shall be properly and sufficiently sealed and other excavations filled in and levelled, any topsoil removed being replaced as the uppermost layer.

Column (1)

Description of Development

Class XXI.—Uses of aerodrome buildings

The use of buildings on an aerodrome which is vested in or under the control of the British Airports Authority for purposes connected with the air transport services or other flying activities at such aerodrome.

Column (2)

Conditions

Column (1)

Description of Development

Class XXII.—Use as a caravan site

The use of land, other than a building, as a caravan site in any of the circumstances specified in paragraph 2 to 9 (inclusive) of Schedule 1 to the Caravan Sites and Control of Development Act 1960 or in the circumstances (other than those relating to winter quarters) specified in paragraph 10 of the said Schedule.

Column (2)

Conditions

The use shall be discontinued when the said circumstances cease to exist, and all caravans on the site shall then be removed.

Column (1)

Description of Development

Class XXIII.—Development on licensed caravan sites

Development required by the conditions of a site licence for the time being in force under Part I of the Caravan Sites and Control of Development Act 1960.

Column 2

Conditions

Column (1)

Description of Development

"*Class XXIV.—Development by Telecommunications Code System Operators*

The carrying out of development by or on behalf of a telecommunications code system operator where the development is being carried out either—

(a) on land occupied by the operator in respect of which he is the estate owner in respect of the fee simple or he holds a lease granted for a term of not less than 10 years; or

(b) in pursuance of a right conferred on the operator under the telecommunications code, and in accordance with any conditions relating to the application of that code which have been imposed by the terms of his licence,

and for the purposes of the operator's telecommunication system; and where the development is within any of the following descriptions:—

(1) the installation, alteration or replacement in, on, over or under land of any telecommunication apparatus where—

(a) in the case of the installation of apparatus (other than on a building or other structure), the apparatus does not exceed a height of 15 metres above ground level;

(b) in the case of the alteration or replacement of apparatus already installed (other than apparatus installed on a building or other structure), the apparatus does not when altered or replaced exceed the height of the existing apparatus or a height of 15 metres above ground level whichever is the greater;

(c) in the case of the installation, alteration or replacement of apparatus on a building or other structure, the height of the apparatus (taken by itself) does not exceed:—

    (i) 15 metres where it is installed, or is to be installed, on a building or other structure which has a height of 30 metres or more; or

    (ii) 10 metres in any other case,

(d) in the case of the installation, alteration or replacement of apparatus on a building or other structure, the highest part of the apparatus when installed, altered or replaced does not exceed the height of the highest part of the existing building or structure by more than—

    (i) 10 metres in the case of a building or structure which is 30 metres or more high;

    (ii) 8 metres in the case of a building or structure which is more than 15 metres but less than 30 metres high; or

    (iii) 6 metres in any other case;

(e) in the case of the installation, alteration or replacement of any apparatus other than a mast, any kind of antenna, a public call box or any apparatus which does not project above the level of the surface of the ground, the ground or base area of the structure does not exceed 1·5 square metres;

(f) in the case of the installation, alteration or replacement of any microwave antenna, or any apparatus which includes or is intended for the support of such an antenna, on a building or other structure—

    (i) the building or other structure on which the antenna is installed or is to be installed exceeds a height of 15 metres;

    (ii) the size of the antenna, when measured in any dimension, does not exceed 1·3 metres (excluding any projecting feed element);

    (iii) the development does not result in the presence on the building or structure of more than two microwave antennas;

Column (2)

Conditions

1. In the case of the installation, alteration or replacement on a building of an antenna of any kind, or any apparatus which is intended to support an antenna, the antenna or apparatus shall so far as practicable be sited so as to minimise its effect on the external appearance of the building.

Column (1)

Description of Development

(2) the use of land in case of emergency, for a period not exceeding six months, for the stationing and operation of moveable telecommunication apparatus required for the replacement of unserviceable telecommunication apparatus, and the erection or placing of moveable structures on the land for the purposes of that use.

Column (2)

Conditions

2. Where development within paragraph (2) in column (1) has been carried out, then at the expiration of the period of six months from commencement of the use, or when the need for the use of the land for the stationing and operation of moveable telecommunication apparatus ceases (whichever first occurs), all such apparatus, and all moveable structures erected or placed on the land for the purpose of the use, shall be removed and the land shall be restored to its condition before development took place.

Column (1)

Description of Development

Class XXV.—Other telecommunications development

The installation, alteration or replacement on any building or other structure (except a dwellinghouse), in circumstances other than those set out in class XXIV of this Schedule, of a microwave antenna and any structures intended for the support of such an antenna where—

(a) the building or other structure on which the antenna is installed or is to be installed exceeds a height of 15 metres;

(b) in the case of a terrestrial microwave antenna—

    (i) the size of the antenna, when measured in any dimension, does not exceed 1·3 metres (excluding any projecting feed element); and

    (ii) the highest part of the antenna or its supporting structure is not more than 3 metres higher than the highest part of the existing building or structure on which it is installed;

(c) in the case of a satellite antenna, the size of the antenna, taken together with its supporting structure (but excluding any projecting feed element), does not exceed 90 centimetres;

(d) the development does not result in the presence on the building or structure of more than two microwave antennas."

Column (2)

Conditions

1. The antenna shall, so far as practicable, be sited so as to minimise its effect on the external appearance of the building or other structure on which it is installed.

2. When an antenna is no longer needed for the reception or transmission of microwave radio energy it shall be removed from the building or structure.

Column (1)

Description of Development

Class XXVI.—Mineral exploration

1. The carrying out of any of the following operations, namely:—

(i) the drilling of boreholes for the purpose of ascertaining the presence, extent or quality of a deposit of a mineral with a view to the exploitation of that mineral;

(ii) operations required for the carrying out of seismic surveys designed for the purpose of ascertaining the presence, extent or quality of a deposit of a mineral with a view to the exploitation of that mineral;

(iii) the making of other excavations for the purpose of ascertaining the presence, extent or quality of a deposit of a mineral with a view to the exploitation of that mineral;

on any land during a period not exceeding 28 consecutive days, and the erection, assembly or construction on the land, or adjoining land, of buildings, plant or machinery, or other structures, which are required in connection with any of those operations, where:—

(a) no operations are carried out in, on, over or under land which is within 50 metres of any part of an occupied residential building or a building which is occupied and used as a hospital or a school;

(b) no operations are carried out on land which is within a National Park, an area of outstanding natural beauty or a site of archaeological interest or special scientific interest;

(c) in the case of operations carried out under sub-paragraph (ii) above, no explosive charge of more than 1 kilogram is used:

(*d*) in the case of operations carried out under sub-paragraph (iii) above—

   (i) no excavation made during the carrying out of the operations exceeds 10 metres in depth or 12 square metres in surface area; and

   (ii) the operations do not result in the making of more than 10 excavations over any period of 24 months within any area of 1 hectare within the land;

(*e*) in the case of the erection, assembly or construction of buildings, plant or machinery or other structures—

   (i) no such building, plant or machinery or other structure exceeds a height of 12 metres; and

   (ii) no building, plant or machinery or other structure which exceeds a height of 3 metres is erected, assembled or constructed on any land which is within 3 kilometres of the perimeter of an aerodrome.

Column (2)

Conditions

1. No operations shall be carried out between the hours of 6 pm and 7 am.

2. No trees on the land shall be removed, felled, lopped or topped except insofar as the mineral planning authority may otherwise have agreed in writing and no operations shall be carried out (or any other thing done on the land) which is likely to have any detrimental effect on the trees.

3. Before any operation consisting of an excavation is carried out the topsoil shall be removed from the area of land excavated and shall be stored separately from other excavated material; and the subsoil shall then be removed and stored separately from other excavated material (including the topsoil).

4. Within a 28 day period following the cessation of the operations the following action shall be taken (unless, in any particular case, the mineral planning authority have otherwise agreed in writing):—

   (*a*) all buildings, plant, machinery and other structures and any waste materials, shall be removed from the land;

   (*b*) all boreholes shall be adequately sealed or (as the case may be) all other excavations shall be filled in with material from the site; the surface shall be levelled and the topsoil shall be replaced as the uppermost layer; and

   (*c*) the land shall (so far as it is practicable to do so) be restored to its condition before the development took place (with the carrying out of seeding and replanting so far as may be necessary).

Column (1)

Description of Development

2.—(1) The carrying out of any of the following operations, namely:—

(i) the drilling of boreholes for the purpose of ascertaining the presence, extent or quality of a deposit of a mineral with a view to the exploitation of that mineral;

(ii) operations required for the carrying out of seismic surveys designed for the purpose of ascertaining the presence, extent or quality of a deposit of a mineral with a view to the exploitation of that mineral;

(iii) the making of other excavations for the purpose of ascertaining the presence, extent or quality of a deposit of a mineral with a view to the exploitation of that mineral;

on any land during a period not exceeding 4 months, and the erection, assembly or construction on that land, or on adjoining land, of buildings, plant or machinery or other structures, which are required in connection with any of those operations, where:—

   (*a*) in the case of operations carried out under sub-paragraph (ii) above, no explosive charge of more than 2 kilograms is used;

(b) in the case of operations carried out under sub-paragraph (iii) above, no excavation made during the carrying out of the operations exceeds 10 metres in depth or 12 square metres in surface area; and

(c) in the case of the erection, assembly or construction of buildings, plant or machinery or other structures, no such building, plant or machinery or other structure exceeds a height of 12 metres,

so long as the developer has previously notified the mineral planning authority in writing of his intention to carry out development under this paragraph (specifying the nature of the development), and the relevant period has elapsed.

2. The relevant period elapses:—

(a) where the mineral planning authority do not issue a direction under article 4A:—

(i) 28 days after the notification referred to in paragraph (1) above, or

(ii) if earlier, on the date on which the mineral planning authority notify the developer in writing that they will not issue such a direction;

(b) where the mineral planning authority issue a direction under article 4A:—

(i) 28 days from the date on which notice of it is sent to the Secretary of State, or

(ii) if earlier, the date on which the mineral planning authority notify the developer in writing that the Secretary of State has disallowed the direction.

Column (2)

Conditions

1. The development shall be carried out in accordance with the details specified in the written notice given to the mineral planning authority, except insofar as the mineral planning authority have otherwise agreed in writing.

2. No trees on the land shall be removed, felled, lopped or topped except insofar as the mineral planning authority may otherwise have agreed in writing, and no operations shall be carried out (or any other thing done on the land) which is likely to have any detrimental effect on the trees.

3. Before any operation consisting of an excavation is carried out, the topsoil shall be removed from the area of land excavated and shall be stored separately from other excavated material; and the subsoil shall then be removed and stored separately from other excavated material (including the topsoil).

4. Within a 28 day period following the cessation of the operations, the following action shall be taken (unless in any particular case, the mineral planning authority have otherwise agreed in writing):—

(a) all buildings, plant, machinery and other structures and any waste materials, shall be removed from the land;

(b) all boreholes shall be adequately sealed or (as the case may be), all other excavations shall be filled in with other material from the site; the surface shall be levelled and the topsoil shall be replaced as the uppermost layer; and

(c) the land shall (so far as it is practicable to do so) be restored to its condition before development took place (with the carrying out of seeding and replanting so far as may be necessary).

Column (1)

Description of Development

Class XXVII.—Removal of material from mineral-working deposits

1. The removal of material of any description from a mineral-working deposit, where material has been extracted from the deposit, otherwise than in breach of planning

control, at any time during the period of 12 months immediately preceding the date of the coming into operation of section 1 of the 1981 Act:

Provided that—

(1) this permission does not authorise the carrying out of development after the end of the period of six months from the date of the coming into operation of section 1 of the 1981 Act, unless an application has been made, before the end of that period, for planning permission to continue to remove material from the deposit;

(2) where an application for permission to continue to remove material from the deposit has been made before the end of the period described in proviso (1), this permission does not authorise the carrying out of any development after the date when that application is determined by the mineral planning authority or, in the event of an appeal to the Secretary of State, the date when that appeal is finally determined;

(3) where an application for permission to continue to remove material from the deposit has been made before the end of the period described in proviso (1), this permission does not authorise the carrying out of any development other than the development described in the application.

Column (2)

Conditions

Column (1)

Description of Development

2.—(1) The removal of material of any description from a stockpile or a mineral-working deposit other than a stockpile which either—

(i) covers a ground area not exceeding 2 hectares; or

(ii) contains no mineral or other material which was deposited on the land more than 5 years before the date of removal;

Provided that:

(a) this permission does not authorise the removal of material from any stockpile or other mineral-working deposit which derives from the carrying out of any operations permitted under class VI; and

(b) no material shall be removed from a mineral-working deposit which is not a stockpile unless the developer has notified the mineral planning authority in writing of his intention to carry out development within this class, specifying the nature of that development, the exact location of the mineral-working deposit from which material is to be removed, the proposed means of vehicular access to the site at which the development is to be carried out and the earliest date at which any material presently contained in the deposit was deposited on the land, and the relevant period has elapsed.

(2) The relevant period elapses:—

(a) where the mineral planning authority do not issue a direction under article 4A:—

(i) 28 days after the notification referred to in paragraph (b) of the proviso above, or

(ii) if earlier, on the date on which the mineral planning authority notify the developer in writing that they will not issue such a direction;

(b) where the mineral planning authority issue a direction under article 4A:—

(i) 28 days from the date on which the notice of it is sent to the Secretary of State, or

(ii) if earlier, on the date on which the mineral planning authority notify the developer in writing that the Secretary of State has disallowed the direction.

Column (2)

Conditions

Where the development consists of the removal of material from a mineral-working deposit which is not a stockpile—

(1) it shall be carried out in accordance with the details given in the notice sent to the mineral planning authority in accordance with proviso (*b*) in column (1) except where the authority have otherwise agreed in writing;

(2) if the mineral planning authority so require, the developer shall submit to them for approval a scheme making provision for the restoration and aftercare of the site, such scheme to be submitted within such period as the authority may specify (which shall not be less than 3 months from the date when the requirement is made); and

(3) where submission of a scheme of restoration and aftercare has been required, the site shall be restored and aftercare shall be carried out in accordance with the provisions of such scheme (as those provisions are approved).

Column (1)

Description of Development

Class XXVIII.—Warehouses

The extension or alteration of a building (whether erected before or after 1st July 1948) which is lawfully used as a warehouse, and which is to be used for that purpose, so long as:—

(*a*) the height of the original building is not exceeded;

(*b*) the cubic content of the original building (as ascertained by external measurement) is not increased by more than 25%, and its aggregate floor space is not increased by more than 1000 square metres;

(*c*) the external appearance of the premises is not materially affected;

(*d*) no part of the building is, as a result of the development, within a distance of 5 metres from any boundary of the curtilage of the premises; and

(*e*) the development does not result in a decrease in the extent of any existing vehicle parking area or area laid out for the turning of vehicles;

Provided that the erection on land within the curtilage of an existing warehouse of an additional building to be used in connection with that warehouse shall be treated as an extension of the existing warehouse and, where any two or more existing buildings in the same curtilage are used as one unit for warehouse purposes, the references in paragraph (*b*) above to the cubic content and to the aggregate floor space shall be construed as references to the aggregate cubic content and the total floor space (respectively) of those buildings.

Column (2)

Conditions

Column (1)

Description of Development

Class XXIX.—Amusement Parks

The carrying out of any of the following operations on land (or on a seaside pier) which is lawfully used on an amusement park:—

(*a*) the erection of any booths, stalls, other similar buildings or structures, or the installation of any plant or machinery (which expression, in this class, includes structures or erections in the nature of plant or machinery) to be used for or in connection with the provision in the amusement park of entertainment or amusement for the public;

    (*b*) the extension, alteration or replacement of any plant or machinery, building or other structure so used;

so long as—

    (i) no plant or machinery installed, extended, altered or replaced pursuant to this permission exceeds a height of 25 metres above ground level (or, if the land or pier is within 3 kilometres of the perimeter of an aerodrome, 25 metres or the height of the highest existing structure, whichever is the lesser), and

    (iii) no other building or structure erected pursuant to this permission exceeds the height of 5 metres above ground level (or, in the case of an extension to a building or structure, 5 metres or the height of the roof of the existing building or of the structure, whichever is the greater),

and so long as no such operation is carried out within 25 metres of the curtilage of a dwelling.

Column (2)

Conditions

Column (1)

Description of Development

Class XXX.—Development by the Historic Buildings and Monuments Commission for England

Development of the following descriptions, by or on behalf of the Historic Buildings and Monuments Commission for England, required for the purpose of securing the preservation of any building or monument in the ownership, or under the guardianship, or otherwise under the control or management of the Commission:—

    (*a*) the maintenance, repair or restoration (but excluding the extension) of any such building or monument;

    (*b*) (insofar as the development is not permitted by sub-paragraph (*a*) above) the erection of structures of the nature of screens or covers, designed or intended to protect or safeguard such buildings or monuments (including any fencing which may be necessary for that purpose);

    (*c*) the carrying out of works for stabilising ground conditions of any cliff, water-course or the coastline."

Column (2)

Conditions

Such structures as are referred to in (*b*) shall be removed at the expiration of 6 months (or such longer period as the local authority may agree in writing) from the date on which work was commenced to erect them.

NOTES

    Commencement: 29 March 1977.

    Class III: new Class III substituted for Class III above by SI 1987 No 765, art 2, Schedule. See Appendix.

    Class XII: amended by SI 1986 No 435, art 2, Sch 1, para 12.

    Class XVIII: item D amended by SI 1986 No 435, art 2, Sch 1, para 12; in item E first and second amendments made by SI 1985 No 1981, art 2; final amendment made by SI 1986 No 435, art 2, Sch 1, para 12; item F substituted by SI 1983 No 1615; item I substituted by SI 1985 No 1011, art 2(*b*); item J, together with condition added by SI 1985 No 1891, art 2.

    Classes XIV, XIX, XX: amended by SI 1986 No 435, art 2, Sch 1, para 12.

    Classes XXIV, XXV added by SI 1985 No 1011, art 2(*b*).

    Classes XXVI-XXX added by SI 1985 No 1981, art 2.

    Other amendments made by SI 1981 No 245 and by SI 1985 No 1981, art 2.

    This schedule modified for certain purposes by the Town and Country Planning (National Parks, Areas of Outstanding Natural Beauty and Conservation Areas, etc.) Special Development Order 1985, SI 1985 No 1012, art 3.

SCHEDULE 2

PART I

TOWN AND COUNTRY PLANNING ACT 1971

Notification to be sent to applicant on receipt of his application

Your application dated   was received on (a)

*[Examination of the form of application and accompanying plans and documents to ascertain whether your application complies with the statutory requirements has not been completed.

If on further examination it is found that the application is invalid for failure to comply with such requirements (or for any other reason) a further communication will be sent to you as soon as possible.]

*[Your application relates to a county matter and [will be] [has been] passed to the county planning authority for determination.] [A further notification will be sent to you if it is decided in the light of further consideration that your application relates to a county matter and that it is necessary to pass the application to the county planning authority for determination.] [As the land which is the subject of the application lies within (b) .... National Park, the application [will be] [has been] passed to the (c) .... for determination.]

If by (d) .... *[you have not received notification that your application is invalid and] the authority dealing with your application have not given you notice of their decision (and you have not agreed with them in writing that the period within which their decision shall be given may be extended) you may appeal to the Secretary of State in accordance with sections 36 and 37 of the Town and Country Planning Act 1971 by notice sent within six months from that date (unless the application has already been referred by this authority to the [Secretary of State for the Environment] [Secretary of State for Wales]). Appeals must be made on a form which is obtainable from the [Department of the Environment] [Welsh Office].

*Delete where inappropriate.

(a) Insert date when relevant document(s) referred to in article 7(2) were received.
(b) Insert name of National Park.
(c) Insert name of county council or planning board.
(d) Insert date eight weeks from date of receipt of application (as given at (a)).

[579]

NOTES

Commencement: 29 March 1977.

PART II

Notification to be sent to applicant on refusal of planning permission or on the grant of permission subject to conditions. (To be endorsed on notices of decision).

(1) If the applicant is aggrieved by the decision of the local planning authority to refuse permission or approval for the proposed development, or to grant permission or approval subject to conditions, he may appeal to the [Secretary of State for the Environment] [Secretary of State for Wales] in accordance with section 36 of the Town and Country Planning Act 1971 within six months of receipt of this notice. (Appeals must be made on a form which is obtainable from the [Department of the Environment] [Welsh Office]). The Secretary of State has power to allow a longer period for the giving of a notice of appeal but he will not normally be prepared to exercise this power unless there are special circumstances which excuse the delay in giving notice of appeal. The Secretary of State is not required to entertain an appeal if it appears to him that permission for the proposed development could not have been granted by the local planning authority, or could not have been so granted otherwise than subject to the

conditions imposed by them, having regard to the statutory requirements, to the provisions of the development order, and to any directions given under the order. He does not in practice refuse to entertain appeals solely because the decision of the local planning authority was based on a direction given by him.

(2) If permission to develop land is refused or granted subject to conditions, whether by the local planning authority or by the [Secretary of State for the Environment] [Secretary of State for Wales], and the owner of the land claims that the land has become incapable of reasonably beneficial use in its existing state and cannot be rendered capable of reasonably beneficial use by the carrying out of any development which has been or would be permitted he may serve on the Common Council, or on the Council of the [London borough or] district in which the land is situated, as the case may be, a purchase notice requiring that council to purchase his interest in the land in accordance with the provisions of Part IX of the Town and Country Planning Act 1971.

(3) In certain circumstances, a claim may be made against the local planning authority for compensation, where permission is refused or granted subject to conditions by the Secretary of State on appeal or on a reference of the application to him. The circumstances in which such compensation is payable are set out in section 169 of the Town and Country Planning Act 1971.   **[580]**

NOTES
   Commencement: 29 March 1977.

SCHEDULE 3

PART I

TOWN AND COUNTRY PLANNING ACT 1971
Notice under section 26(2)

Proposed development at (a) ....

Notice is hereby given that application is being made to the (b) ....

.... Council by (c) ....

....

for planning permission in respect of (d) ....

   A copy of the application and of the plans and other documents submitted with it may be inspected at

(e) .... at

all reasonable hours until (f) ....

   Any person who wishes to make representations to the above-mentioned Council about the application should make them in writing by that date to the Council at

(g) ....

Signed ....

*On behalf of ....

Date ....

* Delete where inappropriate.
   (a) Insert address or location of proposed development.
   (b) Insert name of Council.
   (c) Insert name of applicant.
   (d) Insert description of proposed development.
   (e) Insert address within locality in which land proposed to be developed is situated.
   (f) Insert date not less than 20 days later than the date on which the notice is published.
   (g) Insert address of Council.

[581]

NOTES
Commencement: 29 March 1977.

PART II

TOWN AND COUNTRY PLANNING ACT 1971
Certificate under section 26(2)

Certificate A*

I hereby certify that:—

    *I

————————— posted on the land to which the accompanying application dated
The applicant

(a) .... relates the notice required by section 26(3)
of the Act, and such notice was left in position for not less than seven days in the
period of not more than one month immediately preceding the making of this
application.

Or:—

Certificate B*

I hereby certify that:—

*   I have

————————— been unable to post on the land to which the accompanying
The applicant has

application dated (a) .... relates the notice required

                   *   I have
by section 26(3) of the Act, because ————————— no such rights of access or
                   the applicant has

                    *   me
other rights in respect of the land as would enable ————————— to do so.
                        the applicant

*   I have
————————————— taken the following steps, namely:—
The applicant has

(b) ....

....

                  *have
to acquire those rights and —— been unable to acquire them.
                  has

Or:—

Certificate C*

I hereby certify that:—

*   I

————————— posted on the land to which the accompanying application dated
The applicant

(a) .... relates the notice required by section 26(3) of the
Act, but such notice was left in position for less than seven days in the period of
not more than one month immediately preceding the making of this application

                    *   mine   *   removed
because it was, without any fault or intent of —————————, —————————
                          the applicant's obscured or defaced
before seven days had elapsed in the said period of not more than one month.

      I
————————— took the following steps for the protection and, where necessary,
*The applicant

replacement of the notice, namely:—

(b) ....

....

Signed ....

*On behalf of ....

Date ....

* Delete where inappropriate.
    (a) Insert date of application.
    (b) Insert steps taken.

[582]

NOTES
　　Commencement: 29 March 1977.

Part III

Town and Country Planning Act 1971
Notice under section 26(3) of the Act

Proposed development at (a) ....

TAKE NOTICE that application is being made to the

(b) ....

Council by (c) ....

for planning permission to carry out the following development on the above land, namely:—

(d) ....

....

....

A copy of the application for planning permission and of all plans and other documents relating thereto may be inspected by members of the public at (e)..

....

at all reasonable hours until (f) ....

....

Any person who wishes to make representations to the above mentioned Council about the application should make them in writing by that date to the Council at (g) ....

Signed ....

*On behalf of ....

Date ....

* Delete where inappropriate.
  (a) Insert address or location of proposed development.
  (b) Insert name of Council.
  (c) Insert name of applicant.
  (d) Insert description of proposed development.
  (e) Insert address of place where the application is available for inspection.
  (f) Insert date not less than 20 days later than the date on which the notice is posted.
  (g) Insert address of Council.

[583]

NOTES
  Commencement: 29 March 1977.

SCHEDULE 4

PART I

TOWN AND COUNTRY PLANNING ACT 1971
Certificate under section 27

Certificate A*

(a) "owner" means a person having a freehold interest or a leasehold interest the unexpired term of which was not less than 7 years.

I hereby certify that:—

1. No person other than the $\frac{\text{*applicant}}{\text{appellant}}$ was an owner (a) of any part of the land to which the $\frac{\text{*application}}{\text{appeal}}$ relates at the beginning of the period of 20 days before the date of the accompanying $\frac{\text{*application;}}{\text{appeal;}}$

or:—

Certificate B*

I hereby certify that:—

$\frac{\text{I have}}{}$

1. $\frac{\text{*The applicant has}}{\text{The appellant has}}$ given the requisite notice to all the persons other than

$\frac{\text{myself}}{}$
$\frac{\text{*the applicant}}{\text{the appellant}}$ who, 20 days before the date of the accompanying $\frac{\text{*application,}}{\text{appeal}}$

†See Note (a) to Certificate A.   were owners† of any part of the land to which the $\frac{\text{*application}}{\text{appeal,}}$ relates, viz.--

Name of owner   Address   Date of service of notice

or:—

Certificate C*

I hereby certify that:—

$\frac{\text{I am}}{}$

1. (i) $\frac{\text{*The applicant is}}{\text{The appellant is}}$ unable to issue a certificate in accordance with either

paragraph (a) or paragraph (b) of section 27(1) of the Act in respect of the

(a) Insert ate of pplication or peal.

accompanying $\frac{\text{*application}}{\text{appeal}}$ dated (a) ....

    (ii) $\frac{\text{I have}}{\frac{\text{*The applicant has}}{\text{The appellant has}}}$ given the requisite notice to the following persons

other than $\frac{\text{myself}}{\frac{\text{*the applicant}}{\text{the appellant}}}$ who, 20 days before the date of the $\frac{\text{*application,}}{\text{appeal}}$ were

ee Note (a) to rtificate A.

owners† of any part of the land to which the $\frac{\text{*application}}{\text{appeal}}$ relates, viz.—

Name of owner	Address	Date of service of notice

    (iii) $\frac{\text{I have}}{\frac{\text{*The applicant has}}{\text{The appellant has}}}$ taken the steps listed below, being steps reasonably

open to $\frac{\text{*me,}}{\text{him,}}$ to ascertain the names and addresses of the other owners of the

land or part thereof and $\frac{\text{*have}}{\text{has}}$ been unable to do so:

(b) ....

(b) Insert description of steps taken.

....

(c) Insert name of local newspaper circulating in the locality in which the land is situated.

    (iv) Notice of the $\frac{\text{*application}}{\text{appeal}}$ as set out below has been published in the

(c) ....

(d) Insert date of publication (which must not be earlier than 20 days before the application or appeal).

....

on (d)..

Copy of notice as published

or:—

Certificate D*

I hereby certify that:—

  1. (i) $\frac{\text{I am}}{\frac{\text{*The applicant is}}{\text{The appellant is}}}$ unable to issue a certificate in accordance with

section 27(1)(a) of the Act in respect of the accompanying $\frac{\text{*application}}{\text{appeal}}$ dated

(a) ....

(a) Insert date of application or appeal.

and $\frac{\text{*have}}{\text{has}}$ taken the steps listed below, being steps reasonably open to $\frac{\text{*me}}{\text{him,}}$ to

ascertain the names and addresses of all the persons, other than $\frac{\text{*myself}}{\text{himself,}}$ who,

†See Note (a) to Certificate A

20 days before the date of the $\frac{\text{*application,}}{\text{appeal}}$ were owners† of any part of the land

to which the $\frac{\text{*application}}{\text{appeal}}$ relates and $\frac{\text{*have}}{\text{has}}$ been unable to do so:

(b) ....

(b) Inser
description
steps taker

(ii) Notice of the $\frac{*application}{appeal}$ as set out below has been published in the

(c) Insert
name of local
newspaper
circulating
in the locality
in which the
land is
situated.

(c) ....

on (d) ....

(d) Insert
date of
publication
(which must
not be earlier
than 20 days
before the
application or
appeal).
[Whichever is
appropriate of
these alterna-
tives should
form part of
any certificate
A, B, C or
D above.]

Copy of notice as published

*2. None of the land to which the $\frac{*application}{appeal}$ relates constitutes or forms part of an agricultural holding;

or:—

*2. $\frac{\text{I have}}{\text{*The applicant has}}$ given the requisite notice to every person other than
The appellant has

$\frac{*myself}{himself}$ who, 20 days before the date of the $\frac{*application}{appeal}$, was a tenant

of any agricultural holding any part of which was comprised in the land to which

the $\frac{*application}{appeal}$ relates, viz.—

(e) If you
are the sole
agricultural
tenant enter
"None".

Name of tenant (e)   Address   Date of service of notice

Signed ....

*On behalf of ....

Date ....

* Delete where inappropriate.

[584]

NOTES
Commencement: 29 March 1977.

PART II

[Notice for
service on
individuals]

TOWN AND COUNTRY PLANNING ACT 1971

Notice under section 27 of application for planning permission

(a) Insert
address or
location of
proposed
development.

Proposed development at (a) ....

(b) Insert
name of
Council.

TAKE NOTICE that application is being made to the (b) ....

.... Council by (c) .... for planning

(c) Insert
name of
applicant.

permission to (d) ....

(d) Insert
description of
proposed
development.

If you should wish to make representations about the application, you

should make them in writing not later than (e)................................... to the

(e) Insert
ate not less
han 20 days
ter than the
ate on which
ne notice is
rved.

(f) Insert
ddress of
ouncil.

Council at (f)...

Signed ....

*On behalf of ....

Date ....

* Delete where inappropriate.

lotice for
ablication in
cal newspaper]

(a) Insert
dress or
cation of
oposed
velopment.

(b) Insert
me of
uncil.

(c) Insert
me of
plicant.

(d) Insert
scription of
oposed
velopment.

(e) Insert
te not less
n 20 days
er than the
te on which
notice is
olished.

f) Insert
dress of
uncil.

TOWN AND COUNTRY PLANNING ACT 1971

Notice under section 27 of application for planning permission

Proposed development at (a) ....

NOTICE is hereby given that application is being made to the (b)....................

.... Council by (c)............................... for planning

permission to (d)..

Any owner of the land (namely a freeholder or a person entitled to an unexpired term of at least seven years under a lease) who wishes to make representations to the above-mentioned Council about the application should make them

in writing not later than (e) ....to the Council at

(f) ....

Signed ....

*On behalf of ....

Date ....

* Delete where inappropriate.

[585]

NOTES
Commencement: 29 March 1977.

PART III

TOWN AND COUNTRY PLANNING ACT 1971

Notice under sections 27 and 36 of appeal

Proposed development at (a)..

TAKE NOTICE that an appeal is being made to the [Secretary of State for
the Environment] [Secretary of State for Wales] by (b)................................

*(i) against the decision of the (c)..Council

*(ii) on the failure of the (c)..Council
to give notice of a decision

on an application to (d)...

[Notice for
service on
individuals]

(a) Insert
address or
location of
proposed
development.

(b) Insert
name of
appellant.

(c) Insert
name of
Council.

(d) Insert
description of
proposed
development.

If you should wish to make representations to the Secretary of State about
the appeal you should make them not later than (e)...

to the Secretary [Department of the Environment] [Welsh Office] at........................

Signed ....

*On behalf of ....

Date ....

* Delete where inappropriate.

(e) Insert
date not less
than 20 days
later than the
date on which
the notice is
served.

TOWN AND COUNTRY PLANNING ACT 1971
Notice under sections 27 and 36 of appeal

Proposed development at (a)..

NOTICE is hereby given that an appeal is being made to the [Secretary of
State for the Environment] [Secretary of State for Wales] by (b)............................

*(i) against the decision of the (c).......................................Council

*(ii) on the failure of the (c)....................................Council
to give notice of a decision

on an application to (d)..

....

[Notice for
publication in
local news-
paper]

(a) Insert
address or
location of
proposed
development

(b) Insert
name of
appellant.

(c) Insert
name of
Council.

(d) Insert
description of
proposed
developmen

Any owner of the land (namely, a freeholder or a person entitled to an
unexpired term of at least seven years under a lease) who wishes to make
representations to the Secretary of State about the appeal should make them

in writing not later than (e) ....to the Secretary

[Department of the Environment] [Welsh Office] at ....

Signed ....

*On behalf of ....

Date ....

* Delete where inappropriate.

(e) Insert
date not less
than 20 days
later than the
date on which
the notice is
published.

[586]

NOTES
  Commencement: 29 March 1977.

SCHEDULE 5

PART I

TOWN AND COUNTRY PLANNING ACT 1971

TOWN AND COUNTRY PLANNING GENERAL DEVELOPMENT ORDER 1977
Certificate under article 22(2) in relation to an application for an established use certificate

Certificate A*

(a) "owner" means—
(i) a person having a freehold interest or a leasehold interest the unexpired term of which was not less than 7 years; or
(ii) an occupier of any part of the land.

I hereby certify that:—

1. No person other than the $\frac{\text{*applicant}}{\text{appellant}}$ was an owner (a) of any part of the

land to which the $\frac{\text{*application}}{\text{appeal}}$ relates at the beginning of the period of 20 days

before the date of the accompanying $\frac{\text{*application}}{\text{appeal}}$;

or:—

Certificate B*

I hereby certify that:—

1. $\frac{\text{I have}}{}$
   $\frac{\text{*The applicant has}}{\text{The appellant has}}$ given the requisite notice to all the persons other than

$\frac{\text{myself}}{}$
$\frac{\text{*the applicant}}{\text{the appellant}}$ who, 20 days before the date of the accompanying $\frac{\text{*application}}{\text{appeal}}$,

See Note to tificate A.

were owners† of any part of the land to which the $\frac{\text{*application}}{\text{appeal}}$ relates, viz.—

Name of owner   Address   Date of service of notice

or:—

ificate C*

I hereby certify that:—

1. (i) $\frac{\text{I am}}{}$ $\frac{\text{*The applicant is}}{\text{The appellant is}}$ unable to issue a certificate in accordance with either

sub-paragraph (a) or sub-paragraph (b) of article 22(2) of the Town and Country Planning General Development Order 1977 in respect of the accompanying

Insert of cation or al.

$\frac{\text{*application}}{\text{appeal}}$ dated (a) ....

(ii) $\frac{\text{I have}}{}$ $\frac{\text{*The applicant has}}{\text{The appellant has}}$ given the notice required by the said article 18 to the

following persons other than $\frac{\text{myself}}{\frac{\text{*the applicant}}{\text{the appellant}}}$ who, 20 days before the date of

See Note cate A.

the $\frac{\text{*application}}{\text{appeal}}$, were owners(†) of any part of the land to which the $\frac{\text{*application}}{\text{appeal}}$

relates, viz.—

Name of owner (†)   Address   Date of service of notice

(iii) $\overline{\begin{array}{c}\text{I have}\\ \text{*The applicant has}\\ \text{The appellant has}\end{array}}$ taken the steps listed below, being steps reasonably

open to $\dfrac{\text{*me}}{\text{him}}$, to ascertain the names and addresses of the other owners

of the land, or part thereof, and $\dfrac{\text{*have}}{\text{has}}$ been unable to do so:

(b) ....

....

....

(iv) Notice of the $\dfrac{\text{*application}}{\text{appeal}}$ as set out below has been published in the

(c) ....

....

on (d) ....

Copy of notice as published

or:—

I hereby certify that:—

1. (i) $\overline{\begin{array}{c}\text{I am}\\ \text{*The applicant is}\\ \text{The appellant is}\end{array}}$ unable to issue a certificate in accordance with

sub-paragraph (a) of article 22(2) of the Town and Country Planning General

Development Order 1977 in respect of the accompanying $\dfrac{\text{*application}}{\text{appeal}}$ dated

(a) ....

....

and $\dfrac{\text{*have}}{\text{has}}$ taken the steps listed below, being steps reasonably open to $\dfrac{\text{*me}}{\text{him}}$,

to ascertain the names and addresses of all the persons other than $\dfrac{\text{*myself}}{\text{*himself}}$

who, 20 days before the date of the $\dfrac{\text{*application}}{\text{appeal}}$, were owners (†) of any part

of the land and $\dfrac{\text{*have}}{\text{has}}$ been unable to do so:

(b) ....

....

....

(ii) Notice of the $\dfrac{\text{*application}}{\text{appeal}}$ as set out below has been published in the

(c) ....

....

on (d) ....

Copy of notice as published

*2. None of the land to which the $\dfrac{\text{*application}}{\text{appeal}}$ relates constitutes or forms
part of an agricultural holding;

Marginal notes:

(b) Insert description of steps taken.

(c) Insert name of local newspaper circulating in the locality in which the lan is situated.

(d) Insert date of publication (which must be earlier tha 20 days befor the applicatio or appeal).

Certificate D

(a) Insert date of application appeal.

† See Note (to Certificat

(b) Insert description steps taken.

(c) Insert name of loc newspaper circulating i the locality which the la is situated.

(d) Insert date of publication (which mus not be earli than 20 day before the application appeal).

[Whichever appropriate these altern tives should form part any certific A, B, C or above.]

or:—

*2. $\frac{\text{I have}}{\text{*The applicant has}}$ given the requisite notice to every person other than
$\frac{}{\text{The appellant has}}$

$\frac{\text{*myself}}{\text{himself}}$ who, 20 days before the date of the $\frac{\text{*application}}{\text{appeal}}$, was a tenant of any

agricultural holding any part of which was comprised in the land to which the
$\frac{\text{*application}}{\text{appeal}}$ relates, viz.—

(*e*) If you
e the sole
gricultural
nant, enter
None".

Name of tenant (*e*)	Address	Date of service of notice

Signed ....

*On behalf of ....

Date ....

* Delete where inappropriate.

                                         [587]

NOTES

Commencement: 29 March 1977.

PART II
TOWN AND COUNTRY PLANNING ACT 1971
TOWN AND COUNTRY PLANNING GENERAL DEVELOPMENT ORDER 1977
Notice under article 22 of application for established use certificate

[Notice for service on individuals]

*) Insert
1e of
1ncil.

TAKE NOTICE that application is being made to the

(*a*) ....Council by

*) Insert
1e of
icant.

(*b*) ....

) Insert
ress or
tion of
.

for an established use certificate relating to the use of land at (*c*).............................

....

*) Insert use
ned to be
olished.

for the purposes of (*d*) ....

) Insert
not less
20 days
than the
on which
notice is
d.

If you should wish to make representations about the application, you should

make them in writing not later than (*e*)...

to the Council at (*f*)..

....

) Insert
ess of
ncil.

Signed ....

*On behalf of ....

Date ....

*Delete where inappropriate.

TOWN AND COUNTRY PLANNING ACT 1971
TOWN AND COUNTRY PLANNING GENERAL DEVELOPMENT ORDER 1977
Notice under article 22 of application for established use certificate

[Notice for publication in local newspaper]

Insert
of
cil.

NOTICE is hereby given that application is being made to the (*a*).............................

(b) Insert
name of
applicant.
.... Council by

(b) ....

(c) Insert
address or
location of
land.
for an established use certificate relating to the use of land at (c)..............

(d) Insert use
claimed to be
established.
for the purpose of (d)..

Any person who, in respect of the land or part thereof, is an owner (i.e. is a freeholder or a person entitled to an unexpired term of at least 7 years under a lease) or an occupier and who wishes to make representations to the above-mentioned Council about the application should make them in writing not

later than (e)...

(e) Insert
date not less
than 20 days
later than the
date on which
the notice is
published.

to the Council at (f)...

(f) Insert
address of
Council.

....

Signed ....

*On behalf of ....

Date ....

* Delete where inappropriate.

[588]

NOTES
Commencement: 29 March 1977.

PART III

TOWN AND COUNTRY PLANNING ACT 1971

TOWN AND COUNTRY PLANNING GENERAL DEVELOPMENT ORDER 1977

Notice under article 22 of appeal against refusal of an established use certificate

[Notice for service on individuals]

TAKE NOTICE that an appeal is being made to the [Secretary of State for the Environment] [Secretary of State for Wales] by (a) ....

(a) Insert
name of
appellant.

*(i) against the decision of the (b)...Council

(b) Insert
name of
Council.

*(ii) on the failure of the (b)...Council
to give notice of a decision

on an application for an established use certificate relating to the use of

(c) ....

(c) Insert
address or
location of
land.

....

for the purpose of (d)...

(d) Insert
claimed to
established

If you should wish to make representations to the Secretary of State about the appeal you should make them in writing not later than (*e*).. .... to the Secretary [Department of the Environment] [Welsh Office] at..

(*e*) Insert date not less than 20 days later than the date on which the notice is served.

Signed ....

*On behalf of ....

Date ....

*Delete where inappropriate.

TOWN AND COUNTRY PLANNING ACT 1971

TOWN AND COUNTRY PLANNING GENERAL DEVELOPMENT ORDER 1977

Notice under article 22 of appeal against refusal of an established use certificate

[Notice for publication in local newspaper]

NOTICE is hereby given that an appeal is being made to the [Secretary of State for the Environment] [Secretary of State for Wales] by (*a*).....................................

(*a*) Insert name of appellant.

(*b*) Insert name of Council.

* (i) against the decision of the (*b*) ....Council

*(ii) on the failure of the (*b*)..Council

to give notice of a decision on an application for an established use certificate

Insert description and address or ion of relating to the use of (*c*) ....

....

Insert use ...ed to be ...lished. for the purpose of (*d*) ....

Any person who, in respect of the land or part thereof, is an owner (i.e. is a freeholder or a person entitled to an unexpired term of at least 7 years under a lease) or is an occupier and who wishes to make representations to the Secretary of State about the appeal should make them in writing not later than (*e*) ....

Insert not less ... 20 days than the on which ...otice is ...shed.

....

to the Secretary [Department of the Environment] [Welsh Office] at ....

Signed ....

*On behalf of ....

Date ....

*Delete where inappropriate.

[589]

NOTES

Commencement: 29 March 1977.

SCHEDULE 6

PART I

TOWN AND COUNTRY PLANNING ACT 1971

Notification to be sent to applicant on receipt of his application for an established use certificate

Your application dated..has been received.
*[Your application relates to a county matter and is being passed to the county planning authority for determination] [A further notification will be sent to you if it is decided in the light of further consideration that your application relates to a county matter and that it is necessary to pass the application to the county planning authority for determination] [As the land which is the subject of the application lies within the

(a)   ....National Park, the application has been passed

to the (b)..for determination].

If on (c) ....
the authority dealing with your application have not given you notice of their decision, and you have not agreed with them in writing that the period within which their decision shall be given may be extended, you are entitled to appeal to the Secretary of State in accordance with section 95(2) of the Town and Country Planning Act 1971 by notice served within six months from that date (unless the application has already been referred by the authority to the [Secretary of State for the Environment] [Secretary of State for Wales]). Appeals must be made on a form which is obtainable from the [Department of the Environment] [Welsh Office].

* Delete where inappropriate.
(a) Insert name of national park.
(b) Insert name of county council or planning board.
(c) Insert date of expiry of the period of two months after receipt of the application.

[590]

NOTES
Commencement: 29 March 1977.

PART II

TOWN AND COUNTRY PLANNING ACT 1971
Established Use Certificate

Land at (a) ....

....

more particularly shown　　　edged
　　　　　　　　　　　　　　　*coloured (b)..
　　　　　　　　　　　　　　　hatched

on the plan attached hereto.

The (c) .... Council hereby certify that the use of the above

　　　　*as
land ──── (d) ....
　　　　for

....

was on (e)..

established within the meaning of (t) ....
of section 94(1) of the Town and Country Planning Act 1971.

Signed ....

*On behalf of ....

Date ....

NOTE: This certificate is issued for the purposes of section 94 of the Town and Country Planning Act 1971 only. It certifies that the use of the land for the purpose named is not liable to enforcement action under section 87 of that Act, but it is not a grant of planning permission and does not necessarily entitle the owner or occupier of the land to any consequential statutory rights which may be conferred where planning permission has been granted, under Part III of the Town and Country Planning Act 1971, for a use of land.

* Delete where inappropriate.

(a) Insert location or address of land.
(b) Insert colour.
(c) Insert name of Council.
(d) Insert description of use.
(e) Insert date of application for established use certificate.
(f) Insert "paragraph (a)", "paragraph (b)", or "paragraph (c)" as appropriate.

[591]

NOTES
　Commencement: 29 March 1977.

TOWN AND COUNTRY PLANNING (DETERMINATION OF APPEALS BY APPOINTED PERSONS) (PRESCRIBED CLASSES) REGULATIONS 1981
(SI 1981 NO 804)

NOTES
Made: 3 June 1981
Authority: Town and Country Planning Act 1971, s 287, Sch 9, para 1

ARRANGEMENT OF REGULATIONS

1. Application, citation and commencement

(1) These regulations may be cited as the Town and Country Planning (Determination of appeals by appointed persons) (Prescribed Classes) Regulations 1981 and shall come into operation of 1st July 1981.

(2) These regulations apply to appeals within the classes prescribed in regulation 3 of which notice is given on or after the date when they come into operation.   **[592]**

NOTES
Commencement: 1 July 1981.

2. Interpretation

In these regulations, unless the context otherwise requires—

"the Act" means the Town and Country Planning Act 1971;

"local planning authority" means—

(a) a district [council] or a London borough council;

(b) an urban development corporation which is the local planning authority for its area, for the purposes of determining applications for planning permission under Part III of the Act, by virtue of the provisions of an order made under section 149 of the Local Government, Planning and Land Act 1980; or

(c) an enterprise zone authority which is the local planning authority for an enterprise zone, for the purposes of determining applications for planning permission under Part III of the Act, by virtue of the provisions of an order made under paragraph 5 of Schedule 32 to the Local Government, Planning and Land Act 1980;

"statutory undertakers" means persons authorised by any enactment to carry on any railway, light railway, tramway, road transport, water transport, canal, inland navigation, dock, harbour, pier or lighthouse undertaking or any undertaking for the supply of electricity, gas, hydraulic power or water and includes the British Airports Authority, the Civil Aviation Authority, the Post Office and companies which are deemed to be statutory undertakers by virtue of section 141(2) of the Transport Act 1968.   **[593]**

NOTES
Commencement: 1 July 1981.
Amended by SI 1986 No 443, reg 2, Sch 1, para 7.

3. Classes of appeal for determination by appointed persons

Subject to the provisions of regulation 4 of these regulations, the following classes of appeal are prescribed for the purposes of paragraph 1(1) of Schedule 9 to the Act as appeals to be determined by a person appointed by the Secretary of State instead of by the Secretary of State:—

(*a*) appeals under section 36 of the Act (appeals against planning decision), including appeals under that section as applied by section 37 (appeals in default of planning decision) of the Act;

(*b*) appeals under section 88 of the Act (appeals against enforcement notices).

[(*c*) appeals under section 97 of the Act (listed building enforcement notices), including appeals under that section as having effect by virtue of section 277A of the Act (conservation areas); and

(*d*) appeals under paragraph 8 of Schedule 11 to the Act (listed building consent) including appeals under that paragraph as having effect by virtue of section 277A).]   **[594]**

NOTES
Commencement: 1 July 1981.
Amended by SI 1986 No 623, reg 2(2).

4. Classes of appeal reserved for determination by the Secretary of State

The following classes of case are prescribed for the purposes of paragraph 1(1) of Schedule 9 to the Act as appeals which are not to be determined in the manner set out in that paragraph:—

(*a*) appeals under section 36 of the Act, or under that section as applied by section 37 of the Act, by statutory undertakers where the relevant application related to land to which section 225(1) of the Act applies;

(*b*) appeals by statutory undertakers under section 88 of the Act where the breach of planning control alleged in the enforcement notice consists in the carrying out of development of land to which section 225(1) of the Act applies, or failure to comply with a condition or limitation on a grant of planning permission for development of any such land.

[(*c*) appeals relating to applications to demolish listed buildings or enforcement notices concerned with the demolition of such buildings;

(*d*) appeals relating to applications to alter or extend Grade I or Grade II* listed buildings or to enforcement notices concerned with the alteration or extension of such buildings;

(*e*) appeals relating to buildings for which grants have been made under sections 3A or 4 of the Historic Buildings and Ancient Monuments Act 1953, and

(*f*) appeals referred to in regulation 3(*c*) or (*d*) above relating to buildings in Wales.]   **[595]**

NOTES
Commencement: 1 July 1981.
Amended by SI 1986 No 623, reg 2(3).

5. Publicity for directions under paragraph 1(1) of Schedule 9 to the Act

On the making by the Secretary of State of a direction under paragraph 1(1) of Schedule 9 to the Act he may by notice in writing enclosing a copy of the direction require the local planning authority for every area in respect of which the direction has effect to publish as soon as may be a notice in at least one newspaper circulating in the area; and such notice shall contain a concise statement of the effect of the direction and shall specify the place or places where a copy of the direction may be seen at all reasonable hours.   **[596]**

NOTES
    Commencement: 1 July 1981.

TOWN AND COUNTRY PLANNING (ENFORCEMENT NOTICES AND APPEALS) REGULATIONS 1981
(SI 1981 NO 1742)

NOTES
    Made: 3 December 1981
    Authority: Town and Country Planning Act 1971, ss 87(12), 88(5), 97(4), 287(2)

ARRANGEMENT OF REGULATIONS

PART I
CITATION, COMMENCEMENT AND INTERPRETATION

PART II
ENFORCEMENT NOTICES UNDER SECTION 87

PART III
APPEALS

PART IV
NOTICES ISSUED BY THE SECRETARY OF STATE

PART I

CITATION, COMMENCEMENT AND INTERPRETATION

1. Citation and commencement

These regulations may be cited as the Town and Country Planning (Enforcement Notices and Appeals) Regulations 1981 and shall come into operation on 11th January 1982.   **[597]**

NOTES
Commencement: 11 January 1982.

2. Interpretation

In these regulations, unless the context otherwise requires—

"the 1971 Act" means the Town and Country Planning Act 1971;

"enforcement notice" means a notice issued under section 87(1) or section 96(1) of the 1971 Act;

"local planning authority" means the local authority or other body who issue the relevant enforcement notice.   **[598]**

NOTES
Commencement: 11 January 1982.

PART II

ENFORCEMENT NOTICES UNDER SECTION 87

3. Matters to be specified in enforcement notice

Local planning authorities are directed to specify in any enforcement notice which they issue under section 87 of the 1971 Act—

(a) the reasons why they consider it expedient to issue the notice; and
(b) the precise boundaries of the land to which the notice relates, whether by reference to a plan or otherwise.   **[599]**

NOTES
Commencement: 11 January 1982.
1971 Act: Town and Country Planning Act 1971.

4. Explanatory note to accompany copy enforcement notices

Every copy of an enforcement notice served by a local planning authority under section 87(5) of the 1971 Act shall be accompanied by an explanatory note which shall include the following—

(a) a copy of sections 87 to 88B of the 1971 Act, or a summary of those sections including the following information—
    (i) that there is a right of appeal to the Secretary of State against the enforcement notice;
    (ii) that an appeal must be made in writing to the Secretary of State before the date specified in the enforcement notice as the date on which it is to take effect;
    (iii) the grounds on which an appeal may be brought under section 88;

(*b*) notification that an appellant must submit to the Secretary of State, either when giving notice of appeal or within 28 days from the date on which the Secretary of State sends him a notice so requiring him, a statement in writing specifying the grounds on which he is appealing against the enforcement notice and stating briefly the facts on which he proposes to rely in support of each of those grounds.   **[600]**

NOTES
Commencement: 11 January 1982.
1971 Act: Town and Country Planning Act 1971.

PART III
APPEALS

5. Statement by appellant

A person who gives notice to the Secretary of State under section 88(3) or 97(2) of the 1971 Act appealing against an enforcement notice and who does not send with it a statement in writing specifying the grounds on which he is appealing against the notice and stating briefly the facts on which he proposes to rely in support of each of those grounds, shall deliver such a statement to the Secretary of State not later than 28 days from the date on which the Secretary of State sends him a notice so requiring him.   **[601]**

NOTES
Commencement: 11 January 1982.
1971 Act: Town and Country Planning Act 1971.

6. Statement by local planning authority

(1) Where an appeal has been made to the Secretary of State against an enforcement notice issued by a local planning authority, the authority shall serve on the Secretary of State and on the appellant a statement indicating the submissions which they propose to put forward on the appeal and including the following matters—

(*a*) a summary of the authority's response to each ground of appeal pleaded by the appellant;

(*b*) a statement whether the authority would be prepared to grant planning permission for the development alleged in the enforcement notice to have been carried out, or listed building consent for the works to which the listed building enforcement notice relates, as the case may be, and, if so, particulars of the conditions, if any, which they would wish to attach to such permission or consent.

(2) Any statement which is required to be served by paragraph (1) of this regulation shall be served—

(*a*) where a local inquiry is to be held, not later than 28 days before the date of the inquiry or such later date as may be agreed in writing by the Secretary of State, the appellant and the local planning authority;

(*b*) in any other case, not later than 28 days from the date on which the Secretary of State sends to the authority a notice requiring the statement.   **[602]**

NOTES
Commencement: 11 January 1982.

7. Public notification of appeal

(1) Where an appeal has been made to the Secretary of State against an enforcement notice issued by a local planning authority and he proposes not to hold a local inquiry, the authority shall give notification of the appeal to occupiers of properties in the locality of the site to which the enforcement notice relates and to any other persons who in the opinion of the authority are affected by the breach of planning control or contravention of listed building control which is alleged in the enforcement notice.

(2) Any notification given under paragraph (1) of this regulation shall include—

    (*a*) a description of the alleged breach of control;

    (*b*) in the case of an appeal against an enforcement notice issued under section 87 of the 1971 Act, a statement of the reasons specified in the notice under regulation 3(*a*) of these regulations;

    (*c*) the grounds on which the appellant appealed against the enforcement notice; and

    (*d*) a statement that interested persons may submit comments in writing to the local planning authority within such time as may be specified in the notification. **[603]**

NOTES
Commencement: 11 January 1982.
1971 Act: Town and Country Planning Act 1971.

8. Local planning authority to send copy of notice to Secretary of State

Where an appeal has been made to the Secretary of State against an enforcement notice the local planning authority who issued the notice shall if so required by the Secretary of State send to him, not later than 14 days from the date on which the Secretary of State gives them notice that the appeal has been made, a copy of the enforcement notice and a list of the names and addresses of the persons on whom a copy of the notice was served under section 87(5) or 96(3) of the 1971 Act, as the case may be. **[604]**

NOTES
Commencement: 11 January 1982.
1971 Act: Town and Country Planning Act 1971.

PART IV

NOTICES ISSUED BY THE SECRETARY OF STATE

9. Application of regulations

These regulations, except regulation 8, shall apply with respect to enforcement notices issued by the Secretary of State under section 276(5A) of the 1971 Act and to appeals made to the Secretary of State against such notices as they apply with respect to such notices issued by local planning authorities and to appeals made against them as if—

    (*a*) for references to a local planning authority there were substituted references to the Secretary of State;

    (*b*) in regulation 3, for "section 87" there were substituted "section 276(5A)";

    (*c*) in regulation 4, paragraph (*a*), after "sections 87 to 88B" there were inserted "and section 276(5A)";

(*d*) for regulation 6 the following were substituted—

"6.—(1) Where an appeal has been made to the Secretary of State against an enforcement notice or a listed building enforcement notice which he has issued the Secretary of State shall serve on the appellant a statement indicating the submissions which he proposes to put forward on the appeal including a summary of his response to each ground of appeal pleaded by the appellant.

(2) Any statement which is required to be served by paragraph (1) of this regulation shall, where a local inquiry is to be held, be served not later than 28 days before the date of the inquiry.". **[605]**

NOTES
Commencement: 11 January 1982.
1971 Act: Town and Country Planning Act 1971.

TOWN AND COUNTRY PLANNING (ENFORCEMENT) (INQUIRIES PROCEDURE) RULES 1981
(SI 1981 NO 1743)

NOTES
Made: 3 December 1981
Authority: Tribunals and Inquiries Act 1971, s 11

ARRANGEMENT OF RULES

1. Citation and commencement

(1) These Rules may be cited as the Town and Country Planning (Enforcement) (Inquiries Procedure) Rules 1981.

(2) These Rules shall come into operation on 11th January 1982 but shall not apply to any appeal brought before that date. **[606]**

NOTES
Commencement: 11 January 1982.

2. Application of Rules

(1) These Rules apply—

    (*a*) to local inquiries caused by the Secretary of State to be held for the purpose of appeals against enforcement notices made to him under section 88 of the Town and Country Planning Act 1971;

    (*b*) to local inquiries held by a person appointed by the Secretary of State for the purpose of appeals to the Secretary of State under section 88 of the Town and Country Planning Act 1971, where such appeals fall to be determined by the said person instead of by the Secretary of State by virtue of the powers contained in Schedule 9 to the Act and of regulations made thereunder;

    (*c*) to local inquiries caused by the Secretary of State to be held for the purpose of appeals against listed building enforcement notices made to him under section 97 of the Town and Country Planning Act 1971;

    [(*d*) to local inquiries held by a person appointed by the Secretary of State under Schedule 9 to the Town and Country Planning Act 1971 to determine appeals under section 97 (listed building enforcement notices) or under that section as extended by section 277A (buildings in conservation areas); and

    (*e*) to local inquiries caused by the Secretary of State to be held in connection with the determination by him of applications or appeals under section 95 of the Town and Country Planning Act 1971 (established use certificates).]   **[607]**

NOTES

Commencement: 11 January 1982.
Sub-paras (*d*) and (*e*): substituted for existing sub-para (*d*) by SI 1986 No 420, Sch 3.
The Act: Town and Country Planning Act 1971.

3. Interpretation

In these Rules, unless the context otherwise requires—

"the Act" means the Town and Country Planning Act 1971;

"appellant", in the case of an application of the kind referred to in rule 2(1)(*d*), means the applicant;

"appointed person" means—

    (i) in relation to an inquiry caused by the Secretary of State to be held, the person appointed by the Secretary of State to hold the inquiry; and

    (ii) in relation to an inquiry held by a person appointed by the Secretary of State for the purpose of a transferred appeal, that person;

"enforcement notice" has the meaning assigned to it by section 87(1) of the Act;

"enterprise zone" and "enterprise zone authority" have the meanings assigned to them by Schedule 32 to the Local Government, Planning and Land Act 1980;

"established use certificate" has the meaning assigned to it by section 94(2) of the Act;

"inquiry" means a local inquiry to which these Rules apply;

"listed building enforcement notice" has the meaning assigned to it by section 96(2) of the Act;

"the land" means the land to which the relevant enforcement notice, the relevant listed building enforcement notice or the application for an established use certificate (as the case may be) relates;

"local authority" has the meaning assigned to it by section 290(1) of the Act;

["local planning authority" means the body who issued the relevant enforcement notice or listed building enforcement notice or the body to whom it fell to determine the relevant application for an established use certificate;]

"National Park Committee" has the meaning assigned to it by paragraph 5 of Schedule 17 to the Local Government Act 1972;

"transferred appeal" means an appeal which falls to be determined by a person appointed by the Secretary of State pursuant to the provisions of Schedule 9 to the Act and of regulations made thereunder;

"the relevant enforcement notice" means the enforcement notice which is the subject of the appeal;

"the relevant listed building enforcement notice" means the listed building enforcement notice which is the subject of the appeal;

"urban development area" and "urban development corporation" have the meanings assigned to them by section 134 and section 135 respectively of the Local Government, Planning and Land Act 1980. **[608]**

NOTES
Commencement: 11 January 1982.
Amended by SI 1986 No 420, Sch 3.

4. Notification of inquiry

(1) A date, time and place for the holding of the inquiry shall be fixed and may be varied by the Secretary of State, who shall give not less than 42 days' notice in writing of such date, time and place to the appellant and to the local planning authority:

Provided that—

    (i) with the consent of the appellant and of the local planning authority, the Secretary of State may give such lesser period of notice as shall be agreed with them, and in that event he may specify a date for service of the statements referred to in paragraphs (1), (4) and (5) of rule 6 and of the list of documents referred to in rule 6(2) later than the date therein prescribed;

    (ii) where it becomes necessary or advisable to vary the time or place fixed for the inquiry, the Secretary of State shall give such notice of the variation as may appear to him to be reasonable in the circumstances.

(2) Without prejudice to the foregoing provisions of this rule, the Secretary of State may require the local planning authority to take one or more of the following steps—

    (*a*) to publish in one or more newspapers circulating in the locality in which the land is situated such notices of the inquiry as he may direct;

(b) to serve notice of the inquiry in such form and on such persons or classes of persons as he may specify;

(c) to post such notices of the inquiry as he may direct in a conspicuous place or places near to the land;

but the requirements as to the period of notice contained in paragraph (1) of this rule shall not apply to any such notices.

(3) Where the land is under the control of the appellant, he shall, if so required by the Secretary of State, affix firmly to some object on the land, in such a manner as to be readily visible to and legible by the public, such notice of the inquiry as the Secretary of State may specify, and thereafter for such period before the inquiry as the Secretary of State may specify, the appellant shall not remove the notice, or cause or permit it to be removed.   **[609]**

NOTES
Commencement: 11 January 1982.

5. Notification of identity of appointed person

In the case of a transferred appeal, the Secretary of State shall give to the appellant and to the local planning authority written notice informing them of the name of the appointed person:

Provided that, where, in exercise of his powers under paragraph 4 of Schedule 9 to the Act, the Secretary of State has appointed another person to determine the appeal in the place of a person previously appointed for that purpose and it is not practicable to give written notice of the new appointment before the inquiry is held, in lieu of the Secretary of State's giving such notice the person holding the inquiry shall, at the commencement thereof, announce his own name and the fact of his appointment.   **[610]**

NOTES
Commencement: 11 January 1982.
The Act: Town and Country Planning Act 1971.

6. Service of statements and inspection of documents before inquiry

(1) Where either a government department or a local authority has—

(a) in the case of an appeal of the kinds referred to in rule 2(1)(a), (b) or (c), expressed in writing—

(i) a view as to the expediency of issuing an enforcement notice or listed building enforcement notice in respect of the land;

(ii) an opinion on any of the terms of the relevant enforcement notice, or of the relevant listed building enforcement notice (as the case may be); or

(iii) a view as to whether planning permission should be granted for the development to which the relevant enforcement notice relates or whether listed building consent should be granted for the works to which the relevant listed building enforcement notice relates (as the case may be); or

(b) in the case of an application or appeal of the kinds referred to in rule 2(1)(d), expressed in writing the view that an established use certificate should not be granted on the application, or that such a certificate should be granted only in respect of part of the land or only in respect of some one or more of the uses specified in the application,

and the local planning authority propose to rely on such expression of view or opinion in their submissions at the inquiry they shall, not later than 28 days before the date of the inquiry (or such later date as the Secretary of State may specify under proviso (i) to paragraph (1) of rule 4), serve on the appellant a statement to that effect, together with a copy of the expression of view or opinion in question.

(2) Where the local planning authority intend to refer to, or put in evidence, at the inquiry documents (including maps and plans), they shall serve on the appellant, not later than 28 days before the date of the inquiry (or such later date as the Secretary of State may specify under proviso (i) to paragraph (1) of rule 4), a list of such documents, together with a notice stating the times and place at which the documents may be inspected by the appellant; and the local planning authority shall afford him a reasonable opportunity to inspect and, where practicable, to take copies of the documents.

(3) The local planning authority shall afford any other person interested a reasonable opportunity to inspect and, where practicable, to take copies of any statement served under paragraph (1) of this rule, any of the documents referred to in paragraph (2) of this rule and any statement served on them under paragraph (5) of this rule.

(4) In the case of an application or appeal of the kinds referred to in rule 2(1)(*d*), the local planning authority shall, not later than 28 days before the inquiry (or such later date as the Secretary of State may specify under proviso (i) to paragraph (1) of rule 4)—

    (*a*) serve on the appellant a written statement of any submission which the local planning authority propose to put forward at the inquiry; and

    (*b*) supply a copy of the statement to the Secretary of State;

and the authority shall afford any other person interested a reasonable opportunity to inspect and, where practicable, to take copies of the statement.

(5) In the case of any appeal or application of the kinds referred to in rule 2, the apellant shall, if so required by the Secretary of State, serve on the local planning authority and on the Secretary of State, within such time before the inquiry as the Secretary of State may specify, a written statement of the submissions which he proposes to put forward at the inquiry; and such statement shall be accompanied by a list of any documents (including maps and plans) which the appellant intends to refer to, or put in evidence, at the inquiry, and he shall, if so required by the Secretary of State, afford the local planning authority a reasonable opportunity to inspect and, where practicable, to take copies of such documents. **[611]**

NOTES
Commencement: 11 January 1982.

7. Appointed person acting in place of Secretary of State

Where the appeal is a transferred appeal, the appointed person may himself, in place of the Secretary of State, take such steps as the Secretary of State is required or enabled to take under or by virtue of rule 4, rule 9(2) or rule 10(2).
[612]

NOTES
Commencement: 11 January 1982.

8. Appearances at inquiry

[(1) The persons entitled to appear at the inquiry are—

    (*a*) the appellant;

    (*b*) the local planning authority;

    (*c*) any person on whom the Secretary of State has required notice to be served under rule 4(2)(*b*);

    (*d*) a body of any of the following descriptions where the relevant land is in the area in which that body has responsibilities and it is not otherwise entitled to appear—

        (i) a county council,

        (ii) a London borough council,

        (iii) a district council,

        (iv) a National Park Committee,

        (v) a joint or special planning board,

        (vi) a new town development corporation,

        (vii) an urban development corporation,

        (viii) an enterprise zone authority;

    (*e*) where the inquiry relates to a listed building enforcement notice concerning a building in Greater London and it is not otherwise entitled to appear, the Historic Buildings and Monuments Commission for England.

    In this paragraph "London borough council" includes the Common Council of the City of London and "district council" includes the Council of the Isles of Scilly.]

(2) Any other person may appear at the inquiry at the discretion of the appointed person.

(3) A local authority may appear by their clerk or by any other officer appointed for the purpose by the local authority, or by counsel or solicitor; and any other person may appear on his own behalf or be represented by counsel, solicitor or any other person.

(4) Where there are two or more persons having a similar interest in the matter under inquiry, the appointed person may allow one or more persons to appear for the benefit of some or all persons so interested.   **[613]**

NOTES
Commencement: 11 January 1982.
Para (1): substituted for existing para (1) by SI 1986 No 420, Sch 3.
The Act: Town and Country Planning Act 1971.

9. Representatives of government departments at inquiry

(1) Where the local planning authority have served on the appellant a statement of the kind referred to in paragraph (1) of rule 6 which relates to an expression of view or opinion by a government department, the appellant may, not later than 14 days before the date of the inquiry, apply in writing to the Secretary of State for a representative of the government department concerned to be made available at the inquiry.

(2) Where an application is made to the Secretary of State under the last foregoing paragraph he shall—

    (*a*) in the case of a view or opinion expressed by his own department, make a representative of his department available to attend the inquiry; or (*b*) in any other case, transmit the application to the other government department concerned, who shall make a representative of that department available to attend the inquiry.

(3) A representative of the Secretary of State's department who, in pursuance of this rule, attends an inquiry shall state the reasons for the view or opinion expressed by his department and shall give evidence and be subject to cross-examination to the same extent as any other witness.

(4) A representative of a government department other than the Secretary of State's department who, in pursuance of this rule, attends an inquiry shall be called as a witness by the local planning authority and shall state the reasons for the view expressed by his department, and shall give evidence and be subject to cross-examination to the same extent as any other witness.

(5) Nothing in either of the last two foregoing paragraphs shall require a representative of a government department to answer any question which in the opinion of the appointed person is directed to the merits of government policy, and the appointed person shall disallow any such question.   **[614]**

NOTES
Commencement: 11 January 1982.

10. Representatives of local authorities at inquiry

(1) Where the local planning authority have served on the appellant a statement of the kind referred to in paragraph (1) of rule 6 which relates to an expression of view or opinion by a local authority, the appellant may, not later than 14 days before the date of the inquiry, apply in writing to the Secretary of State for a representative of the authority concerned to be made available to attend the inquiry.

(2) Where an application is made to the Secretary of State under the last foregoing paragraph he shall transmit the application to the authority concerned, who shall make a representative of the authority available to attend the inquiry.

(3) A representative of a local authority who, in pursuance of this rule, attends an inquiry shall be called as a witness by the local planning authority and shall state the reasons for the view or opinion expressed by the authority and shall give evidence and be subject to cross-examination to the same extent as any other witness.   **[615]**

NOTES
Commencement: 11 January 1982.

11. Procedure at inquiry

(1) Except as otherwise provided in these Rules, the procedure at the inquiry shall be such as the appointed person shall in his discretion determine.

(2) Unless in any particular case the appointed person with the consent of the appellant otherwise determines, the appellant shall begin and shall have the right of final reply; and the other persons entitled or permitted to appear shall be heard in such order as the appointed person may determine.

(3) The appellant and the local planning authority shall be entitled to call evidence and cross-examine persons giving evidence, but any other person appearing at the inquiry may do so only to the extent permitted by the appointed person.

(4) The appointed person shall not require or permit the giving or production of any evidence, whether written or oral, which would be contrary to the public interest; but save as aforesaid and without prejudice to the provisions of rule 9(5) any evidence may be admitted at the discretion of the appointed person, who may direct that documents tendered in evidence may be inspected by any person entitled or permitted to appear at the inquiry and that facilities be afforded him to take or obtain copies thereof.

(5) The appointed person may allow the appellant or the local planning authority—

(a) to alter or add to the submissions contained in any statement served under rule 6 of these Rules or under any other enactment requiring the serving of a statement before the inquiry;

(b) to alter or add to any list of documents which accompanied any such statement,

so far as may be necessary for the purpose of determining the questions in controversy between the parties, but shall (if necessary by adjourning the inquiry) give the local planning authority or the appellant, as the case may be, an adequate opportunity of considering any such fresh submission or document; and the appointed person may make a recommendation to the Secretary of State as to the payment of any additional costs occasioned by such adjournment.

(6) If any person entitled to appear at the inquiry fails to do so, the appointed person may proceed with the inquiry at his discretion.

(7) The appointed person shall be entitled (subject to disclosure thereof at the inquiry) to take into account any written representations or statements received by him before the inquiry from any person.

(8) The appointed person may from time to time adjourn the inquiry and, if the date, time and place of the adjourned inquiry are announced before the adjournment, no further notice shall be required.   **[616]**

NOTES
Commencement: 11 January 1982.

12. Site inspections

(1) The appointed person may make an unaccompanied inspection of the land before or during the inquiry without giving notice of his intention to the persons entitled to appear at the inquiry.

(2) The appointed person may, and shall if so requested by the appellant or the local planning authority before or during the inquiry, inspect the land after the close of the inquiry and shall, in all cases where he intends to make such an inspection, announce during the inquiry the date and time at which he proposes to do so.

(3) The appellant and the local planning authority shall be entitled to accompany the appointed person on any inspection after the close of the inquiry; but the appointed person shall not be bound to defer his inspection if any person entitled to accompany him is not present at the time appointed.

[617]

NOTES
Commencement: 11 January 1982.

13. Report of inquiry

Where—

    (*a*) the appeal is not a transferred appeal; or

    (*b*) the appeal is a transferred appeal but the Secretary of State has, under paragraph 3 of Schedule 9 to the Act, directed that the appeal shall be determined by the Secretary of State,

the appointed person shall after the close of the inquiry make a report in writing to the Secretary of State which shall include the appointed person's findings of fact, his conclusions and his recommendations, if any (or his reason for not making any recommendation). **[618]**

NOTES

Commencement: 11 January 1982.
The Act: Town and Country Planning Act 1971.

14. Procedure after inquiry

(1) Where, in a case where a report is made to the Secretary of State by the appointed person in accordance with the requirement in rule 13, the Secretary of State—

    (*a*) differs from the appointed person on a finding of fact; or

    (*b*) after the close of the inquiry takes into consideration any new evidence (including expert opinion on a matter of fact) or any new issue of fact (not being a matter of government policy) which was not raised at the inquiry,

and by reason thereof is disposed to disagree with a recommendation made by the appointed person, he shall not come to a decision which is at variance with any such recommendation without first notifying the appellant and the local planning authority of his disagreement and the reasons for it and affording them an opportunity of making respresentations in writing within 21 days or (if the Secretary of State has taken into consideration any new evidence or any new issue of fact, not being a matter of government policy) of asking within 21 days for the reopening of the inquiry.

(2) If, in the case of a transferred appeal, the appointed person proposes, after the close of the inquiry, to take into consideration any new evidence (including expert opinion on a matter of fact) or any new issue of fact (not being a matter of government policy) which was not raised at the inquiry and which he considers to be material to his decision, he shall not come to a decision without first notifying the appellant and the local planning authority of the substance of the new evidence or of the new issue of fact and affording them an opportunity of making representations thereon in writing within 21 days or of asking within that time for the reopening of the inquiry.

(3) The Secretary of State or, in the case of a transferred appeal, the appointed person may, in any case if he thinks fit, cause the inquiry to be reopened, and shall cause it to be reopened if asked to do so in accordance with paragraph (1) or paragraph (2) of this rule (as the case may be); and if the inquiry is reopened, paragraphs (1) and (2) of rule 4 shall apply as they applied to the original inquiry, with the following modifications:—

    (*a*) for the figure "42" in paragraph (1), there shall be substituted the figure "28";

(*b*) in the case of a transferred appeal, for references to the Secretary of State, wherever they occur, there shall be substituted references to the appointed person.   **[619]**

NOTES

Commencement: 11 January 1982.

15. Costs

Where any person makes application at the inquiry for an award of costs, the appointed person shall report in writing the proceedings on such application to the Secretary of State and draw attention to any considerations which appear to him to be relevant to the Secretary of State's decision and he may include in his report a recommendation on the matter.   **[620]**

NOTES

Commencement: 11 January 1982.

16. Notification of decision

(1) In the case of a tranferred appeal, the appointed person shall (unless the Secretary of State has, under paragraph 3 of Schedule 9 to the Act, directed that the appeal shall be determined by the Secretary of State) notify his decision and his reasons therefor in writing to the appellant, to the local planning authority and to any person who, having appeared at the inquiry, has asked to be notified of the decision.

(2) In the case of an appeal which falls to be determined by the Secretary of State, the Secretary of State shall notify his decision, and his reasons therefor, in writing to the appellant, to the local planning authority and to any person who, having appeared at the inquiry, has asked to be notified of the decision.

(3) Where a decision is notified in accordance with paragraph (2) of this rue and a copy of the appointed person's report is not sent with the notification of decision, the notification shall be accompanied by a summary of the appointed person's conclusions and recommendations; and if any person entitled to be notified of the Secretary of State's decision under the said paragraph (2) has not received a copy of the appointed person's report, he shall be supplied with a copy thereof on written application made to the Secretary of State within one month from the date of his decision.

(4) For the purposes of paragraph (3) of this rule "report" does not include documents, photographs or plans appended to the appointed person's report, but any person entitled to be supplied with a copy of the report under that paragraph may apply to the Secretary of State in writing within six weeks of the notification to him of the decision or the supply to him of the report, whichever is the later, for an opportunity of inspecting such documents, photographs and plans and the Secretary of State shall afford him an opportunity accordingly.

(5) In the case of a transferred appeal, any person entitled to be notified of the decision of the appointed person under paragraph (1) of this rule may apply to the Secretary of State in writing within six weeks of the notification to him of the decision for an opportunity of inspecting any documents, photographs or plans listed in the notification and the Secretary of State shall afford him an opportunity accordingly.   **[621]**

NOTES

Commencement: 11 January 1982.

The Act: Town and Country Planning Act 1971.

17. Service of notices by post

Notices or documents required or authorised to be served or sent under the provisions of any of these Rules may be sent by post. **[622]**

NOTES
Commencement: 11 January 1982.

18. Application to Greater London

In their application to Greater London these Rules shall apply with the following modifications:—

    (*a*) in rule 2—

        (i) after the definition of "the Act" there shall be added:—

        ""the Act of 1963" means the London Government Act 1963"; and

        (ii) for the definition of "local planning authority", the following definition shall be substituted:—

        ""local planning authority" means—

            (*a*) in relation to the appeals referred to in rule 2(1)(*a*), (*b*) and (*c*), the local authority or other body who issued the relevant enforcement notice or listed building enforcement notice; or

            (*b*) in relation to the applications and appeals referred to in rule 2(1)(*d*), the Common Council of the City of London or the council of the London borough in which the land is situated, as the case may be;";

    (*b*) for rule 7(1)(*c*) and (*d*) there shall be substituted the following:—

        "(*c*) the Greater London Council, if not the local planning authority;

        (*d*) the council of the London borough in which the land is situated, if not the local planning authority;". **[623]**

NOTES
Commencement: 11 January 1982.

TOWN AND COUNTRY PLANNING (FEES FOR APPLICATIONS AND DEEMED APPLICATIONS) REGULATIONS 1983
(SI 1983 NO 1674)

NOTES
Made: 14 November 1983
Authority: Local Government, Planning and Land Act 1980, s 87

ARRANGEMENT OF REGULATIONS

APPLICATION, CITATION AND COMMENCEMENT

Regulation   Para

APPLICATION, CITATION AND COMMENCEMENT

1. (1) These Regulations may be cited as the Town and Country Planning
(Fees for Applications and Deemed Applications) Regulations 1983 and shall
come into operation on 1st December 1983.

(2) These Regulations apply—

(*a*) to applications for planning permission made on or after the date
when they come into operation;

(*b*) to applications for approval of reserved matters made on or after the
date when they come into operation;

(*c*) to applications for consent for the display of advertisements made on
or after the date when they come into operation;

(*d*) to applications for planning permission deemed to have been made,
by virtue of section 88B(3) of the Town and Country Planning Act
1971, in connection with an enforcement notice issued on or after the
date when they come into operation; and

(e) to applications for planning permission deemed to have been made, by virtue of section 95(6) of the Town and Country Planning Act 1971, in connection with an application for an established use certificate made on or after the date when they come into operation.

[624]

NOTES

Commencement: 1 December 1983.

INTERPRETATION

2. (1) In these Regulations, unless the context otherwise requires—

"the 1971 Act" means the Town and Country Planning Act 1971;

"the General Development Order" means the Town and Country Planning General Development Order 1977;

"dwellinghouse" means a building or part of a building which is used as a single private dwellinghouse, and for no other purpose;

"glasshouse" means a building which—

(a) has not less than three-quarters of its total external area comprised of glass or other translucent material;

(b) is designed for the production of flowers, fruit, vegetables, herbs or other horticultural produce; and

(c) is used, or is to be used, solely for the purposes of agriculture;

"reserved matters" has the same meaning as in the General Development Order;

"use for residential purposes" means use as a dwellinghouse;

"use of land" includes use of land for the winning and working of minerals.

(2) Subject to the provisions of paragraph (3) below, expressions used in these Regulations have, unless the contrary intention appears, the meaning which they bear in the 1971 Act.

(3) Expressions used in regulation 9 and Schedule 2 have, unless the contrary intention appears, the meaning which they bear in the Town and Country Planning (Control of Advertisements) Regulations 1969.

(4) References in regulation $7(2)(f)$, in regulation 8(5) and in paragraph 4(1) of Schedule 1 to particular provisions contained in these Regulations shall be construed as including references to the provisions of the Town and Country Planning (Fees for Applications and Deemed Applications) Regulations 1981 which are re-enacted in those provisions.

(5) A regulation or Schedule referred to in these Regulations only by number means the regulation or Schedule so numbered in these Regulations. **[625]**

NOTES

Commencement: 1 December 1983.

FEES FOR PLANNING APPLICATIONS

3. (1) Subject to the provisions of regulations 4 to 7, where an application is made to a local planning authority for planning permission for the development of land or for the approval of reserved matters, a fee shall be paid to that authority in accordance with the provisions of these Regulations.

(2) The amount of the fee payable in respect of the application shall be calculated in accordance with the provisions of Schedule 1.

(3) The fee due in respect of an application shall be paid at the time when the application is made; and (subject to the provisions of paragraph 6(2) of Schedule 1) the amount of the fee shall be sent to the local planning authority with whom the application is lodged, together with the application.

(4) Where the local planning authority who receive the fee in accordance with the provisions of paragraphs (1) to (3) above are not the local planning authority to whom it falls to determine the application, they shall remit the amount of the fee to that authority at the same time as they forward the application to them. |626|

NOTES
Commencement: 1 December 1983.
New para (5) inserted by SI 1987 No 101, reg 3, Sch 1, para 1. See Appendix.

EXCEPTIONS

4. (1) The provisions of regulation 3 shall not apply where the local planning authority to whom the application is made are satisfied that it relates solely to:—

   (a) the carrying out of operations for the alteration or extension of an existing dwellinghouse; or
   (b) the carrying out of operations (other than the erection of a dwellinghouse) in the curtilage of an existing dwellinghouse,

for the purpose, in either case, of providing means of access to or within the dwellinghouse for a disabled person who is resident in, or is proposing to take up residence in, that dwellinghouse, or of providing facilities designed to secure his greater safety, health or comfort.

(2) The provisions of regulation 3 shall not apply where the local planning authority to whom the application is made are satisfied that it relates solely to the carrying out of operations for the purpose of providing means of access for disabled persons to or within a building or premises to which members of the public are admitted (whether on payment or otherwise).

(3) In this regulation, "disabled person" means a person who is within any of the descriptions of persons to whom section 29 of the National Assistance Act 1948 applies. |627|

NOTES
Commencement: 1 December 1983.

5. (1) The provisions of regulation 3 shall not apply where the local planning authority to whom the application is made are satisfied—

(*a*) that the application relates to development which is within one or more of the classes specified in Schedule 1 to the General Development Order and solely to such development; and

(*b*) that the permission granted by article 3 of that Order does not apply in respect of that development by reason of (and only by reason of):—

    (i) a direction made under article 4 of that Order which is in force on the date when the application is made; or

    (ii) the requirements of a condition imposed on any permission granted or deemed to be granted under Part III of the 1971 Act otherwise than by that Order.

(2) The reference in subparagraph (1)(*a*) above to an application which relates to development which is within one or more of the classes specified in Schedule 1 to the General Development Order shall be construed as including an application for planning permission for the continuance of a use of land, or the retention of buildings or works on land, without compliance with a condition subject to which a previous planning permission has been granted, where the condition in question prohibits or limits the carrying out of any development which is within one or more of the said classes.   **[628]**

NOTES
Commencement: 1 December 1983.
1971 Act: Town and Country Planning Act 1971.

5A. [The provisions of regulation 3 shall not apply where the local planning authority to whom the application is made are satisfied:—

(*a*) that the application relates to the use of a building or other land for a purpose of any class specified in the Schedule to the Town and Country Planning (Use Classes) Order 1972 and solely to such use; and

(*b*) that the existing use of that building or other land is for another purpose of the same class; and

(*c*) that the making of an application for planning permission in respect of the use to which the application relates is necessary by reason of (and only by reason of) the requirements of a condition imposed on a permission granted, or deemed to have been granted, under Part III of the 1971 Act.]   **[629]**

NOTES
Commencement: 26 August 1985.
Added by SI 1985 No 1182, reg 2.

6. (1) Where all of the conditions set out in paragraph (2) below are satisfied, the provisions of regulation 3 shall not apply to:—

(*a*) an application for planning permission which is made following the granting of planning permission (whether by the local planning authority or by the Secretary of State on appeal or following the reference of the application to him for determination) for development which the local planning authority are satisfied is development of the same character or description as the development to which the application relates, on an application for planning permission made by or on behalf of the same applicant; or

(b) an application for approval of one or more reserved matters which is made following the granting of approval (whether by the local planning authority or by the Secretary of State on appeal, or following the reference of the application to him for determination) of details relating to the same reserved matters authorised by the same outline planning permission, on an application made by or on behalf of the same applicant.

(2) The conditions referred to in paragraph (1) above are:—

(a) that the application is made before the end of the period of 12 months following the date of the relevant grant of planning permission or grant of approval of details of reserved matters, as the case may be;

(b) that the application relates—

(i) in the case of an application for planning permission, to the same site as that to which the grant of planning permission related, or to part of that site, and to no other land (save that in a case where additional land is included in the application solely for the purpose of providing a means of access to the site which differs from that authorised by the planning permission, that land shall be disregarded for the purpose of this paragraph); or

(ii) in the case of an application for approval of reserved matters, to the same land as that in respect of which the approval was granted, or to part of that land (and no other land);

(c) in the case of an application for planning permission which is not made in outline, that the planning permission which has been granted is not an outline planning permission (within the meaning of that term as defined in the General Development Order);

(d) that no previous application has at any time been made by or on behalf of the same applicant which related to the site to which the relevant grant of planning permission or grant of approval of reserved matters, as the case may be, relates (or which related wholly or in part to any part of that site) and which was exempted from the provisions of regulation 3 by the provisions of this regulation.   **[630]**

NOTES

Commencement: 1 December 1983.

---

7. (1) Where all of the conditions set out in paragraph (2) below are satisfied, the provisions of regulation 3 shall not apply to:—

(a) an application for planning permission which is made following the withdrawal (before notice of decision was issued) of an application for planning permission made by or on behalf of the same applicant;

(b) an application for planning permission which is made following the refusal of planning permission (whether by the local planning authority or by the Secretary of State on appeal or following the reference of the application to him for determination) on an application for planning permission made by or on behalf of the same applicant;

(c) an application for planning permission which is made following the making of an appeal to the Secretary of State under section 37 of the 1971 Act (appeal in default of planning decision) in relation to an application for planning permission made by or on behalf of the same applicant;

(*d*) an application for approval of one or more reserved matters which is made following the withdrawal (before notice of decision was issued) of an application made by or on behalf of the same applicant for approval of details relating to the same reserved matters authorised by the same outline planning permission;

(*e*) an application for approval of one or more reserved matters which is made following the refusal (whether by the local planning authority or by the Secretary of State on appeal or following reference of the application to him for determination) to approve details relating to the same reserved matters which were submitted in an application made by or on behalf of the same applicant and in relation to the same outline planning permission; or

(*f*) an application for approval of one or more reserved matters which is made following the making of an appeal to the Secretary of State under section 37 of the 1971 Act in relation to an application made by or on behalf of the same applicant for approval of details relating to the same reserved matters authorised by the same outline planning permission.

(2) The conditions referred to in paragraph (1) above are:—

(*a*) that the application is made before the end of the period of 12 months following:—

   (i) the date when the earlier application was made, in the case of a withdrawn application;

   (ii) the date when (by virtue of the relevant provisions of the General Development Order) the period for the giving of notice of a decision on the earlier application expired, in the case of an application which is made following an appeal under section 37 of the 1971 Act; or

   (iii) the date of the refusal, in any other case;

(*b*) that the application relates—

   (i) in the case of an application for planning permission, to the same site as that to which the earlier application related, or to part of that site, and to no other land (save that in a case where additional land is included in the application solely for the purpose of providing a means of access to the site which differs from that proposed in the earlier application, that land shall be disregarded for the purposes of this paragraph); or

   (ii) in the case of an application for approval of reserved matters, to the same land as that to which the earlier application related, or to part of that land (and no other land);

(*c*) in the case of an application for planning permission, that the local planning authority to whom the application is made are satisfied that it relates to development of the same character or description as the development to which the earlier application related (and to no other development);

(*d*) in the case of an application for planning permission which is not made in outline, that the earlier application was also not made in outline;

(*e*) that the amount of the fee payable in respect of the earlier application was paid; and

(f) that no previous application has at any time been made by or on behalf of the same applicant which related to the site to which the earlier application related (or which related wholly or in part to any part of that site) and which was exempted from the provisions of regulation 3 by the provisions of the regulation. **[631]**

NOTES
Commencement: 1 December 1983.
1971 Act: Town and Country Planning Act 1971.

(New reg 7A inserted by SI 1987 No 101, reg 3, Sch 1, para 2. See Appendix.)

FEES FOR DEEMED APPLICATIONS

8. (1) [Subject to the provisions of paragraphs (3), (5) and (5A) below], a fee shall be paid to the Secretary of State in every case where an application for planning permission is deemed to have been made:—

(a) by virtue of the provisions of section 88B(3) of the 1971 Act (in consequence of an appeal under section 88 of the 1971 Act against an enforcement notice); or

(b) by virtue of the provisions of section 95(6) of the 1971 Act (in consequence of an appeal under section 95(2) against a decision of a local planning authority on an application for an established use certificate, or in consequence of an application for an established use certificate, which has been referred to the Secretary of State under section 95(1)).

(2) The amount of the fee payable in respect of a deemed application shall be calculated in accordance with the provisions of Schedule 1.

[(3) In the case of an application deemed to have been made by virtue of section 88B(3) of the 1971 Act, a fee shall be paid in respect of that deemed application by every person who has made a valid appeal against the relevant enforcement notice and whose appeal has not been withdrawn before the date on which the Secretary of State issues a notice under paragraph (4) below.

(4) The fee due in respect of a deemed application shall be paid at such time as the Secretary of State may in the particular case specify by notice in writing to the appellant or applicant.

(5) In the case of an application deemed to have been made by virtue of section 88B(3) of the 1971 Act, this regulation shall not apply where the person who has appealed against the relevant enforcement notice had, before the date when that notice was issued, made—

(a) an application to the local planning authority for planning permission for the development to which the relevant enforcement notice relates (and had paid to the authority the amount of the fee payable in respect of that application, in accordance with the requirements of regulation 3); or

(b) an appeal to the Secretary of State against the refusal of the local planning authority to grant such permission,

and that application or appeal had not been determined on or before the date when the relevant enforcement notice was issued.

(5A) In the case of an application deemed to have been made by virtue of section 95(6) of the 1971 Act, this regulation shall not apply in any case where—

(a) the relevant application or appeal has been withdrawn; or

(b) the applicant or appellant (as the case may be) has been informed that the Secretary of State declines jurisdiction on his application or appeal,

before the Secretary of State issues a notice under paragraph (4) above.]

(6) [The provisions of regulations 4, 5 and 5A] shall apply to a deemed application as they apply to an application for planning permission made to the local planning authority, with the following modifications:—

(a) references to the local planning authority to whom the application is made shall be construed as references to the Secretary of State; and

(b) references to the development to which the application relates shall be construed as references to the use of land or the operations (as the case may be) to which the relevant enforcement notice relates, or to the use of land in respect of which the relevant application for an established use certificate was made, as the case may be.

(7) In the case of an application deemed to have been made by virtue of section 88(B)(3) of the 1971 Act, in the event that the Secretary of State—

(a) declines jurisdiction on the relevant appeal under section 88 of the 1971 Act on the grounds that it does not comply with one or more of the requirements of subsections (1) to (3) of that section;

(b) dismisses the relevant appeal in exercise of the powers contained in section 88(6)(a) of the 1971 Act (on the grounds that the appellant has failed to comply with subsection (4) of that section); or

(c) allows the relevant appeal and quashes the relevant enforcement notice in exercise of the powers contained in section 88(6)(b) of the 1971 Act (on the grounds that the local planning authority have failed to comply with a requirement of any regulations made under subsection (5) of that section),

[the amount of any fee paid] in respect of the deemed application shall be refunded to the appellant by the Secretary of State.

(8) In the event of the relevant appeal under section 88 or 95, or the relevant application which has been referred to the Secretary of State under section 95(1), being withdrawn at any time before the date appointed for the holding of an inquiry into that appeal or application or, in the case of an appeal or application which is being dealt with by way of written representations, the date appointed for an established use certificate relates, [the amount of any fee paid] in respect of the deemed application shall be refunded to the appellant or the applicant (as the case may be) by the Secretary of State.

(9) The reference in paragraph (8) above to an appeal or application being dealt with by way of written representations shall be construed as a reference to an appeal or application in respect of which neither the appellant or applicant (as the case may be) nor the local planning authority has asked for an opportunity of appearing before and being heard by a person appointed by the Secretary of State and in respect of which no local inquiry is to be held under section 282 of the 1971 Act.

(10) In the case of an application which is deemed to have been made by virtue of section 88B(3) of the 1971 Act, [the amount of any fee paid] by an appellant shall be refunded to him by the Secretary of State in the event of the local planning authority withdrawing the relevant enforcement notice before it takes effect.

(11) Save in the case of an application deemed to have been made in connection with an enforcement notice alleging a breach of planning control by the use of land as a caravan site, the amount of the fee paid by an appellant in respect of an application deemed to have been made by virtue of section 88B(3) of the 1971 Act shall be refunded to him by the Secretary of State in the event of the Secretary of State allowing the appeal against the relevant enforcement notice on—

(a) any of the grounds (b) to (f) set out in section 88(2) of the 1971 Act; or

(b) the ground that the notice is invalid, or that it contains an informality, defect or error which cannot be corrected in pursuance of his powers under section 88A(2) of the 1971 Act.

(12) In the case of an application which is deemed to have been made by virtue of section 95(6) of the 1971 Act, the fee paid by the applicant or appellant (as the case may be) shall be refunded to him by the Secretary of State in the event of the Secretary of State granting him an established use certificate, or modifying the certificate granted by the local planning authority on the application, in pursuance of the provisions of section 95(1) or section 95(2)(a) of the 1971 Act [or determining that he has no power to grant planning permission under section 95(3) of the 1971 Act.] **[632]**

NOTES
 Commencement: 26 August 1985 (paras (3)-(5A)); 1 December 1983 (remainder).
 Paras (1), (6)-(8), (10), (12): amended by SI 1985 No 1182, reg 2.
 Paras (3)-(5A): substituted for existing paras (3)-(5) by SI 1985 No 1182, reg 2.
 Paras (2), (10), (12): amended by SI 1987 No 101, reg 3, Sch 1, para 3. See Appendix.
 New para (13) inserted by SI 1987 No 101, reg 3, Sch 1, para 3. See Appendix.
 1971 Act: Town and Country Planning Act 1971.

FEES FOR APPLICATIONS FOR CONSENT FOR ADVERTISEMENTS

9. (1) Where an application is made to a local planning authority under regulation 17 of the Town and Country Planning (Control of Advertisements) Regulations 1969 for consent for the display of an advertisement, a fee shall be paid to that authority in accordance with the following provisions of this regulation.

(2) The amount of the fee payable in respect of the application shall be calculated in accordance with the provisions of paragraphs (3) to (6) below and with the table in Schedule 2.

(3) Where the application relates to the display of advertisements on more than one site, the amount of the fee payable in respect of the application shall be the aggregate of the sums payable (calculated in accordance with the provisions of paragraph (4) below and with the table in Schedule 2) in respect of the display of advertisement on each such site.

(4) Where the application relates to the display of more than one advertisement on the same site, a single fee shall be payable in respect of all of the advertisements to be displayed on that site:

Provided that, where one or more of the advertisements on that site is within category 3 set out in the table in Schedule 2, the amount of the single fee referred to in this paragraph shall be the amount specified in the table in respect of category 3.

(5) Where the application relates to the display of advertisements on parking meters, litter bins or bus shelters within a specified area, the whole of

the area to which the application relates shall be treated as one site for the purposes of this regulation.

(6) Where the application is made by or on behalf of a parish council or by or on behalf of a community council, the amount of the fee payable in respect of the application shall be one-half of the amount calculated (in accordance with paragraphs (2) to (5) of this regulation and with the table in Schedule 2) to be appropriate to the display of the advertisement to which the application relates.

(7) The fee due in respect of an application shall be paid at the time when the application is made; and the amount of the fee shall be sent to the local planning authority with whom the application is lodged, together with the application.

(8) In the case of an application made in relation to a site within a National Park, the amount of fee shall be remitted to the county planning authority when the application is forwarded to that authority for determination.

(9) Where all of the conditions set out in paragraph (10) below are satisfied, this regulation shall not apply to:—

(a) an application which is made following the withdrawal (before notice of decision was issued) of an application made by or on behalf of the same person; or

(b) an application which is made following the refusal of consent for the display of advertisements issued on an application made by or on behalf of the same person.

(10) The conditions referred to in paragraph (9) above are:—

(a) that the application is made before the end of the period of 12 months following:—

(i) the date when the earlier application was made, in the case of a withdrawn application; or

(ii) the date of the refusal, in any other case;

(b) that the application relates to the same site as that to which the earlier application related, or to part of that site;

(c) that the local planning authority to whom the application is made are satisfied that it relates to an advertisement, or advertisements, of the same description as the advertisement or advertisements to which the earlier application related;

(d) that the amount of the fee payable in respect of the earlier application was paid; and

(e) that no previous application has at any time been made by or on behalf of the same applicant which related to—

(i) the same site as the site to which the earlier application related; and

(ii) an advertisement of the same description as the advertisement (or any of the advertisements) to which the earlier application related,

and which was exempted from the provisions of this regulation by paragraph (9) above. **[633]**

NOTES

Commencement: 1 December 1983.

Para (1): amended by SI 1987 No 101, reg 3, Sch 1, para 4. See Appendix.

Para (10): new sub-para (a)(ii) substituted by SI 1987 No 101, reg 3, Sch 1, para 4. See Appendix.

New paras (11) and (12) inserted by SI 1987 No 101, reg 3, Sch 1, para 4. See Appendix.

REVOCATION

10. The Town and Country Planning (Fees for Applications and Deemed Applications) Regulations 1981 and the Town and Country Planning (Fees for Applications and Deemed Applications) (Amendment) Regulations 1982 and hereby revoked:

Provided that, notwithstanding such revocation, the said regulations shall continue to apply to applications for planning permission deemed to have been made by virtue of section 88B(3) or section 95(6) of the 1971 Act in connection with an enforcement notice issued before the date when these regulations come into operation or an application for an established use certificate made before the date when these regulations come into operation, as the case may be. [634]

NOTES
Commencement: 1 December 1983.
1971 Act: Town and Country Planning Act 1971.

SCHEDULES

SCHEDULE 1
FEES IN RESPECT OF APPLICATIONS AND DEEMED APPLICATIONS FOR PLANNING PERMISSION
OR FOR APPROVAL OF RESERVED MATTERS

PART I
GENERAL PROVISIONS

1. Subject to the provisions of [paragraphs 1A to 8 below], the amount of the fee payable under regulation 3 or regulation 8 in respect of an application or deemed application shall be calculated in accordance with the table set out in Part II of this Schedule and (where applicable) the provisions of paragraphs 9 to 14 below: Provided that, in the case of an application for approval of reserved matters, references in this Schedule to the category of development to which an application relates shall be construed as references to the category of development authorised by the relevant outline planning permission.

[1A. Where an application or deemed application relates to the retention of buildings or works which were constructed or carried out without planning permission, or to the continuance of a use of land which was instituted without planning permission, the amount of the fee payable shall be calculated in accordance with the table set out in Part II of this Schedule as if the application or deemed application were one for planning permission to construct or carry out those buildings or works or to institute that use.]

2. Where an application or deemed application is made or deemed to be made by or on behalf of a parish council or by or on behalf of a community council, the amount of the fee payable in respect of the application shall be one-half of such amount as is calculated, in accordance with the table set out in Part II of this Schedule (and the following provisions of this Part of this Schedule), to be the amount appropriate to the application, having regard to the development to which it relates and the circumstances in which it is made.

3.—(1) Where an application or deemed application for planning permission is made or deemed to be made by or on behalf of a club, society or other organisation (including any persons administering a trust) which is not established or conducted for profit and whose objects are the provision of facilities for sport or recreation, and the conditions specified in subparagraph (2) below are satisfied, the amount of the fee payable in respect of the application or deemed application shall be [£53].

(2) The conditions referred to in subparagraph (1) above are—

(*a*) that the application or deemed application relates to one or both of the following categories of development:—

      (i) the making of a material change in the use of land to use as a playing field; or

     (ii) the carrying out of operations (other than the erection of a building containing floor space) for purposes ancillary to the use of land as a playing field,

    and to no other development; and

   (b) that the local planning authority with whom the application is lodged, or (in the case of a deemed application) the Secretary of State, is satisfied that the development is to be carried out on land which is, or is intended to be, occupied by the club, society or organisation and used wholly or mainly for the carrying out of its objects.

4.—(1) Where an application for planning permission or an application for approval of reserved matters is made not more than 28 days after the lodging with the local planning authority of an application for planning permission or, as the case may be, an application for approval of reserved matters—

   (a) made by or on behalf of the same applicant;
   (b) relating to the same site; and
   (c) relating to the same development or, in the case of an application for approval of reserved matters, relating to the same reserved matters in respect of the same building or buildings authorised by the relevant outline planning permission,

and a fee of the full amount (calculated in accordance with the provisions of the following paragraphs of this Part of this Schedule and the table set out in Part II of this Schedule) payable in respect of the category or categories of development to which the applications relate has been paid in respect of the later application shall, subject to the provisions of subparagraph (2) below, be one-quarter of the full amount paid in respect of the earlier application.

(2) The provisions of subparagraph (1) above allowing payment of a reduced fee shall apply only in respect of one application made by or on behalf of the same applicant in relation to the same development or in relation to the same reserved matters (as the case may be).

(3) The provisions of subparagraphs (1) and (2) above shall apply where more than one application for planning permission or for approval of reserved matters is made by or on behalf of the same applicant on the same day (provided that all of the conditions specified in subparagraph (1)(a) to (c) are fulfilled) as though one of those applications had been lodged earlier than the other application or applications.

[5. Where application is made for approval of one or more reserved matters and where all of the following conditions are met, namely:—

   (1) one or more applications for approval of reserved matters has or have previously been made under the same outline planning permission; and
   (2) that application was, or all of those applications were (as the case may be), made by or on behalf of the person who has made the present application; and
   (3) the amount of the fee paid in respect of that previous application, or the total amount of the fees paid in respect of those previous applications taken together (as the case may be), was not less than the amount which would have been payable had there been one application for approval of all of the matters reserved by the relevant outline planning permission (and in relation to the whole of the development authorised by that outline permission) and that application had been made on the day on which the present application was made,

the amount of the fee payable in respect of the application shall be the sum of £53.]

6.—(1) Where application for planning permission or for approval of reserved matters is made, or is deemed to be made, in respect of development which is to be carried out in, on, under or over land which is not wholly within the area of one district planning authority or London borough council (so that separate applications have to be made to two or more district planning authorities, or London borough councils, in whose areas parts of the land are situated), the total amount of the fees payable in respect of all the applications shall not exceed:—

(a) where the applications relate (wholly or partly) to a county matter, within the meaning of that term as defined in paragraph 32 of Schedule 16 to the Local Government Act 1972, and the land to which they relate is wholly within the area of a single county planning authority, the amount which, in accordance with the provisions of this Schedule, would be payable if an application were made to a single district planning authority or London borough council in respect of the whole development; or

(b) in any other case, one-and-a-half times the amount referred to in subparagraph (a) above.

(2) In a case to which subparagraph (1) above applies, the total amount payable in respect of all the applications (calculated in accordance with that subparagraph) shall be paid to the district planning authority or London borough council (as the case may be) in whose area the largest part of the land to which the application relates is situated.

7.—(1) Where—

(a) application for planning permission is made in respect of two or more alternative proposals for the development of the same land; or

(b) application for approval of reserved matters is made, pursuant to a condition on an outline planning permission, in respect of two or more alternative proposals for the carrying out of the development authorised by that permission,

and application is made in respect of all of the alternative proposals on the same date [and by or on behalf of the same applicant], the fees payable in respect of all such alternative proposals shall be calculated as provided in subparagraph (2) below.

(2) Separate calculations shall be made, in accordance with the provisions of this Schedule, of the amount of the fee appropriate to each of the alternative proposals; and the total amount of the fees payable in respect of all the alternative proposals shall be in the sum of the following amounts:—

(i) an amount equal to the highest of the amounts calculated in respect of each of the alternative proposals; and

(ii) an amount calculated by adding together the amounts of the fees appropriate to all of the alternative proposals, other than the amount referred to in subparagraph (i) above, and dividing that total by the figure of 2.

8. In the case of an application for planning permission which is deemed to have been made by virtue of section 95(6) of the 1971 Act, the amount of the fee payable shall be the sum of [£53].

9. Where, in respect of any category of development specified in the table set out in Part II of this Schedule, the amount of the fee is to be calculated by reference to the site area:—

(a) that area shall be taken as consisting of the area of land to which the application relates or, in the case of an application for planning permission which is deemed to have been made by virtue of section 88B(3) of the 1971 Act, the area of land to which the relevant enforcement notice relates; and

(b) where the area referred to in paragraph (a) above is not an exact multiple of the unit of measurement specified in respect of the relevant category of development, the fraction of a unit remaining after division of the total area by the unit of measurement shall be treated, for the purpose of calculating the fee payable in respect of the application or deemed application, as a complete unit.

10.—(1) In relation to development within any of the categories 2 to 4 specified in the table in Part II of this Schedule, the area of gross floor space to be created by the development shall be ascertained by external measurement of the floor space, whether or not it is to be bounded (wholly or partly) by external walls of a building.

(2) In relation to development within category 2 specified in the said table, where the

area of gross floor space to be created by the development exceeds 75 sq metres and is not an exact multiple of 75 sq metres, the area remaining after division of the total number of square metres of gross floor space by the figure of 75 shall be treated as being 75 sq metres.

(3) In relation to development within category 3 specified in the said table, where the area of gross floor space exceeds 540 sq metres and the amount of the excess is not an exact multiple of 75 sq metres, the area remaining after division of the number of square metres of that excess area of gross floor space by the figure of 75 shall be treated as being 75 sq metres.

11.—(1) Where an application or a deemed application relates to development consisting of or including the erection of a building or buildings which it is proposed to use in part for residential purposes and in part for other purposes, the provisions of the following subparagraph shall apply for the purpose of calculating the amount of the fee payable in respect of the application or deemed application.

(2) An assessment shall be made of the total amount of gross floor space which is to be created by the development and which it is proposed to use for purposes other than residential purposes (hereafter in this paragraph referred to as "the non-residential floor space"), and the sum payable in respect of the non-residential floor space to be created by the development (calculated in accordance with the table in Part II of this Schedule) shall be added to the sum payable in respect of the number of dwellinghouses to be created by the development (calculated in accordance with the table in Part II of this Schedule):

Provided that, where any of the buildings is to contain floor space which it is proposed to use for the purposes of providing common access or common services or facilities for persons occupying or using that building for residential purposes and for persons occupying or using it for non-residential purposes (such floor space being hereafter referred to as "common floor space"), the amount of non-residential floor space shall be assessed, in relation to that building as including such proportion of the common floor space as the amount of non-residential floor space in the building bears to the total amount of gross floor space in the building to be created by the development.

12. Where an application or deemed application relates to development which is within more than one of the categories specified in the table set out in Part II of this Schedule—

    (*a*) an amount shall be calculated, in accordance with the provisions of this Schedule, in respect of the development which is within each such category (subject to the provisions of paragraph 11 above, where the development to which the application or deemed application relates includes a building or buildings to which subparagraph (1) of that paragraph applies); and

    (*b*) the highest of the amounts so calculated shall be taken as the amount of the fee payable in respect of all of the development to which the application or deemed application relates.

13. In the case of an application for planning permission which is deemed to have been made by virtue of section 88B(3) of the 1971 Act where the breach (or breaches) of planning control alleged in the relevant enforcement notice does not (or do not) relate solely to one use of land or the carrying out of one type of operation, paragraph 12 above shall not apply; but

    (*a*) an amount shall be calculated, in accordance with the provisions of this Schedule, in respect of each use of land or type of operation to which the relevant enforcement notice relates (subject to the provisions of paragraph 11 above, where the relevant enforcement notice relates to a building or buildings to which subparagraph (1) of that paragraph applies); and

    (*b*) the highest of the amounts so calculated shall be taken as the amount of the fee payable in respect of the deemed application.

14. In the case of an application for planning permission which is deemed to have been made by virtue of section 88B(3) of the 1971 Act, references in this Schedule to the development to which an application relates shall be construed as references to the use

of land or the operations (as the case may be) to which the relevant enforcement notice relates, references to the amount of floor space or the number of dwellinghouses to be created by the development shall be construed as references to the amount of floor space or the number of dwellinghouses to which that enforcement notice relates, and references to the purposes for which it is proposed that floor space be used shall be construed as references to the purposes for which floor space was stated to be used in the enforcement notice.   **[635]**

NOTES

Commencement: 26 August 1985 (paras 1A, 5); 1 December 1983 (remainder).

Paras 1, 3, 7, 8: amended by SI 1985 No 1182, reg 2.

Para 1A: added by SI 1985 No 1182, reg 2.

Para 5: substituted by SI 1985 No 1182, reg 2; new paras 5 and 5A substituted for para 5 above by SI 1987 No 101, reg 3, Sch 1, para 5. See Appendix.

Para 6: new paras 6 and 6A substituted for para 6 above by SI 1987 No 101, reg 3, Sch 1, para 6. See Appendix.

Paras 3, 5, 8: £53: amended by SI 1987 No 101, reg 2(1), (2). See Appendix.

1971 Act: Town and Country Planning Act 1971.

PART II

SCALE OF FEES

Category of development	Fee payable

I. Operations

1. The erection of dwelling-houses (other than development within category 6 below).

(*a*) Where the application is for outline planning permission, £47 for each 0.1 hectare of the site area, subject to a maximum of £1,175;

(*b*) in other cases, £47 for each dwelling-house to be created by the development, subject to a maximum of £2,350.

2. The erection of buildings (other than dwellinghouses, buildings coming within category 3, category 4 or category 7 or buildings in the nature of plant or machinery).

(*a*) Where the application is for outline planning permission, £47 for each 0.1 hectare of the site area, subject to a maximum of £1,175;

(*b*) in other cases:—

(i) where no floor space is to be created by the development, £24;

(ii) where the area of gross floor space to be created by the development does not exceed 40 sq metres, £24;

(iii) where the area of gross floor space to be created by the development exceeds 40 sq metres but does not exceed 75 sq metres, £47; and

(iv) where the area of gross floor space to be created by the development exceeds 75 sq metres, £47 for each 75 sq metres, subject to a maximum of £2,350.

3. The erection, on land used for the purposes of agriculture, of buildings (other than glasshouses) to be used for agricultural purposes.

(*a*) Where the application is for outline planning permission, £47 for each 0.1 hectare of the site area, subject to a maximum of £1,175;

(*b*) in other cases:—

(i) where the area of gross floor space to be created by the development does not exceed 465 sq metres, nil;

(ii) where the area of gross floor space to be created by the development exceeds 465 sq metres but does not exceed 540 sq metres, £47;

(iii) where the area of gross floor space to be created by the development exceeds 540 sq metres, £47 for the first 540 sq metres and £47 for each 75 sq metres in excess of that figure, subject to a maximum of £2,350.

4. The erection of glasshouses on land used for the purposes of agriculture.

(*a*) Where the area of gross floor space to be created by the development does not exceed 465 sq metres, nil;

(*b*) where the area of gross floor space to be created by the development exceeds 465 sq metres, £280.

SCALE OF FEES *(continued)*

Category of development	Fee payable
I. Operations **5.** The erection, alteration or replacement of plant or machinery.	£47 for each 0.1 hectare of the site area, subject to a maximum of £2,350.
6. The enlargement, improvement or other alteration of existing dwellinghouses.	(*a*) Where the application relates to one dwellinghouse, £24; (*b*) where the application relates to 2 or more dwellinghouses, £47.
7.(*a*) The carrying out of operations (including the erection of a building) within the curtilage of an existing dwellinghouse, for purposes ancillary to the enjoyment of the dwellinghouse as such, or the erection or construction of gates, fences, walls or other means of enclosure along a boundary of the curtilage of an existing dwellinghouse; or (*b*) the construction of car parks, service roads and other means of access on land used for the purposes of a single undertaking, where the development is required for a purpose incidental to the existing use of the land.	£24.
8. The carrying out of any operations not coming within any of the above categories.	£24 for each 0.1 hectare of the site area, subject to a maximum of:— (*a*) in the case of operations for the winning and working of minerals, £3,600; (*b*) in other cases, £240.
II. Uses of Land **9.** The change of use of a building to use as one or more separate dwellinghouses.	(*a*) Where the change is from a previous use as a single dwellinghouse to use as two or more single dwellinghouses, £47 for each additional dwellinghouse to be created by the development, subject to a maximum of £2,350; (*b*) in other cases, £47 for each dwellinghouse to be created by the development, subject to a maximum of £2,350.
10.(*a*) The use of land for the disposal of refuse or waste materials or for the deposit of material remaining after minerals have been extracted from land; or (*b*) the use of land for the storage of minerals in the open.	£24 for each 0.1 hectare of the site area, subject to a maximum of £3,600.

SCALE OF FEES *(continued)*

Category of development	Fee payable

11. Uses of Land
　11.(*a*) The making of a material　　　£47.
change in the use of a building or
land (other than a material change of
use coming within any of the above
categories); or

(*b*) the continuance of a
use of land, or the retention of
buildings or works on land, without
compliance with a condition subject
to which a previous planning
permission has been granted (including
a condition requiring the discontinuance
of the use or the removal of the
building or works at the end of a
specified period).　　　　　　　　　　　　　　　　　**[636]**

NOTES
　Commencement: 26 August 1985.
　Substituted by SI 1985 No 1182, reg 2, Schedule.
　Amended by SI 1987 No 101, reg 2(1), (3). See Appendix.
　New item 7A inserted by SI 1987 No 101, reg 3, Sch 1, para 7. See Appendix.
　New Part II substituted in relation to fees due on or after 1 July 1987 by SI 1987 No 101, reg 4,
Sch 2. See Appendix.

SCHEDULE 2

SCALE OF FEES IN RESPECT OF APPLICATIONS FOR CONSENT TO DISPLAY ADVERTISEMENT

Category of advertisement	*Fee payable*

　1. Advertisement displayed on business premises, on the forecourt　　£12.
of business premises or on other land within the curtilage of business
premises, wholly with reference to all or any of the following matters:—

> (*a*) the nature of the business or other activity carried on on the
> premises;
> (*b*) the goods sold or the services provided on the premises; or
> (*c*) the name and qualifications of the person carrying on such
> business or activity or supplying such goods or services.

　2. Advertisements for the purpose of directing members of the public　　£12.
to, or otherwise drawing attention to the existence of, business premises
which are in the same locality as the site on which the advertisement is
to be displayed but which are not visible from that site.

　3. All other advertisements.　　　　　　　　　　　　　　　　　£47.

　　　　　　　　　　　　　　　　　　　　　　　　　　　　　　[637]

NOTES
　Commencement: 1 December 1983.
　Amended by SI 1985 No 1182, reg 2.
　Amended by SI 1987 No 101, reg 2(1), (4). See Appendix.

TOWN AND COUNTRY PLANNING (CONTROL OF ADVERTISEMENTS) REGULATIONS 1984
(SI 1984 No 421)

NOTES
Made: 23 March 1984.

ARRANGEMENT OF REGULATIONS

PART I

CITATION, COMMENCEMENT, INTERPRETATION, APPLICATION AND REVOCATION

PART II

GENERAL PROVISIONS

PART III

ADVERTISEMENTS WHICH MAY BE DISPLAYED WITHOUT EXPRESS CONSENT

PART IV

APPLICATIONS FOR EXPRESS CONSENT

PART V

SPECIAL CASE

PART I

CITATION, COMMENCEMENT, INTERPRETATION, APPLICATION AND REVOCATION

1. Citation and Commencement

These Regulations may be cited as the Town and Country Planning (Control of Advertisements) Regulations 1984 and shall come into operation on 2nd May 1984.   [638]

2. Interpretation

(1) In these Regulations—

"the Act" means the Town and Country Planning Act 1971;

"advertisement" means any word, letter, model, sign, placard, board, notice, device or representation, whether illuminated or not, in the nature of, and employed wholly or partly for the purposes of, advertisement, announcement or direction (excluding any such thing employed wholly as a memorial or as a railway signal), and (without prejudice to the preceding provisions of this definition) includes any hoarding or similar structure or any balloon used, or adapted for use, for the display of advertisements, and references to the display of advertisements shall be construed accordingly;

"advertiser" means a person who himself, or by his servant or agent, undertakes or maintains the display of an advertisement;

"area of outstanding natural beauty" means an area designated as such by an order made under section 87 of the National Parks and Access to the Countryside Act 1949;

"area of special control" means an area defined by an order made under regulation 26 as an area of special control in respect of the display of advertisements;

"balloon" means a tethered balloon or similar object;

"building" includes any structure or erection, and any part of a building as so defined;

"business premises" has the meaning assigned to it by regulation 14(3);

"the Common Council" means the Common Council of the City of London;

"conservation area" means an area designated under section 277 of the Act;

"development plan" means:—

(*a*) a development plan within the meaning of section 20 of the Act;
(*b*) the development plan approved under Part I of Schedule 5 to the Act, or under any enactment which is re-enacted in that Schedule; or
(*c*) an old development plan within the meaning of Schedule 7 to the Act;

"illuminated advertisement" means an advertisement which is designed or adapted to be illuminated by artificial lighting, directly or by reflection, and which is so illuminated for the purposes of advertisement, announcement or direction at any time after the date on which these Regulations come into operation;

"land" includes buildings, and land covered with water;

"local authority" means the council of a county or district, the Common Council, the council of a London borough and any other authority (except the Receiver for the Metropolitan Police District) who are a local authority within the meaning of the Local Loans Act 1875, and includes any drainage board and any joint board or joint committee if all the constituent authorities are such local authorities as aforesaid;

"National Park" has the meaning assigned to it by section 5 of the National Parks and Access to the Countryside Act 1949;

"site", in relation to an advertisement, means any land, or any building other than an advertisement as herein defined, on which an advertisement is displayed;

"specified classes" means the classes of advertisements specified in regulation 14(1);

"standard conditions" means the standard conditions set out in Schedule 1;

"statutory undertakers" means persons authorised by any enactment to carry on any railway, light railway, tramway, road transport, water transport, canal, inland navigation, dock, harbour, pier or lighthouse undertaking, or any undertaking for the supply of electricity, gas, hydraulic power or water, and "statutory undertaking" shall be construed accordingly, and, in relation to the display of advertisements of descriptions specified in Class I in regulation 14(1), shall be deemed to include any undertaking carried on by the National Coal Board for the winning or supply of coal, and any undertaking carried on by the British Airports Authority, by the Civil Aviation Authority, by the Post Office or by British Telecommunications for the purposes of their respective functions;

"urban development area" means an area designated as such by virtue of an order made under section 134 of the Local Government, Planning and Land Act 1980.

(2) Subject to paragraph (2A) below, any reference in these regulations to a local planning authority shall, in respect of land in an area outside London and the metropolitan counties, be construed as a reference to the district planning authority for that area or, where such land is within a National Park, to the county planning authority for that area.

(2A) In respect of land in an urban development area, any reference in these regulations to a local planning authority other than any such reference in regulation 26(6) shall be construed as a reference to the urban development corporation for the area if that corporation is a local planning authority by virtue of an order made under section 149 of the Local Government, Planning and Land Act 1980 and the powers relating to the control of advertisements contained in sections 63 and 109 of the Act are vested in it.

(3) Any reference in these Regulations to the person displaying an advertisement shall be construed as a reference to the advertiser, and shall be deemed to include —

(a) the owner and occupier of the land on which the advertisement is displayed; and

(b) any person to whose goods, trade, business or other concerns publicity is given by the advertisement.

(4) Subject to the provisions of regulation 3(3) and (4), references in these Regulations to the land, the building, the site or premises on which the advertisement is displayed shall be construed, in the case of an advertisement which is displayed on, or which consists of, a balloon, as references to the land, the building, the site or other premises (as the case may be) to which the balloon is attached.

(5) A regulation or Schedule referred to only by number in these Regulations means the regulation or Schedule so numbered in these Regulations. **[639]**

NOTES
> Para 1: definition "local authority" revoked in part by SI 1986 No 443, reg 2, Sch 1.
> Para (2), (2A): substituted for existing para (2) by SI 1986 No 443, reg 2, Sch 1.

3. Application

(1) Subject to the provisions of paragraph (3) of this regulation, these Regulations shall apply to the display on sites in England and Wales of all advertisements, except any advertisement—

> (a) displayed on enclosed land, and not readily visible from land outside that enclosure or from any part of any public right of way over such enclosure or from any land on such enclosure to which the public have a right of access;
> (b) displayed within a building, other than an advertisement of a description specified in regulation 12;
> (c) displayed on or in a vehicle;
> (d) displayed on, or which consists of, a balloon flown at a height of more than 60 metres above ground level;
> (e) incorporated in, and forming part of, the fabric of a building, other than a building used principally for the display of such advertisements or a hoarding or similar structure;
> (f) displayed on an article for sale or on the package or other container in which an article is sold, or displayed on the pump, dispenser or other container from which an article is sold, being an advertisement wholly with reference to the article for sale, which is not an illuminated advertisement and does not exceed 0·1 square metre in area.

(2) For the purposes of paragraph (1) of this regulation—

> (a) "article" includes a gas or liquid;
> (b) the expression "enclosed land" means land which is wholly or for the most part enclosed within a hedge, fence, or wall or similar screen or structure, and shall be deemed to include any railway station (and its yards) or bus station, together with their forecourts, whether enclosed or not; but shall not include any public park, public garden or other land held for the use or enjoyment of the public, or (save as herein specified) any enclosed railway land normally used for the carriage of passengers or goods by rail;
> (c) "vehicle" means a vehicle normally employed as a moving vehicle on any highway or railway, or a vessel normally employed as a moving vessel on any inland waterway, but shall not include any such vehicle or vessel during any period when it is used primarily for the display of advertisements;
> (d) no advertisement shall be deemed to be displayed within a building unless there is access to the advertisement from inside the building;
> (e) no advertisement shall be deemed to form part of the fabric of a building by reason only of being affixed to, or painted on, the building.

(3) These Regulations shall not apply to the display of an advertisement on, or which consists of, a balloon on a site (as defined in paragraph (4) of this regulation) which is not within an area of special control, a conservation area, a National Park or an area of outstanding natural beauty, so long as the following conditions are complied with:—

  (*a*) not more than one such advertisement shall be displayed at any one time on the site; and

  (*b*) the site shall not be used for the display of such advertisements on more than 10 days in total in any one calendar year (taking into account all occasions on which such an advertisement is displayed on any part of the site by any person for any purpose).

(4) For the purposes of paragraph (3) of this regulation, "site" means—

  (*a*) in a case where the advertisement is being displayed by a person (other than the occupier of the land) who is using or proposing to use the land, building or other premises to which the balloon is attached for a particular activity (other than the display of advertisements) for a temporary period only, the whole of the land, building or other premises used or to be used by that person for the carrying on of that activity; or

  (*b*) in any other case, the land, building or other premises to which the balloon is attached and all land, buildings or other premises normally occupied together therewith.   [640]

4. Revocation

The Regulations specified in Schedule 6 are hereby revoked:

Provided that where, immediately before the coming into operation of these Regulations, an advertisement was being displayed with consent deemed to be granted under the Town and Country Planning (Control of Advertisements) Regulations 1960 (by virtue of regulation 4 of the Town and Country Planning (Control of Advertisements) Regulations 1969) that advertisement shall be treated, for the purposes of regulations 14 and 16 of these Regulations, as being an advertisement of one of the specified classes which is being displayed in accordance with the provisions of regulation 14.   [641]

PART II

GENERAL PROVISIONS

5. Control of advertisements to be exercised in the interests of amenity and public safety

(1) The powers conferred by these Regulations with respect to the grant or refusal of consent for the display of advertisements, the revocation or modification of such consent, and the discontinuance of the display of advertisements with consent deemed to be granted, shall be exercisable only in the interests of amenity and public safety.

(2) When exercising such powers a local planning authority—

  (*a*) shall, in the interests of amenity, have regard to the suitability of the use of a site for the display of advertisements in the light of the general characteristics of the locality, including the presence therein of any feature of historic, architectural, cultural or similar interest; and when assessing the general characteristics of a locality the authority may disregard any advertisements being displayed therein;

(b) shall, in the interests of public safety, have regard to the safety of persons who may use any road, railway, waterway (including any coastal waters), dock, harbour or airfield affected or likely to be affected by any display of advertisements; and shall in particular consider whether any such display is likely to obscure, or hinder the ready interpretation of, any road traffic sign, railway signal, or aid to navigation by water or air;

but without prejudice to their power to have regard to any other material factor.

(3) In determining an application for consent for the display of advertisements, or considering whether to make an order revoking or modifying a consent, the local planning authority may have regard to any material change in circumstances likely to occur within the period for which the consent is required or granted.

(4) Subject to the provisions of these Regulations, express consent for the display of advertisements shall not contain any limitation or restriction relating to any particular subject matter or class of subject matter or to the content or design of any subject matter to be displayed, but shall take effect as consent to the use of the site for the purpose of displaying advertisements in the manner authorised by the consent whether by the erection of structures on the site or otherwise, as the case may be:

Provided that nothing in this paragraph shall affect the duty of the local planning authority, when dealing with an application for consent for the display of a particular advertisement, to have regard to the effect on amenity and public safety of the display of that advertisement.   **[642]**

6. Consent required for the display of advertisements

(1) No advertisement may be displayed without consent granted by the local planning authority or by the Secretary of State on an application in that behalf (referred to in these Regulations as "express consent"), or deemed to be granted under paragraph (2) below.

(2) Consent shall be deemed to be granted for the display of any advertisement displayed in accordance with any provision of these Regulations whereby advertisements of that description may be displayed without express consent; and where the display of such advertisements is allowed subject to the power of the local planning authority to require the discontinuance of the display under regulation 16, the consent so deemed to be granted shall be consent limited until such time as a notice served under regulation 16 takes effect; without prejudice however to the provisions of regulation 27 as respects the removal of advertisements which are being displayed in an area of special control, a conservation area, a National Park or an area of outstanding natural beauty.

(3) In so far as the nature of the consent permits, consent for the display of advertisements shall enure for the benefit of the site to which the consent relates and of all persons for the time being interested in that site; without prejudice however to the provisions of these Regulations as respects the revocation or modification of an express consent.

(4) Save where an advertisement of the description specified in regulation 9(1)(b) is required to be displayed, it shall be a condition (whether expressly imposed or not) of every consent granted by or under these Regulations that

before any advertisement is displayed on a site in pursuance of the consent the permission of the owner of that site or other person entitled to grant permission in relation thereto shall be obtained. **[643]**

7. The standard conditions

Without prejudice to the power of the local planning authority to impose additional conditions upon a grant of consent under these Regulations, the standard conditions set out in Schedule 1 shall, subject to the provisions of these Regulations, apply to the display of all advertisements; and in the case of advertisements being displayed with consent deemed to be granted by these Regulations or granted under regulation 23, the conditions set out in Part II of that Schedule shall also apply. **[644]**

8. Contravention of Regulations

A person displaying an advertisement in contravention of these Regulations shall be liable on summary conviction of an offence under section 109(2) of the Act to a fine of £200 and, in the case of a continuing offence, £20 for each day during which the offence continues after conviction. **[645]**

PART III

ADVERTISEMENTS WHICH MAY BE DISPLAYED WITHOUT EXPRESS CONSENT

9. Election notices, statutory advertisements and traffic signs

(1) Advertisements of the following descriptions may be displayed without express consent—

    (*a*) any advertisement relating specifically to a pending parliamentary, European Assembly or local government election;

    (*b*) advertisements required to be displayed by an enactment for the time being in force, or by Standing Orders of either House of Parliament, including (but without prejudice to the generality hereof) advertisements the display of which is so required as a condition of the valid exercise of any other power, or proper performance of any function, given or imposed by an enactment;

    (*c*) advertisements which are traffic signs employed wholly for the control, guidance or safety of traffic, and displayed by, or with permission of, a local highway, traffic or police authority in accordance with regulations and general directions made by the Secretary of State or in accordance with an authorisation and any relevant direction given by him.

(2) Consent deemed to be granted by virtue of these Regulations for the display of advertisements of the foregoing descriptions shall be subject to the following conditions in addition to the standard conditions—

    (*a*) where advertisements of the description specified in paragraph (1)(*b*) above could, apart from this regulation, be displayed pursuant to regulation 14 as advertisements of a specified class they shall conform with any provision of that regulation as respects size, number or height in relation to the display of advertisements of that class, and otherwise shall not exceed in those respects what is necessary to achieve the purpose for which the display is required; without prejudice, however, to the express requirements with regard to size, number or height as aforesaid of any enactment or Standing Orders under which such advertisements are displayed;

(b) an advertisement of the description specified in paragraph (1)(a) above shall be removed within fourteen days after the close of the poll in the election to which the advertisement relates; and any other advertisement displayed for a temporary purpose in accordance with this regulation shall be removed as soon as may be after the expiry of the period during which such advertisement is required or authorised to be displayed, or, if no such period is specified, shall be removed within a reasonable time after the purpose for which such advertisement was required or authorised to be displayed is satisfied.

(3) With respect to the display of advertisements of the description specified in paragraph (1)(a) above standard condition 1 in Schedule 1 shall not apply.

[646]

10. Display of advertisements by local planning authorities

(1) Subject to paragraph (2) of this regulation, a local planning authority may without express consent display advertisements on land in their area; but shall not display in an area of special control any advertisement for the display of which they could not, by virtue of regulation 27, grant express consent.

(2) The Secretary of State shall have power to serve a notice requiring the discontinuance of the display of any advertisement for which consent is deemed to be granted under paragraph (1) of this regulation, and regulation 16 shall apply to such a notice as though it were a discontinuance notice served by a local planning authority under that regulation.   **[647]**

11. Advertisements on sites used for the display of advertisements on 1st August 1948

(1) Subject to paragraph (3) below, where a site was being used for the display of advertisements on 1st August 1948 the site may continue to be so used after the date of the coming into operation of these Regulations without express consent, subject to the power of the local planning authority to require the discontinuance of the use of that site under regulation 16.

(2) Consent deemed to be granted for the continued use of a site for the display of advertisements pursuant to paragraph (1) above shall be subject to the following conditions and limitations—

(a) there shall be no substantial increase in the extent, or substantial alteration in the manner, of the use of the site as it was used for the display of advertisements on 1st August 1948;

(b) where a building or structure on which advertisements were being displayed on 1st August 1948 is removed (whether in pursuance of a requirement under any enactment or otherwise) the consent deemed to be granted under this regulation shall not extend to the erection of any building or structure on which to continue the display of such advertisements.

(3) Nothing in this regulation shall restrict the exercise by a local planning authority of any power hereinafter conferred on them to decide any application which may be made to them in respect of the display of advertisements on a site to which paragraph (1) above applies or to take action in respect of any contravention of these Regulations.   **[648]**

12. Control of advertisements displayed within buildings

(1) The display of an advertisement within a building so as to be visible from outside that building shall be subject to these Regulations if the advertisement is—

(a) an illuminated advertisement; or

(b) an advertisement displayed within any building used principally for the display of advertisements; or

(c) an advertisement any part of which is within a distance of one metre from any external door, window, or other opening through which the advertisement is visible from outside the building.

(2) Any advertisement the display of which is made subject to these Regulations by paragraph (1) above may be displayed without express consent, subject, except where the advertisement is of a description specified in regulation 9, to the power of the local planning authority to require the discontinuance of the display under regulation 16.

(3) For the purpose of the exercise of any of the powers conferred by these Regulations, the display of any advertisement made subject to these Regulations by paragraph (1) above shall be treated as if it were the display in accordance with regulation 14 of an advertisement of a specified class. **[649]**

13. Display of advertisements after the expiration of express consent

(1) Except where the local planning authority, when granting express consent, impose a condition to the contrary, or where the renewal of consent is applied for and is refused, advertisements displayed with express consent granted under these Regulations may on the expiration of the consent continue to be displayed without express consent, subject to the power of the local planning authority to require the discontinuance of the display under regulation 16.

(2) Consent deemed by virtue of regulation 6(2) to be granted in respect of the continuance of such display shall be subject to the like conditions as those to which the immediately preceding express consent was subject, and, unless previously brought to an end under these Regulations, shall expire when the site ceases to be used for such display. **[650]**

14. The specified classes

(1) Advertisements of the following classes may be displayed without express consent, subject to the provisions of this regulation and to the power of the local planning authority to require the discontinuance of the display under regulation 16 —

CLASS I—Functional advertisements of local authorities, statutory undertakers and public transport undertakers.

Advertisements employed wholly for the purposes of announcement or direction in relation to any of the functions of a local authority or to the operation of a statutory undertaking or of a public transport undertaking engaged in the carriage of passengers in a manner similar to that of a statutory undertaking, being advertisements which are reasonably required to be displayed in the manner in which they are displayed in order to secure the safe or efficient performance of those functions, or operation of that undertaking, and which cannot be displayed as such, or in such a manner, under the provisions of this regulation relating to advertisements of any other of the specified classes.

CLASS II—Miscellaneous advertisements relating to premises on which they are displayed.

(a) Advertisements not exceeding 0·2 square metre in area displayed for the purpose of identification, direction or warning with respect to the land or buildings on which they are displayed.

(b) Advertisements relating to any person, partnership or company separately carrying on a profession, business or trade at the premises where they are displayed; limited to one advertisement, not exceeding 0·3 square metre in area, in respect of each such person, partnership or company, or, in the case of premises with entrances on different road frontages, one such advertisement at each of two such entrances.

(c) Advertisements relating to any institution of a religious, educational, cultural, recreational or medical or similar character, or to any hotel, inn or public house, block of flats, club, boarding house or hostel at the premises where they are displayed; limited to one advertisement, not exceeding 1·2 square metres in area, in respect of each such premises or, in the case of premises with entrances on different road frontages, two such advertisements displayed on different road frontages of the premises.

CLASS III—Certain advertisements of a temporary nature.

(a) Advertisements relating to the sale or letting of the land on which they are displayed; limited, in respect of each such sale or letting, to one advertisement consisting of a board (whether or not attached to a building) not exceeding 2 square metres in area, or of two conjoined boards, together not exceeding 2·3 square metres in area; no such advertisement, when displayed on a building, to project further than one metre from the face of the building.

(b) Advertisements announcing sales of goods or livestock, and displayed on the land where the goods or livestock are situated or where the sales are held, not being land which is normally used, whether at regular intervals or otherwise, for the purposes of holding such sales; limited to one advertisement not exceeding 1·2 square metres in area at each site where such advertisements may be displayed.

(c) Advertisements relating to the carrying out of building or similar work on the land on which they are displayed, not being land which is normally used, whether at regular intervals or otherwise, for the purpose of carrying out such work; limited to one advertisement (on each road frontage of the land) in respect of each separate development project, being an advertisement not exceeding in aggregate, in the case of an advertisement referring to one person, 2 square metres, or, in the case of an advertisement referring to more than one person, 2 square metres together with an additional 0·4 square metre in respect of each additional person referred to, and, in either case, together with one-fifth of the area permitted above for the name, if any, of the particular development project:

Provided that—

(i) where such an advertisement is displayed more than 10 metres from a highway, there shall be substituted for the references to 2 square metres references to 3 square metres, and for the reference to 0·4 square metre a reference to 1·6 square metres;

(ii) any person carrying out such work may, if an advertisement displayed in accordance with the preceding provisions of this paragraph does not refer to him, display a separate advertisement which does so, not exceeding 0·5 square metre in area, for a period not exceeding three months, on each road frontage of the land.

(*d*) Advertisements announcing any local event of a religious, educational, cultural, political, social or recreational character, and advertisements relating to any temporary matter in connection with an event or local activity of such a character, not in either case being an event or local activity promoted or carried on for commercial purposes; limited to a display of advertisements occupying an area not exceeding a total of 0·6 square metre on any site.

(*e*) Advertisements relating to any demonstration of agricultural methods or processes on the land on which they are displayed; limited, in respect of each such demonstration, to a display of advertisements occupying an area not exceeding a total of 1·2 square metres, no one of which exceeds 0·4 square metre in area, the maximum period of display for any demonstration to be six months in any period of twelve months.

CLASS IV—Advertisements on business premises.

Advertisements displayed on business premises wholly with reference to all or any of the following matters, namely, the business or other activity carried on, the goods sold or services provided, and the name and qualifications of the person carrying on such business or activity, or supplying such goods or services, on those premises:

Provided that—

(*a*) no such advertisement may be displayed on the wall of a shop, unless the wall contains a shop window;

(*b*) no such advertisement may be displayed so that the highest part of the advertisement is above the level of the bottom of any first-floor window in the wall on which it is displayed;

(*c*) the space which may be occupied by such advertisements on any external face of a building in an area of special control shall not exceed one-tenth of the overall area of that face up to a height of 3·6 metres from ground level; and the area occupied by any such advertisement shall, notwithstanding that it is displayed in some other manner, be computed as if the advertisement as a whole were displayed flat against the face of the building.

CLASS V—Advertisements on the forecourts of business premises.

Advertisements displayed on any forecourt of business premises wholly with reference to all or any of the matters specified in Class IV above; limited, as respects the aggregate area of the advertisements displayed under this class on any such forecourt, to 4·5 square metres:

Provided that a building with a forecourt on two or more frontages shall be treated as having a separate forecourt on each of those frontages.

CLASS VI—Flag advertisements.

An advertisement in the form of a flag which is attached to a single flagstaff fixed in an upright position on the roof of a building, and which bears no inscription or emblem other than the name or device of a person or persons occupying the building.

CLASS VII—Certain advertisements displayed on hoardings.

Advertisements on hoardings enclosing, either wholly or in part, land on which building operations are taking or are about to take place and which is allocated in any development plan for the time being in force primarily for use for commercial, industrial or business purposes:

Provided that—

    (a) no such advertisements shall be displayed on hoardings enclosing land situated within a conservation area, an area of special control, a National Park or an area of outstanding natural beauty; and

    (b) the display of such advertisements shall be subject to the limitations specified in Schedule 2, but without prejudice to the provisions of paragraph (2) of this regulation.

(2) Consent deemed to be granted by virtue of these Regulations for the display of advertisements of the foregoing classes shall be subject to the following conditions in addition to the standard conditions—

    (a) no such advertisement, other than an advertisement of Class I, shall contain letters, figures, symbols, emblems or devices of a height exceeding 0·75 metre or, in an area of special control, 0·3 metre;

    (b) no such advertisement, other than an advertisement of Class I or Class VI, shall be displayed so that the highest part of the advertisement is above 4·6 metres from ground level, or, in an area of special control, above 3·6 metres from ground level:

        Provided, in the case of an advertisement of Class III(a) relating to the sale or letting of part of a building, that where that part of the building is above the height limit specified above, the advertisement shall be displayed on the building at the lowest level above the specified limit at which it is reasonably practicable to display the advertisement;

    (c) no such advertisement shall be illuminated except as follows—

        (i) an advertisement of Class I may be illuminated in a manner reasonably required to achieve the purpose of the advertisement;

        (ii) advertisements of Class II or Class IV may be illuminated for the purpose of indicating that medical or similar services or supplies are available at the premises on which they are displayed, provided that they are illuminated in a manner reasonably required for that purpose;

    (d) no advertisement of Class III relating to a sale or other matter which is due to begin or take place on a specified date shall be displayed earlier than twenty-eight days before that date and every advertisement of that class shall be removed within fourteen days after the conclusion of the event or other matter to which it relates;

    (e) an advertisement of Class III relating to the carrying out on land of building or similar works may be displayed only while such works are in progress.

(3) In this regulation:—

"business premises" means any building normally used for the purpose of carrying on therein any professional, commercial or industrial undertaking, or any building (other than an institution in respect of which advertisements of Class II(c) may be displayed) normally used for the purpose of providing therein services to members of the public or of any association, and includes public restaurants, licensed premises and places of public entertainment; but—

(*a*) in the case of any building normally used only partly for such purposes, the expression means only the part of the building normally used for such purposes; and

(*b*) the expression does not include—

(i) any building designed for use as one or more separate dwellings, unless the building was normally used immediately before 1st September 1949 for the purpose of carrying on therein any such undertaking or providing therein any such service as aforesaid, or unless the building has been, or is at any time, adapted for use as business premises by the construction of a shop front or the making of a material alteration of a similar kind to the external appearance of the building;

(ii) any forecourt or other land forming part of the curtilage of a building;

(iii) any fence, wall or similar screen or structure, unless it forms part of the fabric of a building constituting business premises;

"forecourt" for the purposes of Class V includes any fence, wall or similar screen or structure enclosing a forecourt and not forming part of the fabric of a building constituting business premises;

"ground level", in relation to the display of advertisements on any building, means the ground-floor level of that building.

(4) The reference in Class III(*d*) of paragraph (1) above to events of a recreational character shall not be construed as including the carrying on of sports, games or physical training primarily as a commercial undertaking.

(5) On the determination of an application for express consent made in respect of an advertisement of a specified class, the provisions of this regulation whereby advertisements may be displayed without express consent shall cease to apply with respect to the advertisement; and, in the event of refusal of consent, the provisions of this regulation whereby the display of advertisements may be undertaken without express consent shall not apply to the subsequent display on the same site of any advertisement by, or on behalf of, the person whose application was so refused.

(6) Where an application is made for consent to display an advertisement of a specified class and such consent is granted subject to conditions in the nature of restrictions as to the site on which, or the manner in which, the display may be undertaken, or both, the provisions of this regulation whereby the display of advertisements may be undertaken without express consent shall not apply to the subsequent display, by or on behalf of the person to whom that consent was granted subject to such conditions, of any advertisement on the same site unless such advertisement is displayed in conformity with the requirements of those conditions.

(7) The conditions and limitations specified in this regulation apply only to the display without express consent of an advertisement within any class or description therein mentioned, and shall not restrict the powers of a local planning authority with regard to the determination in accordance with these Regulations of any application for express consent for the display of advertisements. **[651]**

15. Power to exclude the application of regulation 14

(1) If the Secretary of State is satisfied, upon representations made to him by the local planning authority, that the display of advertisements of a class or

description specified in regulation 14 should not be undertaken in any particular area or in any particular case without express consent, he may direct that the provisions of that regulation shall not apply to the display of such advertisements in that area or in that case.

(2) Before making a direction under this regulation, the Secretary of State shall—

(a) where the representations for such a direction relate to a particular area, publish, or cause to be published, in at least one newspaper circulating in the locality in which the area is situated, and on the same date or a subsequent date in the London Gazette, a notice indicating that representations for such a direction have been made to him and naming a place or places in the locality where a map or maps defining that area may be inspected at all reasonable hours; and

(b) where the representations for such a direction relate to a particular case, serve, or cause to be served, on the owner and occupier of the land in respect of which the representations have been made, and on any other person who, to the knowledge of the Secretary of State, proposes to display on such land an advertisement of the class or description referred to in the said representations, a notice indicating that representations have been made to him and specifying the land and the class or description of advertisement to which those representations relate;

and in each instance the notice shall state that any objection to the making of a direction under this regulation shall be made to the Secretary of State in writing within such period (not being less than 21 days from the date when the notice is given) as may be specified in the notice.

(3) The Secretary of State shall not make a direction under this regulation until after the expiration of the period specified in the notice referred to in paragraph (2) above, and in determining whether to make such a direction he shall take into account any objections made in accordance with that paragraph.

(4) Where the Secretary of State makes a direction under this regulation he shall send it to the local planning authority with a statement in writing of his reasons for making it, and shall send a copy of that statement to any person who has made an objection in accordance with paragraph (2) above.

(5) Notice of any direction given by the Secretary of State under this regulation with respect to a particular area shall be published by the local planning authority in at least one newspaper circulating in the locality in which the area is situated, and, unless the Secretary of State otherwise directs, on the same date or a subsequent date in the London Gazette, and such notice shall—

(a) contain a concise statement of the effect of the direction;

(b) name a place or places in that locality where a copy of the direction and of a map defining the area to which it relates may be seen at all reasonable hours; and

(c) specify a date when such direction shall come into force, being a date not less than fourteen and not more than twenty-eight days after the first publication of the notice.

(6) Notice of any direction given by the Secretary of State under this regulation in a particular case shall be served by the local planning authority on the owner and on any occupier of the land to which the direction relates, and on any other person who, to the knowledge of the authority, proposes to display on

such land an advertisement of the class or description referred to in the direction.

(7) A direction given under this regulation with respect to an area shall come into force on the date specified in the notice given under paragraph (5) above; and a direction given under this regulation in a particular case shall come into force on the date on which notice thereof is served on the occupier or, if there is no occupier, on the owner of the land to which the direction relates.

[652]

16. Power to require the discontinuance of the display of advertisements displayed with deemed consent

(1) The local planning authority, if they consider it expedient to do so in the interests of amenity or public safety, may serve a notice under this regulation (referred to in these Regulations as a "discontinuance notice") requiring the discontinuance of the display of an advertisement which is displayed with consent deemed to be granted under these Regulations, other than an advertisement of a description specified in regulation 9, or requiring the discontinuance of the use of a site for the display of such an advertisement:

Provided that, in relation to the display in accordance with the provisions of regulation 14 of an advertisement of a specified class, the authority shall not serve a discontinuance notice unless they are satisfied that the service of such a notice is required to remedy a substantial injury to the amenity of the locality or a danger to members of the public.

(2) Where the local planning authority serve a discontinuance notice, the notice—

(a) shall be served on the advertiser and on the owner and occupier of the site on which the advertisement is displayed; and

(b) may, if the local planning authority think fit, also be served on any other person displaying the advertisement.

(3) A discontinuance notice shall—

(a) specify the advertisement or the site to which it relates;

(b) specify a period within which the display or the use of the site (as the case may be) is to be discontinued; and

(c) contain a full statement of the reasons why the authority consider it expedient in the interests of amenity or public safety that the display or the use of the site (as the case may be) should be discontinued.

(4) Subject to paragraph (5) below, a discontinuance notice shall take effect at the end of such period (not being less than two months after the service thereof) as may be specified in the notice:

Provided that if an appeal is made to the Secretary of State under regulation 22 the notice shall be of no effect pending the final determination or withdrawal of the appeal.

(5) The local planning authority, by a notice served on the advertiser, may withdraw a discontinuance notice at any time before it takes effect or may, where no appeal to the Secretary of State is pending under regulation 22, from time to time vary a discontinuance notice by extending the period specified therein for the taking effect of the notice; and on any such variation the period for appeal to the Secretary of State under regulation 22(2) shall be increased by the number of days by which the period specified was extended or further extended.

(6) The local planning authority shall, on serving on the advertiser a notice of withdrawal or variation under paragraph (5) above, send a copy thereof to every other person who was served with the discontinuance notice.   **[653]**

PART IV

APPLICATIONS FOR EXPRESS CONSENT

17. How to apply for consent

(1) Subject to the provisions of paragraph (6) below, an application for consent to display advertisements shall be made on a form issued by the authority to whom the application is to be made and obtainable from that authority, and shall include the particulars required by such form and shall be accompanied by such plans, together with such additional number of copies (not exceeding two) of the form and plans, as may be required by the authority:

Provided that, where the Secretary of State has issued a direction under paragraph (5) below which relates to the application (or to a class in which the application is included), the particulars and plans furnished by the applicant shall be such as may be specified in that direction.

(2) Subject to paragraph (3) below, the application shall be made to the local planning authority.

(3) Where the application relates to land in a National Park [outside a metropolitan county], it shall be made to the district planning authority, who shall transmit it to the county planning authority; and an application so made shall be treated for the purposes of these Regulations as an application made to the local planning authority and received by the local planning authority on the date when it is received by the county planning authority.

(4) On receipt of the application the local planning authority shall send an acknowledgement to the applicant, and the authority may by a direction in writing addressed to the applicant require the applicant—

(a) to supply such further information, in addition to that contained in the application, as may be requisite to enable the authority to determine it; or

(b) to produce to an officer of the authority such evidence as may be reasonably called for to verify the particulars and information contained in the application or given to the authority.

(5) The Secretary of State may give directions to a local planning authority, either generally or in relation to a particular case or class of case, specifying the kinds of particulars, plans or information which an applicant may be required to furnish in an application made under this regulation.

(6) Notwithstanding the provisions of paragraph (1) above a local planning authority may accept an application in writing made otherwise than on the form therein referred to, in any case in which the information provided is sufficient to enable the authority to determine the application.   **[654]**

NOTES

Para 3: words in brackets inserted by SI 1986 No 443, reg 2, Sch 1.

18. Duty to consult with respect to an application

(1) A local planning authority shall, before granting consent for any display of advertisements, consult with the following authorities, persons or bodies, namely—

(*a*) with any neighbouring local planning authority whose area, or any part thereof, appears likely to be affected by the display of advertisements to which the application relates;

(*b*) where it appears to the local planning authority that the display of advertisements to which the application relates may affect the safety of persons using any trunk road (within the meaning of that term as defined in section 329 of the Highways Act 1980 in England, with the Secretary of State for Transport;

(*c*) where it appears to the local planning authority that the display of advertisements to which the application relates may affect the safety of persons using any railway, waterway (including any coastal waters), dock, harbour or aerodrome (civil or military), with the authority, statutory undertaker, body or person responsible for the operation thereof, and, in the case of coastal waters, with the Corporation of Trinity House also.

(2) The local planning authority shall give to any authority, person or body with whom they are required to consult as aforesaid not less than fourteen days' notice that the relevant application is to be considered and shall, in determining the application, take into account any representation made by such authority, person or body. **[655]**

19. Power of local planning authority to deal with applications

(1) Subject to the provisions of these Regulations, where application for consent for the display of advertisements is made to the local planning authority, that authority may grant consent subject to the standard conditions specified in Part I of Schedule 1 and to such additional conditions (if any) as they think fit, or may refuse consent:

Provided that where the application relates to the display (in accordance with the relevant provisions of regulation 14) of an advertisement of a specified class the authority shall not refuse consent, or impose a condition more restrictive in effect than any provision of that regulation in relation to advertisements of that class, unless they are satisfied that such refusal or condition is required to prevent or remedy a substantial injury to the amenity of the locality or a danger to members of the public.

(2) Without prejudice to the generality of paragraph (1) above and subject always to the provisions of regulation 5, conditions may be imposed on the grant of consent under this regulation—

(*a*) regulating the display of advertisements to which the consent relates, or the use of land by the applicant for the display of advertisements (whether it is land in respect of which the application was made or adjacent land under the control of the applicant), or requiring the carrying out of works on any such land, so far as appears to the local planning authority to be expedient for the purposes of or in connection with the display of advertisements authorised by the consent;

(*b*) requiring the removal of any advertisement authorised by the consent, or the discontinuance of any use of land so authorised, at the expiration of a specified period, and the carrying out of any works required for the reinstatement of land at the expiration of that period.

(3) Consent under this regulation may be—

(*a*) for the display of a particular advertisement or advertisements with or without illumination, as the application specifies; or

(b) for the use of a particular site for the display of advertisements in a specified manner, whether by reference to the number, siting, size or illumination of the advertisements or the structures intended for such display, or the design or appearance of any such structure, or otherwise.

(4) The power to grant consent for the display of advertisements under these Regulations shall include power to grant consent for the retention on a site of any advertisement being displayed thereon before the date of the application or for the continuance of any use of a site for the display of advertisements begun before that date; and reference in these Regulations to consent for the display of advertisements and to applications for such consent shall be construed accordingly.   **[656]**

20. Consent to be limited

(1) Subject to paragraph (4) of this regulation, every grant of express consent shall operate for a period of five years from the date of the granting of consent:

Provided that the local planning authority may, in the document granting consent, specify such shorter or longer period as they may consider expedient having regard to the provisions of regulation 5 and any period specified in the application for consent.

(2) The limitation on the duration of an express consent (whether specified by the local planning authority when granting consent or imposed by the provisions of paragraph (1) above) shall, for the purposes of these Regulations, be deemed to be a condition imposed upon the grant of consent.

(3) Where the local planning authority grant consent for a period of less than five years they shall (unless the application specified such shorter period) state in writing their reasons for doing so.

(4) Where, at the time when a consent is granted for the display of advertisements, the display to which the consent relates has not already begun, the local planning authority may express the specified period as a period running, in the alternative, from the date of commencement of the display or from a date not later than six months after the date on which the consent is granted, whichever is the earlier.

(5) At any time within a period of six months before the expiry of a consent granted under these Regulations, application may be made for the renewal thereof, and the provisions of these Regulations relating to applications for consent and to the determination thereof shall apply where the application is made for such renewal.   **[657]**

21. Notification of local planning authority's decision

(1) The grant or refusal by a local planning authority of consent for the display of advertisements shall be in writing and, where the authority decide to grant consent subject to conditions in addition to the standard conditions, or to refuse consent, the reasons for their decision shall be stated in writing.

(2) The local planning authority shall, within two months from the date of receipt of the application, give notice to the applicant of their decision:

Provided that such period of two months may, at any time before the expiration thereof, be extended by agreement in writing made between the authority and the applicant.   **[658]**

22. Appeals to the Secretary of State

(1) Where an application under these Regulations for consent to display an advertisement is refused by the local planning authority or is granted subject to conditions, the provisions of sections 36 and 37 of the Act shall apply for the purposes of these Regulations as if the decision of the authority were a decision to refuse planning permission or to grant planning permission subject to conditions, but subject to the modifications set out in paragraphs (2) and (3) below.

(2) In section 36 of the Act, as applied by paragraph (1) above:—

(*a*) in subsection (1), for the words from "for planning permission" to "permission, consent, agreement or approval", there shall be substituted the words "for consent under the Town and Country Planning (Control of Advertisements) Regulations 1984 to display an advertisement and that consent";

(*b*) for subsection (2) there shall be substituted the following subsections:—

"(2) Notice of appeal shall be given in writing to the Secretary of State within two calendar months from the date of receipt of notification of the local planning authority's decision, or such longer period as the Secretary of State may at any time allow, and the notice shall be accompanied by a copy of each of the following documents:—

(*a*) the application made to the local planning authority;
(*b*) all relevant plans and particulars submitted to them;
(*c*) the notice of decision; and
(*d*) all other relevant correspondence with the authority.

(2A) Where an appeal is brought under this section, the Secretary of State may require the appellant or the local planning authority to submit to him, within such period as he may specify, a statement in writing in respect of such matters relating to the application as he may specify; and if, after considering the grounds of appeal and any such statement, the Secretary of State is satisfied that he has sufficient information to enable him to determine the appeal he may, with the agreement in writing of both the appellant and the local planning authority, determine the appeal without complying with subsection (4) of this section.";

(*c*) the following subsection shall be inserted after subsection (3):—

"(3A) The Secretary of State may, in granting consent for the display of advertisements, specify that the term thereof shall run for such longer or shorter period than the period of five years specified in regulation 20(1) of the Town and Country Planning (Control of Advertisements) Regulations 1984 as he considers expedient having regard to the provisions of regulation 5 of those regulations and to any period specified in the application for consent.";

(*d*) subsection (5) shall be omitted;

(*e*) at the end of subsection (6) there shall be added the words "and shall otherwise have effect as if it were a decision of the local planning authority";

(*f*) in subsection (7), for the words from "in respect of an application for planning permission" to "planning permission for that development", there shall be substituted the words "in respect of an application under the Town and Country Planning (Control of Advertisements) Regulations 1984, the Secretary of State forms the opinion that, having regard to the provisions of those regulations and to any direction given under them, consent for the display of the advertisement in respect of which the application was made".

(3) In section 37, as applied by paragraph (1) above:—

(a) for the words from the beginning of the section to the word "order" in the first place where it appears there shall be substituted the words "Where any such application as is mentioned in section 36(1) of this Act (as applied by paragraph (1) and modified by paragraph (2)(a) of regulation 22 of the Town and Country Planning (Control of Advertisements) Regulations 1984) is made to a local planning authority then unless within the period of two calendar months from the date when the application was received by the local planning authority";

(b) for the words from "either" to "section 35 of this Act" there shall be substituted the words "give notice to the applicant of their decision on the application";

(c) after the words "of this Act" there shall be inserted the words "(as so modified)"; and

(d) for the words "at the end of the period prescribed by the development order" there shall be substituted the words "at the end of the period referred to above".

(4) The provisions of section 36 of the Act (as applied by paragraph (1) above and modified by paragraph (2) above) are set out in Part I of Schedule 3, and the provisions of section 37 (as applied and modified by paragraph (3) above) are set out in Part II of that Schedule.

(5) Where a local planning authority serve a discontinuance notice on any person under regulation 16, the provisions of section 36 of the Act, as modified by paragraph (2) above, shall apply as if—

(a) that person had made an application for consent for the display of the advertisements, or for the use of the site, to which the notice relates and the local planning authority had refused consent for the reasons stated in the notice; and

(b) the notice constituted notification of a decision to refuse consent,

and subject to the following further modifications:—

(a) in subsection (2):—

(i) the following subparagraphs shall be substituted for subparagraphs (a) to (d)—

"(a) the discontinuance notice;
(b) any notice of variation thereof;
(c) any relevant correspondence with the authority."; and

(ii) the period prescribed for giving notice of appeal is varied as set out in paragraph (5) of regulation 16 in any case where notice varying a discontinuance notice has been served by the local planning authority under that paragraph;

(b) the following subsection shall be added after subsection (5):—

"(5A) On the determination of an appeal under this section as applied by regulation 22(5) of the Town and Country Planning (Control of Advertisements) Regulations 1984, the Secretary of State shall give such directions as may be necessary for giving effect to his determination, including, where appropriate, directions for quashing the discontinuance notice or for varying the terms of the discontinuance notice in favour of the appellant.". **[659]**

PART V

SPECIAL CASE

23. Advertisements relating to travelling circuses and fairs

(1) On application in that behalf being made to them, a local planning authority may grant consent for the temporary display, on unspecified sites in their area, of placards, posters or bills relating to the visit of a travelling circus, fair or similar travelling entertainment to any specified place in the district; and for the purposes of this regulation the expression "in the district" means in the area of the local planning authority to whom application for such consent is made or in the area of any neighbouring local planning authority.

(2) Consent granted under this regulation shall be subject to the following conditions in addition to the standard conditions set out in Parts I and II of Schedule 1 :—

 (*a*) no such advertisement shall exceed 0·6 square metre in area or be displayed so that any part of the advertisement is above 3·6 metres from ground level;

 (*b*) no such advertisement shall be displayed earlier than fourteen days before the first performance or opening of the circus, fair or other entertainment in the district at a place specified in the advertisement, and every such advertisement shall be removed within seven days after the last performance or closing of the circus, fair or other entertainment in the district at a place specified in the advertisement;

and it shall be the duty of the local planning authority, when granting consent for the display of such advertisements, to inform the applicant that consent does not extend to the display of any advertisement on a site without the prior permission of the owner of the land or other person entitled to grant permission in relation thereto.

(3) Without prejudice to the right to apply under Part IV of these Regulations for consent to display advertisements of the foregoing description on specified sites, the provisions of that Part shall not apply to an application for consent under this regulation, and the decision of a local planning authority on any such application shall be final. **[660]**

PART VI

REVOCATION AND MODIFICATION OF EXPRESS CONSENT

24. Revocation and modification of consent

(1) Subject to regulation 5 and this regulation, if it appears to the local planning authority that it is expedient that any express consent for the display of advertisements should be revoked or modified, they may by order revoke the consent or modify it to such extent as appears to them to be expedient:

Provided that no such order shall take effect unless it is confirmed by the Secretary of State, and the Secretary of State may confirm any order submitted to him either without modification or subject to such modifications as he considers expedient.

(2) Where a local planning authority submit an order to the Secretary of State for confirmation under this regulation, that authority shall serve notice on the person on whose application the consent was granted, on the owner and on the occupier of the land affected, and on any other person who in their opinion will be affected by the order; and if within the period specified in the notice (not being less than twenty-eight days from the service thereof) any person on whom the notice is served so requires, the Secretary of State shall, before confirming the order, afford to that person and to the local planning authority an opportunity of appearing before and being heard by a person appointed by the Secretary of State for the purpose.

(3) The power conferred by this regulation to revoke or modify consent for the display of advertisements may be exercised—

(a) where the consent relates to a display which involves the carrying out of building or similar operations, at any time before those operations have been completed;

(b) where the consent relates to a display which involves no such operations as aforesaid, at any time before the display is begun:

Provided that the revocation or modification of consent for a display which involves the carrying out of building or similar operations shall not affect so much of those operations as has been previously carried out.   **[661]**

25. Supplementary provisions as to revocation and modification

(1) Where express consent for the display of advertisements is revoked or modified by an order made under regulation 24 then if, on a claim made to the local planning authority in writing and served in the manner indicated in paragraph (3) below within six months after the confirmation of the order, it is shown that any person has incurred expenditure in carrying out work, in connection with the display in question, which is rendered abortive by the revocation or modification, or has otherwise sustained loss or damage which is directly attributable to the revocation or modification, that authority shall pay to that person compensation in respect of that expenditure, loss or damage:

Provided that no compensation shall be payable under this paragraph in respect of loss or damage consisting of the depreciation in value of any interest in the land by virtue of the revocation or modification.

(2) For the purposes of this regulation, any expenditure incurred in the preparation of plans for the purposes of any work or upon other similar matters preparatory thereto shall be deemed to be included in the expenditure incurred in carrying out that work, but no compensation shall be paid under this regulation in respect of any work carried out before the grant of the consent which is revoked or modified, or in respect of any other loss or damage arising out of anything done or omitted to be done before the grant of that consent.

(3) A claim for compensation made to a local planning authority under paragraph (1) above shall be served on that authority by delivering it at the offices of the authority or by sending it by pre-paid post to those offices.   **[662]**

PART VII

AREAS OF SPECIAL CONTROL

26. Definition of areas of special control

(1) Every local planning authority shall from time to time consider whether any part or additional part of their area should be defined as an area of special control.

(2) An area of special control shall be defined by an order made by the local planning authority and approved by the Secretary of State in accordance with the provisions of Schedule 4.

(3) An order made under this regulation defining an area of special control may be revoked or modified by a subsequent order made by the local planning authority and approved by the Secretary of State in accordance with the provisions of Schedule 4.

(4) Where an order is made under this regulation, the local planning authority shall consider, at least once in every five years while the order remains in force, whether it should be revoked or modified.

(5) Where an order defining an area of special control is in force at the date of the coming into operation of these Regulations, the appropriate local planning authority shall consider the question of whether that order should be revoked or modified:—

(a) within five years from the date on which the order came into force or within five years from the date on which such matters were last considered, whichever period last expires; and

(b) thereafter, at least once in every five years while the order remains in force.

(6) For the purposes of paragraph (5) above, the appropriate local planning authority in respect of an area of special control shall be the local planning authority within whose area that area is situated; and where the area of special control is situated within the area of more than one local planning authority, each such authority shall be the appropriate local planning authority in so far as the order defining the area of special control relates to the area of that authority.

(7) Before making an order under this regulation a local planning authority shall consult—

(a) where it appears to them that the order will be likely to affect any part of the area of a neighbouring local planning authority, with that authority;

(b) where the order will relate to any land within the boundary of a National Park, with any district planning authority within whose area any of that land is situated.

(8) A local planning authority shall exercise their functions under this regulation only in the interests of amenity and for this purpose shall have regard to the general characteristics of their area, including the presence therein of any feature of historic, architectural or cultural interest. **[663]**

NOTES

Para (6): substituted for existing para (6) by SI 1986 No 443, reg 2, Sch 1.

27. Display of advertisements in areas of special control, conservation areas, National Parks and areas of outstanding natural beauty

(1) No display of advertisements may be undertaken in an area of special control except—

(a) the display of advertisements of the classes and descriptions specified in regulations 9, 12, 14 and 23; or

(b) the display of advertisements in accordance with the provisions of paragraph (2) below.

(2) Without prejudice to the provisions of these Regulations with respect to advertisements of the descriptions referred to in paragraph (1)(a) above, advertisements of the following descriptions may be displayed in an area of special control with express consent granted in accordance with these Regulations—

(a) hoardings or similar structures to be used only for the display of notices relating to local events, activities or entertainments;

(b) any advertisement for the purpose of announcement or direction in relation to buildings or other land in the locality, being an advertisement which, in the opinion of the local planning authority or of the Secretary of State on appeal, is reasonably required having regard to the nature and situation of such buildings or other land;

(c) any advertisement which, in the opinion of the local planning authority or of the Secretary of State on appeal, is required to be displayed in the interests of public safety;

(d) any advertisement which could be displayed as an advertisement of a specified class but for some non-compliance with a condition or limitation as respects size, height from the ground, number or illumination imposed by regulation 14 in relation to the display thereunder of advertisements of that class, being an advertisement which, in the opinion of the local planning authority or of the Secretary of State on appeal, may in all the circumstances reasonably be allowed to be displayed notwithstanding that it does not comply with that condition or limitation.

(3) The power conferred on local planning authorities by regulation 19 to grant consent for the display of advertisements shall, in relation to the display of advertisements in an area of special control, be limited to advertisements of the descriptions mentioned in paragraphs (1) and (2) above, including illuminated advertisements of those descriptions.

(4) On the coming into force of an order defining an area of special control or modifying an existing order by the definition of an additional area of special control, advertisements then being displayed in accordance with these Regulations in the area may continue to be displayed as follows:—

(a) advertisements of the descriptions specified in regulations 9, 12 and 23 may continue to be displayed in accordance with the provisions of those regulations respectively;

(b) advertisements of the specified classes and advertisements of the description specified in paragraph (2)(d) above may continue to be displayed with or without express consent, subject, after the term of any express consent has expired, to the power of the local planning authority to require the discontinuance of the display of any such advertisement under regulation 16;

(c) any other advertisement may continue to be displayed—

(i) in a case where express consent has been granted, for a period of six months from the date on which the order defining the area comes into force or for the remainder of the term of the express consent, whichever is the longer; or

(ii) in a case where no express consent has been granted, for a period of six months from the date on which the order defining the area comes into force and then for a further two months,

and, in either case, the advertisement shall, at the end of the relevant period, be forthwith removed, unless consent is granted for its continued display in accordance with this regulation.

(5) On the designation of an area as a conservation area, National Park or area of outstanding natural beauty, advertisements of Class VII specified in regulation 14 which are then being displayed in the area may continue to be displayed until the expiration of two years from the date of commencement of the display, or one year from the date of designation of the relevant area (whichever period last expires), subject to the power of the local planning authority to require the discontinuance of the display of any such advertisement under regulation 16.

(6) Nothing in the foregoing provisions of this regulation shall—

(a) affect a notice served under regulation 16 before the coming into force of an order defining an area of special control or designating a National Park or area of outstanding natural beauty, or before the designation of an area as a conservation area;

(b) override any condition attached to a consent, whereby an advertisement is required to be removed;

(c) restrict the powers of a local planning authority, or of the Secretary of State, in regard to any contravention of these Regulations;

(d) restrict the power of the local planning authority, or of the Secretary of State, to consent to the display in an area of special control of advertisements of the specified classes in respect of which a direction under regulation 15 is in force. **[664]**

PART VIII

MISCELLANEOUS

28. Powers of the Secretary of State

(1) The Secretary of State may, if he thinks fit, give a direction to a local planning authority, or to local planning authorities generally, requiring them to furnish him with such information as he may require for the purpose of exercising any of his functions under these Regulations.

(2) If it appears to the Secretary of State, after consultation with the local planning authority, to be expedient that an order should be made under regulation 26 defining an area of special control or revoking or modifying such an order, or that a notice should be served under regulation 16, he may himself make such an order or serve such a notice; and any reference in these Regulations to the power of the local planning authority under regulation 16 shall be deemed to include a reference to the power of the Secretary of State.

(3) Where the Secretary of State proposes to make an order under regulation 26 he shall prepare a draft of the order in the form in which he proposes to make it, defining an area of special control, or the modifications to be made to the

existing order, by reference to a map and in all other respects the provisions of Schedule 4 shall apply, with such modifications as may be necessary, to the making of the order by the Secretary of State as they apply to the making of such an order by the local planning authority.   **[665]**

29. Extension of time

Subject to the provisions of the Act and of these Regulations—

    (a) the Secretary of State may if he thinks fit, in any particular case, extend the time within which anything is required under these Regulations to be done, or within which any objection, representation or claim for compensation may be made thereunder;

    (b) the local planning authority may, on reasonable cause being shown to them, extend the time within which an application for consent is required to be, or may be, made to them under these Regulations,

and any such extension may be granted either unconditionally or subject to such conditions as the Secretary of State or the local planning authority, as the case may be, think fit to impose:

Provided that nothing in this regulation shall authorise a local planning authority to grant an extension of the time within which the authority is required, under regulation 21, to notify an applicant of the manner in which his application has been dealt with, otherwise than in the manner expressly provided in that regulation.   **[666]**

30. Recovery of compensation under section 176 of the Act

(1) Where, for the purpose of complying with these Regulations, works are carried out by any person—

    (a) for removing an advertisement which was being displayed on 1st August 1948; or

    (b) for discontinuing the use for the display of advertisements of a site used for that purpose on that date,

and that person desires to recover compensation under section 176 of the Act in respect of any expenses reasonably incurred by him in that behalf, he shall submit a claim in writing to the local planning authority within six months after the completion of those works; and that claim shall contain sufficient information to enable the local planning authority to give proper consideration thereto.

(2) If the local planning authority consider that the information furnished by any claimant under this regulation is insufficient to enable them properly to determine the claim, they may call for such further particulars as they require for that purpose.   **[667]**

31. Register of applications

(1) Every local planning authority shall keep a register containing the following information in respect of land within their area namely:—

    (a) particulars of any application made to them for consent for the display of advertisements on any such land, including the name and address of the applicant, the date of the application, and brief particulars of the type of advertisement forming the subject of the application;

    (b) particulars of any direction given under these Regulations in respect of the application;

    (c) the decision (if any) of the local planning authority in respect of the application and the date of such decision;

(*d*) the date and effect of any decision of the Secretary of State in respect of the application given on appeal.

(2) Such register shall include an index for enabling a person to trace any entry in the register.

(3) Such register shall be kept at the office of the local planning authority:

Provided that so much of the register as relates to land within a particular part of the area of a local planning authority may be kept at a place within or convenient to that part of their area.

(4) Every entry in such register consisting of particulars of an application shall be made within fourteen days of the receipt of such application.

(5) The provisions of section 34(3) of the Act shall apply to every register kept under paragraph (1) above. **[668]**

32. Directions and notices

(1) Any power conferred by these Regulations to give a direction shall be construed as including power to cancel or vary that direction by a subsequent direction.

(2) Any notice to be served or given under these Regulations may be served or given in the manner prescribed by section 283 of the Act and by regulation 15 of the Town and Country Planning General Regulations 1976. **[669]**

33. Other statutory obligations unaffected

Without prejudice to section 64 of the Act, nothing in these Regulations, or in a consent granted under these Regulations, shall operate so as to affect any obligation or liability imposed or incurred under any other enactment in relation to anything involved in the display of advertisements. **[670]**

SCHEDULES

SCHEDULE 1

Regulation 7

THE STANDARD CONDITIONS

PART I

Conditions attaching to all consents granted or deemed to be granted for the display of advertisements

1. All advertisements displayed, and any site used for the display of advertisements, shall be maintained in a clean and tidy condition to the reasonable satisfaction of the local planning authority.

2. Any hoarding or similar structure, or any sign, placard, board or device erected or used principally for the purpose of displaying advertisements shall be maintained in a safe condition.

3. Where any advertisement is required under these Regulations to be removed, the removal thereof shall be carried out to the reasonable satisfaction of the local planning authority. **[671]**

PART II

*Conditions attaching to consent deemed to be granted, or to consent granted under regulation
23*

4. Advertisements shall not be sited or displayed so as to obscure, or hinder the ready
interpretation of, any road traffic sign, railway signal or aid to nevigation by water or air,
or so as otherwise to render hazardous the use of any highway, railway, waterway
(including any coastal waters) or aerodrome (civil or military).   **[672]**

SCHEDULE 2

Regulation 14

LIMITATIONS ON THE DISPLAY OF ADVERTISEMENTS ON HOARDINGS UNDER THE
PROVISIONS OF REGULATION 14(1) CLASS VII

1. Advertisements shall not be displayed earlier than one month before the date of
commencement of building operations.

2. The consent shall not apply to advertisements which are less than 1·5 metres in
height and 1·00 metre in length or more than 3·1 metres in height and 6·1 metres in
length.

3. The advertiser shall, not less than 14 days before the commencement of the display
of an advertisement, notify the local planning authority in writing of the date of the
commencement of the display of the advertisement and such notification shall be sent by
recorded delivery.

4. No advertisement shall be displayed for more than two years from the date of the
commencement of the display of the advertisement.   **[673]**

SCHEDULE 3

Regulation 22

APPEALS TO THE SECRETARY OF STATE

PART I

Provisions of section 36 of the Town and Country Planning Act 1971 (as modified)

"**36.**—(1) Where an application is made to a local planning authority for consent
under the Town and Country Planning (Control of Advertisements) Regulations 1984
to display an advertisement and that consent is refused by that authority or is granted
by them subject to conditions, the applicant, if he is aggrieved by their decision, may
by notice under this section appeal to the Secretary of State.

(2) Notice of appeal shall be given in writing to the Secretary of State within two
calendar months from the date of receipt of notification of the local planning authority's
decision, or such longer period as the Secretary of State may at any time allow, and the
notice shall be accompanied by a copy of each of the following documents:—

  (*a*) the application made to the local planning authority;
  (*b*) all relevant plans and particulars submitted to them;
  (*c*) the notice of decision; and
  (*d*) all other relevant correspondence with the authority.

(2A) Where an appeal is brought under this section, the Secretary of State may
require the appellant or the local planning authority to submit to him, within such
period as he may specify, a statement in writing in respect of such matters relating to
the application as he may specify; and if, after considering the grounds of appeal and
any such statement, the Secretary of State is satisfied that he has sufficient information
to enable him to determine the appeal he may, with the agreement in writing of both
the appellant and the local planning authority, determine the appeal without complying
with subsection (4) of this section.

(3) Where an appeal is brought under this section from a decision of a local
planning authority, the Secretary of State, subject to the following provisions of this
section, may allow or dismiss the appeal, or may reverse or vary any part of the

decision of the local planning authority, whether the appeal relates to that part thereof or not, and may deal with the application as if it had been made to him in the first instance.

(3A) The Secretary of State may, in granting consent for the display of advertisements, specify that the term thereof shall run for such longer or shorter period than the period of five years specified in regulation 20(1) of the Town and Country Planning (Control of Advertisements) Regulations 1984 as he considers expedient having regard to the provisions of regulation 5 of those regulations and any period specified in the application for consent.

(4) Before determining an appeal under this section, other than an appeal referred to a Planning Inquiry Commission under section 48 of this Act, the Secretary of State shall, if either the applicant or the local planning authority so desire, afford to each of them an opportunity of appearing before, and being heard by, a person appointed by the Secretary of State for the purpose.

(6) The decision of the Secretary of State on any appeal under this section shall be final and shall otherwise have effect as if it were a decision of the local planning authority.

(7) If, before or during the determination of an appeal under this section in respect of an application under the Town and Country Planning (Control of Advertisements) Regulations 1984, the Secretary of State forms the opinion that, having regard to the provisions of those regulations and to any direction given under them, consent for the display of the advertisement in respect of which the application was made—

(a) could not have been granted by the local planning authority; or
(b) could not have been granted by them otherwise than subject to the conditions imposed by them,

he may decline to determine the appeal or to proceed with the determination of it.

(8) Schedule 9 to this Act applies to appeals under this section, including appeals under this section as applied by or under any other provision of this Act". **[674]**

Part II

Provisions of section 37 of the Town and Country Planning Act 1971 (as modified)

"**37.** Where any such application as is mentioned in section 36(1) of this Act (as applied by paragraph (1) and modified by paragraph (2)(a) of regulation 22 of the Town and Country Planning (Control of Advertisements) Regulations 1984) is made to a local planning authority then unless within the period of two calendar months from the date when the application was received by the local planning authority, or within such extended period as may at any time be agreed upon in writing between the applicant and the local planning authority, the local planning authority give notice to the applicant of their decision on the application, the provisions of section 36 of this Act (as so modified) shall apply in relation to the application as if the permission or approval to which it relates had been refused by the local planning authority, and as if notification of their decision had been received by the applicant at the end of the period referred to above, or at the end of the said extended period, as the case may be". **[675]**

SCHEDULE 4

Regulation 26

Procedure for Defining Areas of Special Control

Part I

Procedure for defining areas of special control or modifying orders defining areas of special control

1. Where a local planning authority propose to define an area of special control they shall make an order defining the area by reference to a map annexed thereto, and where they propose to modify an existing order defining an area of special control they shall

make an order defining the modifications by reference to a map annexed thereto showing the modifications either in relation to the whole boundary of the existing area of special control or in relation only to such parts thereof as it is proposed to modify. Any order made in accordance with the provisions of this paragraph may contain descriptive matter in relation to the area to be defined or the modifications to be made, and in the case of any discrepancy between that descriptive matter and the map, the descriptive matter shall prevail except insofar as may be otherwise provided by the order.

2. An soon as may be thereafter the authority shall submit the order to the Secretary of State for approval, together with two certified copies of the order and a statement of their reasons for proposing that the area to which the order relates should be defined as an area of special control or their reasons for proposing that an existing order should be modified. In the case of an order modifying an existing order, except where the map annexed to the order shows the modifications in relation to the whole boundary of the existing area of special control, the statement of reasons shall be accompanied by a plan showing both the existing area of special control and the modifications which are to be made thereto. Where it appears expedient to the Secretary of State in any particular case so to do, he may direct the authority to send to him an additional certified copy of the order, map and any descriptive matter.

3. The authority shall forthwith publish in the London Gazette, and in each of two successive weeks in one or more newspapers circulating in the locality in which the area is situated—

(*a*) in the case of an order defining an area of special control, a notice in the appropriate form prescribed in Schedule 5, or in a form substantially to the like effect, describing the area, stating that an order defining it as an area of special control for the purposes of these Regulations has been submitted to the Secretary of State for approval, naming a place or places where a copy of the order and of the statement of reasons mentioned in paragraph 2 above may be seen at all reasonable hours without payment of fee and specifying the time, not being less than 28 days from the date of first publication of the local advertisement, within which objections or representations with respect to the order may be sent in writing to the Secretary of State;

(*b*) in the case of an order modifying an existing order, a notice in the appropriate form prescribed in Schedule 5, or in a form substantially to the like effect, describing the modifications which it is proposed to make to the existing order, stating that an order making the necessary modifications to the existing order for the purposes of these Regulations has been submitted to the Secretary of State for approval, naming a place or places where a copy of the order and of the statement of reasons and any accompanying plan mentioned in paragraph 2 above may be seen at all reasonable hours without payment of fee and specifying the time, not being less than 28 days from the date of first publication of the local advertisement, within which objections or representations with respect to the order may be sent in writing to the Secretary of State.

4. If any objection is duly made as aforesaid and is not withdrawn the Secretary of State shall, before approving the order, either cause a local inquiry to be held or afford to the person making the objection an opportunity of appearing before and being heard by a person appointed by the Secretary of State for the purpose, and if any such person avails himself of the opportunity of being heard, the Secretary of State shall afford to the local planning authority, and to any other person to whom it appears to the Secretary of State expedient to afford it, an opportunity of being heard on the same occasion.

5. After considering any representation or objection duly made and not withdrawn and the report of the person by whom any inquiry or hearing was held, the Secretary of State may approve the order with or without modifications:

Provided that if the Secretary of State proposes to approve the order subject to any modification involving the inclusion therein of any area of land not included in the order as submitted and, in the case of an order modifying an existing order, not defined as an area of special control in the existing order, he shall publish prior notice of his intention so to do and shall afford an opportunity for the making of objections and representations with respect to the proposed modification and for such further hearing as may appear to him, in the light of any such objections or representations, to be necessary or expedient.

6. As soon as may be after the order has been approved, the local planning authority shall publish in the London Gazette, and in each of two successive weeks in one or more newspapers circulating in the locality in which the area is situated, a notice in the appropriate form prescribed in Schedule 5, or a form substantially to the like effect, stating that the order has been approved and naming a place or places where a copy or copies thereof may be seen at all reasonable hours without payment of fee; and any such order shall come into force on the date on which notice of the approval thereof is published in the London Gazette. **[676]**

PART II

Procedure for revoking existing orders defining areas of special control

7. Where a local planning authority propose to make an order revoking an existing order defining an area of special control, a map showing the existing area of special control shall be annexed to the order, and the procedure prescribed in paragraphs 2 to 6 of Part I of this Schedule in relation to an order modifying an existing order shall be followed, subject to the modification that the statement submitted to the Secretary of State, and all notices published in accordance with paragraph 3 of the said Part I, shall set out the local planning authority's reasons for proposing that the existing order be revoked. **[677]**

SCHEDULE 5

FORMS OF NOTICES

FORM 1

Form of notice of submission for approval of an order defining an area of special control or modifying an existing order

TOWN AND COUNTRY PLANNING ACT 1971

Town and Country Planning (Control of Advertisements) Regulations 1984

Notice is hereby given that the (1)   in exercise of their powers under regulation 26 of the Town and Country Planning (Control of Advertisements) Regulations 1984 have submitted for the approval of the Secretary of State for the Environment/Secretary of State for Wales (2) an order defining as an area of special control for the purposes of the said Regulations/an order modifying the (3) order by adding thereto/removing therefrom (2) an area of land situated at   and described in the Schedule hereto, which land is shown coloured   on the map accompanying the order, and that order is about to be considered by the Secretary of State.

A copy of the order and of a statement of reasons submitted therewith have been deposited at   and will be available for inspection free of charge between the hours of

Any objection to the order must be made in writing, stating the grounds of the objection, and addressed to the Secretary, Department of the Environment/Welsh Office (2) at   before (4)   19 .

SCHEDULE

(Here insert description of land comprised in the order)

19   (Signature)

Directions for completing this form

(1) Insert name of authority.

(2) Delete words inapplicable.

(3) Insert details of order defining area of special control.

(4) Insert a date not less than 28 days from the date of first publication of local advertisement. **[678]**

FORM 2

Form of notice of the approval of an order defining an area of special control or modifying an existing order

TOWN AND COUNTRY PLANNING ACT 1971

Town and Country Planning (Control of Advertisements) Regulations 1984

Notice is hereby given that the Secretary of State for the Environment/Secretary of State for Wales (1), in exercise of his powers under section 63 of the Town and Country Planning Act 1971 and regulation 26 of the Town and Country Planning (Control of Advertisements) Regulations 1984, has approved [with modifications] (2) an order defining as an area of special control for the purposes of the said Regulations/an order modifying the (3)

order by adding thereto/removing therefrom (1) an area of land situated at and described in the Schedule hereto, which land is shown coloured   on the map referred to in the order.

The order comes into force on   19   . (4)

A copy of the approved order has been deposited at
                and will be available for inspection free of charge between the hours of

SCHEDULE

(Here insert description of land comprised in the order)

19   .   (Signature)

IMPORTANT

Attention is directed to the provisions of regulation 27 of the above-mentioned Regulations which specify the advertisements which may be displayed in areas of special control and which require the removal in certain circumstances of advertisements already being displayed in the area at the time of its designation as an area of special control.

Directions for completing this form

(1) Delete words inapplicable.

(2) Delete words in square brackets if inapplicable.

(3) Insert details of order defining area of special control.

(4) Insert date of publication in London Gazette. **[679]**

FORM 3

Form of notice of submission for approval of an order revoking an existing order

TOWN AND COUNTRY PLANNING ACT 1971

Town and Country Planning (Control of Advertisements) Regulations 1984

Notice is hereby given that the   (1), in exercise of their powers under regulation 26 of the Town and Country Planning (Control of Advertisements) Regulations 1984, have submitted for the approval of the Secretary of State for the Environment/Secretary of State for Wales (2) an order revoking the (3) order.

A copy of the order and of a statement of reasons submitted therewith have been deposited at   and will be available for inspection free of charge between the hours of

Any objection to the order must be made in writing, stating the grounds of the

objection and addressed to the Secretary, Department of the Environment/Welsh Office
(2) at   before (4)   19 .

19 .   (Signature)

Directions for completing this form

(1) Insert name of authority.

(2) Delete words inapplicable.

(3) Insert details of order defining an area of special control.

(4) Insert a date not less than 28 days from the date of first publication of local
advertisement.   **[680]**

FORM 4

Form of notice of the approval of an order revoking an existing order

TOWN AND COUNTRY PLANNING ACT 1971

Town and Country Planning (Control of Advertisements) Regulations 1984

Notice is hereby given that the Secretary of State for the Environment/Secretary of State
for Wales (1), in exercise of his powers under section 63 of the Town and Country
Planning Act 1971 and regulation 26 of the Town and Country Planning (Control of
Advertisements) Regulations 1984, has approved an order revoking the (2)
order.

The order comes into force on   19 . (3)

A copy of the approved order has been deposited at
            and will be available for inspection free of charge between the hours of

19 .   (Signature)

Directions for completing this form

(1) Delete words in applicable.

(2) Insert details of the order.

(3) Insert date of publication in London Gazette.   **[681]**

SCHEDULE 6
Regulation 4

Regulations revoked	References
The Town and Country Planning (Control of Advertisements) Regulations 1969.	SI 1969/1532.
The Town and Country Planning (Control of Advertisements) (Amendment) Regulations 1972.	SI 1972/489.
The Town and Country Planning (Control of Advertisements) (Amendment) Regulations 1974.	SI 1974/185.
The Town and Country Planning (Control of Advertisements) (Amendment) Regulations 1975.	SI 1975/898.

[682]

APPENDIX
NEW LEGISLATION

HOUSING AND PLANNING ACT 1986
(1986 c 63)

ARRANGEMENT OF SECTIONS

* * * * *

PART II
SIMPLIFIED PLANNING ZONES

England and Wales

PART III
FINANCIAL ASSISTANCE FOR URBAN REGENERATION

PART IV
HAZARDOUS SUBSTANCES

England and Wales

* * * * *

PART VI
MISCELLANEOUS PROVISIONS

England and Wales

* * * * *

Provisions common to England and Wales and Scotland

PART VII
GENERAL PROVISIONS

An Act to make further provision with respect to housing, planning and local inquiries; to provide financial assistance for the regeneration of urban areas; and for connected purposes [7 November 1986]

PART II

SIMPLIFIED PLANNING ZONES

England and Wales

25. Simplified planning zones in England and Wales

(1) In Part III of the Town and Country Planning Act 1971 (general planning control), after section 24 insert—

"Simplified planning zone schemes

24A. Simplified planning zones

(1) A simplified planning zone is an area in respect of which a simplified planning zone scheme is in force.

(2) The adoption or approval of a simplified planning zone scheme has effect to grant in relation to the zone, or any part of it specified in the scheme, planning permission for development specified in the scheme or for development of any class so specified.

(3) Planning permission under a simplified planning zone scheme may be unconditional or subject to such conditions, limitations or exceptions as may be specified in the scheme.

(4) Every local planning authority—

(*a*) shall consider, as soon as practicable after this section comes into operation, the question for which part or parts of their area a simplified planning zone scheme is desirable, and shall thereafter keep that question under review; and

(*b*) shall prepare a scheme for any such part for which they decide, as a result of their original consideration or of any such review, that it is desirable to do so.

(5) The provisions of Schedule 8A to this Act have effect with respect to the making and alteration of simplified planning zone schemes and other related matters.

(6) The functions of local planning authorities under the provisions of

this Act relating to simplified planning zone schemes shall be performed in non-metropolitan counties by the district planning authorities.

24B. Simplified planning zone schemes: conditions and limitations on planning permission

(1) The conditions and limitations on planning permission which may be specified in a simplified planning zone scheme may include—

    (*a*) conditions or limitations in respect of all development permitted by the scheme or in respect of particular descriptions of development so permitted, and

    (*b*) conditions or limitations requiring the consent, agreement or approval of the local planning authority in relation to particular descriptions of permitted development;

and different conditions or limitations may be specified for different cases or classes of case.

(2) Nothing in a simplified planning zone scheme shall affect the right of any person—

    (*a*) to do anything not amounting to development, or

    (*b*) to carry out development for which planning permission is not required or for which permission has been granted otherwise than by the scheme;

and no limitation or restriction subject to which permission has been granted otherwise than under the scheme shall affect the right of any person to carry out development for which permission has been granted under the scheme.

24C. Duration of simplified planning zone scheme

(1) A simplified planning zone scheme shall take effect on the date of its adoption or approval and shall cease to have effect at the end of the period of ten years beginning with that date.

(2) Upon the scheme's ceasing to have effect planning permission under the scheme shall also cease to have effect except in a case where the development authorised by it has been begun.

(3) The provisions of section 44(2) to (6) of this Act (which provide for the termination of planning permission if the completion of development is unreasonably delayed) apply to planning permission under a simplified planning zone scheme where development has been begun but not completed by the time the area ceased to be a simplified planning zone.

(4) The provisions of section 43(1) to (3) of this Act apply in determining for the purposes of this section when development shall be taken to be begun.

24D. Alteration of simplified planning zone scheme

(1) The adoption or approval of alterations to a simplified planning zone scheme has effect as follows.

(2) The adoption or approval of alterations providing for the inclusion of land in the simplified planning zone has effect to grant in relation to that land or such part of it as is specified in the scheme planning permission for development so specified or of any class so specified.

(3) The adoption or approval of alterations providing for the grant of planning permission has effect to grant such permission in relation to the

simplified planning zone, or such part of it as is specified in the scheme, for development so specified or development of any class so specified.

(4) The adoption or approval of alterations providing for the withdrawal or relaxation of conditions, limitations or restrictions to which planning permission under the scheme is subject has effect to withdraw or relax the conditions, limitations or restrictions forthwith.

(5) The adoption or approval of alterations providing for—

(a) the exclusion of land from the simplified planning zone,
(b) the withdrawal of planning permission, or
(c) the imposition of new or more stringent conditions, limitations or restrictions to which planning permission under the scheme is subject,

has effect to withdraw permission, or to impose the conditions, limitations or restrictions, with effect from the end of the period of twelve months beginning with the date of the adoption or approval.

(6) The adoption or approval of alterations to a scheme does not affect planning permission under the scheme in any case where the development authorised by it has been begun.

The provisions of section 43(1) to (3) of this Act apply in determining for the purposes of this subsection when development shall be taken to be begun.

24E. Exclusion of certain descriptions of land or development

(1) The following descriptions of land may not be included in a simplified planning zone—

(a) land in a National Park;
(b) land in a conservation area;
(c) land in an area designated under section 87 of the National Parks and Access to the Countryside Act 1949 as an area of outstanding natural beauty;
(d) land identified in the development plan for the district as part of a green belt;
(e) land in respect of which a notification or order is in force under section 28 or 29 of the Wildlife and Countryside Act 1981 (areas of special scientific interest).

(2) Where land included in a simplified planning zone becomes land of such a description, subsection (1) does not have effect to exclude it from the zone.

(3) The Secretary of State may by order provide that no simplified planning zone scheme shall have effect to grant planning permission—

(a) in relation to an area of land specified in the order or to areas of land of a description so specified, or
(b) for development of a description specified in the order.

(4) An order under subsection (3) has effect to withdraw such planning permission under a simplified planning zone scheme already in force with effect from the date on which the order comes into force, except in a case where the development authorised by the permission has been begun.

The provisions of section 43(1) to (3) of this Act apply in determining for the purposes of this subsection when development shall be taken to be begun.".

(2) After Schedule 8 to the Town and Country Planning Act 1971 insert as Schedule 8A the Schedule set out in Part I of Schedule 6 to this Act which contains provision with respect to the making and alteration of simplified planning zone schemes and other related matters.

(3) The Town and Country Planning Act 1971 also has effect subject to the consequential amendments specified in Part II of Schedule 6 to this Act.   **[683]**

NOTES
Commencement: to be appointed.

*   *   *   *   *

PART III

FINANCIAL ASSISTANCE FOR URBAN REGENERATION

27. Power to give assistance

(1) The Secretary of State may, with the consent of the Treasury, give financial assistance to any person in respect of qualifying expenditure incurred in connection with activities contributing to the regeneration of an urban area by bringing land and buildings into effective use, creating an attractive environment, providing employment for people who live in the area or ensuring that housing and social facilities are available to encourage people to live and work in the area.

(2) Expenditure incurred in connection with any of the following qualifies for assistance—

    (*a*) the acquisition of land or buildings;
    (*b*) the reclamation, improvement or refurbishment of land or buildings;
    (*c*) the development or redevelopment of land, including the conversion or demolition of existing buildings;
    (*d*) the equipment or fitting out of buildings or land;
    (*e*) the provision of means of access, services or other facilities for buildings or land;
    (*f*) environmental improvements.   **[684]**

NOTES
Commencement: 7 January 1987.

28. Forms of assistance

(1) Financial assistance under section 27 may be given in any form.

(2) Assistance may, in particular, be given by way of—

    (*a*) grants,
    (*b*) loans,
    (*c*) guarantees, or
    (*d*) incurring expenditure for the benefit of the person assisted.

(3) The Secretary of State shall not in giving financial assistance under section 27 purchase loan or share capital in a company.   **[685]**

NOTES
Commencement: 7 January 1987.

29. Terms on which assistance is given

(1) Financial assistance under section 27 may be given on such terms as the Secretary of State, with the consent of the Treasury, considers appropriate.

(2) The terms may, in particular, include provision as to—

(*a*) circumstances in which the assistance must be repaid, or otherwise made good, to the Secretary of State, and the manner in which that is to be done; or

(*b*) circumstances in which the Secretary of State is entitled to recover the proceeds or part of the proceeds of any disposal of land or buildings in respect of which assistance was provided.

(3) The person receiving assistance shall comply with the terms on which it is given and compliance may be enforced by the Secretary of State. **[686]**

NOTES
Commencement: 7 January 1987.

PART IV

HAZARDOUS SUBSTANCES

England and Wales

30. Hazardous substances authorities

The following sections shall be inserted after section 1 of the Town and Country Planning Act 1971—

"1A. Hazardous substances authorities—general

(1) Subject to subsections (2) to (4) below, in this Act "hazardous substances authority", in relation to any land other than land to which section 1B below applies, means the council of the district or London borough in which it is situated.

(2) Subject to subsection (3) below, the county council are the hazardous substances authority if the land is in a non-metropolitan county and—

(*a*) is situated in a National Park;

(*b*) is used for the winning and working of minerals (including their extraction from a mineral-working deposit); or

(*c*) is situated in England and used for the disposal of refuse or waste materials.

(3) A joint planning board or special planning board for a National Park are the hazardous substances authority for the Park.

(4) An urban development corporation are the hazardous substances authority for their area, if they are the local planning authority in relation to all kinds of development.

1B. Hazardous substances authorities—statutory undertakers

(1) In this Act "hazardous substances authority", in relation to land to which this section applies, means the appropriate Minister.

(2) This section applies—

(a) to operational land of statutory undertakers;

(b) to land in which statutory undertakers hold, or propose to acquire, an interest with a view to the land being used as operational land.

(3) For the purposes of this section any land to which this subsection applies but which is not operational land of statutory undertakers authorised to carry on a harbour shall be treated as if it were such operational land.

(4) Subsection (3) above applies—

(a) to a wharf; and

(b) to harbour land,

as defined in the Harbours Act 1964.

(5) Any question whether subsection (3) above applies to land shall be determined by the Secretary of State and the Minister who is the appropriate Minister in relation to operational land of statutory undertakers who are authorised to carry on harbour undertakings.". **[687]**

NOTES
Commencement: to be appointed.

31. Hazardous substances

The following shall be inserted after section 58A of the Town and Country Planning Act 1971—

"Hazardous substances

58B. Requirement of hazardous substances consent

(1) Subject to the provisions of this Part of this Act, the presence of a hazardous substance on, over or under land requires the consent of the hazardous substances authority (in this Act referred to as "hazardous substances consent") unless the aggregate quantity of the substance—

(a) on, under or over the land;

(b) on, under or over other land which is within 500 metres of it and controlled by the same person; or

(c) in or on a structure controlled by the same person any part of which is within 500 metres of it,

is less than the controlled quantity.

(2) The temporary presence of a hazardous substance while it is being transported from one place to another is not to be taken into account unless it is unloaded.

(3) The Secretary of State—

(a) shall by regulations specify—

(i) the substances that are hazardous substances for the purposes of this Act;

(ii) the quantity which is to be the controlled quantity of any such substance;

(b) may by regulations provide that hazardous substances consent is not required or is only required—

(i) in relation to land of prescribed descriptions;

(ii) by reason of the presence of hazardous substances in prescribed circumstances;

(c) may by regulations provide that, except in such circumstances as may be prescribed, all hazardous substances falling within a group specified in the regulations are to be treated as a single substance for the purposes of this Act.

(4) Regulations which—

(a) are made by virtue of sub-paragraph (i) of subsection (3)(a) above; or

(b) are made by virtue of sub-paragraph (ii) of that paragraph and reduce the controlled quantity of a substance,

may make such transitional provision as appears to the Secretary of State to be appropriate.

(5) The power to make such transitional provision includes, without prejudice to its generality, power to apply section 34 of the Housing and Planning Act 1986 subject to such modifications as appear to the Secretary of State to be appropriate.

(6) Regulations under this section may make different provisions for different cases or descriptions of cases.

(7) Bodies corporate which are inter-connected for the purposes of the Fair Trading Act 1973 are to be treated as being one person for the purposes of this section and sections 58C to 58K and 101B below.

58C. Applications for hazardous substances consent

(1) Provision may be made by regulations with respect to—

(a) the form and manner in which applications for hazardous substances consent are to be made;

(b) the particulars which they are to contain and the evidence by which they are to be verified;

(c) the manner in which they are to be advertised; and

(d) the time within which they are to be dealt with.

(2) Regulations may provide that an application for hazardous substances consent, or an appeal against the refusal of such an application or against the imposition of a condition on such a consent, shall not be entertained unless it is accompanied by a certificate in the prescribed form and corresponding to one or other of those described in section 27(1)(a) to (d) of this Act; and any such regulations may—

(a) include requirements corresponding to sections 27(2) and (4) and 29(3) of this Act; and

(b) make provision as to who is to be treated as the owner of land for the purposes of any provision of the regulations.

(3) If any person issues a certificate which purports to comply with the requirements of regulations made by virtue of subsection (2) above and which contains a statement which he knows to be false or misleading in a material particular, or recklessly issues a certificate which purports to comply with those requirements and which contains a statement which is false or misleading in a material particular, he shall be guilty of an offence and liable on summary conviction to a fine of an amount not exceeding level 3 on the standard scale.

(4) Regulations—

(a) may require an applicant for hazardous substances consent or the hazardous substances authority or both to give publicity to an application for hazardous substances consent in such manner as may be prescribed;

(b) may require hazardous substances authorities to conduct appropriate consultations before determining applications for hazardous substances consent;

(c) may provide for the manner in which such a consultation is to be carried out and the time within which—

(i) such a consultation;
(ii) any stage in such a consultation, is to be completed;

(d) may require hazardous substances authorities to determine applications for hazardous substances consent within such time as may be prescribed;

(e) may require hazardous substances authorities to give prescribed persons or bodies prescribed information about applications for hazardous substances consent, including information as to the manner in which such applications have been dealt with.

(5) In subsection (4) above "appropriate consultation" means—

(a) consultations—

(i) in the case of a hazardous substances authority other than the appropriate Minister, with the Health and Safety Executive; and
(ii) in the case of the appropriate Minister, with the Health and Safety Commission; and

(b) consultations with such persons or bodies as may be prescribed.

(6) Regulations under this section may make different provision for different cases or descriptions of cases.

58D. Determination of applications for hazardous substances consent

(1) Subject to the following provisions of this Act, where an application is made to a hazardous substances authority for hazardous substances consent, that authority, in dealing with the application, shall have regard to any material considerations, and—

(a) may grant hazardous substances consent, either unconditionally or subject to such conditions as they think fit; or

(b) may refuse hazardous substances consent.

(2) Without prejudice to the generality of subsection (1) above, in dealing with an application the authority shall have regard—

(a) to any current or contemplated use of the land to which the application relates;

(b) to the way in which land in the vicinity is being used or is likely to be used;

(c) to any planning permission that has been granted for development of land in the vicinity;

(d) to the provisions of the development plan; and

(e) to any advice which the Health and Safety Executive or Health and Safety Commission have given following consultations in pursuance of regulations under section 58C(4) above.

(3) If an application relates to more than one hazardous substance, the authority may make different determinations in relation to each.

(4) It shall be the duty of a hazardous substances authority, when granting hazardous substances consent, to include in that consent—

    (*a*) a description of the land to which the consent relates;

    (*b*) a description of the hazardous substance or substances to which it relates; and

    (*c*) in respect of each hazardous substance to which it relates, a statement of the maximum quantity permitted by the consent to be present at any one time and of all conditions relating to that substance subject to which the consent is granted.

(5) Without prejudice to the generality of subsection (1) above, a hazardous substances authority may grant hazardous substances consent subject to conditions with respect to any of the following—

    (*a*) how and where any hazardous substance to which the consent relates is to be kept or used;

    (*b*) times between which any such substance may be present;

    (*c*) the permanent removal of any such substance—

        (i) on or before a date specified in the consent; or

        (ii) before the end of a period specified in it and commencing on the date on which it is granted;

    (*d*) the consent being conditional on the commencement or partial or complete execution of development on the land which is authorised by a specified planning permission;

but an authority who are a hazardous substances authority by virtue of section 1A above may only grant consent subject to conditions as to how a hazardous substance is to be kept or used if the conditions are conditions to which the Health and Safety Executive have advised the authority that any consent they might grant should be subject.

58E. References to Secretary of State and appeals

(1) Subject to subsections (2) and (3) below, sections 35 to 37 of this Act shall have effect in relation to applications for hazardous substances consent and to decisions on such applications as though they were applications for planning permission.

(2) In the application of sections 35 to 37 of this Act to hazardous substances consent—

    (*a*) references to the local planning authority shall be construed as references to the hazardous substances authority;

    (*b*) section 35(4) and section 36(5) and (7) shall be omitted;

    (*c*) the words "and in such manner as may be prescribed" shall be substituted for the words in section 36(2) following "time";

    (*d*) in section 37, the words "by the development order" shall be omitted from both places where they occur.

(3) Subsections (1) and (2) above do not have effect in relation to applications for hazardous substances consent relating to land to which section 1B of this Act applies or to decisions on such applications.

58F. Deemed hazardous substances consent by virtue of authorisation of government department

(1) Where—

   (a) the authorisation of a government department is required by virtue of an enactment in respect of development to be carried out by a local authority, or by statutory undertakers not being a local authority; and

   (b) the development would involve the presence of a hazardous substance in circumstances requiring hazardous substances consent,

the department may, on granting that authorisation, also direct that hazardous substances consent shall be deemed to be granted subject to such conditions (if any) as may be specified in the directions.

(2) The department shall consult the Health and Safety Commission before issuing any such directions.

(3) The provisions of this Act (except Parts VII and XII) shall apply in relation to any hazardous substances consent deemed to be granted by virtue of directions under this section as if it had been granted by the Secretary of State on an application referred to him under section 35 of this Act, as applied by section 58E of this Act.

(4) The reference in subsection (1) above to the authorisation of a government department is to be construed in accordance with section 40(3) of this Act.

58G. Grants of hazardous substances consent without compliance with conditions previously attached

(1) This section applies to an application for hazardous substances consent without a condition subject to which a previous hazardous substances consent was granted.

(2) On such an application the hazardous substances authority shall consider only the question of the conditions subject to which hazardous substances consent should be granted, and—

   (a) if they determine that hazardous substances consent should be granted subject to conditions differing from those subject to which the previous consent was granted, or that it should be granted unconditionally, they shall grant hazardous substances consent accordingly; and

   (b) if they determine that hazardous substances consent should be granted subject to the same conditions as those subject to which the previous consent was granted, they shall refuse the application.

(3) Where—

   (a) hazardous substances consent has been granted or is deemed to have been granted for the presence on, over or under land of more than one hazardous substance; and

   (b) an application under this section does not relate to all the substances,

the hazardous substances authority shall only have regard to any condition relating to a substance to which the application does not relate to the extent that it has implications for a substance to which the application does relate.

(4) Where—

(a) more than one hazardous substances consent has been granted or is deemed to have been granted in respect of the same land; and

(b) an application under this section does not relate to all the consents,

the hazardous substances authority shall only have regard to any consent to which the application does not relate to the extent that it has implications for consent to which the application does relate.

(5) Regulations may make provision in relation to applications under this section corresponding to any provision that may be made by regulations under section 58C above in relation to applications for hazardous substances consent.

58H. Power to revoke or modify hazardous substances consent

(1) If it appears to the hazardous substances authority that—

(a) there has been a material change of use of land to which a hazardous substances consent relates; or

(b) planning permission has been granted for development the carrying out of which would involve a material change of use of such land and the development to which the permission relates has been commenced,

they may by order—

(i) if the consent relates only to one substance, revoke it;

(ii) if it relates to more than one, revoke it or revoke it so far as it relates to a specified substance.

(2) The hazardous substances authority may by order—

(a) revoke a hazardous substances consent which relates to only one substance if it appears to them that that substance has not for at least 5 years been present on, under or over the land to which the consent relates in a quantity equal to or exceeding the controlled quantity; and

(b) revoke a hazardous substances consent which relates to a number of substances if it appears to them that none of those substances has for at least 5 years been so present.

(3) The hazardous substances authority may by order revoke a hazardous substances consent or modify it to such extent as they consider expedient if it appears to them, having regard to any material consideration, that it is expedient to revoke or modify it.

(4) An order under this section shall specify the grounds on which it is made.

(5) An order under this section, other than an order relating to land to which section 1B of this Act applies, shall not take effect unless it is confirmed by the Secretary of State, and the Secretary of State may confirm any such order submitted to him either without modification or subject to such modification as he considers expedient.

(6) Where a hazardous substances authority submit an order under this section to the Secretary of State for his confirmation under this section, the authority shall serve notice of the order—

(a) on any person who is an owner of the whole or any part of the land to which the order relates;

(b) on any person other than an owner who appears to them to be in control of the whole or any part of that land;

(c) on any other person who in their opinion will be affected by the order;

and if within the period specified in that behalf in the notice (not being less than 28 days from the service thereof) any person on whom the notice is served so requires, the Secretary of State, before confirming the order, shall afford to that person and to the hazardous substances authority an opportunity of appearing before, and being heard by, a person appointed by the Secretary of State for that purpose.

(7) Where an order under this section has been confirmed by the Secretary of State, the hazardous substances authority shall serve a copy of the order on every person who was entitled to be served with notice under subsection (6) above.

(8) Section 170 of this Act shall have effect where a hazardous substances consent is revoked or modified by an order made in the exercise of the power conferred by subsection (3) above as it has effect where an order is made under section 51 of this Act, but as if any reference in it to the local planning authority were a reference to the hazardous substances authority.

58J. Provisions as to effect of hazardous substances consent and change of control of land

(1) Without prejudice to the provisions of this Part of this Act, any hazardous substances consent shall (except in so far as it otherwise provides) enure for the benefit of the land to which it relates and of all persons for the time being interested in the land.

(2) A hazardous substances consent is revoked if there is a change in the person in control of part of the land to which it relates, unless an application for the continuation of the consent has previously been made to the hazardous substances authority.

(3) Regulations may make provision in relation to applications under section (2) above corresponding to any provision that may be made by regulations under section 58C of this Act in relation to applications for hazardous substances consent.

(4) When such an application is made, the authority, having regard to any material consideration—

(a) may modify the consent in any way they consider appropriate; or

(b) may revoke it.

(5) Without prejudice to the generality of subsection (4) above, in dealing with an application the authority shall have regard—

(a) to the matters to which a hazardous substances authority are required to have regard by section 58D(2)(a) to (d) above; and

(b) to any advice which the Health and Safety Executive or Health and Safety Commission have given following consultations in pursuance of regulations under subsection (3) above.

(6) If an application relates to more than one consent, the authority may make different determinations in relation to each.

(7) If a consent relates to more than one hazardous substance, the authority may make different determinations in relation to each.

(8) It shall be the duty of a hazardous substances authority, when continuing hazardous substances consent, to attach to the consent one of the following—

(a) a statement that it is unchanged in relation to the matters included in it by virtue of section 58D(4) above;
(b) a statement of any change in respect of those matters.

(9) The modifications which a hazardous substances authority may make by virtue of subsection (4)(a) above include, without prejudice to the generality of that paragraph, the making of the consent subject to conditions with respect to any of the matters mentioned in section 58D(5) above.

(10) Subject to subsection (11) below, sections 35 to 37 of this Act shall have effect in relation to applications under subsection (2) above and to decisions on such applications as though they were applications for planning permission.

(11) In the application of sections 35 to 37 of this Act by virtue of subsection (10) above—

(a) references to the local planning authority shall be construed as references to the hazardous substances authority;
(b) section 35(4) and section 36(5) and (7) shall be omitted;
(c) the words "and in such manner as may be prescribed" shall be substituted for the words in section 36(2) following "time";
(d) in section 37—

(i) the words "by the development order" shall be omitted from the first place where they occur; and
(ii) the words "the application shall be deemed to have been granted" shall be substituted for the words following paragraph (b).

(12) Where the authority modify or revoke the consent, they shall pay to the person in control of the whole of the land before the change compensation in respect of any loss or damage sustained by him and directly attributable to the modification or revocation.

58K. Offences

(1) Subject to this Part of this Act, if there is a contravention of hazardous substances control, the appropriate person shall be guilty of an offence.

(2) There is a contravention of hazardous substances control—

(a) if a quantity of a hazardous substance equal to or exceeding the controlled quantity is or has been present on, under or over land and either—

(i) there is no hazardous substances consent for the presence of the substance; or
(ii) there is hazardous substances consent for its presence but the quantity present exceeds the maximum quantity permitted by the consent;

(b) if there is or has been a failure to comply with a condition subject to which a hazardous substances consent was granted.

(3) In subsection (1) above "the appropriate person" means—

(a) in relation to a contravention falling within paragraph (a) of subsection (2) above—

(i) any person knowingly causing the substance to be present on, over or under the land;

(ii) any person allowing it to be so present; and

(b) in relation to a contravention falling within paragraph (a) or (b) of that subsection, the person in control of the land.

(4) A person guilty of an offence under this section shall be liable—

(a) on summary conviction, to a fine not exceeding the statutory maximum; or

(b) on conviction on indictment, to a fine,

and if the contravention is continued after the conviction he shall be guilty of a further offence and liable on summary conviction to a fine not exceeding £200 for each day on which it continues, or on conviction on indictment to a fine.

(5) In any proceedings for an offence under this section it shall be a defence for the accused to prove—

(a) that he took all reasonable precautions and exercised all due diligence to avoid commission of the offence, or

(b) that commission of the offence could be avoided only by the taking of action amounting to a breach of a statutory duty.

(6) In any proceedings for an offence consisting of a contravention falling within subsection (2)(a) above, it shall be a defence for the accused to prove that at the time of the alleged commission of the offence he did not know, and had no reason to believe,—

(a) if the case falls within paragraph (a)(i)—

(i) that the substance was present; or

(ii) that it was present in a quantity equal to or exceeding the controlled quantity;

(b) if the case falls within paragraph (a)(ii), that the substance was present in a quantity exceeding the maximum quantity permitted by the consent.

(7) In any proceedings for an offence consisting of a contravention falling within subsection (2)(b) above, it shall be a defence for the accused to prove that he did not know, and had no reason to believe, that there was a failure to comply with a condition subject to which hazardous substances consent had been granted.

58L. Emergencies

(1) If it appears to the Secretary of State—

(a) either—

(i) that the community or part of it is being or is likely to be deprived of an essential service or commodity; or

(ii) that there is or is likely to be a shortage of such a service or commodity affecting the community or part of it; and

(b) that the presence of a hazardous substance on, over or under land specified in the direction in circumstances such that hazardous substances consent would be required, is necessary for the effective provision of that service or commodity,

he may direct that, subject to such conditions or exceptions as he thinks fit, the presence of the substance on, over or under the land is not to constitute a contravention of hazardous substances control so long as the direction remains in force.

(2) A direction under this section—

(*a*) may be withdrawn at any time;

(*b*) shall in any case cease to have effect at the end of the period of three months beginning with the day on which it was given, but without prejudice to the Secretary of State's power to give a further direction.

(3) Subject to subsection (4) below, the Secretary of State shall send a copy of any such direction to the authority which are the hazardous substances authority in relation to the land.

(4) Where the land is land to which section 1B of this Act applies, the Secretary of State shall send the copy to the authority which would be the hazardous substances authority in relation to the land but for that section.

58M. Registers, etc

(1) Every authority which is a hazardous substances authority by virtue of section 1A of this Act shall keep, in such manner as may be prescribed, a register containing such information as may be prescribed with respect—

(*a*) to applications for hazardous substances consent—

(i) made to that authority; or

(ii) made to the appropriate Minister with respect to land in relation to which, but for section 1B of this Act, that authority would be the hazardous substances authority;

and including information as to the manner in which such applications have been dealt with;

(*b*) to hazardous substances consent deemed to be granted under section 34 of the Housing and Planning Act 1986 with respect to land in relation to which that authority is, or but for section 1B of this Act would be, the hazardous substances authority;

(*c*) to revocations or modifications of hazardous substances consent granted with respect to such land; and

(*d*) to directions under section 58L of this Act sent to the authority by the Secretary of State.

(2) Where with respect to any land the appropriate Minister exercises any of the functions of a hazardous substances authority, he shall send to the authority which but for section 1B of this Act would be the hazardous substances authority in relation to the land any such information as appears to him to be required by them for the purposes of maintaining a register under this section.

(3) Every register kept under this section shall be available for inspection by the public at all reasonable hours.

58N. Health and safety requirements

(1) Nothing in—

(*a*) any hazardous substances consent granted or deemed to be granted under—

(i) the preceding provisions of this Act; or

(ii) section 34 of the Housing and Planning Act 1986; or

(*b*) any hazardous substances contravention notice issued under section 101B of this Act,

shall require or allow anything to be done in contravention of any of the relevant statutory provisions or any prohibition notice or improvement notice served under or by virtue of any of those provisions; and to the extent that such a consent or notice purports to require or allow any such thing to be done, it shall be void.

(2) Where it appears to a hazardous substances authority who have granted, or are deemed to have granted, a hazardous substances consent or who have issued a hazardous substances contravention notice that the consent or notice or part of it is rendered void by subsection (1) above, the authority shall, as soon as is reasonably practicable, consult the appropriate body with regard to the matter.

(3) If the appropriate body advise the authority that the consent or notice is rendered wholly void, the authority shall revoke it.

(4) If they advise that part of the consent or notice is rendered void, the authority shall so modify it as to render it wholly operative.

(5) In this section—

"the appropriate body" means—

(*a*) in relation to a hazardous substances authority other than the appropriate Minister, the Health and Safety Executive; and

(*b*) in relation to the appropriate Minister, the Health and Safety Commission; and

"relevant statutory provisions", "improvement notice" and "prohibition notice" have the same meanings as in Part I of the Health and Safety at Work etc Act 1974.".   **[688]**

NOTES
Commencement: to be appointed.

32. Hazardous substances contravention notices

The following shall be inserted after section 101A of the Town and Country Planning Act 1971—

"Hazardous substances

101B. Power to issue hazardous substances contravention notice

(1) Subject to subsection (2) below, where it appears to the hazardous substances authority that there is or has been a contravention of hazardous substances control, they may issue a hazardous substances contravention notice if they consider it expedient to do so having regard to any material consideration.

(2) A hazardous substances authority shall not issue a hazardous substances contravention notice where it appears to them that a contravention of hazardous substances control can be avoided only by the taking of action amounting to a breach of a statutory duty.

(3) In this Act "hazardous substances contravention notice" means a notice—

(*a*) specifying an alleged contravention of hazardous substances control; and

(b) requiring such steps as may be specified in the notice to be taken to remedy the contravention.

(4) A copy of a hazardous substances contravention notice shall be served—

(a) on the owner of the land to which it relates;
(b) on any person other than the owner who appears to the hazardous substances authority to be in control of that land; and
(c) on such other persons as may be prescribed.

(5) A hazardous substances contravention notice shall also specify—

(a) a date not less than 28 days from the date of service of copies of the notice as the date on which it is to take effect;
(b) in respect of each of the steps required to be taken to remedy the contravention of hazardous substances control, the period from the notice taking effect within which the step is to be taken.

(6) Where a hazardous substances authority issue a hazardous substances contravention notice the steps required by the notice may, without prejudice to the generality of subsection (3)(b) above, if the authority think it expedient, include a requirement that the hazardous substance be removed from the land.

(7) Where a notice includes such a requirement, it may also contain a direction that at the end of such period as may be specified in the notice any hazardous substances consent for the presence of the substance shall cease to have effect or, if it relates to more than one substance, shall cease to have effect so far as it relates to the substance which is required to be removed.

(8) The hazardous substances authority may withdraw a hazardous substances contravention notice (without prejudice to their power to issue another) at any time before it takes effect.

(9) If they do so, they shall forthwith give notice of the withdrawal to every person who was served with a copy of the notice.

(10) The Secretary of State may by regulations—

(a) specify matters which are to be included in hazardous substances contravention notices, in addition to those which are required to be included in them by this section;
(b) provide—
  (i) for appeals to him against hazardous substances contravention notices;
  (ii) for the persons by whom, grounds upon which and time within which such an appeal may be brought;
  (iii) for the procedure to be followed on such appeals;
  (iv) for the directions that may be given on such an appeal;
  (v) for the application to such appeals, subject to such modifications as the regulations may specify, of any of the provision of sections 88 to 88B, 243 and 246 of this Act;
(c) direct that any of the provisions of sections 89 to 93 of this Act shall have effect in relation to hazardous substances contravention notices subject to such modifications as he may specify in the regulations;
(d) make such other provision as he considers necessary or expedient in relation to hazardous substances contravention notices.

(11) If any person appeals against a hazardous substances contravention notice, the notice shall be of no effect pending the final determination or the withdrawal of the appeal.

(12) Regulations under this section may make different provision for different cases or descriptions of cases.".   [689]

NOTES
Commencement: to be appointed.

33. Consequential amendments

The enactments mentioned in Part I of Schedule 7 to this Act shall have effect with the amendments there specified, being amendments consequential on the provisions of this Part of this Act.   [690]

NOTES
Commencement: to be appointed.

34. Transitional

(1) Until the end of the transitional period—

    (*a*) no offence is committed under section 58K of the Town and Country Planning Act 1971; and

    (*b*) no hazardous substances contravention notice may be issued, in relation to a hazardous substance which is on, under or over any land,

if the substance was present on, under or over the land at any time within the establishment period and—

    (i) in a case in which at the commencement date notification in respect of the substance was required by any of the Notification Regulations, both the conditions specified in subsection (2) below were satisfied; and

    (ii) in a case in which at that date such notification was not so required, the condition specified in paragraph (*b*) of that subsection is satisfied.

(2) The conditions mentioned in subsection (1) above are—

    (*a*) that notification required by the Notification Regulations was given before the commencement date; and

    (*b*) that the substance has not been present during the transitional period in a quantity greater in aggregate than the established quantity.

(3) Where a hazardous substance was present on, under or over any land at any time within the establishment period, hazardous substances consent may be claimed in respect of its presence.

(4) A claim shall be made in the prescribed form before the end of the transitional period and shall contain the prescribed information as to the presence of the substance during the establishment period and as to how and where it was kept and used immediately before the commencement date.

(5) Subject to subsections (6) to (8) below, the hazardous substances authority shall be deemed to have granted any hazardous substances consent which is claimed under subsection (3) above.

(6) If at the commencement date notification in respect of the substance was required by regulation 3 or 5 of the Notification Regulations, hazardous substances consent is only to be deemed to be granted under this section if

notification in respect of the substance was given before that date in accordance with those regulations.

(7) If at the commencement date such notification was not so required, hazardous substances consent is only to be deemed to be granted under this section if an aggregate quantity of the substance not less than the controlled quantity was present at any one time within the establishment period.

(8) If it appears to the hazardous substances authority that a claim for hazardous substances consent does not comply with subsection (4) above, it shall be their duty, before the end of the period of two weeks from their receipt of the claim,—

   (a) to notify the claimant that in their opinion the claim is invalid; and
   (b) to give him their reasons for that opinion.

(9) Hazardous substances consent which is deemed to be granted under this section is subject to the conditions that—

   (a) the maximum aggregate quantity of the substance that may be present—

      (i) on, under or over the land to which the claim relates;
      (ii) on, under or over other land which is within 500 metres of it and controlled by the same person; or
      (iii) in or on a structure controlled by the same person any part of which is within 500 metres of it,

      at any one time shall not exceed the established quantity; and
   (b) the substance shall be kept and used in the place and manner in which information supplied in pursuance of regulations made by virtue of subsection (4) above shows that it was kept and used immediately before the commencement date, and
   (c) none of the substance shall be kept or used in a container greater in capacity than the container, or the largest of the containers, in which the substance was kept or used immediately before the commencement date.

(10) In this section—

"commencement date" means the date on which this Part of this Act comes into force;
"the establishment period" means the period of 12 months immediately preceding the commencement date;
"established quantity" means, in relation to any land—

   (a) where before the commencement date there has been a notification in respect of a substance in accordance with any of the Notification Regulations—

      (i) the quantity notified or last notified before the commencement date; or
      (ii) a quantity equal to twice the quantity which was so notified or last notified before the start of the establishment period,

      whichever is the greater;
   (b) where a notification was not required before that date by any of those regulations, a quantity exceeding by 50 per cent, the maximum quantity which was present on, under or over the land at any one time within the establishment period;

"Notification Regulations" means the Notification of Installations Handling Hazardous Substances Regulations 1982;

"the transitional period" means the period of 6 months beginning with
the commencement date;

and other expressions have the same meanings as in the Town and Country
Planning Act 1971.   [691]

NOTES
Commencement: to be appointed.

* * * * *

PART VI

MISCELLANEOUS PROVISIONS

England and Wales

40. Listed buildings and conservation areas

The enactments relating to listed buildings and conservation areas are amended
in accordance with Part I of Schedule 9 with respect to the following matters—

    (a) the treatment of free-standing objects and structures within the
        curtilage of a listed building;

    (b) the scope of the exception for urgent works to a listed building;

    (c) the grant of listed building consent subject to the subsequent approval
        of detail;

    (d) applications for the variation or discharge of conditions attached to
        listed building consent;

    (e) the extent of the exemption accorded to ecclesiastical buildings;

    (f) dangerous structure orders in respect of listed buildings;

    (g) the power of a local authority, the Secretary of State or the Historic
        Buildings and Monuments Commission for England to carry out
        urgent works for the preservation of a building;

    (h) the control of demolition in a conservation area;

    (i) the form of an application for listed building consent; and

    (j) the powers of the Secretary of State with respect to applications for
        listed building consent.   [692]

NOTES
Commencement: 1 April 1987.

41. Local plans and unitary development plans

(1) In Part II of the Town and Country Planning Act 1971 (development plans),
the sections set out in Part I of Schedule 10 are substituted, except as to Greater
London, for sections 10C to 15B (local plans), the main changes being—

    (a) to provide for the co-ordination by county planning authorities, in
        conjunction with the district planning authorities, of the process of
        making, altering, repealing or replacing local plans;

    (b) to provide a short procedure for altering a local plan where the issues
        are not of sufficient importance to warrant the full procedure; and

    (c) to enable the Secretary of State to direct a local planning authority to
        reconsider proposals for making, altering, repealing or replacing a
        local plan; and

    (d) to omit provisions which are spent in consequence of the approval of
        structure plans for the whole of England and Wales.

(2) The substituted sections have effect in relation to metropolitan counties until the coming into force of Part I of Schedule 1 to the Local Government Act 1985 (unitary development plans), but subject to the provisions of Part II of that Schedule. **[693]**

* * * * *

NOTES
Commencement: to be appointed.

* * * * *

45. Control of advertisements: experimental areas

In section 63 of the Town and Country Planning Act 1971 (control of advertisements), for subsection (3) (power to make different provision for different areas) substitute—

"(3) Regulations made for the purposes of this section may make different provision with respect to different areas, and in particular may make special provision—

(a) with respect to conservation areas.

(b) with respect to areas defined for the purposes of the regulations as experimental areas, and

(c) with respect to areas defined for the purposes of the regulations as areas of special control.

(3A) An area may be defined as an experimental area for a prescribed period for the purpose of assessing the effect on amenity or public safety of advertisements of a prescribed description.

(3B) An area may be defined as an area of special control if it is—

(a) a rural area, or

(b) an area which appears to the Secretary of State to require special protection on grounds of amenity;

and, without prejudice to the generality of subsection (3), the regulations may prohibit the display in an area of special control of all advertisements except advertisements of such classes (if any) as may be prescribed.". **[694]**

NOTES
Commencement: 7 January 1987.

46. Land adversely affecting amenity of neighbourhood

For section 65 of the Town and County Planning Act 1971 (proper maintenance of waste land), and the heading preceding it, substitute—

"Land adversely affecting amenity of neighbourhood

65. Power to require proper maintenance of land

(1) It if appears to the local planning authority that the amenity of a part of their area, or of an adjoining area, is adversely affected by the condition of land in their area, they may serve on the owner and occupier of the land a notice under this section.

(2) The notice shall require such steps for remedying the condition of the

land as may be specified in the notice to be taken within such period as may be so specified.

(3) Subject to the provisions of Part V of this Act, the notice shall take effect at the end of such period (not being less than 28 days after the service of the notice) as may be specified in the notice.

(4) In non-metropolitan counties the functions of the local planning authority under this section are exercisable by the district planning authorities.".   [695]

NOTES
Commencement: 7 January 1987.

47. Areas which may be designated urban development areas

In section 134 of the Local Government, Planning and Land Act 1980 (power to designate urban development areas), omit subsection (2) (which restricts the power to land in metropolitan districts and certain land in or adjacent to inner London).   [696]

NOTES
Commencement: 7 January 1987.

48. Repeal of unnecessary enactments

(1) The following enactments are repealed—

* * * * *

    (b) sections 66 to 72 of the Town and Country Planning Act 1971 (special control over industrial development);

    (c) sections 250 to 252 of that Act (grants to local authorities for development of land, &c).

(2) The repeal does not affect the operation—

* * * * *

    (b) of sections 250 to 252 of the 1971 Act in relation to land for which approval for the purposes of regulations under section 250 was sought before 1st April 1986.   [697]

NOTES
Commencement: 7 January 1987.

49. Minor and consequential amendments; repeals

(1) The Town and Country Planning Act 1971, and certain related enactments, are amended in accordance with Part I of Schedule 11 with respect to the following matters—

    (a) the operation of the Use Classes Order on the subdivision of the planning unit;

    (b) the provision which may be made by development orders;

    (c) the construction of references to certain documents relating to access for the disabled;

    (d) applications to vary or revoke conditions attached to planning permission;

    (e) the procedure on appeals and applications disposed of without a local inquiry or hearing;

    (f) purchase notices;

(*g*) local inquiries;
(*h*) the determination of appeals by inspectors; and
(*i*) daily penalties for offences;

and that Part also contains amendments consequential on the provisions of this Part.

(2) The enactments specified in Part III of Schedule 12 are repealed to the extent specified. **[698]**

NOTES
Commencement: 7 November 1986 (certain purposes); 7 January 1987 (certain purposes); 2 March 1987 (certain purposes); 1 April 1987 (certain purposes); to be appointed (remaining purposes).

*   *   *   *   *

Provisions common to England and Wales and Scotland

54. Effect of modification or termination of enterprise zone scheme

(1) In Schedule 32 to the Local Government, Planning and Land Act 1980 (enterprise zones), for paragraphs 21 and 22 (effect of modification or termination of scheme on planning permission) substitute—

"*Effect on planning permission of modification or termination of scheme*

21. Modifications to a scheme do not affect planning permission under the scheme in any case where the development authorised by it has been begun before the modifications take effect.

22.—(1) Upon an area ceasing to be an enterprise zone planning permission under the scheme shall cease to have effect except in a case where the development authorised by it has been begun.

(2) The following provisions (which provide for the termination of planning permission if the completion of development is unreasonably delayed) apply to planning permission under the scheme where development has been begun but not completed by the time the area ceases to be an enterprise zone—

(*a*) in England and Wales, subsections (2) to (6) of section 44 of the 1971 Act;
(*b*) *   *   *   *   *.".

(2) In paragraph 26 of that Schedule (interpretation of Part III of the Schedule), after sub-paragraph (1) insert—

"(1A) The following provisions apply in determining for the purposes of this Schedule when development shall be taken to be begun—

(*a*) in England and Wales, subsections (1) to (3) of section 43 of the 1971 Act;
(*b*) *   *   *   *   *.". **[699]**

NOTES
Commencement: 7 January 1987.

*   *   *   *   *

PART VII

GENERAL PROVISIONS

56. Financial provisions

(1) There shall be paid out of money provided by Parliament any expenses of the Secretary of State under this Act and any increase attributable to this Act in the sums so payable under any other enactment.

(2) Any sums received by the Secretary of State under this Act shall be paid into the Consolidated Fund.

(3) There shall be paid out of or into the Consolidated Fund or the National Loans Fund any increase attributable to this Act in the sums so payable under any other enactment. **[700]**

NOTES
Commencement: 7 November 1986.

57. Commencement

(1) The following provisions of this Act come into force on the day this Act is passed—

      *   *   *   *   *

this Part.

(2) The other provisions of this Act come into force on such day as may be appointed by the Secretary of State by order made by statutory instrument and—

  (*a*) different days may be appointed for different provisions or different purposes; and

  (*b*) an order may make such transitional provision as the Secretary of State thinks appropriate.

      *   *   *   *   *

[701]

NOTES
Commencement: 7 November 1986.

58. Extent

(1) The following provisions of this Act extend to England and Wales—

Part I (housing), except section 3, paragraphs 10(7), 14 and 17 of Schedule 5 and the associated repeals in Part I of Schedule 12;

in Part II (simplified planning zones), section 25 and Parts I and II of Schedule 6;

Part III (financial assistance for urban regeneration);

in Part IV (hazardous substances), sections 30 to 34 and Part I of Schedule 7;

      *   *   *   *   *

in Part VI (miscellaneous provisions), sections 40 to 49, 54 and 55, Part I of Schedule 9, Schedule 10, Part I of Schedule 11 and Part III of Schedule 12;

this Part.

* * * * * **[702]**

NOTES
Commencement: 7 November 1986.

59. Short title

This Act may be cited as the Housing and Planning Act 1986. **[703]**

NOTES
Commencement: 7 November 1986.

SCHEDULES

* * * * *

SCHEDULE 6

Sections 25(2), (3), 26(2), (3)

SIMPLIFIED PLANNING ZONES: FURTHER PROVISIONS

PART I

SCHEDULE TO BE INSERTED IN THE TOWN AND COUNTRY PLANNING ACT 1971

SCHEDULE 8A

SIMPLIFIED PLANNING ZONES

General

1. A simplified planning zone scheme shall consist of a map and a written statement, and such diagrams, illustrations and descriptive matter as the local planning authority think appropriate for explaining or illustrating the provisions of the scheme, and shall specify—

   (*a*) the development or classes of development permitted by the scheme,
   (*b*) the land in relation to which permission is granted, and
   (*c*) any conditions, limitations or exceptions subject to which it is granted;

and shall contain such other matters as may be prescribed.

Proposals to make or alter scheme

2.—(1) A local planning authority may at any time decide to make a simplified planning zone scheme or to alter a scheme adopted by them or, with the consent of the Secretary of State, to alter a scheme approved by him.

(2) An authority who decide to make or alter a simplified planning zone scheme shall—

   (*a*) notify the Secretary of State of their decision as soon as practicable, and
   (*b*) determine the date on which they will begin to prepare the scheme or the alterations.

Power of Secretary of State to direct making or alteration of scheme

3.—(1) If a person requests a local planning authority to make or alter a simplified planning zone scheme but the authority—

   (*a*) refuse to do so, or
   (*b*) do not within the period of three months from the date of the request decide to do so,

he may, subject to sub-paragraph (2), require them to refer the matter to the Secretary of State.

(2) A person may not require the reference of the matter to the Secretary of State if—

    (*a*) in the case of a request to make a scheme, a simplified planning zone scheme relating to the whole or part of the land specified in the request has been adopted or approved within the twelve months preceding his request;

    (*b*) in the case of a request to alter a scheme, the scheme to which the request relates was adopted or approved, or any alteration to it has been adopted or approved, within that period.

(3) The Secretary of State shall, as soon as practicable after a matter is referred to him—

    (*a*) send the authority a copy of any representations made to him by the applicant which have not been made to the authority, and

    (*b*) notify the authority that if they wish to make any representations in the matter they should do so, in writing, within 28 days.

(4) The Secretary of State may, after—

    (*a*) considering the matter and any written representations made by the applicant or the authority, and

    (*b*) carrying out such consultations with such persons as he thinks fit,

give the authority a simplified planning zone direction.

(5) The Secretary of State shall notify the applicant and the authority of his decision and of his reasons for it.

4.—(1) A simplified planning zone direction is—

    (*a*) if the request was for the making of a scheme, a direction to make a scheme which the Secretary of State considers appropriate; and

    (*b*) if the request was for the alteration of a scheme, a direction to alter it in such manner as he considers appropriate.

(2) In either case the direction may extend to—

    (*a*) the land specified in the request to the authority,

    (*b*) any part of the land so specified, or

    (*c*) land which includes the whole or part of the land so specified;

and, accordingly, may direct that land shall be added to or excluded from an existing simplified planning zone.

Publicity and consultation: general

5.—(1) A local planning authority who propose to make or alter a simplified planning zone scheme shall proceed in accordance with this paragraph, unless paragraph 6 applies (short procedure for certain alterations).

(2) They shall take such steps as will in their opinion secure—

    (*a*) that adequate publicity for their proposals is given in the area to which the scheme relates,

    (*b*) that persons who may be expected to wish to make representations about the proposals are made aware that they are entitled to do so, and

    (*c*) that such persons are given an adequate opportunity of making such representations;

and they shall consider any representations made to them within the prescribed period.

(3) They shall then, having prepared the relevant documents, that is, the proposed scheme or alterations—

    (*a*) make copies of the documents available for inspection at their office, and

    (*b*) send a copy of them to the Secretary of State.

(4) Each copy of the documents made available for inspection shall be accompanied by a statement of the time within which objections may be made.

(5) The local planning authority shall before preparing the proposed scheme or alterations consult the Secretary of State having responsibility for highways as to the

effect of their proposals on existing or future highways; and when they have prepared the proposed scheme or alterations they shall send him a copy.

(6) A district planning authority in a non-metropolitan county shall also, before preparing the proposed scheme or alterations, consult the county council as planning authority and as to the effect of their proposals on existing or future highways; and when they have prepared the scheme or alterations they shall send the county council a copy.

Publicity and consultation: short procedure for certain alterations

6.—(1) Where a local planning authority propose to alter a simplified planning zone scheme and it appears to them that the issues involved are not of sufficient importance to warrant the full procedure set out in paragraph 5, they may proceed instead in accordance with this section.

(2) They shall prepare the proposed alterations and shall—

(*a*) make copies of them available for inspection at their office, and
(*b*) send a copy of them to the Secretary of State.

(3) Each copy of the documents made available for inspection shall be accompanied by a statement of the time within which representations or objections may be made.

(4) They shall then take such steps as may be prescribed for the purpose of—

(*a*) advertising the fact that the proposed alterations are available for inspection and the places and times at which, and the period during which, they may be inspected, and
(*b*) inviting the making of representations or objections in accordance with regulations;

and they shall consider any representations made to them within the prescribed period.

(5) The local planning authority shall send a copy of the proposed alterations to the Secretary of State having responsibility for highways.

(6) A district planning authority in a non-metropolitan county shall also send a copy of the proposed alterations to the county council.

Powers of Secretary of State to secure adequate publicity and consultation

7.—(1) The documents sent by the local planning authority to the Secretary of State under paragraph 5(3) shall be accompanied by a statement—

(*a*) of the steps which the authority have taken to comply with paragraph 5(2), and
(*b*) of the authority's consultations with other persons and their consideration of the views of those persons.

(2) The documents sent by the local planning authority to the Secretary of State under paragraph 6(2) shall be accompanied by a statement of the steps which the authority are taking to comply with paragraph 6(4).

(3) If, on considering the statement and the proposals and any other information provided by the local planning authority, the Secretary of State is not satisfied with the steps taken by the authority, he may, within 21 days of the receipt of the statement, direct the authority not to take further steps for the adoption of the proposals without—

(*a*) if they have proceeded in accordance with paragraph 6, proceeding instead in accordance with paragraph 5, or
(*b*) in any case, taking such further steps as he may specify, and satisfying him that they have done so.

(4) A local planning authority who are given directions by the Secretary of State shall—

(*a*) forthwith withdraw the copies of the documents made available for inspection as required by paragraph 5(3)(*a*) or 6(2)(*a*), and
(*b*) notify any person by whom objections to the proposals have been made to the authority that the Secretary of State has given such directions.

Objections: local inquiry or other hearing

8.—(1) The local planning authority may cause a local inquiry or other hearing to be held for the purpose of considering objections to their proposals for the making or alteration of a simplified planning zone scheme.

(2) They shall hold such a local inquiry or other hearing in the case of objections made in accordance with regulations unless all the persons who have made such objections have indicated in writing that they do not wish to appear.

(3) A local inquiry or other hearing shall be held by a person appointed by the Secretary of State or, in such cases as may be prescribed, by the authority themselves.

(4) Regulations may—

    (a) make provision with respect to the appointment, and qualifications for appointment, of persons to hold a local inquiry or other hearing;

    (b) include provision enabling the Secretary of State to direct a local planning authority to appoint a particular person, or one of a specified list or class of persons;

    (c) make provision with respect to the remuneration and allowances of the person appointed.

(5) Subsections (2) and (3) of section 250 of the Local Government Act 1972 (power to summon and examine witnesses) apply to an inquiry held under this paragraph.

(6) The Tribunals and Inquiries Act 1971 applies to a local inquiry or other hearing held under this paragraph as it applies to a statutory inquiry held by the Secretary of State, with the substitution in section 12(1) (statement of reasons for decision) for the references to a decision taken by the Secretary of State of references to a decision taken by a local authority.

Adoption of proposals by local planning authority

9.—(1) After the expiry of the period afforded for making objections to proposals for the making or alteration of a simplified planning zone scheme or, if such objections were duly made within that period, after considering the objections so made, the local planning authority may, subject to the following provisions of this paragraph and to paragraph 10 (calling in of proposals by Secretary of State), by resolution adopt the proposals.

(2) They may adopt the proposals as originally prepared or as modified so as to take account of—

    (a) any such objections as are mentioned in sub-paragraph (1) or any other objections to the proposals, or

    (b) any other considerations which appear to the authority to be material.

(3) After copies of the proposals have been sent to the Secretary of State and before they have been adopted by the local planning authority, the Secretary of State may, if it appears to him that the proposals are unsatisfactory, direct the authority to consider modifying the proposals in such respects as are indicated in the direction.

(4) An authority to whom a direction is given shall not adopt the proposals unless they satisfy the Secretary of State that they have made the modifications necessary to conform with the direction or the direction is withdrawn.

Calling in of proposals for approval by Secretary of State

10.—(1) After copies of proposals have been sent to the Secretary of State and before they have been adopted by the local planning authority, the Secretary of State may direct that the proposals shall be submitted to him for his approval.

(2) In that event—

    (a) the authority shall not take any further steps for the adoption of the proposals, and in particular shall not hold or proceed with a local inquiry or other hearing in respect of the proposals under paragraph 8; and (*b*) the proposals shall not have effect unless approved by the Secretary of State and shall not require adoption by the authority.

Approval of proposals by Secretary of State

11.—(1) The Secretary of State may after considering proposals submitted to him under paragraph 10 either approved them, in whole or in part and with or without modifications, or reject them.

(2) In considering the proposals he may taken into account any matters he thinks are relevant, whether or not they were taken into account in the proposals as submitted to him.

(3) Where on taking the proposals into consideration the Secretary of State does not determine then to reject them, he shall, before determining whether or not to approve them—

(*a*) consider any objections to them made in accordance with regulations,
(*b*) afford to any person who made such an objection which has not been withdrawn an opportunity of appearing before and being heard by a person appointed by him for the purpose, and
(*c*) if a local inquiry or other hearing is held, also afford such an opportunity to the authority and such other persons as he thinks fit,

except so far as objections have already been considered, or a local inquiry or other hearing into the objections has already been held, by the authority.

(4) In considering the proposals the Secretary of State may consult with, or consider the views of, any local planning authority or any other person; but he is under no obligation to do so, or to afford an opportunity for the making of representations or objections, or to cause a local inquiry or other hearing to be held, except as provided by sub-paragraph (3).

Default powers

12.—(1) Where by virtue of any of the preceding provisions of this Schedule—

(*a*) a simplified planning zone scheme or proposals for the alteration of such a scheme are required to be prepared, or
(*b*) steps are required to be taken for the adoption of any such scheme or proposals,

then, if the Secretary of State is satisfied, after holding a local inquiry or other hearing, that the local planning authority are not taking the steps necessary to enable them to prepare or adopt such a scheme or proposals within a reasonable period, he may make the scheme or the alterations, as he thinks fit.

(2) Where under this paragraph anything which ought to have been done by a local planning authority is done by the Secretary of State, the preceding provisions of this Schedule apply, so far as practicable, with any necessary modifications, in relation to the doing of that thing by the Secretary of State and the thing so done.

(3) Where the Secretary of State incurs expenses under this paragraph in connection with the doing of anything which should have been done by a local planning authority, so much of those expenses as may be certified by the Secretary of State to have been incurred in the performance of functions of that authority shall on demand be repaid by the authority to the Secretary of State.

Regulations and directions

13.—(1) Without prejudice to the preceding provisions of this Schedule, the Secretary of State may make regulations with respect to the form and content of simplified planning zone schemes and with respect to the procedure to be followed in connection with their preparation, withdrawal, adoption, submission, approval, making or alteration.

(2) Any such regulations may in particular—

(*a*) provide for the notice to be given of, or the publicity to be given to, matters included or proposed to be included in a simplified planning zone scheme and the adoption or approval of such a scheme, or of any alteration of it, or any other prescribed procedural step, and for publicity to be given to the procedure to be followed in these respects;

(b) make provision with respect to the making and consideration of representations as to matters to be included in, or objections to, any such scheme or proposals for its alteration;

(c) without prejudice to paragraph (b), provide for notice to be given to particular persons of the adoption or approval of a simplified planning zone scheme, or an alteration to such a scheme, if they have objected to the proposals and have notified the local planning authority of their wish to receive notice, subject (if the regulations so provide) to the payment of a reasonable charge;

(d) require or authorise a local planning authority to consult with, or consider the views of, other persons before taking any prescribed procedural step;

(e) require a local planning authority, in such cases as may be prescribed or in such particular cases as the Secretary of State may direct, to provide persons making a request in that behalf with copies of any document which has been made public for the purpose mentioned in paragraph 5(2) or 6(3) or has been made available for inspection under paragraph 5(3) or 6(2), subject (if the regulations so provide) to the payment of a reasonable charge;

(f) provide for the publication and inspection of a simplified planning zone scheme which has been adopted or approved, or any document adopted or approved altering such a scheme, and for copies of any such scheme or document to be made available on sale.

(3) Regulations under this paragraph may extend throughout England and Wales or to specified areas only and may make different provision for different cases.

(4) Subject to the preceding provisions of this Schedule and to any regulations under this paragraph, the Secretary of State may give directions to any local planning authority or to local planning authorities generally—

(a) for formulating the procedure for the carrying out of their functions under this Schedule;

(b) for requiring them to give him such information as he may require for carrying out any of his functions under this Schedule.   **[704]**

NOTES
Commencement: to be appointed.

PART II

CONSEQUENTIAL AMENDMENTS—ENGLAND AND WALES

1. In section 34(1) of the Town and Country Planning Act 1971 (registers to be kept by local planning authorities) at the end add "and also containing such information as may be so prescribed with respect to simplified planning zone schemes relating to zones in the authority's area".

2. In section 41 of the Town and Country Planning Act 1971 (limit of duration of planning permission), in subsection (3) (exceptions) after paragraph (aa) insert—

"(ab) to any planning permission granted by a simplified planning zone scheme;".

3. In section 53(1) of the Town and Country Planning Act 1971 (application to determine whether planning permission required) after "scheme" insert "or simplified planning zone scheme".

4. In section 242(1) of the Town and Country Planning Act 1971 (validity of certain instruments to be questioned under that Act and not otherwise), after paragraph (a) insert—

"(aa) a simplified planning zone scheme or an alteration of such a scheme whether before or after the adoption or approval of the scheme or alteration;".

5. In section 244 of the Town and Country Planning Act 1971 (procedure for questioning certain instruments), after subsection (6) insert—

"(7) Subsections (1) and (2) of this section apply to a simplified planning zone scheme or an alteration of such a scheme as they apply to a structure plan and an alteration of such a plan, with the following modifications—

(a) for the references to Part II of this Act substitute references to Part III of this Act, and

(b) for the reference to regulations under section 18(1) of this Act substitute a reference to regulations under paragraph 13 of Schedule 8A to this Act,

and with any other necessary modifications.".

6. In section 287 of the Town and Country Planning Act 1971 (general provisions as to regulations and orders)—

(a) in subsection (4) (orders to be made by statutory instrument) after "24," insert "24E,", and

(b) in subsection (5)(b) (orders subject to negative resolution procedure), after "section" insert "24E,".

7. In section 290(1) of the Town and Country Planning Act 1971 (interpretation), at the appropriate place insert—

"simplified planning zone" and "simplified planning zone scheme" shall be construed in accordance with section 24A of this Act;". [705]

NOTES

Commencement: to be appointed.

* * * * *

SCHEDULE 7

Sections 33 and 37

HAZARDOUS SUBSTANCES: CONSEQUENTIAL AMENDMENTS

PART I

ENGLAND AND WALES

* * * * *

Town and Country Planning Act 1971 (c 78)

2. In subsection (3) (action on the part of the Secretary of State that may be questioned in legal proceedings) of section 242 of the Town and Country Planning Act 1971, the following paragraph shall be inserted after paragraph (d)—

"(dd) any decision by the Secretary of State relating to an application for hazardous substances consent;".

3. In subsection (2)(a) of section 266 of that Act (orders which, in relation to Crown land, may only be made with consent of appropriate authority)—

(a) after "51B" there shall be inserted "58H"; and

(b) for "or 96" there shall be substituted "96 or 101B".

4. Section 269 of that Act (application to Isles of Scilly) shall have effect as if sections 58B to 58N and 101B were included among the provisions specified in Part III of Schedule 21 (provisions that may be applied to Isles as if they were a district).

5. The following section shall be inserted after section 271 of that Act—

"271A Application to certain hazardous substances authorities of provisions as to hazardous substances control

(1) The provisions of this Act relating to hazardous substances shall have effect subject to such exceptions and modifications as may be prescribed in relation to

granting hazardous substances consent for authorities who are hazardous substances authorities by virtue of section 1A of this Act.

(2) Subject to the provisions of section 58F of this Act, any such regulations may in particular provide for securing—

(*a*) that any application by such an authority for hazardous substances consent in respect of the presence of a hazardous substance on, over, or under land shall be made to the Secretary of State and not to the hazardous substances authority;

(*b*) that any order or notice authorised to be made, issued or served under those provisions shall be made, issued or served by the Secretary of State and not by the hazardous substances authority."

6. In section 280 of that Act (rights of entry)—

(*a*) the following subsection shall be inserted after subsection (1)—

"(1A) Any person duly authorised in writing by the Secretary of State or by a hazardous substances authority may at any reasonable time enter any land for the purpose of surveying it in connection with—

(*a*) any application for hazardous substances consent;

(*b*) any proposal to issue a hazardous substances contravention notice.";

(*b*) at the end of subsection (4) there shall be added the words "and any person duly authorised in writing by the Secretary of State or by a hazardous substances authority may at any reasonable time enter any land for the purpose of ascertaining whether an offence appears to have been committed under section 58K of this Act.";

(*c*) the following subsection shall be inserted after subsection (6)—

"(6A) Subsection (6) above shall have effect for the purposes of a claim for compensation made by virtue of section 58H(8) or 58J(12) of this Act as if a reference to a local planning authority were a reference to a hazardous substances authority."; and

(*d*) in subsection (8), after the word "section" there shall be inserted the words "or a hazardous substances contravention notice has been issued".

7. In section 290(1) of that Act (Interpretation)—

(*a*) the following shall be inserted after the definition of "conservation area"—

""contravention of hazardous substances control" has the meaning assigned to it by section 58K(2) of this Act;";

(*b*) the following shall be inserted after the definition of "the Greater London development plan"—

""hazardous substances authority" is to be construed in accordance with sections 1A and 1B of this Act;

"hazardous substances consent" means consent required by section 58B of this Act;

"hazardous substances contravention notice" has the meaning assigned to it by section 101B(3) of this Act;"; and

(*c*) the following shall be inserted after the definition of "tree preservation order"—

""urban development area" and "urban development corporation" have the same meaning as in Part XVI of the Local Government, Planning and Land Act 1980;".

Town and Country Planning Act 1984 (c 10)

8. In section 1 of the Town and Country Planning Act 1984 (applications in anticipation of disposal of Crown interest)—

(*a*) in subsection (1)(*a*), after the words "listed building consent" there shall be inserted the words ", hazardous substances consent"; and

(b) the following subsection shall be inserted after subsection (3)—

"(3A) Any hazardous substances consent granted by virtue of this section shall apply only—

(a) to the presence of the substance to which the consent relates after the land in question has ceased to be Crown land; and

(b) so long as that land continues to be Crown land, to the presence of the substance by virtue of a private interest in the land.".

*   *   *   *   *

[706]

NOTES
  Commencement: to be appointed.

*   *   *   *   *

SCHEDULE 9
Sections 40 and 50

LISTED BUILDINGS AND CONSERVATION AREAS

PART I

ENGLAND AND WALES

*Free-standing objects and structures within curtilage of
listed building*

1.—(1) In section 54(9) of the Town and Country Planning Act 1971 (definition of "listed building"), for the words from "and for the purposes" to the end substitute—

"and, for the purposes of the provisions of this Act relating to listed buildings and building preservation notices, the following shall be treated as part of the building—

(a) any object or structure fixed to the building;

(b) any object or structure within the curtilage of the building which, although not fixed to the building, forms part of the land and has done so since before 1st July 1984.".

(2) Where by virtue of this paragraph an object or structure ceases to be treated as part of a listed building—

(a) liabilities incurred before the commencement of this paragraph by reason of the object or structure being so treated cease to have effect, and

(b) a condition attached to a listed building consent ceases to have effect if, or to the extent that, it could not have been attached if this paragraph had been in force;

except for the purposes of criminal proceedings begun before the commencement of this paragraph.

NOTES
  Commencement: 1 April 1987.

Scope of exception for urgent works

2.—(1) In section 55 of the Town and Country Planning Act 1971 (control of works for demolition, alteration or extension of listed buildings), for subsection (6) (exception for certain urgent works) substitute—

"(6) In proceedings for an offence under this section it shall be a defence to prove the following matters—

(a) that works to the building were urgently necessary in the interests of safety or health or for the preservation of the building,

(b) that it was not practicable to secure safety or health or, as the case may be, the preservation of the building by works of repair or works for affording temporary support or shelter,

(c) that the works carried out were limited to the minimum measures immediately necessary, and

(d) that notice in writing justifying in detail the carrying out of the works was given to the local planning authority as soon as reasonably practicable.".

(2) In section 97 of the Town and Country Planning Act 1971 (appeal against listed building enforcement notice) in subsection (1) (grounds of appeal), for paragraph (d) substitute—

(d) that works to the building were urgently necessary in the interests of safety or health or for the preservation of the building, that it was not practicable to secure safety or health or, as the case may be, the preservation of the building by works of repair or works for affording temporary support or shelter, and that the works carried out were limited to the minimum measures immediately necessary;".

NOTES
Commencement: 1 April 1987.

Grant of listed building consent subject to subsequent approval of detail

3.—(1) In section 56 of the Town and Country Planning Act 1971 (supplementary provisions with respect to listed building consent), after subsection (4A) insert—

"(4B) Listed building consent may be granted subject to a condition reserving specified details of the works (whether or not set out in the application) for subsequent approval by the local planning authority or, in the case of consent granted by the Secretary of State, specifying whether the reserved details are to be approved by the local planning authority or by him.".

(2) In paragraph 8(1) of Schedule 11 to the Town and Country Planning Act 1971 (listed building consent: appeal against decision), for the words from the beginning to "and the consent is refused" substitute—

"Where an application is made to the local planning authority—

(a) for listed building consent, or

(b) for approval of the authority required by a condition imposed on the granting of listed building consent with respect to details of the works,

and the consent or approval is refused".

(3) Renumber paragraph 9 of Schedule 11 to the Town and Country Planning Act 1971 (appeal in default of decision) as sub-paragraph (1) of that paragraph and after it insert—

"(2) Sub-paragraph (1) of this paragraph applies to an application to the local planning authority for approval by the authority required by a condition imposed on the granting of listed building consent with respect to details of the works as it applies to an application for listed building consent, with the following modifications—

(a) for references to the prescribed period substitute references to the period of eight weeks from the date of the receipt of the application, and

(b) omit paragraph (b) and the word 'or' preceding it.".

NOTES
Commencement: 1 April 1987.

Application to modify or discharge conditions attached to listed building consent

4. After section 56A of the Town and Country Planning Act 1971 insert—

"56B Application for variation or discharge of conditions

(1) Any person interested in a listed building with respect to which listed building consent has been granted subject to conditions may apply to the local planning authority for the variation or discharge of the conditions.

(2) The application shall indicate what variation or discharge of conditions is applied for and the provisions of Part I of Schedule 11 to this Act apply to such an application as they apply to an application for listed building consent.

(3) On such an application the local planning authority or, as the case may be, the Secretary of State may vary or discharge the conditions attached to the consent, and may add new conditions consequential upon the variation or discharge, as they or he thinks fit.".

NOTES
Commencement: 1 April 1987.

Extent of exemption accorded to ecclesiastical buildings

5.—(1) After section 58A of the Town and Country Planning Act 1971 insert—

"58AA Power to restrict exemption of certain ecclesiastical buildings

(1) The Secretary of State may by order provide for restricting or excluding in such cases as may be specified in the order the operation in relation to ecclesiastical buildings of sections 56(1) and 58(2) of this Act (buildings excepted from provisions relating to listed buildings and building preservation notices).

(2) An order under this section may—

(a) make provision for buildings generally, for descriptions of building or for particular buildings;

(b) make different provision for buildings in different areas, for buildings of different religious faiths or denominations or according to the use made of the building;

(c) make such provision in relation to a part of a building (including, in particular, an object or structure falling to be treated as part of the building by virtue of section 54(9) of this Act) as may be made in relation to a building and make different provision for different parts of the same building;

(d) make different provision with respect to works of different descriptions or according to the extent of the works;

(e) make such consequential adaptations or modifications of the operation of any other provision of this Act, or of any instrument made under this Act, as appear to the Secretary of State to be appropriate.".

(2) In section 287 of the Town and Country Planning Act 1971 (regulations and orders)—

(a) in subsection (4) (orders to be made by statutory instrument), after "55(3)" insert "58AA";

(b) in subsection (5) (orders subject to negative resolution), after "section" insert "58AA";

(c) in subsection (9) (power to include supplementary and incidental provisions), after "section" insert "58AA".

NOTES
Commencement: 1 April 1987.

Dangerous structure orders in respect of listed buildings

6.—(1) In the Town and Country Planning Act 1971, after the section inserted by paragraph 4 above insert—

"56C Dangerous structure orders in respect of listed buildings

(1) Before taking any steps with a view to the making of a dangerous structure order in respect of a listed building, a local planning authority shall consider whether they should instead exercise their powers under—

(a) section 101 of this Act (power to carry out urgent works for preservation of building), or

(b) sections 114 and 115 of this Act (power to acquire building in need of repair).

(2) In this section "dangerous structure order" means an order or notice under section 77(1)(a) or 79(1) of the Building Act 1984 or section 62(2), 65 or 69(1) of the London Building Acts (Amendment) Act 1939.".

*   *   *   *   *

NOTES

Commencement: 1 April 1987.

Works for preservation of buildings

7. For section 101 of the Town and Country Planning Act 1971 (urgent works for preservation of unoccupied buildings) substitute—

"101 Urgent works to preserve building

(1) Where it appears to the local authority or the Secretary of State that works are urgently necessary for the preservation of—

(a) a listed building, or

(b) a building in respect of which a direction has been given by the Secretary of State that this section shall apply,

they or he may, subject to the following provisions of this section, execute the works, which may consist of or include works for affording temporary support or shelter for the building.

(2) The ground on which the Secretary of State may give a direction that this section shall apply to a building is that the building is in a conservation area and it appears to him that its preservation is important for maintaining the character or appearance of the conservation area.

(3) If the building is occupied works may be carried out only to those parts which are not in use; and no action may be taken in respect of an excepted building within the meaning of section 58(2) of this Act.

(4) The owner of the building shall be given not less than seven days' notice in writing of the intention to carry out the works and the notice shall describe the works proposed to be carried out.

(5) The Historic Buildings and Monuments Commission for England have the following functions under this section—

(a) as respects buildings in Greater London the Commission have concurrently with the relevant London borough council the functions of a local authority;

(b) the Secretary of State shall consult the Commission before giving a direction under subsection (1)(b) in respect of a building in England; and

(c) if it appears to the Secretary of State in accordance with subsection (1) that works are required for the preservation of a building in England, he shall not himself carry out the works but shall instead authorise the Commission to do so, specifying the works in the authorisation, and it shall be for the Commission to give notice to the owner under subsection (4).

101A Recovery of expenses of works under s 101

(1) This section has effect for enabling the expenses of works executed under section 101 of this Act to be recovered by the authority who carried out the works, that is, the local authority, the Historic Buildings and Monuments Commission for England or the Secretary of State or, in the case of works carried out by the Historic Buildings and

Monuments Commission for England on behalf of the Secretary of State, by the Secretary of State.

(2) The authority or, as the case may be, the Secretary of State may give notice to the owner of the building requiring him to pay the expenses of the works.

(3) Where the works consist of or include works for affording temporary support or shelter for the building—

    (*a*) the expenses which may be recovered include any continuing expenses involved in making available the apparatus or materials used, and

    (*b*) notices under subsection (2) in respect of any such continuing expenses may be given from time to time.

(4) The owner may within 28 days of the service of the notice represent to the Secretary of State—

    (*a*) that some or all of the works were unnecessary for the preservation of the building,

    (*b*) in the case of works for affording temporary support or shelter, that the temporary arrangements have continued for an unreasonable length of time, or

    (*c*) that the amount specified in the notice is unreasonable or that the recovery of it would cause him hardship,

and the Secretary of State shall determine to what extent the representations are justified.

(5) The Secretary of State shall give notice of his determination, the reasons for it and the amount recoverable—

    (*a*) to the owner of the building, and

    (*b*) to the local authority or the Historic Buildings and Monuments Commission for England, if they carried out the works.".

NOTES
Commencement: 1 April 1987.

Control of demolition in conservation areas

8.—(1) Section 277A of the Town and Country Planning Act 1971 (control of demolition in conservation areas) is amended as follows.

(2) For subsection (8) (application of provisions relating to listed buildings) substitute—

"(8) The following provisions of this Act have effect in relation to buildings to which this section applies as they have effect in relation to listed buildings, subject to such exceptions and modifications as may be prescribed by regulations—

sections 55 to 56C and 58AA and Parts I and II of Schedule 11 (requirement of consent to works: application for and revocation of consent),
sections 96 to 100 (enforcement),
section 172 (compensation where consent revoked or modified),
section 190 and Schedule 19 (purchase notice on refusal of consent),
sections 242, 243, 245 and 246 (validity of orders, proceedings for review and appeals),
section 255 (contributions by local authorities and statutory undertakers);
section 266(1)(*b*), (4) and (5) (application to Crown land), and
section 271 and Part VI of Schedule 21 (application of provisions to works by local planning authority).".

(3) In subsection (11) (authorities exercising functions of local planning authority), in paragraph (*c*) (non-metropolitan counties, excluding areas in National Parks) omit "the county planning authority and".

NOTES
Commencement: 1 April 1987.

Form of application for listed building consent

9. For paragraph 1(1) of Schedule 11 to the Town and Country Planning Act 1971 (regulations as to form and manner of application for listed building consent) substitute—

"(1) An application for listed building consent shall be made in such form as the local planning authority may require and shall contain—

(a) sufficient particulars to identify the building to which it relates, including a plan, and

(b) such other plans and drawings as are necessary to describe the works which are the subject of the application,

and such other particulars as may be required by the local planning authority.

(1A) Provision may be made by regulations under this Act with respect to the manner in which applications for listed building consent are to be made, the manner in which such applications are to be advertised and the time within which they are to be dealt with by local planning authorities or, as the case may be, by the Secretary of State.".

NOTES
Commencement: 1 April 1987.

Listed building consent: consideration whether to call in application

10.—(1) In paragraph 5(2) of Schedule 11 to the Town and Country Planning Act 1971 (notice to local planning authority that Secretary of State requires further time to consider whether to call in an application for listed building consent), for the words from "and sub-paragraph (1)" to the end substitute "; and if he gives such a notice the authority shall not grant the listed building consent until he has notified them that he does not intend to require the reference of the application.".

(2) In paragraph 6(4) of Schedule 11 to the Town and Country Planning Act 1971 (notice to Historic Buildings and Monuments Commission that Secretary of State requires further time to consider whether to call in an application for listed building consent), for the words from "and sub-paragraph (3)" to the end substitute "; and if he gives such a notice the Commission shall not authorise the local planning authority as mentioned in sub-paragraph (2)(a) of this paragraph, nor under sub-paragraph (2)(b) of this paragraph direct them to grant listed building consent, until he has notified them that he does not intend to require the reference of the application.".

(3) In paragraph 6(6) of Schedule 11 to the Town and Country Planning Act 1971 (notice to local planning authority that Secretary of State requires further time to consider whether to call in application for listed building consent which the Historic Buildings and Monuments Commission have directed the authority to refuse), for the words from "and sub-paragraph (5)(a)" to the end substitute "; and if he gives such a notice the authority shall not give effect to the Commission's direction until he has notified them that he does not intend to require the reference of the application.".

NOTES
Commencement: 1 April 1987.

Listed building consent: directions as to which applications need
not be notified to the Secretary of State

11.—(1) Paragraph 7 of Schedule 11 to the Town and Country Planning Act 1971 (directions as to which applications need not be notified to Secretary of State) is amended as follows.

(2) In paragraph 7(1) (power to direct that certain descriptions of application need not be notified) omit, "other than such consent for the demolition of a building" and after that sub-paragraph insert—

"(1A) Before giving a direction under sub-paragraph (1) of this paragraph in respect of any description of application for consent to the demolition of a building in England, the Secretary of State shall consult the Historic Buildings and Monuments Commission for England.".

(3) For paragraph 7(1A) and (1B) (power to except applications from direction under sub-paragraph (1)) substitute—

"(1B) Where a direction is in force under sub-paragraph (1) of this paragraph, the Secretary of State may give to a local planning authority a direction that paragraph 5 or (as the case may be) paragraph 6 of this Schedule shall nevertheless apply—

    (*a*) to a particular application for listed building consent, or

    (*b*) to such descriptions of application for listed building consent as are specified in the direction;

and such a direction has effect in relation to any such application which has not been disposed of by the authority by their granting or refusing consent.".

(4) At the end of the paragraph add—

"(3) Directions under sub-paragraph (1) or (2) of this paragraph may be given to authorities generally or to particular authorities or descriptions of authority.".

NOTES
    Commencement: 1 April 1987.

*Application to local planning authorities of provisions
relating to listed buildings*

12. In Part VI of Schedule 21 to the Town and Country Planning Act 1971 (provisions of Act applying to applications by local planning authorities with respect to listed buildings), at the appropriate place insert "Sections 242, 243, 245 and 246.".   **[707]**

NOTES
    Commencement: 1 April 1987.

*   *   *   *   *

SCHEDULE 10
Section 41(1) and (3)

LOCAL PLANS AND UNITARY DEVELOPMENT PLANS

PART I

SECTIONS 11 TO 15B OF THE TOWN AND COUNTRY PLANNING ACT 1971 (C 78), AS SUBSTITUTED

ARRANGEMENT OF SECTIONS

Local Plans

15B   Conformity between plans: local plan prevails

* * * * *

Local plans

11 Local plans

(1) A local plan shall consist of—

(a) a written statement formulating in such detail as the local planning authority think appropriate their proposals for the development or other use of land in their area, or for any description of development or other use of such land, including such measures as the authority think fit for the improvement of the physical environment and the management of traffic;

(b) a map showing those proposals; and

(c) such diagrams, illustrations or other descriptive matter as the authority think appropriate to explain or illustrate the proposals in the plan, or as may be prescribed.

(2) Different local plans may be prepared for different purposes for the same area.

(3) In formulating their proposals in a local plan the local planning authority shall have regard to any information and any other considerations which appear to them to be relevant or which may be prescribed or which the Secretary of State may in any particular case direct them to take into account.

(4) The proposals in a local plan shall be in general conformity with the structure plan.

(5) A local planning authority may prepare a local plan for a part of their area (an "action area") which they have selected for the commencement during a prescribed period of comprehensive treatment, by development, redevelopment or improvement of the whole or part of the area selected, or partly by one method and partly by another; and a local plan prepared for such an action area shall indicate the nature of the treatment selected for the area.

(6) For the purpose of discharging their functions with respect to local plans a district planning authority may, in so far as it appears to them necessary to do so having regard to the survey made by the county planning authority under section 6 of this Act, examine the matters mentioned in subsections (1) and (3) of that section so far as relevant to their area.

(7) In preparing a local plan a local planning authority shall take into account the provisions of any scheme under paragraph 3 of Schedule 32 to the Local Government, Planning and Land Act 1980 relating to land in their area which has been designated under that Schedule as an enterprise zone.

11A Local plan schemes

(1) A local plan scheme for each county shall be maintained in accordance with this section setting out a programme for the making, alteration, repeal or replacement of local plans for areas in the county, except any part of the county included in a National Park.

(2) The scheme shall, as regards each local plan for which it provides—

(a) specify the title and nature of the plan and the area to which it is to apply and give an indication of its scope,

(b) indicate where appropriate its relationship with the other local plans provided for by the scheme, and

(c) designate the local planning authority, whether county or district, responsible for the plan;

and may contain any appropriate incidental, consequential, transitional and supplementary provisions.

(3) The district planning authorities shall keep under review the need for, and adequacy of, local plans for their area and may make recommendations to the county planning authority for incorporation into the local plan scheme.

(4) The county planning authority shall, in the light of the recommendations of the

district planning authorities and in consultation with those authorities, make and thereafter keep under review and from time to time amend the local plan scheme.

(5) As soon as practicable after making or amending a local plan scheme the county planning authority shall send a copy of the scheme, or the scheme as amended, to the Secretary of State.

(6) If a district planning authority make representations to the Secretary of State that they are dissatisfied with a local plan scheme, the Secretary of State may amend the scheme.

(7) A local planning authority may prepare proposals for the making, alteration, repeal or replacement of a local plan—

    (a) in any case, except in the case of proposals relating only to land in a National Park, only where authorised to do so by the local plan scheme, and

    (b) in the case of proposals for the alteration, repeal or replacement of a local plan approved by the Secretary of State, only with the consent of the Secretary of State;

but subject to any direction of the Secretary of State under section 11B.

11B Power of Secretary of State to direct making of local plan, &c

(1) The Secretary of State may, after consulting a local planning authority, direct them to make, alter, repeal or replace a local plan with respect to their area or part of it.

(2) A direction for the making, alteration or replacement of a local plan shall specify the nature of the plan or, as the case may be, the nature of the alteration required.

(3) The authority shall comply with the direction as soon as possible.

(4) The county planning authority shall make such amendments of the relevant local plan scheme as appear to them appropriate in consequence of the direction.

12 Publicity and consultation: general

(1) A local planning authority who propose to make, alter, repeal or replace a local plan shall proceed in accordance with this section, unless section 12A applies (short procedure for certain alterations, &c).

(2) They shall take such steps as will in their opinion secure—

    (a) that adequate publicity is given to the proposals in the area to which the plan relates,

    (b) that persons who may be expected to wish to make representations about the proposals are made aware that they are entitled to do so, and

    (c) that such persons are given an adequate opportunity of making such representations;

and they shall consider any representations made to them within the prescribed period.

(3) They shall consult the county planning authority or, as the case may be, the district planning authority with respect to their proposals, shall afford that authority a reasonable opportunity to express their views and shall take those views into consideration.

(4) They shall then, having prepared the relevant documents, that is, the proposed plan, alterations, instrument of repeal or replacement plan, as the case may be, and having obtained any certificate required by section 15 (certificate of conformity with structure plan)—

    (a) make copies of the documents available for inspection at their office,

    (b) send a copy of them to the Secretary of State, and

    (c) send a copy of them to the district or county planning authority, as the case may require.

(5) Each copy of the documents made available for inspection shall be accompanied by a statement of the time within which objections may be made.

12A Publicity and consultation: short procedure for certain alterations, &c

(1) Where a local planning authority propose to alter, repeal or replace a local plan and it appears to them that the issues involved are not of sufficient importance to warrant

the full procedure set out in section 12, they may proceed instead in accordance with this section.

(2) They shall prepare the relevant documents, that is, the proposed alterations, instrument of repeal or replacement plan, as the case may be, and, having obtained any certificate required by section 15 (certificate of conformity with structure plan) shall—

(a) make copies of the documents available for inspection at their office,
(b) send a copy of them to the Secretary of State, and
(c) send a copy of them to the county or district planning authority, as the case may require.

(3) Each copy of the documents made available for inspection shall be accompanied by a statement of the time within which representation or objections may be made.

(4) They shall then take such steps as may be prescribed for the purpose of—

(a) advertising the fact that the documents are available for inspection and the places and times at which, and period during which, they may be inspected, and
(b) inviting the making of representations or objections in accordance with regulations;

and they shall consider any representations made to them within the prescribed period.

12B Powers of Secretary of State to secure adequate publicity and consultation

(1) The documents sent by the local planning authority to the Secretary of State under section 12 shall be accompanied by a statement—

(a) of the steps which the authority have taken to comply with subsection (2) of that section, and
(b) of the authority's consultations with other persons and their consideration of the views of those persons.

(2) The documents sent by the local planning authority to the Secretary of State under section 12A shall be accompanied by a statement of the steps which the authority are taking to comply with subsection (4) of that section.

(3) If, on considering the statement and the proposals and any other information provided by the local planning authority, the Secretary of State is not satisfied with the steps taken by the authority, he may, within 21 days of the receipt of the statement, direct the authority not to take further steps for the adoption of the proposals without—

(a) if they have proceeded in accordance with section 12A, proceeding instead in accordance with section 12, or
(b) in any case, taking such further steps as he may specify,

and satisfying him that they have done so.

(4) A local planning authority who are given directions by the Secretary of State shall—

(a) forthwith withdraw the copies of the documents made available for inspection as required by section 12(4) or 12A(2), and
(b) notify any person by whom objections to the proposals have been made to the authority that the Secretary of State has given such directions.

13 Objections: local inquiry or other hearing

(1) The local planning authority may cause a local inquiry or other hearing to be held for the purpose of considering objections to their proposals for the making, alteration, repeal or replacement of a local plan.

(2) They shall hold such a local inquiry or other hearing in the case of objections made in accordance with regulations unless all the persons who have made such objections have indicated in writing that they do not wish to appear.

(3) A local inquiry or other hearing shall be held by a person appointed by the Secretary of State or, in such cases as may be prescribed, by the authority themselves.

(4) Regulations may—

    (*a*) make provision with respect to the appointment, and qualifications for appointment, of persons to hold a local inquiry or other hearing;

    (*b*) include provision enabling the Secretary of State to direct a local planning authority to appoint a particular person, or one of a specified list or class of persons;

    (*c*) make provision with respect to the remuneration and allowances of the person appointed.

(5) Subsections (2) and (3) of section 250 of the Local Government Act 1972 (power to summon and examine witnesses) apply to an inquiry held under this section.

(6) The Tribunals and Inquiries Act 1971 applies to a local inquiry or other hearing under this section as it applies to a statutory inquiry held by the Secretary of State, with the substitution in section 12(1) (statement of reasons for decision) for the references to a decision taken by the Secretary of State of references to a decision taken by a local authority.

14 Adoption of proposals

(1) After the expiry of the period afforded for making objections to proposals for the making, alteration, repeal or replacement of a local plan or, if such objections were duly made within that period, after considering the objections so made, the local planning authority may, subject to the following provisions of this section and to section 14A (calling in of proposals by Secretary of State), by resolution adopt the proposals.

(2) They may adopt the proposals as originally prepared or as modified so as to take account of—

    (*a*) any such objections as are mentioned in subsection (1) or any other objections to the proposals, or

    (*b*) any other considerations which appear to the authority to be material.

(3) The authority shall not adopt any proposals which do not conform generally to the structure plan.

(4) After copies of the proposals have been sent to the Secretary of State and before they have been adopted by the local planning authority, the Secretary of State may, if it appears to him that the proposals are unsatisfactory, direct the authority to consider modifying the proposals in such respects as are indicated in the direction.

(5) An authority to whom a direction is given shall not adopt the proposals unless they satisfy the Secretary of State that they have made the modifications necessary to conform with the direction or the direction is withdrawn.

(6) Where an objection to the proposals has been made by the Minister of Agriculture, Fisheries and Food and the local planning authority do not propose to modify their proposals to take account of the objection—

    (*a*) the authority shall send particulars of the objection to the Secretary of State, together with a statement of their reasons for not modifying their proposals to take account of it, and

    (*b*) they shall not adopt the proposals unless the Secretary of State authorises them to do so.

14A Calling in of proposals for approval by Secretary of State

(1) After copies of proposals have been sent to the Secretary of State and before they have been adopted by the local planning authority, the Secretary of State may direct that the proposals shall be submitted to him for his approval.

(2) In that event—

    (*a*) the authority shall not take any further steps for the adoption of the proposals, and in particular shall not hold or proceed with a local inquiry or other hearing in respect of the proposals under section 13; and

    (*b*) the proposals shall not have effect unless approved by the Secretary of State and shall not require adoption by the authority.

(3) Where particulars of an objection made by the Minister of Agriculture, Fisheries and Food have been sent to the Secretary of State under section 14(6), then, unless the

Secretary of State is satisfied that that Minister no longer objects to the proposals, he shall give a direction in respect of the proposals under this section.

14B Approval of proposals by Secretary of State

(1) The Secretary of State may after considering proposals submitted to him under section 14A either approve them, in whole or in part and with or without modifications or reservations, or reject them.

(2) In considering the proposals he may take into account any matters he thinks are relevant, whether or not they were taken into account in the proposals as submitted to him.

(3) Where on taking the proposals into consideration the Secretary of State does not determine then to reject them, he shall, before determining whether or not to approve them—

(a) consider any objections to them made in accordance with regulations,
(b) afford to any person who made such an objection which has not been withdrawn an opportunity of appearing before and being heard by a person appointed by him for the purpose, and
(c) if a local inquiry or other hearing is held, also afford such an opportunity to the authority and such other persons as he thinks fit,

except so far as the objections have already been considered, or a local inquiry or other hearing into the objections has already been held, by the authority.

(4) In considering the proposals the Secretary of State may consult with, or consider the views of, any local planning authority or any other person; but he is under no obligation to do so, or to afford an opportunity for the making of representations or objections, or to cause a local inquiry or other hearing to be held, except as provided by subsection (3).

15 Conformity between plans: certificate of conformity

(1) A district planning authority who have prepared proposals for the making, alteration, repeal or replacement of a local plan shall not take the steps mentioned in section 12(4) or 12A(2) (deposit of documents for inspection, &c) unless a certificate that the proposals conform generally to the structure plan has been issued in accordance with this section.

(2) The district planning authority shall request the county planning authority to certify that their proposals so conform and that authority shall, within a month of receiving the request, or such longer period as may be agreed between the authorities, consider the matter and, if satisfied that the proposals do so conform, issue a certificate to that effect.

(3) If it appears to the county planning authority that the proposals do not so conform in any respect, they shall, during or as soon as possible after the end of that period, refer the question whether they so conform in that respect to the Secretary of State to be determined by him.

(4) The Secretary of State may in any case by direction to a county planning authority reserve for his own determination the question whether proposals for the making, alteration, repeal or replacement of a local plan conform generally to the structure plan.

(5) On determining a question so referred to or reserved for him, the Secretary of State—

(a) if he is of opinion that the proposals do so conform, may issue, or direct the county planning authority to issue, a certificate to that effect, and
(b) if he is of the contrary opinion, may direct the district planning authority to revise their proposals in such respects as he thinks appropriate so that they will so conform.

15A Conformity between plans: alteration of structure plan

(1) Where proposals for the alteration or replacement of a structure plan have been prepared and submitted to the Secretary of State, he may, on the application of a local planning authority proposing to make, alter, repeal or replace a local plan, direct that it

shall be assumed for that purpose that the structure plan proposals have been approved by him, subject to such modifications as may from time to time be proposed by him and notified to the county planning authority.

(2) A direction ceases to have effect if the Secretary of State rejects the proposals for the alteration or replacement of the structure plan.

(3) Before giving a direction the Secretary of State shall consult—

(a) in the case of an application by a county planning authority, any district planning authority whose area is affected by the relevant local plan proposals;

(b) in the case of an application by a district planning authority, the county planning authority.

(4) A county planning authority shall, on the approval of proposals for the alteration or replacement of a structure plan, consider whether the local plans for areas affected conform generally to the structure plan as altered or to the new plan, as the case may be.

(5) Within the period of one month from the date on which they receive notice of the Secretary of State's approval of the proposals, the county planning authority shall send—

(a) to the Secretary of State, and

(b) to every district planning authority responsible for such a local plan,

lists of the local plans so affected which, in their opinion, do and do not so conform.

15B Conformity between plans: local plan prevails

(1) Where there is a conflict between any of the provisions of a local plan in force for an area and the provisions of the relevant structure plan, the provisions of the local plan shall be taken to prevail for all purposes.

(2) Where the structure plan is altered or replaced and the local plan is specified in a list under section 15A(5) as a plan which does not conform to the structure plan as altered or replaced, subsection (1) above does not apply until a proposal for the alteration of the local plan, or for its repeal and replacement, has been adopted or approved by the Secretary of State and the alteration, or replacement plan, has come into force.   **[708]**

NOTES

Commencement: to be appointed.

PART II

UNITARY DEVELOPMENT PLANS

1. Part I of Schedule 1 to the Local Government Act 1985 (unitary development plans) is amended as follows.

2. After paragraph 6 insert—

"*Direction to reconsider proposals*

6A.—(1) After a copy of a unitary development plan has been sent to the Secretary of State and before it is adopted by the local planning authority, the Secretary of State may, if it appears to him that the plan is unsatisfactory, direct the authority to consider modifying the proposals in such respects as are indicated in the direction.

(2) An authority to whom a direction is given shall not adopt the plan unless they satisfy the Secretary of State that they have made the modifications necessary to conform with the direction or the direction is withdrawn.".

3. In paragraph 10(2) (provisions applicable to making of unitary development plan also apply to alteration or replacement of plan), at the beginning insert "Subject to paragraph 10A below,".

4. After paragraph 10 insert—

"Short procedure for certain alterations

10A.—(1) Where a local planning authority propose to alter or replace a unitary development plan and it appears to them that the issues involved are not of sufficient importance to warrant the full procedure set out in paragraph 3(1) and (2), they may instead proceed as follows.

(2) They shall prepare the relevant documents, that is, the proposed alterations or replacement plan, and shall make a copy of them available for inspection at their office and at such other places as may be prescribed and send a copy to the Secretary of State.

(3) Each copy of the documents made available for inspection shall be accompanied by a statement of the time within which representations or objections may be made.

(4) They shall then take such steps as may be prescribed for the purpose of—

(*a*) advertising the fact that the documents are available for inspection, and the places and times at which and period during which they may be inspected, and

(*b*) inviting the making of representations or objections in accordance with regulations;

(5) The documents sent by the local planning authority to the Secretary of State under sub-paragraph (2) above shall be accompanied by a statement of the steps which the authority are taking to comply with sub-paragraph (4) above.

(6) If, on considering the statement submitted with and the matters contained in the documents sent to him under sub-paragraph (2) above and any other information provided by the local planning authority, the Secretary of State is not satisfied with the steps taken by the authority he may, within twenty-one days of the receipt of the statement, direct the authority not to take further steps for the adoption of their proposals without—

(*a*) proceeding in accordance with paragraph 3(1) and (2) above, or

(*b*) taking such further action as he may specify,

and satisfying him that they have done so.

(7) A local planning authority who are given directions by the Secretary of State under sub-paragraph (6) above shall—

(*a*) forthwith withdraw the copies of documents made available for inspection as required by sub-paragraph (2) above; and

(*b*) notify any person by whom objections to the proposals have been made to the authority that the Secretary of State has given such directions as aforesaid.

(8) Where a local planning authority proceed in accordance with this paragraph, the references in paragraphs 4(2)(*a*) and (4) and 7(1) to copies made available or sent to the Secretary of State under paragraph 3(2) shall be construed as references to copies made available or sent to the Secretary of State under sub-paragraph (2) of this paragraph.". **[709]**

NOTES
Commencement: to be appointed.

SCHEDULE 11

Sections 49 and 53

PLANNING: MINOR AND CONSEQUENTIAL AMENDMENTS

PART I

ENGLAND AND WALES

Operation of Use Classes Order on subdivision of planning unit

1. In section 22(2) of the Town and Country Planning Act 1971 (operations and changes of use not amounting to development), in paragraph (*f*) (use of same prescribed

class as existing use) for "the use thereof" substitute "the use of the buildings or other land or, subject to the provisions of the order, of any part thereof".

Development orders

2.—(1) In section 24 of the Town and Country Planning Act 1971 (development orders), for subsection (3) (general and special orders) substitute—

"(3) A development order may be made either—

(*a*) as a general order applicable, except so far as the order otherwise provides, to all land, but which may make different provision with respect to different descriptions of land, or

(*b*) as a special order applicable only to such land or descriptions of land as may be specified in the order.".

(2) In paragraph 17 of Schedule 16 to the Local Government Act 1972 (inclusion of provision in development orders empowering local highway authority to impose restrictions on grant of planning permission in certain cases) for "shall include in a development order under section 24 provision" substitute "may include in a development order under section 24 such provision as he thinks fit".

Disabled persons; construction of references to certain documents

3.—(1) In section 29A of the Town and Country Planning Act 1971 (duty to draw attention to certain provisions for the benefit of the disabled: public buildings and places of work), in subsection (1) for paragraph (ii) substitute—

"(ii) the Code of Practice for Access of the Disabled to Buildings (British Standards Institution code of practice BS 5810:1979) or any prescribed document replacing that code.".

(2) In section 29B of the Town and Country Planning Act 1971 (duty to draw attention to certain provisions for the benefit of the disabled: educational buildings), in subsection (1) for paragraph (ii) substitute—

"(ii) to Design Note 18 'Access for Disabled People to Educational Buildings' published in 1984 on behalf of the Secretary of State, or any prescribed document replacing that Note.".

Applications to vary or revoke conditions attached to planning permission

4. After section 31 of the Town and Country Planning Act 1971 insert—

"31A Permission to develop land without compliance with conditions previously attached

(1) This section applies to applications for planning permission for the development of land without complying with conditions subject to which a previous planning permission was granted.

(2) Special provision may be made with respect to such applications—

(*a*) by regulations under section 25 of this Act as regards the form and content of the application, and

(*b*) by a development order as regards the procedure to be followed in connection with the application.

(3) On such an application the local planning authority shall consider only the question of the conditions subject to which planning permission should be granted, and—

(*a*) if they decide that planning permission should be granted subject to conditions differing from those subject to which the previous permission was granted, or that it should be granted unconditionally, they shall grant planning permission accordingly, and

(*b*) if they decide that planning permission should be granted subject to the same conditions as those subject to which the previous permission was granted, they shall refuse the application.

(4) This section does not apply where the application is made after the previous

planning permission has become time-expired, that is to say, the previous permission having been granted subject to a condition as to the time within which the development to which it related was to be begun, that time has expired without the development having been begun.".

Purchase notices: transmission of documents to Secretary of State

5.—(1) In section 181 of the Town and Country Planning Act 1971 (action by council on whom purchase notice is served)—

    (a) in subsection (1)(c) (notice of unwillingness to comply with purchase notice: contents of notice) for the words from "and that they have transmitted" to the end substitute "and that they have transmitted to the Secretary of State a copy of the purchase notice and of the notice under this subsection";

    (b) in subsection (3) (duty of council to transmit documents to Secretary of State) for the words from "they shall transmit" to the end substitute "then, before they take steps to serve that notice, they shall transmit to the Secretary of State a copy of the purchase notice together with a copy of the notice which they propose to serve".

(2) In paragraph 1 of Schedule 19 to the Town and Country Planning Act 1971 (action by council on whom listed building purchase notice is served)—

    (a) in sub-paragraph (1)(c) (notice of unwillingness to comply with purchase notice: contents of notice) for the words from "and that they have transmitted" to the end substitute "and that they have transmitted to the Secretary of State a copy of the purchase notice and of the notice under this sub-paragraph";

    (b) in sub-paragraph (3) (duty of council to transmit documents to Secretary of State) for the words from "they shall transmit" to "reasons" substitute "then, before they take steps to serve that notice, they shall transmit to the Secretary of State a copy of the purchase notice together with a copy of the notice which they propose to serve under sub-paragraph (1)(c)".

Purchase notice relating to land where use restricted by virtue of previous planning permission

6. In section 184 of the Town and Country Planning Act 1971 (power to refuse to confirm purchase notice where land has restricted use by virtue of previous planning permission)—

    (a) in subsection (1) (cases to which the section applies) for "land which has a restricted use" substitute "land which consists in whole or in part of land which has a restricted use"; and

    (b) in subsection (3) (power of Secretary of State to refuse to confirm purchase notice), for the words "the land ought, in accordance with the previous planning permission', substitute "the land having a restricted use by virtue of a previous planning permission ought, in accordance with that permission,".

Consideration of purchase notice concurrently with related planning appeal

7.—(1) In section 186(3) of the Town and Country Planning Act 1971 (relevant period at end of which purchase notice is deemed to have been confirmed) after "relevant period is" insert ", subject to subsection (3A) of this section,", and after that subsection insert—

    "(3A) The relevant period does not run if the Secretary of State has before him at the same time both a copy of the purchase notice transmitted to him under section 181(3) of this Act and an appeal notice under any of the following provisions of this Act relating to any of the land to which the purchase notice relates—

        section 36 (appeal against refusal of planning permission, &c),

        section 88 (appeal against enforcement notice),

        section 95 (appeal against refusal of established use certificate),

        section 97 (appeal against listed building enforcement notice), or

        paragraph 8 or 9 of Schedule 11 (appeal against refusal of listed building consent, &c).".

(2) In paragraph 3(3)(*b*) of Schedule 19 to the Town and Country Planning Act 1971 (relevant period at end of which listed building purchase notice is deemed to have been confirmed) after "'the relevant period' is" insert ", subject to sub-paragraph (3A) of this paragraph,", and after that sub-paragraph insert—

"(3A) The relevant period does not run if the Secretary of State has before him at the same time both a copy of the listed building purchase notice transmitted to him under paragraph 1(3) of this Schedule and an appeal notice under any of the following provisions of this Act relating to any of the land to which the purchase notice relates—

> section 97 (appeal against listed building enforcement notice), or
> paragraph 8 or 9 of Schedule 11 (appeal against refusal of listed building consent, &c).".

Local inquiries: application of general provisions of Local Government Act

8.—(1) In section 282 of the Town and Country Planning Act 1971 (local inquiries held by Secretary of State), for subsection (2) substitute—

"(2) The provisions of subsections (2) to (5) of section 250 of the Local Government Act 1972 (local inquiries: evidence and costs) apply to an inquiry held by virtue of this section.".

(2) In Schedule 9 to the Town and Country Planning Act 1971 (determination of certain appeals by person appointed by the Secretary of State), in paragraph 5 (local inquiries and hearings held by appointed person) for sub-paragraph (3) substitute—

"(3) The provisions of subsections (2) to (5) of section 250 of the Local Government Act 1972 (local inquiries: evidence and costs) apply to an inquiry held by virtue of this paragraph, with the following adaptations—

> (*a*) for the references in subsection (4) (recovery of costs of holding the inquiry) to the Minister causing the inquiry to be held, substitute the Secretary of State; and
> (*b*) for the reference in subsection (5) (orders as to the costs of the parties) to the Minister causing the inquiry to be held, substitute a reference to the person appointed to determine the appeal or the Secretary of State.".

Orders as to costs of parties where no local inquiry held

9.—(1) After section 282 of the Town and Country Planning Act 1971 (local inquiries: application of general provisions of Local Government Act) insert—

"282A Orders as to costs of parties where no local inquiry held

(1) The Secretary of State has the same power to make orders under section 250(5) of the Local Government Act 1972 (orders with respect to the costs of the parties) in relation to proceedings to which this section applies which do not give rise to a local inquiry as he has in relation to a local inquiry.

(2) This section applies to proceedings under this Act where the Secretary of State is required, before reaching a decision, to afford any person an opportunity of appearing before and being heard by a person appointed by him.".

(2) In Schedule 9 to the Town and Country Planning Act 1971 (determination of certain appeals by persons appointed by the Secretary of State), in paragraph 5 (local inquiries and hearings held by appointed person) at the end add—

"(4) The person appointed to determine the appeal or the Secretary of State has the same power to make orders under section 250(5) of the Local Government Act 1972 (orders with respect to the costs of the parties) in relation to proceedings under this Schedule which do not give rise to an inquiry under this paragraph as he has in relation to such an inquiry.".

Procedure on applications and appeals disposed of without inquiry or hearing

10. After section 282A of the Town and Country Planning Act 1971 insert—

"282B   Procedure on certain appeals and applications

(1) The Secretary of State may by regulations prescribe the procedure to be followed in connection with proceedings under this Act where he is required, before reaching a decision, to afford any person an opportunity of appearing before and being heard by a person appointed by him and which are to be disposed of without an inquiry or hearing to which rules under section 11 of the Tribunals and Inquiries Act 1971 apply.

(2) The regulations may in particular make provision as to the procedure to be followed—

(a) where steps have been taken with a view to the holding of such an inquiry or hearing which does not take place, or

(b) where steps have been taken with a view to the determination of any matter by a person appointed by the Secretary of State and the proceedings are the subject of a direction that the matter shall instead be determined by the Secretary of State, or

(c) where steps have been taken in pursuance of such a direction and a further direction is made revoking that direction,

and may provide that such steps shall be treated as compliance, in whole or in part, with the requirements of the regulations.

(3) The regulations may also—

(a) provide for a time limit within which any party to the proceedings must submit representations in writing and any supporting documents;

(b) prescribe the time limit (which may be different for different classes of proceedings) or enable the Secretary of State to give directions setting the time limit in a particular case or class of case;

(c) empower the Secretary of State to proceed to a decision taking into account only such written representations and supporting documents as were submitted within the time limit; and

(d) empower the Secretary of State after giving the parties written notice of his intention to do so, to proceed to a decision notwithstanding that no written representations were made within the time limit, if it appears to him that he has sufficient material before him to enable him to reach a decision on the merits of the case.".

Power to return appeal for determination by inspector

11. In Schedule 9 to the Town and Country Planning Act 1971 (determination of certain appeals by persons appointed by the Secretary of State), after paragraph 3 (power of Secretary of State to direct that appeal should be determined by him) insert—

"3A.—(1) The Secretary of State may by a further direction revoke a direction under paragraph 3 of this Schedule at any time before the determination of the appeal.

(2) A direction under this paragraph shall state the reasons for which it is given and shall be served on the person, if any, previously appointed to determine the appeal, the applicant or appellant, the local planning authority and any person who has made representations relating to the subject matter of the appeal which the authority are required to take into account under section 29(3)(a) of this Act.

(3) Where a direction under this paragraph has been given, the provisions of this Schedule relevant to the appeal shall apply, subject to sub-paragraph (4), as if no direction under paragraph 3 had been given.

(4) Anything done by or on behalf of the Secretary of State in connection with the appeal which might have been done by the person appointed to determine the appeal (including any arrangements made for the holding of a hearing or local inquiry) shall, unless that person directs otherwise, be treated as having been done by him.".

Appointment of assessors

12. In Schedule 9 to the Town and Country Planning Act 1971 (determination of certain appeals by persons appointed by the Secretary of State), in paragraph 5 (local inquiries and hearings) after sub-paragraph (1) insert—

"(1A) Where a person appointed under this Schedule to determine an appeal—

(a) holds a hearing by virtue of paragraph 2(2)(b) of this Schedule, or

(b) holds an inquiry by virtue of this paragraph,

an assessor may be appointed by the Secretary of State to sit with the appointed person at the hearing or inquiry to advise him on any matters arising notwithstanding that the appointed person is to determine the appeal.".

Increase of daily penalties for offences

13.—(1) In the provisions of the Town and Country Planning Act 1971 listed in column 1 of the following Table, which impose daily penalties for certain offences whose general nature is indicated in column 2, for the amount shown in column 3 substitute the amount shown in column 4.

TABLE

Provision of 1971 Act	Nature of offence	Present maximum daily fine	New maximum daily fine
Section 57(3)	Damage to listed building	£20	£40
Section 89(4)	Non-compliance with enforcement notice.	£100	£200
Section 89(5)	Use of land in contravention of enforcement notice.	£100	£200
Section 90(7)	Non-compliance with stop notice.	£100	£200
Section 98(4)	Failure to secure compliance with listed building enforcement notice.	£100	£200
Section 104(7)	Failure to secure compliance with notice as to condition of land.	£20	£40
Section 109(2)	Contravention of advertisement control regulations.	£20	£40

(2) The increased amounts applicable by virtue of sub-paragraph (1) apply to every day after the commencement of this paragraph, notwithstanding that the offence began before.

Consequential amendments of the Town and Country Planning Act 1971

14. In section 1 of the Town and Country Planning Act 1971 for subsection (2A) substitute—

"(2A) References in this Act to a local planning authority in relation to a non-metropolitan county shall be construed, subject to any express provision to the contrary as references to both the county planning authority and the district planning authorities.".

15. In section 18(1)(f) of that Act, except as respects Greater London—

(a) for "section 12(1)(a)" substitute "section 12(2)(a)", and

(b) for "section 12(2)" substitute "section 12(4) or 12A(2)".

16. In section 29(1)(a) of that Act for "sections 41, 42, 70 and 77 to 80" substitute "sections 41 and 42".

17. In sections 35(4) and 36(5) of that Act for "and 30A" substitute ", 30A and 31A".

18. In sections 36(7) of that Act for "sections 29(1), 30(1), 67 and 74" substitute "sections 29(1) and 30(1)".

19. In section 55(4) of that Act omit "under section 56 of this Act".

20. In section 105 of that Act—

(a) in paragraph (a) for "seriously injure" substitute "adversely affect",

(b) omit paragraph (c), and

(c) in paragraph (d) for "seriously injuring" substitute "adversely affecting".

21. In Schedule 21, in Parts I and V for "Sections 63 to 68" substitute "Sections 63 to 65".

Consequential amendments of other enactments

22. In section 182(5) of the Local Government Act 1972 (functions exercisable in National Park concurrently by county planning authority and district planning authority), for the words "(waste land)", which describe the subject-matter of section 65 of the Town and Country Planning Act 1971, substitute "(power to require proper maintenance of land)".

23.—(1) Part I of Schedule 16 to the Local Government Act 1972 (functions under and modification of Town and Country Planning Act 1971) is amended as follows.

(2) For paragraphs 10 to 12 (joint local plans) substitute, except as respects Greater London—

"10.—(1) This paragraph applies where two or more local planning authorities jointly prepare proposals for the making, alteration, repeal or replacement of a local plan.

(2) The local planning authorities are jointly responsible for taking the steps required by section 12 or 12A, except that they each have the duty imposed by section 12(4)(a) or 12A(2)(a) of making copies of the relevant documents available for inspection and objections to the proposals may be made to any of those authorities and the statement required by section 12(5) or 12A(3) to accompany the relevant documents shall state that objections may be so made.

(3) It shall be for each of the local planning authorities to adopt the proposals under section 14(1) and they may do so as respects any part of their area to which the proposals relate, but any modifications subject to which the proposals are adopted must have the agreement of all those authorities.

11. Where in a non-metropolitan county—

(a) a structure plan has been jointly prepared by two or more county planning authorities, or

(b) a local plan has been jointly prepared by two or more district planning authorities,

a request for a certificate under section 15 that the local plan conforms generally to the structure plan shall be made by each district planning authority to the county planning authority for the area comprising the district planning authority's area and it shall be for that county planning authority to deal with the request.

12. Where a local plan has been made jointly, the power of making proposals for its alteration, repeal or replacement may be exercised as respects their respective areas by any of the authorities by whom it was made, in accordance with the provisions of the relevant local plan scheme, and the Secretary of State may under section 11B direct any of them to make proposals as respects their respective areas.".

(3) In paragraph 19(2) (planning applications subject to duty to consult county planning authority)—

(a) in sub-paragraph (vi), for the words from "section 12" to the end substitute "section 12 or 12A (publicity and consultation regarding local plans)", and

(b) in sub-paragraph (vii), for the words from "the said section 12" to the end substitute "section 12 or 12A (publicity and consultation regarding local plans)".

*   *   *   *   *

26. In Part I of Schedule 1 to the Local Government Act 1985 (unitary development plans), in paragraph 12 (joint plans), for sub-paragraph (7) substitute—

"(7) In relation to any proposals made jointly under paragraph 10 above, the references—

(a) in sub-paragraph (2) of that paragraph to paragraphs 2 to 9 above, and (*b*) in paragraph 10A(1) above to paragraph 3(1) above,

shall include a reference to sub-paragraph (2) above.

(7A) In relation to such joint proposals the references in paragraph 10A above to the local planning authority shall be construed as references to the authorities acting jointly, except that—

    (*a*) each of the authorities shall have the duty under sub-paragraph (2) of making copies of the relevant documents available for inspection, and

    (*b*) representations or objections may be made to any of the authorities, and the statement required by sub-paragraph (3) of that paragraph shall state that objections may be so made."

27.—(1) In Part II of Schedule 1 to the Local Government Act 1985 (transitional provisions), paragraph 20 (local plans between abolition date and commencement of unitary planning provisions) is amended as follows.

(2) In sub-paragraph (2) (application of provisions of Part II of Town and Country Planning Act 1971) omit the words from "and in respect of those matters" to the end.

(3) After that sub-paragraph insert—

"(2A) In respect of the matters referred to in sub-paragraph (2) the following provisions (which relate to county planning authorities) do not apply to metropolitan district councils, namely, sections 11A, 11B(4), 12(3) and (4)(*c*), 12A(2)(*c*), 15, 15A and 15B(2).".

(4) For sub-paragraph (3) substitute—

"(3) In section 15(1) and (2) (alteration of local plans), as applying in Greater London, the reference to a local plan adopted by a local planning authority includes, in the case of a London borough council, a local plan adopted by the Greater London Council and in force in respect of the area of that authority on the abolition date.

(3A) A metropolitan district council may at any time—

    (*a*) make proposals for the preparation, alteration, repeal or replacement of a local plan adopted by them or adopted by the metropolitan county council and in force in the area of that authority on the abolition date;

    (*b*) with the consent of the Secretary of State, make proposals for the alteration, repeal or replacement of a local plan approved by him.".   **[710]**

NOTES

    Commencement: 7 January 1987 (except paras 8–9, 15, 19, 23, 26–27); 1 April 1987 (para 8); to be appointed (remainder).

---

*   *   *   *   *

SCHEDULE 12
Sections 24(3), 39(4), 49(2) and 53(2)

REPEALS

*   *   *   *   *

PART III
MISCELLANEOUS (ENGLAND AND WALES)

Chapter	Short title	Extent of repeal
1971 c 78	Town and Country Planning Act 1971	In section 29A— (*a*) in subsection (2), the definition of "the Code of Practice for Access of the Disabled to Buildings";

Chapter	Short title	Extent of repeal

1971 c 78—*cont*	Town and Country Planning Act 1971—*cont*	(*b*) subsection (3).
		Section 29B(2) and (3).
		In section 32(2), in the proviso, the words "of sections 66 to 86".
		In section 55(4), the words "under section 56 of this Act".
		Sections 66 to 86.
		Section 88B(4).
		Section 105(1)(*c*).
		Section 110(1).
		In section 147(3), the words from "or in respect of" to the end.
		Section 151.
		Section 165(4).
		In section 169—
		  (*a*) subsection (5);
		  (*b*) in subsection (7), the words from "and no compensation" to the end.
		In section 180(4), the words from "and no account" to the end.
		Section 185.
		Section 191(2).
		In section 237(5), the words from "and no compensation" to the end.
		Sections 250 to 252.
		In section 260(1)(*d*), the words "grants in accordance with regulations made under section 250 of this Act or".
		In section 287—
		  (*a*) in subsection (4), the words "69, 73(6), 74(4), 75(8)";
		  (*b*) in subsection (5)(*b*), the words "69, 73(6), 75(8) or" and the words from "or an order under section 74(4)" to the end;
		  (*c*) subsection (7);
		  (*d*) subsection (9).
		In section 290(1)—
		  (*a*) in the definition of "building", the words in parenthesis;
		  (*b*) the definition of "industrial development certificate".
		In Schedule 21—
		  (*a*) in Part I, the references to sections 250, 251(1) and 252;

Chapter	Short title	Extent of repeal
1971 c 78—*cont*	Town and Country Planning Act 1971—*cont*	(*b*) in Part II, the references to sections 79 to 81; (*c*) in Part III, the references to sections 72 and 251(2) to (5); (*d*) in Part V, the references to sections 72 and 73 to 86.
1972 c 70	Local Government Act 1972	In section 182(1), the words from "(2A)" to the end. Section 183(2). In Schedule 16, paragraphs 1 to 3.
1980 c 65	Local Government, Planning and Land Act 1980	In section 134— (*a*) in subsection (1), the words "Subject to subsection (2) below,"; (*b*) subsection (2). In Part I of Schedule 29, in the entry relating to section 65, the word "waste".

[711]

NOTES

Commencement: 7 January 1987 (except repeal of or in the Town and Country Planning Act 1971, ss 55(4), 110, 287(9), and the Local Government Act 1972, s 183(2), Sch 16, paras 1–3); 1 April 1987 (repeal in s 55(4) of the 1971 Act); to be appointed (remainder).

*   *   *   *   *

THE TOWN AND COUNTRY PLANNING (FEES FOR APPLICATIONS AND DEEMED APPLICATIONS) (AMENDMENT) REGULATIONS 1987
(SI 1987 No 101)

NOTES
Made: 28 January 1987
Commencement: 25 February 1987.

1. Citation and commencement

(1) These regulations may be cited as the Town and Country Planning (Fees for Applications and Deemed Applications) (Amendment) Regulations 1987.

(2) These regulations shall come into force on the twenty-eighth day after the day on which they are made.   **[712]**

2. General increase in fees

(1) The Town and Country Planning (Fees for Applications and Deemed Applications) Regulations 1983 ("the 1983 regulations") shall have effect with the amendments relating to the amounts of fees that are set out in this regulation.

(2) In Part I of Schedule 1 there shall be substituted for "£53"—

(*a*) in relation to fees due after the commencement of these regulations but before 1st July 1987, "£60"; and

(*b*) in relation to fees due on or after 1st July 1987, "£66".

(3) The scale of fees set out in Part II of Schedule 1 shall have effect with the substitution for a reference to a sum mentioned in the first column of the Table below—

(i) in relation to fees due after the commencement of these regulations but before 1st July 1987, of a reference to the relevant sum specified in the second column; and

(ii) in relation to fees due on or after 1st July 1987, of a reference to the relevant sum specified in the third column.

Sum currently specified	Increased sum for the period until 1st July 1987	Increased sum from 1st July 1987
Fees and multipliers		
£27	£30	£33
£53	£60	£66
Maxima		
£270	£300	£330
£315	£355	£390
£1,325	£1,500	£1,650
£2,650	£3,000	£3,300
£4,050	£4,500	£4,950

(4) In Schedule 2,—

(*a*) in relation to fees due after the commencement of these regulations but before 1st July 1987, "£16" shall be substituted for "£14" and "£60" for "£53"; and

(*b*) in relation to fees due on or after 1st July 1987, "£18" shall be substituted for "£14" and "£66" for "£53".   **[713]**

3. Miscellaneous amendments

The 1983 regulations shall also have effect subject to the miscellaneous amendments set out in Schedule 1 hereto.   **[714]**

4. Substitution of a new fee Schedule

In relation to fees due on or after 1st July 1987 there shall be substituted for Part II of Schedule 1 to the 1983 regulations the new Part II set out in Schedule 2 hereto (which reflects the increased amounts mentioned in column 3 of the Table in regulation 2 and other amendments made to Part II by these regulations).   **[715]**

5. Revocations

(1) In the Town and Country Planning (Fees for Applications and Deemed Applications) (Amendment) Regulations 1985, regulations 2(*c*)(iii), (iv) and (vi) and (*e*) are revoked from the commencement of these regulations, and regulation 2(*d*) and the Schedule are revoked on 1st July 1987.

(2) Regulations 2(2)(*a*), (3) and (4)(*a*) of, and paragraph 7 of Schedule 1 to, these regulations cease to have effect on 1st July 1987.   **[716]**

SCHEDULE 1

Regulation 3

MINOR AMENDMENTS TO THE 1983 REGULATIONS

1. Invalid application: refund of fees

In regulation 3, there shall be added as paragraph (5),—

"(5) Any fee paid pursuant to this regulation shall be refunded if the relevant application is rejected as invalidly made.".

2. Consolidation of permissions for mineral working: exemption from fee

There shall be inserted as regulation 7A—

"**7A.** Regulation 3 shall not apply to impose a fee in relation to an application to a local planning authority for permission to carry out development consisting of the winning and working of minerals where the application—

(a) is for a permission which consolidates two or more subsisting permissions; and
(b) does not seek permission for development which is not authorised by a subsisting permission.".

3. Refund of fees on deemed applications

In regulation 8,—

(a) at the beginning of paragraph (2) there shall be inserted, "Subject to paragraph (13)";
(b) at the end of paragraph (10) there shall be added "or if the Secretary of State decides that the enforcement notice is a nullity";
(c) at the end of paragraph (12) there shall be added "(whether because there is no subsisting use of the land in relation to which he may grant planning permission or for any other reason)"; and
(d) there shall be added as paragraph (13),—

"(13)(a) Where planning permission is deemed to have been applied for by virtue of section 88B(3) of the 1971 Act and—

(i) an enforcement notice is varied under section 88A otherwise than to take account of a grant of planning permission under section 88B; and
(ii) the amount of the fee calculated in accordance with Schedule 1 would have been a lesser amount if the original notice had been in the terms of the varied notice,

the fee payable shall be that lesser amount; and any excess amount already paid shall be refunded.

(b) In determining a fee under sub-paragraph (a) no account shall be taken of any change in fees which takes effect after the making of the deemed application.".

4. Advertisement consent: exemption from, and refund of, fees

In regulation 9,—

(a) in paragraph (1) for "1969" there shall be substituted "1984 ("the 1984 regulations")";
(b) in paragraph (10) (conditions for exemption) there shall be substituted for subparagraph (a)(ii)—

"(ii) in any other case, the date of refusal, or where an appeal is made to the Secretary of State pursuant to regulation 22 of the 1984 regulations, the date on which the appeal is determined,"; and

(c) there shall be added as paragraphs (11) and (12),—

"(11) No fee is payable under this regulation in respect of an application for consent to display an advertisement if the application is occasioned by a direction under regulation 15 of the 1984 regulations disapplying regulation 14 in relation to the advertisement in question.

(12) Any fee paid pursuant to this regulation shall be refunded if the relevant application is rejected as invalidly made.".

5. Multiple applications for approval of reserved matters

Paragraph 5 of Part I of Schedule 1 shall be omitted and there shall be inserted the following two paragraphs—

"**5.**—(1) This paragraph applies where—

(a) an application is made for approval of one or more reserved matters ("the current application"); and

(b) the applicant has previously applied for such approval under the same outline planning permission and paid fees in relation to one or more such applications; and

(c) no application has been made under that permission other than by or on behalf of the applicant.

(2) Where this paragraph applies and the amount of the fees paid as mentioned in sub-paragraph (1)(b) is not less than the amount which would be payable if the applicant were by his current application seeking approval of all the matters reserved by the outline permission (and in relation to the whole of the development authorised by the permission), the amount of the fee payable in respect of the current application shall be—

(a) if the fee is due after the commencement of these regulations but before 1st July 1987, £60;

(b) if the fee is due on or after 1st July 1987, £66.

(3) Where—

(i) this paragraph applies;

(ii) a fee has been paid as mentioned in sub-paragraph (1)(b) at a rate lower than that prevailing at the date of the current application; and

(iii) sub-paragraph (2) would apply if that fee had been paid at the rate applying at that date,

the amount of the fee in respect of the current application shall be the relevant amount specified in sub-paragraph (2).

5A. Applications under section 31A of the 1971 Act

Where application is made pursuant to section 31A of the 1971 Act the amount of the fee payable in respect of the application shall be £30 if the fee is due before 1st July 1987, and £33 if it is due on or after that date.".

6. Land in the area of two or more authorities

Paragraph 6 of Part I of Schedule 1 shall be omitted and there shall be inserted the following two paragraphs—

"**6.**—(1) This paragraph applies where applications are made for planning permission or for the approval of reserved matters in respect of the development of land lying in the areas of—

(a) two or more local planning authorities in a metropolitan county or in Greater London; or

(b) two or more district planning authorities in a non-metropolitan county; or

(c) one or more such local planning authorities and one or more such district planning authorities.

(2) Where this paragraph applies a fee shall be payable under these regulations only to the local planning authority or district planning authority in whose area the largest part of the relevant land is situated: and the amount of that fee shall be—

(i) where the applications relate wholly or partly to a county matter within the meaning of paragraph 32 of Schedule 16 to the Local Government Act 1972, and all the land is situated in a single non-metropolitan county, the amount which would have been payable if application had fallen to be made to one authority in relation to the whole development;

(ii) in any other case, one and a half times the amount which would have been payable if application had fallen to be made to a single authority.

6A.—(1) This paragraph applies where application for planning permission is deemed to have been made by virtue of section 88B(3) of the 1971 Act in respect of such land as is mentioned in paragraph 6(1).

(2) Where this paragraph applies, the fee payable to the Secretary of State shall be a fee of the amount which would be payable by virtue of paragraph 6(2) if application for the like permission had been made to the relevant local or district planning authority on the date on which notice of appeal was given in accordance with section 88(3) of the 1971 Act.".

7. Development in connection with oil or gas exploration
In Part II of Schedule 1 there shall be inserted as item 7A—

"**7A.** The carrying out of any operations connected with exploratory drilling for oil or natural gas.

(a) Where application is made before 1st July 1987, £60 for each 0.1 hectare of the site area subject to a maximum of £4,500;

(b) in any other case, £66 for each 0.1 hectare of the site area subject to a maximum of £4,950.".

[717]

SCHEDULE 2
Regulation 4

NEW PART II OF SCHEDULE 1 TO THE 1983 REGULATIONS
SCALE OF FEES PAYABLE ON OR AFTER 1ST JULY 1987

Category of development	*Fee payable*
1. Operations **1.** The erection of dwellinghouses (other than development within category 6 below).	(a) Where the application is for outline planning permission, £66 for each 0.1 hectare of the site area, subject to a maximum of £1,650; (b) in other cases, £66 for each dwellinghouse to be created by the development, subject to a maximum of £3,300.
2. The erection of buildings (other than dwellinghouses, buildings coming within category 3, category 4 or category 7 or buildings in the nature of plant or machinery).	(a) Where the application is for outline planning permission, £66 for each 0.1 hectare of the site area, subject to a maximum of £1,650; (b) in other cases— (i) where no floor space is to be created by the development, £33;

Category of development	Fee payable

<table>
<tr><td></td><td>(ii) where the area of gross floor space to be created by the development does not exceed 40 sq metres, £33;
(iii) where the area of gross floor space to be created by the development exceeds 40 sq metres but does not exceed 75 sq metres, £66; and
(iv) where the area of gross floor space to be created by the development exceeds 75 sq metres, £66 for each 75 sq metres, subject to a maximum of £3,300.</td></tr>
<tr><td>3. The erection, on land used for the purposes of agriculture, of buildings (other than glasshouses) to be used for agricultural purposes.</td><td>(a) Where the application is for outline planning permission, £66 for each 0.1 hectare of the site area, subject to a maximum of £1,650;
(b) in other cases—
(i) where the area of gross floor space to be created by the development does not exceed 465 sq metres, nil;
(ii) where the area of gross floor space to be created by the development exceeds 465 sq metres but does not exceed 540 sq metres, £66;
(iii) Where the area of gross floor space to be created by the development exceeds 540 sq metres, £66 for the first 540 sq metres and £66 for each 75 sq metres in excess of that figure, subject to a maximum of £3,300.</td></tr>
<tr><td>4. The erection of glasshouses on land used for the purposes of agriculture.</td><td>(a) Where the area of gross floor space to be created by the development does not exceed 465 sq metres, nil;
(b) where the area of gross floor space to be created by the development exceeds 465 sq metres, £390.</td></tr>
<tr><td>5. The erection, alteration or replacement of plant or machinery.</td><td>£66 for each 0.1 hectare of the site area, subject to a maximum of £3,300.</td></tr>
<tr><td>6. The enlargement, improvement or other alteration of existing dwellinghouses.</td><td>(a) Where the application relates to one dwellinghouse, £33;
(b) where the application relates to 2 or more dwellinghouses, £66.</td></tr>
<tr><td>7. (a) The carrying out of operations (including the erection of a building) within the curtilage of an existing dwellinghouse, for purposes ancillary to the enjoyment of the dwellinghouse as such, or the erection or construction of gates, fences, walls or other means of enclosure along a boundary of the curtilage of an existing dwellinghouse; or</td><td>£33.</td></tr>
</table>

Category of development	Fee payable
(b) the construction of car parks, service roads and other means of access on land used for the purposes of a single undertaking, where the development is required for a purpose incidental to the existing use of the land.	
8. The carrying out of any operations connected with exploratory drilling for oil or natural gas.	£66 for each 0.1 hectare of the site area, subject to a maximum of £4,950.
9. The carrying out of any operations not coming within any of the above categories.	£33 for each 0.1 hectare of the site area, subject to a maximum of— (a) in the case of operations for the winning and working of minerals, £4,950; (b) in other cases, £330.

II. Uses of Land

10. The change of use of a building to use as one or more separate dwellinghouses.	(a) Where the change is from a previous use as a single dwellinghouse to use as two or more single dwellinghouses, £66 for each additional dwellinghouse to be created by the development, subject to a maximum of £3,300; (b) in other cases, £66 for each dwellinghouse to be created by the development, subject to a maximum of £3,300.
11. (a) The use of land for the disposal of refuse or waste materials or for the deposit of material remaining after minerals have been extracted from land; or (b) the use of land for the storage of minerals in the open.	£33 for each 0.1 hectare of the site area, subject to a maximum of £4,950.
12. The making of a material change in the use of a building or land (other than a material change of use coming within any of the above categories).	£66.
13. The continuance of a use of land, or the retention of buildings or works on land, without compliance with a condition subject to which a previous planning permission has been granted (including a condition requiring the discontinuance of the use or the removal of the building or works at the end of a specified period).	£33.

THE TOWN AND COUNTRY PLANNING (LISTED BUILDINGS AND BUILDINGS IN CONSERVATION AREAS) REGULATIONS 1987
(SI 1987 No 349)

NOTES
Made: 4 March 1987.
Commencement: 1 April 1987.

ARRANGEMENT OF REGULATIONS

1. Citation and Commencement

These Regulations may be cited as the Town and Country Planning (Listed Buildings and Buildings in Conservation Areas) Regulations 1987 and shall come into force on 1st April 1987. **[719]**

2. Interpretation

In these Regulations, unless the context otherwise requires—

"the Act" means the Town and Country Planning Act 1971;
"conservation area consent" means consent required by section 277A(2) of the Act;
"local planning authority" means—

 (a) in regulation 11, the council of a district, the council of a London borough or (as respects Greater London) the Historic Buildings and Monuments Commission for England;
 (b) in regulation 13, the council of a district or county or the council of a London borough; and
 (c) elsewhere in these Regulations, the council of a district or the council of a London borough. **[720]**

3. Applications for listed building consent or for conservation area consent

(1) An application to a local planning authority for listed building consent or for conservation area consent shall be made on a form issued by the local planning authority and obtainable from that authority and shall, subject to regulation 7, be lodged with the local planning authority together with two further copies of the form, plans and drawings.

(2) On receipt of any such application with a certificate under regulation 6 the local planning authority shall send to the applicant an acknowledgement thereof in the terms (or substantially in the terms) set out in Part I of Schedule 1 hereto.

(3) Where, after the sending of an acknowledgement as required by paragraph (2) above, the local planning authority form the opinion that the application is invalid by reason of failure to comply with the requirements of paragraph (1) above or with any other statutory requirement, they shall as soon as may be notify the applicant that his application is invalid.

(4) Where a valid application under paragraph (1) above has been received by a local planning authority, the period within which the authority shall give notice to an applicant of their decision or of the reference of an application to the Secretary of State shall be 8 weeks from the date when the form of application and the certificate under regulation 6 were lodged with the local planning authority or (except where the applicant has already given notice of appeal to the Secretary of State) such extended period as may at any time be agreed upon in writing between the applicant and the local planning authority.

(5) Every such notice of decision or reference to the Secretary of State shall be in writing and where the local planning authority decide to grant listed building consent or conservation area consent subject to conditions or to refuse it, the notice shall state the reasons for the decision and shall be accompanied by a notification in the terms (or substantially in the terms) set out in Part II of Schedule 1 hereto. **[721]**

4. Applications to vary or discharge conditions attached to listed building consent or conservation area consent

(1) An application to a local planning authority by a person interested in a building for the variation or discharge of conditions attached to a listed building consent or conservation area consent granted in respect of that building, shall be made on a form issued by the local planning authority and obtainable from that authority, and shall, subject to regulation 7, be lodged with the local planning authority together with two further copies of the form, plans and drawings.

(2) Regulations 3(2) to 3(5) shall have effect in relation to an application under this regulation as they have effect in relation to an application under regulation 3(1), except that for the reference in regulation 3(5) to a notification in the terms set out in Part II of Schedule 1, there shall be substituted a reference to a notification in the terms set out in Part III of that Schedule **[722]**

5. Advertisement of applications

(1) Subject to paragraph (3) below, where an application under regulation 3 or 4 is made to a local planning authority in respect of any building the authority shall—

(a) publish in a local newspaper circulating in the locality in which the building is situated a notice indicating the nature of the works which are the subject of the application and naming a place within the locality where a copy of the application, and of all plans and other documents submitted with it, will be open to inspection by the public at all reasonable hours during the period of 21 days beginning with the date of publication of the notice; and

(b) for not less than 7 days display on or near the said building a notice containing the same particulars as are required to be contained in the notice to be published in accordance with sub-paragraph (a) above.

(2) Subject to paragraph (3) below, an application under regulation 3 or 4 shall not be determined by the local planning authority before both of the following periods have elapsed, namely—

(a) the period of 21 days referred to in sub-paragraph (a) of paragraph (1) above; and

(b) the period of 21 days beginning with the date on which the notice required by sub-paragraph (b) of the said paragraph (1) was first displayed;

and in determining the application the authority shall take into account any representations relating to the application which are received by them before both of those periods have elapsed.

(3) Paragraphs (1) and (2) above shall not apply to any application for—

(a) listed building consent to carry out works affecting only the interior of a building which when last notified to the authority by the Secretary of State as a building of special architectural or historic interest was classified as a Grade II (unstarred) listed building; or

(b) the variation or discharge of conditions attached to a listed building consent in respect of the interior of such a Grade II (unstarred) listed building.   **[723]**

6. Certificates to accompany applications and appeals

(1) A local planning authority shall not entertain any application under regulation 3 or 4 unless it is accompanied by one or other of the following certificates signed by or on behalf of the applicant, that is to say—

(a) a certificate stating that at the beginning of the period of 21 days ending with the date of the application, no person (other than the applicant) was the owner of the building to which the application relates;

(b) a certificate stating that the applicant has given the requisite notice of the application to all persons (other than the applicant) who, at the beginning of the period of 21 days ending with the date of the application, were owners of the building to which the application relates, and setting out the names of those persons, the addresses at which notice of the application was given to them respectively, and the date of service of each such notice;

(c) a certificate stating that the applicant is unable to issue a certificate in accordance with either of the preceding sub-paragraphs, that he has given the requisite notice of the application to such one or more of the persons mentioned in the last preceding sub-paragraph as are specified in the certificate (setting out their names, the addresses at which notice of the application was given to them respectively, and the date of service of each such notice) that he has taken such steps as are reasonably open to him (specifying them) to ascertain the names and addresses of the remainder of those persons and that he has been unable to do so;

(d) a certificate stating that the applicant is unable to issue a certificate in accordance with sub-paragraph (a) above, that he has taken such steps as are reasonably open to him (specifying them) to ascertain the names and addresses of the persons mentioned in sub-paragraph (b) of this paragraph and that he has been unable to do so.

(2) Any such certificate as is mentioned in sub-paragraph (c) or sub-paragraph (d) of paragraph (1) above shall also contain a statement that the requisite notice of the application, as set out in the certificate, has on a date specified in the certificate (being a date not earlier than the beginning of the period mentioned in sub-paragraph (b) of paragraph (1) above) been published in a local newspaper circulating in the locality in which the building is situated.

(3) Where an application under regulation 3 or 4 is accompanied by such a certificate as is mentioned in sub-paragraph (b), sub-paragraph (c), or sub-paragraph (d) of paragraph (1) above, the local planning authority shall not determine the application before the end of the period of 21 days beginning with the date appearing from the certificate to be the latest of the dates of service of notices as mentioned in the certificate, or the date of publication of a notice as therein mentioned, whichever is the later.

(4) Where an application under regulation 3 or 4 is accompanied by such a certificate as is mentioned in sub-paragraph (b), sub-paragraph (c), or sub-paragraph (d) of paragraph (1) above, the local planning authority—

(a) in determining the application, shall take into account any represen-tations relating thereto which are made to them, before the end of the period mentioned in paragraph (3) above, by any person who satisfies them that he is an owner of the building to which the application relates, and

(b) shall give notice of their decision to every person who has made representations which they were required to take into account in accordance with the preceding sub-paragraph.

(5) For the purposes of this regulation, "owner" in relation to any building, means a person who is for the time being the estate owner in respect of the fee simple in the building or who is entitled to a tenancy of the building granted or extended for a term of years certain of which not less than seven years remain unexpired.

(6) The provisions of this regulation shall apply, with any necessary modifications, where an application under regulation 3 or 4 is referred (or is deemed to have been referred) to the Secretary of State under paragraph 4 of Schedule 11 to the Act or in relation to an appeal to the Secretary of State under paragraph 8 or paragraph 9 of that Schedule as they apply in relation to an application which falls to be determined by the local planning authority.

(7) Certificates issued for the purposes of this regulation shall be in the forms set out in Part I of Schedule 2 hereto.

(8) The requisite notices for the purposes of the provisions of this regulation in relation to applications shall be in the forms set out in Part II of Schedule 2 hereto.

(9) The requisite notices for the purposes of the provisions of this regulation

in relation to appeals shall be in the forms set out in Part III of Schedule 2
hereto.   [724]

7. Applications in National Parks

(1) An application under regulation 3 or 4 as respects a building situated in an
area of a National Park outside a metropolitan county shall be made to the
council of the district who shall send it on, together with all accompanying
documents required by these Regulations, to the body authorised to exercise the
functions relating to such application (being the council of the county, the joint
planning board or the special planning board, as the case may be).

(2) An application under regulation 3 or 4 as respects a building situated in
an area of a National Park within a metroplitan county shall be made to the
joint planning board.   [725]

8. Appeals

(1) An applicant who desires to appeal—

    (a) against a decision of a local planning authority—

        (i) refusing listed building consent or conservation area consent or
granting either such consent subject to conditions, or

        (ii) refusing to vary or discharge the conditions attached to a listed
building consent or a conservation area consent, or in respect of
the addition of new conditions consequential upon any such
variation or discharge or

    (b) on the failure of a local planning authority to give notice of their
decision or of the reference of the application to the Secretary of
State;

shall give notice of appeal to the Secretary of State (on a form obtained from
the Secretary of State) within six months of notice of the decision or of the
expiry of the appropriate period allowed under regulation 3(4), as the case may
be, or such longer period as the Secretary of State may at any time allow.

(2) Such a person shall also furnish to the Secretary of State a copy of each
of the following documents—

        (i) the application;

        (ii) all relevant plans, drawings, particulars and documents submitted
with the application, including a copy of the certificate given in
accordance with regulation 6;

        (iii) the notice of the decision, if any;

        (iv) all other relevant correspondence with the local planning
authority.   [726]

9. Claims for compensation and listed building purchase notices

(1) A claim for compensation made to a local planning authority under sections
171(2), 172(1), 173(3) of the Act, or a listed building purchase notice served on
the council of a district, or on the Common Council or on the council of a
London borough under section 190 of the Act, shall be in writing and shall be
served on that authority or council by delivering it at the offices of the authority
or council addressed to the clerk thereof, or by sending it so addressed by
prepaid post.

(2) The time within which any such claim or notice as is mentioned in
paragraph (1) above shall be served shall be—

(*a*) in the case of a claim for compensation, 6 months; and

(*b*) in the case of a listed building purchase notice, 12 months from the date of the decision in respect of which the claim or notice is made or given, or such longer period as the Secretary of State may allow in any particular case. **[727]**

10. Advertisement of unopposed revocation or modification order

Where by virtue of the provisions of paragraph 12(2) of Schedule 11 to the Act the making of an order under paragraph 10 of that Schedule in respect of works to a building is required to be advertised, the local planning authority shall publish the advertisement in a local newspaper circulating in the area in which the building is situated. **[728]**

11. Application of the Public Health Act 1936 to listed building enforcement notices

The provisions of sections 276, 289 and 294 of the Public Health Act 1936 shall apply in relation to steps required to be taken by a listed building enforcement notice, as if—

(*a*) references to a local authority were references to a local planning authority;

(*b*) references (in whatever form) to the execution of works under the said Act of 1936 were references to the taking of steps required to be taken under the notice;

(*c*) references in the said section 289 to the occupier were references to a person having an interest in the premises other than the owner; and

(*d*) the reference in the said section 294 to "expenses under this Act" were a reference to expenses incurred in the taking of such steps as aforesaid. **[729]**

12. Demolition of unlisted buildings in conservation areas

In their application to buildings to which section 277A of the Act applies, the provisions of the Act which are set out in column (1) of Schedule 3 hereto shall have effect as they have effect in relation to listed buildings subject to—

(*a*) the substitution of "conservation area consent" for any reference to "listed building consent", the substitution of "conservation area enforcement notice" for any reference to "listed building enforcement notice", and the substitution of "conservation area purchase notice" for any reference to "listed building purchase notice"; and

(*b*) the exceptions and additional modifications (if any) set out opposite such provisions in column 2 of that Schedule. **[730]**

13. Applications by local planning authorities

(1) In relation to applications by local planning authorities relating to the execution of works for the demolition, alteration or extension of listed buildings or for the demolition of unlisted buildings in conservation areas, the provisions of the Act specified in Part VI of Schedule 21 to the Act shall have effect subject to the exceptions and modifications prescribed in this regulation.

(2) Where a local planning authority require listed building consent for the demolition, alteration or extension of a listed building in their area or conservation area consent for the demolition of a building within a conservation area in their area, the authority shall, subject to paragraph (7) below, make application to the Secretary of State for that consent.

(3) Any such application shall be in the form of an application to the local planning authority, and shall be deemed to have been referred to the Secretary of State under paragraph 4 of Schedule 11 to the Act and the provisions of the said paragraph shall apply to the determination of the application by the Secretary of State.

(4) Where a local planning authority have made an application for consent under paragraph (2) above they shall, before sending it to the Secretary of State—

(a) publish in a local newspaper circulating in the locality in which the building is situated a notice indicating the nature of the works which are the subject of the application and naming a place within the locality where a copy of the application, and of all the plans and other documents which it is intended to submit to the Secretary of State with it, will be open to inspection by the public at all reasonable hours during the period of 21 days beginning with the date of publication of the notice; and

(b) for not less than 7 days display on or near the said building a notice containing the same particulars as are required to be contained in the notice to be published in accordance with sub-paragraph (a) above.

(5) Paragraph (4) above does not apply to any application by a local planning authority relating to works affecting only the interior of a building which when last notified to the authority by the Secretary of State as a building of special architectural or historic interest was classified as a Grade II (unstarred) listed building.

(6) An application by a local planning authority to the Secretary of State under paragraph (2) above shall be accompanied by a copy of all representations duly made in relation thereto.

(7) An application by the council of a county to the Secretary of State under paragraph (2) above, together with any accompanying documents required by this regulation, shall be made to the council of the district who shall forthwith send it on to the Secretary of State.

(8) In relation to a listed building, or a building in a conservation area, belonging to a local planning authority, the Secretary of State may serve any notice authorised to be served by a local planning authority in relation to a listed building or a building in a conservation area.   **[731]**

14. Form of notice that a building has become, or ceased to be, listed

The forms set out in Schedule 4 hereto (or forms substantially to the like effect) are the prescribed forms of notice for the purposes of section 54(7) of the Act.
                                                                              [732]

15. Consequential amendments

The Town and Country Planning (Crown Land Applications) Regulations 1984 shall be amended as follows—

(a) in regulation 2, for "Regulations 1977" there shall be substituted "Regulations 1987";

(b) in the right hand column of the Schedule (opposite the reference to "Regulation 3(2)"), for the words "regulation 5" in each of the places where they occur there shall be substituted "regulation 6"; and

(c) in the left hand column of the Schedule, for "Regulation 5" there shall be substituted "Regulation 6", and in the inserted paragraph "(1A)" in the appropriate modification in the opposite part of the right hand column of that Schedule, after the words "listed building consent" there shall be inserted the words "or conservation area consent".

[733]

16. Revocations

The Town and Country Planning (Listed Buildings and Buildings in Conservation Areas) Regulations 1977 and paragraphs 5 and 6 of Schedule 1 to the Town and Country Planning (Local Government Reorganisation) (Miscellaneous Amendments) Regulations 1986 are hereby revoked.   [734]

SCHEDULE 1

Regulations 3 and 4

PART I

NOTIFICATION TO BE SENT TO APPLICANT ON RECEIPT OF APPLICATION

Your application dated   was received on   (a). *[Examination of the form of application and accompanying plans and documents to ascertain whether your application complies with the statutory requirements has not been completed.

If on further examination it is found that the application is invalid for failure to comply with such requirements (or for any other reason) a further communication will be sent to you as soon as possible.]

If by   (b) *[you have not received notification that your application is invalid and] this authority have not given you notice of their decision (and you have not agreed with them in writing that the period within which their decision shall be given may be extended) you may appeal to the Secretary of State in accordance with paragraphs 8 and 9 of Schedule 11 to the Town and Country Planning Act 1971 by notice sent within six months from that date (unless the application has already been referred by this authority to the [Secretary of State for the Environment] [Secretary of State for Wales]). Appeals must be made on a form which is obtainable from the [Department of the Environment] [Welsh Office].

Notes

(a) Insert date when relevant document(s) referred to in regulation [3(1)], [4(1)]* were received.

(b) Insert date 8 weeks from date of receipt of application (as given at (a)).

* Delete where inappropriate.   [735]

PART II

NOTIFICATION TO BE SENT TO APPLICANT ON REFUSAL OF LISTED BUILDING CONSENT OR CONSERVATION AREA CONSENT, OR GRANT OF CONSENT SUBJECT TO CONDITIONS (TO BE ENDORSED ON NOTICES OF DECISION)

(1) If the applicant is aggrieved by the decision of the local planning authority to refuse listed building consent or conservation area consent for the proposed works, or to grant consent subject to conditions, he may appeal to the [Secretary of State for the Environment] [Secretary of State for Wales] in accordance with paragraph 8 of Schedule 11 to the Town and Country Planning Act 1971 within six months of receipt of this notice. (Appeals must be made on a form which is obtainable from the [Department of the Environment] [Welsh Office]). The Secretary of State has power to allow a longer period for the giving of a notice of appeal but he will not normally be prepared to exercise this power unless there are special circumstances which excuse the delay in giving notice of appeal.

(2) If listed building consent or conservation area consent is refused, or granted subject to conditions, whether by the local planning authority or by the [Secretary of

State for the Environment] [Secretary of State for Wales], and the owner of the land claims that the land has become incapable of reasonably beneficial use in its existing state and cannot be rendered capable of reasonably beneficial use by the carrying out of any works which have been or would be permitted, he may serve on the council of the district, or London borough in which the land is situated (or, where appropriate, on the Common Council of the City of London) a purchase notice requiring that council to purchase his interest in the land in accordance with the provisions of section 190 of the Town and Country Planning Act 1971.

(3) In certain circumstances a claim may be made against the local planning authority for compensation where permission is refused or granted subject to conditions by the Secretary of State on appeal or on a reference of the application to him. The circumstances in which such compensation is payable are set out in section 171 of the Town and Country Planning Act 1971. **[736]**

PART III

NOTIFICATION TO BE SENT TO APPLICANT ON REFUSAL TO VARY OR DISCHARGE CONDITIONS ATTACHED TO LISTED BUILDING CONSENT OR CONSERVATION AREA CONSENT, OR ON THE ADDITION OF NEW CONDITIONS CONSEQUENTIAL UPON VARIATION OR DISCHARGE

If the applicant is aggrieved by the decision of the local planning authority—

(a) to refuse to vary or discharge the conditions attached to a listed building consent or a conservation area consent; or

(b) to add new conditions consequential upon any such variation or discharge,

he may appeal to the [Secretary of State for the Environment] [Secretary of State for Wales] in accordance with paragraph 8 of Schedule 11 to the Town and Country Planning Act 1971 within six months of receipt of this notice. (Appeals must be made on a form which is obtainable from the [Department of the Environment] [Welsh Office]). The Secretary of State has power to allow a longer period for the giving of a notice of appeal but he will not normally be prepared to exercise this power unless there are special circumstances which excuse the delay in giving notice of appeal. **[737]**

SCHEDULE 2

Regulation 6

PART I

TOWN AND COUNTRY PLANNING ACT 1971

Certificate A*

I hereby certify that no person other than [myself] [the applicant] [the appellant]* was an owner (a) of the building to which the [application] [appeal]* relates at the beginning of the period of 20 days before the date of the accompanying [application] [appeal]*.

or

Certificate B*

I hereby certify that:

[I have] [The applicant has] [The appellant has]* given the requisite notice to all the persons other than [myself] [the applicant] [the appellant]* who, 20 days before the date of the accompanying [application] [appeal]*, were owners (a) of the building to which the [application] [appeal] relates, viz:—

Name of owner	Address	Date of service of notice

or

Certificate C*

I hereby certify that:

1. [I am] [The applicant is] [The appellant is]* unable to issue a certificate in accordance

with either sub-paragraph (*a*) or sub-paragraph (*b*) of regulation 6(1) of the Town and Country Planning (Listed Buildings and Buildings in Conservation Areas) Regulations 1987 in respect of the accompanying [application] [appeal]* dated

2. [I have] [The applicant has] [The appellant has]* given the requisite notice to the following persons other than [myself] [the applicant] [the appellant]* who, 20 days before the date of the [application] [appeal]*, were owners (*a*) of the building to which the [application] [appeal] relates, viz:—

Name of owner   Address   Date of service
                                                                    of notice

3. [I have] [The applicant has] [The appellant has]* taken the steps listed below, being steps reasonably open to [me] [him]* to ascertain the names and addresses of the other owners (*a*) of the building and [have] [has]* been unable to do so: (*b*).

4. Notice of the [application] [appeal]* as set out below has been published in the (*c*) on   (*d*).

Copy of notice as published

or

*Certificate D**

I hereby certify that:

1. [I am] [The applicant is] [The appellant is]* unable to issue a certificate in accordance with sub-paragraph (*a*) of regulation 6(1) of the Town and Country Planning (Listed Buildings and Buildings in Conservation Areas) Regulations 1987 in respect of the accompanying [application] [appeal]* dated   and [have] [has]* taken the steps listed below, being steps reasonably open to [me] [him]*, to ascertain the names and addresses of all the persons other than [myself] [himself]* who, 20 days before the date of the [application] [appeal]*, were owners (*a*) of the building to which the [application] [appeal]* relates and [have] [had]* been unable to do so: (*b*).

2. Notice of the [application] [appeal]* as set out below has been published in the (*c*) on   (*d*).

Copy of notice as published

Signed........................
[On behalf of...................]*
Date ....

*Delete where inappropriate.

Notes

(*a*) "Owner" means a person having a freehold interest or a leasehold interest the unexpired term of which not less than 7 years remain unexpired.
(*b*) Insert description of steps taken.
(*c*) Insert name of local newspaper circulating in the locality in which the land is situated.
(*d*) Insert date of publication (which must not be earlier than 20 days before the application or appeal).   [738]

PART II

TOWN AND COUNTRY PLANNING ACT 1971

NOTICE FOR SERVICE ON INDIVIDUALS

Proposal for [demolishing] [altering] [extending] [varying or discharging conditions]*

(*a*).

TAKE NOTICE that application is being made to the   (*b*) Council by (*c*) for [listed building consent] [conservation area consent] [variation or discharge of conditions]*   (*d*).

If you wish to make representations about the application, you should make them in writing, not later than   (e) to the Council at   (f).

Signed.........................
[On behalf of...................]*
Date ....

TOWN AND COUNTRY PLANNING ACT 1971

NOTICE FOR PUBLICATION IN LOCAL NEWSPAPERS WHERE NOT ALL THE OWNERS ARE KNOWN, PURSUANT TO REGULATION 6(2) OF THE TOWN AND COUNTRY PLANNING (LISTED BUILDINGS AND BUILDINGS IN CONSERVATION AREAS) REGULATIONS 1987

Proposal for [demolishing] [altering] [extending] [varying or discharging conditions]*

(a).

Notice is hereby given that application is being made to the   (b) Council by
        (c) for [listed building consent] [conservation area consent] [variation or discharge of conditions]*

(d).

Any owner of the building (namely a freeholder, or a leaseholder entitled to an unexpired term of at least seven years) who wishes to make representations to the above-mentioned Council about the application should make them in writing not later than   (e) to the Council at   (f).

Signed.........................
[On behalf of...................]*
Date ....

*Delete where inappropriate.

Notes

(a) Insert name, address or location of building with sufficient precision to ensure identification of it.

(b) Insert name of council.

(c) Insert name of applicant.

(d) Insert description of proposed works and name, address or location of building, or in the case of an application to vary or discharge conditions, insert description of the proposed variation or discharge.

(e) Insert date not less than 20 days later than the date on which the notice is served or published.

(f) Insert address of council.   **[739]**

PART III

TOWN AND COUNTRY PLANNING ACT 1971

NOTICE FOR SERVICE ON INDIVIDUALS

Proposal for [demolishing] [altering] [extending] [varying or discharging conditions]*

(a).

TAKE NOTICE that an appeal is being made to the [Secretary of State for the Environment] [Secretary of State for Wales]* by   (b) [against the decision of the
        (c) Council] [on the failure of the   (c) Council to give notice of a decision]* on an application to   (d).

If you should wish to make representations to the Secretary of State about the appeal you should make them not later then   (e), to the [Secretary of State for the Environment] [Secretary of State for Wales]* at

Signed.........................
[On behalf of...................]*
Date ....

TOWN AND COUNTRY PLANNING ACT 1971

NOTICE FOR PUBLICATION IN LOCAL NEWSPAPERS

Proposal for [demolishing] [altering] [extending] [varying or discharging conditions]*

(*a*).

Notice is hereby given that an appeal is being made to the [Secretary of State for the Environment] [Secretary of State for Wales]* by   (*b*)

[against the decision of the   (*c*) Council]
[on the failure of the   (*c*) Council to give notice of a decision]*
on an application to   (*d*).

Any owner of the building [namely, a freeholder, or a leaseholder entitled to an unexpired term of at least seven years) who wishes to make representations to the Secretary of State about the appeal should make them in writing, not later than   (*e*), to the [Secretary of State for the Environment] [Secretary of State for Wales]* at   .

Signed.........................
[On behalf of...................]*
Date ....

*Delete where inappropriate.

Notes

(*a*) Insert name, address or location of building with sufficient precision to ensure identification of it.
(*b*) Insert name of appellant.
(*c*) Insert name of council.
(*d*) Insert description of proposed works and name, address or location of building, or in the case of an application to vary or discharge conditions, insert description of the proposed variation or discharge.
(*e*) Insert date not less than 20 days later than the date on which the notice is served or published.   **[740]**

SCHEDULE 3

Regulation 12

(1) Provisions of the Act relating to listed building control	(2) Exceptions and additional modifications (if any)
Section 55	1. In subsection (1), omit the words "or for its alteration or extension in any manner which would affect its character as a building of special architectural or historic interest".
	2. In subsection (2)—
	(i) omit the words "or for its alteration or extension";
	(ii) omit paragraph (*b*).
	3. In subsection (2A), omit the words "or for its alteration or extension,".
	4. Omit subsection (3).
	5. For subsection (3A) substitute the following subsection—
	"(3A) Consent under subsection (2) or (2A) of this section is referred to in this Part of this Act as "conservation area consent.".

(1) *Provisions of the Act relating to listed building control*	(2) *Exceptions and additional modifications (if any)*
Section 56	Omit subsection (3).
Section 56A	None.
Section 56B	None.
Section 56C	In subsection (1), omit paragraph (b).
Section 58AA	None.
Section 96	In subsection (1), for the words "the character of the building as one of special architectural or historic interest", substitute the words "the character or appearance of the conservation area in which the building is situated".
Section 97	In subsection (1)— (i) substitute the following paragraph for paragraph (a)— "(a) that retention of the building is not necessary in the interests of preserving or enhancing the character or appearance of the conservation area in which it is situated;". (ii) omit paragraph (i).
Section 97A	Omit subsection (4)(c).
Sections 98 to 100	None.
Section 172	None.
Section 190	None.
Sections 242, 243, 245 and 246	None.
Section 255	None.
Section 266(1)(b), (4) and (5)	None.
Section 271	Omit the words "alteration or extension".
Schedule 11, Parts I and II	In Part I, omit paragraphs 5, 7(1) to 7(1B), 8(2) and (3)(b), and substitute the following paragraph for paragraph 6— "6. Where application for conservation area consent is made as respects a building situated in Greater London, the local planning authority shall notify the Historic Buildings and Monuments Commission for England of that application, shall not determine such application until the expiry of a period of 28 days from such notification, shall take into account any representations made by the Commission within such period in respect of that application, and shall notify the Commission of their decision on that application.".
Schedule 19	None.
Schedule 21, Part VI	The exceptions and modifications mentioned in regulation 13 and also as mentioned above in this column, shall have effect in relation to the appropriate provision in Part VI of Schedule 21.

SCHEDULE 4

Regulation 14

NOTICE THAT A BUILDING HAS BECOME LISTED

IMPORTANT—
THIS COMMUNICATION AFFECTS YOUR PROPERTY

TOWN AND COUNTRY PLANNING ACT 1971
BUILDINGS OF SPECIAL ARCHITECTURAL OR HISTORIC INTEREST

To:

NOTICE IS HEREBY GIVEN that the building known as
situated in   has been included in a list of buildings of special architectural
or historic interest compiled by the [Secretary of State for the Environment] [Secretary
of State for Wales] under section 54 of the Town and Country Planning Act 1971 on
         19   .

Date   19   [Town Clerk]
                                                   [Clerk of the Council]
                                                   [Chief Executive]

Note

Listing of Buildings of Special Architectural or Historic Interest

The above notice is addressed to you as owner or occupier of the building named,
which has been included in one of the lists of buildings of special architectural or historic
interest under section 54 of the Town and Country Planning Act 1971 by the [Secretary
of State for the Environment] [Secretary of State for Wales]. The lists are compiled by
the Secretary of State as a statutory duty after consultation with [the Historic Buildings
and Monuments Commission for England and with such other]* persons or bodies as
appear to him appropriate as having special knowledge of, or interest in, buildings of
architectural or historic interest.

This notice does not call for any action on your part unless you propose at any time to
demolish the building or to do any works (either to the exterior or the interior) which
would affect its character. In that event you will need to seek "listed building consent",
that is to say, the consent of the local planning authority (the   Council) to the
work you wish to do.

You should however note that it is an offence to carry out any of these works without
obtaining listed building consent. A conviction for this offence could result in a fine or
even imprisonment. Nevertheless where works which were urgently necessary in the
interests of safety or of health or for the preservation of the building were carried out
without consent it is a defence to prove that—

(a) it was not practicable to secure safety or health or the preservation of the
    building by works of repair or works for affording temporary support or shelter;
(b) the works carried out were limited to the minimum measures immediately
    necessary; and
(c) notice in writing justifying in detail the carrying out of the works was given to
    the local planning authority as soon as reasonably practicable.

Certain buildings are exempt from the requirement to obtain listed building consent,
notably ecclesiastical buildings which are for the time being used for ecclesiastical
purposes (but it should also be noted that this exemption does not apply to a building
used or available for use as a residence by a minister of religion and that the exemption
may be restricted or excluded by an order of the Secretary of State under section 58AA
of the 1971 Act).

Although there is no statutory right of appeal as such against the listing of a building,
you are not precluded at any time from writing to the Secretary of State claiming that the

building should cease to be listed, on the ground that it is not in fact of special architectural or historic interest; and any such claim, with the evidence supporting it, will be carefully considered by the Secretary of State in consultation with his statutory advisers. A guidance note on the procedure is available from the Secretary of State. In addition, where listed building consent is refused by a local planning authority or is granted subject to conditions, there is a right of appeal to the [Secretary of State for the Environment] [Secretary of State for Wales]; and one of the grounds for an appeal may be that the building is not of special architectural or historic interest.

If at any time you propose to take any action which may affect the character of your building, you would be well advised to refer to the provisions of the Town and Country Planning Act 1971, Part IV and Schedule 11, and of the Town and Country Planning (Listed Buildings and Buildings in Conservation Areas) Regulations 1987 (SI 1987/349). Further details can be obtained from your local planning authority.

NOTICE THAT A BUILDING HAS CEASED TO BE LISTED

IMPORTANT—
THIS COMMUNICATION AFFECTS YOUR PROPERTY

TOWN AND COUNTRY PLANNING ACT 1971
BUILDINGS OF SPECIAL ARCHITECTURAL OR HISTORIC INTEREST

To:

NOTICE IS HEREBY GIVEN that the building known as
situated in   has, by an amendment made by the [Secretary of State for the Environment] [Secretary of State for Wales] under section 54(1) of the Town and Country Planning Act 1971 on   19 , been excluded from the list of buildings of special architectural or historic interest compiled by the Secretary of State.

Date: 19

> [Town Clerk]
> [Clerk of the Council]
> [Chief Executive]

Note
The building referred to in the above notice has been excluded from the list because*

*Insert reason for exclusion.   **[742]**

THE TOWN AND COUNTRY PLANNING (APPEALS) (WRITTEN REPRESENTATIONS PROCEDURE) REGULATIONS 1987
(SI 1987 No 701)

NOTES
Made: 9 April 1987.
Commencement: 5 May 1987.

1. Citation and commencement

These Regulations may be cited as the Town and Country Planning (Appeals) (Written Representations Procedure) Regulations 1987 and shall come into force on 5th May 1987.   **[743]**

2. Interpretation

In these Regulations, unless the context otherwise requires—

"the Act" means the Town and Country Planning Act 1971;
"appeals questionnaire" means a document in the form supplied by the Secretary of State to local planning authorities for the purpose of proceedings under these Regulations; and
"local planning authority" means the body who were responsible for dealing with the application occasioning the appeal. **[744]**

3. Application

(1) These Regulations apply where, after they come into force, a person giving notice of appeal to the Secretary of State under section 36 of the Act ("the appellant") informs the Secretary of State in the notice that he wishes the appeal to be disposed of on the basis of written representations and other documents.

(2) Where an appeal under section 36 of the Act is being disposed of otherwise than on the basis of written representations and other documents and the appellant and the local planning authority inform the Secretary of State that they wish it to be disposed of on that basis, these Regulations thereafter apply to the proceedings to such extent as the Secretary of State may specify having regard to any steps already taken in relation to those proceedings.

(3) These Regulations cease to apply as respects proceedings if the Secretary of State informs the appellant and the local planning authority that he will afford to them an opportunity of appearing before being heard by a person appointed by him for the purpose.

(4) In this regulation references to section 36 of the Act include a reference to that section as applied by section 37. **[745]**

4. Notification of receipt of appeal

The Secretary of State shall forthwith upon receipt of the notice of appeal advise the appellant and the local planning authority of—

(*a*) the date of receipt ("the starting date");
(*b*) the enforcement number allocated to the appeal; and
(*c*) the address to which written communications to the Secretary of State about the appeal are to be sent. **[746]**

5. Notice to interested persons

(1) The local planning authority shall not later than 5 working days after receiving notification of the appeal give written notice of it to—

(*a*) any authority or any person notified or consulted in accordance with the Act or a development order about the application which has given rise to the appeal; and
(*b*) any other person who made representations to the local planning authority about that application.

(2) A notice under paragraph (1) shall—

(*a*) state the name of the appellant and the address of the site to which the appeal relates;
(*b*) describe the application;
(*c*) set out the matters notified to the authority under regulation 4;

(*d*) state that copies of any representations made by any authority or person mentioned in paragraph (1), other than representations which the maker has asked to be treated as confidential, will be sent to the Secretary of State and the appellant; and will be considered by the Secretary of State when determining the appeal unless, within 28 days of the starting date, the authority or person who made the representation asks the Secretary of State to disregard them;

(*e*) state that further written representations may be submitted to the Secretary of State within 28 days of the starting date. [747]

6. Appeals questionnaire

(1) The local planning authority shall not later than 14 days after the starting date submit to the Secretary of State—

(*a*) an appropriately completed appeals questionnaire;

(*b*) a copy of all documents relating to the case which are referred to in the completed questionnaire other than any written representations which the maker has asked to be treated as confidential.

(2) The appeals questionnaire shall state the date on which it is submitted and the local planning authority shall simultaneously send to the appellant a copy of the questionnaire and of all documents submitted to the Secretary of State under paragraph (1). [748]

7. Representations

(1) The notice of appeal and the documents accompanying it shall comprise the appellant's representations in relation to the appeal.

(2) The local planning authority may elect to treat the appeals questionnaire and the documents submitted with it as their representations in relation to the appeal; and, where they do so, they shall notify the Secretary of State and the appellant accordingly when submitting the questionnaire or sending the copy in accordance with regulation 6.

(3) Where the local planning authority do not elect as described in paragraph (2), they may submit representations to the Secretary of State not later than 28 days after the starting date.

(4) The appellant may make further representations by way of reply to the local planning authority not later than 17 days after—

(*a*) in a case where the authority have elected as described in paragraph (2), the date stated on the appeals questionnaire as the date on which it was submitted to the Secretary of State; or

(*b*) in a case where the authority have not so elected, the date of submission of the authority's representations in accordance with paragraph (3).

(5) Any representations made by the local planning authority or the appellant shall be dated and submitted to the Secretary of State on the date they bear; and the local planning authority shall on that date send to the appellant a copy of any representations they make and the appellant shall similarly send to the local planning authority a copy of any further representations he makes.

(6) Any interested party may submit representations to the Secretary of State not later than 28 days after the starting date; and where the Secretary of State sends to the appellant and the local planning authority a copy of any such

representations, he shall allow them a period of not less than 7 days in which to reply to them.

(7) In this regulation references to representations include a reference to supporting documents.   [749]

8. Power to set later time limits

The Secretary of State may in a particular case give directions setting later time limits than those prescribed by these Regulations.   [750]

9. Decision on appeal

(1) The Secretary of State may proceed to a decision on an appeal taking into account only such written representations and supporting documents as have been submitted within the relevant time limits.

(2) The Secretary of State may, after giving the appellant and the local planning authority written notice of his intention to do so, proceed to a decision on an appeal notwithstanding that no written representations have been made within the relevant time limits if it appears to him that he has sufficient material before him to enable him to reach a decision on the merits of the case.

(3) In this regulation, "relevant time limits" means the time limits prescribed by these Regulations or, where the Secretary of State has given directions under regulation 8, the time limits set by those directions.   [751]

THE TOWN AND COUNTRY PLANNING GENERAL DEVELOPMENT (AMENDMENT) ORDER 1987
(SI 1987 No 702)

NOTES
Made: 9 April 1987.
Commencement: 5 May 1987.

1. Citation and commencement

This Order may be cited as the Town and Country Planning General Development (Amendment) Order 1987 and shall come into force on 5th May 1987.   [752]

2. Amendment of existing order

The Town and Country Planning General Development Order 1977 shall be amended by substituting for article 20 (appeals), the following—

"**20.**—(1) An applicant who desires to appeal to the Secretary of State under section 36 of the Act, or under that section as applied by section 37 or 53 of the Act, shall give notice of appeal to the Secretary of State, by completing a form obtained from him, within six months of the decision or determination giving rise to the appeal or of the expiry of the appropriate period allowed under article 7(6) or 7A (as the case may be) or such longer period as the Secretary of State may at any time allow.

(2) A notice of appeal shall be accompanied by a copy of such of the following documents as are relevant to the appeal—

(a) the application made to the local planning authority which has occasioned the appeal;

(b) all plans, drawings and documents sent to the authority in connection with the application;

(c) all correspondence with the authority relating to the application;

(d) any notice provided to the authority in accordance with section 26 of the Act;

(e) any certificate provided to the authority under section 26 or 27 of the Act;

(f) any other plans or drawings relating to the application which were not sent to the authority;

(g) the notice of the decision or determination, if any;

(h) if the appeal relates to an application for approval of reserved matters, the application for outline planning permission, the plans submitted with that application and the outline planning permission granted.

(3) An applicant shall send a copy of the notice of appeal, and of any such plans or drawings mentioned in paragraph 2(f) as accompany it, to the local planning authority on the same date as he gives notice to the Secretary of State.". [753]

THE TOWN AND COUNTRY PLANNING (USE CLASSES) ORDER 1987
(SI 1987 No 764)

NOTES
Made: 28 April 1987.
Commencement: 1 June 1987.

1. Citation and commencement

This Order may be cited as the Town and Country Planning (Use Classes) Order 1987 and shall come into force on 1st June 1987. [754]

2. Interpretation

In this Order, unless the context otherwise requires;

"care" means personal care for people in need of such care by reason of old age, disablement, past or present dependence on alcohol or drugs or past or present mental disorder, and in class C2 also includes the personal care of children and medical care and treatment;

"day centre" means premises which are visited during the day for social or recreational purposes or for the purposes of rehabilitation or occupational training, at which care is also provided;

"hazardous substance" and "notifiable quantity" have the meanings assigned to those terms by the Notification of Installations Handling Hazardous Substances Regulations 1982;

"industrial process" means a process for or incidental to any of the following purposes:—

(a) the making of any article or part of any article (including a ship or vessel, or a film, video or sound recording);

(*b*) the altering, repairing, maintaining, ornamenting, finishing, cleaning, washing, packing, canning, adapting for sale, breaking up or demolition of any article; or

(*c*) the getting, dressing or treatment of minerals;

in the course of any trade or business other than agriculture, and other than a use carried out in or adjacent to a mine or quarry;

"Schedule" means the Schedule to this Order;

"site" means the whole area of land within a single unit of occupation.

[755]

3. Use Classes

(1) Subject to the provisions of this Order, where a building or other land is used for a purpose of any class specified in the Schedule, the use of that building or that other land for any other purpose of the same class shall not be taken to involve development of the land.

(2) References in paragraph (1) to a building include references to land occupied with the building and used for the same purposes.

(3) A use which is included in and ordinarily incidental to any use in a class specified in the Schedule is not excluded from the use to which it is incidental merely because it is specified in the Schedule as a separate use.

(4) Where land on a single site or on adjacent sites used as parts of a single undertaking is used for purposes consisting of or including purposes falling within any two or more of classes B1 to B7 in the Schedule, those classes may be treated as a single class in considering the use of that land for the purposes of this Order, so long as the area used for a purpose falling either within class B2 or within classes B3 to B7 is not substantially increased as a result.

(5) No class specified in the Schedule includes any use for a purpose which involves the manufacture, processing, keeping or use of a hazardous substance in such circumstances as will result in the presence at one time of a notifiable quantity of that substance in, on, over or under that building or land or any site of which that building or land forms part.

(6) No class specified in the Schedule includes use—

(*a*) as a theatre,

(*b*) as an amusement arcade or centre, or a funfair,

(*c*) for the washing or cleaning of clothes or fabrics in coin-operated machines or on premises at which the goods to be cleaned are received direct from the visiting public,

(*d*) for the sale of fuel for motor vehicles,

(*e*) for the sale or display for sale of motor vehicles,

(*f*) for a taxi business or business for the hire of motor vehicles,

(*g*) as a scrapyard, or a yard for the storage or distribution of minerals or the breaking of motor vehicles. **[756]**

4. Change of use of part of building or land

In the case of a building used for a purpose within class C3 (dwellinghouses) in the Schedule, the use as a separate dwellinghouse of any part of the building or of any land occupied with and used for the same purposes as the building is not, by virtue of this Order, to be taken as not amounting to development. **[757]**

5. Revocation

The Town and Country Planning (Use Classes) Order 1972 and the Town and Country Planning (Use Classes) (Amendment) Order 1983 are hereby revoked.

[758]

SCHEDULE

PART A

Class A1. Shops

Use for all or any of the following purposes—

(*a*) for the retail sale of goods other than hot food,
(*b*) as a post office,
(*c*) for the sale of tickets or as a travel agency,
(*d*) for the sale of sandwiches or other cold food for consumption off the premises,
(*e*) for hairdressing,
(*f*) for the direction of funerals,
(*g*) for the display of goods for sale,
(*h*) for the hiring out of domestic or personal goods or articles,
(*i*) for the reception of goods to be washed, cleaned or repaired,

where the sale, display or service is to visiting members of the public.

Class A2. Financial and professional services

Use for the provision of—

(*a*) financial services, or
(*b*) professional services (other than health or medical services), or
(*c*) any other services (including use as a betting office) which it is appropriate to provide in a shopping area,

where the services are provided principally to visiting members of the public.

Class A3. Food and drink

Use for the sale of food or drink for consumption on the premises or of hot food for consumption off the premises.

PART B

Class B1. Business

Use for all or any of the following purposes—

(*a*) as an office other than a use within class A2 (financial and professional services),
(*b*) for research and development of products or processes, or
(*c*) for any industrial process,

being a use which can be carried out in any residential area without detriment to the amenity of that area by reason of noise, vibration, smell, fumes, smoke, soot, ash, dust or grit.

Class B2. General industrial

Use for the carrying on of an industrial process other than one falling within class B1 above or within classes B3 to B7 below.

Class B3. Special Industrial Group A

Use for any work registrable under the Alkali, etc. Works Regulation Act 1906 and which is not included in any of classes B4 to B7 below.

Class B4. Special Industrial Group B

Use for any of the following processes, except where the process is ancillary to the getting, dressing or treatment of minerals and is carried on in or adjacent to a quarry or mine:—

 (a) smelting, calcining, sintering or reducing ores, minerals, concentrates or mattes;
 (b) converting, refining, re-heating, annealing, hardening, melting, carburising, forging or casting metals or alloys other than pressure die-casting;
 (c) recovering metal from scrap or drosses or ashes;
 (d) galvanising;
 (e) pickling or treating metal in acid;
 (f) chromium plating.

Class B5. Special Industrial Group C

Use for any of the following processes, except where the process is ancillary to the getting, dressing or treatment of minerals and is carried on in or adjacent to a quarry or mine:—

 (a) burning bricks or pipes;
 (b) burning lime or dolomite;
 (c) producing zinc oxide, cement or alumina;
 (d) foaming, crushing, screening or heating minerals or slag;
 (e) processing pulverized fuel ash by heat;
 (f) producing carbonate of lime or hydrated lime;
 (g) producing inorganic pigments by calcining, roasting or grinding.

Class B6. Special Industrial Group D

Use for any of the following processes:—

 (a) distilling, refining or blending oils (other than petroleum or petroleum products);
 (b) producing or using cellulose or using other pressure sprayed metal finishes (other than in vehicle repair workshops in connection with minor repairs, or the application of plastic powder by the use of fluidised bed and electrostatic spray techniques);
 (c) boiling linseed oil or running gum;
 (d) process involving the use of hot pitch or bitumen (except the use of bitumen in the manufacture of roofing felt at temperatures not exceeding 220°C and also the manufacture of coated roadstone);
 (e) stoving enamelled ware;
 (f) producing aliphatic esters of the lower fatty acids, butyric acid, caramel, hexamine, iodoform, naphthols, resin products (excluding plastic moulding or extrusion operations and producing plastic sheets, rods, tubes, filaments, fibres or optical components produced by casting, calendering, moulding, shaping or extrusion), salicylic acid or sulphonated organic compounds;
 (g) producing rubber from scrap;
 (h) chemical processes in which chlorphenols or chlorcresols are used as intermediates;
 (i) manufacturing acetylene from calcium carbide;
 (j) manufacturing, recovering or using pyridine or picolines, any methyl or ethyl amine or acrylates.

Class B7. Special Industrial Group E

Use for carrying on any of the following industries, businesses or trades:—

 Boiling blood, chitterlings, nettlings or soap.
 Boiling, burning, grinding or steaming bones.
 Boiling or cleaning tripe.
 Breeding maggots from putrescible animal matter.
 Cleaning, adapting or treating animal hair.
 Curing fish.
 Dealing in rags and bones (including receiving, storing, sorting or manipulating rags in, or likely to become in, an offensive condition, or any bones, rabbit skins, fat or putrescible animal products of a similar nature).

Dressing or scraping fish skins.
Drying skins.
Making manure from bones, fish, offal, blood, spent hops, beans or other putrescible animal or vegetable matter.
Making or scraping guts.
Manufacturing animal charcoal, blood albumen, candles, catgut, glue, fish oil, size or feeding stuff for animals or poultry from meat, fish, blood, bone, feathers, fat or animal offal either in an offensive condition or subjected to any process causing noxious or injurious effluvia.
Melting, refining or extracting fat or tallow.
Preparing skins for working.

Class B8. Storage or distribution

Use for storage or as a distribution centre.

PART C

Class C1. Hotels and hostels

Use as a hotel, boarding or guest house or as a hostel where, in each case, no significant element of care is provided.

Class C2. Residential institutions

Use for the provision of residential accommodation and care to people in need of care (other than a use within class C3 (dwelling houses)).

Use as a hospital or nursing home.

Use as a residential school, college or training centre.

Class C3. Dwellinghouses

Use as a dwellinghouse (whether or not as a sole or main residence)—

    (a) by a single person or by people living together as a family, or
    (b) by not more than 6 residents living together as a single household (including a household where care is provided for residents).

PART D

Class D1. Non-residential institutions

Any use not including a residential use—

    (a) for the provision of any medical or health services except the use of premises attached to the residence of the consultant or practitioner,
    (b) as a crèche, day nursery or day centre,
    (c) for the provision of education,
    (d) for the display of works or art (otherwise than for sale or hire),
    (e) as a museum,
    (f) as a public library or public reading room,
    (g) as a public hall or exhibition hall,
    (h) for, or in connection with, public worship or religious instruction.

Class D2. Assembly and leisure

Use as—

    (a) a cinema,
    (b) a concert hall,
    (c) a bingo hall or casino,
    (d) a dance hall,
    (e) a swimming bath, skating rink, gymnasium or area for other indoor or outdoor sports or recreations, not involving motorised vehicles or firearms.   **[759]**

THE TOWN AND COUNTRY PLANNING GENERAL DEVELOPMENT (AMENDMENT) (NO 2) ORDER 1987
(SI 1987 No 765)

NOTES
Made: 28 April 1987.
Commencement: 1 June 1987.

1.—(1) This Order may be cited as the Town and Country Planning General Development (Amendment) (No 2) Order 1987.

(2) This Order shall come into force on 1st June 1987.   **[760]**

2. The Town and Country Planning General Development Order 1977 is amended by the substitution for Class III in Schedule 1 to that Order of the class set out in the Schedule to this Order.   **[761]**

SCHEDULE

CLASS III.—Changes of use

1. Development consisting of a change of the use of a building to a use falling within class A1 (shops) of the Schedule to the Town and Country Planning (Use Classes) Order 1987 from a use falling within class A3 (food and drink) of the Schedule to that Order, or from a use for the sale (or display for sale) of motor vehicles.

2. Development consisting of a change of the use of a building:—

   (*a*) to a use for any purpose falling within class B1 (business) of the Schedule to that Order from any use falling within class B2 (general industrial) or B8 (storage and distribution) of that Schedule;

   (*b*) to a use for any purpose within class B8 (storage and distribution) from any use within class B1 (business) or B2 (general industrial);

where the total amount of floorspace in the building used for the purposes of the undertaking does not exceed 235 square metres.   **[762]**

INDEX

References are to paragraph number

A

ADVERTISEMENT
balloon, on, [640]
building, displayed within, [649]
building, on, [44]
business premises, on, [651]
compensation for restricting, [208], [667]
consent to display of,
  appeals, [659], [674], [675]
  applications, [654], [656]
    fees, [663], [637]
  conditions attached to, [656]
  consultations, [655]
  contravention of Regulations, [645]
  decision on, notification of, [658]
  deemed, [643], [646]
  expiration of, [650]
  limited, to be, [657]
  local planning authority dealing with, [656]
  modification of, [661], [662]
  not required, where, [646], [651]
  register of applications, [668]
  requirement of, [643]
  revocation of, [661], [662]
  site, enuring for benefit of, [643]
  standard conditions, [644], [671], [672]
  travelling circuses and fairs, relating to, [660]
  unconditional, [642]
control of, [98]
  amenity, in interests of, [642]
  appeals, [455]
  area of outstanding natural beauty, in, [664]
  area of special control, in, [664]
  conservation area, in, [664]
  enforcement, [137]
  National Park, in, [664]
  public safety, in interests of, [642]
  Secretary of State,
    direction of, [652]
    powers of, [665], [666]
deemed planning permission for display, [99]
directions, [669]
discontinuance of display, power to require, [653]
flag, [651]
functional, [651]
hoardings, on, [651], [673]
illuminated, [639], [651]
local inquiries, [439]
local planning authority, displayed by, [647]
meaning, [326], [639]
notices, service of, [670]
operational land, on, [275]
person displaying, reference to, [137], [639]
placard or poster, removal of, [138]
premises on which displayed, relating to, [651]
purchase notice, [226]
regulations controlling display of, 8
site,
  consent enuring for benefit of, [643]
  continuing use of, [648]
  meaning, [639]

ADVERTISEMENT—*continued*
  special control, areas of, [98]
    meaning, [639]
    order defining, [663], [676]
    notices, [678], [679]
    prohibition of display in, [664]
    revocation of order, [663], [677]
    notices, [680], [681]
  temporary, [651]
  validity of orders, [276], [279]

AMENITY
adversely affected, remedy for, 9
advertisements, display of, 8, [642]
meaning of, 7

B

BETTERMENT
compensation for loss of, 10
taxation of, 10

BLIGHT NOTICE
appropriate authority, [241]
appropriate enactment, meaning, [242]
claimant, [229]
  death of, [236]
  whole heriditament, right to sell, [238]
compulsory acquisition following, [232], [233]
compulsory purchase order, land subject to, [233], [235]
counter-notice, [231], [529]
  further, [370]
Crown land, in respect of, [300]
forms, [524], [527]–[529]
land affected by provisions, [228]
Lands Tribunal, reference of objection to, [231]
mortgagee's, [237], [527]
objection to, [230]
  money advanced for purchase, [290]
partnership, provisions applying to, [240]
personal representative's, [380], [528]
power to serve, [229]
public authority, service on, 10
urban development area, land within, [397]
valid, effect of, [232]
whole agricultural unit, requiring purchaser of, [381]–[383]
withdrawal of, [234]
withdrawal of plan, service after, [370]

BRIDLEWAY
development, affected by, order on, [246], [354], [355]
highway charging to, [248]

BUILDING
advertisement in, [649]
advertisement on, [44]
agreement, acquisition by, [148]
alteration or removal, local planning authority ordering, [76]
easements, etc, power to override, [156]

1